FEDERAL PRACTICE SERIES

FEDERAL APPEALS

Jurisdiction and Practice
Second Edition

Michael E. Tigar
Joseph C. Jamail Chair in Law
University of Texas at Austin

SHEPARD'S/McGRAW-HILL, INC.
P.O. Box 35300
Colorado Springs, CO 80935-3530

McGRAW-HILL, INC.
New York • St. Louis • San Francisco • Auckland • Bogotá
Caracas • Colorado Springs • Hamburg • Lisbon • London • Madrid
Mexico • Milan • Montreal • New Delhi • Panama • Paris
San Juan • São Paulo • Singapore • Sydney • Tokyo • Toronto

Revised edition of *Federal Appeals: Jurisdiction and Practice* by Michael E. Tigar (Shepard's/McGraw-Hill 1987)

12345678910 SHLB 932109876543

Library of Congress Cataloging-in-Publication Data

Tigar, Michael E., 1941-
Federal appeals : jurisdiction and practice / Michael E. Tigar.—2nd ed.
p. cm. — (Federal practice series)
Includes index.
ISBN 0-07-172390-0
1. Appellate procedure—United States. I. Title. II. Series.
KF9050.T54 1993
347.73'8—dc20
[347.3078] 93-41056
CIP

ISBN 0-07-172390-0
FAJP3

The Publisher was Mary Kay LaRue and the Sponsoring Editor for this book was J. Patrick McCahill.

Introduction to the Second Edition

The Second Edition was made necessary by extensive and sometimes dramatic changes in the law relating to the jurisdiction and procedures of the United States Courts of Appeals. I welcomed the opportunity, however, to review the First Edition and to make changes and improvements in the book.

I did not change the order of chapters. Readers of the First Edition will find topics dealt with in about the same places. I have rearranged some sections, and added sections where necessary. Throughout, I have tried to make the book more accessible, to make it easier to find what you are looking for. Chapter One contains an overview of the book and of the appellate process, and at **§1.01** you will find helpful information on how to use the book.

The text of the Federal Rules of Appellate Procedure, and of relevant Federal Rules of Civil Procedure, Federal Rules of Criminal Procedure, and statutes are in Appendixes. Each Appendix is annotated with the sections of the book where that rule or statute is cited or discussed. This supplements the Index and Table of Cases. I have added dozens of pages of material, drawn from my experience and that of lawyers and judges who have made helpful suggestions, to help the advocate face and deal with practical problems in handling an appeal. Since the First Edition appeared, I have briefed and argued dozens of cases in the United States courts of appeals, and several in the United States Supreme Court. I have appeared on dozens of programs on appeals law and practice. From these experiences, I have tried to distill some fresh insights for this edition. In addition to changes in the law, the book deals at many points with the increased use of computers in litigation.

For this edition, I have helpful comments from—among many others—the late Alvin B. Rubin of the Fifth Circuit, Patrick E. Higginbotham of the Fifth Circuit, Leonard I. Garth of the Third Circuit, and Deanell R. Tacha of the Tenth Circuit. Loren Kieve not only read the book and reviewed it, but sent me many valuable and detailed suggestions for material to add; I have adopted all of his proposed changes, and hope I have done them justice.

Several of the annual supplements were co-authored by Jon S. Tigar, now a Deputy Public Defender in San Francisco. This collaboration began when

Jon was Articles Editor of the California Law Review, continued during his judicial clerkship, and ended only when the demands of his law practice required it. Jon is my son, and nobody could ask for a better one. His contributions have been incorporated into this edition.

Susan C. Casey worked as research assistant on this edition; her assistance was invaluable. Caroline Dickinson Avery, Esq., read the entire manuscript for content and style, and made many excellent suggestions. Misty Farris's eagle eyes and able pen helped us move from page proofs to final production. My secretary James J. Patterson has every year contended with the production process for the annual supplements, and then supervised all aspects of producing this Second Edition. Pat McCahill of Shepard's kept this project on the rails.

Again my thanks to the University of Texas School of Law, to its valiant library staff, and above all to its Dean, Mark G. Yudof, who has supported my research and writing. I repeat my thanks to those acknowledged in the Introduction to the First Edition.

Michael E. Tigar
Austin, Texas
August 1993

Introduction to the First Edition

This book is based on 20 years of being an advocate in trial and appellate courts across the United States. I have briefed and argued cases in most of the United States courts of appeals and in the Supreme Court.

I have tried to combine, in a single volume, the complex lore of federal appellate jurisdiction and the practical knowledge of effective advocacy. The footnotes contain references to more complete treatment of most issues.

As I wrote this book, I was constantly reminded of the debts I owe to colleagues, teachers, writers, and judges. I have acknowledged some of these debts in the footnotes and text. At law school, my intense wish to be an advocate was nurtured by Professors Geoffrey C. Hazard, David W. Louisell, and Preble Stolz. I began practice with Edward Bennett Williams in 1966, and he has been my godfather in the law ever since; he is, in my view, the greatest trial and appellate advocate of this century.

My colleague Edward Sherman reviewed the entire draft and made many helpful comments, suggestions, and corrections. My colleague Charles Alan Wright willingly shared his mastery of this subject.

Three outstanding research assistants at the University of Texas School of Law contributed immensely to this project: Elizabeth Bosworth Ulmer, John Paul Flores, and Susan Koegel. My secretary, Catherine P. Haggard, contended with word processing, cite-checking and myriad other complex and difficult tasks.

The University of Texas School of Law and the University of North Carolina School of Law each made research facilities available.

My wife, Amanda G. Birrell, encouraged this project and lent constructive advice, despite the pressures of her own busy federal litigation practice.

I will not try to list the lawyers and judges with and against whom I have practiced, for risk of offending by an unintentional omission. In the same spirit, I extend thanks to the clerks and deputy clerks in the Supreme Court and the courts of appeals where I have appeared. They represent an invaluable source of knowledge about appellate practice, and they have been uniformly helpful.

Finally, my thanks to the clients that I have been honored to represent. They have provided me the opportunity to be an advocate. More important, they are the consumers of what is called justice, and the vigorous and effective defense of their interests is the advocate's highest goal.

Michael E. Tigar
Austin, Texas
July 1987

Contents

Summary

Detailed

2 Federal Appellate Jurisdiction—What Is an Appealable Order?

3 Extraordinary Writs: The Original Jurisdiction of the Courts of Appeals

4 Where to Appeal: The Twelve Circuits and the Specialized Courts of Appeals

6 Notice of Appeal and Other Postjudgment Proceedings in the District Court, Tax Court, or Agency

7 Handling the Record in the Court of Appeals

8 Motions Practice in the Court of Appeals

9 The Brief on Appeal: Timing and Content

1 The Art, Science, and Tactics of Appellate Advocacy

§1.01 The Organization of This Treatise

This book is organized to give the reader a quick answer or an in-depth discussion with equal facility. The Table of Contents provides an overview. The Index and Tables of Cases at the end of the volume will direct the reader to more specific subjects. Cross-references appear at many points in the text, and should be followed up for a thorough discussion of a given point. In **§1.02,** the reader will find a Checklist on Appellate Review that will also serve as a guide to relevant sections of this treatise.

The Federal Rules of Appellate Procedure, relevant Federal Rules of Civil Procedure and Criminal Procedure, and key federal statutes are reproduced in the Appendix, with a detailed indication of where to find discussion of their application and use. The annotated rules and statutes are an alternative and supplemental way of finding information in this treatise, in addition to the Index and Table of Contents.

In addition to the statutes and rules, practice in the courts of appeals is governed by each court's local rules, sometimes supplemented by published internal operating procedures. Most of these compilations are numbered to correspond to the Federal Rules of Appellate Procedure to make it easier to find a local rule bearing upon a particular subject. For example, Fed R App

P 28(g) sets a 50-page limit for principal briefs. However, most courts of appeals have adopted special rules regulating brief length, depending on whether the brief is printed, copied from a word processing document with standard 10-pitch type, or done on a word processor with justified type.[1] Because local rules are various and ever-changing, the advocate must keep up with them through the clerk's office or the annotated rules in, for example, United States Code Annotated.

The chapters are organized in the order in which the advocate confronts decisions in the appellate process. Chapter 1 introduces the federal appellate process and the advocate's role in it. It describes the kinds of decisions the advocate must make and the tools necessary to carry out those decisions. It also contains, at **§1.02,** a summary checklist of decisions that confront the advocate who is handling a federal appeal.

Chapters 2, 3, and 4 provide an overview of the subject matter and geographical jurisdiction of the federal courts of appeals, beginning with appellate jurisdiction (Chapter 2), and continuing with writ practice as an alternative to appeal (Chapter 3), and the geographical and subject matter jurisdiction of the courts of appeals (Chapter 4).

Chapter 5 presents a series of expanded checklists to help the advocate decide whether an appeal is possible, cost-effective, and meritorious. Chapter 5 discusses alternatives to appeal such as settlement, and suggests what can and must be done in the agency or lower court to position the case for appeal. Chapter 5 also shows how to compute the fee for appeal in a fee-paying case, or the costs that will be incurred by an institutional or pro bono advocate who does not set a fee.

The remaining chapters take the advocate step-by-step through the appeal process: the procedural steps of noticing the appeal, ordering the record, and obtaining stays and related orders in the agency or lower court (Chapter 6); handling the record in the court of appeals (Chapter 7); motions practice (Chapter 8); writing persuasive briefs (Chapter 9); oral argument, the court's decisional process, judgment, and mandate (Chapter 10); and, finally, rehearing and other additional review (Chapter 11).

The advocate should read Chapters 1 and 2 before beginning work on a federal appeal, and Chapter 5 to resolve questions of whether to take an appeal, how to select issues, and how to set a fee. Then, she or he can safely browse the remaining chapters, focusing on the sections that are directly relevant to the issue at hand.

The sheer volume of federal appellate caselaw has grown dramatically in the past decade. In order to reduce their workload, streamline their procedures and make the decisional process more efficient, appellate courts are paying ever-increasing attention to appellate procedural issues. In every edition of Federal 2d—and now Federal 3d—there are several reported opinions dismissing cases without reaching the merits, for failure to comply with the rules that govern and regulate appellate power and practice. Judges and their staffs comb

---

[1] *See* **§9.04.** Local rules are authorized by Fed R App P 47.

briefs and appellate records to find a basis to dismiss appeals, to decline decision due to procedural default, or to shunt the case onto a summary track to a decision rendered without oral argument and perhaps without a published opinion. Judges defend this heightened concern with procedure by pointing to their workload.

There are some notable examples of judges invoking procedural bars. In *United States v Vontsteen,*[2] the defendant had been resentenced after appeal more severely than after conviction, and challenged the enhanced sentence on appeal. The case presented a significant constitutional issue, which a panel of the Fifth Circuit had resolved in Vontsteen's favor. The court voted rehearing en banc on the government's suggestion. At oral argument, government counsel asserted for the first time that Vontsteen's counsel had not made a contemporaneous objection to the enhancement in the trial court. On rehearing, the court of appeals held that Vontsteen's claim had been waived. Months of litigation and countless hours of lawyer and judge time were thereby short-circuited.

In *United States v Dunkel,*[3] the court reached the merits of a claim, but only after a detour over the rough road of waiver. Dunkel claimed that the trial judge erred in his tax evasion trial by refusing to recognize his claim that he lacked criminal intent. He appealed his conviction, lost,[4] and then sought certiorari. The Supreme Court held in another case, *United States v Cheek,*[5] that claims like Dunkel's had merit, and remanded Dunkel's case to the court of appeals.[6] The court of appeals explained its detour:

> The government contends that Dunkel's conviction is not affected by *Cheek.* First, the prosecutor contends, Dunkel waived any objection to the district court's ruling by burying it in a single unreasoned paragraph of his brief on appeal. A skeletal "argument," really nothing more than an assertion, does not preserve a claim . . . [e]specially not when the brief presents a passel of other arguments, as Dunkel's did. Judges are not like pigs, hunting for truffles buried in briefs. But claims of waiver may themselves be waived, . . . and the United States did just that—not in this court, but in the Supreme Court of the United States.[7]

The court went on to note that when Dunkel petitioned for certiorari on the intent issue, the government neglected to claim that his contention had been waived.

Some may see the trend towards procedural particularity as an undue constriction of access to courts. Whether or not one agrees with this assessment, the lessons are clear: advocates must pay increased attention to the procedural law of appeals and to strategies that gain and hold the attention of busy judges.

---

[2] 950 F2d 1086 (5th Cir), *cert denied,* 112 S Ct 3039 (1992).

[3] 927 F2d 955 (7th Cir 1991), *affd,* 986 F2d 1425 (7th Cir 1993).

[4] United States v Dunkel, 900 F2d 105 (7th Cir 1990).

[5] 498 US 192 (1991).

[6] 498 US 1043 (1991).

[7] *Dunkel,* 927 F2d at 956 (citations omitted).

This book is designed to fill both needs, for it contains a thorough discussion of legal principles and a step-by-step guide to technique.

In discussing legal principles, treatment of any given issue in this treatise begins with the relevant constitutional provision, statute, or rule. Analysis of caselaw begins with relevant Supreme Court authority, usually in detail. Court of appeals cases have been selected according to several criteria. To merit inclusion, a court of appeals decision must (a) be generally recognized as authoritative; (b) contain extensive analysis and citation of other relevant authority; (c) contain quotable and pertinent language; or, (d) if there is a conflict among circuits, state the conflict and cite cases from other circuits on both sides of it.

This selection method gives the reader *lighthouse cases.* Reading the cited cases will usually provide additional research help in the form of citations to other pertinent authority, which the constraints of a single-volume treatise make impracticable to provide in the text. Shepardizing the case merits more than the usual counsel of prudence; cases selected because they have become accepted statements of rule or doctrine will prove themselves by the number and quality of additional references turned up in Shepard's.

Section **1.07** discusses additional references and source materials for the appellate advocate, including electronic databases. The reader will also find citations to other, more specialized works throughout this treatise. With this book and access to a basic federal library and either Westlaw or Lexis, the advocate should have a ready answer to any procedural issue arising in the federal appellate process.

§1.02 A Checklist on Appellate Review

Appellate review begins with an adverse order or judgment in a district court or administrative agency.[8] Guidance on each of these items can be found by referring to the Table of Contents and Index.

1. How the lawyer evaluates the case.

   - Is the investment in appeal worth it?
   - Avoiding sanctions for frivolous appeal.
   - Identifying potential errors and standards of review.
   - Estimating fees, evaluating appeal.
   - Motions that improve the position on appeal.
   - Exploring settlement as alternative.

2. Is the order reviewable under general principles of federal appellate jurisdiction and practice?

   - Is the order adverse to the party seeking review?

---

[8] To be reviewable, the order must be adverse. *See* **§2.02.**

- Does the party seeking review have standing?
- Is the order moot?
- Has the alleged error been preserved in the record?
- If the alleged error has not been preserved in the record, is it reviewable under some exception such as *plain error?*
- What standard of review will the court apply?

3. The finality principle—does a court of appeals have jurisdiction (power) to give appellate review?

   - Is the order *final*?
   - Is the order properly entered?
   - If not, can it be made final, for example, by application to the issuing judge or agency?
   - If the order is not and cannot be made final, is there a statutory exception to finality based on the subject matter, for example, admiralty, bankruptcy, receivership proceedings, or certain orders involving a government party?
   - If the order is not and cannot be made final, is there an exception to finality based on the kind of order, for example, preliminary injunction or collateral order?
   - If the order is not and cannot be made final, is it reviewable by extraordinary writ, such as mandamus or prohibition?
   - Is there a bar to appeal, such as a statutory limitation, for example on review of orders remanding removed cases to state court or (for government appeals) double jeopardy? *See* Chapter 2.

4. Cross-appeals.

   - Seeking review when one's opponent has done so.

5. Where to appeal.

   - Does one or more of the geographically defined courts of appeals (1st through 11th and D.C. Circuit) have jurisdiction over the appeal?
   - Does a specialized court of appeals, such as the United States Court of Appeals for the Federal Circuit, have jurisdiction?
   - Is there a choice of courts of appeals?
   - Can an appeal be transferred from one court of appeals to another?

6. How to initiate review.

   - Timing of the notice of appeal and consequences of missing deadlines.
   - How to recover from a missed deadline.
   - How a valid notice of appeal can evaporate and become a nullity.
   - Putting the correct names in the notice of appeal.
   - Identifying the issues in the notice of appeal.

- For review of some nonfinal orders, a petition is filed and not an appeal.
- To obtain review by writ, a petition is filed and not an appeal.
- To obtain review of administrative agency orders, a petition is filed and not an appeal.
- What to file to review a Tax Court decision.

7. The mechanics of handling an appeal.

   - Handling the record on appeal.
   - Making motions in the court of appeals.

8. Writing the appellate brief.
9. Arguing the appeal.
10. How the court will decide the appeal.
11. After the court decides.

    - Seeking or resisting a rehearing.
    - Issuance of the mandate.

§1.03 How Appellate Advocacy Differs from Trial Advocacy and Nonadversary Settings Generally

A venerable but questionable maxim is that good trial advocates are not good appellate advocates. This maxim is based upon an image of the trial lawyer as a barn-burning, stem-winding spellbinder, at home with the facts and impatient with the law. Edward Bennett Williams tells a story of his first years in the law, arguing a legal point in a trial. This was before the days of photocopy machines, and he was struggling up the courthouse steps with an armload of books. An old denizen of the courthouse, in a rumpled three-piece suit, called out, "Throw away those books, son, and get yourself a witness."

In addition, the image of appellate advocacy has changed in ways that seem to make the maxim true. The magnificent arguments of Daniel Webster before the Supreme Court or of the Irish, English, or Scottish barristers in appellate courts are masterpieces of rhetoric in a classic tradition that has almost faded away. Courts of appeals receive written briefs.[9] Oral argument is rationed and, when granted, is limited to a relatively few minutes.[10] Advocates of today have neither their predecessors' luxury of hours to develop a theme, nor even the same amount of time a trial lawyer colleague would be granted to argue before a jury.

---

[9] The differences between communications with appellate judges in a brief and communicating with other deciders are discussed at **§§9.06** and **9.07.**

[10] See **§§10.09-10.11** for a discussion of oral argument strategies.

This book argues that a candle can be lit in this gloom and that there is such a thing as a good advocate, without the adjectives *trial* or *appellate.* We are talking about federal appeals. Since the overwhelming majority of federal cases—civil and criminal—are resolved by settlement or plea bargain, the pool of potential appeal cases is small. If a case is worth appealing, it will usually present some legal issue worthy of in-depth consideration, even if that issue is the legal sufficiency of the evidence.

Though there is no difference in the skills required of the advocate, the appellate tribunal is different from the trial court or the arbitral arena. To be sure, there are similarities. All judges (including arbitrators for this purpose) are professional deciders. Federal appellate judges either come to understand this truth or suffer its consequences. Any professional decider adopts techniques to understand the issues being presented for decision, and for ruling on them quickly and efficiently.

A trial judge makes many decisions in the course of a day, but most of them lie within the realm of discretion and are bound up with facts and legal arguments that relate to an immediate event in the ongoing trial. The paradigmatic trial judge decision, illustrating this point, is a ruling to admit or exclude trial evidence. While trial judges occasionally tackle large issues requiring study of extensive briefs and records, this is not their day-to-day work. The best trial judges are those who move their calendar by a combination of docket control, case management, settlement pressure, respect for the advocates and parties, and a sense of justice.

Arbitrators seek a result that harmonizes parties' positions, the extent of which depends on whether the arbitrator occupies an ongoing role in adjusting differences or is simply providing an alternative adjudicatory setting.

Appellate professional deciders work differently. True, they are busy. Counting motions for stay, emergency applications, and other procedural rulings in addition to decisions on entire cases, a federal appellate judge makes five or six appellate decisions per day. This treatise discusses how to influence such decisions, principally in the chapter on motions practice.[11]

Some of the daily appellate decisions on procedural issues move a case towards a certain result, sometimes irretrievably. A decision to dispense with oral argument or to issue a short nonpublished opinion usually puts the case on a one-way street to affirmance. Thus, a good advocate must work to obtain oral argument and to persuade the court that the issues require serious consideration. Seeking oral argument,[12] and underscoring the importance of the issues presented,[13] are dealt with in other sections of this treatise.

Aside from purely formal decisions about such things as calendaring and the length of briefs—many of which are delegated to personnel in the court

---

[11] *See* **ch 8.**

[12] *See* **§10.02.**

[13] *See* **§§9.08, 9.10.**

clerk's office[14]—the federal appellate judge looks at the issues differently from a trial judge. The decisions appellate judges make have a formal precedental effect that district court decisions lack.[15] Given the Supreme Court's limited resources to hear cases, the appeal often represents the parties' last practical chance to get a fair decision of their claims. Case-resolving decisions of federal appellate judges are generally reflected in an opinion that spells out a factual basis and legal reasons, and judges know when deciding that the decision usually must be justified or defended in this fashion.

If the paradigmatic trial court decision is within a zone of legally defined discretion, the appellate decision is made in a matrix determined more clearly by precedent. This fact must influence the advocate's style of argument and presentation.

Judge Patrick Higginbotham has written that the great majority of cases filed in court are destined from the moment of filing to come out one way. If this speculation is true, then advocates and judges are wasting valuable resources on disputes that should have been settled short of litigation. One may be led to doubt that the 90 per cent figure is entirely accurate. Certainly, lawyers often misjudge the strength of their cases.

When advocates see the formal constraints of precedent, opinion writing, and a field of decision narrower than the trial judge's, they often wrongly conclude that their arguments must be technical, legalistic, and even complex. Their briefs are filled with lists of issues, each supported by a legal argument. Their presentation lacks coherence. They have no clear, short statement of why their client should win. They fail to tie issues together and they fail to select among issues for maximum impact.

In short, they forget a lesson that every trial lawyer knows, and that is no less valid in appellate practice: Deciders perceive whole stories. Appellate judges decide cases, not just issues.[16] A court of appeals may dismiss an appeal for want of jurisdiction, or find that the interplay of federal preemption and state law leaves a litigant without a remedy. But it will seldom do so without understanding the impact of the decision on the litigants and seeking to measure the result by some canon of fairness. The lawyer with a case-winning jurisdictional argument will find the path to victory easier if he or she takes such concerns seriously.

This is not to say there is a unitary and idealistic concept of fairness shared by every appeals judge. Judges of different ideological temperament will view, and state, the dictates of fairness quite differently. Consider, for example, the opinions in *Federated Department Stores v Moitie.*[17] Seven private antitrust actions, all based on the same set of facts, were filed in federal district court. The district judge dismissed all seven. Plaintiffs in five of the actions appealed, and the

---

[14] *See* **§§8.02, 8.03.**

[15] *See* Starbuck v City & County of San Francisco, 556 F2d 450, 457 n13 (9th Cir 1977); Evan T. Lee, *Deconstitutionalizing Justiciability: The Example of Mootness,* 105 Harv L Rev 603, 668 n320 (1992).

[16] *See* Michael E. Tigar, Examining Witnesses 1-28 (1993).

[17] 452 US 394 (1981).

other two sets of plaintiffs refiled in state court. While the federal appeals were pending, the Supreme Court announced a new rule that benefited the plaintiffs and the court of appeals remanded the five cases with directions to reinstate the complaints. The nonappealing plaintiffs sought to take advantage of this decision, but a majority of the Supreme Court held them barred by res judicata.

For six members of the Court, Justice Rehnquist took this approach:

> The Court of Appeals also rested its opinion in part on what it viewed as "simple justice." But we do not see the grave injustice which would be done by the application of accepted principles of res judicata. "Simple justice" is achieved when a complex body of law developed over a period of years is evenhandedly applied.[18]

Justice Blackmun, joined by Justice Marshall, concurred in the result, but wrote separately to emphasize that, in his view, "Just as res judicata is occasionally qualified by an overriding, competing principle of public policy, so occasionally it needs an equitable tempering."[19]

Able advocacy sees and accommodates different judicial stances towards fairness and equity.

The entire federal appellate process is, however, dominated by the judges' perception that their workload is increasing faster than they can efficiently manage it. The number of appellate cases per panel of judges per year was 599 in 1981, and 751 in 1991. This represents an increase of about 25 per cent. By comparison, the federal district court caseload per judge stayed about the same from 1981 to 1991, although in some judicial districts the caseloads are much greater than in others.[20]

§1.04 —How Appellate Judges Decide Issues and Cases

Federal appellate judges, in addition to being professional deciders, dwell within the rather strict limits on their power set by constitution and statute. Their power to decide an issue must be found, if at all, in a statute passed by Congress within the constitutional boundaries of Article Three.

Federal courts of appeals are creatures of statute and derive no power directly from the Constitution.[21] For appellate judges, the maxim that federal courts have limited subject matter jurisdiction means that an appeal must be dismissed at any procedural hour when a want of jurisdiction becomes apparent.[22]

---

[18] *Id* 401.

[19] *Id* 403 (quoting 1B James William Moore & Thomas S. Currier, Moore's Federal Practice ¶0.405[12], at 791 (1980)).

[20] Administration Office of US Courts, Annual Report of the Director 80-81, 86 (1991).

[21] *See* **§2.01.**

[22] *See* **§§2.01-2.02.**

Federal judges generally react to this fact of their professional life by setting up a more or less formal decision tree in their chambers, defining the order in which the issues in any appeal will be resolved. Some judges will describe this process in a memorandum to their law clerks.

The order in which most judges approach the issues is as follows:

First, does the court have jurisdiction under a federal statute conferring power on this court to hear this case at this time?[23]

Second, is there a constitutional or prudential bar to my hearing the case, for example because the appellant is the wrong party, or the case is moot, or (in a criminal case) the double jeopardy clause forbids me to hear it?[24]

Third, if the case survives these hurdles, is the case easy or hard? Some believe, as noted above, that the great majority of lawsuits filed are destined from the beginning to come out one way.[25] Perhaps this is an overstatement, but in these days of increasing appellate workload, a case on appeal will be screened at least once and more likely several times to see whether it can be decided without argument or without published opinion.

Whether a case is easy or hard cannot be argued as an issue. Rather, the advocate's initial brief must show the court into which category the case fits. Most appellants want to convince the court that the case is hard, in the sense that one should stop to consider whether the lower court was wrong. The easy v. hard decision is different for each case and each judge. For example, many federal judges still regard the law as settled and only rarely overturn jury verdicts. However, Eric Schnapper has surveyed the appellate literature and concluded that federal judges are more willing today than 25 years ago to reverse jury verdicts in at least some types of civil cases.[26] Whether or not one agrees with Schnapper's conclusions, there is clearly much room for a judge to express ideological preferences in deciding issues of appellate jurisdiction and practice. The decision to allow an interlocutory appeal[27] or to issue a prerogative writ[28] is expressly subject to fairly broad discretion. In reviewing a district court's final judgment, the court can find a broader scope of review by characterizing the issue as one of law subject to de novo review, rather than one of fact.[29]

The growth in appellate caseloads has had a major influence on the way in which the initial easy or hard screening decisions are made. It appears that an increasing amount of judicial workload is being deflected away from judges, particularly as to threshold issues. Law clerks play a much more important role in evaluating such issues in some judges' chambers than in others. Almost every

---

[23] *See* **§§2.01-2.17.**

[24] *See* **§§2.11, 2.18,** and **2.19.**

[25] *See* Patrick Higginbotham, *Text and Precedent in Constitutional Adjudication,* 73 Cornell L Rev 411 (1988).

[26] Eric Schnapper, *Judges Against Juries—Appellate Review of Federal Civil Jury Verdicts,* 1989 Wis L Rev 237, 246-59.

[27] *See* **§§2.09, 6.05.**

[28] *See* **§3.02.**

[29] *See* **§5.05.**

court of appeals also uses staff attorneys to screen cases. Staff attorneys are recruited from the same pool of law graduates as are law clerks, although some of them have had prior experience in public service or private practice. Their functions vary from circuit to circuit, even with respect to screening decisions.[30]

The staff attorney's or law clerk's focus will be on the difficulty of the issues presented, the complexity of the record, and the possibility of summary disposition without oral argument. The role of this initial audience gives the issues presented, statement of the case, and request for oral argument heightened importance.[31]

Fourth, the appellate judge—having taken care of the three preliminary matters—will focus on the issues presented by the appeal. Again, the style of judicial work tends to vary more depending on the judge's habits and temperament.[32]

Some judges will prefer to read the issues presented and then the statement of facts, to get a feel for the case and how it should come out. Chapter Two of this treatise contains a detailed outline of the categories of appellate issues, with discussion about the standard of review applicable to each. Regardless of the order in which the judge approaches the issues on the merits, he or she will array every issue against its appropriate standard of review, and never forget to ask whether the issue is fairly raised on the record.

Judges rely to greatly varying extents upon their law clerks to summarize briefs and appellate records, but judges are reticent on this subject. Over the years, however, one who argues often before a given judge will have an insight into how thoroughly that judge studies the briefs and record as opposed to relying upon law clerk summaries.

Most court of appeals judges have three law clerks, selected by the judge from dozens of applicants. Law clerks probably have little impact on the major outlines of decisions reached by their judge. The judge's judicial and political philosophy will be too well-formed to permit influence to any great degree.

Law clerks can and do influence the judge, however, by choosing particular cases and issues for extra attention, or by pointing out arguments or controlling precedent that the advocates might have overlooked or downplayed.[33] The busy judge cannot possibly read every case cited in every brief, let alone ponder the additional issues that might have been raised in every case. And to the extent that the judge chooses to play the role in chambers of administrative senior partner rather than active manager, the law clerks will have correspondingly more influence.

---

[30] *See* **§10.02.**

[31] *See* **§§9.09-9.11, 10.02.**

[32] Insight into particular judges' styles can be gained at appellate seminars and from professional journals.

[33] Arthur M. Boley, *Pretrial Motions in a U.S. District Court: The Role of the Law Clerk,* 74 Judicature 44 (1990); Kevin D. Swan, Comment, *Protecting the Appearance of Judicial Impartiality in the Face of Law Clerk Employment Negotiations,* 62 Wash L Rev 813 (1987); J. Daniel Mahoney, *Law Clerks: For Better or For Worse?,* 54 Brook L Rev 321 (1988); Kenneth C. Broodo & Douglas D. Haloftis, *Practice in the Federal District Courts from the Law Clerk's Perspective: The Rules Behind the Rules,* 43 Baylor L Rev 333 (1991).

Judge Patrick Higginbotham once remarked that a bright law clerk is like a well-tuned power lawnmower. The mower cuts straight, true, and fine, but when it comes to a rosebush it will mow that down as well, unless properly guided.

§1.05 —Depth of Research into Points of Law

On appeal, the advocate usually has the luxury of time for research.[34] The appellate process is thus adapted to the institutional role of appellate courts and to the way in which appellate judges make decisions after considering the parties' briefs and arguments.

The advocate can posit a hierarchy of decisional style from district court to court of appeals to Supreme Court. The district judge will often be concerned simply with moving the case forward. For example, it is usually more important to have an evidentiary issue decided than to have the decision be right in an abstract sense. Most cases on the trial docket are settled. The outcome of any particular case is unlikely to affect anyone beyond the litigants, so they are or should be the primary focus of concern.

District court judges are also aware that they will seldom be reversed for rulings on evidence or procedure, or for findings of fact, because the appellate courts afford them considerable deference in these areas. They also know that they are bound only by appellate decisions, and not by the views expressed by any other district judge, even one in their own district.[35] Their discretion, and their awareness of it, means that argument to district judges is more concrete, more overtly oriented towards common sense and justice, than is argument to an appellate tribunal.

The Supreme Court, at the apex of the federal judicial pyramid, selects 100 to 125 cases per year for briefing and argument.[36] Its announced criteria of selection look to broad-ranging issues that require resolution, rather than to remedying injustice to a particular litigant. Since the Supreme Court may disregard its own precedent, and is not bound by decisions of any other court, briefs and argument focus upon formulating relatively broad-gauge rules, and upon the likely impact of such rules in situations other than those before the Court. The advocate arguing before the Supreme Court can expect to be tested with hypothetical questions, to which the answer can never be "that is not this case."

Authority based on precedent is content-independent, in the sense that the obligation to follow it does not rest upon logic or persuasiveness but upon the authority's position as binding. Professor Schauer gives an example from the nonlegal world. If the sergeant tells the private to stop, and points to a mine, the private seeing the mine decides based on content (experience) to

---

[34] *See* **§5.14.**

[35] *See* Starbuck v City & County of San Francisco, 556 F2d 450, 457 n13 (9th Cir 1977); Evan T. Lee, *Deconstitutionalizing Justiciability: The Example of Mootness,* 105 Harv L Rev 603, 668 n320 (1992).

[36] *See generally* Robert L. Stern, Eugene Gressman, & Stephan M. Shapiro, Supreme Court Practice (6th ed 1986).

heed the admonition. However, the private commanded by the sergeant to stop must obey irrespective of the reason.[37]

The Supreme Court, since it may overrule its own precedents,[38] is relatively unconcerned with content-independent commands of prior judicial decisions. It must, of course, obey statutes and may defer under certain circumstances to executive discretion.[39] It also has near-absolute power to refuse to decide cases, by denying certiorari.

The courts of appeals possess little, if any, discretionary power to refuse to decide. By summary procedures, a court of appeals can issue dispositive rulings that affect only the litigants. While some have wondered if judges from time to time bury difficult cases in an unpublished opinion in order to achieve a certain result without making precedent, the evidence for such claims is fairly slim. The unpublished opinions are available in Lexis and Westlaw, which provides some control of the process and may help the appellate advocate research the judicial attitude of particular judges.

The majority of cases are decided by written opinion which becomes precedent, cannot by law depart from prior circuit authority unless issued by an en banc court,[40] and analyzes the legal principles on which it is based. The opinions in such cases are issued weeks or months after briefs are filed and argument is held, and if authored by one judge are usually joined by one or two other judges. Indeed, one consequence of increasing judicial workload seems to be a decline in the number of dissenting opinions.

The time spent crafting published opinions reflects more than judicial styles of work and the pressure of crowded dockets. The writing judge, and the other judges and law clerks who edit that judge's drafts, are concerned with making the opinion consistent with the circuit's settled law, if possible. The judge will also seek to harmonize the result with the views of other circuits, if possible, to avert an intercircuit conflict.[41] She or he will usually have thought about the impact of the rule announced or applied on future cases.

To have maximum effect in this decisional process, the advocate on appeal must broaden the scope of research beyond that appropriate in most trial court settings. Research will take place in five stages: first, search for applicable constitutional, statutory, or federal rule provisions; second, look for relevant Supreme Court cases; third, focus on circuit precedent; fourth, look to other circuits;[42] and fifth, seek out other authorities whose work may summarize the law, cast a critical glance, make a prediction, or talk about the effect of legal rules on an entire class of litigants. Doing research in these five stages requires

---

[37] Frederick Schauer, *The Authority of Legal Scholarship,* 139 U Pa L Rev 1003, 1005-06 (1991).

[38] Payne v Tennessee, 111 S Ct 2597, 2618 (1991).

[39] Michael E. Tigar, *Judicial Power, the "Political Question Doctrine," and Foreign Relations,* 17 UCLA L Rev 1135 (1970).

[40] One panel of a court of appeals cannot ignore an opinion issued by another panel. **§11.04.**

[41] *See* **§11.04.**

[42] *See* **§9.13.**

a research plan for each case, and a sense of what authority is likely to persuade judges. A detailed discussion of research techniques appears at Chapter 9.

The results of research stages one, two, and three are content-independent, in the sense that the court must follow relevant authority irrespective of whether it disagrees. But in many—perhaps most—cases, there is a fair argument whether a given authority applies, or whether it is broad enough to cover the situation before the court. The results of research stages four and five must persuade based on their content.

§1.06 —Making Hard Choices About Points on Appeal

Both the appellant who seeks to overturn an adverse decision, and the appellee who seeks to sustain it, must resist the temptation to replay the trial.

Counsel for the appellant must perform two tasks: first, rethink the case from the beginning, without prejudice based on theories and points already raised; second, dare to focus on a few strong points and jettison all the others.[43] Each task is important.

Rethinking the case would seem an obvious step, but many advocates overlook it, often because they are so convinced that they began with the right theory. The fact that one is now an appellant ought to provoke a little self-reflective humility, but may not. Many advocates—and many clients who litigate frequently—insist that new counsel come into a case on appeal, precisely to reexamine the premises on which the case has been built up to that point. Whether new counsel or not, one must decouple one's view that the case has merit from any particular way of thinking through and stating the issues.

Rethinking is also important because many issues that loom large in the trial court will have no significance on appeal. For example, much trial time may have been spent trying to admit or exclude important items of evidence. Yet if the trial judge's decision to admit or exclude was within the realm of discretion, an appeal will seldom lie.[44] If the case was tried to a jury, trial counsel may not have focused clearly upon the most persuasive presentation of legal issues that will come to dominate the appeal.

Of course, one must remember in rethinking the case that points on appeal usually must have been raised and preserved in the trial court.[45] However, this rule is not invariable, for some errors not raised are harmful enough to require

---

[43] This counsel is subject to a caveat: in some settings, such as federal habeas corpus review, and particularly in death penalty cases, the penalty for abandoning a point at any procedural hour is so severe that counsel will often err on the side of including a debatably meritorious but marginal issue. *See* **§6.08.**

[44] This is an example, and a general principle. There are, of course, exceptions. *See, e.g.*, United States v Salerno, 974 F2d 231 (2d Cir 1992) (erroneous exclusion of hearsay evidence requires reversal of RICO conviction), panel opinion vacated & case remanded to panel, __ F3d __ (2d Cir Nov 1, 1993).

[45] Lyons v Jefferson Bank & Trust, 994 F2d 716 (10th Cir 1993); *see also* **§5.03.**

appellate action. Too, an issue may be held to have been preserved even though not specifically identified in the trial court.[46]

The goal of rethinking is to present the most coherent possible set of issues. The appellate advocate seeks to rediscover a short, persuasive way of saying why the judgment must be reversed; the only way to do that is by retracing the steps taken by trial counsel, who in preparing for trial identified the main themes that then required a certain outcome.

The second task is selection. As later sections discuss in more detail,[47] an appellate brief freighted with subsidiary issues sinks of its own weight. Putting weak issues with strong ones saps the latter, and does not infuse the former. Lawyers are supposed to have the courage, skill, and knowledge to make choices. The test of a strong issue is whether a simple, powerful statement of it can be made in concluding the sentence, "The judgment must be reversed because. . . ."

Counsel for the appellee sometimes think they have only to defend the judgment below, which means telling the appellate court the same thing they told the trial court, and adding how right the trial court was. Counsel who think this way are wrong. Countless cases have been reversed because appellee's counsel failed to rethink the case and refused to acknowledge possible vulnerability.

An example will illustrate. Suppose the trial judge has granted summary judgment for a defendant. Federal Rule of Civil Procedure 56, and the caselaw construing it, set out in detail the procedure for considering a summary judgment motion.[48] The trial judge will most likely have pored over the affidavits and exhibits, perhaps bringing to the task long familiarity with the case. The order granting summary judgment may be accompanied by findings of fact and conclusions of law.

To win summary judgment, the advocate will have had to master detail and even highly technical law and lore. Having followed the advice above, the defeated plaintiff will rethink the case and focus on dispositive issues.

The rule most important to the plaintiff-appellant will be that court of appeals review of the grant of summary judgment is de novo. Under current law, no matter how much time the district judge has spent, nor how carefully she or he has found the facts, the court of appeals makes an independent judgment of whether the case should be tried based upon a set of briefs, study of the record portions that the parties cite, and oral argument.[49]

---

[46] Examples include acquittal and directed verdict points.

[47] *See* **§§9.08, 9.10.**

[48] *E.g.*, Celotex Corp v Catrett, 477 US 317 (1986); Anderson v Liberty Lobby, Inc, 477 US 242 (1986); Matsushita Elec Indus Co v Zenith Radio Corp, 475 US 574 (1986). This trilogy of cases redefined summary judgment standards and practice. *See* Samuel Issacharoff & George Lowenstein, *Second Thoughts About Summary Judgment,* 100 Yale LJ 73 (1990).

[49] *E.g.*, Abercrombie v City of Catoosa, 896 F2d 1228, 1230 (10th Cir 1990) (court of appeals reviews the grant or denial of summary judgment de novo, applying the same standard as the district court; inferences to be drawn, regardless of whether summary

The appellant will be stressing the need for a trial. If the appellee burrows into the minutiae that were so important in the district court, she or he risks supporting the appellant's position by making the case seem hard and complicated enough that summary disposition is inappropriate.

So while "the district court (or agency, or Tax Court) was right," is no doubt a consistent and worthwhile appellee's theme, it must be brigaded with "my client is right."

§1.07 The Appellate Advocate's Library—Basic Research Tools

Decisions on what to buy for a law library are highly personal and affected by budget, access to public library facilities, and areas of practice specialization. This section presents a coherent view of the minimum library resources for a firm that does federal appellate work. The list assumes that the office has this treatise and its annual supplements.

The Computer and Legal Research

Computer-assisted legal research is considered first because the investment one makes in books and library access will be shaped by initial decisions about the kind of computer system to have.

The ideal computer system for a law office will be able to handle word processing for brief writing, desktop publishing for reproducing briefs, high speed computer-assisted legal research through Westlaw or LEXIS, CD-ROM access to treatises and other materials that are available in this format, and fax capability. In addition, the lawyer may want to use the computer for calendaring, timekeeping, accounting, and billing.

The law office will necessarily consider whether to have stand-alone computers or any of several versions of a network. Once hardware is chosen, the software options are myriad. The following checklist should be helpful.[50]

1. IBM-compatible 386 or 486 chip-based computer central processing unit, with send and receive fax modem rated at least at 9600 baud and data modem no slower than 2400 baud. With this equipment, the attorney can send and receive faxes from the desktop PC and have access to Westlaw or Lexis at data transmission speeds that are generally available

---

judgment was granted or denied, in favor of party opposing the motion); Christopher v Mobil Oil Corp, 950 F2d 1209, 1213-14 (5th Cir 1992) (semble).

[50] One hesitates to recommend particular brands, particularly in so fast-moving and volatile a market. Recommendations in the text and footnotes are based on experience, and on recommendations of the American Bar Association Legal Technology Committee (LTAC), which evaluates computer hardware and software. Winning With Computers: Trial Practice in the Twenty-First Century (John C. Tredennick, Jr & James A. Eidelman eds 1991) and Winning With Computers, Part 2 (John C. Tredennick, Jr & James A. Eidelman eds 1993).

throughout the country. In addition, data files can be transferred from one computer to another.

2. Lawyers who are computer-trained should have access to laptop PCs with hard disks and data-fax modem capabilities.
3. A laser printer that supports desktop publishing software sophisticated enough for the particular law office. If the printer is to be used for trial graphics, more sophistication is required than if its most complex function will be producing briefs for the court of appeals.
4. CD-ROM (Compact Disc—Read Only Memory) attachment. The entire text of some treatises and caselaw collections are now available on compact discs that resemble the ones in record stores. The disc player is hooked up to the computer serial port, providing access to the entire text of the treatise or reporter. The CD-ROM is an advantage because of its light weight and portability.[51] Moreover, the reader can search the ROM for particular word combinations.
5. Word processing and spreadsheet software, discussed in more detail in Chapter 9.
6. Westlaw or LEXIS, or both. The choice is to some extent a matter of personal preference. I prefer Westlaw. The libraries, at least for United States materials, are more complete. The command structure seems easier to use. West has invested heavily in making it easier to consult, research, and download from its databases. Moreover, West has developed citechecking software under the name WestCheck that can be integrated with your word processing program. This software runs citation verifications at the chosen level of detail, improving accuracy and saving valuable lawyer and paralegal time.

Basic Library

1. Annotated United States Code, either USCA or FCA. In addition, each advocate's office should contain the latest West pamphlet edition of Titles 18 and 28 of the United States Code, with the current Rules of Civil Procedure, Criminal Procedure, Evidence, and Appellate Procedure. Although the annotated codes contain current texts of court of appeals rules, the law office whose practice is primarily in one or more courts of appeals should have the current edition of the rules as published by the Clerk of Court.[52]

2. *Federal Practice and Procedure* is a multivolume set authored by Charles Alan Wright, Arthur Miller, and Mary Kay Kane (1990). Published by West Publishing, it is greatly superior to the competing product, and every law firm that does any federal litigation should have a set in its library or nearby. The treatise also is available on CD-ROM.

3. Thomas E. Baker, *A Primer on the Jurisdiction of the U.S. Courts of Appeals* (1989), published by the Federal Judicial Center, Dolley Madison House, 1520

---

[51] Bookshelves take up a lot of expensive floor space in the typical law office.

[52] Addresses of courts of appeals are given in **ch 4.**

H St., N.W., Washington, D.C. 20005. This introductory volume supplements the discussion of jurisdictional issues in this book.

4. Charles Alan Wright, *Federal Courts* (4th ed 1983). This book belongs in the office of every lawyer who does any federal practice. It provides quick answers and valuable research insights.

5. David Knibb, *Federal Court of Appeals Manual* (2d ed 1990), is a valuable reference, but most of the information in it is found in this treatise.

6. Federal Reporter, 2d Series. Having one's own library of Federal Supplement is less important, as such cases are available on Westlaw. The only district court opinions of consequence to the appellate practitioner are those certifying matters for appeal under 28 USC §1292(b) or Fed R Civ P 54(b).[53]

7. An edition of Supreme Court Reports, either Lawyer's Edition or West.

8. Shepard's Citators. These indispensable works are available on line from Westlaw, and I find less need than formerly to have paper editions.

Other Library Materials

1. A source of information on current trends in federal appellate litigation. ALR Fed deals with both substantive and procedural federal law, so may not be worth the cost. United States Law Week is a good investment for the federal practitioner. It identifies significant cases from around the country. More importantly, it keeps one informed of current issues before the Supreme Court, including, of course, federal jurisdictional matters. Browsing Law Week can help the lawyer identify potential issues on appeal.

2. Steven A. Childress & Martha S. Davis, *Federal Standards of Review* (2d ed 1992).

3. Edward J. Devitt, Charles B. Blackmar, Michael A. Wolff, & Kevin O'Malley, *Federal Jury Practice and Instructions: Civil and Criminal* (4th ed 1992). This valuable research tool identifies the elements of federal civil and criminal causes of action, and contains pattern instructions on procedural and evidentiary issues that often arise in federal litigation. Each pattern charge is supported by careful research. Thus, the set helps one to identify issues on appeal and begin research. West Publishing Company also publishes pattern jury instruction pamphlets for many of the circuits. Some of these are valuable.

4. *Appellate Practice Manual* (Priscilla A. Schwab ed 1992).

Specialized Works

For the lawyer whose practice concentrates on particular areas, there are valuable specialized treatises. Among these are:

1. James S. Liebman, *Federal Habeas Corpus Practice & Procedure* (1988). This three-volume set is regularly updated.

2. Wayne R. LaFave & Austin W. Scott, Jr, *Criminal Law* (2d ed 1986). There is also a multi-volume set by the same authors, entitled *Substantive Criminal Law.*

---

[53] *See* §§2.09, 2.10.

3. Wayne R. LaFave & Jerold H. Israel, *Criminal Procedure* (2d ed 1992). This treatise is available in a single-volume student edition as well as in a more complete multivolume format under the same title.

4. Stephen A. Saltzburg & Michael M. Martin, *Federal Rules of Evidence Manual* (5th ed 1990). This treatise is a valuable introduction to any evidence issue. In addition to the text of the Federal Rules of Evidence, the Advisory Committee Notes and any legislative history, the book consists principally of case summaries from the courts of appeals.

5. Lissa Griffin, *Federal Criminal Appeals* (1992).

6. Joel M. Androphy, *White Collar Crime* (Shepard's/McGraw-Hill 1992).

Other Sources

Larger law offices and those that specialize in particular fields will identify law journals and treatises appropriate to their practice.

All litigating lawyers should become members of the American Bar Association Section of Litigation. Members receive the section's quarterly publication, *Litigation,* and regular news on litigation matters. In addition, section members can join as many section committees as they wish. Many of these committees publish newsletters with valuable information and legal research. The Appellate Practice Committee has a particularly fine newsletter on current developments.

Specialized bar groups such as the American Trial Lawyers Association, Federal Bar Association, and the National Lawyers Guild have valuable programs and publications. The American Inns of Court chapters provide important opportunities to meet and learn from colleagues of the bench and bar.

Many of the courts of appeals have bar associations. The lawyer who practices regularly in one or more circuits should join. Some of the circuits, such as the Fifth, publish journals with guides to current circuit law and practical articles on appellate practice.

§1.08 —The Lore and Literature of Advocacy

Persuading an appellate tribunal requires more than thorough research and shrewd evaluation of issues. Appellate advocacy—as a kind of argument to the court—has its own lore and literature. The wise advocate will make these the objects of careful study. There are four ways to do this.

First, read the speeches and writings of great orators and advocates, and delve into the theory and history of rhetoric. The craft of advocacy has been studied, taught, and collected for millenia. Modern advocates are using devices and techniques that trace long roots. There is a distressing modern tendency to dismiss the study of rhetoric, and even the search for eloquence and elegance of expression, as unnecessary. It is true that the term *rhetoric* is sometimes used to describe orotund and exaggerated modes of expression.[54] Rightly described, rhetoric is the study of persuasive speech.

Robert Hanley, one of the great advocates of the 20th century, titled his 1986 article in Litigation magazine, *Brush Up Your Aristotle.* His theme will be familiar to anyone who pages through this treatise. Hanley said he was addressing trial advocates, but the basic techniques are the same in any court. Here is an excerpt:

> Demosthenes of Athens was the greatest orator of ancient Greece. His eloquence, says Professor Epiphanius Wilson, was of unique power.
>
> According to Professor Wilson: "It is the intellectual grasp, the trenchant vehemence, the face and vigor of the orator that affect us." Demosthenes scorned mere ornaments of rhetorical finish. "Yet his language has all the living glow, all the purity, all the transparency that belongs to the best age of Attic Greek. . . ."
>
> How did he do it? Can he light the fires of today's advocates?
>
> Demosthenes' oratory was simple and unadorned. He used it in a lifelong struggle against Philip II of Macedonia (hence the term "philippic"). Demosthenes justifiably feared that Philip intended to extinguish Greek liberty.
>
> By his words, Demosthenes drew the Thebans into a confederacy against Philip. The Thebans at the time were the best soldiers in the world, but, according to Plutarch, they had before their eyes the terrors of war and their losses in the Phocean troubles were still recent; but such was the force and power of the orator [Demosthenes] fanning up . . . their courage and firing their emulation that casting away every thought of prudence, fear or obligation in a sort of divine possession, they chose the path of honor, to which his words invited them, and this success, thus accomplished by an orator, was thought to be so glorious and of such consequence that Philip immediately sent his heralds to entreat and petition for a peace. . . .
>
> Nice result.
>
> What Demosthenes was to Greek advocacy, Marcus Tullius Cicero was to Roman advocacy.
>
> Plutarch tells us: "For Cicero, it may be said, was the one man, above all others, who made the Romans feel how great a charm eloquence lends to what is good."
>
> These were powerful advocates.
>
> In a school for trial lawyers, Cicero's De *Oratore* and Demosthenes' *Orations* should be required reading.
>
> The students' heads should be filled with excellent advocacy—from the classics to the trials of Edward Bennett Williams—and with the literature

---

[54] For a longer discussion of the modern uses of insights from the study of rhetoric, see Michael E. Tigar, Examining Witnesses 1-28 (1993). *Examining Witnesses* is primarily devoted to trial technique. The first chapter, however, sets out a theory of advocacy and persuasion.

> of trials—from Aristophanes, Tacitus, and Shakespeare's *Julius Caesar, Henry V,* and *Richard II* to Wordsworth's *Character of the Happy Warrior.* The students would read great speeches too: Henry George's "The Curse of Poverty," Abraham Lincoln's "A House Divided," and Adlai Stevenson's "There Are No Gibraltars."
>
> They would discover power through simplicity, grace, and unadorned sincerity.
>
> Then, when they are panting to learn how to duplicate these masterpieces, they should be hit with a good solid dose of Aristotle's *Rhetoric* and Quintilian's *Institutes of Oratory.*
>
> These were geniuses who knew how to make language work. There were few writers of rhetoric before them. There were few teachers. What they had was a magnificently sensitive power of observation. They learned by raw observation of human behavior what makes arguments tell—how to persuade, how to change the minds of biased listeners.
>
> Lane Cooper, in his book *The Rhetoric of Aristotle,* says that Aristotle's treatise on rhetoric is one of the world's best and wisest books. It is a book to be chewed and digested. It is the greatest of all books on the philosophy and technique of persuasion. The work is "a textbook of human feeling; a storehouse of taste; an example of condensed and accurate, but uniformly clear and candid, reasoning."[55]

To Hanley's list one might add the two-volume set *The World of Law,* edited by Ephraim London and published by Simon & Schuster.[56] Darrow's great arguments and speeches are collected in *Attorney for the Damned.*[57] *Litigation* magazine, the quarterly where Hanley's article appeared, contains regular features on great advocacy. Notable cases of former days have been collected in several series, available in any large law library; these include collections called *Howell's State Trials,* and *Notable British Trials.*[58]

It is possible to obtain texts of United States Supreme Court arguments. Many of these repay study. For example, Edward Bennett Williams's argument in *Alderman v United States*[59] is a masterpiece of rhetorical style and appellate advocacy. To find an oral argument that may provide inspiration and instruction, one can choose a Supreme Court case and then look up the argument transcript in the law library. Or, one can run a Westlaw or LEXIS search for

---

[55] Robert F. Hanley, *Brush Up Your Aristotle,* 12 Litig No 2, at 39 (Winter 1986) (reprinted by permission).

[56] The World of Law (Ephraim London ed 1960).

[57] Clarence Darrow, Attorney for the Damned (Arthur Weinberg ed 1957).

[58] A Complete Collection of State Trials (Thomas B. Howell ed 1816). Notable British Trials Series (1927). Freedom of Expression: A Collection of Best Writings (Kent Middleton & Roy M. Mersky eds 1981).

[59] Reargument, Alderman v United States, 394 US 165 (1968) (No 133), microformed on Oral Arguments of the Supreme Court of the United States: The Warren Court, 1953 Term-1968 Term, Case 133, Reargument 1967 term, Fiche 1 (Univ Publications of America).

the name of an advocate in whose work one is interested and find cases in that way.

Robert Bolt's play, *A Man For All Seasons,* contains stirring examples of the advocate's art, taken mostly from surviving records of Sir Thomas More's trial. The reader with access to a first-class law library ought to read some of Erskine's speeches in defense of seditious libel cases and, of course, Andrew Hamilton's defense of the colonial newspaper editor, John Peter Zenger.[60]

Second, volunteer to work with good advocates and to observe them as they prepare for and argue cases. In a law firm, in a public interest office, as a pro bono lawyer—the process will differ from setting to setting. Yet, watching a good advocate put together the prepared part of an argument, and anticipate questions, is an unmatched learning experience.

In some law firms and government agencies, advocates who are to present oral argument are *mooted* by their colleagues. Attend these sessions. In a law firm, try to attend oral arguments presented by firm members. The experience is valuable enough that one might offer to assist in argument preparation and not bill the client for the time, nor expect the time spent to count towards one's quota of hours.

Sensible firms and sensible clients encourage the participation of younger lawyers in this way, and their attendance at arguments. In complex litigation, where teamwork is essential, team morale and team understanding of the common problems are greatly enhanced by this sort of involvement.

At the very least, seize any opportunity to listen to several sessions of federal court of appeals or United States Supreme Court arguments. Indeed, at least one court of appeals requires applicants to its bar to attend argument sessions before being admitted.

Third, one can participate in appellate training programs and seminars. The value of these varies greatly. Until recently, law school courses and intermural and intramural competitions on appellate advocacy stressed debate skills. The record from which students argued was derisorily short. Oral presentation was stressed to the detriment of written briefs. Judging was based on debate competition criteria, rather than criteria derived from the practice of winning advocates and the experience of judges.

These inadequate offerings have been reformed, largely through efforts of the Appellate Judges Conference of the ABA Judicial Administration Division, and the Law Student Division entities responsible for intermural advocacy competitions. In addition, the Appellate Judges Conference has created a library of appellate records that can be used for law school courses and in competitions give participants a more realistic picture of appellate work.

The ABA Section of Litigation and the Appellate Judges Conference also sponsor appellate practice institutes, usually every other year. Those enrolled

---

[60] For discussion of and citations to advocacy in these celebrated cases, see Michael E. Tigar, *Crime Talk, Rights Talk, and Double-Talk: Thoughts on Reading Encyclopedia of Crime and Justice,* 65 Tex L Rev 101 (1986). Some cases containing excellent examples of advocacy include *Rex v Zenger,* 17 Howell's State Trials 675 (1735); *Rex v Woodfall,* 20 Howell's State Trials 895 (1770); *Rex v Miller,* 20 Howell's State Trials 880 (1770); and *Rex v Shipley,* 21 Howell's State Trials 847 (1783).

are required to submit a brief before the institute begins. The brief is intensively edited by a judge, advocate, or academic. At the institute, lectures on basic principles are followed by small group instruction. In the small groups, enrollees will make one or more oral arguments and be critiqued.

Less intensive, but still valuable, are appellate advocacy sessions presented by bar groups and law schools. In several of the circuits, seminars are sponsored by circuit bar associations; these sessions often feature significant participation by sitting federal judges.

Except for law students who already have paid their tuition, these seminars can be expensive. The best ones follow the principles suggested above:

First, choose a learning setting that stresses the full range of research, preparation, and communication skills required of an advocate, and stay away from those that replicate debate society methods.

Second, choose a seminar that either gives enrollees a chance to perform and be evaluated, or at the least stresses demonstrations rather than lectures.

Third, remember that if you want to catch fish, a candid fish is a better authority than even the wisest fisherperson. Choose a seminar in which judges talk about how they organize their work, evaluate arguments, and respond to written and oral advocacy.

Fourth, do it. Brief and argue appeals. In every jurisdiction, dozens of indigents need appellate representation. Sources of these cases include bar associations, including the ABA Section of Litigation; local pro bono referral agencies; public interest and public service entities; and judges and clerks.

In this way, the lawyer fulfills a professional obligation while sharpening vital skills.

2 Federal Appellate Jurisdiction—What Is an Appealable Order?

§2.01 The Constitutional and Statutory Bases of Federal Appellate Jurisdiction

The courts of appeals, and their powers, are creatures of statute under the constitutional provision that "[t]he judicial power of the United States, shall be vested in one supreme Court, and in such inferior Courts as Congress shall from time to time ordain and establish."[1] The courts of appeals, as an intermediate judicial step between the district court and the Supreme Court, were created by the Evarts Act in 1891,[2] part of significant reforms of the federal judicial system. When first established, there was one circuit court of appeals for each then-existing judicial circuit. The Evarts Act established that circuit courts would sit in panels of three.

The court of appeals is, in almost all cases, the court of last resort for litigants. Congress has progressively narrowed the Supreme Court's compulsory jurisdiction; that is, the kinds of cases the Court must hear because a litigant has the right to review by appeal. The distinction between appeals and petitions for certiorari (appeals formerly fell under the mandatory jurisdiction of the Court, which was therefore required to hear them, while the Court granted certiorari in its discretion) has largely evaporated. Almost every case now falls under the Court's discretionary jurisdiction.[3]

In 1925, the Congress established the Supreme Court's discretionary certiorari jurisdiction, and limited the right of review to a fairly narrow class of cases.[4] The Congress has also progressively limited the Supreme Court's power to review trial court decisions directly without an intervening hearing in the court of appeals.[5]

A 1988 statute abolished virtually all remaining categories of Supreme Court review of right.[6] The Congress eliminated direct appeal to the Court in civil

---

[1] US Const art III, §1.

[2] The Circuit Court of Appeals Act of 1891, ch 517, 26 Stat 826. *See generally* Henry Hart & Herbert Wechsler, The Federal Courts and the Federal System 42-47 (1st ed 1953). An excellent assessment of the first 100 years of the federal courts of appeals is ABA, Standing Committee on Federal Judicial Improvements, The United States Courts of Appeals: Reexamining Structure and Process after a Century of Growth (1989), available from the American Bar Association.

[3] *See* Robert L. Stern, Eugene Gressman, & Stephan M. Shapiro, *Epitaph for Mandatory Jurisdiction,* 74 ABAJ 66 (Dec 1988); Bennett Boskey & Eugene Gressman, *The Supreme Court Bids Farewell to Mandatory Appeals,* 109 S Ct LXXXI (1988).

[4] Act of February 13, 1925, ch 229, 43 Stat 936. The Supreme Court's jurisdiction is now defined at 28 USC §§1251-1254, 1257-1259. For the background of this legislation, see Charles A. Wright, Federal Courts 1, 4 (4th ed 1983). In this treatise, discussion is limited to the cases in the United States courts of appeals. Such cases reach the Supreme Court under 28 USC §1254, which provides for review by certiorari before or after judgment in the court of appeals, or by the almost never used power of the court of appeals to certify a question to the Supreme Court.

[5] *See* **§2.15.**

[6] Review of Cases by the Supreme Court Act, Pub L No 100-352, 102 Stat 662 (1988) (repealing 28 USC §§1252) (appeals involving federal statutes), and amending §1254(2) (state statutes), and of 28 USC §1257(1), (2) (highest state court appeals, including Dis-

cases in which a federal statute is declared unconstitutional and the United States is a party, and in cases where state statutes are declared unconstitutional. The Court does retain the power to grant certiorari before judgment in the court of appeals[7] as a means of bringing important cases to it quickly for authoritative resolution. The Court exercised this power in *United States v Mistretta,*[8] a case involving the constitutionality of the federal sentencing guidelines; the issue was clearly of great and immediate significance, and the United States sought review. Direct appeals to the Supreme Court in three-judge court cases are still authorized,[9] as are some antitrust appeals.[10]

The Supreme Court will hear only 125 or so cases per year on full briefing and argument. It selects these from the more than 5,000 certiorari petitions it receives each year in cases from federal courts of appeals and state courts of last resort.[11] Even these figures overstate the odds of obtaining Supreme Court review for a private litigant, because the federal government, as petitioner, is more likely to obtain a grant of certiorari. Therefore, in the overwhelming majority of cases, the court of appeals is the highest federal tribunal where a litigant may receive a hearing on the merits.

Although the courts of appeals and their jurisdiction are creatures of statute, distinguishing between appellate and original jurisdiction of the courts of appeals presents the same issue decided in *Marbury v Madison,*[12] in which the Supreme Court construed the appellate jurisdiction versus original jurisdiction language in article III of the Constitution. The courts of appeals are, like all federal courts, of limited jurisdiction.[13] This means that a court may well inquire on its own motion into its power to hear a case.[14]

---

trict of Columbia), and §1258 (parallels changes made in §1257 as applicable to the Supreme Court of Puerto Rico).

[7] 28 USC §1254 and Sup Ct R 11 (Jan 1, 1990). *See also* James Lindgren & William P. Marshall, The Supreme Court's Extraordinary Power to Grant Certiorari Before Judgment in the Court of Appeals, [1986] Sup Ct Rev 259.

[8] 486 US 1054 (1988).

[9] 28 USC §1253.

[10] 15 USC §29(b).

[11] The standards applied by the Supreme Court in accepting cases on certiorari are ably discussed in Charles G. Cole, *Petitioning for Certiorari in the Big Case,* 12 Litig No 3, at 33 (Spring 1986). The standard work on Supreme Court practice is Robert L. Stern, Supreme Court Practice (6th ed 1986).

[12] 5 US (1 Cranch) 137 (1803).

[13] *See, e.g.,* Firestone Tire & Rubber Co v Risjord, 449 US 368, 379 (1981) ("finality requirement embodied in §1291 is jurisdictional in nature"; court of appeals has no discretion to waive it). The court of appeals obligation to inquire into its jurisdiction even if the question is not raised by the parties is discussed in, e.g., United States v Pan Am Management Co, 789 F2d 632, 635-36 (8th Cir 1986) (citing Liberty Mut Ins Co v Wetzel, 424 US 737, 740 (1976)).

[14] Some jurisdictional errors are curable. For example, if a litigant arrives in the court of appeals only to discover a fatal jurisdiction error was committed in the district court, the court of appeals has some limited authority to remedy the matter. If the allegations of jurisdiction are defective, 28 USC §1653 permits amendment in the trial or appellate court. If, however, jurisdiction is lacking because a nondiverse party is present, the court

The advocate must understand well the basic outlines of federal appellate court power, and take seriously the obligation to invoke that jurisdiction by acting timely and appropriately. This obligation is underscored by cases holding that Congress has broad power to control and allocate the jurisdiction of the federal courts and to restrict and condition the right to review.[15]

The congressional power to prescribe the jurisdiction of the courts of appeals is not, however, limitless. This is illustrated by two Supreme Court cases, *United States v Klein,*[16] and *Ex parte McCardle.*[17] Klein filed suit in the Court of Claims seeking recovery of property captured during the Civil War. The statute under which he sued required him to prove either that he had never given aid and comfort to the rebel states, or that he had taken and obeyed an oath of allegiance and had received a general amnesty and pardon. Klein had received a pardon, but it stated that he had been disloyal. He won in the Court of Claims. While his case was pending on appeal in the Supreme Court, the Congress passed a statute providing that in any war claim case involving an appeal by one whose pardon recited previous disloyalty, the Supreme Court was without jurisdiction and should dismiss the appeal. The Court invalidated the act, holding that the Congress had attempted to prescribe a rule of decision retroactively and had thereby invaded the judicial power.

By contrast, McCardle was arrested during the Civil War for publishing disloyal articles and was held in military custody. He sought habeas corpus from a trial court. He appealed the denial of his petition to the Supreme Court. The Congress, fearful that the Court might invalidate military jurisdiction in such cases, hastily passed a statute repealing the portions of the habeas statute that authorized an appeal to the Supreme Court. The Court acquiesced and dismissed the appeal for want of jurisdiction.

The rule of these cases has come to be that Congress may prescribe the jurisdiction of the inferior federal courts, but may not tell the courts how that jurisdiction is to be exercised. This formulation probably begs more questions than it answers, but fortunately Congress has provided few occasions for the courts to consider the issue.

This book's discussion of federal court of appeals jurisdiction proceeds as follows:

This chapter, Chapter 2, sets out the statutory basis for court of appeals review by appeal of orders of courts and administrative agencies, and the case law interpretation of these statutes. Review by appeal is the statutory descen-

---

of appeals has the authority to dismiss the nondiverse party. It need not remand to the district court for this purpose. Newman-Green, Inc v Alfonzo-Larrain, 490 US 826 (1989). A valuable guide is *Staff Attorneys' Instructions to Case Managers Re: Checking for Jurisdictional Defects,* 10 Fifth Cir Rep 609 (1993).

[15] *See generally* Yakus v United States, 321 US 414 (1944). An example of Congress's exercise of this power is the creation and operation of specialized courts of appeals such as the Temporary Emergency Court of Appeals, discussed at **§4.15,** and the United States Court of Appeals for the Federal Circuit, discussed at **§§2.16, 4.14.**

[16] 80 US (13 Wall) 128 (1871).

[17] 74 US (7 Wall) 506 (1868).

dant of the common law writs of error and certiorari. It reviews a record of a proceeding that occurred in some other tribunal.

Chapter 3 deals with extraordinary writs. These are original proceedings in the court of appeals, undertaken under the authority of the All Writs Act, 28 USC §1651.

Other chapters also contain valuable basic information on lodging and maintaining an appellate proceeding. The advocate must decide where (Chapter 4), when (Chapter 6), and what (again Chapter 6) papers to file. The rules discussed in these chapters are mainly jurisdictional, in that failure to comply with them will result in an appeal being dismissed with no further chance of reviving it.

Other rules are discussed in the remaining chapters, dealing with filing motions (Chapter 8) and briefs (Chapter 9). Failure to observe these rules may cause the court of appeals to impose sanctions, including dismissal of an appeal.

§2.02 Final Judgments in Civil Cases: 28 USC §1291

28 USC §1291 is the basic provision of federal law for appeals from final judgments in the district courts. It provides:

> The courts of appeals (other than the United States Court of Appeals for the Federal Circuit) shall have jurisdiction of appeals from all final decisions of the district courts of the United States, the United States District Court for the District of the Canal Zone, the District Court of Guam, and the District Court of the Virgin Islands, except where a direct review may be had in the Supreme Court. The jurisdiction of the United States Court of Appeals for the Federal Circuit shall be limited to the jurisdiction described in sections 1292(c) and (d) and 1295 of this title.[18]

---

[18] The provision "except when a direct review may be had in the Supreme Court" is now largely anachronistic, because direct review has been narrowed by the Congress. *See* Charles A. Wright, Federal Courts 105 (4th ed 1983). Direct review may be obtained in certain ICC and antitrust cases, when the district judge makes the appropriate certification. 15 USC §29; 49 USC §45. Direct review is also available from three-judge court determinations holding an Act of Congress unconstitutional, if the United States or one of its officers or agencies is a party. 28 USC §1252. *See generally* Walters v National Assn of Radiation Survivors, 473 US 305 (1985). The Supreme Court's jurisdiction in cases where such direct review is available is exclusive of the court of appeals. However, the Court may remand the case to the appropriate court of appeals if it does not have a qualified quorum to hear the appeal. 28 USC §2109. *See* **§2.15.**

For discussion of certiorari before judgment, see **§2.01.**

The Federal Circuit's powers are discussed in **§2.12** and **§4.14.**

This statute raises the following questions: *What* is a final judgment[19] for purposes of appeal? *When* is a judgment final for purposes of appeal? This section deals with *what.* The question of *when* is important primarily for purposes of timely filing a notice of appeal and is principally dealt with in Chapter 6.[20]

A final judgment must be *adverse, documented,* and *dispositive.*

Adverse means that the judgment must be hostile to the interests of the appellant. One may not appeal a judgment to which one has consented,[21] or that grants all the relief for which one has asked. For example, if the plaintiff moves for voluntary dismissal under Fed R Civ P 41(a)(1), and the judge grants the motion on condition that the plaintiff pay the defendant's attorney fees, the court of appeals will likely hold that the plaintiff has no right of appeal.[22] The proper remedy would be to move to withdraw the motion to dismiss and appeal the denial as an abuse of discretion.[23]

On the other hand, the collateral consequences of a favorable judgment may permit the judgment winner to appeal. In *Aetna Casualty & Surety Co v Cunningham,*[24] Aetna was permitted to appeal a judgment in its favor for the exact amount prayed in its complaint. The district judge had upheld Aetna on its contract theory, but held Cunningham not guilty of fraud. Aetna claimed that

---

[19] The statute speaks of final decisions. Caselaw speaks indifferently of final judgment and final order. As noted in the text below, Fed R Civ P 58 refers to judgment. The terms are for most purposes interchangeable.

[20] *See* **§§6.03, 6.04.**

[21] Swift & Co v United States, 276 US 311, 328 (1928); United States v Bechtel Corp, 648 F2d 660, 663 (9th Cir), *cert denied,* 454 US 1083 (1981). As discussed in **§5.15,** one must be wary of the consent problem when the court dismisses a complaint with leave to amend. Standing on the dismissal complaint and appealing risks a holding that the appellant could have solved the problem by amending, and therefore is foreclosed from appeal.

One can also expressly waive the right of appeal, and such waivers are enforceable. *See* DeGarmo v Collins, 984 F2d 142, 143 (5th Cir 1993) (court enforces state's written stipulation that it would not appeal grant of habeas relief and dismisses state's appeal, warning of sanctions on this "dismal record").

[22] In Unioil, Inc v EF Hutton & Co, 809 F2d 548 (9th Cir 1986), the district judge told the plaintiff that she would grant their motion for voluntary dismissal but would impose a condition that plaintiffs reimburse defendants for costs and attorneys' fees. Plaintiff did not withdraw its motion, but took the voluntary dismissal and appealed. The court of appeals held that the order appealed from did not involve *legal prejudice.* Agreement, even reluctantly, to entry of the order makes the order not adverse. The opinion contains extensive discussion of holdings by various courts of appeals on this issue. *See also* St Paul Fire & Marine Ins Co v United States, 959 F2d 960 (Fed Cir 1992) (plaintiff's dismissal of its complaint was not truly voluntary; court of appeals therefore had jurisdiction).

[23] *Cf* Mortgage Guar Ins Corp v Richard Carlyon Co, 904 F2d 298 (5th Cir 1990) (*legal prejudice* may be found if conditions of dismissal are unduly onerous; plaintiff must be given a reasonable time to withdraw motion to dismiss).

[24] 224 F2d 478 (5th Cir 1955). See also the discussion in **§2.03** of Parr v United States, 351 US 513 (1956).

a contract judgment would be dischargeable in bankruptcy, and on this basis the court heard the appeal on the merits.[25]

"Every judgment shall be set forth on a *separate document*,"[26] according to Fed R Civ P 58. A judgment is not, therefore, the same thing as a memorandum opinion. The separate document[27] called for by Fed R Civ P 58 must then be entered on the docket as provided in Fed R Civ P 79(a).

The *separate document* requirement has been extensively litigated, and illustrates that sometimes the question of "what is a final judgment" may overlap with "when is a judgment final." For example, in *United States v Indrelunas,*[28] a docket entry was made on March 21, 1969, noting jury verdicts in favor of the respondent and another in favor of the government. The formal judgment specifying the amount of the verdicts was entered on February 25, 1971. The government began, and then abandoned, an appeal from the 1969 docket entry, and then began a new appeal from the 1971 order. The Supreme Court held that Fed R Civ P 58 meant that the 1971 order was properly appealed from, and that the government did not forfeit its appeal right by having taken and then aborted the earlier appeal. This decision was disavowed by *Bankers Trust Co v Mallis*:[29] The Court upheld the court of appeals jurisdiction to hear an appeal even though Fed R Civ P 58 had not been complied with and there was no separate document. The Court regarded the Rule 58 requirement as waivable by the parties.

Fed R Civ P 58 serves an important purpose, by requiring a prevailing party to obtain a clear signal, on the record, that the district judge has finished the work of deciding the case.[30] But the rule can become a trap. Suppose a party

---

[25] There is some authority that a party may consent to a judgment and reserve the right to appeal, provided it does so unequivocally. Coughlin v Regan, 768 F2d 468, 470 (1st Cir 1985); Bash v Firstmark Standard Life Ins Co, 861 F2d 159, 163 (7th Cir 1988).

[26] Fed R Civ P 58 (emphasis supplied).

[27] Fed R Civ P 58 is discussed in Amoco Oil Co v Jim Heiling Oil & Gas, Inc, 479 US 966 (Blackmun & O'Connor, JJ, dissenting from denial of certiorari), *cert denied,* 786 F2d 1163 (6th Cir 1986). *See also* Wood v Coast Frame Supply, Inc, 791 F2d 802 (9th Cir), *amending* 779 F2d 1441 (9th Cir 1986) (where one party has not waived Fed R Civ P 58 requirement, and district court may not have concluded ruling on all issues in the case, court of appeals lacks jurisdiction of appeal); Ellender v Schweiker, 781 F2d 314, 318 (2d Cir 1986) (determining factor under *Mallis* is whether district judge intended the order embodied in the separate document to be the final judgment, even though it may not have set out the precise relief awarded).

Of course, a Fed R Civ P 58 judgment, or the order accompanying it, must be specific enough under Fed R Civ P 52(a) so that a reviewing court can tell what has been decided. Warner Bros v Wilkinson, 782 F2d 136 (10th Cir 1985).

[28] 411 US 216 (1973) (per curiam).

[29] 435 US 381 (1978) (per curiam).

[30] Blazak v Ricketts, 971 F2d 1408 (9th Cir 1992). In Foremost Sales Promotions, Inc v Bureau of Alcohol, Tobacco & Firearms, 812 F2d 1044 (7th Cir 1987), *as amended,* 860 F2d 229 (7th Cir 1988), the district court had held for the plaintiff on cross-motions for summary judgment and entered a minute order to that effect. However, the court had noted that a further memorandum and order were to be entered. Held, the entry was not a final judgment and the court of appeals had no jurisdiction. *See also* National

wins in the district court, but fails to see that a separate document is entered containing the judgment. The time for appeal is not running, and the judgment will not, in theory, become final. Some courts of appeals allow this kind of stalemate to continue for a time, then dispense with the Rule 58 requirement.[31]

The separate document trap can be sprung the other way, however. In *Hollywood v City of Santa Maria*,[32] the Ninth Circuit held that the Rule 58 requirement could not be applied to render the district court's memorandum order denying a new trial ineffective to start the time for appeal running. Therefore, a notice of appeal filed more than 30 days after the order denying new trial was untimely.

To avoid the Rule 58 trap and put the appeal safely on track, the parties in the district court must seek entry of judgment in compliance with Fed R Civ P 58 and 79(a), and must regularly check the docket to make sure the request has been complied with.[33]

The most basic meaning of finality is that the judgment being appealed effectively ends the litigation in the district court or agency. In *Cobbledick v United States*,[34] Justice Frankfurter wrote of the origins and justification of the finality principle:

> Finality as a condition of review is an historic characteristic of federal appellate procedure. It was written into the first Judiciary Act and has been departed from only when observance of it would practically defeat the right to any review at all. Since the right to a judgment from more than one court is a matter of grace and not a necessary ingredient of justice, Congress from the very beginning has, by forbidding piecemeal disposition on appeal of what for practical purposes is a single controversy, set itself against enfeebling judicial administration.[35]

RR Passenger Corp v City of New York, 882 F2d 710 (2d Cir 1989); Frank Rosenberg, Inc v Tazewell County, 882 F2d 1165 (7th Cir 1989), *cert denied*, 493 US 1023 (1990). Where the district court judge has retained jurisdiction to enforce compliance with an injunction, that order is final and appealable even in the absence of a Rule 58 judgment order; an interim decree that assumes the entry of a further order is not appealable. Patterson v Portch, 853 F2d 1399, 1403 (7th Cir 1988).

[31] Fiore v Washington County Community Mental Health Ctr, 960 F2d 229 (1st Cir 1992) (en banc) (in the 1st Circuit, Rule 58 will be strictly enforced and requires that orders denying or granting postjudgment motions must be set forth on a separate document; the time for appeal will not begin to run unless and until that separate document is obtained and entered; court of appeals imposes a three-month window for this process, and held that after the expiration of three months, the judgment should be treated as final to avoid the prospect of long dormant cases suddenly being revived and taken to the court of appeals).

[32] 886 F2d 1228 (9th Cir 1989).

[33] The docket check also will give notice of motions, the filing of which suspends the operation of the judgment or otherwise affects the timing or validity of a notice of appeal. *See* **§6.03.**

[34] 309 US 323 (1940) (district court order denying motions to quash grand jury subpoenas and directing appearance and document production was not a final order).

[35] *Id* 324-25.

This passage echoes the familiar principle that there is no constitutional right to an appeal, although of course there is a right to equal protection and due process for all litigants if appeals are allowed.[36]

In *Catlin v United States,*[37] the Court held that a final judgment "ends the litigation on the merits and leaves nothing for the court to do but execute the judgment." Thus, in a civil case, judgment on the merits of all claims in the action will usually be final.

In a diversity proceeding, federal law governs the question of what constitutes a final judgment for the purposes of §1291.[38]

Among easily identifiable *nonfinal* decisions are those denying summary judgment motions,[39] settling discovery disputes,[40] disqualifying counsel,[41] and consolidating or severing actions and claims.[42] Grant of a new trial is almost never an appealable order,[43] even if coupled with a remittitur; that is, if the trial judge reduces the jury's award and gives the prevailing party the option of accepting the reduced amount or submitting to a new trial, the party cannot hold on to the reduced amount and take an appeal.[44]

---

[36] Jones v Barnes, 463 US 745, 751 (1983); Griffin v Illinois, 351 US 12, 18, (1956); Douglas v California, 372 US 353, 355-56, (1963).

[37] 324 US 229, 233 (1945).

[38] Budinich v Becton Dickinson & Co, 486 US 196, 198-99 (1988) (applying the test of Hanna v Plumer, 380 US 460 (1965)).

[39] *See, e.g.,* Pacific Union Conference of Seventh Day Adventists v Marshall, 434 US 1305 (1977) (Rehnquist, J, in chambers); Forsyth v Kleindeinst, 599 F2d 1203 (3d Cir 1979), *cert denied,* 453 US 913 (1981). Of course, a denial of summary judgment may present an appealable order if the issue is one on which interlocutory appeals are routinely available, see **§2.04;** or if the denial is made the subject of a 1292(b) certificate, see **§2.09;** or if the order is in effect the denial of a preliminary injunction, see **§2.06.** Review also may be available, in a rare case, by extraordinary writ. *See* **§§3.01-3.03.** In the usual case, however, denial of a summary judgment motion means only that the case has enough merit to warrant a trial at which the movant may win or lose.

[40] Milton Roberts, Annotation, *Appealability of Discovery Order as "Final Decision" under 28 USC 1291,* 36 ALR Fed 763 (1978). While a discovery order with respect to a party is usually not appealable, nonparty discovery orders stand on a different footing. See the discussion in **§2.04.** *See also* Heat & Control, Inc v Hester Indus, 785 F2d 1017 (Fed Cir 1986) (in patent infringement action, West Virginia district court's quashing of subpoena for witness over whom California court, where action was pending, had no jurisdiction was immediately appealable because there would be no effective means of challenging the order on appeal from a final judgment).

[41] Firestone Tire & Rubber Co v Risjord, 449 US 368 (1981).

[42] Gary D. Spivey, Annotation, *Appealability of Federal Court Order Granting or Denying Consolidation, Severance or Separate Trials,* 30 ALR Fed 393 (1976).

[43] *See* Smith v National RR Passenger Corp, 856 F2d 467, 470 (2d Cir 1988) (order granting new trial appealable when issued in conjunction with the grant or denial of judgment nov and the new trial is conditional upon appellate reversal of that judgment).

[44] *See, e.g.,* Seltzner v RDK Corp, 756 F2d 51 (7th Cir 1985) (if plaintiff is not satisfied with the outcome of the new trial, he can appeal from the judgment entered at that trial and seek reinstatement of the original jury award). The remittitur rules were applied and discussed in Hattaway v McMillian, 903 F2d 1440 (11th Cir 1990). After a jury verdict for $500,000 in this civil rights case, the trial judge granted additur, raising the amount to $843,603, but giving the defendants the option of a new trial on damages

In addition, some orders are made nonappealable, nonreviewable, or nonfinal by statute. Examples include certain orders remanding removed civil cases to state court,[45] orders in the conduct of multidistrict litigation,[46] and some types of orders compelling arbitration.[47]

A party disappointed by a decision that is ostensibly nonfinal or nonreviewable may nonetheless have other avenues to the appeals court than §1291. These are discussed elsewhere in this chapter and in Chapter 3.[48]

Beyond the clear categories established by caselaw, the finality rule has proven difficult to apply. As the Supreme Court remarked in *Eisen v Carlisle & Jacquelin,*[49] "[N]o verbal formula yet devised can explain prior finality decisions with unerring accuracy or provide an utterly reliable guide for the future."[50]

---

only. The defendants accepted the additur and appealed. The court of appeals recognized that additur violates the Seventh Amendment, but held that acceptance of it, even under protest, waived the defendants' right of appeal. Their proper course was, as in the case of remittitur, Donovan v Penn Shipping Co, 429 US 648 (1977), to go through a new trial and then appeal. The *Hattaway* decision seems questionable. Granted that a new trial on damages might moot the issue, but additur is clearly impermissible and remittitur is not. Perhaps the court should have treated the appeal as a petition for writ of mandamus. Better yet, the defendants should have sought mandamus or prohibition (to confine the court to the lawful exercise of its jurisdiction).

[45] *See* **§2.15.** The FDIC is permitted to appeal remand orders under a special statutory provision of FIRREA, 12 USC §1819(b)(2). *See In re* Resolution Trust Corp, 888 F2d 57 (8th Cir 1989). The extraordinary power of the FDIC to remove state litigation to federal court has created problems of interpretation and appealability. *In re* Meyerland Co, 960 F2d 512 (5th Cir 1992) (en banc), *cert denied,* 113 S Ct 967 (1993).

[46] *See* **§§3.04, 3.05,** and **4.01.**

[47] *See* **§2.15.**

[48] *See* **§§2.09, 2.10, 2.15-2.17,** and **3.04-3.14.**

[49] 417 US 156, 170 (1974). The Court repeated, 417 US at 171, that the requirement of finality is to be given a "practical rather than a technical construction" (quoting Cohen v Beneficial Indus Loan Corp, 337 US 541, 546 (1949)) (discussed in detail in **§2.04**). *See also* Ellender v Schweiker, 781 F2d 314, 317-18 (2d Cir 1986) (final judgment on the merits is not made less final by inclusion of provision deciding collateral matter of attorneys' fees).

[50] 417 US at 170. Only a review of appellate decisions can enable counsel to develop a sense of what will satisfy the finality requirement. *See, e.g.,* Hicks v NLO, Inc, 825 F2d 118 (6th Cir 1987) (plaintiff who suffered summary judgment as to all but one of her claims dismissed the remaining claim without prejudice and appealed; held, the dismissal made the earlier grant of summary judgment a final appealable order); Benjamin v United States, 833 F2d 669 (7th Cir 1987) (dismissal of complaint alone is not an appealable order); Sherpell v Humnoke Sch Dist No 5, 814 F2d 538 (8th Cir 1987) (order finding violation of students' and parents' rights under 42 USC §§1983 and 1985 and requiring defendant to initiate affirmative action plan not final and appealable); Plasterers Local Union No 346 v Wyland Enters, 819 F2d 217 (9th Cir 1987) (stipulated judgment not appealable where stipulation is entered merely to gain review); Kearns v Shillinger, 823 F2d 399 (10th Cir 1987) (order refusing appointment of special master not appealable). For a perceptive treatment of appellate review issues arising in the forum non conveniens context, see David W. Robertson, *Forum Non Conveniens in America and England: "A Rather Fantastic Fiction,"* 103 Law Q Rev 398, 415-16 (1987).

In *Brown Shoe Co v United States,*[51] the district court had concluded that a merger violated the antitrust laws, and had ordered divestiture and other remedies. However, the court had directed the parties to file a detailed plan for carrying out the divestiture order. Both parties contended that the judgment was final for purposes of review. The Supreme Court declined to accept this concession, however, because "consent . . . cannot, by itself, confer jurisdiction" and "a review of the sources of the Court's jurisdiction is a threshold inquiry appropriate to the disposition of every case that comes before us."[52]

The Court, using a pragmatic approach, found the order was final. It noted that the district court had disposed of the entire complaint. Divestiture had been ordered and there was no turning back from that decision. The detailed divestiture order, the Court noted, would require negotiation in light of fluctuating market conditions. Insisting that such an order be entered before review could be obtained might be futile, in that the order being reviewed would with the passage of time become "impractical or otherwise unenforceable."[53]

Gillespie v United States Steel Corp[54] represents a controversial extension of the finality principle. The plaintiff sued under the Jones Act as administratix of her son's estate. The son had been killed while working on a US Steel ship. The complaint also included claims under Ohio law and claims of unseaworthiness under general maritime law. The district judge struck all the state law and unseaworthiness claims. This, said Justice Black for seven justices, was a final judgment: ". . . in deciding the question of finality the most important competing considerations are 'the inconvenience and costs of piecemeal review on the one hand and the danger of denying justice by delay on the other.' " Justice Black gave some deference to the court of appeals' decision to hear the appeal and then noted that "now that the case is before us . . . the eventual costs . . . will certainly be less if we now pass on the questions presented here rather than send the case back with those issues undecided."[55]

The Court's analysis has been criticized for its ad hoc, case-by-case character,[56] and was sharply limited in a later decision.[57] Moreover, Justice Black's

---

[51] 370 US 294 (1962). On appealability of orders in antitrust cases, see generally John P. Luddington, Annotation, *Appealability of Orders in Government Antitrust Actions,* 10 ALR Fed 607 (1972).

[52] 370 US at 305-06. The direct appeal statute involved in Brown has been repealed. Charles A. Wright, Federal Courts §105 (4th ed 1983). However, the principles of finality set out in Brown retain their vitality. *See also* **§2.15.**

[53] 370 US at 309. Division of liability and remedy issues will not always so easily yield an appealable order. In Way v Reliance Ins Co, 815 F2d 1033 (5th Cir 1987) the parties had agreed that, in the event of a liability finding, they would arbitrate the issue of damages. Liability having been found, the loser appealed. Held, no final judgment. Quaere, whether a §1292(b) certification would have solved the problem.

[54] 379 US 148 (1964).

[55] *Id* 152-53.

[56] Criticism is summarized in Charles A. Wright, *supra* note 52, §101, at 705-07.

[57] Criticism of Gillespie is summarized in Charles A. Wright, *supra* note 52, §101, at 705-07. Gillespie was limited to its unique facts in Coopers & Lybrand v Livesay, 437 US 463, 477 n30 (1978) and distinguished into almost certain oblivion by the unani-

judicial economy argument is subject to question. Once a case has been in the appellate process for some time, it will usually be possible to argue that the appellate court might as well resolve all the issues now rather than waiting. However, this reasoning contains several flaws. First, depending on the ultimate outcome in the trial court, it may be unnecessary for any appellate court to ever review the questions presented. For example, if Gillespie had recovered a judgment on her Jones Act claim, the dismissed claims would merge in it and there would be no need to review them unless the opponent had successfully attacked the Jones Act judgment.

Moreover, the finality rule serves to prevent courts of appeals from committing the constitutional and prudential sin of issuing an advisory opinion.[58] If the nonfinal order is subject to revision by the court that entered it, or may never actually prejudice the appellant, there are serious constitutional questions in a court opining on it. As a prudential matter, deciding complex issues of law without the full record that might accompany a final judgment is risky business.[59]

A less controversial and less expansive finality holding is *Goodall-Sanford, Inc v United Textile Workers,*[60] which held final a decision compelling arbitration

---

mous opinion ("if Gillespie is extended beyond the unique facts of that case, 1291 would be stripped of all significance"). However, in Granberry v Greer, 481 US 129 (1987), the Court held that in a habeas corpus case, when the state contends for the first time in the court of appeals that the petitioner failed to exhaust state remedies, the court of appeals has the option of addressing the merits forthwith or remanding the case for further proceedings.

In Mallory v Eyrich, 922 F2d 1273, 1279 (6th Cir 1991), the Sixth Circuit applied the *Gillespie* doctrine to uphold the appealability of an order granting relief under Fed R Civ P 60(b)(6) from a judgment entered under Fed R Civ P 68. The court also held that Fed R Civ P 68 judgments are generally final. The discussion is confusing, because a Rule 68 judgment may be entered with respect to less than all the issues in a case, leaving the question of finality unresolved.

[58] The rule against advisory opinions is based upon the constitutional command that the judicial power is limited to cases and controversies. *See generally* Charles A. Wright, *supra* note 52, §12. However, the prudential and discretionary aspect of the doctrine appears in such cases as Muskrat v United States, 219 US 346 (1911). *See also* FCC v Sanders Bros Radio Station, 309 US 470 (1940) (radio station that will suffer economic, as opposed to signal interference, harm from grant of license to rival may not have standing to be a party in FCC proceeding, but is a *party aggrieved* for judicial review purposes).

[59] As the Court recognized in Firestone Tire & Rubber Co v Risjord, 449 US 368, 374 (1981), the preference for finality is a mark of deference to the district judge, who has the primary responsibility for developing the factual record. As a practical matter, appeal of an order entered before the lawsuit has run its course cuts off the district judge's opportunity to reconsider the challenged order or to take corrective action.

However, it is equally true that when the district judge makes it unequivocally clear that he or she has disposed of the entire case, an order is a final judgment. Ellender v Schweiker, 781 F2d 314, 318 (2d Cir 1986).

[60] 353 US 550 (1957).

under a labor agreement when that was the only relief sought.[61] However, a 1988 amendment to the Federal Arbitration Act specifically denies appealability to any "interlocutory order . . . directing arbitration,"[62] no doubt in the interest of forcing parties to go through with arbitration before prolonging court litigation by appeal. Because the order in Goodall-Sanford was final in the sense that it disposed of the entire action, the Act might not apply. Moreover, arbitration under a labor agreement might not be *under* the Arbitration Act. Appealability issues in the arbitration context are discussed at **§2.15.**

The Supreme Court has wrestled with the problem of orders that ostensibly leave the litigation alive but, realistically viewed, prevent a party from ever prevailing on reasonable terms. Several courts of appeals had found such orders appealable under what came to be known as the death knell doctrine. However, the Supreme Court killed the doctrine in *Coopers & Lybrand v Livesay.*[63] The Livesays and others brought a class action against an accounting firm and a corporation, alleging federal securities law violations. The district court first certified, then, after further hearings, decertified a class. The court of appeals held that it could review the decertification order because it removed the economic incentive for the plaintiffs to pursue their lawsuit.

The Supreme Court unanimously reversed, holding that a decertification order was not final under §1291, and that it was not appealable under the collateral order doctrine.[64] The Court first held that the death knell doctrine was inherently arbitrary in its application to class action decertification orders. If special rules of appellate review should be enacted for class actions, the Court reasoned, Congress should provide them. The Court noted that the contours of the doctrine appeared to turn upon speculative calculations about the value of a class action in permitting aggregation of small individual claims. Moreover, the doctrine was uniquely applied to plaintiffs seeking certification. The courts of appeals had held that a defendant objecting to certification could not immediately appeal.

The principal vice of the death knell doctrine, said the Court, was that it authorized indiscriminate interlocutory review without the screening process

---

[61] *Id.*

[62] Judicial Improvements and Access to Justice Act of 1988, Pub L No 100-702, 102 Stat 7671 (codified as amended at 9 USC §15(b) (1988), later redesignated 9 USC §16(b)(2) by Pub L No 101-650, __ Stat 5120 (1990)).

[63] 437 US 463 (1978). *Coopers & Lybrand* signals the end of any rational contention that the courts of appeals are free to fashion discretionary and loosely constructed exceptions to the finality principle. The Court's decision was unanimous in rejecting several theories upon which such doctrines have been constructed. The decision surprised some observers because the Second Circuit had upheld the death knell theory in Eisen v Carlisle & Jacquelin, 370 F2d 119, 121 (2d Cir 1966), *cert denied,* 386 US 1035 (1967), and this holding was cited with apparent approval when the *Eisen* litigation eventually reached the Supreme Court, 417 US 156, 162 (1974).

[64] Discussed at **§2.04.**

provided for in 28 USC §1292(b).[65] That section, discussed in **§2.09,** requires that the district judge consent to an interlocutory appeal, and that the court of appeals agree to hear it. This procedure ensures that appeals courts retain their distinct role, and not be "thrust . . . indiscriminately into the trial process."[66] Moreover, courts of appeals ought not be burdened with having to determine, in every case, the particular facts supporting or denying appealability.

In 1983, the Court again considered the finality problem and found an order appealable over the dissenters' objection that the majority was ignoring the teaching of *Coopers & Lybrand.* In *Moses H. Cone Memorial Hospital v Mercury Construction Corp,*[67] the hospital sued Mercury in state court under a construction contract. Mercury invoked a contractual provision mandating arbitration, but to no avail. Mercury then filed a diversity suit in federal district court, seeking an order compelling arbitration under §4 of the Federal Arbitration Act. The hospital moved to stay the federal lawsuit, and the district judge stayed the federal action pending the outcome of the state action. Was the stay order a final judgment? Yes, said Justice Brennan for six justices.

The stay would have permitted the state court to resolve all the issues between the parties, including that of arbitrability. Its decision would be res judicata and the federal action would simply be dismissed. Therefore, the stay order meant that Mercury was "effectively out of court."[68] True, Mercury had its state remedy, but it was out of federal court, where, under a well-settled rule, it had every right to be. Thus, "this stay order amounts to a dismissal of the suit."[69]

---

[65] 437 US at 474-75.

[66] *Id* 476. Some circuits have extended the holding of *Coopers & Lybrand* to bar immediate review of all certification decisions, affirmative or negative. *See* Lusardi v Lechner, 855 F2d 1062, 1067 (3d Cir 1988).

[67] 460 US 1 (1983).

[68] *Id* 10 (quoting Idlewild Bon Voyage Liquor Corp v Epstein, 370 US 713, 715 n2 (1962)).

[69] *Id. Moses H. Cone* was distinguished in Hartford Financial Sys v Florida Software Servs, 712 F2d 724, 726 (1st Cir 1983). The court of appeals, in an opinion that reviewed cases from other circuits, held that the rule of *Moses H. Cone* and kindred cases is limited to situations in which the stay order effectively denies the appellant any judicial remedy at all. In most cases in which a district court grants or denies a stay to permit arbitration, the order will not be reviewable.

A dismissal from federal court is final even if litigation will continue in state court. "[A]n order that ends litigation in one dispute-resolution system is final and appealable even though it kicks off litigation in another." Disher v Information Resources, Inc, 873 F2d 136, 139 (7th Cir 1989). In *Disher,* the plaintiff brought securities claims in both state and federal court on the same basic facts. After he prevailed in state court, he activated his federal suit. The district judge granted summary judgment for defendants on all but two state law counts, which he dismissed without prejudice, noting that these claims should properly be tried in the state courts. The defendants, believing they were entitled to a dismissal with prejudice, appealed. The Seventh Circuit found jurisdiction.

Effectively out of court is not so broad as *death knell,* for the former requires that the district court have taken a procedural step that makes the lawsuit legally nonviable, as opposed to unduly financially burdensome. The distinction may be unintelligible to a litigant, for whom a financial barrier to the federal courts is as onerous as a procedural one, but *Coopers & Lybrand* was unanimous and the courts of appeals have not rushed to broaden the meaning of finality.[70] To maintain any semblance of consistent meaning to *final,* it seems preferable to limit the term to judgments that dispose of the entire action and to remit reviewability issues for other orders to the settled categories of certified questions,[71] collateral orders,[72] prerogative writs,[73] and the special statutory treatment given some classes of orders and claims.[74]

Sometimes, however, it is difficult to say where the entire action ends, and a new proceeding begins. For example, statutes and caselaw give parties the right to recover attorney fees in some types of lawsuits. The claim for attorney fees typically does not arise until a judgment is entered on the merits. Then, the trial judge must begin an often complicated inquiry into the proper fee.

In *White v New Hampshire Department of Employment Security,*[75] the Court held that a claim "for attorney's fees under [42 USC] §1988 raises legal issues collateral to the main cause of action." Based on this reasoning, the Court found that the district judge's ruling on a fee request made after the main part of the action was over did not deprive the merits judgment of finality for appeal purposes. *White* thus settled the issue of finality for a fee request made under a statutory provision separate from that on which the lawsuit is based.

In such a case, the judgment settling the lawsuit is final and appealable without waiting for resolution of the fee issue. By the same token, the fee issue may be the subject of a separate appeal.[76]

---

[70] *See, e.g.,* Barnes v Bosley, 790 F2d 718 (8th Cir 1986) (order granting employee reinstatement and ordering back pay but not fixing amount not appealable, discussing *Coopers & Lybrand*). The variety of situations calling for finality analysis is too great to permit more than a brief overview in this treatise. *See, e.g.,* Ohio-Sealy Mattress Mfg Co v Duncan, 714 F2d 740 (7th Cir 1983) (denial of arbitration not a final order; court can always reconsider), *cert denied,* 464 US 1044 (1984); Shore v Parkland Hosiery Co, 606 F2d 354 (2d Cir 1979) (order limiting intervention to proposed class settlement a grant of intervention and not appealable); Hawaii-Pacific Venture Capital Corp v Rothbard, 564 F2d 1343 (9th Cir 1977) (order denying intervention not appealable); New York Pub Interest Research Group, Inc v Regents of the Univ, 516 F2d 350 (2d Cir 1975) (denial of intervention appealable); Weiser v White, 505 F2d 912 (5th Cir) (order denying intervention not appealable), *cert denied,* 421 US 993 (1975). The appealability of orders granting or denying transfer is discussed in 15 Charles A. Wright & Arthur R. Miller, Federal Practice and Procedure 3194 (1977). *See also* **§3.07.**

[71] *See* **§§2.09, 2.10.**

[72] *See* **§§2.04, 2.05.**

[73] *See* **ch 3.**

[74] *See* **§§2.13-2.17.**

[75] 455 US 445, 451 (1982).

[76] *See* Sidag Aktiengesellschaft v Smoked Foods Prods Co, 813 F2d 81 (5th Cir 1987) (attorney fee award to defendant will usually be collateral issue; order establishing right to fees, but not fixing amount, is not final and cannot be made final by Fed R Civ P

The Supreme Court clarified matters in *Budinich v Becton Dickinson & Co,*[77] holding that "[a]s a general matter . . . a claim for attorney's fees is not part of the merits of the action to which the fees pertain."[78] Therefore, a judgment on the underlying claim that does not resolve the attorney fee issue is final under §1291. The finality rule is unyielding in the sense that the time for taking an appeal from the merits judgment begins to run and the losing party does not have the option of waiting for the attorney fee award and appealing all questions at the same time. As a practical matter, however, if the attorney fee award can be made expeditiously, the separate appeal from that decision can be consolidated with the merits appeal by motion in the court of appeals.[79]

Despite *Budinich,* problems of finality, and therefore of timely appeal, remain in attorney fee cases. For example, if a creditor sues to collect a debt, and the debt instrument entitles it to attorney fees, as is often the case, the debt judgment and attorney fee award could be regarded as a single decision for §1291 purposes.[80] Counsel's only recourse is to file a notice of appeal in reliance on *Budinich,* then to file a second notice when the attorney fee issue is decided. The parties and the court of appeals can then sort out whether one notice or two is necessary.

The attorney fee cases are one aspect of a broader problem created by the liberal joinder, consolidation, and severance provisions of the Federal Rules of Civil Procedure. A federal civil suit may be a Hydra-headed beast, either at its inception or by virtue of case management orders uniting separate cases or severing issues for separate trial. The courts of appeals are split on appeala-

---

54(b) certificate), *appeal after remand,* 854 F2d 799 (5th Cir 1988), *appeal after remand,* 960 F2d 564 (5th Cir 1992).

[77] 486 US 196 (1988).

[78] *Id* 200.

[79] For motions practice, see **ch 8.**

[80] *See, e.g.,* Barrington Press, Inc v Morey, 816 F2d 341 (7th Cir) (judgment upholding promissory notes and reciting that prevailing party was entitled to attorney's fees resolved both merits and fee issue), *cert denied,* 484 US 906 (1987) (White, J, dissenting from denial of certiorari). *See also* Alter Fin Corp v Citizens & S Intl Bank, 817 F2d 349 (5th Cir 1987) (district court did not exceed scope of remand order by imposing attorney fees as sanction on losing appellant); Jaffe v Sundowner Properties, Inc, 808 F2d 1425 (11th Cir 1987) (order imposing sanction not final until amount of attorney fees determined); First Nationwide Bank v Sumer House Joint Venture, 902 F2d 1197 (5th Cir 1990) (clear explanation of *Harcon* and *Budinich* rules; judgment is final when entered despite reservation of attorney fee issue and later amendment to correct spelling of one party's name; therefore, new trial motion filed more than ten days later was untimely under Fed R Civ P 59 and would be construed as Fed R Civ P 60(b) motion; in consequence, new trial motion did not extend time for filing notice of appeal from original judgment; only issue on appeal is propriety of denying Fed R Civ P 60(b) motion, which is tested by forgiving abuse of discretion standard). *But see* Justine Realty Co v American Natl Can Co, 945 F2d 1044 (8th Cir 1991), *revd on the merits,* 976 F2d 385 (8th Cir 1992). The Eighth Circuit disagrees with the Fifth Circuit's decision in *First Nationwide,* and holds that *Budinich* applies only to fees incurred in litigation. Fees due under a contract and "incurred in pre-litigation performance of the contract" are tied to the merits. Therefore, a motion to set those contract fees was made under Rule 59(e) and tolled the time for appeal.

bility from dispositive orders in cases consolidated under Fed R Civ P 42(a).[81] When circuit law denies a §1291 appeal, the disappointed litigant may find review under other provisions.[82] Where an appeal is permitted, however, it must be taken timely.

While a final decision is a necessary precondition of appeal under §1291, the appeal brings before the court of appeals all interlocutory orders in the lawsuit that can be said to have affected the outcome. For example, an appeal from a money judgment permits the loser to argue that evidentiary rulings made by the trial judge were prejudicially wrong.[83]

§2.03 —Defendant's Appeals in Criminal Cases

A criminal defendant may not, with exceptions discussed in **§2.05,** appeal except from a final judgment of conviction.[84] In *Cobbledick v United States,*[85] the Supreme Court stressed the special importance of the final judgment rule in criminal cases. This rule is straightforward. As the Supreme Court has said repeatedly, "Final judgment in a criminal case means sentence. The sentence is the judgment."[86]

Thus, a defendant is usually precluded from appealing orders denying various forms of pretrial relief, including dismissal. For example, in *DiBella v United*

---

[81] *Compare* Kamerman v Steinberg, 891 F2d 424 (2d Cir 1989) (when district court enters final judgment on one of several actions consolidated in that court, no appeal lies unless Fed R Civ P 54(b) certification is entered) *with* Albert v Maine Cent RR, 898 F2d 5 (1st Cir) (time for appeal in one of several consolidated actions runs from grant of summary judgment, and not from final disposition of all consolidated cases; appeal dismissed as untimely), *cert denied,* 498 US 807 (1990).

[82] *See* **§§2.09, 2.10, 2.15-2.17,** and **3.04-3.14.**

[83] Hill v Bache Halsey Stuart Shields, Inc, 790 F2d 817 (10th Cir 1986); Whalen v Unit Rig, Inc, 974 F2d 1248 (10th Cir 1992), *cert denied,* No 92-1236, 1993 WL 22848 (US 1993). The appellate court may disregard this rule, however, where adherence would reward a party for dilatory and bad faith tactics. *See* Sere v Board of Trustees, 852 F2d 285 (7th Cir 1988).

The party who prevailed below will not, however, be permitted to claim error from interlocutory rulings, because the *judgment* is not adverse to it. The appeals court will review such lower court rulings only if necessary to provide guidance to the trial judge in the event a new trial is ordered. See **§6.10** for discussion of when the judgment winner should file a protective cross-appeal.

[84] This section deals with defendants' appeals only. The government's right to appeal, which is limited by statute (principally 18 USC §3731), and by the double jeopardy clause of the Fifth Amendment, is discussed in **§2.11.**

[85] 309 US 323 (1940).

[86] Berman v United States, 302 US 211, 212-13 (1937) (even if accused is given a suspended sentence of imprisonment or a fine, he still has been convicted and sentenced and is entitled to appeal from the judgment). The language in *Berman* was cited in Parr v United States, 351 US 513, 518 (1956).

If probation is revoked under Fed R Crim P 32.1, the order is appealable. *See* 3 Charles A. Wright, Federal Practice and Procedure, Criminal 2d 542, at 234 (1982 & Supp 1993).

States,[87] the Court held that the district judge's denial of a motion to suppress evidence obtained in violation of the Fourth Amendment was not appealable. *DiBella* put an end to the Second Circuit's practice of hearing appeals from such orders.

Despite *DiBella,* a civil proceeding to challenge an unlawful seizure procedure remains available under Fed R Crim P 41(e).[88] Denial of a preindictment motion for return of property Rule 41(e) challenge to unlawful search and seizure may be appealed by the challenger, provided no indictment has been returned.[89]

In *United States v Hollywood Motor Car Co,*[90] the Court held that denial of a defendant's motion to dismiss based on prosecutorial vindictiveness was not appealable. The Court distinguished cases, discussed in **§2.05,** permitting interlocutory appeal of refusals to dismiss based upon double jeopardy. In the double jeopardy case, the defendant is asserting a right not to be tried at all. Following *Hollywood,* the courts of appeals have been quite hesitant to hear appeals other than from judgments of conviction, rightly believing that the Supreme Court's tolerance for such appeals is limited.

This rationale has been used to deny appealability to orders dismissing cases without prejudice under the Speedy Trial Act.[91] The defendant arguably is aggrieved by such orders, because they permit the prosecution to start again. However, the prospect of such further litigation is taken to mean that the dismissal is but a step towards an eventual judgment. Moreover, the prosecution might not bring the case again or the defendant might be acquitted.

Because of the short time allowed the defendant to appeal a criminal judgment—usually ten days[92]—finality questions often must be resolved quickly. The advocate uncertain on the point should file a protective notice of appeal. The issue of finality can be troublesome when the defendant has been convicted of multiple counts and is not sentenced on all counts at the same time.[93] Under Fed R Crim P 11(a)(2), a defendant can enter a plea of guilty conditioned on the right to appeal one or more issues, usually search and seizure issues.[94]

---

[87] 369 US 121 (1962).

[88] A civil action for return of property also may be available.

[89] For citation of authorities, see **§2.05.**

[90] 458 US 263 (1982).

[91] United States v Kelly, 849 F2d 1345 (11th Cir 1988); United States v Tsosie, 966 F2d 1357 (10th Cir), *cert denied,* 113 S Ct 358 (1992); United States v Ford, 961 F2d 150 (9th Cir 1992).

[92] Fed R App P 4(b), discussed in **§6.04.**

[93] *See also* United States v Patel, 835 F2d 708 (7th Cir 1987) (defendant sentenced at separate times on counts indicted and tried together may wait until the last sentence is imposed, then have 10 days to file notice of appeal).

[94] Rule 11 was amended in 1983 to end a circuit split on the appealability of judgments of conviction entered on conditional pleas of guilty. Some courts had held that such a judgment was not adverse to the defendant, because it had been consented to. *See* **§2.02.** *See also* Advisory Committee Notes to 1983 Amendment of Rule 11. The Supreme Court had approved the concept of conditional please in Lefkowitz v Newsome, 420 US 283, 193 (1975) (discussing New York practice).

There is some authority that the acceptance of the plea is final for appeal purposes.[95]

The teaching of the cases discussed above has been applied to appeals from orders directing compliance with grand jury subpoenas. The grand jury investigation is regarded as part of the criminal process and deserving of the same deference towards finality.[96] *Cobbledick* itself involved a grand jury subpoena for testimony and documents that the movants had been directed to obey. The Supreme Court held that the denial of the motion was not an appealable order. It held that the movant would have to appear in response to the subpoena or be held in contempt. The contempt order would be final and therefore appealable.[97] This is now accepted law, although in extraordinary cases mandamus relief may be available from an order denying a motion to quash,[98] and **§2.05** suggests how the collateral order doctrine may be invoked to obtain appeal of an order arising in a grand jury investigation.

Finality questions may also arise when a defendant is facing multiple or successive proceedings. In *Parr v United States,*[99] the defendants were indicted in the Southern District of Texas, where they resided, for tax fraud. They obtained a transfer to a division of the district where the government thought it would not receive a fair trial. So the government reindicted in the Western District of Texas, where the returns were filed, for the same offenses. It then moved to dismiss the Southern District case. The district judge granted the motion over the defendants' vigorous opposition. The defendants appealed the dismissal. The Supreme Court held that the Parrs had no right of appeal unless and until a final judgment of conviction was entered in the Western District prosecution. If the Southern District case were considered by itself, the defendants were not aggrieved by the order and could not appeal.[100] If the Southern and Western District cases were considered together, the dismissal was simply

---

[95] United States v Green, 847 F2d 622 (10th Cir 1988) (notice of appeal may be filed after conditional plea of guilty and before sentencing).

[96] An extensive discussion of the finality principle in the context of grand jury litigation appears in *In re* Grand Jury Investigation (Lance), 610 F2d 202, 221-28 (5th Cir 1980) (Kravitch, J, dissenting). *See also* National Lawyers Guild, Representation of Witnesses Before Federal Grand Juries 2-26 to -38 (1985).

[97] This was the situation in, e.g., Gelbard v United States, 408 US 41 (1972). The witness presented a live controversy by being held in contempt.

[98] *See* **§3.13.**

[99] 351 US 513 (1956).

[100] For a discussion of the requirement that the appellant be aggrieved by the order, see **§§2.02, 2.19.** A leading speedy trial denial case is United States v Grabinski, 674 F2d 677 (8th Cir) (en banc) (per curiam), *cert denied,* 459 US 829 (1982). *See also* United States v Mehrmanesh, 652 F2d 766 (9th Cir 1980). A related issue, that of an alleged broken plea bargain, is United States v Bird, 709 F2d 388 (5th Cir 1983) (accused claiming prosecution barred by immunity agreement must await conviction to challenge denial of motion to dismiss).

a "step toward final disposition of the merits of the case" and would be "merged in the final judgment."[101]

While the sentence is a final judgment for almost all claims arising from the trial and pretrial, there may be some claims not yet ripe for presentation on the first appeal. For example, claims of ineffective assistance of counsel at a federal criminal trial may usually be raised only on collateral attack under 28 USC §2255 for both practical and jurisdictional reasons. A practical reason is that trial counsel is often the one who argues the appeal, and one can hardly be expected to argue his or her own ineffectiveness. The jurisprudential reason is that most claims of ineffective assistance require development of a record on the reasons for trial counsel's decisions, and such record has usually not been made in the district court. Indeed, the issue itself has usually not been raised in the district court while the case is on direct appeal. Some ineffectiveness claims must be raised on direct appeal, however, on pain of being barred from raising them in collateral proceedings. These claims include those in which the defendant is no longer represented by trial counsel on direct appeal and the ineffectiveness claim therefore would not be aided by further development of the record.[102]

As in any case, the district court in a criminal matter may be called upon to construe or apply its judgment and decision. For example, in *United States v Beech-Nut Nutrition Corp,*[103] a probationer under federal sentence sought permission to travel in Europe to pursue job opportunities and the district court denied relief. The court of appeals held the denial an appealable order, even though the defendant did not appeal his original sentence imposing probation. The court distinguished cases in which the defendant is belatedly seeking to challenge the conditions of probation as opposed to their application; that sort of challenge must be raised on direct appeal of the sentence and judgment.[104]

Under the Sentencing Guidelines legislation passed in 1984 and, for the most part, effective beginning in 1987, a defendant may appeal a sentence on certain grounds that were not available before the Act took effect.[105] Under 18 USC §3742(a), the defendant may appeal a sentence that was imposed in violation of the sentencing guidelines, that was greater than the guideline range sentence, or that was a plainly unreasonable sentence for which there is no guide-

---

[101] *Parr,* 351 US at 519 (quoting Cohen v Beneficial Indus Loan Corp, 337 US 541, 546 (1949)). *See also* United States v Day, 806 F2d 1240 (5th Cir 1986) (order dismissing indictment without prejudice not final and therefore not appealable).

[102] See Beaulieu v United States, 930 F2d 805 (10th Cir 1991), which discusses the principles involved. The court notes, *id* 807 n2, "in close cases, prudent defense attorneys will raise ineffectiveness assistance claims on direct appeal."

[103] 925 F2d 604 (2d Cir 1991).

[104] *See* United States v Ofchinick, 937 F2d 892 (3d Cir 1991), holding that a probationer's claim that the district court improperly calculated monthly income when entering an order requiring restitutionary payment is ripe for appellate review when entered. Probationer need not wait until failure to make the payment and subsequent revocation of probation.

[105] Thus, the appeal provisions do not apply to pre-Guidelines sentences.

line. Section 3742(a) restates the appealability of a sentence imposed in violation of law, and of course procedural errors in sentence continue to be appealable as before.[106]

Under §3742, the defendant has no right of appeal if the district judge has discretion and exercises it adversely to the defendant. A defendant may, however, appeal a departure from the guidelines.[107]

The Supreme Court clarified the issue in two cases decided during the 1991 Term. In *Wade v United States,*[108] the Court held that a defendant is entitled to challenge, on constitutional grounds, the government's refusal under 18 USC §3553(e) to move for a downward departure of the defendant's guideline sentence in exchange for "substantial assistance." Therefore, the district court's denial of relief would be subject to appeal. In *Williams v United States,*[109] the Court held that a sentence imposed under a mistaken interpretation of a Sentencing Commission policy statement is "imposed as a result of an incorrect application of the sentencing guidelines" within the meaning of 18 USC §3742(f)(1) and therefore is appealable. *Williams* expands appealability beyond claims based on the terms of the guidelines themselves.

Appealability will, in this area as in others, depend upon counsel's ability to make a record that the judge engaged in an error of law rather than a discretionary refusal to depart.[110]

Where the defendant or his or her attorney has disputed a matter in the presentencing report, however, the trial court cannot simply guess at the true state

---

[106] 18 USC §3742(a). The government also has the right to appeal, under §3742(b). *See* **§2.11.**

[107] *Compare* United States v Burch, 873 F2d 765, 768 (5th Cir 1989) (a sentencing judge departing from the guidelines "must state the reasons for the departure, and the sentence imposed must be reasonable") *with* United States v Paulino, 873 F2d 23, 25 (2d Cir 1989) (the decision to depart from Guidelines is within the sound discretion of the trial judge); Schetz v United States, 901 F2d 85 (7th Cir 1990) (court of appeals has no jurisdiction to review discretionary refusal to depart downward from guidelines). *See also* United States v Aubrey, 878 F2d 825, 828 (5th Cir) (sentencing judge could not resolve discrepancy between defendant's contentions and presentencing report by simply guessing at the true facts), *cert denied,* 493 US 922 (1989).

[108] 112 S Ct 1840 (1992).

[109] 112 S Ct 1112, 1119 (1992).

[110] *Compare* United States v Castellanos, 904 F2d 1490 (11th Cir 1990) (fact that district judge denied government's motion for downward departure from guidelines did not establish that court failed to follow guideline direction to accord weight to motion) *with* United States v Sharpsteen, 913 F2d 59 (2d Cir 1990) (defendant may appeal district court refusal to downwardly depart from guideline where district court may have been under mistaken impression that it had no authority to depart; where record is ambiguous as to basis for refusal to depart, court of appeals will remand for clarification). *See also* United States v Higgins, 967 F2d 841 (3d Cir 1992) (while court of appeals has no jurisdiction to review discretionary refusal to depart downward under the Guidelines, it exercises *de novo* plenary review if district court states it lacks authority to depart).

of the facts. Rather, the judge must make the explicit finding required by Fed R Crim P 32(c)(3)(d) or state why none is required.[111]

§2.04 Exceptions to Finality Rule—Collateral Orders in Civil Cases

Some orders entered during litigation and before final judgment are reviewable under 28 USC §1291 as *collateral.*[112] This section discusses the origins of the collateral order rule, sets out categories of orders generally recognized as reviewable, notes the kinds of orders generally denied review, and concludes with a discussion of the general principles by which new and untried collateral order claims will be judged by the courts of appeals and the Supreme Court. The Supreme Court's candid admission[113] that its finality jurisprudence makes it difficult to predict results is aptly applied to the collateral order doctrine.

The doctrine in its present form originated in *Cohen v Beneficial Industrial Loan Corp,*[114] a stockholder derivative suit in which federal jurisdiction was founded solely on diversity of citizenship. The defendant corporation invoked a state statute requiring certain derivative plaintiffs to post security for court costs. The district court held the statute inapplicable to federal diversity plaintiffs. Was this an appealable order, or did the defendants have to wait until the lawsuit was over, and a final judgment entered, before appealing?

The Supreme Court held, without dissent on this point, that the order was appealable because:

> This decision appears to fall in that small class [of cases] which finally determine claims of rights separable from, and collateral to, rights asserted in the action, too important to be denied review and too independent of the cause itself to require that appellate consideration be deferred until the whole case is adjudicated. This Court has long given this provision of the statute [§1291] this practical rather than a technical construction.

---

[111] *See* United States v Aubrey, 878 F2d 825, 828 (5th Cir), *cert denied,* 493 US 922 (1989).

[112] This section deals only with orders appealable under the caselaw collateral order exception to finality. Orders denied collateral status may nonetheless be appealable under the approaches outlined in **§§2.09, 2.10, 2.15,** and **2.17,** or reviewable by extraordinary writ as discussed in **ch 3.** Another device for bestowing appellate jurisdiction is to claim that the district court has in effect denied a preliminary injunction. *See* **§2.06.** Such an effort is often futile. *See, e.g.,* Uehlein v Jackson Natl Life Ins Co, 794 F2d 300 (7th Cir 1986) (order refusing to turn over life insurance proceeds to widow pending dispute over whether they should be awarded to alleged victims of decedent's fraud not appealable as denial of preliminary injunction or otherwise), *cert denied,* 479 US 1034 (1987).

[113] Eisen v Carlisle & Jacquelin, 417 US 156, 170 (1974) discussed in **§2.02.**

[114] 337 US 541, 546 (1949). *See* Bruce I. McDaniel, Annotation, *Appealability Under "Collateral Order" Doctrine of Order Staying or Dismissing, or Refusing to Stay or Dismiss, Proceedings in United States District Court Pending Federal or State Administrative Determination,* 40 ALR Fed 740 (1978).

In *Swift & Co Packers v Compania Colombiana Del Caribe, SA,*[115] the Supreme Court held that the collateral order doctrine makes appealable an order in admiralty vacating attachment of a vessel. The Court reasoned that appellate review at a later date would be "an empty rite" because restoration of the attachment would be only a theoretical possibility.

Eisen v Carlisle & Jacquelin[116] was a class suit by odd lot securities traders against brokerage firms and the New York Stock Exchange. Each named plaintiff had a stake in the controversy of at most $70. Therefore, the action had to proceed as a class suit or not at all. After years of litigation on the issue, the district court certified a class and made provisions for allocating the costs of notice to class members. Was this order appealable?

The Supreme Court found the order appealable under the collateral order doctrine.[117] The Court viewed *Cohen* as imposing a two-part test. First, the challenged order must not be " 'tentative, informal or incomplete;' " it must "settle conclusively" the matter to which it was addressed.[118] This part of the test was satisfied because the district judge in *Eisen* had completely determined the class certification and notice issue. Second, the decision was not merely a " 'step toward final disposition of the merits of the case.' . . . Rather, it concerned a collateral matter that could not be reviewed effectively on appeal from the final judgment."[119]

Based on *Cohen* and its progeny, federal appellate courts have fashioned a list of orders that will generally be appealable.[120]

In *Mitchell v Forsyth,*[121] the Supreme Court held that an order denying a public official's motion to dismiss a civil case or for summary judgment based upon qualified immunity from suit is appealable as a collateral order. The rationale is that immunity doctrine protects the official against even having to respond to certain kinds of allegations; this right is best protected by preliminary review of such claims.[122] Thus, the former Attorney General, though not entitled to the absolute immunity from suit that would shield the President, was entitled

---

[115] 339 US 684 (1950).

[116] 417 US 156 (1974).

[117] *Id* 171-72.

[118] *Id* (partially quoting 337 US at 546).

[119] *Id.*

[120] The cases that follow illustrate the difficulty of finding a coherent pattern of collateral order decision. The fact that the challenged decision is clearly a threshold matter, as in Cohen, is not dispositive. *Compare* Perpetual Am Bank v Terrestrial Sys, 811 F2d 504 (9th Cir 1987) (grant of prejudgment writ of attachment not appealable as a collateral order, though denial of an order vacating an attachment would be appealable) *with* Grune v Coughlin, 913 F2d 41 (2d Cir 1990) (court of appeals has collateral order jurisdiction over appeal from denial of bail to habeas corpus petitioner, provided district court has ruled on application for certificate of probable cause).

[121] 472 US 511 (1985).

[122] *Mitchell* was prefigured by Nixon v Fitzgerald, 457 US 731 (1982), and Harlow v Fitzgerald, 457 US 800 (1982), in which the Court upheld the president's absolute immunity but denied such immunity to his aides. Both cases reached the Court by collateral order appeal.

to interlocutory appeal of a denial of his immunity claim in a lawsuit arising from the conduct of unlawful electronic surveillance. To meet this requirement, public officials raise immunity defenses on Fed R Civ P 12(b)(6) motions to dismiss or by summary judgment motion if factual matters must be explored.[123] The courts of appeals generally have regarded any immunity question capable of resolution on summary judgment as sufficiently law-bound to permit immediate appeal.[124] Indeed, when a district judge permits broad discovery into the factual basis of an immunity claim, the court of appeals may hear an interlocutory appeal from discovery orders, saying that too much discovery undercuts the values that *Mitchell v Forsyth* is designed to protect.[125]

The public official must timely raise the immunity issue in the district court to protect the right of appeal[126] and must appeal the denial within the time provided by Fed R App P 4.[127] If the district court rejects the immunity claim on motion or on summary judgment without certifying that it was frivolous or forfeited, and the public official appeals, the district court loses jurisdiction

---

[123] 472 US at 526-27.

[124] *See* Duran v City of Douglas, 904 F2d 1372 (9th Cir 1990) (court of appeals has jurisdiction over appeal from denial of summary judgment on qualified immunity; on the merits, court holds that the moving finger not only writes, but is constitutionally protected). Scott v Lacy, 811 F2d 1153 (7th Cir 1987) (order denying official immunity from damages appealable, even though claim for injunction is pending and will be tried regardless of outcome of appeal); Theis v Smith, 827 F2d 260 (7th Cir 1987) (collateral order doctrine does not permit plaintiff to appeal from grant of public official defendant's motion to dismiss on grounds of immunity; plaintiff must prosecute action to final judgment and then take appeal or cross-appeal). *But see* White v Frank, 855 F2d 956 (2d Cir 1988) (entitlement to immunity turned on a question of fact—degree to which appellants might have initiated underlying prosecution—and therefore denial of immunity not appealable).

[125] Lugo v Alvarado, 819 F2d 5 (1st Cir 1987) (public official not entitled to stay discovery pending decision on immunity issue; order limiting discovery held unappealable); Graham v Gray, 827 F2d 679 (10th Cir 1987) (discovery orders ordinarily not appealable, but denial of motion to dismiss based on qualified official immunity is appealable; in this case, the official appealed from the denial of his motion to bar discovery, rather than clearly invoking jurisdiction by appealing from orders denying dispositive motions); Boulos v Wilson, 834 F2d 504 (5th Cir 1987) (order granting limited discovery to determine validity of official immunity claim not appealable; decision makes clear that review would be available if the discovery was too broadly permitted).

[126] Edwards v Cass County, 919 F2d 273 (5th Cir 1990) (defendants did not move for leave to file for summary judgment on immunity until after the time set by the district court for filing all dispositive motions; district court denied the motion and would not entertain the immunity claim; held, appeal dismissed; the district court's trial management authority must be respected; if a district judge should abuse the discretion to set time limits for immunity motions, the proper remedy would be either a §1292(b) appeal or mandamus).

[127] Nicoletti v City of Waco, 947 F2d 190 (5th Cir 1991) (district court denied defendant police officer's qualified immunity motion; defendant went to trial and lost; district judge then granted a new trial on damages only; defendant appealed; held, failure to appeal when the immunity defense was first rejected waives the right to take an interlocutory appeal). *See* **§6.03.**

to proceed further and any trial it holds is a nullity.[128] It is uncertain whether the district court would have power to try claims on which the official did not assert immunity.[129] The district judge must give the public official defendant an opportunity to raise the immunity issue and have it decided pretrial.[130]

Mitchell v Forsyth confers only one opportunity for early appeal and the defendant must decide whether to pursue appeal after denial of a motion to dismiss or to make a factual record and seek summary judgment before appealing. In *Abel v Miller,*[131] the court held that *Mitchell v Forsyth* "does not contemplate sequential appeals" by public officials claiming official immunity.[132] Once a public official has taken an appeal in any procedural context, that right is exhausted. Otherwise, reasoned the court, a defendant might appeal denial of a motion to dismiss under Fed R Civ P 12(b)(6), then appeal denial of summary judgment, and finally appeal on the merits. The doctrine of law of the case, and the need to resolve cases expeditiously, suggests this result, although the court said there was no prior decision directly on point. In *Abel,* plaintiffs had prevailed in a 1984 jury trial, but had their judgment reversed on appeal, with directions to grant a new trial on only one of their claims. On remand, the district court denied the public officials motion for summary judgment on that remaining claim. The officials appealed, claiming that the district court had failed to give sufficient weight to their right under *Mitchell* to an early judicial determination of immunity. The court of appeals dismissed the appeal for want of jurisdiction.[133]

The Supreme Court has applied the *Cohen/Mitchell/Eisen* analysis to hold that Eleventh Amendment claims of sovereign immunity are appealable under the collateral order doctrine. In *Puerto Rico Aqueduct & Sewer Authority v Metcalf & Eddy, Inc,*[134] respondent engineering firm sued a Puerto Rican government instrumentality in diversity for a declaration of rights under a contract. The Court reasoned that: (1) the order denying an Eleventh Amendment claim conclusively determined that the agency has no right not to be sued in federal

---

[128] Stewart v Donges, 915 F2d 572 (10th Cir 1990).

[129] *See* Green v Brantley, 941 F2d 1146 (11th Cir 1991) (en banc); prior opinion, 895 F2d 1387 (11th Cir 1990), (vacated) (denial of summary judgment based on a qualified immunity claim is appealable, even when the defendant must still face trial on another claim arising from the same occurrence). The decision seems to encourage unnecessary delay in the resolution of disputes; this problem would be exacerbated if one held that the entire case had to await appellate review of those portions subject to immunity claims.

[130] Helton v Clements, 787 F2d 1016 (5th Cir 1986) (district judge's deferral of the immunity claim until trial was appealable; held, the defendant is entitled to a pretrial ruling on the issue; remanded to district judge for decision).

[131] 904 F2d 394 (7th Cir 1990).

[132] *Id* 395.

[133] *Id* 397. This ground may require explanation. *Mitchell* is an exception to the jurisdictional finality rule of 28 USC §1291. Thus, the court of appeals' invocation of the law of the case amounts to a holding that the judgment is not within the narrow finality exception.

[134] 113 S Ct 684 (1993).

court; (2) the Eleventh Amendment confers a fundamental constitutional right unrelated to the ultimate merits of the lawsuit; (3) as with the immunity considered in *Mitchell* the benefits of immunity are lost by forcing the agency to endure litigation; and (4) determination of an Eleventh Amendment claim typically does not involve factual difficulty.

The rationale of *Puerto Rico Aqueduct* could be applied to any sovereign immunity determination, including those under the Foreign Sovereign Immunities Act.[135]

There are a few other categories of orders to which collateral order status has been applied, though the precise contours of these categories may at times be difficult to discern.[136] Discovery orders in civil cases generally are not appealable, although a few such orders may qualify as collateral.[137] If a nonparty witness fails to obey a discovery order and is held in civil contempt, an immediate appeal lies, and there are some cases permitting appeal without the nonparty suffering contempt.[138] Such orders are reviewable on the theory that the challenged order is final as to the aggrieved party. However, the nonparty can only raise issues in which it has a legitimate interest, such as the trial court's subject matter jurisdiction or the validity of the order requiring testimony; the appellant lacks standing to raise issues that do not affect the order or process

---

[135] *See* Segni v Commercial Office of Spain, 816 F2d 344 (7th Cir) (order rejecting defense based on First Amendment right of petition not immediately appealable, but order denying immunity under the Foreign Sovereign Immunities Act, 28 USC §1601 *et seq,* is appealable).

[136] The DC Circuit held that an administrative agency to which a dispute has been remanded may appeal the legal standard imposed by the district court under the collateral order doctrine. Occidental Petroleum Corp v SEC, 873 F2d 325, 331 (DC Cir 1989). In its opinion, the court discusses exhaustively the opinions of other circuits on the topic, all of which reach the identical conclusion. *Id* 328-32. The Eighth Circuit has ruled that the cancellation of a lis pendens (known as expungement in some jurisdictions) is appealable under the collateral order exception. SB McLaughlin & Co v Tudor Oaks Condominium Project, 877 F2d 707, 708 (8th Cir 1989).

[137] *See* Reise v Board of Regents, 957 F2d 293 (7th Cir 1992) (mental examination under Fed R Civ P 35 is not final decision under 28 USC §1291; disagreeing with Fifth Circuit).

[138] United States v Sciarra, 851 F2d 621 (3d Cir 1988) (nonparty witness may only appeal discovery order absent contempt if there is no real possibility of disrupting an underlying action); (nonparty has no means to defend his or her rights on appeal from a final judgment); Heat & Control, Inc v Hester Indus, 785 F2d 1017 (Fed Cir 1986). *But see* United States Catholic Conference v Abortion Rights Mobilization, Inc, 487 US 72 (1988) (nonparty witness may challenge court lack of subject matter jurisdiction in defense of a civil contempt citation), *cert denied,* 495 US 918 (1990); Estate of Domingo v Republic of Philippines, 808 F2d 1349 (9th Cir 1987) (former Philippine President Marcos could not appeal order denying motion to terminate deposition because he had not placed himself in contempt of subpoena); *In re* Subpoena Served on the Cal PUC, 813 F2d 1473 (9th Cir 1987) (expressly disagreeing with Federal and Eleventh Circuits) (Kennedy, J, on panel). In the latter case, the court denied appealability to a district court decision quashing a subpoena, even though the district court that entered the order was not the court before which the underlying litigation was pending.

being challenged.[139]

If a party seeks, and is denied, discovery in a different judicial district than that in which the case is pending, an appeal may lie under the collateral order doctrine. If the different district is in the same circuit, however, the party may have to wait until final judgment in the main action and then appeal from that judgment and the adverse discovery order.[140]

By similar reasoning, an otherwise interlocutory order directing the immediate payment of money or other transfer of property may be held appealable as a collateral order.[141] The courts of appeals are divided on whether and when an attorney subjected to a midtrial monetary sanction may take an immediate appeal.[142]

Attorney-client privilege issues continue to enjoy a special status. For example, in *Conkling v Turner,*[143] civil RICO defendants sought discovery from the

---

[139] United States Catholic Conference v Abortion Rights Mobilization, Inc, 487 US 72, 76-77 (1988), *cert denied,* 495 US 918 (1990).

[140] *E.g.*, Hooker v Continental Life Ins Co, 965 F2d 903 (10th Cir 1992); Periodical Publishers Serv Bureau, Inc v Keys, 981 F2d 215 (5th Cir 1993).

[141] A variation on this theme is the practical finality doctrine in which review of an order before entry of judgment in the underlying case is permissible whenever the order directs "immediate delivery of physical property and subjects the losing party to irreparable harm" if the court delays review until the conclusion of the case. Ortho Pharmaceutical Corp v Sona Distribs, 847 F2d 1512, 1515 (11th Cir 1988) (quoting *In re* Martin Bros Toolmakers, Inc, 796 F2d 1435, 1437 (11th Cir 1986)) (order of pretrial sanctions, payable immediately, appealable under this doctrine).

[142] The question of appealability arises frequently in the context of midtrial sanctions against lawyers and parties. The courts of appeals are divided. *Compare* Sanko SS Co v Galin, 835 F2d 51 (2d Cir 1987) (Rule 11 sanctions against attorney for advancing frivolous motion immediately appealable as collateral order); Aetna Life Ins Co v Alla Medical Servs, 855 F2d 1470 (9th Cir 1988) (imposition of Rule 11 sanctions immediately appealable); Ortho Pharmaceutical Corp v Sona Distribs, 847 F2d 1512 (11th Cir 1988) (order of pretrial sanctions, payable immediately, appealable under *Cohen*) *with* Thomas v Capital Sec Servs, 836 F2d 866 (5th Cir 1988) (en banc) (citing Click v Abilene Natl Bank, 822 F2d 544, 545 (5th Cir 1987)), *disagreed with by,* Kale v Combined Ins Co of Am, 861 F2d 746 (1st Cir 1988) (district courts were cautioned to abjure imposing sanctions that in effect foreclosed access to the courts, because doing so would be unfair given the Fifth Circuit's rule that sanctions orders entered prior to a final judgment are not appealable). In the circuit of its origin, *Click* has been modified to permit a sanctioned attorney to appeal under some circumstances. Markwell v County of Bexar, 878 F2d 899 (5th Cir 1989). Thomas E. Hoar, Inc v Sara Lee Corp, 882 F2d 682 (2d Cir 1989) (monetary discovery sanction imposed jointly and severally on nonparty lawyer and party appealable as collateral order, even though no appeal would lie if sanction was imposed on party only). The Seventh Circuit will hear appeals from orders awarding attorney's fees and other sanctions, because the award is independent of the merits, and there is a risk that a party prevailing at the end of the case will be unable to recoup the money once it has been paid. However, denial for a request for fees or sanctions will not be reviewed until the end of the case. Cassidy v Cassidy, 950 F2d 381 (7th Cir 1991). *Compare* Atlantic Fed Sav & Loan Assn v Blythe Eastman Paine Webber, Inc, 890 F2d 371 (11th Cir 1989) (discovery sanctions nonappealable).

[143] 883 F2d 431 (5th Cir 1989). However, in Texaco, Inc v Louisiana Land & Exploration Co, 995 F2d 43 (5th Cir 1993), the court held that a discovery order allegedly requiring turnover of attorney-client privileged documents was not appealable. The panel stated

plaintiff's attorney on statute of limitations issues. The Fifth Circuit held the order compelling the attorney's testimony to be appealable, without requiring the attorney to suffer a contempt citation by refusing to testify.[144]

Beyond the fairly well-settled categories permitting collateral order appeals, the Supreme Court's decisions since 1978 counsel that collateral order appealability is sharply rationed. In the wake of these decisions, it is a rare case in which reversal on appeal is not an adequate remedy, or in which a trial record will not be useful in assessing prejudice. Given the exclusion from collateral order status of rulings that have a practical, as distinguished from legal, fatal impact on the plaintiff's case, the collateral order rule must be regarded as only rarely available.[145]

Transfer orders, no matter how onerous an impact they are claimed to have, will not generally be appealable.[146] Denial of forum non conveniens dismissal is also unlikely to be reviewed on appeal.[147] The courts of appeals are divided on the appealability of orders refusing to appoint counsel in indigent civil cases.[148]

The second *Eisen* test, that the issue not be reviewable on appeal from a final judgment, has spelled defeat in the Supreme Court for a number of collateral order claims since *Eisen* was decided. In *Coopers & Lybrand v Livesay,* decided

---

that prior opinions reaching a different result on appealability were not the law of the Circuit. The opinion does not, however, preclude appeal by a nonparty witness or by a nonparty privilege holder. Moreover, mandamus would still be a viable option, as discussed in **§3.06.** *See also* **§§2.03, 2.05.**

[144] On the merits, the court affirmed the discovery order. Other courts of appeals more readily entertain mandamus petitions when attorney-client issues are involved. *See* **§3.06.**

[145] The Tenth Circuit continues to grant collateral order review when "the issue is not 'collateral' but justice may require immediate review." Bender v Clark, 744 F2d 1424, 1427 (10th Cir 1984), applied in United States v PHE, Inc, 965 F2d 848 (10th Cir 1992), discussed at **§2.05.**

[146] *See* Alimenta (USA), Inc v Lyng, 872 F2d 382 (11th Cir 1989) (order transferring case to Claims Court not appealable); Jesko v United States, 713 F2d 565 (10th Cir 1983) (order transferring case to Claims Court not appealable). *See also* **§3.07** (discussing review by mandamus of transfer orders).

[147] *See* Carlenstolpe v Merck & Co, 819 F2d 33 (2d Cir 1987) (denial of forum non conveniens dismissal not appealable; mandamus refused).

[148] *See* Holt v Ford, 828 F2d 1523 (11th Cir), *rehg granted & panel opinion vacated* (en banc), 833 F2d 1437 (11th Cir 1987), *on rehg,* 862 F2d 850 (11th Cir 1989) (order denying appointment of counsel in an indigent's civil rights action not appealable); Welch v Smith, 810 F2d 40 (2d Cir), *cert denied,* 484 US 903 (1987); Miller v Simmons, 814 F2d 962 (4th Cir) (denial of motion for appointment of counsel under 28 USC §1915(d) to indigent civil litigant not appealable as collateral order), *cert denied,* 484 US 903 (1987); Justices White and Blackmun dissented from denial of certiorari, contrasting the appealability of such orders in the Ninth Circuit; *compare* Wilborn v Escalderon, 789 F2d 1328 (9th Cir 1986) (order denying appointment not appealable under *Cohen,* but review granted incident to review of final judgment); *with* Bradshaw v Zoological Socy, 662 F2d 1301 (9th Cir 1981) (order denying counsel in Title VII action is immediately appealable).

in 1978,[149] the district court had certified, then decertified, a class. The named plaintiffs claimed this was tantamount to dismissal. Their claim for appealability under the collateral order doctrine was certainly plausible. In *Cohen,* an order to post security for costs did not formally end the action; it would, at most, have required the plaintiffs to come up with cash in order to proceed. In *Eisen,* the district judge's order that plaintiffs pay 90 per cent of the costs of notice to the class (which would have cost millions of dollars) did not say the plaintiffs were out of court. But the practical effect in each case would be to burden the lawsuit so heavily that plaintiffs would be without remedy.

In *Coopers,* the Court expressed the test as follows: "[T]he order must [1] conclusively determine the disputed question, [2] resolve an important issue completely separate from the merits of the action, and [3] be effectively unreviewable on appeal from a final judgment."[150] This formulation divides the second *Eisen* test into two subparts.

In finding the decertification order not appealable, the Court reasoned that orders granting or denying class status are tentative, because Fed R Civ P 23(c)(1) gives the district court power to amend them. Second, certification questions are bound up with the merits of the underlying claim, and are not separate. Third, an order denying class certification can be challenged on appeal from the final judgment.[151]

The same reasoning was applied to deny appealability to an order refusing to disqualify an attorney in a civil case. In *Firestone Tire & Rubber Co v Risjord,*[152] a civil defendant claimed the plaintiff's counsel was disqualified because he also represented defendant's insurance carrier in some matters. The district judge refused to disqualify the lawyer, provided the carrier and the plaintiffs consented to his continuing in the case. This condition was met. The defendant appealed the refusal to disqualify.

The Supreme Court held that the order met the first part of the three-part *Coopers & Lybrand* test. The Court assumed, without deciding, that the order met the second test, in that it was arguably separate from the merits. However, not only could the matter be reviewed on appeal from a final judgment, but waiting until that time would permit development of a record that would show whether the aggrieved party was prejudiced. The Court did, however, hold open the possibility that a party might demonstrate irreparable harm from denial of a disqualification motion and therefore be entitled to seek certification under 28 USC §1292(b)[153] or relief by mandamus.[154]

---

[149] The case is also discussed at **§2.02.**

[150] Coopers & Lybrand v Livesay, 437 US 463, 468 (1978).

[151] The Court did not foreclose §1292(b) review of a class certification order, but noted that such review requires the district judge and the court of appeals to concur on the propriety of an interlocutory appeal. 437 US at 474-75. *See* **§2.09.**

[152] 449 US 368 (1981).

[153] *See* **§2.09.**

[154] *Risjord,* 449 US at 378 n13. *See* **§3.04.** *See* Christensen v United States Dist Court, 844 F2d 694 (9th Cir 1988) (mandamus available to correct erroneous order disqualifying counsel in civil case). The same rule will apply in administrative cases, Law Offices

Firestone Tire may reflect an unspoken opinion that disqualification motions are often dilatory tactics. When a party, particularly a civil defendant, can obtain a lengthy delay by making a motion and then appealing it, the risks of abuse are great.

The teaching of *Firestone* was applied and extended in *Richardson-Merrell, Inc v Koller.*[155] Plaintiff's counsel in a protracted and emotion-laden products liability suit was disqualified for alleged misconduct. The court of appeals, distinguishing *Firestone Tire* and a more recent Supreme case dealing with orders disqualifying counsel in criminal cases,[156] held the order appealable and reversed.

The Supreme Court, with only Justice Stevens dissenting, acknowledged that the right to choose one's own counsel is precious. The Court concluded, however, that while a disqualification order might satisfy the first part of the *Coopers & Lybrand* formulation, it did not meet the other two criteria. If a showing of prejudice were required to reverse a judgment after erroneous disqualification of counsel—a point the Court did not reach—the order would be effectively reviewable on appeal. If prejudice were required, the trial record would be of invaluable aid in assessing it and therefore the issue was bound up with the facts of the underlying litigation.[157]

In *Stringfellow v Concerned Neighbors in Action,* 480 US 370 (1987), the Court again refused to extend the boundaries of collateral order review. CNA, a citizens' group, sought leave to intervene in a suit brought by the federal and state governments against operators of a toxic waste dumpsite. The district court denied intervention of right, but granted permissive intervention under a set of limiting conditions. CNA appealed, claiming that the court had, in effect, either denied intervention completely or refused an injunction. The first argument invoked the settled rule that the district court's denial of intervention

---

of Seymour M. Chase, PC v FCC, 843 F2d 517 (DC Cir 1988) (FCC order disqualifying counsel not reviewable as final order), and admiralty actions, Cement Div, Natl Gypsum Co v City of Milwaukee, 915 F2d 1154 (7th Cir 1990) (order disqualifying counsel in admiralty action nonappealable as in ordinary civil case), *cert denied,* 111 S Ct 1583 (1991).

[155] 472 US 424 (1985). However, in Pan E Exploration Co v Hufo Oils, 798 F2d 837 (5th Cir 1986), the court refused to entertain an appeal by Canadian banks from an order denying dismissal based upon international comity. A Canadian court had entered an order staying all litigation against the banks. The court of appeals held that the banks had at most a "defense to liability," not "a recognized protection from the burdens of trial." *Id* 841. To similar effect is Group Health, Inc v Blue Cross Assn, 793 F2d 491 (2d Cir 1986) (fiscal intermediaries in medicare provider suit have no right to interlocutory appeal on their immunity claim), *cert denied,* 480 US 930 (1987). *Group Health* recognizes that once an interlocutory appeal is properly before the court of appeals, the doctrine of pendent appellate jurisdiction permits the court to hear related nonappealable issues. *Id* 497.

[156] Flanagan v United States, 465 US 259 (1984), discussed at **§2.05.**

[157] The Court declined to consider the disqualified lawyer's interest in vindication as relevant. *Koller,* 472 US at 433. The Court recognized that the lawyer might have a remedy under exceptional circumstances.

of right is an appealable order.[158] The latter argument invoked 28 USC §1292(a)(1).[159]

Cases construing *Mitchell v Forsyth* establish just how clearly the *Mitchell* result was driven by concerns about *official* immunity. In *Van Cauwenberghe v Biard,* 486 US 517 (1988) the Court held denial of motion to dismiss that claimed an extradited person to be immune from civil process is not appealable as a collateral order. The Court distinguished *Mitchell* on two grounds. First, it said that the doctrine of specialty[160] did not implicate the petitioner's right to be protected from a civil trial because the receiving state's role in a civil suit is merely to provide a forum for the resolution of a private dispute, rather than to prosecute the suit as it would in a criminal case. The petitioner's claims that the court lacked jurisdiction and that his due process rights were violated, asserted only a right to be free from a binding judgment, not a right to avoid a civil trial. As such, these rights could be protected on appeal from a final decision. Second, the Court said that claims of specialty amounted are often fact-bound and therefore better resolved on the full record that a trial would produce.[161]

The strength of the Court's concern with restricting the collateral order doctrine is also manifested by the unanimous opinion in *Lauro Lines SRL v Chasser.*[162] Sophie Chasser and the other plaintiffs were passengers on the cruise ship *Achille Lauro,* travelling in the Mediterranean and based in Naples, Italy. The ship was hijacked. One passenger was killed and others injured. After the passengers and their representatives sued Lauro Lines in New York, Lauro invoked the forum selection clause printed on the passenger ticket, dictating trial in Naples.

The district court denied Lauro's motion to dismiss. The court of appeals held the denial nonappealable and the Supreme Court affirmed, resolving a conflict among the circuits.

The Court's opinion retraces the path of collateral order jurisprudence, and concludes that the "right not to be haled for trial before tribunals outside the

---

[158] Denial of a motion under Fed R Civ P 24(a) for intervention of right is appealable, but, barring a clear abuse of discretion, denial of a motion for permissive intervention under Fed R Civ P 24(b) is not. *See* Worlds v Department of Health & Rehabilitation Servs, 929 F2d 591 (11th Cir 1991) (while an order denying intervention of right is appealable, a holding that the denial was proper causes jurisdiction to evaporate as to all other claims because "the proper denial of leave to intervene is not a final decision" (quoting Stallworth v Monsanto Co, 558 F2d 257, 263 (5th Cir 1977); thus, upon such a finding, the appeals will be dismissed)).

[159] *See* **§2.06.**

[160] The specialty doctrine forbids trial of a fugitive for any crime other than that for which he was extradited. United States v Rauscher, 119 US 407 (1886).

[161] *See also* Nemours Found v Manganaro Corp, 878 F2d 98 (3d Cir 1989) (district court order certifying state law question to state supreme court is not appealable as a form of "abstention," citing *Van Cauwenberghe*).

[162] 490 US 495 (1989).

agreed forum"[163] is sufficiently vindicable by a postjudgment appeal. The Court draws an analogy to personal jurisdiction issues which typically are appealable only after final judgment. Justice Scalia's brief concurrence states that the Court inevitably assesses the importance of the right being asserted by a collateral order appellant and, in this case, finds the right "not sufficiently important to overcome the policies militating against interlocutory appeals."[164]

Despite the Supreme Court's skeptical approach to collateral order claims, the courts of appeals, often in disagreement with one another, continue to grant appealability to an extent that makes it necessary to evaluate the prospects of appeal in almost every instance where an important right is adjudicated by interlocutory order. Several cases recognize the right of immediate appeal from an order denying effect to a release or settlement agreement, on the theory that the appellant is claiming a right not to be in court at all.[165] Other cases granting[166] or denying[167] appealability are too various to be classified.

§2.05 —Defendant's Appeal of Collateral Orders in Criminal Cases

The Supreme Court has often said that the doctrine of finality applies with special force to criminal cases.[168] Permitting interlocutory appeals of postindictment orders may compromise the speedy trial provisions of the Sixth Amendment.[169] Assertedly, there is a strong interest in insulating the criminal process from premature judicial interference.[170] Applications of the collateral order doctrine in criminal cases are therefore few, narrow, and well-defined.

---

[163] *Id* 500 (quoting Brief for Petitioner 38-39).

[164] *Id* 502.

[165] *E.g.*, Forbus v Sears Roebuck & Co, 958 F2d 1036 (11th Cir) (order denying motion for reconsideration of denial of summary judgment was appealable under collateral order doctrine; plaintiff employees had at the time they left Sears signed documents that Sears claimed released it from liability; therefore, Sears was asserting a right not to go to trial at all, and was entitled to an interlocutory appeal), *cert denied,* 113 S Ct 412 (1992); Grillet v Sears, Roebuck & Co, 927 F2d 217 (5th Cir 1991) (order denying summary judgment in employment discrimination case appealable, when issue is validity of released signed by employee at the time she left the company's employ); Janneh v GAF Corp, 887 F2d 432 (2d Cir 1989) (distinguishing *Lauro Lines,* an order denying effect to a settlement agreement is immediately appealable under the collateral order doctrine; settlement implicates the right not to be sued at all, not simply a right not to be held in a particular forum; settlement is important as a means of clearing clogged dockets), *cert denied,* 498 US 865 (1990).

[166] Aliota v Graham, 984 F2d 1350 (3d Cir 1993).

[167] Chaput v Unisys Corp, 964 F2d 1299 (2d Cir 1992); United States v Santtini, 963 F2d 585 (3d Cir 1992).

[168] *E.g.*, Will v United States, 389 US 90, 96-98 (1967).

[169] *Id* 98. In this section, the focus is upon appeals by a defendant under 28 USC §1291. The government's right of appeal is conferred by a number of statutes that limit interlocutory appeal to certain specified types of orders. *See* **§2.15.**

[170] United States v Calandra, 414 US 338 (1974) (grand jury witness not permitted to refuse to answer questions based on evidence obtained from illegal search and sei-

This section deals with appealability of: (1) orders issued after indictment that are incidental to the charges against the defendant; (2) orders issued after indictment denying defense motions to dismiss or for other significant relief directed at the merits of or defense against the charges; and (3) orders issued before there is an indictment, for example during a grand jury investigation.

First, an indicted defendant usually seeks release on bail. In *Stack v Boyle,*[171] defendants charged under the Smith Act were held by the district court on excessive bail. The Supreme Court held their remedy to be a motion to the district judge to reduce the amount of bail, followed by an appeal under 28 USC §1291 to the appropriate court of appeals. While the Court recognized that a separate action for habeas corpus was theoretically a remedy, such collateral attacks should necessarily give way to a direct appeal. The Court cited *Cohen* without extensive discussion and the rule of *Stack* is now codified. According to 18 USC §3145(c), a criminal defendant has the right to appellate review of an order denying bail pending trial under 28 USC §1291.[172] The procedure for such appeals is dictated by Fed R App P 9(a).

The rationale of *Stack* would apply to any pretrial order, separable from the merits of the charges, that affects a significant interest of the defendant. For example, if the trial judge finds a defendant mentally incompetent[173] or orders the defendant to submit to a mental examination, the order should be reviewable as meeting the *Cohen* standard.

A similar example is *United States v Ford,*[174] in which the court held that a gag order imposed by the district judge on the defendant-Congressman was immediately appealable in order to review First Amendment issues. On the merits, the court held the order to be invalid as overbroad. In such circumstances, mandamus also should be available, as discussed at **§3.09.**[175]

The second category of reviewable orders includes those that meet the same standards on which the Court relied in *Mitchell v Forsyth,*[176] the defendant is asserting the right not to be tried at all, rather than a right to be free of a binding judgment. Moreover, the legal issue can be determined without a time-

---

zure); Gelbard v United States, 408 US 41 (grand jury witness can invoke statutory prohibition under 28 USC §2515 as defense to civil contempt charges brought after their refusal to testify regarding information obtained through illegal interceptions of communication), *cert denied,* 408 US 922 (1972); Branzburg v Hayes, 408 US 665 (1972) (requiring newsman to appear and testify before a grand jury regarding information obtained from confidential sources does not violate his First Amendment rights).

[171] 342 US 1 (1951), citing Cohen, discussed in **§2.04.**

[172] The government may appeal an order granting bail under 18 USC §3731. *See* **§2.11.**

[173] *See* United States v Gold, 790 F2d 235 (2d Cir 1986) (defendant found under 18 USC §4241 to be suffering from a mental disease that rendered him mentally incompetent to stand trial; held, the order is appealable).

[174] 830 F2d 596 (6th Cir 1987).

[175] In United States v Stemm, 835 F2d 732 (10th Cir 1987), the court upheld its authority to issue a rule authorizing consolidation of appeal from denial of bail after conviction with appeal on the merits and summary disposition of the entire case. The court, however, held summary determination was improper without a record on appeal.

[176] 472 US 511 (1985).

consuming factual inquiry. Under this analysis, the defendant has the right of interlocutory appeal from an order denying dismissal based upon double jeopardy[177] and from an order refusing to accord the defendant the protection of the speech or debate clause of article I of the Constitution.[178]

The double jeopardy case is *Abney v United States*. The Court applied the collateral order test as follows:

> [F]irst . . . such orders constitute a complete, formal, and, in the trial court, final rejection of a criminal defendant's double jeopardy claim. . . . Moreover, the very nature of a double jeopardy claim is such that it is collateral to, and separable from the principal issue at the accused's impending criminal trial, i.e., whether or not the accused is guilty of the offense charged. . . . [H]e is contesting the very authority of the Government to hale him into court to face trial on the charge against him. . . . Finally, the rights conferred . . . by the Double Jeopardy Clause would be significantly undermined if appellate review . . . were postponed until after conviction and sentence. . . . [T]he Double Jeopardy Clause protects . . . against being twice put to trial for the same offense.[179]

The value of *Abney* has been eroded by decisions denying stay of trial pending appeal of a double jeopardy point when the appeal is assertedly frivolous. The appellant must be prepared to make a threshold showing that the double jeopardy claim has merit.[180]

The rationale of *Abney* was applied in *Helstoski v Meanor*.[181] The accused had been a member of Congress, accused of introducing private immigration bills in exchange for bribes. He claimed the indictment charged conduct protected by the speech or debate clause. The Supreme Court held that denial of his motion was redressable by appeal and not by mandamus or other extraordinary writ. Following its *Abney* analysis, the Court noted that the clause protected a member against "be[ing] questioned in any other Place" for legislative conduct. Thus, interlocutory appeal was necessary to preserve the member's right not to be tried at all.[182]

---

[177] Abney v United States, 431 US 651 (1977).

[178] Helstoski v Meanor, 442 US 500 (1979) (mandamus not an appropriate remedy for denial of speech or debate clause motion to dismiss criminal case; appeal is sole remedy). *See also* United States v Helstoski, 442 US 477 (1979) (on merits, government precluded from using certain evidence in former Congressman's trial).

[179] Abney v United States, 431 US 651, 659-61 (1977).

[180] United States v Ragins, 840 F2d 1184, 1192 (4th Cir 1988).

[181] 442 US 500 (1979).

[182] *Id* 501. Helstoski did not benefit from this holding, because he did not appeal the denial of his motion to dismiss on *speech or debate* grounds. He sought mandamus. The Court held that he should have taken an appeal, but that it was too late to do so because the time for filing a notice of appeal had expired. The case illustrates the wisdom of taking an appeal and filing for an extraordinary writ as alternative remedies where there is any doubt about which is appropriate.

The Supreme Court and the courts of appeals have rejected efforts to recognize additional collateral order exceptions to the finality requirement. When the government allegedly breaches a plea bargain and indicts a defendant, denial of a motion to dismiss based on the plea bargain has been held nonappealable despite the close analogy between broken plea bargain and double jeopardy analysis.[183] The Court held in *United States v Hollywood Motor Car Co,*[184] that denial of a motion to dismiss based upon vindictive prosecution was not appealable under the collateral order doctrine. Denial of either constitutional or statutory speedy trial motions also will not be appealable.[185]

In *Flanagan v United States,*[186] a unanimous Supreme Court held that an order

---

[183] *See* United States v Thompson, 814 F2d 1472 (10th Cir) (district court held that a defendant's plea agreement was rendered void by the defendant's conduct; defendant appealed; held, appeal dismissed: defendant, by pleading guilty, had not been placed in such jeopardy as to trigger *Abney* rights), *cert denied,* 484 US 830 (1987).

[184] 458 US 263 (1982). The Court reversed the Ninth Circuit's decision to permit an interlocutory appeal in vindictive prosecution cases. The courts of appeals have taken *Hollywood Motor Car* as a signal that they should be sparing in permitting appeals before final judgment in criminal cases. *See, e.g.,* United States v Caparros, 800 F2d 23 (2d Cir 1986) (district court order forbidding defendant to disclose documents received in pretrial discovery not appealable; precedent from "prior restraint" cases rejected); United States v Gurary, 793 F2d 468 (2d Cir 1986) (district judge continuance of indictment and preliminary hearing date not appealable and mandamus not available; court recognizes defendant prejudiced and may have no other remedy); United States v French, 787 F2d 1381 (9th Cir 1986) (retransfer of indictment after aborted Fed R Crim P 20 plea bargain not appealable and mandamus not available; extensive review of appealability precedent).

[185] United States v Mehrmanesh, 652 F2d 766 (9th Cir 1980). Denial of a motion to dismiss for want of subject matter jurisdiction has been held not appealable. United States v Layton, 645 F2d 681 (9th Cir), *cert denied,* 452 US 972 (1981). Therefore, even though the failure of an indictment to state an offense is jurisdictional, Fed R Crim P 12(b)(2), denial of a motion to dismiss on such a ground will not be appealable absent special circumstances such as the presence of a speech or debate or double jeopardy issue.

The Tenth Circuit has applied its own collateral order exception to review denial of a motion to dismiss an indictment on first amendment/prosecutorial misconduct grounds. United States v PHE, Inc, 965 F2d 848 (10th Cir 1992). A federal task force targeted defendants and other alleged purveyors of obscene materials in a series of state and federal prosecutions. The defendants sought injunctive relief against government tactics, with mixed success. The government brought a criminal prosecution in Utah. The defendants moved to dismiss the indictment, arguing that the decision to prosecute them was motivated by a desire to suppress protected speech, and in retaliation for their having litigated against the government in other forums. The district judge denied the motion.

On appeal the Tenth Circuit, one judge dissenting, held that it had jurisdiction to review the order denying dismissal, because the defendants were asserting a First Amendment based right not to be tried, holding that Dombrowski v Pfister, 380 US 479 (1965) and other first amendment cases established the right in this setting.

On the merits, the court held that the district court's conclusion that the prosecution was improperly motivated was wrong "as a matter of law." 965 F2d at 859-60. It remanded for a hearing conducted according to the standards it announced.

[186] 465 US 259 (1984).

disqualifying an accused's retained counsel on grounds of possible conflict of interest was not appealable. Flanagan and other Philadelphia police officers jointly charged with civil rights violations retained the same law firm to represent them. They were thoroughly interrogated by the trial judge and understood the potential for conflicting interests as the pretrial and trial process wore on. Their counsel was paid by their labor organization and was familiar with the case from lengthy participation in grand jury and other related proceedings. Thus, the defendants clearly suffered prejudice from a wrongful denial of their rights to counsel of their choice and to waive conflict-free representation.

The Court noted that the accused's claims would be fully vindicated by an acquittal on the merits. Moreover, the Court held that, if the disqualification were found on appeal from a conviction and sentence to have been erroneous, the accused would be entitled to reversal without any showing of prejudice.[187] This amounts to an assertion that the accused is not harmed by waiting until final judgment and therefore that the third part of the *Coopers & Lybrand*[188] test is not met.

The *Flanagan* rationale seems flawed. Some disqualification orders are surely reviewable without extensive factual inquiry, after a hearing that is analytically separable from the merits of the case. In *Flanagan* itself, this was so since the disqualification issue arose because the defendants desired joint representation and had made a thorough record waiving any prejudice from possible conflict of interest.

As for the adequacy of review following final judgment, the mere pendency of criminal charges—let alone the expense and anguish of trial and appeal—inflicts serious costs on a defendant and others.[189]

The Court's reluctance to countenance pretrial appeals was again underscored in *Midland Asphalt Corp v United States.*[190] The Court held that denial of a motion to dismiss predicated upon abuse of the grand jury process in violation of Fed R Crim P 6(e) is not appealable. The Court said that for an order to be "effectively unreviewable"[191] and therefore appealable under the collateral order doctrine, it must involve "an asserted right the legal and practical

---

[187] The Court did not expressly decide the prejudice issue; however, it noted that prior decisions involving denial of Sixth Amendment rights have been held reversible without a showing of prejudice. *Id* 268.

[188] The *Coopers & Lybrand* test is discussed at **§2.02.**

[189] Klopfer v North Carolina, 386 US 213 (1967) (although solicitor's taking of nolle prosequi with leave permitted defendant to go "whither soever he would," it did not relieve defendant of limitations placed on his life and liberty, thereby denying him of his right to a speedy trial); Smith v Hooey, 393 US 374 (1969) (federal prisoner who had additional charges pending in another state may suffer as much oppression as an individual jailed without bail upon an untried charge; held, state must make a diligent, good faith effort to bring him to trial).

[190] 489 US 794 (1989), *affg* 840 F2d 1040 (2d Cir 1988), *disagreeing with* United States v Dederich, 825 F2d 1317 (9th Cir 1987).

[191] *Id* 799.

value of which would be destroyed if it were not vindicated before trial."[192] The Court noted that it has "interpreted the collateral order exception 'with the utmost strictness' in criminal cases."[193] By a parity of reasoning, other orders denying relief from alleged prosecutorial misconduct have been held not immediately appealable.[194]

The third category of collateral order involves preindictment activity such as grand jury proceedings or government-conducted searches. Here again the caselaw cautions district judges to avoid interference with the criminal process before it yields formal charges.

A grand jury witness may, of course, resist a subpoena by motion to quash, although judicial review will probably be unavailable unless and until the witness suffers a contempt citation.[195] At that point, the proceedings are final as to that witness, and review is available. The interest in finality is enforced even in such proceedings by restricting the issues that the witness may present on appeal. For example, a witness has a statutory right to challenge grand jury inquiry based on unlawful electronic surveillance, but no right to prevent questions based on other kinds of illegal searches.[196]

Suppose, however, that the person subpoenaed is an attorney who is directed by the client to invoke the attorney-client privilege. It has been held that, in such a case, the privilege holder (the client) may intervene in the district court and appeal directly from the order overruling the claim of privilege. The order is final with regard to the client, because nothing remains for the client to do with respect to his or her claim.[197]

By similar reasoning, orders granting or denying access to grand jury minutes are appealable. For example, in *Illinois v Abbott & Associates,*[198] the Attorney General of Illinois moved under Fed R Crim P 6(e) and a 1976 amendment to the Clayton Act for access to minutes of an antitrust federal grand jury. The district judge denied the motion, holding that the Attorney General must show

---

[192] *Id* (quoting United States v MacDonald, 435 US 850, 860 (1978), *cert denied,* 440 US 961 (1979)). United States v Mechanik, 475 US 66 (1986).

[193] *Midland Asphalt Corp,* 489 US at 799 (quoting Flanagan, 465 US at 265).

[194] *E.g.,* United States v Moreno-Green, 881 F2d 680 (9th Cir 1989); United States v Shah, 878 F2d 272 (9th Cir 1989).

[195] *In re* Sealed Case, 827 F2d 776 (DC Cir 1987) (order denying motion to quash grand jury subpoena became appealable only when witness found in contempt of order). 28 USC §1826(b).

[196] Gelbard v United States, 408 US 41, *cert denied,* 408 US 922 (1972). United States v Calandra, 414 US 338 (1974). *See also* Branzburg v Hayes, 408 US 665 (1972); *In re* Grand Jury Subpoenas (Barrett), 818 F2d 330 (5th Cir) (order denying application to terminate grand jury not appealable), *cert denied,* 484 US 856 (1987).

[197] *E.g.,* Velsicol Chem Corp v Parsons, 561 F2d 671 (7th Cir 1977), *cert denied,* 435 US 942 (1978). *In re* Oberkoetter, 612 F2d 15 (1st Cir 1980); *In re* Grand Jury Proceedings Subpoena (Wire), 841 F2d 230 (8th Cir 1988). *But see In re* Grand Jury Proceedings (Doe), 831 F2d 222 (11th Cir 1987) (denial of client's motions to quash grand jury subpoena directed to attorney and to deliver documents seized by the IRS is nonappealable). From the point of view of the client appellant, this is also an issue of standing. *See* **§2.19.**

[198] 460 US 557 (1983).

particularized need for disclosure.[199] Even though the order did not preclude a further application based upon such a showing, the order at issue terminated the controversy with regard to all the Attorney General's claims and contemplated that further applications would be heard by other judges.

Other claims relating to grand jury proceedings may be appealable under the *Abbott* rationale. In the pre-*Abbott* case of *In re Grand Jury Investigation (Lance),*[200] Lance was the target of a federal grand jury investigation. He moved in the district court for contempt sanctions against government lawyers who allegedly had breached Fed R Crim P 6(e) by leaking grand jury information to the media. The district judge had found Lance's prima facie showing insufficient. The court of appeals reversed, holding that the order was appealable, because Lance was seeking civil contempt sanctions. If he were denied appellate review, he would be without a meaningful remedy. Further, the order was analogous to an interlocutory civil order. The court also held that the case was not mooted by the subsequent indictment of Lance.[201]

Closely related to grand jury litigation is that challenging allegedly unlawful searches and seizures. An indicted defendant has the right to move under Fed R Crim P 12 for suppression of unlawfully obtained evidence. If the motion is denied, the defendant can challenge the denial on appeal after trial, or can enter a conditional plea of guilty and appeal from the judgment entered on the plea. If the motion is granted, the government has a right of appeal under 18 USC §3731, discussed in **§2.11.** However, not all searches result in formal charges, and there is often a considerable gap between the search and a governmental decision regarding whether or not to bring charges.

Federal Rule of Criminal Procedure 41(e) permits the object of a search and seizure to file a motion for return of property. Denial of the motion is appealable, though the appeal will be dismissed if the movant is indicted.[202]

The Tenth Circuit held in *In re 6455 South Yosemite,*[203] that it did not have jurisdiction over an individual's appeal from denial of the motion for return of property, because he had been indicted and his motion had become one to suppress under the express terms of Fed R Crim P 41(e). The court did, however, assert jurisdiction over the corporate party's appeal because it had

---

[199] Fed R Crim P 6(e).

[200] 610 F2d 202 (5th Cir 1980).

[201] Judge Kravitch dissented, reasoning that the proposed contempt sanction was criminal and not civil. "This distinction is important because a criminal contempt action is governed by the rules applicable to criminal proceedings generally; no appeal may be taken from a judgment in favor of the alleged contemnor, including a denial of the motion." *Id* 221. *But see In re* Grand Jury Subpoena Dated June 5, 1985, 825 F2d 231 (9th Cir 1987) (appeal from order denying motion concerning grand jury production mooted by indictment of production witness; attorney's appeal not moot, but denial of attorney's motion to quash grand jury subpoena duces tecum not appealable).

[202] *See* United States v Mid-States Exch, 815 F2d 1227 (8th Cir 1987) (order denying a motion to return property rendered interlocutory and nonappealable by return of indictment against defendant after oral argument in court of appeals; defendant could raise issue in motion to suppress before district court).

[203] 897 F2d 1549 (10th Cir 1990).

not been indicted. Pendency of a grand jury proceeding in which the corporation might be indicted was irrelevant, the court said. The court of appeals remanded the corporation's case to the district court for a determination of whether the corporation met the irreparable injury and inadequate remedy at law requirements for invoking the essentially equitable Rule 41(e) remedy. *6455 South Yosemite* counsels advocates to include all persons with standing among the Fed R Crim P 41(e) movants to minimize the risk that the case will be sidetracked by an indictment.

§2.06 —28 USC §1292(a)(1): Grant or Denial of Preliminary Injunction

Title 28 USC §1292(a)(1) grants the courts of appeals "jurisdiction of appeals from . . . [i]nterlocutory orders . . . granting, continuing, modifying, refusing or dissolving injunctions, or refusing to dissolve or modify injunctions, except where a direct review may be had in the Supreme Court."[204]

Appealability turns upon whether the trial judge's action concerned an injunction, and upon whether the judge did one of the enumerated actions.

If the district court's order is entered after a hearing conducted under Fed R Civ P 65(a), it will almost surely be a preliminary injunction and therefore appealable. However, the court that issues an injunctive order under Fed R Civ P 65 must also make its order effective by setting a bond as the Rule requires. Otherwise, its order is not an injunction.[205]

By generally accepted definition, an injunction represents the exercise of equitable power to compel a person to do or refrain from doing an act. Under a broad interpretation of this definition, some nonfinal orders will be considered the equivalent of an injunction and therefore reviewable under 1292(a)(1).[206]

Defining *injunction* was arguably easier before the fusion of law and equity under Fed R Civ P 2, the one form of action rule. In the old days, an injunction was something that a chancellor, rather than a common law judge, had power to issue. This was true even if the federal judge served in both capacities.

Technical distinctions abounded, however, based on the historic distinction between law and equity. For example, if a party sued on a contract on the law side of the federal court and the defendant claimed mutual mistake, the defendant might very well file a separate action on the equity side and seek to have

---

[204] The full text of 28 USC §1292 is in **app E.** Direct Supreme Court review is a rara avis. *See* **§2.01.**

[205] *See, e.g.*, Coquina Oil Corp v Transwestern Pipeline Co, 825 F2d 1461 (10th Cir 1987) (district court's refusal to consider motion to set preliminary injunction bond rendered injunction unenforceable and deprived court of appeals of jurisdiction to review).

[206] *See, e.g.*, Continuum Co v Incepts, Inc, 883 F2d 333 (5th Cir 1989) (order increasing security bond for injunction, though usually interlocutory, becomes appealable if coupled with an order directing that the injunction be dissolved if the additional security is not posted).

the action at law stayed until the mutual mistake claim could be heard without a jury. The Supreme Court held under the old *Enelow-Ettelson* doctrine that such a stay was really an injunction, because a chancellor issued it in a court of equity. This was the rule even when the chancellor was also the judge to whom the stay was directed.[207]

The technical virtuosity of such distinctions is illustrated by *City of Morgantown v Royal Insurance Co.*[208] The insurance company sued to reform an insurance policy, alleging mutual mistake. The insured counterclaimed, seeking to recover under the policy as written, and demanded a jury trial. The district judge granted the insurance company's motion to strike the jury demand and set the case for nonjury trial. The Supreme Court held that the order was not appealable, because the case was not at all similar to a chancellor enjoining a judge. Rather, the order was just one step in the trial court's control of a lawsuit filed in the first instance on the equity side of the court. The Court distinguished its earlier decisions because, in those cases, the insured had filed an action at law, and the insurance company counterclaimed on the basis of mutual mistake. Thus, the order setting the counterclaim for a priority nonjury trial was in effect a stay of an action at law and, therefore, was an injunction.

The Supreme Court overruled the *Enelow-Ettelson* doctrine in *Gulfstream Aerospace Corp v Mayacamas Corp,* calling the doctrine "a total fiction" and noted that modern federal court procedures made the rule unworkable.[209]

In *Gulfstream,* petitioner filed a breach of contract action in Georgia state court. Respondent answered this complaint, but one-and-a-half months later filed a diversity action in federal court alleging breach of the same contract. Petitioner moved the district court to stay or dismiss the federal action. The motion was denied. The court of appeals dismissed petitioner's appeal for lack of jurisdiction, holding that neither 28 USC §1291 nor §1292(a)(1) permitted an intermediate appeal from the district court's order.

Petitioners based their §1292(a)(1) claim on the *Enelow-Ettelson* doctrine, arguing that stay of an action pending the resolution of similar proceedings in state court constituted an equitable order, thus fulfilling *Enelow-Ettelson's* second requirement.

The Court marked out four paths to the court of appeals that remain open after the *Enelow-Ettelson* gate is closed. First, §1292(a)(1) continues to provide appellate jurisdiction over orders that "have the practical effect of granting or denying injunctions and have "serious, perhaps irreparable, consequence.' "[210] Second, parties subject to onerous interlocutory orders can

---

[207] This was the rule in Ettelson v Metropolitan Life Ins Co, 317 US 188 (1942) and Enelow v New York Life Ins Co, 293 US 379 (1935), *overruled* Gulfstream Aerospace Corp v Mayacamas Corp, 485 US 271 (1988).

[208] 337 US 254 (1949).

[209] 485 US 271, 283 (1988).

[210] *Id* 287-88 (citing Carson v American Brands, Inc, 450 US 79, 84 (1981)) (quoting Baltimore Contractors, Inc v Bodinger, 348 US 176, 181 (1955)).

attempt to appeal under the collateral order doctrine of §1291 or, third, seek certification for immediate appeal under 28 USC §1292(b). Fourth, in exceptional cases, a party can apply for a writ of mandamus.[211]

The question whether an order resembles an injunction, or has the same practical effect, was addressed in *Baltimore Contractors, Inc v Bodinger,*[212] which remains a valuable source of legislative history for §1292(a)(1). In this diversity case, the plaintiff sought an accounting under a construction contract, alleging fraud and other improper practices. The defendant Baltimore Contractors invoked what they claimed to be an arbitration clause in the contract and sought a stay pending arbitration. The district court refused the stay. The Supreme Court, affirming the court of appeals, held that the denial of a stay was not appealable under §1292(a)(1) as a denial of an injunction.

Under the one form of action rule,[213] the order was simply one step in the conduct of the lawsuit. If such orders are appealable at all, they must satisfy the tests of the collateral order doctrine or be of such a nature that an extraordinary writ is available.[214]

In *United States v Ryan,*[215] the respondent's motion to quash a grand jury subpoena duces tecum was denied. Under *Cobbledick v United States,*[216] such an order would not be final, but Ryan claimed that the denial constituted an injunction because the district judge had ordered him to seek leave from the government of Kenya to bring the documents that were located there to the United States. If such permission was denied, the order directed Ryan to permit United States officials to see the documents in situ. A unanimous Court said that "the District Court's order did nothing more than inform respondent before the event of what efforts the District Court would consider sufficient attempts to comply

---

[211] *Gulfstream* has led a number of courts of appeals to rethink their precedents construing orders directing a party to do or refrain from doing something as equivalent to an injunction. *See, e.g.,* Feldspar Trucking Co v Greater Atlanta Shippers Assn, 849 F2d 1389 (11th Cir 1988) (order denying motion for stay of action pending referral of questions to ICC not appealable under either statute providing jurisdiction for appeals of interlocutory orders concerning injunctions or the collateral order doctrine). A too-sweeping reading of *Gulfstream* is Hamilton v Robertson, 854 F2d 740 (5th Cir 1988), which disallowed an appeal from a district court order that required the plaintiff to seek leave of the court before filing any further suits within the district. Although the order severely restricted plaintiff's conduct, the Circuit Court labeled it " 'merely a calendar order issued under the court's inherent power to regulate the administration of its own business.' " *Id* 741 (citing Anderson v United States, 520 F2d 1027, 1028 (5th Cir 1975) (quoting Penoro v Rederi A/B Disa, 376 F2d 125, 128 (2d Cir), *cert denied,* 389 US 852 (1967)).

[212] 348 US 176 (1955).

[213] Fed R Civ P 2: "There shall be one form of action to be known as 'civil action.' "

[214] *See* **§§2.04, 3.04.** For criticism of difficulties introduced by the subtle distinction between legal and equitable remedies and by rewarding the winner of the race to the courthouse, see Charles A. Wright, Federal Courts §102, at 727-28 (4th ed 1983) (citing and discussing cases).

[215] 402 US 530 (1971).

[216] 309 US 323 (1940), discussed at **§2.03.**

with the subpoena. . . . [It] did not convert denial of a motion to quash into an appealable injunctive order."[217]

Nor will an order that *affects* an injunction, present or future, necessarily *be* an injunction. An order construing a prior injunction, as distinct from modifying it, usually will not be appealable.[218] The Supreme Court held in *Gardner v Westinghouse Broadcasting Co*[219] that an order refusing to certify a class in an action seeking injunctive relief was not appealable under 1292(a)(1). The plaintiff argued that the injunctive relief available to the class was far broader than she could obtain as an individual. The Court found this argument unpersuasive, noting that the district court had not acted on the plaintiff's claim for injunctive relief.

Drawing upon *Baltimore Contractors,* the Court described narrowly the intended scope of §1292(a)(1): "[T]he statute creates an exception from the long-established policy against piecemeal appeals, which this Court is not authorized to enlarge or extend. The exception is a narrow one and is keyed to the 'need to permit litigants to effectually challenge interlocutory orders of serious, perhaps irreparable, consequence.' "[220]

This language was seized upon by the Court in a 1981 case as a basis for holding an order refusing to approve a consent decree to be appealable. In *Carson v American Brands, Inc,*[221] the petitioners represented a class of black employees challenging employment discrimination. The parties negotiated a settlement, which included a permanent injunction against discrimination and provided for race-conscious remedies. The district court refused to approve the settlement, claiming that it would violate constitutional and statutory limits on race-conscious remedies. The court of appeals held the refusal nonappealable, rejecting claims that it was a collateral order and that it was a denial of an injunction.

Justice Brennan's unanimous opinion for the Court held that "[a]lthough the District Court's order declining to enter the proposed consent decree did not in terms 'refus[e]' an 'injunctio[n],' it nonetheless had the practical effect of doing so."[222] The Court then quoted the "serious, perhaps irreparable" language from *Baltimore Contractors* and *Gardner,* and held that an order that has the practical effect of refusing an injunction, and that meets this further test, will be appealable under §1292(a)(1).

The principle that an order will be appealable, regardless of its label, if it has the practical effect of denying a preliminary injunction, has been estab-

---

[217] 402 US at 534.

[218] See discussion below in this section.

[219] 437 US 478 (1978).

[220] *Id* 480 (quoting Baltimore Contractors, Inc v Bodinger, 348 US 176, 181 (1955)).

[221] 450 US 79 (1981).

[222] *Id* 83.

lished in a number of cases.[223] For example, in *Cohen v Board of Trustees of the University of Medicine,*[224] a medical school professor sued the university and faculty members, challenging her denial of tenure. The district judge granted plaintiff's motion for partial summary judgment under Fed R Civ P 56(d). The court also "ordered that plaintiff remain in her position until such time as a hearing be held."[225] The court of appeals held that ordinarily a grant of partial summary judgment is similar to a pretrial order under Fed R Civ P 16, and simply narrows the issues for trial. To the extent it performs that function, it is not appealable under 28 USC §1291,[226] nor certifiable under Fed R Civ P 54(b).[227] The order would be appealable, if at all, only if certified under 28 USC §1292(b).[228] However, the order in this case went on to compel the defendants to do something. The "something" corresponded closely to relief requested by the plaintiff in her motion for preliminary injunction, which the district court did not in terms decide. Under these circumstances, the court of appeals held that the order was in form a preliminary injunction. Overruling prior authority, the court of appeals held that to be immediately appealable as an injunction, an order must adjudicate some relief sought in the complaint and must be of such a nature that if it grants relief it could be enforced during

---

[223] The cases are summarized in *Carson,* 450 US at 82 n6. To invoke the court of appeals' power, the appellant usually must show "serious, perhaps irreparable injury" from the denial. *See also* Durrett v Housing Auth of Providence, 896 F2d 600 (1st Cir 1990) (court of appeals has jurisdiction under Carson 450 US 79 (1981) and §1292(a)(1)) to review interlocutory order refusing to enter consent decree providing for injunctive relief); Sierra Club, Inc v Electronic Controls Design, Inc, 909 F2d 1350 (9th Cir 1990) (district court refusal to enter consent decree providing for injunctive relief appealable under §1292(a)); Volvo N Am Corp v Men's Intl Professional Tennis Council, 839 F2d 69 (2d Cir) (order dismissing antitrust complaint had the practical effect of denying injunctive relief from antitrust violations and therefore was immediately reviewable under §1292(a)(1)), *cert denied,* 487 US 1219 (1988); Bailey v Systems Innovation, Inc, 852 F2d 93 (3d Cir 1988) (gag order had effect of preliminary injunction and was appealable); EEOC v Pan Am World Airways, 796 F2d 314 (9th Cir 1986) (disapproval of proposed consent decree not appealable because it did not have practical effect of denying injunction and did not have serious, irreparable consequences), *cert denied,* 479 US 1030 (1987); Gillis v Department of Health & Human Servs, 759 F2d 565 (6th Cir 1985) (court had jurisdiction over interlocutory appeal of order dismissing defendant, despite District Court refusal to certify no reason for just delay, where remaining elements of case were finally disposed of prior to disposition of appeal). *See also* Charles A. Wright, *supra* note 214. *See also* Woodard v Sage Prods, Inc, 818 F2d 841 (Fed Cir 1987) (en banc) (order granting summary judgment of noninfringement in favor of one of several defendants in a patent infringement action does not wreak the kind of harm that would justify appellate review under the guise that the court refused an injunction; review available only by §1292(b) certification or under Fed R Civ P 54(b)); Ross v Zavarella, 916 F2d 898 (3d Cir 1990) (plaintiff seeking to appeal denial of order that has the practical effect of denying a preliminary injunction under §1292(a)(1) must show that order has a serious, perhaps irreparable consequence that can be averted only by immediate appeal).

[224] 867 F2d 1455 (3d Cir 1989).

[225] *Id.*

[226] *See* **§2.02.**

[227] *See* **§2.10.**

[228] *See* **§2.09.**

the litigation by contempt if necessary. Even an order such as the one under review, which could be characterized as a grant of specific performance pending the outcome of the litigation, would be treated as an injunction.

Equally valid is the principle that grant of a temporary restraining order that works so sweeping a change of the parties' relations as to be in effect a preliminary injunction rather than simple maintenance of the status quo will be appealable under §1292(a)(1).[229] Similarly, denial of a temporary restraining order will sometimes, though rarely, be reviewable as having the practical effect of denying an injunction.[230]

In addition to satisfying the requirement that the order appealed from be an injunction, the appellant must show that the action taken was one "granting, continuing, modifying, refusing, or dissolving" an injunction, or "refusing to dissolve or modify" one.[231] An order that merely interprets or applies a previous injunction is not appealable, and a party cannot use such an order to gain review of an injunction from which the party did not timely appeal in the first instance.[232]

If an order is appealable under §1292(a)(1), the entire order may be

---

[229] *See* Nordin v Nutri/System, Inc, 897 F2d 339 (8th Cir 1990) (court of appeals can review grant of TRO that unlawfully extends beyond 10-day period authorized by Fed R Civ P 65, because TRO is in effect a preliminary injunction); Haitian Refugee Ctr, Inc v Baker, 950 F2d 685 (11th Cir 1991) (TRO held appealable under exceptional circumstances; court of appeals will review TRO where it has the effect of a preliminary injunction, and is not bound by the district court's designation of the order; case stretches the concept of appealability at the government's behest); Teradyne, Inc v Mostek Corp, 797 F2d 43 (1st Cir 1986) (order restricting defendant in contract action from dispersal or encumbrance of assets tantamount to injunction because more than minimally coercive, treated by parties as an injunction, and goes beyond requiring posting of security); Charles A. Wright, *supra* note 214, at 102 n15 and accompanying text.

[230] Vuitton v White, 945 F2d 569 (3d Cir 1991) (denial of application for an ex parte order authorizing seizure of alleged counterfeit goods is immediately appealable under §1292(a)(1); court distinguishes cases holding denial of TRO not appealable); Woods v Wright, 334 F2d 369 (5th Cir 1964) (denial of TRO to black pupil expelled from school for participating in lawful protest appealable); Office of Personnel Management v American Fedn of Govt Employees, 473 US 1301 (1985) (Burger, CJ, in chambers) (denial of temporary restraining order not, on facts of this case, tantamount to denial of a preliminary injunction).

[231] 28 USC §1292(a)(1).

[232] The determination is often difficult to make. *See, e.g.*, Bradley v Milliken, 772 F2d 266 (6th Cir 1985) (in determining whether an injunction has been modified, so as to permit appellate review under §1292(a)(1), courts must look at whether there exists an underlying order injunctive in nature, whether the order being appealed in some way modified the initial order, and the practical consequences of the challenged order); International Assn of Machinists & Aerospace Workers v Eastern Airlines, 849 F2d 1481, 1485-86 (DC Cir 1988); Sierra Club v Marsh, 907 F2d 210, 212 (1st Cir 1990) (in determining whether an order is appealable as modifying a preliminary injunction, "a reviewing court must examine whether there was an underlying decree of an injunctive character, and if so, whether the ruling appealed from can fairly be said to have changed the underlying decree in a jurisdictionally significant way"). On timeliness of appeal, see **§6.03.**

reviewed, and not simply the parts of it that grant or deny an injunction.[233] In addition, related orders in the same case may be appealable concurrently with the preliminary injunction in the interest of conserving judicial resources.[234]

§2.07 —28 USC §1292(a)(2): Receivership Appeals

Title 28 USC §1292(a)(2) provides that the courts of appeals "shall have jurisdiction of appeals from:

> Interlocutory orders appointing receivers, or refusing orders to wind up receiverships or to take steps to accomplish the purposes thereof, such as directing sales or other disposals of property.[235]

Most of the scant caselaw on §1292(a)(2) deals with whether the order in question involved a true receiver; that is, one who steps into the shoes of the title holder with power seriously to affect property interests.[236] A receiver may be a guardian ad litem or someone appointed to administer the estate of an incompetent person.[237] A receiver may be appointed to administer the affairs of a corporation in the interests of its stockholders.[238] Under the Racketeer Influenced and Corrupt Organizations Act (RICO),[239] the district court may appoint a receiver in connection with a government civil suit.[240] The laws of many states permit appointment of a receiver to protect the public interest in the operation of corporations whose operations are regulated closely.[241] Thus, despite the paucity of appellate lore, §1292(a)(2) is of some potential importance.

---

[233] Kohn v American Metal Climax, Inc, 458 F2d 255 (3d Cir), *cert denied,* 409 US 874 (1972).

[234] *See, e.g.,* O'Halloran v University of Wash, 856 F2d 1375, 1378 (9th Cir 1988) (appeal from order denying a motion to remand joined with an appeal from an order denying an injunction). For discussion of pendent appellate jurisdiction, see **§2.18.** *Cf* Henco, Inc v Brown, 904 F2d 11 (7th Cir 1990) (expiration of preliminary injunction moots appeal, despite prospect that damages will be sought for having had to post injunction bond; issues can be resolved if district court in fact awards damages; neither party sought to expedite the appeal to obtain resolution before the injunction terminated); the general issue of mootness is discussed in **§2.18.**

[235] The full text of 28 USC §1292(a)(2) is in **app E.**

[236] *See generally* 16 Charles A. Wright, Arthur R. Miller, E. Cooper, & Eugene Gressman, Federal Practice and Procedure §3925 (1977 & Supp 1986).

[237] *E.g.,* Lyman v Spain, 774 F2d 495 (DC Cir 1985) (receiver for incompetent elderly person; order appointing receiver for corporation appealable and summarily affirmed).

[238] *Id.*

[239] 18 USC §1964.

[240] *See, e.g.,* United States v Ianniello, 824 F2d 203 (2d Cir 1987) (upholding order appointing receiver under 18 USC §1964 to collect and pay taxes on restaurants allegedly victimized by skimming).

[241] *See* People *ex rel* Hartigan v Peters, 861 F2d 164 (7th Cir 1988) (state and federal motor vehicle laws invoked to put car dealer in receivership).

A receiver is a creature of equity; appellate review is therefore permitted based upon a clear analogy to §1292(a)(1), which grants review of preliminary injunctions. Indeed, the injunction review and receiver review provisions now codified at §1292(a)(1) and (2) were both part of the same statutory section, which was designed to confer appellate jurisdiction over district court orders that were considered essentially equitable in nature.[242] The receivership/injunction analogy is mentioned in some of the cases[243] and judges have even suggested that an order appointing a receiver for no more than 10 days, with a hearing to be held at that time on whether the appointment should be continued, would not be appealable because such an order is analogous to a nonreviewable grant of a temporary restraining order.[244]

There is a major difference, however, between §1292(a)(1) and §1292(a)(2): the latter provision does not permit appeal if the court refuses to act; orders refusing to appoint a receiver are not appealable, nor are like orders such as those vacating an appointment or refusing to vacate an appointment already made.[245]

An order refusing to vacate an appointment cannot be appealed on the theory that the district judge refused to wind up the receivership. The *winding up* language refers to situations in which the receivership has been properly in operation, but which due to "changed circumstances ought not to be continued."[246] Moreover, appellate jurisdiction is limited to orders taking steps to

---

[242] Act of Feb 13, 1925, ch 229, §1, 43 Stat 937.

[243] A receiver is an "ordinary equity receiver" or some official of similar statutory authority and not a collection agent or special master. *See* Martin v Partridge, 64 F2d 591, 592 (8th Cir 1933). However, a receiver by any other name is still a receiver, and the appointment will be reviewable. United States v Sylacauga Properties, Inc, 323 F2d 487 (5th Cir 1963). The standard of review is abuse of discretion. Skirvin v Mesta, 141 F2d 668 (10th Cir 1944).

[244] Marion Mortgage Co v Edmunds, 64 F2d 248, 250-51 (1933). *See also* Charles A. Wright, *supra* note 236, §3925, at 95-96.

[245] Warren v Bergeron, 831 F2d 101 (5th Cir 1987) (Rubin, J) (order vacating appointment of receiver not appeable absent certification, citing cases from other circuits).

[246] Grand Beach Co v Gardner, 34 F2d 836, 838 (6th Cir 1929), *quoted in* People *ex rel* Hartigan v Peters, 861 F2d 164, 165 (7th Cir 1988). The Ninth Circuit, in Mitchell v Lay, 48 F2d 79, 85 (9th Cir 1930), *cert denied*, 238 US 864 (1931), suggested that a party who was "brought into the court after the receiver is appointed and who has had no opportunity and no right to appeal from the order appointing a receiver" might be permitted to make a motion to vacate the appointment and to appeal from the denial. This notion was referred to with apparent approval by Judge Posner in *Hartigan*, 861 F2d at 166. The better avenue to appeal would be to wait until the receiver orders the new party to do something to which the party objects, then appeal under the collateral order doctrine or on the theory that the order is an injunction. *See* **§§2.04, 2.06.**

SEC v Bartlett, 422 F2d 475, 477 (8th Cir 1970), permitted an appeal from an order refusing to vacate a receivership, but upheld appellate jurisdiction by misquoting §1292(a)(2). In SEC v Lincoln Thrift Assn, 577 F2d 600, 602 (9th Cir 1978), the court said that the *practical effect* doctrine (discussed in **§2.06**) would permit appeal of an order that had the effect of refusing to wind up a receivership. The analysis was disagreed with in *Hartigan*, 861 F2d at 165, and would create an exception that swallows the rule.

accomplish the purposes of winding up receiverships, not orders refusing to take such steps.[247]

Orders *involving* receivers, not appealable under §1292(a)(1),[248] may be reviewable by mandamus or under §1292(b).[249] Particular orders *by a receiver,* when upheld by a district judge, may amount to grant or denial of a preliminary injunction and be appealable on that basis.[250] A district judge's order granting or denying a stay in connection with a receivership will be appealable under §1291(a)(1).[251]

§2.08 —28 USC §1292(a)(3): Admiralty Appeals

Title 28 USC §1292(a)(3)[252] provides that, except for cases where jurisdiction lies with the Court of Appeals for the Federal Circuit, the courts of appeals for the various circuits have jurisdiction of appeals from:

> Interlocutory decrees of such district courts or the judges thereof determining the rights and liabilities of the parties to admiralty cases in which appeals from final decrees are allowed.

In essence, the loser on liability in an admiralty case has the right, though not the obligation, to appeal before damages are determined. However, §1292(a)(3) antedates the unification of admiralty procedure with federal civil procedure generally[253] and therefore may raise difficult problems of interpretation. These problems are compounded by judicial opinions, even from the same court, saying that the subsection is to be interpreted broadly[254] or narrowly.[255]

There are some clear guidelines. An admiralty case is one that contains an

---

[247] SEC v American Principals Holdings, Inc, 817 F2d 1349 (9th Cir 1987).

[248] *See* **§2.06.**

[249] *See* **§§2.09, 3.04.**

[250] *See* **§2.06.**

[251] SEC v Universal Fin, 760 F2d 1034 (2d Cir 1985).

[252] The full text of 28 USC §1292(a)(3) is in **app E.**

[253] The background to the present statute is discussed in Schoenamsgruber v Hamburg Am Line, 294 US 454 (1935). Federal judges sitting in admiralty cases may, as in any other case, issue many interlocutory orders. Despite the 1966 merger of admiralty practice with civil practice generally, one must continue to apply the *Schoenamsgruber* teaching that "Congress did not intend to make appealable any other interlocutory decrees in admiralty" beyond those specified in §1292(a)(3). *See* Hollywood Marine, Inc v M/V Artie James, 755 F2d 414, 416 (5th Cir 1985) (dismissing appeal and analyzing statute; discussed in text below); Constructora Subacuatica Diavaz, SA v M/V Hiryu, 718 F2d 690, 692-93 (5th Cir 1983) (citing *Schoenamsgruber*). *See generally* 16 Charles A. Wright, Arthur R. Miller, Edward H. Cooper, & Eugene Gressman, Federal Practice and Procedure §3927 (1977 & Supp 1993).

[254] Walter E. Heller & Co v O/S Sonny V, 595 F2d 968, 971 (5th Cir 1979).

[255] Hollywood Marine, Inc v M/V Artie James, 755 F2d 414 (5th Cir 1985).

admiralty claim. An admiralty claim is defined by Fed R Civ P 9(h)[256] as being either (1) one cognizable in admiralty at the plaintiff's option and also within the district court's jurisdiction on nonadmiralty grounds and identified as an admiralty claim in the pleadings, or (2) a claim cognizable only in admiralty whether or not so identified in the pleadings.

Another clear rule is that §1292(a)(3) provides an opportunity to appeal, but not the compulsion to do so. A party may await entry of a final judgment and invoke §1291 as the basis for appeal. Similarly, the provisions of Fed R Civ P 54(b) are as available to an admiralty litigant as to any other, although Rule 54(b) certification is not a prerequisite to appealing under §1292(a)(3).[257]

Beyond these basic principles, the potential appellant may have difficulty identifying the point at which §1292(a)(3) confers appellate jurisdiction. As the Eighth Circuit said in *Slatton v Martin K. Eby Construction Co,*[258] "[T]he primary purpose of 1292(a)(3) was to provide an immediate appeal in those situations where liability had been determined, but reference to a commissioner for the determination of damages was made." The term *liability* means, so the cases teach, "one party's liability to another."[259] For example, an interlocutory order which finally determines the liability of one party to a maritime suit is appealable under §1293(a)(3) even if damages have not been finally computed.[260]

Instructive are the cases involving an insurance company that is added as a party after denying coverage for the event that triggers admiralty jurisdiction. If the carrier is dismissed on pretrial motion as not liable, its liability is then settled in the district court with regard to the suing party and its insured. Therefore, an appeal will lie under §1292(a)(3).[261]

Similarly, if the district court holds the insurance company liable for statutory penalties and costs, the order will be appealable even though other issues

---

[256] Fed R Civ P 9(h) provides:

> A pleading or count setting forth a claim for relief within the admiralty and maritime jurisdiction that is also within the jurisdiction of the district court on some other ground may contain a statement identifying the claim as an admiralty or maritime claim for the purposes of Rules 14(c), 38(e), 82, and the Supplemental Rules for Certain Admiralty and Maritime Claims. If the claim is cognizable only in admiralty, it is an admiralty or maritime claim for those purposes whether so identified or not. The amendment of a pleading to add or withdraw an identifying statement is governed by the principles of Rule 15. The reference in Title 28, USC §1292(a)(3), to admiralty cases shall be construed to mean admiralty and maritime claims within the meaning of this subdivision (h).

[257] *In re* Intercontinental Properties Management, SA, 604 F2d 254, 258 n2 (4th Cir 1979); Walter E. Heller & Co v O/S Sonny V, 595 F2d 968, 971 (5th Cir 1979); O'Donnell v Latham, 525 F2d 650, 652 (5th Cir 1976).

[258] For discussion of Fed R Civ P 54(b), see **§2.10.**

[259] Hollywood Marine, Inc v M/V Artie James, 755 F2d 414, 416 (5th Cir 1985).

[260] Stoot v Fluor Drilling Servs, 851 F2d 1514, 1516 (5th Cir 1988) (intent of §1292(a)(3) is "to permit a party found liable to take an immediate appeal from that finding and thereby possibly avoid an oftentimes costly and protracted trial of the damages issue, quoting 9 Moore's Federal Practice §110.19[3], at 209-10 (1985)).

[261] O'Donnell v Latham, 525 F2d 650 (5th Cir 1976).

remain in the litigation.[262] As illustrated by *Hollywood Marine, Inc v M/V Artie James,*[263] however, an insurance carrier that is held liable to its insured if and when a judgment is obtained against the latter cannot appeal. The nature and extent of its liability remains to be determined, depending upon the fate of its insured in the ensuing litigation. This decision rests, the Fifth Circuit explained, upon the same principle as those cases holding that district court orders rejecting defenses and exceptions in admiralty cases are not appealable.[264]

In *Walter E. Heller & Co v O/S Sonny V,*[265] the district court had held two parties liable to the plaintiff; it had not adjudicated one of those parties' counterclaim against the plaintiff. The judgment might have been appealable under 18 USC §1291 if certified under Fed R Civ P 54(b),[266] but no Rule 54(b) certification was entered. The court of appeals held it had jurisdiction under §1292(a). While the district court's order did not dispose of all the defendants' claims against the plaintiff, it did dispose of all the plaintiffs claims, which is enough to satisfy the statute.

In admiralty cases, the Supreme Court's decision in *Schoenamsgruber v Hamburg American Line*[267] often has been cited by the courts of appeals as governing appealability of stays and conditional dismissals. In that case, the district court stayed the action pending arbitration under an arbitration clause and retained jurisdiction to enter judgment on the award. The Supreme Court held that the stay was not an injunction, because admiralty courts could not at that time issue injunctions; hence, it was not appealable under the predecessor to §1292(a)(1). The decision was not final because it did not meet the standards of §1291. Nor was appeal available under the predecessor to §1292(a)(3), because the order did not determine the rights and liabilities of any party.[268]

Schoenamsgruber has been invoked to deny appealability to a dismissal—for example, on forum non conveniens grounds—conditioned upon a party posting security and waiving the statute of limitations in the new forum.[269] Such

---

[262] Offshore Logistics Servs v Mutual Marine Office, Inc, 639 F2d 1168 (5th Cir 1981). *See also In re* Talbott Big Foot, Inc, 854 F2d 758 (5th Cir 1988) (the parties may appeal an order increasing the amount of required security in a limitation of liability action); Afram Lines Intl, Inc v M/V Capetan Yiannis, 905 F2d 347 (11th Cir 1990) (court of appeals has jurisdiction to review countersecurity order entered under Admiralty Rule E(7)).

[263] 755 F2d 414 (5th Cir 1985).

[264] *Id* 416.

[265] 595 F2d 968 (5th Cir 1979).

[266] **§2.10.**

[267] 294 US 454 (1935).

[268] *Id* 458. The Schoenamsgruber discussion of the *Enelow-Ettleson* doctrine, and of the appealability of orders affecting arbitration, must be read in light of the overruling of *Enelow-Ettleson,* discussed in **§2.06,** and the statutory provisions concerning arbitration under the Federal Arbitration Act, discussed in **§2.15.**

[269] Constructora Subacuatica Diavaz, SA v M/V Hiryu, 718 F2d 690, 693 (5th Cir 1983) (holding nonappealable an order of dismissal conditioned upon waiver of statute of limitations, and remitting the case to an arbitrator).

an order is appealable under §1291 only if and when the district judge also releases the vessel seized at the inception of the action (as discussed at **§2.02**). However, if the case is properly before the court of appeals under §1292(a)(3), the court may consider issues beyond the particular order that confers jurisdiction.[270]

If a party chooses the interlocutory appeal route, there is a risk of being trapped by the effect that a notice of appeal will have on the district court's jurisdiction. A notice of appeal in an admiralty case divests the district court of jurisdiction only if the order is appealable, and only to the extent of that order. This problem is illustrated by *Offshore Logistics Services v Mutual Marine Office, Inc.*[271] In an admiralty case, the district court ordered insurance company A to pay a statutory penalty to parties G and O, and by a later order refused to reconsider its decision. A appealed. Thereafter, the district judge changed his mind, and entered an order that A was not liable to G and O. They appealed.[272] The court of appeals dismissed G's and O's appeal because the district court lacked jurisdiction to change its mind, A's appeal having been properly and timely filed under §1292(a)(3). The proper course would have been for A to secure remand from the court of appeals so that the district judge could enter a new order.

§2.09 —28 USC §1292(b): Appeals by Permission

With the permission of the district judge and the approval of the court of appeals, otherwise interlocutory orders can be immediately appealed under 28 USC §1292(b). Section 1292(b) provides a limited escape valve from finality rules, jealously monitored by trial and appellate courts. This section discusses the statutory standards for certification from the district judge and court of appeals grant of permission to appeal, describes the procedures in the trial and appellate court, and finally deals with the scope of review in §1292(b) cases.

Section 1292(b) provides that a district judge may certify an order not otherwise appealable if the judge is

> of the opinion that such order involves a [1] controlling question of law [2] as to which there is substantial ground for difference of opinion and [3] that an immediate appeal from the order may materially advance the ultimate termination of the litigation. . . .[273]

---

[270] Salazar v Atlantic Sun, 881 F2d 73 (3d Cir 1989) (order confirming sale of arrested vessel appealable under §1292(a)(3) and court will hear all points involved in appeal because underlying due process issues affect validity of sale). *Cf* Cement Div, Natl Gypsum Co v City of Milwaukee, 915 F2d 1154 (7th Cir 1990) (order disqualifying counsel in admiralty action nonappealable as in ordinary civil case, but order apportioning liability among alleged wrongdoers is appealable), *cert denied,* 111 S Ct 1583 (1991).

[271] 462 F Supp 485 (ED La 1978), *vacated & dismissed,* 639 F2d 1168 (5th Cir 1981).

[272] A apparently abandoned its appeal after the district judge's new order.

[273] Numbers supplied for ease of reference.

The judge must make these findings in writing and in the order from which an appeal is to be taken.

The party aggrieved by the order then has 10 days within which to file a "Petition for Permission to Appeal" under Fed R App P 5, in the "Court of Appeals which would have jurisdiction of an appeal of such action."[274] The opponent may file a response to the petition within seven days.[275]

In the first 20 years after enactment of 1292(b) in 1958, there were about 100 district court certifications per year, of which about half have led a court of appeals to grant permission to appeal. The number has increased somewhat in proportion to the increase in the number of federal appeals generally. As explained in *Coopers & Lybrand v Livesey,*[276] §1292(b) rations review of nonfinal orders:

> . . . Congress carefully confined the availability of such review. Nonfinal orders could never be appealed as a matter of right. Moreover, the discretionary power to permit an interlocutory appeal is not, in the first instance, vested in the courts of appeals. A party seeking review of a nonfinal order must first obtain the consent of the trial judge. This screening procedure serves the dual purpose of ensuring that such review will be confined to appropriate cases and avoiding time-consuming jurisdictional determinations in the court of appeals. Finally, even if the district judge certifies the order under §1292(b), the appellant still "has the burden of persuading the court of appeals that exceptional circumstances justify a departure from the basic policy of postponing appellate review until after the entry of a final judgment." . . . The appellate court may deny the appeal for any reason, including docket congestion.[277]

Given the double hurdle of district court certification and court of appeals discretion, it is not surprising that few appeals are decided under §1292(b). The advocate faced with a troublesome order that disposes of less than all the claims in a case should first consider using Fed R Civ P 54(b).[278] Next, consideration should turn to the collateral order doctrine.[279] Counsel also should evaluate the prospects of an extraordinary writ.[280] These various devices can be used in combination. For example, if an order is arguably final, the advocate can

---

[274] 28 USC §1292(b). *See* **ch 4.**

[275] The full text of Fed R App P 5 is in **app A.** The procedure for invoking §1292(b) jurisdiction in the court of appeals is discussed in **§2.09.**

[276] 437 US 463 (1978).

[277] *Id* 474-75. *See generally* Note, *Interlocutory Appeals in the Federal Courts under 28 USC §1292(b),* 88 Harv L Rev 607 (1975) (an excellent reference). The procedure for invoking the court of appeals jurisdiction under §1292(b) is discussed at **§6.05.**

[278] Discussed at **§2.10.**

[279] Discussed at **§2.04.**

[280] Stone v Heckler, 722 F2d 464 (9th Cir 1983).

seek 1292(b) certification and also appeal under 1291.[281] Mandamus also may be sought if the standards discussed in Chapter 3 are met.[282]

As noted above in quoting the statute, Section 1292(b) contains three criteria. The procedure for seeking certification is abbreviated. Most courts of appeals' decisions accepting cases under §1292(b) result in an opinion on the merits, usually without discussion of the basis for §1292(b) treatment. Rejection of a certification request or dismissal of the appeal is more likely to yield an opinion. Hence, the reported appellate decisions are skewed. There is a wealth of district court authority, however, in rulings on motions to include a certification in an order.

In support of the application in the district court to certify, and the Fed R App P 5 petition, the advocate must separately establish, with legal authority and support in the record, the three bases for appeal.

Under the first §1292(b) criterion, *controlling question of law,* factual findings are not to be reviewed no matter how important they may be. Once a question of law is present, the factual findings that led to the decision also will be reviewed. Some courts have suggested that rulings within the district court's broad discretionary authority, such as transfer orders, should not be reviewable. The courts of appeals, with the apparent acquiescence of the Supreme Court, generally have agreed that §1292(b) is available to review discretionary class determinations under Fed R Civ P 23.[283] It may be that a decision that one party among several defendants is not liable is appropriate for certification if the other criteria are met.

A controlling question of law will be one that deeply affects the ongoing process of litigation. Such a question may involve an entire theory of liability, the amenability to suit of a defendant, or the standing of plaintiffs. A procedural order of sufficiently onerous effect may, however, meet the *controlling question* test.[284]

Under the second criterion, the district judge must look to the law of the court of appeals with jurisdiction to review the order and determine that the question is novel or difficult. If the court that will have such jurisdiction has

---

[281] With respect to class actions, see Coopers & Lybrand v Livesey, 437 US 463, 474-75 (1978), *reaffd in* Deposit Guar Natl Bank v Roper, 445 US 326, 336 n8 (1980); EEOC v DH Holmes Co, 556 F2d 787 (5th Cir), *rehg denied,* 565 F2d 164 (1977), *cert denied,* 436 US 962 (1978).

As to multiparty cases, see 16 Charles A. Wright, Arthur R. Miller, Edward H. Cooper, & Eugene Gressman, Federal Practice and Procedure §3929, at 147-48 (1977 & Supp 1993).

[282] An unusual §1292(b) case is *In re* McClelland Engrs, Inc, 742 F2d 837 (5th Cir 1984) (district judge's forum non conveniens denial rested on novel premises and judge abused discretion in refusing to certify under §1292(b); mandamus denied with a request that the district judge certify the challenged order under §1292(b)), *cert denied,* 469 US 1228 (1985).

[283] *See* Coopers & Lybrand v Livesey, 437 US 463, 474-75 (1978).

[284] On use of §1292(b) certification to review forum non conveniens issues, see David W. Robertson, *Forum Non Conveniens in America and England: "A Rather Fantastic Fiction,"* 103 Law Q Rev 398, 416 n137 (1987).

clearly decided the issue, but is in disagreement with other courts of appeals, this will be an important but not determinative factor in seeking certification.

The final criterion must be read together with the first. An issue that may speed the litigation would, for example, be a liability determination that leaves out a major defendant. If the order is wrong, then there will have to be another trial. An interlocutory order dealing with issue preclusion on a key element of a party's case also will be appropriate for certification.[285]

The court of appeals, upon petition for permission, will apply the same standards as did the district judge. Thus, cases from the district courts and the courts of appeals are equally relevant in construing §1292(b). In seeking certification and permission to appeal, the same kinds of considerations that might lead a court of appeals to hear an application for extraordinary writ will be relevant.[286]

An example of §1292(b) in action is provided by *Raymond v Mobil Oil Corp.*[287] Plaintiffs filed a class action in Colorado under the Employee Retirement Income Security Act (ERISA) and an opt-in action under the Age Discrimination in Employment Act (ADEA), claiming that Mobil had unlawfully caused them to retire by making changes in its pension plan. An earlier Tenth Circuit case involving the same employment decision has resulted in an opinion holding that the sole plaintiff in that case lacked standing under ERISA. However, the Fifth Circuit had held that standing might obtain for some employees if certain facts could be proved.[288] Relying on the Tenth Circuit case, Mobil moved for summary judgment. The district court denied the motion, but certified the issue under §1292(b). Obviously the issue was controlling because it involved a threshold matter of right to sue.

The disagreement between the Tenth and Fifth Circuits was not irreconcilable, but there was some arguable tension between the two prior cases, heightened by the district judge's decision to adopt the rationale of the Fifth Circuit rather than the Tenth. Finally, if the uncontested facts showed that plaintiffs did not have standing, several hundred plaintiffs would be out of the suit entirely and only ADEA issues would remain to be tried; resolution of the issue therefore would serve judicial economy.

By contrast, Judge Newman's opinion for the Second Circuit in *Isra Fruit, Ltd v Agrexco Agricultural Export Co,*[289] denied §1292(b) appealability to an order

---

[285] When controlling circuit law is doubtful, certification may be granted. Giglio v Farrell Lines, 424 F Supp 927 (SDNY 1977).

On the certification of questions related to the effect of earlier proceedings, see Charles A. Wright, *supra* note 281, at 3931.

[286] *See* **§§3.04-3.10, 3.15.**

[287] 983 F2d 1528 (10th Cir), *cert denied,* 114 S Ct 81 (1993).

[288] Christopher v Mobil Oil Corp, 950 F2d 1209 (5th Cir), *cert denied,* 113 S Ct 68 (1992).

[289] 804 F2d 24 (2d Cir 1986). *See also In re* Coordinated Pretrial Proceedings in Petroleum Prods Antitrust Litig MDL No 150, 788 F2d 1571 (Emer Ct App 1986) (vacating earlier order permitting interlocutory appeal and remanding for entry of judgment in final form).

holding that the plaintiff had standing. The parties were competitors in importing produce into the United States from Israel. The district judge, denying a motion to dismiss the complaint, held that a competitor has standing to sue under the anti-dumping act, and certified this "question" under §1292(b). Judge Newman did not doubt the importance and difficulty of the issue. However, appeal would not materially advance the termination of the litigation because the antitrust claims would be tried in any event and the jury could be asked to render special verdicts on the various statutory theories.

Another illustrative case is *In re Showa Denko KK L-Tryptophan Products Liability Litigation-II.*[290] In a complex multidistrict tort case, the district judge entered a sweeping order on the conduct of discovery and case management. It is quite unusual for such orders to be reviewable on any theory, but the district judge found the §1292(b) standard satisfied and made the appropriate certificate. The court of appeals granted the petition for permission and, on the merits, reversed the order. The court of appeals disagreement with the order appealed from suggests that it might have granted a mandamus if the district court had not certified the issue.[291]

These cases teach that the party seeking certification should persuade the district judge to make relatively detailed findings of why the statutory standards are met, including particularly an analysis of how the litigation will be helped by early review of the certified order. Although §1292(b) permits the district judge to certify an order sua sponte, usually one must move for certification. For example, in *Isra Fruit,* the anti-dumping claim might have been so vital to the plaintiff's position that resolution of it would greatly enhance the prospects of settlement. Or, evidence on anti-dumping issues might have materially lengthened the trial or introduced legal complexities that would make the jury's work more difficult.[292] Indeed, Judge Newman cautioned against district judges issuing §1292(b) certificates in the bare statutory words.[293]

Because the statute requires that the order being certified contain the §1292(b) certification and findings, an advocate may well find it wise to urge certification of an issue when briefing or orally arguing the merits.

Once certification is granted, the 10-day period prescribed in Fed R App P 5(a) is jurisdictional and may not, as Fed R App P 26(b) states, be extended. However, a party may ask the district judge to enter new findings and recertify the order, thus starting the 10 days anew.[294] Counsel should not, however, take for granted that the district court's tardy addition of a §1292(b) controlling question certification will always be sufficient, even given Fed R App P 5(a)'s express authorization to amend the order to start the 10-day clock running again.

---

[290] 953 F2d 162 (4th Cir 1992).

[291] *See* **ch 3.**

[292] See for a thoughtful analysis of considerations leading to certification, Fukuda v County of Los Angeles, 630 F Supp 228 (CD Cal 1986).

[293] Isra Fruit, Ltd v Agrexco Agric Export Co, 804 F2d 24, 25 (2d Cir 1986).

[294] Note, *supra* note 277, at 615.

In *Weir v Propst*,[295] the defendant public officials' claim of immunity was denied on January 29. They had the right to an immediate *Mitchell v Forsyth*[296] appeal under §1291, but did nothing. On April 2, they asked the district court either to reconsider its order or to certify it under §1292(b). The court denied reconsideration but did certify. The court of appeals held that so tardy and unjustified an amendment satisfied neither §1292(b) nor Fed R App P 5(a). The court reaffirmed the teaching of cases that permit counsel a reasonable time to review an order and then seek to have it amended to include a §1292(b) situation, but found this case outside the liberal limits set by those cases.

Section 1292(b) provides for certification of an *order* and not a *question*.[297] The order must meet the statutory criteria. If the order presents more than one question, review may be correspondingly broad. By the same token, the court of appeals is powerless to review matters decided in orders other than the one certified. For example, in *United States v Stanley*,[298] a soldier injured as the result of drug experiments conducted on him while he was in the military sued the United States under the Federal Tort Claims Act. This suit was decided adversely to him, although he was permitted to replead on a constitutional tort theory. A complicated series of proceedings in the district court led to an order upholding Stanley's right to sue for a constitutional tort. The district court certified its order under §1292(b).

The court of appeals accepted the certification and upheld the constitutional tort theory. It also decided that intervening law had revitalized Stanley's Federal Tort Claims Act suit and directed the district court to allow him to replead that claim. The Supreme Court reversed, holding that "[e]ven if the Court of Appeals' jurisdiction is not confined to the precise question certified by the lower court (because the statute brings the 'order,' not the question, before the court), that jurisdiction is confined to the particular order appealed from."[299]

§2.10 —Federal Rule 54(b): Partial Judgment in Case with Multiple Claims or Multiple Parties

Federal Rule of Civil Procedure 54(b) provides another avenue to the court of appeals before a final judgment that resolves all issues as to all parties. The rule provides in part:

> When more than one claim for relief is presented in an action, whether as a claim, counterclaim, cross-claim, or third-party claim, or when multiple parties are involved, the court may direct the entry of a [1] final judg-

---

[295] 915 F2d 283 (7th Cir 1990).

[296] 472 US 511 (1985), discussed in **§§2.02, 2.04.**

[297] Judge Newman reiterates this point in 804 F2d at 25.

[298] 483 US 669 (1987).

[299] *Id* 677.

> ment as to one or more but fewer than all of the claims or parties [2] only upon an express determination that there is no just reason for delay and upon an express direction for the entry of judgment.[300]

Rule 54(b) took its present form in 1961,[301] to allow appeal of orders that do not meet the rigorous standards of §1292(b), but nonetheless finally dispose of part of a multifaceted lawsuit.[302] The district judge must be satisfied that the order to be appealed need not be reconsidered in light of later developments involving the remaining claims and parties. This section describes the circumstances under which Rule 54(b) treatment will be an option for litigators, and illustrates how the district courts and courts of appeals interpret the rule's standards.[303]

The purposes and scope of Rule 54(b) are not difficult to divine. The Federal Rules of Civil Procedure permit, indeed encourage, liberal joinder of parties and claims over which the district court has original jurisdiction.[304] That power is expanded by the availability of pendent and ancillary jurisdiction.[305] Multidistrict cases and mass tort actions are particularly likely to breed complexity.[306]

Recognizing this procedural flexibility, district judges have broad power to

---

[300] Numbers supplied for ease of reference. The full text of Fed R Civ P 54(b) is in **app B.** The rule goes on to provide that: In the absence of such determination and direction, any order or other form of decision, however designated, which adjudicates fewer than all the claims or the rights and liabilities of fewer than all the parties shall not terminate the action as to any of the claims or parties, and the order or other form of decision is subject to revision at any time before the entry of judgment adjudicating all the claims and the rights and liabilities of all the parties.

[301] A 1946 amendment to Fed R Civ P 54(b) had made clear the trial court's power to certify a judgment that disposed of fewer than all the claims in the action. The 1961 amendment was designed to overturn a line of cases that had held the rule inapplicable to an order disposing of fewer than all defendants jointly named in a single claim. For a discussion of the original rule and the amendment, see Sears, Roebuck & Co v Mackey, 351 US 427, 432-35 (1956).

[302] The validity of Rule 54(b) was settled early. *See* Sears, Roebuck & Co v Mackey, 351 US 427, 429 n1 (1956) (collecting cases).

[303] See the Advisory Committee Notes to the 1961 amendment. Although the notes state that the availability of Rule 54(b) treatment to one or more parties in a multiple party lawsuit means that 28 USC §1292(b) certification is not available in such a situation, Rule 54(b) certifications and appeals by permission under 1292(b) continue to coexist in the decided cases. The overlap is discussed, and cases collected, in 16 Charles A. Wright, Arthur R. Miller, Edward H. Cooper, & Eugene Gressman, Federal Practice and Procedure §3929, at 147-49 (1977 & Supp 1993); 10 Charles A. Wright, Arthur R. Miller, & Mary Kay Kane, Federal Practice and Procedure §2657 (1983 & Supp 1993).

[304] Fed R Civ P 13, 14, 18, 19, 20, 21, 22, 23, 23.1, 23.2, and 24 are the principal joinder provisions. *See* Sears, Roebuck & Co v Mackey, 351 US 427, 432-33 (1956).

[305] *See generally* United Mine Workers v Gibbs, 383 US 715 (1966); Aldinger v Howard, 427 US 1 (1976); Finley v United States, 490 US 545 (1989); *cf* Owen Equip & Erection Co v Kroger, 437 US 365 (1978).

[306] 28 USC §1407; *see also* Rules of Procedure of the Judicial Panel on Multidistrict Litigation.

consolidate and sever claims and parties for purposes of trial.[307] Rule 56 envisions partial summary judgment as to one or more claims or parties.[308] All of this is a long way from the common law writ system of one claim at a time.[309] For these reasons, it makes sense to depart from a rule that the entire case must be disposed of on final judgment before any party can appeal any claim. Rule 54(b) appeals are available only in multiclaim or multiparty cases.

Rule 54(b) appealability is triggered by the district judge directing entry of judgment on one or more claims or parties and certifying that there is no just reason to delay appeal from that judgment. Without the entry of such a judgment and such a certification, a party has no right of appeal; the order in question then remains nonfinal and subject to revision during the rest of the lawsuit.[310]

However, the district court's entry of judgment and issuance of the certificate do not guarantee the aggrieved party a hearing on the merits in the court of appeals. First, the judgment entered must, as to the matters it adjudicates, satisfy the same finality requirements as a judgment reviewable under 1291.[311]

---

[307] Fed R Civ P 42. *See In re* Korean Air Lines Disaster of Sept 1, 1983, 829 F2d 1171, 1176 n9 (DC Cir 1987), *affd sub nom* Chan v Korean Air Lines, 490 US 122 (1989).

[308] Fed R Civ P 56(d).

[309] *See* 10 Charles A. Wright, *supra* note 303, at §2653.

[310] Bristol v Fibreboard Corp, 789 F2d 846, 848 (10th Cir 1986); Mooney v Friderich, 784 F2d 875 (8th Cir 1986). Rule 54(b) does not affect the right of a party, in a timely appeal from a final judgment, to challenge orders made during the litigation. For example, in Levron v Gulf Intl Marine, Inc, 854 F2d 777 (5th Cir 1988), the district court dismissed plaintiff's claim against one defendant, but left the remaining defendants in the lawsuit; the court refused to certify this order under Rule 54(b). Several months later, the district judge entered an order dismissing the remaining parts of the lawsuit; this order was clearly final under §1291. The plaintiff was unsure how to proceed and waited more than 30 days to file a notice of appeal. The court of appeals dismissed the appeal. It reasoned that the final order of dismissal started the appellate clock running and in effect made the earlier order appealable. The district court's refusal to grant certification was questionable, because the dismissed defendant and the plaintiff were compelled to wait around until the rest of the action was resolved in order to know whether their dispute belonged in court since the refusal to grant Rule 54(b) certification is not appealable. The court of appeals decision, however, is uncontroversial, and could be reached without reference to Rule 54(b). Many orders and rulings in litigation become subject to challenge in the court of appeals when a final judgment is entered, including rulings on motions for judgment as a matter of law and rulings on admission or exclusion of evidence.

[311] Sears, Roebuck & Co v Mackey, 351 US 427, 437 (1956). Most courts of appeals recognize a limited exception to this rule when the claim being appealed might not itself be a proper subject for Rule 54(b) certification, but by the time the court of appeals considers the case, all other claims in the district court have been dismissed or given a Rule 54(b) certification. *See, e.g.*, FSLIC v Huff, 851 F2d 316 (10th Cir 1988) (en banc) (premature notice of appeal from dismissal order is not appealable absent a Rule 54(b) certification when cross-claims and counterclaims remain pending, even though such claims are substantially dependent upon the dismissal action); Lewis v BF Goodrich Co, 850 F2d 641 (10th Cir 1988) (when filed prematurely, notice of appeal from order disposing of less than all claims is nevertheless effective if certification or final adjudication of the issue is obtained before the appeal is considered on its merits; court found

Second, the judge's certificate of *no just reason for delay* is subject to limited review in the court of appeals.[312] The district court's order should specify the reasons why there is no just cause for delay, and not merely mimic the language of the rule; the party seeking immediate appeal should, in moving for Rule 54(b) certification, provide a proposed order that includes the necessary findings.[313]

The first of these requirements—finality—was discussed in *Sears, Roebuck & Co v Mackey*.[314] Mackey sued Sears on six separate claims, four of which were still at issue by the time the case reached the Supreme Court. The first claim was a federal question Sherman Act allegation. The second was a diversity claim for wilful destruction of business, based upon some of the same events. The third and fourth claims alleged common law inducing breach of contract and unfair competition. The district judge entered a judgment dismissing the first and second claims, and made the required certificate under Rule 54(b). The Supreme Court held that the judgment met the requirements of Rule 54(b) and was appealable.

The Court first held that Rule 54(b) is not inconsistent with the finality requirement of 28 USC §1291. Granted, prior to Rule 54(b), "There was no authority for treating anything less than the whole case as a judicial unit for purposes of appeal. This construction of the judicial unit was developed from the common law which had dealt with litigation generally less complicated than much of that of today."[315] The Court went on to note that the liberal joinder provisions of the federal rules required relaxing the "judicial unit for purposes of appellate jurisdiction."[316] After all, when what is now §1291 made its first appearance—in the Judiciary Act of 1789[317]—each of the claims in the *Sears* case would have required a separate lawsuit.

The Court insisted, however, that "[s]ound judicial administration did not require relaxation of the standard of finality in the disposition of the individual adjudicated claims for the purpose of their appealability."[318] Put another way,

---

the same rule in all other circuits which have considered the issue; when appellants have not obtained dismissal or certification of remaining claims, the court will set a date by which this must be done or appeal will be dismissed); Crowley Maritime Corp v Panama Canal Commn, 849 F2d 951 (5th Cir 1988) (notice of appeal from dismissal of motion to intervene filed prior to certification of judgment was sufficient to confer jurisdiction upon Court of Appeals even though district court failed to comply technically with certification procedure outlined in Fed R Civ P 54(b)).

[312] Curtiss-Wright Corp v General Elec Co, 446 US 1, 9-10 (1980).

[313] See discussion below.

[314] 351 US 427 (1956). See also Cold Metal Process Co v United Engg & Foundry Co, 351 US 445 (1956), decided the same day. Although these cases were decided before the 1961 amendment to the rule, their holding remains valid.

[315] 351 US at 432.

[316] *Id.*

[317] Judiciary Act of 1789, ch 20, §22, 1 Stat 73, 74.

[318] 351 US at 432. Justice Frankfurter doubted the truth of this assertion in his concurrence. *Id* 439.

the finality, as opposed to the unit of suit, requirements of §1291 are fully applicable to the claims adjudicated and certified, and the court of appeals will dismiss an appeal from a judgment certified under Rule 54(b) that does not meet the §1291 test.[319] Rule 54(b) "scrupulously recognizes the statutory requirement of a 'final decision' under §1291 as a basic requirement for an appeal."[320]

The Court noted Rule 54(b)'s positive and negative features. The positive side is that the district judge acts as dispatcher and defines, within the limits set by §1291, the time when a judgment disposing of part of the case may be appealed, thus eliminating uncertainty.[321] The negative side is that there can be no appeal without the certificate of "no just reason for delay."[322]

Following *Sears, Roebuck,* the courts of appeals have carefully examined Rule 54(b) cases under the §1291 standard and dismissed when the finality requirement is found lacking.[323]

The second Rule 54(b) requirement, *no just reason for delay,* was construed in *Curtiss-Wright Corp v General Electric Co.*[324] Curtiss-Wright sued GE over a series of contracts. Curtiss-Wright had many claims related to these contracts, and GE filed a number of counterclaims. One of Curtiss-Wright's claims was for $19 million for work performed; this claim depended upon construction of a release clause in the contracts. The district judge construed the release provision and granted Curtiss-Wright summary judgment for $19 million plus interest. Curtiss-Wright asked for and was granted a Rule 54(b) certification of this judgment.

GE resisted appellate review, and argued in the court of appeals that the district court had abused its discretion in certifying that there was no just reason for delay. The court of appeals agreed with GE that later in the litigation, the district court might order a setoff against the $19 million, as the result of GE's counterclaims. Therefore, the court reasoned, it was unfair to certify Curtiss-Wright's $19 million judgment as final, because the judgment would, if affirmed, become final and collectible in its entirety before GE had a chance to air its claims to a setoff. The court of appeals therefore held the Rule 54(b) certification was improper.

---

[319] Liberty Mut Ins Co v Wetzel, 424 US 737 (1976), and, e.g., American Family Life Assurance Co v United States Fire Ins Co, 794 F2d 629, 630-31 (11th Cir 1986), so hold. The courts of appeals are in some disagreement on whether procedural orders can be the subject of a Rule 54(b) appeal, as distinct from orders that dispose of substantive claims. *See, e.g.,* Black Assn FF (Banoff) v City of New Orleans, 911 F2d 1063 (5th Cir 1990) (absent Fed R Civ P 54(b) certification, order is interlocutory; court declines to decide if discovery order could ever be given Fed R Civ P 54(b) treatment, for discovery orders are not substantive claims, noting Seventh Circuit holds appeal not permissible).

[320] 351 US at 438.

[321] *Id* 435.

[322] *Id.*

[323] *E.g.,* American Family Life Assurance Co v United States Fire Ins Co, 794 F2d 629, 630-31 (11th Cir 1986) (District Court erred in certifying as final and appealable order 54(b) an issue that was not final under §1291).

[324] 446 US 1 (1980).

The Supreme Court reversed the court of appeals and held that the district court had not abused its discretion. The Court rejected the court of appeals' narrow construction of Rule 54(b) and counseled greater deference to district court decisions under the rule. The district court's order of certification, the Court held, must be tested against "the interest of sound judicial administration" and affirmed unless the district court abused its discretion.[325]

The Court suggested some guidelines for exercising the discretion to certify, and gave meaning to the *no just cause for delay* standard:

> Not all final judgments on individual claims should be immediately appealable, even if they are in some sense separable from the remaining unresolved claims. . . . It is left to the sound judicial discretion of the district court to determine the "appropriate time" when each final decision in a multiple claims action is ready for appeal. . . . [A] district court must take into account judicial administrative interests as well as the equities involved. . . . It was therefore proper for the District Judge here to consider such factors as whether the claims under review were separable from the others remaining to be adjudicated and whether the nature of the claims already determined was such that no appellate court would have to decide the same issues more than once even if there were subsequent appeals.[326]

The Supreme Court held that certification was proper. The likelihood of Curtiss-Wright becoming insolvent and unable to pay on any counterclaim liability was remote, and the district judge had clearly given appropriate weight to the parties' contentions.[327]

The deference due the district court's order may evaporate, however, when that court fails to enunciate the reasons for its certification.[328] The courts of

---

[325] *Id* 8, 10 (quoting Sears, Roebuck & Co v Mackey, 351 US 427, 437 (1956)).

[326] *Id* 8. In an able discussion, the Fifth Circuit discussed the court of appeals' dual role in evaluating a Rule 54(b) certification. Samaad v City of Dallas, 940 F2d 925 (5th Cir 1991); review of a Rule 54(b) judgment involves two potential inquiries. The first is a legal question, which is reviewed de novo and may be raised by the court of appeals on its own motion: that is, whether there is more than one claim for relief. Second, there is the question committed to the district court's discretion, whether there is any just reason for delay. The Ninth Circuit elaborated upon the *Curtiss-Wright* rule in Gregorian v Izvestia, 871 F2d 1515 (9th Cir), *cert denied,* 493 US 891 (1989). There the court held that the district court's evaluation of judicial administrative interests such as the relationship between claims should be reviewed de novo as a mixed question of law of fact. *Id* 1519. The district court's assessment of the equities is reviewed for abuse of discretion. *Id.*

[327] *Id* 11-13. *But see* Hardie v Cotter & Co, 819 F2d 181 (8th Cir 1987) (entry of final judgment on fewer than all claims under Rule 54(b) is abuse of discretion where there is no evidence that judicial resources will be conserved by early appellate review).

[328] National Bank v Dolgov, 853 F2d 57, 58 (2d Cir 1988) (per curiam) (District Court's correct usage of Rule 54(b) language, absent explanation of its decision to grant partial final judgment to less than all defendants, was not final and appealable within meaning of 28 USC §1291).

appeals have somewhat inconsistent standards on this point, some saying that if the district judge merely announces that there is no just reason for delay, the certification and the circuit court's jurisdiction will fail.[329] While other courts of appeals take a more relaxed attitude,[330] the expense and uncertainty caused by litigating the validity of a certification should be avoided by seeking and obtaining detailed findings.

The administration of Rule 54(b) has been relatively noncontroversial, given the mandate of *Sears* and *Curtiss-Wright.* The Rule itself tells courts of appeals and parties that a judgment resolving less than all claims, or addressed to the contentions of fewer than all parties, will not be appealable absent the certification.[331]

Difficulty arises under the rule when the claims in the trial court are intertwined, stemming from the same factual and legal issues. In such a case, the court of appeals may well dismiss the appeal despite a Rule 54(b) certification. Waiting until all closely connected claims are resolved minimizes the risk of parallel proceedings—in the district court and court of appeals—which might lead to inconsistent results.[332]

Rule 54(b) does not permit certification of less than an entire claim. In *Liberty Mutual Insurance Co v Wetzel,*[333] the court held that Rule 54(b)'s reference to

---

[329] Knafel v Pepsi Cola Bottlers, Inc, 850 F2d 1155, 1159 (6th Cir 1988).

[330] *Compare* Cullen v Margiotta, 811 F2d 698, 711 (2d Cir) (district judge must give "a reasoned, even if brief, explanation" of why the case is suitable for Rule 54(b) treatment), *cert denied,* 483 US 1021 (1987) *with* Pension Benefit Guar Corp v LTV Corp, 875 F2d 1008, 1014-15 (2d Cir 1989) (district court found in conclusive terms that "there is no just reason for delay;" court of appeals excused the failure to give a more detailed explanation, citing the *Curtiss-Wright* "sound judicial administration" standard, and noting that judicial efficiency dictated deciding the case rather than insisting on strict technical compliance with Rule 54(b)), *revd on other grounds,* 496 US (1990). The Fifth Circuit, sitting en banc, has relaxed the standards, holding that the district court need not recite the *no just reason* formula if it appears with unmistakable clarity from the order appealed from and from the portions of the record referred to in the order that it intended Rule 54(b) action. Kelly v Lee's Old Fashioned Hamburgers, Inc, 908 F2d 1218, 1220-21 (5th Cir 1990) (en banc) (overruling Mills v Zapata, 722 F2d 1170 (5th Cir 1983)). The Seventh Circuit permits a Rule 54 certification to be entered after a notice of appeal has been filed. In Mendrala v Crown Mortgage Co, 955 F2d 1132 (7th Cir 1992), the certification was not completed until after oral argument; the holding makes it a little hard to see how the court of appeals can meaningfully review compliance with the substantive standards of Rule 54(b).

[331] *See* Mooney v Friderich, 784 F2d 875 (8th Cir 1986); Bristol v Fibreboard Corp, 789 F2d 846 (10th Cir 1986).

[332] *E.g.,* Spiegel v Trustees of Tufts College, 843 F2d 38, 44-46 (1st Cir 1988).

[333] 424 US 737 (1976). Sandwiches, Inc v Wendy's Intl, Inc, 822 F2d 707 (7th Cir 1987) (absent a Rule 54(b) order and a showing that issues and parties in one consolidated case were sufficiently separate from the issues and parties in other consolidated cases, appellant not permitted to appeal a district court decision on the only issue as to which it was a party). *See also* Trinity Broadcasting Corp v Eller, 827 F2d 673 (10th Cir) (judgment in a consolidated action that does not dispose of all claims is not final and appealable without certification), *affd on rehg,* 835 F2d 245 (10th Cir 1987), *cert denied,* 487 US 1223 (1988); Mathis v Zant, 903 F2d 1368 (11th Cir 1990) (per curiam) (habeas corpus petitioner has one claim for each conviction and sentence challenged,

claims means *causes of action*. Therefore, a district judge's certification of a decision on liability, having reserved the question of damages, does not give the court of appeals jurisdiction. The Court said: "[T]he only possible authorization for an appeal from the District Court's order would be pursuant to the provisions of 28 USC §1292."[334]

Moreover, the district judge must not only dispatch the appeal as envisioned by the rule, but must be seen to have done so. For example, in *Mooney v Frierdich*,[335] the district court had dismissed a third party complaint for want of jurisdiction. The third party plaintiffs filed a handwritten motion requesting the court to certify its order under Rule 54(b). The district judge endorsed "so ordered" on the motion. The court of appeals held that this alleged certification failed to comply substantially with Rule 54(b). The decision seems sound. If the court of appeals must defer to the district judge's expertise and familiarity with the case, there ought to be something in the record to which that deference may rationally attach.[336]

The advocate seeking guidance on the arguments that might be made in favor of certification, and the judge seeking to know what kind of an order to enter, should examine such cases as *EEOC v Chicago Miniature Lamp Works*.[337]

A party receiving a Rule 54(b) certification must look to the Rules of Appellate Procedure and take timely action to bring the disputed order to the court of appeals.[338]

---

even if he presents multiple grounds for relief on each claim; therefore Fed R Civ P 54(b) certification is required for appeal if less than all claims are decided by district court and losing party wishes to appeal). *But see* Insinga v La Bella, 817 F2d 1469 (11th Cir 1987) (final judgment in favor of medical center, leaving only unserved defendant remaining, was final appealable order; unserved defendant not a party for purposes of Rule 54(b)).

[334] Liberty Mut Ins Co v Wetzel, 424 US 737, 744 (1976). *Compare* Indiana Harbor Belt RR v American Cyanamid Co, 860 F2d 1441 (7th Cir 1988) (Rule 54(b) does not permit certification for appeal of order resolving one of two claims that have significant factual overlap; reasoned dissent by Judge Cudahy). Of course, in an admiralty case, a liability determination would be appealable under §1292(a)(3). *See* **§2.08.**

[335] 784 F2d 875 (8th Cir 1986).

[336] Spiegel v Trustees of Tufts College, 843 F2d 38, 42-44 (1st Cir 1988). There are other decisions requiring that the district judge specify the grounds on which certification is granted. *See, e.g.*, Rider v Pennsylvania, 850 F2d 982, 984 n1 (3d Cir), *cert denied*, 488 US 993 (1988). Counsel should inform the district judge of decisional law requiring specificity, and seek an order that complies.

[337] 110 FRD 120 (ND Ill 1986).

[338] *See* **§6.03.** Johnson v Orr, 897 F2d 128 (3d Cir 1990) (order fixing attorney fees as to claim that is subject of Fed R Civ P 54(b) appeal is itself final when entered; therefore, successful party's challenge of fees as inadequate is untimely; decision turns on court's view of Rule 54(b) policy rather than text of rule or statute).

§2.11 18 USC §§3731 and 3742: Government Appeals in Criminal Cases

The government's right to appellate review in a criminal case is limited by statute, and by the constitutional prohibition against double jeopardy.[339] When the government seeks interlocutory appellate review, it must act expeditiously so as not to burden unduly the defendant's right to speedy trial.[340]

The government's right of appellate review can exist in the following situations, each of which is discussed in this section:

(1) if the district court grants a motion to dismiss the indictment or information before jeopardy attaches, the government may appeal under 18 USC §3731.[341]

(2) if the district judge terminates the case in the defendant's favor, on the defendant's motion and on grounds unrelated to factual innocence, an appeal will lie under §3731.[342]

(3) if the district judge, after verdict or finding of guilty, grants a new trial under Fed R Crim P 33, arrests judgment under Fed R Crim P 34, or grants a postverdict judgment of acquittal under Fed R Crim P 29(c), the government may appeal under §3731.

(4) if the district court grants a motion to suppress or exclude evidence, before jeopardy has attached and before a verdict or finding, the government may appeal under §3731 if it "certifies to the district court that the appeal is not taken for purpose of delay and that the evidence is a substantial proof of a fact material in the proceeding;"

(5) if the district court releases the defendant on bail or changes conditions of release, the government may appeal under §3731 and 18 USC §3145(c).[343]

(6) the government may appeal sentences imposed under the sentencing guidelines legislation enacted in 1984 and effective beginning in 1987, according to 18 USC §3742.[344]

---

[339] US Const amend V. *See* United States v Wilson, 420 US 332, 336 (1975) (reaffirming no government right to appeal unless conferred by statute). For a more complete discussion of government appeals in criminal cases, see Wayne R. LaFave & Jerold H. Israel, Criminal Procedure ch 26 (Hornbook ed 1985). However, in a criminal case removed to federal court from state court, the prosecuting sovereign will have a right to appeal under §1291 from any order that could be appealed by that sovereign in the state court. Arizona v Manypenny, 451 US 232 (1981).

[340] US Const amend VI.

[341] For the full text of 18 USC §3731, see **app D.**

[342] See discussion below, United States v Jenkins, 420 US 358 (1975), *overruled in part sub nom* United States v Scott, 437 US 82 (1978).

[343] For the full text of 18 USC §3145(c), see **app D.**

[344] Sentencing Reform Act of 1984, Pub L No 98-473, tit II, ch 2, §§211-239, 98 Stat 1987, *as amended by* Sentencing Reform Amendments Act of 1985, Pub L No 99-217, 99 Stat 1728, *as amended by* Sentencing Act of 1987, Pub L No 100-182, 101 Stat 1266 (codified as amended in various sections of 18 and 28 USC). For a critical analysis of the sentencing guidelines under the Sentencing Reform Act, see sentencing guidelines under the Jim McHugh, *The United States Sentencing Guidelines: Justice for all or Justice for*

In addition, the government may obtain appellate review of some collateral orders in criminal and quasi-criminal cases by an appeal under §1291.[345] Disclosure orders under the Classified Information Procedures Act are appealable before or after jeopardy attaches.[346] And, as discussed at **§3.12,** the government may sometimes be able to obtain mandamus in criminal cases.

The Congress has expanded the reach of §3731 several times, conferring ever-broader appeal rights on the government.[347] In addition, a 1986 amendment struck out a provision that the defendant must be released pending resolution of a §3731 appeal.[348]

It is well to begin analysis by reviewing the Supreme Court's teaching on the relationship between double jeopardy and government appeals. The Supreme Court addressed this relationship in three cases usually referred to as the *Serfass* trilogy: *Serfass v United States,*[349] *United States v Jenkins,*[350] and *United States v Wilson.*[351] These cases are particularly relevant to categories (1), (2), and (3), above. The Court reaffirmed the principle that the government cannot appeal a not guilty verdict in a criminal case.[352] Nor can the government, having lost a criminal case on the merits of guilty or innocence, seek to relitigate any of the factual issues that led to the judgment.[353]

In *Serfass,* the defendant was charged with failing to submit to induction into the armed forces. He moved to dismiss the indictment. The district judge, in granting the motion, considered the defendant's affidavit, his Selective Service file, and factual representations made by counsel at argument. The Supreme Court held that the dismissal was appealable, because jeopardy had not attached. In a jury trial, jeopardy attaches when the jury is sworn. In a nonjury trial, a defendant is "put to trial before the trier of facts" and therefore in jeopardy no later than when the first witness is sworn.[354]

---

a few?, 36 Vill L Rev 877 (1991). The constitutionality of the Act was upheld in Mistretta v United States, 488 US 361 (1989).

[345] *E.g., In re* Grand Jury Subpoena (Rochon), 873 F2d 170, 173 (7th Cir 1989) (an order disqualifying government counsel in a criminal case is a final collateral order immediately appealable under §1291); United States v Marmolejo, 915 F2d 981 (5th Cir 1990) (government can appeal dismissal of a supervised release revocation proceeding under 28 USC §1291, as such proceedings are not criminal cases).

[346] Pub L No 96-456, 94 Stat 2025 (1980) (codified at 18 USC app III, §7). The Act's constitutionality has been upheld. *See* United States v Wilson, 750 F2d 7 (2d Cir 1984), *cert denied,* 479 US 839 (1986); United States v Smith, 750 F2d 1215 (4th Cir 1984) (affirming district judge on government appeal), *vacated on rehg,* 780 F2d 1102 (4th Cir 1985).

[347] See legislative history in 28 USCA §3731.

[348] Pub L No 99-646, §32, 100 Stat 3598 (1986).

[349] 420 US 377 (1975).

[350] 420 US 358 (1975), *overruled in part sub nom* United States v Scott, 437 US 82 (1978).

[351] 420 US 332 (1975).

[352] *Wilson,* 420 US at 348-49.

[353] United States v Scott, 437 US 82, 87-92 (1978).

[354] *Serfass,* 420 US at 388 (citing United States v Jorn, 400 US 470, 479 (1971)).

The *Serfass* holding sustains that part of §3731 which permits a government appeal from an order, entered before jeopardy attaches, that disposes of the case. A defendant who raises factual issues as part of a pretrial motion to dismiss under Fed R Crim P 12, does not thereby turn the motion into one for acquittal. Federal Rule of Criminal Procedure 12(e) forbids the trial judge to defer ruling on a pretrial motion "if a party's right to appeal is adversely affected." Federal Rule of Criminal Procedure 12(f) requires motions capable of pretrial resolution to be brought before trial. These provisions, taken together with *Serfass,* help to ensure appellate review of almost every dispositive motion decided before jeopardy attached.

The *Serfass* Court did, however, reiterate the rule that once jeopardy has attached, termination of the trial on the merits and in the defendant's favor precludes a government appeal and a retrial.[355] Cases applying this principle abound. For example, in *Fong Foo v United States,*[356] the district judge became impatient with the prosecutor's conduct and directed an acquittal before all the evidence was in. Since jeopardy had attached, the order was unreviewable.[357]

In *Jenkins,* the defendant was also charged with refusing to submit to induction. His claims that his local draft board erred were heard in a nonjury trial rather than on pretrial motion.[358] Jeopardy had attached. The district judge held that the local board had not erred, but that the defendant had relied upon the law as it stood at the time of his refusal to submit to induction and that it would be unfair to convict him. The judge dismissed the indictment and discharged the defendant. The Supreme Court held that the government had no right to appeal this order, which was the practical equivalent of an acquittal even though not named as such.

---

[355] *Id.* If the trial terminates on the defendant's motion for mistrial because of jury disagreement or some event at trial that leads defense counsel to believe that a fresh start is a good idea, a retrial will not violate the double jeopardy clause. *See, e.g.,* United States v Dinitz, 424 US 600 (1976). Even if the defendant objects to a mistrial, a retrial may be possible if there was a manifest necessity for terminating the first trial. United States v Perez, 22 US (9 Wheat) 579, 580 (1924). *See* Illinois v Somerville, 410 US 458 (1973) (trial judge discovered technical error in pleadings); Arizona v Washington, 434 US 497 (1978) (defense counsel misconduct in opening statement); Wayne R. LaFave & Jerold H. Israel, *supra* note 339, at 24.2. However, if the defense is goaded by governmental or prosecutorial misconduct into moving for a mistrial, a retrial will be precluded. Oregon v Kennedy, 456 US 667 (1982); United States v Martinez, 667 F2d 886 (10th Cir 1981), *cert denied,* 456 US 1008 (1982).

[356] 369 US 141 (1962) (per curiam).

[357] *See also* United States v Ellison, 722 F2d 595 (10th Cir), *vacating panel opinion at* 684 F2d 664 (10th Cir 1982) (double jeopardy clause forbids review of midtrial dismissal).

[358] In a Selective Service case, the validity of the local draft board's order is a matter for the judge to decide, and not the jury. In *Jenkins,* the defendant waited until the actual trial began before seeking and obtaining a judicial determination of the local board's action. The distinction makes sense only if one accepts the need for a clear demarcation when jeopardy attaches. *See Serfass,* 420 US at 388-89.

However, in *United States v Scott,*[359] the Court overruled *Jenkins* in part. Scott was tried for drug offenses. Prior to trial he moved for dismissal, claiming that his speedy trial rights had been violated. His counsel renewed that claim during trial, after jeopardy had attached. The trial judge granted the motion. Under a broad reading of *Jenkins,* the government could not appeal the dismissal because jeopardy had attached and reversal of the trial judge's order would have led to further proceedings in the trial court directed to determining guilt or innocence.

The Court held that the order was appealable, because the defendant could properly be saddled with the consequences of seeking dismissal after jeopardy had attached. While the Court declined to term the midtrial motion to dismiss a *waiver* of the right against double jeopardy, the case relies on cases in which the defendant can be retried after a mistrial.[360]

Scott and *Jenkins* have not drawn a clear line. When the district judge terminates a criminal case after jeopardy attaches, the appeals court will have to determine whether the defendant deliberately sought the termination on grounds "unrelated to factual guilt or innocence."[361] If so, the government's appeal is not barred by the double jeopardy clause. In this determination, the label the parties and the district court place on the action will not be controlling.[362] Taken together, *Scott* and *Jenkins* permit government appeals in a limited

---

[359] 437 US 82 (1978).

[360] *See, e.g.,* Lee v United States, 432 US 23 (1977); United States v Perez, 22 US (9 Wheat) 579 (1824); and United States v Dinitz, 424 US 60 (1976).

[361] *Scott,* 437 US at 99. The appeals courts continue to build upon the double jeopardy doctrine's "tortured and inconsistent history." United States v Douglas, 874 F2d 1145, 1149 (7th Cir), *cert denied,* 493 US 841 (1989). In *Douglas,* defendants raised an insufficiency of the evidence claim on appeal from their conspiracy convictions, but the court of appeals refused to resolve that claim and reversed their convictions on the ground of trial error. After defendants were retried and convicted, they claimed on appeal that the refusal of the court of appeals to hear the sufficiency claim subjected them to a second trial in violation of the double jeopardy clause. The Seventh Circuit rejected this position, even though the court noted that at least four sitting Supreme Court justices would not allow a court of appeals to reverse a conviction for trial error and decline to review a claim of insufficiency of the evidence. *Id* 1150. The issue of whether a defendant may be retried following appeal is considered more fully in **§10.15.**

[362] *See* United States v Steed, 646 F2d 136, 138 n2 (4th Cir 1981) (reconciling Scott and Jenkins), *revd on rehg,* 674 F2d 284 (4th Cir), *cert denied,* 459 US 829 (1982). An example of the difficulty posed by *Johnson* and *Scott* is United States v Affinito, 873 F2d 1261 (9th Cir 1989). Defendant was employed by Rockwell International Corporation, a major defense contractor. Defendant allegedly established a subcontracting enterprise and secured certain contracts with his employer in violation of Rockwell policy. After the jury convicted defendant on five counts of mail fraud, the Supreme Court decided McNally v United States, 483 US 350 (1987), holding that the mail fraud statute did not protect the intangible right to honest conduct. Defendant filed a Rule 29 motion for a postverdict judgment of acquittal. The trial court granted the motion. Because the trial judge had not explicitly stated in his order that he found the evidence insufficient under the holding of *McNally,* the court of appeals reversed and remanded for a new trial.

number of cases terminated after jeopardy has attached but before verdict or judgment of conviction or acquittal.

The third case in the trilogy, *United States v Wilson,*[363] dealt with government appeals of orders after verdict or judgment. The jury returned a verdict of guilty in the defendant's trial for converting union funds to his own use. The trial judge granted a postverdict motion to dismiss the indictment for prejudicial preindictment delay. The Supreme Court held that the dismissal was reviewable on the government's appeal. "Since reversal on appeal would merely reinstate the jury's verdict, review of such an order does not offend the policy against multiple prosecution,"[364] that is, there would be no "further proceedings," no "resolution of factual issues," of the kind that the Court held in *Jenkins* would bar review. Thus, if the district judge grants a postverdict motion that terminates the case in the defendant's favor, or awards a new trial, that order will be appealable under §3731 without offending the double jeopardy clause.[365]

Because the text and evident purpose of §3731 confer appellate jurisdiction to the extent permitted by the double jeopardy clause, the statute will permit a government appeal in categories (1), (2), or (3) provided only that there is no double jeopardy violation.[366] However, when the government seeks to appeal after verdict or judgment, it must satisfy both the finality requirements of §1291 and the double jeopardy limitations of §3731.[367] For example, in *United States v General Dynamics Corp,*[368] the district court stayed a defense contract fraud case pending referral of the contract issues to the Armed Services Board of Contract Appeals (ASBCA). The government appealed the stay order, terming it the equivalent of a dismissal under the effectively out-of-court theory discussed at **§2.02.** The court of appeals agreed and considered the merits of the government's appeal. Referral to ASBCA would be followed by an appeal to the Federal Circuit,[369] whose decision might collaterally estop the government on issues in the criminal case. It was clear that, in addition to being final, the district court's order had issued before jeopardy attached.

While §3731 is designedly broad, it will not permit all appeals that the double

---

363 420 US 332 (1975).

364 *Id* 344-450.

365 A related principle is that the double jeopardy clause does not bar a court of appeals from reversing a district judge's reversal of a criminal conviction properly imposed by a magistrate judge. United States v Aslam, 936 F2d 751 (2d Cir 1991) (citing cases from other circuits, held that allowing appeal would require only that judgment be entered on the magistrate's earlier finding, thus case analytically no different from *Wilson;* neither §1291 nor §3731 precludes jurisdiction).

366 For example, the clause of §3731 permitting a government appeal from an order granting a new trial has been held constitutional in light of the *Serfass* trilogy. Nilson Van & Storage Co v Marsh, 755 F2d 362 (4th Cir), *cert denied,* 474 US 818 (1985).

367 United States v Martinez, 763 F2d 1297 (11th Cir 1985).

368 828 F2d 1356 (9th Cir 1987).

369 *See* **§§2.12, 4.14.**

jeopardy clause would allow. For example, in *United States v Hundley*,[370] the district judge sentenced the defendant to a 15-year prison term based on a record of prior convictions. The judge almost immediately granted a motion to set aside the sentence under 28 USC §2255 because one of the prior convictions was constitutionally infirm. The government appealed the granting of the §2255 motion. Usually, §2255 motions to vacate sentence are brought by prisoners to set aside their convictions as a collateral attack after direct appeals are exhausted. In such a case, the government may appeal the grant of relief.

However, in Hundley's case, the government would not have been permitted to appeal if the court simply had found the prior conviction invalid and sentenced Hundley to a lesser term in the first instance. Hence, the court of appeals reasoned, the government had no right of appeal.[371]

Category (4) appeals were first authorized by a 1968 amendment to §3731, which was intended primarily to permit appeals from suppression orders that would assertedly threaten the government's ability to obtain a conviction.[372] The premise for the amendment is that the acquittal that might result from an improvident suppression would be unreviewable.

The statute covers a broader field, however, than motions to suppress evidence under the exclusionary rule. The prosecutor may, by filing the required certificate of good faith and importance, appeal any order excluding evidence, including one based upon the Federal Rules of Evidence.[373] For example, if the district judge excludes statements of a codefendant under the *Bruton* doctrine, the order will be appealable.[374] Even a conditional order of exclusion, as a potential sanction, may be subject to §3731. For example, in *United States v Horwitz*,[375] the court granted the defendant a new trial on tax fraud charges and told the prosecutors that their immunized witnesses would not be permitted to testify unless the government gave use immunity to crucial defense witnesses. The court of appeals held this to be an order excluding evidence and therefore appealable.

It has been held that the language "not made after the defendant has been put in jeopardy" refers to the timing of the district court's decision or order and not to the government's appeal.[376] Therefore, if the district judge suppresses evidence before the trial, and trial begins within 30 days, the government can appeal the suppression ruling during the trial. Of course, if the case

---

[370] 858 F2d 58 (2d Cir 1988).

[371] However, as noted later in this section, the government may have the right to appellate review of orders under the post-1984 version of Fed R Crim P 35, amending sentences.

[372] The legislative history of 3731 is discussed in Serfass v United States, 420 US 377, 383-87 (1975).

[373] *See, e.g.*, United States v Flores, 538 F2d 939 (2d Cir 1976) (order excluding prior acts appealable).

[374] United States v Perry, 624 F2d 29 (5th Cir 1980).

[375] 622 F2d 1101 (2d Cir 1980), *cert denied*, 449 US 1076 (1981).

[376] United States v Shears, 762 F2d 397, 399 (4th Cir 1985).

goes to verdict and judgment while the appeal is pending, and the defendant is acquitted, the appeal will be mooted.[377]

The requirement of §3731 that government counsel certify to the district court that the appeal is not taken for delay and that the evidence is substantial proof has not proven to be a great hindrance to the government.[378] However, an appeal taken without the certification should be dismissed.[379] A pretrial appeal poses some danger to a defendant's speedy trial rights.[380]

As to category (5), the bail appeal provision of §3731 must be read together with the Bail Reform Act of 1984.[381] 18 USC §3145(c) provides for appellate review of bail decisions adverse to the government in all criminal cases. The standards for granting, denying, or modifying bail orders, and the government's obligations in seeking review in the district court before coming to the court of appeals, are dealt with in the Bail Reform Act.[382]

The 30-day provision in §3731 for taking an appeal must be read together with the timing provisions of Fed R App 4(a). If the government files a motion to reconsider a suppression ruling, for example, its 30 days is generally held to run from the denial of its motion to reconsider.[383]

Category (6) refers to the government's right, under 18 USC §3742(b),[384] to appeal sentences imposed in violation of law, sentences imposed contrary to the minimum and maximum provisions of the Sentencing Guidelines mandated by the 1984 Crime Control Act[385] or sentences resulting from an incorrect application of the Sentencing Guidelines. Appellate review under §3742

---

[377] This follows from the rule that the government's appeal is barred if it will result in further proceedings on the merits after jeopardy has attached.

[378] *E.g.*, United States v Kepner, 843 F2d 755 (3d Cir 1988) (trial court suppressed evidence gathered under an overbroad warrant; government indicated that it would not seek review of this decision; when defendant successfully suppressed additional evidence based on the first order, the government appealed both orders; held, government not estopped from violating its representation to the district court). *But cf* DeGarmo v Collins, 984 F2d 142 (5th Cir 1993).

[379] United States v Miller, 952 F2d 866 (5th Cir), *cert denied,* 112 S Ct 3029 (1992) (dismissing appeal); United States v Eccles, 850 F2d 1357 (9th Cir 1988) (permitted certificate to be made after oral argument in court of appeals, but warned that timely certificate would be required in future).

[380] *See* United States v Gatto, 763 F2d 1040 (9th Cir 1985) (while government has conditional right to appeal suppression ruling, such appeals might disrupt trial process and potential for abuse exists; government's right to appeal therefore should be weighted against defendant's right to a speedy trial).

[381] 18 USC §§3141-3148. *See also* Gavino v McMahon, 499 F2d 1191 (2d Cir 1974).

[382] See **§2.15** for a discussion of defendant's appeal from an adverse bail determination. Posttrial bail is discussed at **§6.12.**

[383] United States v Milian-Rodriguez, 759 F2d 1558, 1562 n1 (11th Cir), *cert denied,* 474 US 845 (1985).

[384] The full text of 18 USC §3742(b) is in **app D.**

[385] Departure from the guidelines may, however, be permitted by a plea agreement. 18 USC §3742(b)(3)(B).

is available only for sentences imposed under the act for offenses committed after its effective date,[386] and the act and any guidelines under it are not to be given ex post facto effect.[387]

In order to appeal, the government must have the approval of the attorney general or solicitor general.[388] The government may not appeal unless it has raised and preserved its position in the district court.[389] The court of appeals will hear the appeal on the sentencing record, giving *due regard* to the district judge's opportunity to judge credibility and using a *clearly erroneous* standard to evaluate findings of fact.[390] The court of appeals, if it finds error, may remand or simply resentence. On remand, the district court's duty to correct its sentence is established by Fed R Crim P 35(a), effective as of December 1, 1991.[391]

The combination of complex sentencing guidelines and a new right of appeal has further clogged appellate dockets. However, departures from the guidelines will be accorded appellate deference if the district judge both has and provides a valid reason and explanation for departing.[392]

---

[386] United States v Martinez-Zayas, 857 F2d 122 (3d Cir 1988) (recognizing, however, that mandamus may be available to the government when there is no statutory right of appeal).

[387] United States v Bell, 1993 WL 139799 (8th Cir 1993).

[388] 18 USC §3742(b). *See, e.g.*, United States v Hall, 943 F2d 39 (11th Cir 1991) (18 USC §3742(b) approval by Solicitor General may be filed after the case is in the court of appeals; proof of the approval is not jurisdictional). In United States v Petti, 973 F2d 1441, 1446 n9 (9th Cir 1992), *cert denied*, 113 S Ct 1859 (1993), the court noted that although the Sixth Circuit is the only circuit requiring filing of proof of appeal no later than the government's opening brief, that circuit also decided that late submission of proof of approval does not affect the court's jurisdiction of the matter. *See* United States v Smith, 910 F2d 326, 328 (6th Cir 1990) and United States v Rutana, 932 F2d 1155, 1158 n5 (6th Cir), *cert denied*, 112 S Ct 300 (1991).

[389] United States v Garcia-Pillado, 898 F2d 36 (5th Cir 1990) (government may not appeal sentence unless it objects in the district court); United States v Prichett, 898 F2d 130 (11th Cir 1990) (government's failure to object in district court to alleged departure from guideline is fatal to government's appeal of sentence; rule that contentions raised for first time on appeal will not be considered applies to sentencing appeals).

[390] 18 USC §3742(e).

[391] Fed R Crim P 35 also provides for sentence reductions based on a defendant's cooperation after initial sentence. The circuits are divided over whether the government may appeal from grant of an order under Rule 35, 28 USC §1291 or 18 USC §3731. If the district court plainly exceeds its power in changing a sentence, mandamus is available. *In re* United States, 900 F2d 800 (5th Cir), *cert denied*, 498 US 905 (1990).

[392] *See, e.g.*, United States v Valdez-Gonzalez, 957 F2d 643 (9th Cir 1992) (affirming district court's downward departure from sentencing guidelines) and United States v Jackson, 921 F2d 985 (10th Cir 1990) (en banc) (sentence vacated because district court provided inadequate explanation of its departure from sentencing guidelines).

§2.12 Appeals to the Court of Appeals for the Federal Circuit

The United States Court of Appeals for the Federal Circuit was created in 1982 as a specialized court to hear patent, trademark, and certain governmental claims. Its jurisdiction is defined for the most part by 28 USC §1295,[393] although it also has jurisdiction over certain interlocutory orders under 28 USC §1292(c).[394] Its interlocutory order review power is the same as that of a geographic court of appeals, within the areas of substantive law assigned to the Federal Circuit. That is, the Federal Circuit can review injunctive and receivership matters as defined at **§§2.06**[395] and **2.07,** appeals by permission as described at **§2.09,** and partial final judgments as discussed in **§2.10.** In addition, the Federal Circuit reviews employment discrimination cases involving Senate and Presidential employees.[396] A more detailed discussion in relation to the other courts of appeals appears in Chapter 4.

The Federal Circuit applies the same finality rules as the other circuits, including the collateral order rule of *Cohen v Beneficial Industrial Loan Corporation.*[397]

The Federal Circuit also has the power to issue extraordinary writs to a district court, provided the main action is one over which the Federal Circuit will eventually have appellate jurisdiction.[398] The circuit's nationwide jurisdiction also gives it the power to resolve discovery disputes in cases that may eventually come before it, even though the dispute spans more than one geographic circuit. This is in marked contrast to the confusion that sometimes arises in multicircuit discovery disputes.[399]

---

[393] The text of this statute is reproduced at **§4.14.** See United States v Hohri, 482 US 64 (1987), discussed at **§4.14.**

[394] The text of this statute is reproduced at **§4.14.** However, in ruling upon procedural matters, such as discovery disputes, the Federal Circuit will apply the law of the geographic circuit in which the matter arose. Heat & Control, Inc v Hester Indus, 785 F2d 1017 (Fed Cir 1986) (discovery dispute arising in West Virginia; Fourth Circuit law applied).

[395] *See* Woodard v Sage Prods, Inc, 818 F2d 841 (Fed Cir 1987) (en banc) (order granting summary judgment of noninfringement to one defendant in patent action not appealable as denial of injunction).

[396] Government Employee Rights Act of 1991, passed as tit 3 of the Civil Rights Act of 1991, Pub L No 102-166, 105 Stat 1071, codified to 2 USC §1201 *et seq.* For Federal Circuit review powers, see 2 USC §1209(a) (Senate employees) and 2 USC §1219(a)(3) (presidential employees).

[397] 337 US 541 (1949), discussed at **§2.04.** *See* 15A Charles A. Wright, Arthur R. Miller, Edward H. Cooper, Federal Practice and Procedure: Jurisdiction 2d §3903.1, at 188-89 (1992 & Supp 1993); Symposium, *A Review of Recent Decisions of the United States Court of Appeals for the Federal Circuit,* 40 Am U L Rev 1003 (1991).

[398] *In re* International Medical Prosthetics Research Assocs, 739 F2d 618, 619 (Fed Cir 1984); *In re* Precision Screen Machines, Inc, 729 F2d 1428, 1429 (Fed Cir 1984).

[399] *See, e.g.,* Hooker v Continental Life Ins Co, 965 F2d 903 (10th Cir 1992), discussed in **§2.04.**

A principal reason for creating the Federal Circuit was to ensure consistency in patent and other intellectual property litigation, where certainty is particularly important. The Supreme Court has cautioned the Federal Circuit to use its powers to promote the "strong public interest in the finality of judgments in patent litigation."[400] In *Cardinal Chemical Co v Morton International, Inc,*[401] the Federal Circuit had followed its usual practice and dismissed as moot a holding that a patent was invalid because the circuit affirmed the alternative holding that the patent had not been infringed. The Court held that the invalidity determination was not mooted in any constitutional sense[402] by the affirmance on infringement. It then pointed to the strong public interest in having patent validity resolved, and said that refusing to reach the merits was an abuse of discretion.

§2.13 Review of Tax Court Judgments

Title 26 USC §7482(a)(1) provides that the appropriate court of appeals has exclusive jurisdiction to review decisions of the United States Tax Court "in the same manner and to the same extent as decisions of the district courts in civil actions tried without a jury."

The Tax Court is an article II court that hears petitions filed by taxpayers who have received statutory notices of a deficiency in the payment of tax. Tax Court procedure resembles civil procedure in the district courts[403] in that the jurisdiction of the court is invoked by petition (the equivalent of a complaint),[404] the Commissioner of Internal Revenue is invariably the respondent, discovery is available under the Tax Court rules,[405] and, eventually, a judgment is entered ending the controversy, as a result of either settlement or trial.

With respect to cases that fit this paradigm, appealability is governed by the same finality principles that govern civil cases coming from the district courts. Ordinarily, the final judgment of the Tax Court, leaving nothing to be done but appeal or submit to collection of the tax, is the only occasion to invoke the court of appeals' authority.[406]

---

[400] Cardinal Chem Co v Morton Intl, Inc, 113 S Ct 1967, 1977 (1993).

[401] *Id* 1977-78.

[402] *See* **§2.18.**

[403] See Rules of the Tax Court of the United States, adopted pursuant to 26 USC §7453. Tax Court practice and procedure is covered in Marvin J. Garbis & Allen L. Schwait, Tax Court Practice (1974). *See also* Marvin J. Garbis, Stephen S. Struntz, & Ronald B. Rubin, Tax Procedure and Tax Fraud (2d ed 1987). Review of Tax Court decisions is also discussed at **§§5.11, 6.08.**

[404] Resort to the Tax Court is only one option. A taxpayer who receives a statutory notice of deficiency may pay the tax and sue in the appropriate district court or the United States Claims Court for a refund.

[405] Tax Ct R 70-74, 90 (effective May 1, 1979 & as amended Mar 1, 1983).

[406] Kreider v Commissioner, 762 F2d 580 (7th Cir 1985) (final judgment is one that determines deficiency); Sampson v Commissioner, 710 F2d 262 (6th Cir 1983) (denial of petition to intervene is a final decision as to intervenor and may be appealed); Ryan v

There are, however, exceptions. When the Tax Court's authority is invoked in a special proceeding, and that proceeding is terminated by an order that disposes of all the issues before the court, an appeal is proper. Thus, in *Louisville Builders Supply Co v Commissioner,*[407] the Tax Court granted the Commissioner's application to take the deposition of one of the corporate taxpayer's directors. No statutory notice of deficiency had been issued, much less a taxpayer petition filed in the Tax Court. The Commissioner wanted the deposition to clear up some questions in an ongoing audit, although the parties were certain that the audit would result in a notice of deficiency and most likely a Tax Court proceeding. The court of appeals denied the Commissioner's motion to dismiss the appeal. The court of appeals did not find any precise statutory basis for its jurisdiction, but reasoned that the order was final with respect to the special proceeding in which it was entered, and that the Tax Court should not have unreviewable power to determine its own jurisdiction. The decision seems eminently just as a means of restraining the power of the IRS.

The court of appeals also relied upon *United States v California Eastern Line,*[408] in which the Supreme Court held that the court of appeals could review an order in a nontax proceeding over which Congress had given the Tax Court jurisdiction. The Court reasoned that the basic statutory grant of appellate jurisdiction to the courts of appeals was broad enough to encompass any "justiciable matters entrusted to the Tax Court by Congress."[409]

Louisville Builders might have been decided with less travail by treating the appeal as a petition for mandamus or prohibition, for clearly an abuse of power of this sort triggers the right to an extraordinary writ.[410] The advocate should have sought relief in the alternative.

Commissioner, 680 F2d 324 (3d Cir 1982) (denial of summary judgment motion not appealable).

The principle that one may not appeal a judgment to which one has consented, discussed in **§2.02,** applies to appeals from the Tax Court, as illustrated by Abatti v Commissioner, 859 F2d 115 (9th Cir 1988). The appellants were among many taxpayers who had taken deductions based on participation in limited partnerships. The IRS disallowed the deductions and all affected taxpayers petitioned the Tax Court for redetermination of deficiencies. All taxpayers agreed to be bound by the result of a "lead case" involving five petitioners. The Commissioner won the lead case on summary judgment. The remaining taxpayers consented to judgments against themselves. Meanwhile, the lead case petitioners appealed and won.

The remaining petitioners then asked the Tax Court to vacate the judgments against them. The Tax Court held that the taxpayers had waived their right to appeal and the Ninth Circuit agreed. The court of appeals rejected the argument that finality as to the "tag-along" taxpayers was tied to the judgment in the lead case while also rejecting an assertion that the IRS had so misled the taxpayers that they should be granted relief.

[407] 294 F2d 333 (6th Cir 1961).

[408] 348 US 351 (1955).

[409] *Id* 354.

[410] *See* **§3.04** and *In re* Stone, 569 F2d 156 (DC Cir 1978) (mandamus must be sought in court of appeals that will have jurisdiction over appeal from a final judgment).

In *Commissioner v McCoy,*[411] the Supreme Court stressed that the court of appeals' 26 USC §7482(a) review jurisdiction extends only to correction of errors made by the Tax Court and does not bestow an equitable power of supervision.[412] McCoy was executor of his father's will. He misconstrued some complex provisions of the Internal Revenue Code and the Commissioner asserted a $22,159.72 deficiency against the estate. The Commissioner won in the Tax Court and McCoy did not file an appeal bond that would have stayed assessment and collection of the deficiency. This triggered a demand for payment; when payment was not made within 10 days, a further penalty was added to the tax due.

The court of appeals affirmed the Tax Court and then, on petition for rehearing, entered an unpublished order, nonprecedential under its local rules, directing forgiveness of the penalties and interest. This order, the Supreme Court held (without waiting for full briefing on the merits), exceeded the court of appeals' jurisdiction. The Court held that:

> [I]n reviewing a Tax Court decision, the duty of the court of appeals is to consider whether the Tax Court committed error. Plainly, the court of appeals lacks jurisdiction to decide an issue that was not the subject of the Tax Court proceeding or to grant relief that is beyond the powers of the Tax Court itself.[413]

The Tax Court's decision was simply that there was a deficiency, which was the only issue before it. The penalty and interest are mandated by statute. The taxpayer could obtain relief by paying these amounts and suing for a refund in either the district court or the claims court.

By analogy to civil appeals under §1291, the courts of appeals have accepted jurisdiction of appeals from Tax Court orders finally disposing of a case with regard to one party who appears separately. For example, the denial of a motion to intervene is appealable.[414]

However, there is a split of authority as to appealability of a Tax Court decision that disposes of part of a controversy, leaving the rest to be determined at a later time. The Sixth Circuit held in *Schrader v Commissioner,*[415] that it had no jurisdiction to review the Tax Court's dismissal, as time-barred, of one year of a multiyear petition. The court acknowledged that other circuits had implicitly held such dismissals reviewable.[416]

The *Schrader* holding may be criticized as potentially wasting judicial time, at least as applied to a single year dismissal on timeliness grounds. Review of

---

[411] 484 US 3 (1987).

[412] The court of appeals power is expressly limited by 26 USC §7482(c)(1) and this section provides further support to the *McCoy* result.

[413] Commissioner v McCoy, 484 US 3, (1987).

[414] Sampson v Commissioner, 710 F2d 262 (6th Cir 1983).

[415] 916 F2d 361 (6th Cir 1990) (per curiam).

[416] *Id* at 363. The court followed the holding in Estate of Yaeger v Commissioner, 801 F2d 96, 98 (2d Cir 1986).

such a decision will rarely involve the court of appeals in factual complexities, the issue is segregable from the tax law issues still pending in Tax Court, and an expeditious and orderly determination that results in reversal would send the matter back to Tax Court in time to have all the taxpayer's contentions on the merits reviewed in a single proceeding. Such unified review makes sense in tax cases, which frequently involve multiyear transactions. It is difficult to see why the order dismissing one year of Schrader's petition was not a collateral order under traditional §1291 analysis.[417]

Section 7482(a)(1) expressly provides for appeals by permission under virtually identical standards and procedures as for such appeals from the federal districts under 28 USC §1292(b).[418] Thus, if a significant legal issue arises in a Tax Court case, the court may certify it to the appropriate court of appeals. The court of appeals that hears the appeal will hear any later appeals, unless the parties stipulate otherwise.[419]

As with civil appeals generally,[420] one may not appeal a Tax Court judgment to which one has consented.[421] This principle can be tricky in Tax Court cases, because of the way in which judgment is entered. Usually, a contested case leads to a written decision resolving the legal issues. Then, under Tax Court Rule 155, the parties must either agree on the computation of a deficiency, or submit their disagreement to the Court for resolution. In making a Rule 155 agreement, a party must not seem to be consenting to the deficiency, otherwise any resulting appeal will be dismissed. Rather, the party must agree only that the computations accurately reflect the Court's decision, to which the party will continue to note objection.

Although the subject of to which court of appeals one should appeal is treated in more detail in the next chapter, it is appropriate to discuss it now as applied to Tax Court appeals. 26 USC §7482(b) provides for venue of appeals from the Tax Court. In general, individuals appeal to the court of appeals for the circuit of their residence, corporations to the court of appeals for the circuit of their principal place of business or principal office,[422] and partnerships at their principal place of business. The taxpayer and secretary of the treasury may agree on a different venue, even if the agreement is reached after the appeal is filed, to avoid a claim that the wrong circuit has been chosen.[423]

---

[417] *See* **§2.02.**

[418] For tactics and principles involved in such appeals, see **§2.09.**

[419] 26 USC §7482(b)(2).

[420] *See* **§2.02.**

[421] White v Commissioner, 776 F2d 976, 978 (11th Cir 1985) ("by stipulating to the entry of judgment for the reduced deficiencies, taxpayers waived their right to appeal"); Tapper v Commissioner, 766 F2d 401, 403 (9th Cir 1985) ("[g]enerally, a party cannot appeal a judgment entered with its consent"); Clapp v Commissioner, 875 F2d 1396, 1398 (9th Cir 1989) ("party consenting to entry of judgment generally waives the right to appeal. This rule applies to stipulated judgments of the Tax Court.").

[422] If the entity has no principal place of business in any circuit, it appeals in the circuit where the return was filed. 26 USC §7482(b)(1)(B).

[423] 26 USC §7482(b)(2). Other provisions apply to certain declaratory judgment actions. 26 USC §7482(b)(1)(B).

While there is some authority that a wrong choice of venue is fatal to the appeal,[424] the better view is that the court of appeals to which appeal is taken may order the case transferred to the correct circuit under 18 USC §1631.[425]

Moreover, trial venue for Tax Court cases and appeal venue of the Court's eventual decision may be different. Trial venue is often set by stipulation of the parties, or even by considerations of forum non conveniens. Appeal venue does not necessarily follow trial venue.[426]

Timing of appellate review and standard of review of Tax Court decisions are dealt with in **§§6.07** and **5.12,** respectively.

§2.14 Review in Bankruptcy Matters

Title 28 USC §158(d) provides that "[t]he courts of appeals shall have jurisdiction of all final decisions, judgments, orders, and decrees" entered by (a) a district court on appeal to such court from the bankruptcy judge,[427] or (b) a bankruptcy appellate panel established by order of the judicial council of the circuit to review bankruptcy judge orders.[428] Section 158, amended as part of the Congressional overhaul of bankruptcy practice in 1984, thus establishes a three-tier system of judicial review: bankruptcy judge to district court or bankruptcy panel to court of appeals. Section 158(d) gives the court of appeals jurisdiction only of bankruptcy court orders that have been reviewed by the district judge or bankruptcy panel, whose decision on review must be final. Appeal procedures under §158(d) are governed by Fed R App P 6, and not by Fed R App P 4.[429] Moreover, bankruptcy rules may confer §158(d) finality on an order in the same way as would civil rules such as Fed R Civ P 54(b).[430] In addi-

---

[424] Becker v Commissioner, 716 F2d 285, 286 (5th Cir 1983). If the appeal is timely filed, but in the wrong court, the parties can waive the defect. *See* Industrial Addition Assn v Commissioner, 323 US 310 (1945). The *Becker* court laments the harshness of dismissing the appeal of an obviously well intentioned pro se taxpayer, but neglects to consider the possible application of 28 USC §1631 to transfer the case to the proper court of appeals.

[425] In Dornbusch v Commissioner, 860 F2d 611 (5th Cir 1988), a nonparty witness held in contempt by the Tax Court appealed to the Fifth Circuit rather than to the proper court, the District of Columbia Circuit. The government contended that the appeal must be dismissed on the authority of *Becker* and because the transfer provisions of 18 USC §1631 do not apply when the transferor court has jurisdiction, but not venue. The court of appeals considered that a proper reading of §1631, at least when the appellant acted in good faith, permitted transfer to the appropriate court rather than dismissal. *See* **§4.14.**

[426] Becker v Commissioner, 716 F2d 285, 287 (5th Cir 1983).

[427] 28 USC §158(a) provides for such appeals.

[428] §158(b)(1).

[429] *See* **§6.06.**

[430] See *In re* Chateaugay Corp, 922 F2d 86 (2d Cir 1990), *affd,* 945 F2d 1205 (2d Cir 1991), *cert denied,* 112 S Ct 1167 (1992), in which the party to an adversary proceeding in bankruptcy court obtained a partial summary judgment. The opponent appealed to the district court, which found the order appealable and affirmed. The court of appeals held the order not appealable under less rigid bankruptcy appealability rules.

tion, Congress has foreclosed appeal of some discretionary orders of bankruptcy courts that might otherwise be considered final, such as certain orders of abstention, stay, or even dismissal.[431]

However, §158(d) is not the only avenue to the court of appeals. There are at least three others. First, if a district judge has withdrawn a matter from the bankruptcy court, and is hearing it in the first instance, the judge's actions are reviewable as they would be in any civil case under 28 USC §§1291-92 and the rules discussed in preceding sections of this chapter.[432] In such cases, the notice of appeal is filed as in a civil case.[433]

A second avenue is established under the Supreme Court's decision in *Connecticut National Bank v Germain.*[434] In that case, a bankruptcy trustee sued the bank, which removed the action to bankruptcy court. The trustee filed a jury demand. The bankruptcy judge denied the bank's motion to strike the jury demand, but allowed an appeal of that order to the district court under 28 USC §158(a). The district court affirmed, but certified an interlocutory appeal under 28 USC §1292(b).[435] The Second Circuit held that §1292(b) appeals could only be taken from orders of a district judge sitting as a civil trial court and not from orders issued on appeal from a bankruptcy judge.

The Supreme Court reversed, holding that §1292 interlocutory appeals are available to review actions of a district judge who is hearing a bankruptcy appeal under 28 USC §158(a). Justice Thomas, writing for five justices, rested decisions on the assertedly plain language of §§1292 and 158. Despite the seeming overlap of the two provisions, both must be given effect. No similar problem of statutory construction arises with respect to §1291, because the finality pro-

---

However, the court tempered its dismissal of the appeal by giving the parties 30 days to obtain a certification under Bankruptcy Rule 7054, which is virtually identical to Fed R Civ P 54(b). If certification were obtained, the court held the case would be restored to the docket and decided on the merits.

[431] 11 USC §305(c), *as amended by* Pub L No 102-198, 105 Stat 1623 (1991), makes orders under 11 USC §305(a) (relating to dismissal or suspension of proceedings in the interest of the debtor or creditors, or in deference to other pending proceedings) unreviewable "by appeal or otherwise." §305(c) in its amended form probably undercuts the authority of cases such as *In re* Pan Am Corp, 950 F2d 839 (2d Cir 1991), which held a bankruptcy court order of abstention reviewable under the collateral order doctrine.

[432] *See* Metro Transp Co v North Star Reinsurance Co, 912 F2d 672 (3d Cir 1990) (when bankruptcy case is transferred to district court before trial, appealability from district court's judgment is governed by 28 USC §§1291-92 and Fed R Civ P 54(b) and not by 28 USC §158(d)); *In re* Bishop, Baldwin, Rewald, Dillingham & Wong, Inc, 856 F2d 78 (9th Cir 1988) (per curiam) (appellate review of opinion of district court sitting in bankruptcy (as compared to bankruptcy court) is proper under 28 USC §1291); *In re* Benny, 791 F2d 712 (9th Cir 1986) (extensive discussion of statute and case law).

[433] *See* **§6.03.**

[434] 112 S Ct 1146 (1992).

[435] The procedural facts appear in more detail in the court of appeals' opinion, 926 F2d 191, 191-92 (2d Cir 1991). For discussion of §1292(b) procedure, see **§2.09.**

visions of that statute and §158(d) are identical.[436]

A third route to the court of appeals would be provided by mandamus or prohibition under the All Writs Act, as discussed in Chapter 3. However, as discussed below, the liberality with which appeals courts construe finality in the bankruptcy context may present obstacles to writ practice.[437]

The 1984 amendments to federal bankruptcy law represented the second major reworking in six years, in part because of constitutional considerations governing the status of bankruptcy judges under article III.[438] When an appeal is taken under §158(d), the court of appeals will impose a sort of double finality requirement. It will ask whether or not the order of the district judge or bankruptcy panel is final within the meaning of §158(d). But it will also inquire whether the judge or panel was reviewing an order that is appealable to them under the standards set out in §158(a).[439]

Because §158(a) empowers the district court or bankruptcy panel to hear appeals from interlocutory orders of the bankruptcy court, many district judge appellate decisions will not have the finality required by §158(d) as a prerequisite to court of appeals review; that is, while a party in a bankruptcy proceeding may appeal certain interlocutory orders from the bankruptcy judge to the district court or bankruptcy panel, the right of further review (in the court of appeals) is restricted by §158(d).

In determining whether the order of the district judge or bankruptcy panel is final, the courts of appeals continue the practice, begun well before the 1984 amendments, of construing finality more liberally than in the usual civil case.[440]

---

[436] 112 S Ct at 1149. Appeal procedures in cases relying on §1292 are the same as in any other §1292 appeal. *See* **ch 4.**

[437] *In re* Kaiser Steel Corp, 911 F2d 380 (10th Cir 1990) (§158(d) is so broad that mandamus will rarely, if ever, be available in bankruptcy cases; language in this case concerning the inapplicability of §1292 to bankruptcy cases is no longer effective in light of *Connecticut Natl Bank*).

[438] Northern Pipeline Constr Co v Marathon Pipe Line Co, 458 US 50 (1982). *See generally* 16 Charles A. Wright, Arthur R. Miller, & Edward H. Cooper, Federal Practice and Procedure §3926 (Supp 1993).

[439] *See In re* Abdallah, 778 F2d 75 (1st Cir 1985), *cert denied,* 476 US 1116 (1986) (district court decision on an appeal from final order of bankruptcy judge is not final if case also is remanded for further proceedings and therefore is not appealable). *Cf In re* Continental Airlines, 932 F2d 282 (3d Cir 1991) (if bankruptcy court's order satisfies the finality test, but the district court on review issues an order that would not ordinarily be final, held, finality of bankruptcy court order gives court of appeals jurisdiction in bankruptcy matters; good discussion of case law).

[440] There are varying statements of the finality requirement. *In re* Topco, Inc, 894 F2d 727 (5th Cir 1990) (finality principles discussed with able review of caselaw); *In re* Plaza de Diego Shopping Ctr, Inc, 911 F2d 820 (1st Cir 1990) (liberal finality rules applicable to bankruptcy cases applied regardless of whether court of appeals' jurisdiction is invoked under §1291 or §158(d)); *In re* Chateaugay Corp, 880 F2d 1509, 1511 (2d Cir 1989) (collects cases, reviews the legal principles, and applies the rule that "the concept of finality that has developed in bankruptcy matters is more flexible than in ordinary civil litigation"); *In re* Brown, 916 F2d 120, 123 (3d Cir 1990) (appeal from bankruptcy court denial of motion to dismiss debtor's Chapter 11 petition as bad faith filing is appealable to district court under §158, and hence to court of appeals from

Bankruptcy involves many parties and issues, and decisions that do not dispose of the entire case may nonetheless be a proper subject of review.[441] As the Ninth Circuit has said, "[C]ertain proceedings in a bankruptcy case are so distinct and conclusive either as to the rights of individual parties or the ultimate outcome of the case that final decisions as to them should be appealable as of right."[442]

Because bankruptcy cases may well involve a series of orders directing transfer of money or other property, an otherwise appealable order may become moot and therefore unreviewable if the transfer is irrevocably made before appellate review is concluded.[443]

The liberal construction of the finality requirement that one finds in many bankruptcy appeals is often grounded in a broad interpretation of the collateral order doctrine of *Cohen v Beneficial Industrial Loan Corp.*[444] Even where the *Cohen* doctrine is not specifically mentioned, the basis of review is consistent with its rationale: the claim is separate, final for its own purposes, and otherwise

---

district court, even though effect of denial is to permit bankruptcy proceeding to continue and creditor can renew motion; pragmatic approach to finality in bankruptcy cases); *In re* Bucyrus Grain Co, 905 F2d 1362, 1364 (10th Cir 1990) (district court order reversing bankruptcy court grant of secured creditor's stay motion, and remanding for further proceedings, not appealable because it contemplates significant further proceedings (quoting *In re* Commercial Contractors, 771 F2d 1373, 1375 (10th Cir 1985); extensive discussion and refusal to follow, e.g., Third Circuit); *In re* Watson, 884 F2d 879, 880 (5th Cir 1989) (while finality is flexible in bankruptcy, it is limited by practicality (quoting *In re* Morrell, 880 F2d 855, 856 (5th Cir 1989)); order imposing sanctions on party in ongoing bankruptcy case is interlocutory); *In re* County Management, Inc, 788 F2d 311 (5th Cir 1986) (district judge order reversing and remanding case to bankruptcy court for significant further proceedings not appealable to court of appeals; court expressly notes that in bankruptcy cases, finality rules are more liberal); *In re* TCL Investors, 775 F2d 1516, 1519 (11th Cir 1985) (final order ends litigation on the merits and leaves nothing to do but execute the judgment); *In re* Sambo's Restaurants, Inc, 754 F2d 811, 814-15 (9th Cir 1985) (district court order affirming or reversing a final bankruptcy court order is final for appeal purposes); *In re* Saco Local Dev Corp, 711 F2d 441, 444 (1st Cir 1983) (court of appeals has power to review orders resolving discrete issues within the larger framework of a bankruptcy proceeding); Charles A. Wright, *supra* note 438, 3926 at 131-32 (Supp 1993).

[441] *See, e.g., In re* Moody, 817 F2d 365 (5th Cir 1987) (order compelling debtor to turn over item of property is final and appealable).

[442] *In re* Benny, 791 F2d 712, 718 (9th Cir 1986).

[443] *See, e.g., In re* Holywell Corp, 911 F2d 1539 (11th Cir 1990), *revd on other grounds,* 112 S Ct 1021 (1992). See **§2.18** for a discussion of mootness principles.

[444] 337 US 541 (1949). *See* **§2.04.** Representative cases applying the doctrine include DOE v West Tex Mktg Corp, 763 F2d 1411, 1417 (Emer Ct App 1985); *In re* Cash Currency Exch, Inc, 762 F2d 542, 547 (7th Cir) (matter reviewable on appeal from final judgment; appealability denied), *cert denied,* 474 US 904 (1985); *In re* Pacor, Inc, 743 F2d 984 (3d Cir 1984) (district court order holding bankruptcy court without jurisdiction in products liability case and remanding to state court appealable); *In re* UNR Indus, 725 F2d 1111, 1118 (7th Cir 1984) (matter not effectively reviewable on appeal from final judgment; appealability recognized).

unreviewable.[445] To qualify for review, the party must show that the order complained of is irreversible in future proceedings or that denying an appeal now will cause irreparable harm.[446] On this basis, courts of appeals regularly review decisions allowing or disallowing a particular claim.[447]

However, a decision will not be final if the district judge has, for example, remanded to the bankruptcy court for significant further proceedings.[448] Such an order looks to the development of a more complete factual record and is therefore not regarded as final.

Courts and commentators have recognized that the jurisdictional nuances of appellate bankruptcy practice require a thorough grounding in basic bankruptcy law and procedure.[449] With the complexities engendered by the legislative developments of 1984, this caveat is all the more significant.

§2.15 Other Statutes Conferring or Denying Appealability to Particular Orders

Sections of this chapter have mentioned specific provisions that confer or restrict appellate review in particular kinds of cases. There are, however, statutory and federal rule appealability provisions that require separate discussion.

Remands in Cases Removed to Federal Court[450]

28 USC §§1441-1452 deal with removal from state court of civil and criminal cases over which the federal court would have original jurisdiction or which involve civil rights or bankruptcy questions.[451] 28 USC §1447(d) provides:

---

[445] *See In re* American Mariner Indus, 734 F2d 426, 428-29 (9th Cir 1984) (court of appeals has jurisdiction to review order denying relief from automatic stay). *Compare In re* Johns-Manville Corp, 824 F2d 176 (2d Cir 1987) (order denying request for appointment of shareholders' committee neither final nor appealable as collateral order); British Aviation Ins Co v State Airlines, 822 F2d 1029 (11th Cir 1987) (denial of motion to set aside stay in bankruptcy proceedings not appealable as final order, collateral order, or appealable interlocutory order); *In re* Moody 825 F2d 81 (5th Cir 1987) (order declaring that debtor's bankruptcy had dissolved partnership is not appealable as a final order, under the collateral order doctrine, or as a hardship exception to the final judgment rule).

[446] *In re* UNR Indus, 725 F2d 1111, 1118 (7th Cir 1984).

[447] DOE v West Tex Mktg Corp, 763 F2d 1411, 1416 (Emer Ct App 1985).

[448] *In re* County Management, Inc, 788 F2d 311 (5th Cir 1986). *See also In re* Kemble, 776 F2d 802 (9th Cir 1985) (court of appeals has no jurisdiction over district court's withdrawal of reference to bankruptcy court because this is a discretionary decision). Review also may be available, in an appropriate case, by extraordinary writ. See *In re* Teleport Oil Co, 759 F2d 1376, 1378 (9th Cir 1985), and the discussion in ch 3.

[449] Authorities are collected in the 1993 Supplement to Charles A. Wright, *supra* note 438, §3926, at 144-47 n21.

[450] Federal financial regulatory entities have special rights of removal and of appellate review of remand orders. *See* **§2.02.**

[451] *See generally* Charles A. Wright, Federal Courts §§38-41 (4th ed 1983).

> An order remanding a case to the State court from which it was removed is not reviewable on appeal or otherwise, except that an order remanding a case to the State court from which it was removed pursuant to §1443 of this title shall be reviewable by appeal or otherwise.[452]

Section 1443 deals with removal of civil rights cases, as to which there is a manifest federal interest, protected by permitting appeals from orders sending the case back to state court. 28 USC §1452(b) prohibits appellate review of remand orders in bankruptcy-related matters.

The text of §1447(d) could be read to bar all appellate review of remand orders, but the Supreme Court has held that there are exceptions. From the Court's opinions, and the courts of appeals' interpretation of them, have emerged some fairly clear rules of appealability.

In *Thermtron Products, Inc v Hermansdorfer*[453] two Kentucky citizens sued Thermtron, an Indiana corporation, in Kentucky state court. Thermtron removed the case under 28 USC §1441(a) because the federal court would have had original jurisdiction due to the parties diverse citizenship. The district judge conceded that Thermtron had the right to remove, but remanded the case because the federal docket was so busy that plaintiffs could obtain a speedier trial in state court. Thermtron sought mandamus. The Supreme Court held that appellate review was available. The §1447(d) bar on review is limited to cases in which the remand order is predicated on a ground listed in §1447(c), which at that time provided for remand of cases removed "improvidently and without jurisdiction."

The Supreme Court reasoned that if a remand order is based on grounds wholly different from those authorized by §1447(c), review should be available.[454] The dissenting Justices argued that §1447(d) is unambiguous and contains no language showing that Congress intended to tie nonreviewability to the presence or absence of a jurisdictional issue under §1447(c).[455]

In 1988, Congress amended 28 USC §1446(c) to provide in part:

> A motion to remand the case on the basis of any defect in removal procedure must be made within 30 days of the filing of the notice of removal under section 1446(a). If at any time before final judgment it appears that the district court lacks subject matter jurisdiction, the case shall be remanded.

The courts of appeals continue to follow *Thermtron* by holding that a remand order that is based on the grounds set out in the *amended* §1447(c) is not subject

---

[452] 28 USC §1447(d).

[453] 423 US 336 (1976).

[454] *Id* 344.

[455] 28 USC §1446(c) as amended in part in 1988.

to review, but that an order based on some other ground will be reviewed.[456]

The Supreme Court returned to the review issue in *Carnegie-Mellon University v Cohill.*[457] William and Carrie Boyle sued Carnegie-Mellon in state court, claiming it had discharged William Boyle unlawfully. The Boyles alleged violation of the federal age discrimination laws, and state law discrimination, tort, and contract claims. Carnegie-Mellon removed. The Boyles moved to amend their complaint to delete their federal claim and remand to state court. The district judge granted both motions. Carnegie sought mandamus.

The Supreme Court held that the remand was not based on the grounds set out in §1447(c), so that appellate review was available. On the merits, the Court held that although discretionary remand is not specifically authorized in such cases, the power to remand follows from principles of pendent jurisdiction. If a case involving state and federal claims is filed in federal court in the first instance and the federal law claims are dismissed, the federal court would have had the discretion to dismiss the state claims.[458]

The narrow *Thermtron* exception rests on sound principles. As Chief Judge Merritt of the Sixth Circuit has said:

> This rule of nonreviewability of remand orders, first enacted over one hundred years ago, is important to our system of federalism. Parties to state litigation should not be delayed by procedural fencing over the intricacies and perplexities of removal jurisdiction, and state courts should not be long interrupted in the conduct of their litigation by removal petitions. It makes no difference that the District Court may be wrong in its conclusions concerning jurisdiction or the plausibility of the federal defense asserted. The federalism principle overrides this concern.[459]

To determine whether review is available, one must ask two questions. First, was the remand order based on an asserted lack of jurisdiction, rendering applicable the *Thermtron* rule? Second, should review be sought by appeal or mandamus?

The court of appeals opinions are not in harmony on the first question. Only a review of the cases can give one a sense of the situations in which review has been permitted.[460] The remand order will be more surely insulated from

---

[456] For example, in *In re* Shell Oil Co, 932 F2d 1518, 1523 (5th Cir 1991), *cert denied,* 112 S Ct 914 (1992) (White, J, dissented from denial of certiorari), the court held reviewable an order remanding a case under the 28 USC §1441(b) ban on removal of certain cases in which any party is a citizen of the state in which the suit is brought. *See generally* Joan Steinman, *Removal, Remand, and Review in Pendent Claim and Pendent Party Cases,* 41 Vand L Rev 923 (1988) (extensive discussion of appellate jurisdiction concerning remand orders).

[457] 484 US 343 (1988).

[458] United Mine Workers of Am v Gibbs, 383 US 715 (1966).

[459] Ohio v Wright, 992 F2d 616 (6th Cir 1993) (en banc) (footnote omitted).

[460] *See, e.g., In re* TMI Litig Cases Consol II, 940 F2d 832 (3d Cir 1991) (district court remanded based upon a finding that the statute ostensibly conferring federal jurisdiction was unconstitutional; held, remand order is reviewable, in part to review holding

review if the district judge states on the record that it is applying §1447(c) and remanding on that basis.[461]

The second question also does not have an easy answer. The review in *Thermtron* was by mandamus, although the Court did not discuss a preference for one mode of review over another.[462] The remanded party is out of federal court, and therefore the order is arguably final. The Fifth Circuit has held that remands not authorized by §1447(c) should be reviewed on mandamus, and remands based on forum selection clauses by direct appeal.[463] In another case, however, the Fifth Circuit reviewed a remand order by appeal although the issue was whether remand had been granted under §1447(c).[464] The advocate is advised to file a timely notice of appeal together with a petition for manda-

---

that a federal statute is unconstitutional; extensive discussion of rationale and caselaw), *cert denied,* 112 S Ct 1262 (1992); *In re* Allied-Signal, Inc, 919 F2d 277 (5th Cir 1990) (Louisiana public agency sued Allied-Signal in state court; Allied-Signal removed because of diversity and filed counterclaim in federal court; district judge remanded on sole ground that Louisiana law gave the agency sovereign immunity from suit in federal court; held, since the remand was based on construction of Louisiana law, not §1447(c), appellate jurisdiction existed; mandamus is the proper remedy; on the merits, held that the public agency could be sued in federal court without regard to contrary Louisiana statute); Richards v Federated Dept Stores, Inc, 812 F2d 211 (5th Cir), (applying *Thermtron*), *cert denied,* 484 US 824 (1987); *In re* Adams, 809 F2d 1187 (5th Cir 1987) (bankruptcy court's order reinstating litigation is appealable, unlike one remanding under 28 USC 1452(b)); New Orleans Pub Serv v Majoue, 802 F2d 166, 167 (5th Cir 1986) (once a district court has remanded the case to state court, the court of appeals may not review the order, and indeed the district court is powerless to vacate the order if it becomes convinced it was wrong); Clorox Co v United States Dist Court, 779 F2d 517 (9th Cir 1985) (remand orders reviewable in the Ninth Circuit if based upon a prior interpretation of substantive law; when propriety of remand is based on construction of alleged waiver of right to remove, review by appeal is available); Pelleport Investors, Inc v Budco Quality Theaters, Inc, 741 F2d 273 (9th Cir 1984) (remand order reviewable to test validity of forum selection clause); Allegheny Corp v United States Dist Court, 881 F2d 777 (9th Cir 1989) (failure to comply with time limitation of 28 USC §1446(b) not "wholly different," appeal dismissed for lack of jurisdiction).

[461] Kolibash v Committee on Legal Ethics, 872 F2d 571 (4th Cir 1989) (remand order is immune from review only if the district court invokes the grounds specified in §1447(c); remand on discretionary public policy grounds similar to abstention, because the case concerned the essentially state function of licensure of professionals, is reviewable).

[462] *See* 15A Charles A. Wright, Arthur R. Miller, & Edward H. Cooper, Federal Practice and Procedure §3914.11, at 703 (1992), suggesting that "[i]f review is to be available, it is better to use the more familiar and less cumbersome procedure of appeal than to force reliance on extraordinary writ practice."

[463] McDermott Intl, Inc v Lloyds Underwriters, 944 F2d 1199, 1201-04 (5th Cir 1991) (district court remand order issued under an insurance contract forum selection clause is reviewable by appeal rather than by mandamus), citing cases from other circuits.

[464] Mobil Corp v Abeille Gen Ins Co, 984 F2d 664 (5th Cir 1993) (remand orders are not appealable if district judge holds case was removed without jurisdiction; no exception to nonappealability based on the Foreign Sovereign Immunities Act and one plaintiff's claimed status as an instrumentality of the Republic of Ireland).

mus. The chances of obtaining mandamus are enhanced if the petition is filed expeditiously.[465]

Orders Concerning Arbitration

Federal arbitration statutes restrict appealability of district court orders in ways designed to encourage arbitration agreements and to discourage litigated challenges to arbitration. 9 USC §16, part of the Federal Arbitration Act, establishes a one-way ratchet on appeals involving arbitration. If the district judge stays a lawsuit or takes other action enforcing an arbitration agreement, an appeal will seldom lie. If the judge denies or limits arbitration, however, the order will be appealable.[466]

The courts of appeals have heeded the Congressional call and regulate appellate review accordingly.[467]

---

[465] *See* **ch 3.**

[466] The text is:

> §16 Appeals
> (a) An appeal may be taken from—
> (1) an order—(A) refusing a stay of any action under section 3 of this title, (B) denying a petition under section 4 of this title for arbitration to proceed, (C) denying an application under section 206 of this title to compel arbitration, (D) confirming or denying confirmation of an award or partial award, or (E) modifying, correcting, or vacating an award; (2) an interlocutory order granting, continuing, or modifying an injunction against an arbitration that is subject to this title; or (3) a final decision with respect to an arbitration that is subject to this title. (b) Except as otherwise provided in section 1292(b) of title 28, an appeal may not be taken from an interlocutory order—
> (1) granting a stay of any action under section 3 of this title; (2) directing arbitration to proceed under section 4 of this title; (3) compelling arbitration under section 206 of this title; or (4) refusing to enjoin an arbitration that is subject to this title.

The background to §15 is ably sketched in Richard J. Medalie, *The New Appeals Amendment: A Step Forward for Arbitration,* 44 Arb J 22 (1989).

[467] *E.g.*, Corion Corp v Chen, 964 F2d 55 (1st Cir 1992) (district court order compelling arbitration, staying lawsuit, and determining that an arbitrable claim exists is not appealable; while the district judge's failure to enter a Fed R Civ P 58 order is not fatal to appellate jurisdiction, it appears that the court intended to retain jurisdiction and not to enter a final order and the absence of a Rule 58 judgment is some evidence of this; as a matter of policy, orders compelling arbitration should not be appealable); McDermott Intl v Underwriters at Lloyds, Inc, 981 F2d 744 (5th Cir 1993) (Federal Arbitration Act bars appeal of order directing arbitration and staying action: "The FAA manifests a 'liberal federal policy favoring arbitration,' citing Gilmer v Interstate/Johnson Lane Corp, 111 S Ct 1647, 1651 (1991)). . . . "Section 16 promotes this policy 'by permitting interlocutory appeals of orders favoring litigation over arbitration and precluding review of interlocutory orders that favor arbitration' " (citing Forsythe Intl, SA v Gibbs Oil Co of Tex, 915 F2d 1017, 1020 (5th Cir 1990)); West of England Ship Owners Mut Ins v American Marine Corp, 981 F2d 749 (5th Cir 1993) (district court order compelling arbitration and staying litigation not reviewable due to Federal Arbitration Act; mandamus not available); Britton v Co-op Banking Group, 916 F2d 1405 (9th Cir 1990) (Arbitration Act appeal from denial of arbitration not mooted by district court's later ruling on merits of underlying claim; party who claims right to arbitrate and suffers default judgment by refusal to make discovery on underlying case does not waive right

Magistrate Judge-Decided Civil Cases

Under 28 USC §636(c), parties to civil actions in the district courts may elect to have their cases heard and decided by a federal magistrate judge.

If the parties choose a magistrate judge trial, they have a choice of appeal procedure which must be exercised at the time they consent to the magistrate judge's jurisdiction. If the parties select the option provided by §636(c)(4), there is a right of appeal to "a judge of the district court in the same manner as on an appeal from a judgment of the district court to a court of appeals."[468] The district judge's review of the magistrate judge's judgment "may be reviewed by the appropriate United States court of appeals upon petition for leave to appeal by a party stating specific objections to the judgment."[469] Parties electing this procedure follow the petition and cross-petition procedure under Fed R App P 5.1.

If the parties do not choose the §636(c)(4) route, the magistrate judge's judgment is appealable directly to the court of appeals in the same manner as an appeal from the district court.[470] In such a case, the parties are directed by Fed R App P 3.1 to proceed in the court of appeals exactly as they would have if the judgment had been entered by the district court.

Magistrate Judge-Decided Criminal Cases

Under 18 USC §3401, a misdemeanor defendant may consent to be tried before a United States magistrate judge. The procedure for referral to the magistrate judge, the district judge's discretion to try the case itself, and the government's limited right to bring the trial back to district court, are dealt with in that statute. 18 USC §3402 provides that magistrate judge decisions in referred cases are appealable to the district judge; the appellate rights of the government and the defendant are set out at Fed R Crim P 58(g)(2).

The court of appeals hears appeals from the district judge's decisions reviewing magistrate judge orders under the same rules as apply to appeals from other orders of district judges in criminal cases.[471] However, a district judge's decision to reverse a magistrate judge conviction and ordering acquittal of the

---

to arbitration by such refusal, but default judgment will stand if court of appeals concludes party is not entitled to arbitration). *But see* Swenson v Management Recruiters Intl, Inc, 872 F2d 264 (8th Cir) (order to compel arbitration of discrimination claim appealable because arbitration clause violates public policy; no consideration of §15, so status of case may be questionable), *cert denied,* 493 US 848 (1989).

[468] 28 USC §636(c)(4).

[469] *Id* §636(c)(5). *See* Provident Bank v Manor Steel Corp, 882 F2d 258 (7th Cir 1989) (court applies rule in Thomas v Arn, 474 US 140 (1985), to preclude an appeal from a district court's affirmance of a magistrate judge decision when the appellant has not presented his contentions to the district court as objections to the magistrate judge's report).

[470] 28 USC §636(c)(3).

[471] *See* **§§2.03, 2.05.**

defendant may be appealed by the government without falling afoul of the double jeopardy clause.[472]

Bail Decisions in Criminal Cases

There are three stages at which a decision granting or denying release on bail may be reviewable, and there are different procedures for each stage. The three stages are: before and during trial; while a convicted defendant awaits sentence; and on appeal from the judgment of conviction.

Before and during trial, the standards for release and detention are set out in 18 USC §3142.[473] Review of such orders is provided for by 18 USC §3145. According to that section, the defendant has a right of appeal under 28 USC §1291[474] and the government has a right of appeal under 18 USC §3731.[475] However, Fed R App P 9(a) provides that review of decisions "refusing or imposing conditions of release" shall be determined in an expedited fashion without formal briefs and that "the court of appeals or a judge thereof may order the release of the appellant pending the appeal."[476] The appellant—defendant or government—must be sure to assemble enough of an appellate record to permit informed decision of the issue.

A convicted defendant awaiting sentence is released or detained under the standards set out in 18 USC §3143(c). Review of the district court's decision is governed by the same appellate rules and principles as a decision before or during trial.[477]

Once a judgment of conviction has been entered, the decision to release or detain of a defendant resembles an order granting or refusing a stay pending appeal. The defendant and the government must litigate their positions before the district judge, who will grant or deny release according to the standards set out in 18 USC §3143(b)—a section which establishes a presumption against release.

If the defendant is released, the government may notice a timely appeal of that decision under 18 USC §3731 and 18 USC §3145(c).[478] If release is denied, however, the defendant's preferred route to review is to file a notice of appeal

---

[472] United States v Aslam, 936 F2d 751 (2d Cir 1991) (court of appeals has jurisdiction over the government's appeal from district court order reversing the judgment of conviction entered by the United States magistrate judge; court overcomes objections based on 28 USC §1291, 18 USC §3731, and double jeopardy).

[473] During any interlocutory appeal by the government, the defendant's release or detention is decided by §3142 standards. 18 USC §3143(c).

[474] *See* **§§2.03, 2.05, 6.04.**

[475] *See* **§2.11.**

[476] Fed R App P 9(a).

[477] This principle follows from Stack v Boyle, 342 US 1 (1951), holding that a decision denying bail prior to a final judgment of conviction is an appealable collateral order. *See* 18 USC §3145(c).

[478] The order granting release must be a final order, however. *See* United States v Cheeseman, 783 F2d 38 (2d Cir 1986) (district court order remanding to magistrate judge to fix conditions of release is not a "release order" appealable by the government; appeal dismissed).

from the conviction[479] and a motion for release under Fed R App P 9(b).[480] Such a motion may be made to the court or to a single judge. Counsel should consult the circuit rules and the clerk's office for the proper procedure. The motion may be accompanied by relevant portions of the record, and may be decided speedily.[481]

Antitrust Cases

15 USC §29(a) envisions direct court of appeals jurisdiction of most antitrust judgments. However, on appeal from an antitrust case brought by the United States, any party may seek an order from the district court under §29(b) that immediate Supreme Court review "is of general public importance in the administration of justice."[482] If such an order is entered, the Supreme Court may hear the case or may, in its discretion, remand to the court of appeals.[483]

Direct Supreme Court Review

28 USC §1253 provides for direct Supreme Court review of decisions of three-judge district courts granting or denying injunctive relief. If the three-judge court issues declaratory rather than injunctive relief, appeal should be taken to the court of appeals.[484]

Federal Election Law Constitutional Issues

2 USC §437h provides that a district court "immediately shall certify all questions of constitutionality of th[e Federal Election Campaign] Act to the United States Court of Appeals for the circuit involved, which shall hear the matter sitting *en banc.*"[485] This provision was designed to provide speedy resolution of constitutional questions concerning the act. However, given the Supreme Court's decision in *Buckley v Valeo,*[486] few undecided constitutional issues are likely to be presented. Therefore, a district court need not certify challenges that are frivolous or that involve settled principles of law.[487]

---

[479] The notice of appeal confers jurisdiction over the entire case under §1291.

[480] United States v Zherebchevsky, 849 F2d 1256 (9th Cir 1988).

[481] See **§6.12** for additional discussion of bail pending appeal.

[482] 15 USC §29(b).

[483] Id. *See generally* United States v American Tel & Tel Co, 714 F2d 178 (DC Cir 1983) (per curiam) (after district court certified order for immediate appellate consideration by the Supreme Court, the entire case came under the exclusive jurisdiction of that court and no other appeals from the district court could be taken).

[484] Socialist Workers Party v Hill, 483 F2d 554 (5th Cir 1973).

[485] 2 USC §437h.

[486] 424 US 1 (1976).

[487] California Medical Assn v FEC, 453 US 182, 192 n14 (1981). *See* Khachaturian v FEC, 980 F2d 330 (5th Cir 1992) (en banc) (court of appeals remanded a certified question to the district court with a direction to hold a hearing to determine whether the constitutional issue was frivolous; if issue determined to be frivolous, district court should dismiss; if not, it should recertify the case).

§2.16 Review of Administrative Agency Orders

Final decisions and certain interim and interlocutory orders of dozens of agencies, boards, and individual officers in the federal establishment are reviewable in the courts of appeals;[488] for convenience, this section refers to these individuals and entities by the generic term *agency*. Review of agency decisions constitutes somewhat more than 10 per cent of the cases decided by the courts of appeals each year.[489] The substantive law administered by each officer and agency is a specialized field of its own.

The Administrative Procedure Act (APA) sets out general principles of judicial review.[490] Many, if not most, agency decisions are reviewed in the first instances in the appropriate United States district court, from whose decision an appeal lies under the principles discussed elsewhere in this chapter. However, 28 USC §§2341-51 governs court of appeals review, by petition, of the agencies listed in 28 USC §2342 and of agency action made reviewable under some other specialized statutes. Many agencies have separate statutes calling for review of decisions in the district court or court of appeals. It is beyond the scope of this treatise to detail all of these individual statutes, but most of them are listed in the reference notes to 5 USCA §701 in the United States Code Annotated.

To this legislative patchwork, one must add two other kinds of rules. First, there are judge-made principles of agency review, primarily dealing with finality and the ripeness of the agency decision. Second, Fed R App P 15 through 20 set out a uniform procedure for all agency decisions that the court of appeals is empowered to review.[491] This section deals with the statutory and judge-made jurisdictional principles of administrative review. Timing and procedures for invoking court of appeals jurisdiction are dealt with in Chapter 6. Briefing, argument and decisional process are the same as in any other court of appeals case.

The APA provides that "A person suffering legal wrong because of agency action . . . is entitled to judicial review thereof."[492] This right may be limited if "statutes preclude judicial review"[493] or if the agency's action is "committed to agency discretion by law."[494] There are constitutional limits—under the due process clause—on the extent to which Congress and the courts may refuse

---

[488] *See generally* 16 Charles A. Wright, Arthur R. Miller, Edward H. Cooper, & Eugene Gressman, Federal Practice and Procedure: Jurisdiction §3943 (1977 & Supp 1993).

[489] *See id* §3940, at 301 n3.

[490] 5 USC §§701-706. The general principles of agency review are discussed in, e.g., Louis L. Jaffe, Judicial Control of Administrative Action (1965); another valuable resource is Robert L. Rabin, *Federal Regulation in Historical Perspective,* 38 Stan L Rev 1189 (1986). *See generally* Kenneth C. Davis, Administrative Law Treatise (2d ed 1978).

[491] Procedures under these rules are discussed more fully at **§6.09.**

[492] 5 USC §702.

[493] 5 USC §701(a)(1).

[494] *Id* §701(a)(2). *See, e.g.,* Slyper v Attorney Gen, 827 F2d 821 (DC Cir 1987) (USIA decision not reviewable), *cert denied,* 485 US 941 (1988).

judicial review of agency action that affects individual rights.[495] 5 USC §704 provides that

> Agency action made reviewable by statute and final agency action for which there is no other adequate remedy in a court are subject to judicial review. A preliminary, procedural, or intermediate agency action or ruling not directly reviewable is subject to review on the review of the final agency action.[496]

Section 704 thus establishes a general principle of reviewability.[497] If a statute provides for review, one must follow the path marked by the statute, except in certain narrowly defined circumstances.[498] If there is no explicit provision for review, an aggrieved party must seek redress in federal district court, usually under the federal question[499] or mandamus[500] statutes. The APA does not, of itself, confer jurisdiction on federal courts to review agency action.[501] Given this statutory structure, the court of appeals will directly review agency action only when a statute so provides.

As mentioned above, most court of appeals review is governed by 28 USC §§2341-51. Those sections limit review to final orders,[502] at the instance of a

---

[495] These due process issues are canvassed in, e.g., Louis L. Jaffe, *supra* note 490; Robert L. Rabin, *supra* note 490; and Judah A. Shechter, Note, *De Novo Judicial Review of Administrative Agency Factual Determinations Implicating Constitutional Rights,* 88 Colum L Rev 1483 (1988). They are not uniquely relevant to court of appeals review and therefore are not dealt with in detail in this Treatise.

[496] *See generally* Califano v Sanders, 430 US 99 (1977).

[497] The principles of review are set out at 5 USC §706. *See* **§5.11.**

[498] For example, review of a final Federal Communications Commission order would be by petition under 28 USC §2342 in the court of appeals, but a facial constitutional challenge to a provision of the Communications Act might be within the original jurisdiction of the federal district courts under 28 USC §1331. *See* Sable Communications of Cal v FCC, 827 F2d 640 (9th Cir 1987).

Under the Immigration Reform and Control Act of 1986 (IRCA), Pub L No 99-603, 100 Stat 3359 (codified as amended in scattered sections of 8 USC), as under prior law, an individual alien who seeks review of his or her status has a defined administrative path, usually ending in the court of appeals. However, broad-gauge challenges to immigration practices affecting numbers of aliens may be pursued by an independent action in the district court not limited by these jurisdictional constraints, provided that the issues are ripe for adjudication. Reno v Catholic Social Servs, 113 S Ct 2485 (1993). *See also* McNary v Haitian Refugee Ctr, Inc, 498 US 479 (1991) and Ayuda, Inc v Thornburgh, 498 US 1117 (1991).

In sum, the line is not clear between the cases in which one must first resort to the agency and those in which such resort will be excused.

[499] 28 USC §1331.

[500] *Id* §1361.

[501] Califano v Sanders, 430 US 99 (1977).

[502] Some statutes outside title 28 provide for court of appeals review of orders that do not finally dispose of an entire controversy, but have an immediate coercive effect similar to an injunction. Examples include Health and Human Services orders concerning drug and food products. *See, e.g.,* 21 USC §371 *et seq.*

party aggrieved,[503] in the court of appeals where the petitioner resides or has its principal office, or in the United States Court of Appeals for the District of Columbia Circuit.[504]

The principle of finality, contained in almost all statutes providing for review of agency action, operates with special force in the administrative setting.[505] The agency is presumed to possess a special competence within its defined area of competence and must be allowed the opportunity to exercise its authority fully before judicial intervention is proper.[506] This rule of finality can be tempered in situations involving overriding considerations, such as a claim of constitutional right, or the judiciary's conclusion that a particular matter falls outside the range of agency expertise.[507] Finality analysis forms a large part of the agency review caselaw.[508]

---

[503] 28 USC §2344.

[504] *Id* §2343.

[505] Some statutes expressly provide for review of agency interlocutory orders. However, when a final agency decision is a prerequisite to judicial review, courts are reluctant to provide review at some earlier point. *See, e.g.,* Bell v New Jersey & Pennsylvania, 461 US 773 (1983); Breen v Selective Serv Local Bd No 16, 396 US 460 (1970); Joint Anti-Fascist Refugee Comm v McGrath, 341 US 123, 154-56 (1951) (Frankfurter, J, concurring); Estep v United States, 327 US 114 (1946); Ohio Citizens for Responsible Energy, Inc v NRC, 803 F2d 258, 260 (6th Cir 1986) (NRC denial of reopening of hearing not so "flagrantly wrong" (citing Ecology Action v United States Atomic Energy Commission, 492 F2d 998, 1001 (2d Cir 1974)) as to justify judicial review before a final order).

[506] Despite statutory provisions that seem to limit review to agency action, an order by a lower level administrative official may be reviewable if the official has lawfully been delegated the power vested in a higher officer and acts on the latter's behalf. Southern Cal Aerial Advertisers' Assn v FAA, 881 F2d 672 (9th Cir 1989) (FAA order reviewable because issued in the name of the agency acting under authority delegated from secretary of transportation). However, if a lower level official acts in the agency's name in a way that does not lawfully constitute agency action, then the official's decision is not reviewable. NLRB v United Food & Commercial Workers Union, 484 US 112 (1987) (unfair labor practice complaint diverted under NLRB procedure to a regional director and then, by administrative appeal, to the NLRB General Counsel was not an NLRB decision and hence not reviewable by court of appeals, even though the General Counsel was acting for the NLRB).

[507] Breen v Selective Serv Bd, 396 US 460 (1970), is an example of such a case. *See also* Wolff v Selective Serv Local Bd No 16, 372 F2d 817, 823 (2d Cir 1967) (review of local draft board action without necessity of registrant refusing to submit to induction). In United States v Storer Broadcasting Co, 351 US 192 (1956), the Court permitted a radio station licensee to challenge regulations limiting the number of licenses that one entity could hold without requiring the licensee to undergo a licensing proceeding and be denied relief by a final agency order. The decision was based upon a finding of present harm to Storer from the agency's adoption of the regulation. In addition, as noted above, some statutes confer judicial jurisdiction to review interlocutory agency orders.

[508] *See, e.g.,* Sullivan v Finkelstein, 496 US 617 (1990) (ordinarily, a district court order remanding a social security case to the Secretary of Health and Human Service for further proceedings is not final and appealable under the applicable statute, 42 USC §405(g); however, a determination that the Secretary properly denied relief under the regulation it relied upon, but the regulations themselves are invalid in denying relief, coupled with a remand to fix benefits, is appealable because of the holding that the

The principle of finality was underscored in *ICC v Brotherhood of Locomotive Engineers.*[509] In October 1982, the ICC issued an order permitting railroad companies to lease out rail lines of another carrier. In April 1983, railway unions petitioned the ICC for clarification of the order, seeking a determination that the railroads could not use their own crews on the leased trackage. The ICC denied the petition on May 18, 1983, noting that its October 1982 order did not require clarification because it expressly contemplated that the railroads would use their own crews. The unions filed petitions with the ICC for reconsideration; these petitions were timely responses to the May 18 order. On October 25, 1983, the ICC denied these petitions in a lengthy opinion.

The unions filed a petition in the court of appeals within 60 days of October 25 as provided by 28 USC §2344. This petition was timely with respect to the October 25 and May 18 orders. However, the Supreme Court held that the court of appeals had no jurisdiction to review the October 1982 order.

The Court distinguished three situations. First, if a party to an agency proceeding seeks reconsideration by the agency within the time alloted by statute or agency rule, the time for seeking judicial review of the original decision may be extended.[510] This is by analogy to a petition for rehearing in the court of appeals, which extends the time for seeking further review of the court of appeals action, as noted at **§11.01.**

---

regulations are invalid); Pittston Coal Group v Sebben, 488 US 105, 121 (1988) (administrative law judge denied two coal miners' claims for black lung benefits using regulations later determined to be impermissibly strict; although claimants had declined to appeal the ALJ's initial determination and the time for direct review had expired, they sought mandamus to compel the ALJ to rehear their claims using the proper standard; held, mandamus not available because ALJ did not have a clear duty to reopen; review usually available only of a final decision); Colon v Secretary, 877 F2d 148, 151-52 (1st Cir 1989) (per curiam) (district court order remanding claim to Secretary appealable on the ground that the district court lacked jurisdiction); Westvaco Corp v EPA, 899 F2d 1383 (4th Cir 1990) (EPA Administrator's decisions under Clean Water Act are reviewable under 33 USC §1369(b) only when they constitute final agency action; preliminary, partial actions subject to later review are nonfinal); Abbs v Sullivan, 963 F2d 918 (7th Cir 1992) (procedural rules under which an agency proposes to investigate and make adjudications are not final agency decisions within the meaning of the Administrative Procedure Act; hence, no right to judicial review); Law Offices of Seymour M. Chase, PC v FCC, 843 F2d 517 (DC Cir 1988) (FCC order disqualifying counsel not reviewable as final order); Exportal Ltda v United States, 902 F2d 45 (DC Cir 1990) (court of appeals has jurisdiction under applicable statute, 7 USC §499f(e), to review Secretary of Agriculture's denial of foreign producer's request for waiver of a preadjudication bond requirement; order is final because it effectively precludes further administrative review of petitioner's claim; case truly is an administrative version of the *Cohen* facts); Her Majesty the Queen in Right of Ontario v EPA, 912 F2d 1525, 1530-32 (DC Cir 1990) (held, EPA inaction on petition for issuance of acid rain regulations is final and reviewable under 42 USC §7607(b)(1), particularly as issue involves only statutory interpretation; "agency inaction may represent effectively final agency action that the agency has not frankly acknowledged' " (quoting Sierra Club v Thomas, 828 F2d 783, 793 (DC Cir 1987)).

[509] 482 US 270 (1987).

[510] *Id* 278.

Second, a party may seek reopening of agency action based upon new evidence or changed circumstances.[511] In such a case, judicial review of the agency's refusal to reopen generally will be available. Third, and dispositive in *Locomotive Engineers,* "where a party petitions an agency for reconsideration on the ground of 'material error,' " that is, on the same record that was before the agency when it rendered its original decision, "an order which merely denies rehearing of . . . [the prior] order is not itself reviewable.' "[512] The Court held the ICC action unreviewable despite the ICC's having issued an extensive written justification of its October 25, 1983 action.

Related to finality is the judicially enforced principle that agency action must be ripe for review. Ripeness is established under a two-part test. First, agency action must be sufficiently final so that there is no interest in postponing review until issues are more concrete; and second, there must be an immediate impact so harmful to petitioner that present consideration is warranted.[513] *Beach Communications, Inc v FCC* [514] illustrates the interplay of ripeness principles with the special relationship between reviewing courts of appeals and the agencies whose actions they are to control. Satellite master antenna facility owners sought review of federal communications order that required their facility to be franchised. The court of appeals held that a First Amendment challenge to the FCC's position was not ripe, because neither the FCC nor the Congress had fully defined the broadcast content obligations that the owners would incur if they were subject to franchising. A challenge to the FCC's order on equal protection grounds was held to be ripe, but the court of appeals professed itself unable to decide the issue, because rational basis review of the order required legislative facts that were not in the record. Rather than gather these facts itself, the court of appeals remanded to the Federal Communications Commission to consider the equal protection challenge under the legal standards set out by the court.

---

[511] *Id* 278-79. Compare the discussion in the concurring opinion, *id* 293-95.

[512] *Id* 280 (quoting Microwave Communications, Inc v FCC, 515 F2d 385, 387 n7 (DC Cir 1974).

[513] Abbott Laboratories v Gardner, 387 US 136, 148-49 (1967), *overruled on other grounds sub nom* Califano v Sanders, 430 US 99 (1977). *See also* United Church of Christ v FCC, 911 F2d 813 (DC Cir 1990) (challenge to FCC regulations on trafficking in broadcast licenses ripe because it involves a discrete legal issue unburdened by detailed factual inquiries and regulations; if permitted to operate, will have profound effect on petitioner's interest); TeleSTAR, Inc v FCC, 888 F2d 132, 133 (DC Cir 1989) ("The question . . . is whether a petition for review, unripe because of the pendency of a request for agency reconsideration, ripens so as to vest this court with jurisdiction once the agency issues its final decision on reconsideration." Held, no); Public Citizen v Office of the United States Trade Representatives, 970 F2d 916 (DC Cir 1992) (judicial review not available to compel OTR to prepare environmental impact statements for North American Free Trade Agreement being negotiated; agency action is neither ripe nor final; action can be ripe in the sense that only purely legal issues remain, while not being final under APA).

[514] 959 F2d 975 (DC Cir 1992), *revd on the merits after remand & appeal,* 1993 WL 179242 (US 1993).

The party seeking review of agency action must, in general, have exhausted administrative remedies provided in agency rules or in the governing legislation. This is a rule of deference to agency expertise as well as finality. Most agency review statutes preclude review of claims not first raised before the agency, although sometimes the failure may be excused upon a proper showing.[515] While deference to agency expertise is the hallmark of judicial review, it will sometimes be unclear to whom the appellate court must defer in reviewing administrative agency action. Under the Occupational Safety and Health Act, 29 USC §651 *et seq,* the Secretary of Labor sets standards and the Occupational Safety and Health Review Commission performs adjudicatory functions. In *Martin v Occupational Safety & Health Review Commission,*[516] the Supreme Court held that when the Commission and the Secretary differ on interpretation of a regulation, a reviewing court must defer to the latter's expertise.

A party challenging an agency order must meet the same standing requirements as a party to any other appellate proceeding in the court of appeals.[517] This standing may be conferred upon one who was not a party to the challenged order but who is affected by it, allowing that party to move to intervene in the agency proceedings for the purpose of being able to appeal. If the statute governing agency action does not contain a specific provision for intervention, Fed R App P 15(d) permits a party to file a motion for leave to intervene setting forth its interest in the proceedings.[518] Intervention of interested persons also

---

[515] *Compare* McKart v United States, 395 US 185 (1969) (claim of entitlement to ministerial exemption not raised before Selective Service System; failure excused) *with* EEOC v FLRA, 476 US 19 (1986) (EEOC barred from judicial review of claims not raised before the agency absent "extraordinary circumstances"). *See also* McNeil v United States, 113 S Ct 1980 (1993) (Federal Tort Claims Act claimant must exhaust administrative remedies before starting to litigate; once claimant has commenced litigation, he is forever barred because he cannot meet the statutory requirement of pre-filing exhaustion; extensive discussion of exhaustion theory); Tideland Welding Serv v Department of Labor, 817 F2d 1211 (5th Cir 1987) (court of appeals has no jurisdiction to review administrative law judge award of compensation under Longshore & Harbor Workers Act until Benefits Review Board enters final order reviewing ALJ award). If the governing legislation does not require exhaustion of remedies, however, the courts have no basis for insisting upon it. In Darby v Cisneros, 113 S Ct 2539 (1993), the petitioners had not asked the Secretary of Housing and Urban Development to review an adverse determination by an administrative law judge concerning a school lunch program. The Supreme Court held that federal courts have no authority to require exhaustion of remedies when neither the statute nor agency rules require it. The Administrative Procedure Act does not require exhaustion.

[516] 494 US 144 (1991).

[517] Standing to challenge administrative action depends on the existence of a harm sufficient to satisfy art III, as well as upon statutory considerations. *Compare* Branton v FCC, 993 F2d 906 (DC Cir 1993) (listener has no standing to challenge FCC refusal to take action against indecent broadcast language) *with* Office of Communications of United Church of Christ v FCC, 359 F2d 994 (DC Cir 1966) (listener standing in license renewal). *See generally* Michael E. Tigar, *Judicial Power, the "Political Question Doctrine," and Foreign Relations,* 17 UCLA L Rev 1135, 1138 n10 (1970).

[518] Fed R App P 15 is discussed at **§6.09.**

is permitted for certain agency proceedings under 28 USC §2348.[519] Other doctrines of appealability, such as mootness, also apply in review of agency action.[520]

Agency factfindings will, under most of the statutory review standards, be affirmed if supported by substantial evidence.[521] The advocate must be aware, however, that the review procedure under discussion, and the special provisions of the Federal Rules of Appellate Procedure discussed at **§6.09,** apply in general to review of adjudicative actions after hearing in accordance with the Administrative Procedure Act (APA) or some special procedure that is substituted for it.[522] Even then, the Congress must have provided for review in the court of appeals.[523]

Agency actions that do not fit this framework may be reviewable by other means. If the court of appeals will have jurisdiction to review a final decision of the agency, it will have the power to issue a writ of mandamus or prohibition.[524] Agency investigative action may be reviewable by civil suit in the district court, with eventual review in the court of appeals.[525] As suggested above, if the agency is engaged in a clearly illegal—particularly unconstitutional—course of conduct that will wreak irreparable harm if the parties await a final order, the district court will have injunctive power or the power to issue a statutory order in the nature of mandamus.[526] These actions will be reviewable in the court of appeals like any other civil case.

§2.17 Pendent Appellate Jurisdiction

Where other bases of jurisdiction fail, pendent appellate jurisdiction may be available. Under this doctrine, when an appealable preliminary injunction issue cannot be resolved without reference to an otherwise unappealable

---

[519] In addition, a party may be able to intervene before the agency, a matter governed by the agency's own operating statute and rules. *See generally* United Church of Christ v FCC, 359 F2d 994 (DC Cir 1966).

[520] For a discussion of mootness as a limit on judicial power, see **§2.18.**

[521] **§5.11.** Some agency actions are judged by a different standard. *See, e.g.,* Estep v United States, 327 US 114, 122 (1946) (*no basis in fact* test for Selective Service System).

[522] Agency action that does not fit this mold may be unreviewable until the process grinds on to a final order. However, there are many cases permitting parties harmed by agency action not amounting to a final order to obtain judicial review. See the discussion below.

[523] *See* Califano v Sanders, 430 US 99 (1977), discussed *supra* notes 496 and 501.

[524] This is an instance of the general principles discussed in **ch 3.** *See, e.g.,* Potomac Elec Power Co v ICC, 702 F2d 1026 (DC Cir), *supplemented,* 705 F2d 1343 (DC Cir 1983).

[525] The district court will have jurisdiction under its federal question, 28 USC §1332, or in the nature of mandamus, 28 USC §1361, jurisdiction. A detailed discussion of this issue is beyond the scope of this treatise.

[526] *See, e.g.,* SEC v ESM Govt Sec, Inc, 645 F2d 310 (5th Cir 1981).

issue,[527] or an otherwise nonreviewable claim is inextricably bound up with an appealable interlocutory order,[528] the court of appeals has jurisdiction to hear both claims.[529]

The contours of the doctrine are uncertain, and the courts of appeals have not developed a single, consistent analysis. As one court has noted, the rule receives a narrow construction to avoid "abuse of the tail-wagging-the-dog variety," in which litigants bring appealable claims solely to obtain jurisdiction over nonappealable ones.[530] Judge Posner has said the Court of Appeals "can review an unappealable order only if it is so entwined with an appealable one that separate consideration would involve sheer duplication of effort by the parties and this court."[531] Nor does the doctrine apply when there is not even one issue that is properly before the court;[532] there must be some appealable order to which the otherwise nonappealable one is pendent.

---

[527] Wagner v Taylor, 836 F2d 578, 586 (DC Cir 1987) ("a denial of class certification may be investigated on an appeal from an action taken on a motion for preliminary injunction" because "the availability of provisional relief" is "tightly interwoven into the fabric of class certification"); Kershner v Mazurkiewicz, 670 F2d 440 (3d Cir 1982) (order denying class certification not reviewable because preliminary injunction issue was separable from class certification issue). *See also* **§2.06.**

[528] Liskey v Oppenheimer & Co, 717 F2d 314 (6th Cir 1983) (because issues raised by cross-appeal were unrelated to issues on appeal, there was no jurisdictional basis for the court of appeals to hear the cross-appeal).

[529] *See also* Primas v City of Oklahoma City, 958 F2d 1506, 1512 (10th Cir 1992) (court of appeals would exercise pendent jurisdiction over plaintiff's cross-appeal from interlocutory order denying immunity in civil rights case; hearing cross-appeal contributed to expeditious resolution of case); Avery v Secretary of Health & Human Services, 762 F2d 158, 160 (1st Cir 1985) (orders requiring Secretary to issue certain notices and follow certain procedures were "equivalent to an injunction and therefore appealable under 28 USC §1292(a)(1)"); Cable Holdings of Battlefield, Inc v Cooke, 764 F2d 1466 (11th Cir 1985) (exercising pendent jurisdiction, court of appeals reviews partial summary judgment ruling that provided basis for dissolution of preliminary restraint and denial of preliminary injunction); Intermedics Infusaid, Inc v Regents of Univ of Minn, 804 F2d 129, 134 (Fed Cir 1986) (citing caselaw, court concludes that "the major factor in determining whether to exercise [pendent appellate] jurisdiction is the extent that review of the appealable order will involve consideration of factors relevant to the otherwise nonappealable order").

[530] Parks v Pavkovic, 753 F2d 1397, 1402 (7th Cir) (if district court's order to pay is sufficiently closely related to a permanent injunction, it is reviewable by the court of appeals whether final or not), *cert denied,* 473 US 906 (1985); *see also* Weiss v York Hosp, 745 F2d 786 (3d Cir 1984) (appellate jurisdiction narrowly construed: where there are significant issues involved in the nonappealable orders which are, or may be, different from issues involved in the appealable orders, the court lacks pendent jurisdiction over the former), *cert denied,* 470 US 1060 (1985).

[531] Patterson v Portch, 853 F2d 1399, 1403 (7th Cir 1988) (overlap between appeal and cross-appeal is insufficient to warrant review of cross-appeal by pendent appellate jurisdiction).

[532] Rodriguez v Handy, 802 F2d 817 (5th Cir 1986) (plaintiff's cross-appeal challenging denial of fees not properly before the court since, although final to that issue, it does not end the litigation and leaves other matters unresolved; the cross-appeal therefore cannot confer pendent appellate jurisdiction over defendant's appeal because no issues are properly before the court), *appealed after remand,* 873 F2d 814 (5th Cir 1989).

The Supreme Court has rarely spoken on the question. It has reserved decision on whether a court of appeals reviewing an administrative order would have pendent jurisdiction to review claims not embraced within the order under review.[533] The Court has also confined §1292(b) review to the order certified.[534] In criminal cases, the Court has made clear that it disfavors the exercise of pendent appellate jurisdiction.[535] The contours of the doctrine, and indeed its very existence, are therefore unsettled.

§2.18 Mootness

An appeal properly begun may be derailed if the subject matter becomes moot. Mootness has been variously defined. The Supreme Court has said: "Simply stated, a case is moot when the issues presented are no longer 'live' or the parties lack a legally cognizable interest in the outcome."[536] The doctrine of mootness has a constitutional basis, because article III of the Constitution limits the jurisdiction of federal courts to cases and controversies.[537] This limitation is applicable to appellate courts. A case that presented a substantial controversy at its inception "may become moot on appeal by the occurrence of subsequent events."[538]

---

[533] See, e.g., Cheng Fan Kwok v INS, 392 US 206, 216 n16 (1968) (reserving opinion on whether pendent appellate jurisdiction would lie over denials of discretionary relief presented with a petition for review of deportation decision); *see also* Mohammadi-Motlagh v INS, 727 F2d 1450 (9th Cir 1984) (pendent appellate jurisdiction lies over discretionary decisions "on which final order of deportation is contingent' " (quoting Chadha v INS, 634 F2d 408, 413 (9th Cir 1980), *affd,* 462 US 919 (1983)).

[534] See **§2.09,** discussing United States v Stanley, 483 US 669, 676-77 (1987) (court of appeals has jurisdiction only over certified orders, not over matters ruled upon in other orders).

[535] United States v MacDonald, 435 US 850, 857 n6 (1978) (denying pendent appellate jurisdiction over otherwise nonappealable claims even though they are joined with double jeopardy claims over which the court has interlocutory appellate jurisdiction (citing Abney v United States, 431 US 651, 662-63 (1977)).

[536] Powell v McCormack, 395 US 486, 496 (1969).

[537] US Const art III, 1. *See generally* Charles A. Wright, Federal Courts 12, 55-56 (4th ed 1983).

[538] *In re* Grand Jury Proceedings re Larson, 785 F2d 629, 630 (8th Cir 1986) (witnesses' appeal from contempt for refusing to testify before grand jury mooted by grand jury target pleading guilty to tax evasion; court cites and discusses cases in which mootness argument is rejected). *See also* Continental Trading Servs v Cavazos, 893 F2d 877 (7th Cir 1990) (when the district court enters a permanent injunction while the appeal from the preliminary injunction is pending, the appeal becomes moot); Henco, Inc v Brown, 904 F2d 11 (7th Cir 1990) (expiration of preliminary injunction moots appeal, despite prospect that damages will be sought for having had to post injunction bond; issues can be resolved if district court in fact awards damages; neither party sought to expedite the appeal to obtain resolution before the injunction terminated); Clark Equip Co v Lift Parts Mfg Co, 972 F2d 817 (7th Cir 1992) (when sanctions are made payable to the opposing party, the sanctions order is mooted when the parties settle the litigation; the district court's interest in enforcing its rules is not sufficient to prevent this finding; if the district court wants to impose sanctions that survive a settlement by the parties,

Language in the decided cases[539] and the writings of some commentators[540] have suggested that mootness is a doctrine solely of constitutional dimension. It is clear from reviewing the cases, however, that it may have a prudential and almost discretionary dimension. For example, in *United States v Campos-Serrano,*[541] the respondent was deported after his conviction. The Supreme Court held that "the fact that the respondent is now out of the country does not render this case moot."[542] The Court distinguished a number of cases in which the defendant's voluntary flight or escape led it to decline "to consider the merits of criminal cases in which the party seeking review has escaped 'from the restraints placed upon him pursuant to the conviction.' "[543]

---

it must make them payable to the court or impose some nonmonetary penalty); *In re* Taylor, 916 F2d 1027 (5th Cir 1990) (challenge to sanction imposed on member of district court bar mooted by challenger's resignation from bar; issue of sanctions may be litigated if he seeks reinstatement); United States v $2,490.00, 825 F2d 1419 (9th Cir 1987) (court of appeals jurisdiction over appeal from forfeiture order ends when the money is deposited in United States Treasury); Matson Navigation Co v United States, 825 F2d 502 (DC Cir 1987) (judicial review of Department of Transportation orders permitting two shipping companies to affiliate became moot when one company sold the vessel that formed the basis of the Department's jurisdiction); Wilmington Firefighters Local 1590 v City of Wilmington, 824 F2d 262 (3d Cir 1987) (appeal from grant of summary judgment concerning promotion list in racial discrimination controversy rendered moot when list expired without any promotions having been made from it); *In re* Bunker Ltd Partnership, 820 F2d 308 (9th Cir 1987) (where amended statute gave agency right to administrative warrant, dispute over agency's ability to obtain warrant under original statute rendered moot); United States v Barrett, 837 F2d 1341 (5th Cir 1988) (proceeding to conditionally enforce IRS summons was not mooted by taxpayer's release to IRS, under court order, of names of patients the IRS wished to contact; the IRS had not yet contacted patients and, therefore, information protected by the Internal Revenue Code had not been disclosed to third parties), *called into doubt by* United States v Zolin, 491 US 554, *cert denied,* 492 US 926 (1989); Bahnmiller v Derwinski, 923 F2d 1085, 1088-89 (4th Cir 1991) (held, "[w]ithdrawal or alteration of administrative policies can moot an attack on those policies"; thus, challenge to VA regulations on right to counsel mooted by VA concession while appeal was pending, and amendment of regulations; proper course is to vacate judgment below as to the moot part of the case and decide the remaining live issues on appeal (citing CIA v Holy Spirit Assn, 455 US 997 (1982)). *Compare* United States v Salerno, 481 US 739 (1987), in which the Court reached and decided the constitutionality of pretrial detention based on dangerousness even though both respondents were no longer detained under the challenged denial of bail but under another, concededly valid, process. *See also id* 755-67 (Marshall, J, dissenting).

For a thorough discussion of the mootness effect when the case is settled on appeal, see **§5.16.**

[539] *See, e.g.,* Powell v McCormack, 395 US 486, 496 n7 (1969) and accompanying text.

[540] Charles A. Wright, *supra* note 537.

[541] 404 US 293 (1971), *cert denied,* 404 US 1023 (1972).

[542] *Id* 295 n2.

[543] *Id* (quoting Molinaro v New Jersey, 396 US 365, 366 (1970)). In Ortega-Rodriguez v United States, 113 S Ct 1199 (1993), the Court reaffirmed that dismissal of a fleeing defendant's appeal is a matter of discretion for the court of appeals and is not a mandatory sanction. The doctrine has many faces. For a discussion in the field of habeas corpus, see R. Sokol, Federal Habeas Corpus §§6.01-6.02 (2d ed 1968). It has been

In *Honig v Doe,*[544] respondents Doe and Smith were suspended from a federally funded special educational program for emotionally disturbed children. They sued. The district court granted relief and the court of appeals affirmed. The Court held that the controversy was moot as to Doe, because at 24 years of age, he was no longer eligible to be in the program, which was for individuals aged 3 to 21. The controversy as to Smith, 20 years old, was still alive, for he could seek to continue in the program and might likely suffer the same sort of due process violation.

The majority opinion, by Justice Brennan, regarded a truly moot controversy as beyond the article 3 judicial power.[545] Honig provoked two opinions extensively studied for clues to the Court's future direction on mootness issues. Chief Justice Rehnquist, concurring, reviewed the mootness doctrine from its origins and found no constitutional basis for it:

> The logical conclusion to be drawn from these cases, and from the historical development of the principle of mootness, is that while an unwillingness to decide moot cases may be connected to the case or controversy requirement of Art. III, it is an attenuated connection that may be overrid-

---

recognized that a defendant absent from the United States—and therefore not subject to any punishment a court might impose—may have his or her case considered by the courts and dismissed for procedural error. United States v Weinstein, 511 F2d 622 (2d Cir), *cert denied,* 422 US 1042 (1975), discussed in **§3.12.** *But see* United States v Puzzanghera, 820 F2d 25 (1st Cir) (defendant who escaped from custody while appeal was pending and recaptured more than 30 days later forfeited right of appeal; appeal dismissed with prejudice), *cert denied,* 484 US 900 (1987); Feigley v Fulcomer, 833 F2d 29 (3d Cir 1987) (habeas petitioner waived opportunity to have federal review of double jeopardy claim by escaping from prison during pendency of state postconviction proceeding); United States v DeValle, 894 F2d 133 (5th Cir 1990) (court dismissed appeals from conviction, but not from sentence, because defendant became a fugitive following her conviction; though defendant was recaptured before the appeal was dismissed, court held its power of dismissal to be undiminished). These are not mootness cases in an article III sense. The court acknowledges its power of review, but has decided to punish the litigant by finding waiver by conduct. *See* Michael E. Tigar, *Foreword: Waiver of Constitutional Rights: Disquiet in the Citadel,* 84 Harv L Rev 1 (1970).

It was formerly held that a criminal defendant who conceded the validity of one or more convictions on which concurrent sentence had been imposed could not challenge the other counts on which the defendant was convicted. This doctrine was overruled in Benton v Maryland, 395 US 784 (1969). The courts of appeals are now divided on whether they will review concurrent sentence counts as a matter of discretion or in all cases. *See* Charles A. Wright, Federal Practice and Procedure: Criminal 2d §527 (1982 & Supp 1993). In support of reviewability, see Ray v United States, 481 US 736 (1987) (although petitioner was serving concurrent seven-year terms on the three counts of which he was convicted, his sentence was not concurrent because the district judge imposed a mandatory monetary assessment of $50 on each of the three counts).

[544] 484 US 305 (1988). *Honig* is extensively discussed in Evan Tsen Lee, *Deconstitutionalizing Justiciability: The Example of Mootness,* 105 Harv L Rev 603 (1992).

[545] Honig v Doe, 484 US 305, 318 (1988). Justice Brennan applied the *capable of repetition, yet evading review* standard (discussed below in this section) to find this case reviewable as to Smith.

> den where there are strong reasons to override it. The "capable of repetition, yet evading review" exception[546] is an example. So too is our refusal to dismiss as moot those cases in which the defendant voluntarily ceases, at some advanced stage of the appellate proceedings, whatever activity prompted the plaintiff to seek an injunction.[547]

The Chief Justice then urged the Court to abandon the doctrine of mootness to permit decision of cases on which certiorari had been granted to permit the Court to decide the important issues on which it had made the grant.

Disagreeing with Chief Justice Rehnquist on the constitutional basis for mootness doctrine, and arguing that the case was moot, Justice Scalia parsed the constitutional debates and cases from several periods in the Court's history, and concluded:

> In sum, I cannot believe that it is only our prudence, and nothing inherent in the understood nature of "The judicial Power," U.S. Const., Art. III, §1, that restrains us from pronouncing judgment in a case that the parties have settled, or a case involving a nonsurviving claim where the plaintiff has died, or a case where the law has changed so that the basis of the dispute no longer exists, or a case where conduct sought to be enjoined has ceased and will not recur. Where the conduct has ceased for the time being but there is a demonstrated probability that it will recur, a real-life controversy between parties with a personal stake in the outcome continues to exist, and Art. III is no more violated than it is violated by entertaining a declaratory judgment action. But that is the limit of our power.[548]

Writing for a unanimous Court, Justice Scalia reaffirmed the constitutional basis for at least some aspects of mootness doctrine in *Lewis v Continental Bank Corp.*[549] Continental had sought approval from Florida officials to establish a federally insured bank. When the officials denied permission, Continental sued and won in both the district court and the court of appeals, on the ground that Florida's action violated the commerce clause.

After the court of appeals' decision, Congress amended federal banking law to make clear that the Florida officials had the power they claimed the right to exercise. The Supreme Court held that the judgment of the lower court must be vacated and the case remanded. Justice Scalia wrote:

> This case-or-controversy requirement subsists through all stages of federal judicial proceedings, trial and appellate. To sustain our jurisdiction in the present case, it is not enough that a dispute was very much alive when suit was filed, or when review was obtained in the Court of

---

[546] Discussed below in this section.

[547] 484 US at 331.

[548] *Id* 341.

[549] 494 US 472 (1990).

> Appeals. . . . The parties must continue to have a "personal stake in the outcome" of the lawsuit. . . .[550]

Given the jurisprudential disputes over mootness in the Supreme Court and the courts of appeals, the doctrine is best understood by example. Even at the level of results, and ignoring doctrinal consistency, the cases do not seem to speak with a single voice. In *Weinstein v Bradford,*[551] the Court dismissed as moot an appeal from a holding that the respondent was entitled to certain due process protections in the parole hearing process. While the case was pending on appeal, the respondent was paroled. Therefore, the Court reasoned, he "no longer has any present interest" in the policies he challenged.[552] Similarly, the appeal of a grand jury witness committed for civil contempt for refusal to testify or produce documents will be mooted when the grand jury's term ends and the witness is released from custody.[553]

In *Murphy v Hunt,*[554] a state prisoner was held without bail on sexual assault charges under a Nebraska statute that made such offenses nonbailable. The prisoner sought federal habeas corpus while his state case was pending. While the federal habeas proceeding was pending on appeal, the prisoner was convicted. The Supreme Court held that the court of appeals should have dismissed the prisoner's federal habeas appeal as moot, since he "no longer had a legally cognizable interest in the result in this case."[555] The prisoner was demanding, in the federal action, the right to pretrial bail, and that claim was mooted by his conviction.

Murphy v Hunt recognizes, and other cases apply, an exception to the mootness doctrine when a party seeks something in addition to specific relief, or represents a class under Fed R Civ P 23 or a similar provision.[556] In *Powell v*

---

[550] *Id* 1253-54 (citations omitted). *See also* Clarke v United States, 915 F2d 699 (DC Cir 1990) (en banc) (appeal from holding that appropriations statute is unconstitutionally discriminatory is mooted by expiration of statute; judgment below vacated under United States v Munsingwear, 340 US 36 (1950); extensive discussion in majority and dissenting opinions of mootness doctrine).

[551] 423 US 147 (1975).

[552] *Id* 148.

[553] United States v Johnson, 801 F2d 597 (2d Cir 1986) (Winter, J, discussing many cases); *In re* Grand Jury Proceedings re Larson, 785 F2d 629 (8th Cir 1986). However, if the government will likely convene a new grand jury and seek the same testimony, these cases recognize that the alleged contemnor may obtain review under the capable of repetition standard discussed below.

[554] 455 US 478 (1982).

[555] *Id* 482.

[556] *See also* Karcher v May, 484 US 72 (1987). The Court held that the nominal appellants had no standing to appeal. However, this did not render the case moot and, therefore, the court of appeals decision simply stood unchanged; the Court distinguished cases such as United States v Munsingwear, 340 US 36, 39 (1950) (when a case becomes moot, appellate court should reverse or vacate unreviewable judgment). For discussion of the standing issue in *Karcher,* see **§2.19.**

McCormack,[557] for example, a Congressman sued to challenge his exclusion from the Ninetieth Congress. While his lawsuit was pending on appeal, the Ninetieth Congress was adjourned and Powell was seated in the Ninety-first Congress. The Court held his case not moot because he had a live claim for his salary as Congressman during the Ninetieth Congress.[558]

In the law of federal habeas corpus, the petitioner's claim does not become moot if he or she is released from custody, provided there remain collateral consequences of the underlying basis for detention, such as a felony conviction.[559] Similarly, in a class suit to desegregate a school system, class representatives may graduate, but the underlying claim of those represented by the class will still be viable.[560]

One way to avoid a finding of mootness is to show that relief can still be granted despite the event that is claimed to moot the case. The Supreme Court provided powerful support to this notion in *Church of Scientology v United States.*[561] Under two provisions of the Internal Revenue Code,[562] the district court ordered a state court official to comply with an IRS summons for production of tape recordings containing attorney-client conversations. The church, as holder of the privilege, filed a timely notice of appeal, but was unable to obtain a stay of the summons enforcement order. Copies of the tapes were delivered to the IRS while the appeal was pending. The court of appeals granted the IRS's motion to dismiss the appeal as moot, holding that no controversy existed because the tapes already had been turned over to the IRS.

The Supreme Court reversed. The Court held that compliance with the summons enforcement order did not moot the appeal. Citing *Mills v Green,*[563] the Court held that the test was whether it was being asked to "give opinions upon moot questions or abstract propositions, or to declare principles or rules of law which cannot affect the matter in issue in the case before it."[564] If, therefore,

---

[557] 395 US 486 (1969).

[558] *See also* Board of Pardons v Allen, 482 US 369 (1987), holding that state prisoners' due-process challenge to state parole procedures was not mooted by their release on parole, because "[i]n addition to requesting injunctive and declaratory relief, the complaint sought damages" and 'the validity of respondents' claim for damages . . . is not so insubstantial or so clearly foreclosed by prior decisions that this case may not proceed.' " *Id* 370-71 n1 (quoting Memphis Light, Gas & Water Div v Craft, 436 US 1, 8-9 (1978)).

[559] Prantil v California, 843 F2d 314, 316 n2 (9th Cir) (defendant's release from custody prior to completion of federal habeas corpus proceedings will not render petition moot because a felony conviction may cause defendant to suffer adverse collateral consequences even after serving sentence), *cert denied,* 488 US 861 (1988).

[560] This is because of the special position of the class action. The class representatives may lose their personal interest in the case, but the class members are still affected by the challenged action. *See* Sosna v Iowa, 419 US 393 (1975).

[561] 113 S Ct 447 (1992).

[562] 26 USC §§7402(b), 7604(a).

[563] 159 US 651 (1895).

[564] *Id* 653.

an event occurs while a case is pending on appeal "that makes it impossible for the court to grant 'any effectual relief whatever' to a prevailing party, the appeal must be dismissed."[565]

Of course, it was too late to provide a full remedy for the alleged infringement of the church's interest that occurred when the tapes were turned over. However, a court could still order the tapes returned and all copies destroyed. It could also take steps to prevent IRS use of the information in the tapes and any leads derived from the tapes. The Court also held that there was appellate jurisdiction to review allegedly unlawful IRS summons enforcement orders, noting that similar orders by other agencies are routinely held reviewable and that a line of authority precluding review of summonses by the IRS was not defensible on statutory or decisional grounds.

An in rem proceeding may be mooted when the res is removed from the court's jurisdiction. Usually, parties prevent this from happening by obtaining a stay.[566] In *Republic National Bank v United States,*[567] the Supreme Court clarified the mootness doctrine for in rem forfeiture proceedings, where there is a real danger that the res will be sold or transferred while the case is pending. The government had filed a civil forfeiture action against a residence owned by an alleged narcotics trafficker. The bank held a mortgage on the property and claimed its rights as a good faith innocent owner.[568] While the lawsuit was pending, the government sold the house and transferred the sale proceeds to the United States Treasury. The court of appeals granted the government's motion to dismiss and held that removal of the sale proceeds from the judicial district terminated the district court's in rem jurisdiction. The Supreme Court reversed. The Court held that an in rem action is not necessarily mooted by the transfer of the res from the judicial district where the case is pending. This would be the case only if the transfer would render any judgment useless because the res could neither be delivered to the complainant nor restored to the claimant. In this case, any judgment in favor of the bank would not be useless, because the court could order the United States to return the funds representing the sale proceeds. Legislation purporting to make such a course difficult, if not impossible, did not stand in the way of the Court's decision.

As noted above, there is another avenue of escape from a mootness-based dismissal of an appeal. The Supreme Court has recognized that some controversies are "capable of repetition, yet evading review"[569] and will be heard on the merits even though the underlying dispute has been resolved. This caveat to mootness doctrine was first enunciated in *Southern Pacific Terminal Co v ICC.*[570]

---

[565] 113 S Ct at 449 (quoting Mills v Green 159 US 651, at 653 (1895)).

[566] *See* **§6.11.**

[567] 113 S Ct 554 (1992).

[568] *See* United States v A Parcel of Land, 113 S Ct 1126 (1993).

[569] Weinstein v Bradford, 423 US 147, 148-49 (1975) (discussing doctrine).

[570] 219 US 498 (1911).

In *Weinstein v Bradford,*[571] the terminal company challenged an ICC order of short duration, which expired during the judicial review process. The Court held that appellate jurisdiction would lie, noting that "because of the short duration of the Interstate Commerce Commission order challenged, it was virtually impossible to litigate the validity of the order prior to its expiration."[572] This rationale might save from dismissal an appeal in a grand jury witness case, if the commitment for contempt was close to the end of the grand jury's term and the government evinced an intention to convene a new grand jury and put the witness in the same "answer or go to jail" box as before.[573]

As the Court said in *Weinstein v Bradford:*

> [I]n the absence of a class action, the "capable of repetition, yet evading review" doctrine [is] limited to the situation where two elements combined: (1) the challenged action was in its duration too short to be fully litigated prior to its cessation or expiration, and (2) there was a reasonable expectation that the same complaining party would be subjected to the same action again.[574]

The *capable of repetition, yet evading review* standard is particularly appropriate when constitutional rights are at stake. For example, in *Christian Knights of*

---

[571] 423 US 147 (1975).

[572] *Id* 149. The Court also rejected a mootness claim under the *capable of repetition* standard in California Coastal Commn v Granite Rock Co, 480 US 572 (1987), and again in Brock v Roadway Express, Inc, 481 US 252 (1987) (plurality opinion). *See also* Deposit Guar Natl Bank v Roper, 445 US 326 (1980), holding that appealability of the district court's denial of class certification was not mooted by the defendant's payment to each putative representative of the full amount of their claimed damages. One who claims to be a class representative has a continuing interest in class certification, collateral to the merits, if only because of a desire to shift some litigation costs to the class members.

[573] This position, expressly recognized in *In re* Grand Jury Proceedings re Larson, 785 F2d 629 (8th Cir 1986), is supported by the analysis in Weinstein v Bradford, 423 US 147 (1975).

[574] 423 US 147, 149 (1975). *See also* Brock v Roadway Express, Inc, 481 US 252 (1987) (Secretary of Labor issued preliminary reinstatement order of employee to employer without first holding an evidentiary hearing and employer appealed; district court granted summary judgment motion of employer and Secretary appealed directly to Supreme Court, which used *capable of repetition* doctrine to determine that the Secretary's appeal was not mooted by his subsequent issuance of a final reinstatement order since the preliminary order was too short for employer's challenge to it to be fully litigated and it was reasonable to expect employer to be subjected to similar orders in the future); Ward v City of Portland, 857 F2d 1373 (9th Cir 1988) (*capable of repetition* doctrine applied to police officers' challenge of a rule forbidding officers involved in fatal shootings from conferring with their attorney before filing a report with the department; on the merits, the court upheld the regulations); Air Line Pilots Assn, Intl v UAL Corp, 897 F2d 1394 (7th Cir 1990) (applies *capable of repetition* standard to find dispute between United and union over takeover bid not moot; issue between parties on appeal may be moot, but other issues remain in the case that affect parties' legal rights; such a case is not moot under article III).

KKK v District of Columbia[575] the district judge issued a preliminary injunction requiring the District to give the Klan a parade permit. The District of Columbia and its codefendant, the United States, appealed. While the appeal was pending, the Klan held its march. The United States moved to dismiss the appeal as moot. Such a dismissal would have had the effect of vacating the district court's order. The court evoked the *capable of repetition* doctrine and decided the merits in favor of the Klan's First Amendment contention. The court noted that the parade permit issuance process is long and arduous, and that the Klan and others who might wish to use the public streets to carry their message had an interest in resolution of the merits.

Although not a constitutional case, *IOMM&P v Brown*[576] involved statutory free speech rights that were infringed in a way that threatened future trouble for the speaker even after the immediate dispute had become moot. Respondent unsuccessfully sought to have his union distribute campaign literature to its membership, as required by the Labor-Management Reporting and Disclosure Act.[577] However, by the time the case reached the Supreme Court, the election had been held and respondent had lost by a small margin. The Court held the case not moot because respondent had run for office before and "may well do so again."[578] It was likely that the union's rule against distribution of campaign literature would once again prevent respondent from running.

What happens to a moot case that is not salvaged by some principle such as *capable of repetition*? The Ninth Circuit noted in a perceptive opinion: "The established procedure when a civil case becomes moot on appeal is to 'vacate the judgment below and remand with a direction to dismiss.' "[579] This deprives the challenged judgment of any precedential value.[580] However, if portions of the controversy that were not the subject of the mooted appeal remain alive, the district court will, of course, have jurisdiction to resolve them.[581] The related issue of mootness caused by settlement of case on appeal is discussed at **§5.16.**

---

[575] 972 F2d 365 (DC Cir 1992).

[576] 498 US 466 (1991).

[577] 29 USC §411.

[578] 498 US at 473.

[579] Kitlutsisti v Arco Alaska, Inc, 782 F2d 800, 801 (9th Cir 1986) (appeal from injunction against drilling without permit mooted by issuance of permit (quoting United States v Munsingwear, 340 US 36, 39 (1950)).

[580] *Id* 801-02. *See also* Weinstein, 423 US at 149. *But see* Harris v Board of Governors of Fed Reserve Sys, 938 F2d 720 (7th Cir 1991) (vacatur of a moot order deprives the order of any preclusive effect in subsequent litigation; it does not deprive it of such *stare decisis* effect as it may have had; thorough discussion by Posner, J).

[581] Crowell v Mader, 444 US 505 (1980) (per curiam), discussed at 782 F2d at 802.

§2.19 Standing to Appeal

The literature of standing is extensive and confusing.[582] For purposes of appellate court jurisdiction to hear a particular person's claim, some basic principles may be distilled. The usual rule—to which exceptions are noted below—is that "[t]o have standing to appeal, an appellant ordinarily must have been a party to the proceeding below and have been aggrieved by the order appealed from."[583]

One may be a party below either by being named in the original action or by such litigation expanding devices as third-party practice and intervention.[584] For example, in *United Airlines v McDonald,*[585] flight attendants brought a class suit claiming sex discrimination. The district court refused to hear the matter as a class suit, but eventually entered a judgment for the named plaintiffs on the issues of back pay and reinstatement. The district court thereafter entered an order of dismissal when the parties reached agreement on the amounts due each named plaintiff.[586] Eighteen days after judgment, McDonald moved to intervene in the district court. When the district court denied intervention, McDonald appealed both that denial and the denial of class certification that

---

[582] The term *standing* gives lawyers and judges considerable difficulty. *See generally* Flast v Cohen, 392 US 83 (1968). The term is used to refer to several quite distinct limitations—constitutional, statutory, and discretionary—upon judicial power and willingness to decide cases. *See* Michael E. Tigar, *Judicial Power, the "Political Question Doctrine," and Foreign Relations,* 17 UCLA L Rev 1135, 1138 n11 (1970). Sometimes, standing can be used in the sense of ripeness to deny appealability to an order that has not harmed a party, or at least not yet. *In re* El San Juan Hotel, 809 F2d 151 (1st Cir 1987), provides an example. The United States filed an ex parte application for leave to file a complaint against the debtor's former trustee in bankruptcy. The bankruptcy court granted leave. The trustee appealed first to the district court and then to the court of appeals. The court of appeals held that the order granting leave to file a complaint did not detrimentally affect the former trustee's rights and that he therefore lacked standing to appeal. *See also* Massachusetts Assn of Afro-American Police, Inc v Boston Police Dept, 973 F2d 18 (1st Cir 1992) (challenge to district court's amendment of a prior consent decree is not ripe for judicial review when the amendment has not resulted in any concrete harm to the party seeking an appeal). See the discussion of legal prejudice at **§2.02.**

[583] United States v Little Joe Trawlers, Inc, 780 F2d 158, 161 (1st Cir 1986) (citing and discussing cases). *See also* Whitmore v Arkansas, 495 US 149 (1990) (co-inmate lacks standing to seek review of death sentence on another inmate who has waived his right to pursue appeal; habeas corpus next friend is limited to cases where the prisoner lacks access to courts for some reason); Goos v ICC, 911 F2d 1283 (8th Cir 1990) (court of appeals will consider party's standing before ICC, even though not raised there, as this is a jurisdictional requirement).

[584] *See, e.g.,* Armstrong Rubber Co v United States, 781 F2d 889 (Fed Cir 1986) (intervention in proceeding below does not confer right to participate in appeal; party must also file notice of appeal).

[585] 432 US 385 (1977).

[586] The parties who originally had sought class certification were granted permission to appeal under §1292(b), but the court of appeals refused to hear the matter at that time. These parties then decided not to make any further challenge to the class certification refusal. If McDonald had not been permitted to intervene, there would have been no effective means to obtain class suit treatment, given the passage of time and the potential that claims would have become time-barred.

had occurred early in the lawsuit. The Supreme Court held that McDonald was entitled to intervene and to challenge the district court's denial of class certification. The Court reasoned that McDonald's action was timely, because it was taken within the time for appealing the district court's judgment and because McDonald acted as soon as it became clear that the named class representatives would no longer protect her interests. They, after all, had been the beneficiaries of a judgment in their favor and had no particular motivation to pursue the class certification issue.

McDonald tells the advocate that a party dissatisfied with the district court's action should intervene in that court and then file a notice of appeal. Even if other parties are taking an appeal, a party's right to participate in the court of appeals is conferred only by timely appealing.[587]

The teaching of *McDonald* was reaffirmed in *Marino v Ortiz.*[588] White police officers claimed to have been adversely affected by settlement of an employment discrimination suit. They did not seek to intervene in the district court, but nonetheless appealed the judgment to the court of appeals. That court suggested that a nonparty might appeal when it had an interest affected by the district court's judgment. The Supreme Court, on the procedural issue of the white officers' right to appeal, held that they were not proper parties. As the Court explained, "[w]e think the better practice is for such a nonparty to seek intervention for purposes of appeal; denials of such motions are, of course, appealable."[589]

Exceptions to the rule that one must be a party in order to have standing to appeal are difficult to classify. In *United States Catholic Conference v Abortion Rights Mobilization,*[590] two Catholic organizations had been dismissed as defendants in a suit to revoke the Roman Catholic Church's tax-exempt status. After being dismissed, the two organizations resisted discovery requests and were held in contempt. They sought to defend against the contempt by challenging the district court's subject matter jurisdiction over the lawsuit. The Supreme Court held that a nonparty witness had standing to make such a challenge.

The Court recognized that a nonparty witness would not be able to raise an issue such as lack of personal jurisdiction over one of the parties, for a nonparty has "no legitimate interest"[591] in such matters, which in any case are "waivable defenses."[592]

---

[587] Armstrong Rubber Co v United States, 781 F2d 889 (Fed Cir 1986). See also Deposit Guar Natl Bank v Roper, 445 US 326 (1980), holding that appealability of the district court's denial of class certification was not mooted by the defendant's payment to each putative representative of the full amount of their claimed damages. One who claims to be a class representative has a continuing interest in class certification, collateral to the merits, if only because of a desire to shift some litigation costs to the class members.

[588] 484 US 301 (1988).

[589] *Id* 304.

[590] 487 US 72 (1988).

[591] *Id* 76.

[592] *Id* 77. The Court also held that an interlocutory appeal was available to the nonparties to assert their claim. *See* **§2.04.**

There also are cases in the courts of appeals permitting a nonparty to appeal orders in class actions[593] or to assert the rights of a related party such as a corporate subsidiary or parent.[594] However, even cases that permit such appeals do not set out a clear rule, so the advocate is better advised to seek to intervene in the district court before taking an appeal.[595]

---

[593] Some courts of appeals permit persons who were not parties in the district court to take an appeal, provided that "the equities favor hearing the appeal" and that the parties actually participated in the district court proceedings and have a stake in the lawsuit that is discernable from the record. Binker v Pennsylvania, 977 F2d 738, 745 (3d Cir 1992) (employees represented by the EEOC in an employment discrimination case permitted to appeal from district court's approval of settlement agreement and denial of motion for relief from an order approving the settlement; these employees had participated in the proceedings below at the district court's invitation; settlement formula approved by the district court did not treat all employees evenly).

[594] In such a case, it may be necessary to substitute the new party in the court of appeals under Fed R App P 43(b). Alabama Power Co v Interstate Commerce Commn, 852 F2d 1361 (DC Cir 1988) (one party may litigate on another's behalf, but not where the first party has voluntarily given up the litigation); Evanston Ins Co v Fred A. Tucker & Co, 872 F2d 278, 280 (9th Cir 1989) (party seeking to appeal liability of another must have "direct and immediate" interest, rather than "indirectly pecuniary" interest (quoting Libby, McNeill, & Libby v City Natl Bank, 592 F2d 504, 512 (9th Cir 1978)); Astor Chauffeured Limousine Co v Runnfeldt Inv Corp, 910 F2d 1540 (7th Cir 1990) (parent corporation entitled to file and prosecute appeal, even though it had been dismissed as a party in district court; district judge, despite dismissal, treated parent as proper party and it is named in the judgment); EEOC v Pan American World Airways, 897 F2d 1499 (9th Cir) (nonparty may appeal judgment of district court if it actually participated in proceedings and is adversely affected by the judgment), *cert denied* 498 US 815 (1990); Samuels v American Motors Sales Corp, 969 F2d 573 (7th Cir 1992) (attorney has standing to pursue claim for entitlement to fees under statute, even though statute appears to vest fee claim in client and not attorney; court notes that First Circuit and Second Circuit take a different approach). *See also* Estate of Bishop v Bechtel Power Corp, 905 F2d 1272 (9th Cir 1990) (client has no standing to appeal award of fees assessed against its attorney; attorney has the right and duty to appeal such a collateral order in his or her own right).

Some statutes confer the right to appeal to persons not parties to an adverse decision. These statutes are found in the administrative area and in matters reviewable by the Federal Circuit. *See, e.g.*, LSI Computer Sys v United States Intl Trade Commn, 832 F2d 588 (Fed Cir 1987) (manufacturer of components used in products excluded because of patent infringement entitled to appeal Commission order even though it had not been a party before the Commission because of Trade Act provision).

[595] *See* Croyden Assocs v Alleco, Inc, 969 F2d 675 (8th Cir 1992) (class member who was not a named class representative and who did not intervene in district court cannot appeal district court's approval of settlement, rejecting cases from other circuits that would permit appeal), *cert denied,* 113 S Ct 1251 (1993); Jenkins by Agyei v Missouri, 967 F2d 1245 (8th Cir) (individuals who were not party in the district court have no right of appeal from that court's approval of a partial settlement in a desegregation case; narrow exceptions to this principle do not apply), *cert denied,* 113 S Ct 811 (1992); Mayfield v Barr, 985 F2d 1090 (DC Cir 1993) (class members who retained their right to litigate even after a settlement agreement lack standing to challenge that agreement; they are not adversely affected by it); Walker v City of Mesquite, 858 F2d 1071 (5th Cir 1988) (nonnamed parties to class lack standing to appeal, absent intervention or filing of separate suit challenging adequacy of class representation).

Many if not most of the cases permitting nonparty appeal in class actions involve employment discrimination. The permission to participate seems unwise and indeed unauthorized. *McDonald* sets out liberal standards for an affected employee to intervene in an action under Fed R Civ P 24(a) and thus gain the right to appeal either from the final judgment or from an order denying authorization to intervene as of right. In this way, the district judge's consideration of an individual's claim is clearly reflected on the appellate record, and the status of the individual and the proper timing of his or her notice of appeal are equally clear. The discretionary exercise of equitable power to permit appeal by one not a party in the district court also assumes power to deny such an audience on an equally discretionary and standardless basis.

The other ingredient of standing is that a party must be aggrieved by the judgment. A plaintiff who obtains a dismissal of the action, even one conditioned on payment of attorneys' fees and costs to the other side, is not aggrieved.[596] As noted elsewhere in this chapter,[597] a defendant whose case is dismissed is not aggrieved even when the dismissal may be a pretext for refiling under more advantageous conditions. In such a case, the remedy is by motion to the district court where the matter is refiled.[598]

The standing rules pose particular difficulties when more than one person has an interest that is affected by a district court's order. For example, when an attorney being compelled to testify before a grand jury or in a deposition invokes the attorney-client privilege, he or she has an obvious interest in not being committed for contempt for improperly refusing to answer. However, the attorney does not suffer a final judgment until and unless the contempt sanction is imposed.

The client, who holds the privilege, has no assurance that the attorney's gumption will not fade at the jailhouse door. Thus, most courts have held that the client has the right to intervene in the district court and take an appeal from an order overruling a claim of privilege. The client obtains both standing

---

[596] See discussion at **§2.02.** *See also* Holmes v Silver Wings Aviation, Inc, 881 F2d 939 (10th Cir 1989) (held, bankruptcy debtor lacks standing to appeal an award of attorney's fees to a creditor, when the award simply allocates the debtor's estate, the amount of which already has been determined); United States v Grundhoefer, 916 F2d 788 (2d Cir 1990) (restitution statute, 18 USC §§3663-3664, does not provide standing to victims denied restitution, hence no appeal lies from district judge order that defendant make restitution to one entity rather than another; lack of standing appears under article 3 as well as prudential limits on federal court power; appeal dismissed); United States v Kelley, 997 F2d 806 (10th Cir 1993) (same); *In re* Andreuccetti, 975 F2d 413 (7th Cir 1992) (to appeal a bankruptcy order, a litigant must be a "person aggrieved" by the order; this is a narrower group than those who would have Article III standing; appellant must demonstrate that the order diminishes its property, increases its burdens, or impairs its rights).

[597] **§2.03.**

[598] As noted in the discussion at **§2.03,** if the motion is denied, the issue can be reviewed on appeal from a final judgment of conviction.

to appeal and the right to take that appeal before a final judgment is entered against the attorney.[599]

In a broader sense, the standing of a party to assert rights nominally belonging to another avails equally in the court of appeals and in the district court.[600] The Supreme Court recently canvassed this question in *Bender v Williamsport Area School District.*[601] Students who had been denied a school meeting place for their religious club sued the school district, members of the school board, the superintendent of schools, and the principal. The district court granted the plaintiff students' summary judgment motion, but did not issue an injunction or award damages. The school board began complying with the court's order by permitting the students to hold their meetings.

Bender, a defendant member of the school board, appealed. The Supreme Court held that he lacked standing. The Court said that Bender could not appeal in his individual capacity because, although the complaint named him in that capacity, the record did not disclose that relief was sought or given on that basis. Second, Bender could not appeal in his official capacity because standing on that basis belonged only to the school board of which he was a member. Finally, Bender attempted in the Supreme Court to claim standing because his child attended the school; the Court held that such a basis for standing would have to have been asserted in the district court. A party may not add to the record in the appellate court to confer standing that does not appear from the trial record.

Bender both repeats the traditional rule that a party must have standing in the district court to have it on appeal and reaffirms that "every federal appellate court has a special obligation to 'satisfy itself not only of its own jurisdiction,

---

[599] Conkling v Turner, 883 F2d 431, 433-34 (5th Cir 1989); *In re* Special Grand Jury No 81-1 (Harvey), 676 F2d 1005 (4th Cir), *vacated,* 697 F2d 112 (4th Cir 1982); *In re* Grand Jury Proceedings (Fine), 641 F2d 199 (5th Cir 1981); Velsicol Chem Corp v Parsons, 561 F2d 671 (7th Cir 1977), *cert denied,* 435 US 942 (1978). But see *In re* Grand Jury Matter, 802 F2d 96 (3d Cir 1986), in which standing was denied. A hospital received a grand jury subpoena. It moved to quash and the motion was denied. The hospital, its parent organization (a labor union), the chairman of the hospital's board of directors, and a health and welfare fund with a proprietary interest in certain records all appealed. The court held (1) the hospital could not appeal until its refusal to produce had led to a contempt citation; (2) the parent union did not face a "now or never" situation since it was presumably able to control the hospital's action; (3) the chairman lacked personal interest in the matter; but (4) the health and welfare fund had standing based upon claiming a proprietary interest in some of the subpoenaed records. The case is a thorough study of the interplay of finality and standing law in the grand jury setting.

[600] *See generally* Charles A. Wright, Federal Courts §13 (4th ed 1983); Robert A. Sedler, *Standing to Assert Constitutional Jus Tertii in the Supreme Court,* 71 Yale LJ 599 (1962); Note, *Standing to Assert Constitutional Jus Tertii,* 88 Harv L Rev 423 (1974).

[601] 475 US 534 (1986). *See also* Diamond v Charles, 476 US 54 (1986) (district court declared portions of Illinois anti-abortion statute unconstitutional and enjoined their enforcement; court of appeals affirmed and expanded scope of injunctive relief; State of Illinois did not appeal; physician-intervenor professing opposition to abortion, practicing pediatrician, and parent of unemancipated minor daughter had no standing to appeal; appeal dismissed).

but also that of the lower courts in a cause under review,' even though the parties are prepared to concede it.''[602]

This point was underscored in *Karcher v May.*[603] The Third Circuit had decided a school prayer case, upholding the district court's decision that the statute permitting a moment of silence in school was unconstitutional. When the lawsuit was originally filed, neither the Attorney General of New Jersey, nor any other public agency, would defend it. So the then-presiding Speaker of the Assembly, Karcher, and then-President of the State Senate, Orechio, intervened as defendants and conducted the litigation. Both of these men had lost their posts to others after the court of appeals' decision, but they nonetheless filed notices of appeal in the Supreme Court under 28 USC §1254(2). Their successors in office declined to pursue the appeal. The Court dismissed the appeal, holding that Karcher and Orechio had been parties only in their official capacities and that they therefore could not take an appeal in their personal capacities: "One who is not a party or has not been treated as a party to a judgment has no right to appeal therefrom.''[604]

§2.20 Amicus Curiae Participation on Appeal

An advocate whose case involves an issue of great consequence should seriously consider inviting an amicus brief from organizations and individuals that support his or her position. An amicus brief is rarely disinterested; usually it supports one party or the other. Even when the other side refuses to consent to an amicus filing, most courts of appeals freely grant leave to file, provided the brief is timely and well-reasoned. Summary statements of position without legal or factual research will be rejected.

Amici can sometimes address the implications of a particular rule, or application of a rule, in a broader context than the advocate for a party. Amici can, and should, discuss the impact of a particular result upon parties not before the court. In a complex, multi-issue case, the advocate can often rely upon a specialized amicus to make in detail an argument that the page limitations of the advocate's brief require him or her to develop less fully. On a proper and timely motion, the court of appeals may even permit the amicus to share in oral argument.[605]

For example, a criminal defendant's position on appeal may be supported by the National Association of Criminal Defense Lawyers (NACDL) or the American Civil Liberties Union. The American Bar Association files amicus briefs, though it usually waits until a case reaches the United States Supreme Court. Industry committees and business organizations support litigation positions of corporate defendants. Individual plaintiffs may find that a consumer organization, an interest group such as the American Association of Retired

---

[602] 475 US at 541 (quoting Mitchell v Maurer, 293 US 237, 244 (1934)).

[603] 484 US 72 (1987).

[604] *Id* 77.

[605] Fed R App P 29.

Persons, or a labor organization will file an amicus brief. The array of organizations that seek to advance their positions through litigation is wide.

Because of the time requirements of Fed R App P 29, the search for an amicus must begin early. Counsel should identify potential amici and prepare a brief summary statement of the litigation and its importance. Next, counsel must find out how to approach the organization. Some organizations, such as NACDL, have a committee that reviews amicus curiae requests. Other organizations are best contacted through the general counsel. Many organizations cannot file amicus briefs without going through a lengthy review and approval process; the advocate should find out how that process works.

The procedure for filing an amicus brief is set out in Fed R App P 29,[606] which requires either written consent of the parties or leave of court. In exceptional cases, the court may itself call for amicus briefs.

---

[606] The full text of Fed R App P 29 is in **app A.**

3 Extraordinary Writs: The Original Jurisdiction of the Courts of Appeals

§3.01 Basis and Background of Writ Practice

The All Writs Act,[1] provides: "The Supreme Court and all courts established by Act of Congress may issue all writs necessary or appropriate in aid of their respective jurisdictions and agreeable to the usages and principles of law." This statute, based upon language that has been a part of American law since the

---

[1] 28 USC §1651(a). The alternative writ procedure mentioned in §1651(b) is, in effect, provided for by the Fed R App P 21(b) procedure for directing an answer to a petition for the writ. *See* **§3.17.**

Judiciary Act of 1789,[2] authorizes United States courts of appeals to review and control the exercise of power by federal district courts without the necessity of a final judgment.[3]

The procedure for obtaining a writ is discussed in detail below.[4] Briefly, application for a writ of mandamus or prohibition—the most commonly used—is an original proceeding in the court of appeals. It is begun by filing a petition as described in Fed R App P 21(a). The court may deny the petition outright or call for a response before ruling.[5]

As the discussion below makes clear, the power to issue writs directed to federal district courts is sparingly exercised. The clearest exposition of the availability of appellate review by extraordinary writ must begin with a discussion of the development of controlling Supreme Court authority.[6]

Under the All Writs Act, the most commonly used writ is mandamus, which at common law was designed to compel an inferior tribunal or officer to perform its duty.[7] Other writs used for a similar purpose included prohibition, designed to restrain an unjustified exercise of power,[8] and certiorari, designed to bring up the record to the appellate court for purposes of review.[9] Today, these distinctions are almost meaningless and the general practice is to request

---

[2] Act of Sept 24, 1789, chs 13, 14, 20, 1 Stat 73, 80-81. The mandamus provisions were construed in Marbury v Madison, 5 US (1 Cranch) 137 (1803). The Court, per Chief Justice Marshall, held that the Congress could not authorize the Supreme Court to issue mandamus except in aid of its appellate jurisdiction, because the US Const art III, §2, limited the original jurisdiction of the Court to "Cases affecting Ambassadors, other public Ministers and Consuls and those in which a State shall be a Party." The 1789 Act had authorized the Supreme Court to issue writs to courts and public officers of the United States. Marbury dealt solely with the public officers provision. It is clear that the Supreme Court, in aid of its appellate jurisdiction, would be empowered to issue a writ to an inferior federal court. *See generally Ex parte* Republic of Peru, 318 US 578 (1943); Sup Ct R 20 (Jan 1, 1990) (procedure for issuance of extraordinary writs in Supreme Court).

[3] The final judgment rule, to which writ jurisdiction is an exception, is treated in **ch 2.** The All Writs Act also provides jurisdiction to issue writs other than those discussed here, such as the writ of error coram nobis to review a criminal conviction when the defendant is no longer in custody. *See* United States v Morgan, 346 US 502 (1954). Use of writs in the district court is beyond the scope of this treatise.

[4] **§§3.15-3.17.**

[5] Fed R App P 21(b).

[6] It is beyond the scope of this work to discuss the use of the remedy in the nature of mandamus against a federal officer, which may be sought in the United States district court under 18 USC §1361. *See generally* David A. Johns, Annotation, *Construction and Application of 28 USCS §1361 Conferring on Federal District Courts Original Jurisdiction of Actions in Nature of Mandamus to Compel Federal Officer, Employee, or Agency to Perform Duty Owed Plaintiff,* 13 ALR Fed 145 (1972 & Supp Oct 1992).

[7] *See* 52 Am Jur 2d *Mandamus* 1-11 (1970 & Supp Apr 1993). The older mandamus jurisprudence is chronicled in Annotation, *Mandamus* as the appropriate remedy to control action of federal court in civil case—Supreme Court cases, 98 L Ed 114 (1953), *superseded,* 57 L Ed 2d 1203 (1979).

[8] *See* 63A Am Jur 2d *Prohibition* 1-7 (1984).

[9] *See* 14 Am Jur 2d *Certiorari* 1-13 (1964 & Supp Apr 1993).

relief in the alternative or to seek a writ in the nature of mandamus or prohibition.[10] In the discussion below, the term *mandamus* will be used for convenience and because this is the writ most often used as a substitute for an appeal.

In theory, mandamus is an independent action brought against a federal district court judge by a litigant who is asking the court of appeals to order the judge to act or to refrain from acting in a particular way. In most cases, however, the judge is only a nominal party and the real dispute is between litigants on opposite sides of the controversy in the district court. The Supreme Court suggested in *La Buy* that one reason for limiting access to mandamus is that writ practice puts a burden upon the district judge/respondent to find volunteer counsel and it makes her or him a party.[11] This seems farfetched in most settings. *La Buy* was an unusual case, in that the district judge took action that was opposed by all litigants.

Usually, the litigants are the only real parties in interest. Indeed, the rules of most courts of appeals provide that the district judge must not be named in the caption of the petition.[12] Although the district judge is seldom an active party, when he or she is under direct challenge, the court of appeals may set a date for his or her answer to the petition.[13] A district judge who takes a controversial action that is the subject of mandamus certainly has the right to find volunteer counsel. Indeed, many mandamus actions involve broad-gauge questions as to which volunteer counsel independent of the parties in interest may have a valuable perspective. The burden on the district judge of finding a lawyer to assume that role seems justified by the importance of helping the decisional process.

The older Supreme Court cases sharply restricted the availability of mandamus, stressing that the moving party bears "the burden of showing that its right

---

[10] *See* Comment, *Supervisory and Advisory Mandamus Under the All Writs Act,* 86 Harv L Rev 595, 596 n7 (1973) [hereinafter Harvard Mandamus Comment]. *In re* Halkin, 598 F2d 176, 179 n 1 (DC Cir 1979). The Harvard Mandamus Comment is a recognizedly authoritative work. It has been cited in, for example, *In re* Société Nationale Industrielle Aérospatiale, 782 F2d 120, 123 (8th Cir 1986), *vacated & remanded on other grounds sub nom,* Société Nationale Industrielle Aérospatiale v United States Dist Court, 482 US 222 (1987); *In re* Cement Antitrust Litig, 688 F2d 1297 (9th Cir 1982), *affd per curiam sub nom* Arizona v United States Dist Court, 459 US 1191 (1983); United States v Kane, 646 F2d 4, 9 n7 (1st Cir 1981); Wilk v American Medical Assn, 635 F2d 1295, 1299 n6 (7th Cir 1980) (Wisdom, J, of the Fifth Circuit, sitting by designation); *In re* Vuitton et Fils SA, 606 F2d 1, 3 n5 (2d Cir 1979); *In re* Halkin, 598 F2d 176, 179 n1 (DC Cir 1979). *But see* discussion of *Halkin* at **§3.09;** a party need not specify which writ is sought. *In re Halkin,* 598 F2d at 179 n1. Writ practice is discussed in detail in **§§3.15-3.17.**

[11] La Buy v Howes Leather Co, 352 US 249, 257-58 (1957); *Ex parte* Fahey, 332 US 258 (1947). *See also* United States v Cowan, 524 F2d 504, 505 (5th Cir 1975) (district judge refused to dismiss prosecution despite government motion concurred in by defendants—order held appealable so mandamus not issued), *cert denied,* 425 US 971 (1976).

[12] *See* **§3.15.**

[13] Lefton v City of Hattiesburg, 333 F2d 280 (5th Cir 1964).

to issuance of the writ is 'clear and indisputable' "[14] and suggesting that an appeals court would issue mandamus only to correct a "usurpation of power"[15] by the district court. The Court also suggested that only if the district court had acted beyond its jurisdiction could mandamus or prohibition issue.[16] This language led to some uncertainty about the power of courts of appeals under the All Writs Act.

§3.02 Writ Availability Liberalized: *Roche* and *La Buy*

In 1943, Chief Justice Stone, for a unanimous Court, clarified the courts of appeals' power in *Roche v Evaporated Milk Assn.*[17] He wrote:

> As the jurisdiction of the . . . court of appeals is exclusively appellate, its authority to issue writs of mandamus is restricted by statute to those cases in which the writ is in aid of that jurisdiction. Its authority is not confined to the issuance of writs in aid of a jurisdiction already acquired by appeal but extends to those cases which are within its appellate jurisdiction although no appeal has been perfected. Otherwise the appellate jurisdiction could be defeated and the purpose of the statute authorizing the writ thwarted by unauthorized action of the district court obstructing the appeal.[18]

Despite this language, *Roche* was cited by the Supreme Court as late as 1956 for the proposition that mandamus was to be used when "a court has exceeded or refused to exercise its jurisdiction."[19] In 1957, however, *La Buy v Howes Leather Co*,[20] set the Court upon its present path by repeating that if the court of appeals could "at some stage of the . . . proceedings entertain" an appeal in the action pending in the district court, it has "the naked power" to issue

---

[14] Bankers Life & Casualty Co v Holland, 346 US 379, 384 (1953) (quoting United States v Duell, 172 US 576, 582 (1899)), *quoted with approval in* Will v Calvert Fire Ins Co, 437 US 655, 661 (1978) (plurality opinion).

[15] De Beers Consol Mines, Ltd v United States, 325 US 212, 217 (1945). *See* Harvard Mandamus Comment, *supra* note 10, at 595-96.

[16] "The traditional use of the writ in aid of appellate jurisdiction both at common law and in the federal courts has been to confine an inferior court to a lawful exercise of its prescribed jurisdiction or to compel it to exercise its authority when it is its duty to do so." Roche v Evaporated Milk Assn, 319 US 21, 26 (1943). *See also* Harvard Mandamus Comment, *supra* note 10, at 598-600.

[17] 319 US 21, at 25 (1943).

[18] Id 25.

[19] Parr v United States, 351 US 513, 520 (1956). See also United States v Smith, 331 US 469 (1947), in which the Court seems to make a litigant's right to the writ turn upon whether the challenged action was beyond the power of the district court.

[20] 352 US 249 (1957). See Comment, *Mandamus Proceedings in the Federal Courts of Appeals: A Compromise With Finality*, 52 Cal L Rev 1036 (1964), for a discussion of the application of *La Buy* by the courts of appeals.

a writ of mandamus to reach that case.[21] The Court then warned that its decision was not "intended . . . to authorize the indiscriminate use of prerogative writs as a means of reviewing interlocutory orders."[22] The Court upheld the issuance of mandamus to compel the district judge to vacate an order referring two complex antitrust cases to a special master, over the objections of all the parties; the referral abdicated the judicial function and deprived the parties of a trial.

La Buy stated what has become commonplace in the decisional law governing extraordinary, sometimes called prerogative, writs: in most cases, the question is not one of power but of prudence or discretion. The language of usurpation continues to appear in Supreme Court opinions, and one is reminded that mandamus is an extraordinary remedy.[23] However, these observations are almost invariably used to emphasize that the discretion to issue the writ must be sparingly exercised, rather than to cast doubt upon the power to do so. Study of the Court's decisions yields a fairly clear sense of which cases are appropriate for the issuance of an extraordinary writ.

In *La Buy* itself, only a bare majority of five justices voted to uphold issuance of the writ. This was because, despite its cautionary language, the majority spoke broadly in terms of the "supervisory control of the District Courts by the Courts of Appeals."[24] The dissenters agreed that Judge La Buy's reference of complex cases to a master may well have been wrong; they simply argued that the proper remedy was to let the cases go to judgment and then hear the question on appeal.[25]

The decision in *La Buy* was subjected to some trenchant criticism as authorizing a generalized appellate court intrusion into all phases of discretionary trial court action.[26] Some of these concerns were raised again by the Court's decision in *Schlagenhauf v Holder*.[27] In a bus crash diversity case, the district judge ordered a physical examination of a defendant bus driver on motion of a codefendant. The driver objected that Fed R Civ P 35, authorizing such orders, could not be applied to him. On the merits, the issue was whether one defendant could require another to submit to a physical examination under Rule 35, and what constitutes good cause under the rule. The court of appeals denied mandamus.

---

[21] 352 US at 255. In most cases, it will be obvious which court of appeals has jurisdiction to issue the writ. Exceptions arise when, for example, a district court orders an action transferred to a district court in another circuit; the issue arises regarding which court of appeals has power to issue mandamus "in aid of" its jurisdiction. *See* **§§3.07, 4.01.**

[22] 352 US at 255.

[23] *E.g.*, Allied Chem Corp v Daiflon, Inc, 449 US 33, 34, 35 (1980).

[24] La Buy v Howes Leather Co, 352 US 249, 259-60 (1957).

[25] *Id* 260-69.

[26] Charles A. Wright, *The Doubtful Omniscience of Appellate Courts*, 41 Minn L Rev 751, 771-78 (1957).

[27] 379 US 104 (1964). Professor Wright had wondered in 1957 whether mandamus would lie to correct a district court's decision on *good cause* in a discovery dispute. Charles A. Wright, *supra* note 26, at 775. *Schlagenhauf* answered in the affirmative, at least on its narrow facts.

The Supreme Court held that the case was appropriate for the exercise of mandamus jurisdiction. The Court repeated the *usurpation* and *abuse of discretion* language[28] of earlier cases. It held that usurpation arguably was involved because the trial judge's power to order any examination of a defendant was "an issue of first impression that called for the construction and application of Rule 35 in a new context."[29] Moreover, the Court reasoned, the court of appeals should have reached the merits "so as to avoid piecemeal litigation and to settle new and important problems."[30] The Court went on to establish procedures and guidelines respecting Rule 35.[31] The Court noted "[t]his is not to say, however, that, following the setting of guidelines in this opinion [relating to Fed R Civ P 35], any future allegation that the District Court was in error in applying these guidelines to a particular case makes mandamus an appropriate remedy."[32] In other words, Rule 35 would no longer present a question of first impression.

The Court's observation points up a characteristic of many mandamus cases; the appellate court hears petitions for writs to resolve broad-gauge questions. Once such a question is resolved, the court will revert to considering detailed application of its holding on appeal from final judgment. Where the broad-gauge question relates to discovery, it is likely that few such applications will ever be presented on appeal.

La Buy and *Schlagenhauf* may be read together as creating two categories of mandamus review: supervisory and advisory, although the latter term was not used in either opinion.[33] The former category generated controversy, as discussed above, respecting the ordinary requirements of finality. The latter raised the possibility that the Court was authorizing departure from the constitutionally based limitations upon advisory opinions,[34] by reaching out to clarify a novel statutory or Federal Rules question or resolve a question of first impression, and requiring neither a final judgment nor a concrete factual record as a condition of doing so. Certainly the reference in *Schlagenhauf* to "avoid[ing] piecemeal litigation"[35] could fuel such concerns.

---

[28] 379 US at 110.

[29] *Id* 111.

[30] *Id.*

[31] *Id* 112-22. The defendant claimed that Rule 35 could be applied only to a plaintiff because, by filing an action, he or she waived any right not to be examined. The Court relied upon its earlier decision in Sibbach v Wilson & Co, 312 US 1 (1941), and held that, upon a proper showing of good cause and that physical or mental condition was in controversy, a court could order an examination of a defendant.

[32] 379 US at 112.

[33] *See generally* Comment, *Supervisory and Advisory Mandamus Under the All Writs Act,* 86 Harv L Rev 595 (1973) [hereinafter Harvard Mandamus Comment].

[34] *See* **§2.17.**

[35] Schlagenhauf v Holder, 379 US at 104, 111 (1964).

In *Miller v United States*,[36] the court of appeals declined to go beyond "deciding the case before us." However, a leading work on writ practice advocates that the court of appeals refuse to issue the writ unless it is prepared to "lay down general guidance."[37] An advocate anxious to restrict the issuance of mandamus would point out that the general guidance language of *Schlagenhauf* arose in the context of construing a federal rule of civil procedure issued by the Supreme Court under the Rules Enabling Act.[38] Once the Court decided the rule was valid, it was justified in giving guidance to the lower courts on its application.

The Second Circuit, in *In re Vuitton et Fils SA*,[39] reached and decided the merits of a mandamus petition seeking a determination that a district judge had the power and duty to issue an ex parte restraining order under Fed R Civ P 65 in a trademark and unfair competition case. One defendant below had been dismissed from the action prior to oral argument on the petition. The other defendant had told the appeals court clerk's office that "he had no interest whatsoever in presenting his views on the matter, nor did he care what decision was eventually reached by the panel."[40] The court nevertheless reached and decided the merits, holding that the "question presented here is so obviously 'capable of repetition, yet evading review.' "[41] This case illustrates how far an appellate court may go in the interest of supervising and advising district judges, which is remarkable coming from a court that had said: "[W]e note that this court has been more reluctant than some courts to exercise freely the supervisory or advisory power to issue writs of mandamus."[42]

To be sure, the Supreme Court reaffirmed in other cases that mandamus must be used sparingly.[43] The courts of appeals, however, have taken *La Buy* and *Schlagenhauf* as authorizing them to issue mandamus with greater liberality, if an important issue, or one of first impression, were involved.[44]

---

[36] 403 F2d 77, 81 (2d Cir 1968), *discussed in* Harvard Mandamus Comment, *supra* note 33, at 616 n89, 619 n97.

[37] Harvard Mandamus Comment, *supra* note 33, at 619.

[38] 28 USC §2072.

[39] 606 F2d 1, 2 (2d Cir 1979).

[40] *Id* 2 n2.

[41] *Id* (citing Southern Pac Terminal Co v ICC, 219 US 498, 515 (1911)). On the mootness doctrine generally, see **§2.18.**

[42] *In re* Attorney Gen, 596 F2d 58, 63 (2d Cir), *cert denied,* 444 US 903 (1979) (footnote and citations omitted).

[43] *See* Platt v Minnesota Mining & Mfg Co, 376 US 240, 245 (1964) (if district court applied improper test in ruling on transfer motion in criminal case, court of appeals should at most state proper test and remand so that district court could apply it); Schlagenhauf v Holder, 379 US 104, 110 (1964); *see also* La Buy v Howes Leather Co, 352 US 249, 258 (1957); Van Dusen v Barrack, 376 US 612, 615 n3 (1964) (rejecting challenge to use of mandamus to review 28 USC §1404(a) transfer order).

[44] *See* Harvard Mandamus Comment, *supra* note 33, at 616-18.

§3.03 The Newer Approach: *Calvert Fire Insurance*

The Supreme Court has retrenched from some of the broader language in *La Buy* and *Schlagenhauf,*[45] and has laid renewed stress upon the final judgment rule and the extraordinary character of mandamus. As is discussed below, these limitations are enforced with special vigilance in criminal cases.[46] Despite the retrenchment, there is enough flexibility in the Court's teaching that courts of appeals can—as the remaining sections of this Chapter will show—justify hearing a very broad range of issues on mandamus.

In *Will v Calvert Fire Insurance Co,*[47] a district judge stayed a federal lawsuit under the Securities Exchange Act of 1934 pending resolution of an earlier filed and factually related state court lawsuit involving the same parties and issues. The federal court plaintiff/state court defendant sought mandamus, claiming that the district judge's stay impermissibly diluted its right to have its federal claim, over which federal courts have exclusive jurisdiction, tried in federal court.[48] The court of appeals issued mandamus and the Supreme Court reversed. There was no majority opinion on the mandamus issue. Justice Rehnquist wrote for four justices and Justice Blackmun provided the fifth vote on the basis that the court of appeals had acted prematurely in issuing a mandamus and should have sent the case back to the district judge for reconsideration in light of its conclusion that the judge had wrongly applied the law.[49]

Justice Rehnquist's plurality opinion states, quoting *Roche,* that mandamus is available only to "confine an inferior court to a lawful exercise of its prescribed jurisdiction or to compel it to exercise its authority when it is its duty

---

[45] *See* **§3.02.**

[46] **§3.11.**

[47] 437 US 655 (1978).

[48] Although the pendency of a state court action does not preclude proceedings in the federal court on the same cause of action, McClellan v Carland, 217 US 268, 282 (1910) (mandamus issued to prevent federal district court from declining to exercise jurisdiction over case before it), there are circumstances in which a federal court may abstain from proceeding and let the state court litigation run its course. *See generally* Colorado River Water Conservation Dist v United States, 424 US 800 (1976). The proper interpretation of *Colorado River,* which was decided after District Judge Will stayed the federal action in *Calvert Fire Insurance* and before the court of appeals issued the writ, was the principal point of dispute in the four opinions in the Supreme Court.

[49] Justice Blackmun concurred in the judgment only, Will v Calvert Fire Ins Co, 437 US 655, 667-68 (1978). Because *Colorado River* had been decided after Judge Will's order, Justice Blackmun thought it proper to remand to Judge Will and let him apply the *Colorado River* test in the first instance. Justice Brennan dissented for four justices. Chief Justice Burger joined the Brennan dissent and also wrote separately. However, since on the merits five justices agreed on an interpretation of *Colorado River,* the Rehnquist plurality opinion is not the law of the case. The Court so held in Moses H. Cone Memorial Hosp v Mercury Constr Corp, 460 US 1, 16-17 (1983). This distinction would have immense practical significance in a case involving use of an extraordinary writ to compel a district court to stay or dismiss, or refrain from staying or dismissing, a parallel proceeding. In *Moses H. Cone,* the Court did not reach this issue because it held that the stay order there was a final decision under 28 USC §1291.

to do so."[50] Justice Brennan, also writing for four justices, argued that even under this standard the district judge was wrong for refusing to accord the plaintiff his unqualified right to a federal forum. Justice Brennan also cited the clear abuse of discretion standard of *La Buy* in support of issuing the writ.[51]

Justice Rehnquist's plurality opinion on the mandamus issue was cited by the Court in *Allied Chemical Corp v Daiflon, Inc,*[52] in a per curiam opinion for five justices. The district judge had granted a new trial in an antitrust case where the jury's verdict was $2.5 million in favor of the plaintiff. The defendant claimed that the district judge had erred in evidentiary rulings and that the evidence did not support the amount of the verdict. The court of appeals issued the writ, directing the trial judge to restore the verdict on liability but permitting a new trial on damages. The Supreme Court granted certiorari and reversed on the papers without full briefing and argument.

The per curiam opinion cited *Calvert* only for the limited, and indisputable, proposition that "[w]here a matter is committed to discretion, it cannot be said that a litigant's right to a particular result is 'clear and indisputable.' "[53] The Court said: "In short, our cases have answered the question as to the availability of mandamus in situations such as this with the refrain: 'What never? Well, *hardly* ever!' "[54] The words appear in a song about a sea captain who is "never, never sick at sea." The "hardly ever" refrain is designed to summon an image of the captain doubled over the lee rail at fairly regular intervals. Here the Court quotes Gilbert & Sullivan without attribution. (Understanding the source of the quote reemphasizes how much discretion courts retain to issue a writ.)

While the rationale of *Calvert* and *Allied Chemical* appears less congenial to the issuance of mandamus than earlier cases, the courts of appeals have not interpreted either case as limiting their power to resolve novel and important questions through supervisory or advisory mandamus.[55]

The advocate who must advise a client whether to "run a writ" will, however, have difficulty speaking with confidence about the probable result. The question of power has been decided; if the court of appeals will have jurisdiction of an eventual final judgment, it has jurisdiction to issue the writ. In these days of burgeoning appellate dockets, courts of appeals motions panels may be sym-

---

[50] Will v Calvert Fire Ins Co, 437 US 655, 661 (1978) (quoting Roche v Evaporated Milk Assn, 319 US 21, 26 (1943)).

[51] *Id* 676.

[52] 449 US 33 (1980) (per curiam).

[53] *Id* 36 (citing Will v Calvert Fire Ins Co, 473 US 655, 666 (1978)).

[54] *Id* (emphasis in original).

[55] While *Will v Calvert Fire Ins Co* is often cited by the courts of appeals, e.g., United States v Carrigan, 778 F2d 1454, 1467 (10th Cir 1985); Coastal (Bermuda), Ltd v E.W. Saybolt & Co, 761 F2d 198, 204 n6 (5th Cir 1985); *In re* Bendectin Prod Liab Litig, 749 F2d 300, 303 n7 (6th Cir 1984) (holding that neither *Calvert* nor *Allied Chemical* changes the law regarding "proper use of . . . mandamus"; adopting Ninth Circuit test as discussed in **§3.04**), it has not had the effect of seriously undercutting the *La Buy-Schlagenhauf* standards. Indeed, one court has expressly noted the absence of an opinion for the Court in deciding to issue a mandamus. Southern Pac Transp Co v San Antonio 748 F2d 266, 270 n9 (5th Cir 1984).

pathetic to Justice Rehnquist's narrow reading of the permissible uses of mandamus.[56] This is a matter of tactics and of the unreported jurisprudence of the writ. Counsel must recall that reported writ cases are only those in which the court of appeals has decided to hear the issue on the merits. As noted below, the court may dismiss the petition without calling for a response, and its dismissal will almost never be reported.

Not only does this system skew the reported jurisprudence, but counsel should be aware that appellate judges are reluctant to rebuke their district court colleagues in public print. This means that some decisions granting mandamus are not reported. More significantly, a petition for writ of mandamus may provoke one or more courts of appeals judges to contact the district judge and informally suggest that he or she take steps to correct a problem. There is only anecdotal evidence on the prevalence of this informal mandamus jurisprudence, but it is frequently discussed at judicial conferences.[57]

In deciding whether to seek a writ, the Supreme Court's doctrinal development provides one element of decision. A second element is the classification of the issue involved in a civil or criminal case as worthy of mandamus in light of court of appeals precedent, as discussed in the next two sections.[58] The final element is the investment/advocacy decision, discussed later in this chapter.[59]

§3.04 Mandamus and Prohibition in Civil Cases—General Principles

There are two questions that counsel must answer, and that must be answered in the petition for the writ: First, does the court in which the petition is filed have *jurisdiction* to review an eventual final judgment in this case? If the answer is yes, then that court has jurisdiction—the naked power—to issue the writ.[60] For example, if mandamus is sought to review denial of or refusal to hear a motion to transfer venue under 28 USC §1404(a) or §1406(a), the proper court of appeals will be that for the district court in which the motion

---

[56] Indeed, there is an occasional case citing the plurality opinion in favor of a narrow reading of the mandamus power. *See, e.g., In re* Dalton, 733 F2d 710, 716 (10th Cir 1984), *cert dismissed,* 469 US 1185 (1985); United States v Kane, 646 F2d 4, 9 (1st Cir 1981). See also discussion in §3.04.

[57] *See, e.g., In re* Allied-Signal, Inc, 915 F2d 190, 192, 193 (6th Cir 1990) (unusual case; respondent district judge appeared pro se at oral argument in court of appeals and agreed to modify challenged orders; court denied mandamus; on rehearing, court of appeals found district judge's amended order "problematic," and directed him to vacate and amend those orders; court of appeals nonetheless "declined to issue a writ of mandamus;" quaere, if the detailed orders to the district judge are not a mandamus, what jurisdictional basis would they have?).

[58] **§§3.04, 3.05.**

[59] **§3.15.**

[60] See discussion in **§3.15.**

was made.[61] A difficult issue of jurisdiction could arise if such a motion had been granted and mandamus were sought to challenge such action: the appropriate court probably will depend upon whether the transfer actually has taken place. If the transfer has not taken place or a stay order is obtained, then the proper court of appeals will still be that for the transferor district court.[62] However, if the transfer procedure has been carried out and the transferee district court has the case, then the court of appeals to which an appeal from a final judgment of the transferee court would be taken will be the proper forum.[63] Difficult questions may arise if the underlying case involves an issue within the jurisdiction of the Court of Appeals for the Federal Circuit.[64]

The second question is one of *discretion* or *prudence:* should the court of appeals exercise the power it plainly has? A few general rules have emerged, based upon the broad outlines provided by the Supreme Court's exposition of the history and function of the writ. The Ninth Circuit, in an often cited case,[65] has set out the following guidelines for issuance of mandamus in a civil case:

---

[61] Northern Acceptance Trust 1065 v Gray, 423 F2d 653 (9th Cir), *cert denied,* 398 US 939 (1970). *See* Bankers Life & Casualty Co v Holland, 346 US 379 (1953) (holding mandamus not proper under the circumstances but recognizing that a court of appeals has power to compel a district court to do its duty).

[62] *See generally* General Casualty Co v Grubb, 253 F2d 51 (7th Cir), *cert denied,* 357 US 907 (1958). The use of mandamus in connection with change of venue in federal civil cases is discussed at length in S.R. Shapiro, Annotation, *Mandamus, Prohibition, or Interlocutory Appeal As Proper Remedy to Seek Review of District Court's Disposition of Motion for Change of Venue Under §1404(a) or §1406(a) of Judicial Code,* 2 ALR Fed 573 (1969).

[63] *In re* Sosa, 712 F2d 1479 (DC Cir 1983) (transfer of records and files of case to transferee district in another circuit deprived DC Circuit of power to review propriety of transfer); Drabik v Murphy, 246 F2d 408 (2d Cir 1957). Some courts of appeals have declined to review orders transferring cases to courts in other circuits even when the files and records have not been sent to the transferee district. The rationale is that review may be available from the court of appeals having power over the transferee district. *See, e.g.,* Clayton v Warlick, 232 F2d 699 (4th Cir 1956); Magnetic Engg & Mfg Co v Dings Mfg Co, 178 F2d 866 (2d Cir 1950). It should be noted that this is a purely discretionary decision; the court of appeals with power over the transferor court has the power to issue mandamus if the files and records have not been sent out of the circuit, and there is a strong argument that it should hear the matter on the merits in the interest of judicial economy if the transfer is determined to have been improper. As discussed below, counsel must seek a stay of the transfer order to prevent the actual transfer of files and records from taking place. Also discussed below is the advisability of seeking certification under 28 USC §1292(b) in order to exhaust all nonwrit remedies. *See* **§3.07.** *See also Ex parte* Deepwater Exploration Co, 260 F2d 546 (5th Cir 1958) (mandamus not available until petitioner had requested the district judge to authorize §1292(b) appeal).

[64] *See* **§§2.12, 4.14.**

[65] Bauman v United States Dist Court, 557 F2d 650, 654-55 (9th Cir 1977), applied and discussed in, e.g., *In re* Bendectin Prod Liab Litig, 749 F2d 300, 303 (6th Cir 1984); United States v Harper, 729 F2d 1216, 1221 (9th Cir 1984); *In re* Cement Antitrust Litig, 688 F2d 1297, 1301 (9th Cir 1982), *affd sub nom* Arizona v United States Dist Court, 459 US 1191 (1983) (because five justices were disqualified from hearing the case, the affirmance has the same effect as an affirmance by an equally divided Court).

1. There is no adequate remedy by appeal or otherwise[66]
2. Petitioner will be damaged in a way not correctable on direct appeal
3. The district court's challenged order is erroneous as a matter of law
4. The issue is likely to recur, either because the particular district judge has a practice of making such rulings, or because the problem presented is capable of repetition and may repeatedly evade appellate review
5. The challenged order raises issues that are new and important or of first impression[67]

However, "the guidelines are cumulative and may not all point to the same conclusion. . . . Moreover, all of the guidelines are unlikely to be met in any one case."[68] The Second Circuit has adopted an ostensibly simpler test that restates the same elements in a different form. In *In re United States,*[69] the court set out a three-part test for mandamus: (1) a novel and significant issue of law; (2) inadequacy of other remedies; and (3) presence of a legal issue that will aid in the administration of justice.[70] The court held that a government objection to magistrate conducted voir dire met these standards and issued the writ.

It is instructive to see how these guidelines are used in a particular situation. In *In re Cement Antitrust Litigation,*[71] 21 separate price fixing antitrust suits were assigned in 1977 to a single judge under the multidistrict litigation statute, 28 USC §1407, for consolidated pretrial procedures. The judge held extensive hearings, resulting in more than 75 pretrial orders and rulings on countless motions. Early in 1981, some of the defendants advised the judge that his wife owned stock in seven of the 210,235 members of the plaintiff class; these defendants demanded that the judge recuse himself. After lengthy consideration, he did so.

The judge certified the recusal question under 28 USC §1292(b).[72] The plaintiffs appealed under 28 USC §1291, claiming that the recusal was a final collateral order.[73] They also sought mandamus. The Ninth Circuit denied permission to appeal under §1292(b), dismissed the appeal under §1291, and heard the merits on petition for writ of mandamus.

---

[66] An order may be nonappealable because it is not final or because it is among a class of orders made not appealable by statute. *See* **ch 2.**

[67] *Bauman,* 557 F2d at 654-55.

[68] *In re* Cement Antitrust Litig, 688 F2d 1297, 1301 (9th Cir 1982), *affd sub nom* Arizona v United States Dist Court, 459 US 1191 (1983) (citation omitted). *See also In re* Bendectin Prod Liab Litig, 749 F2d 300, 306 (6th Cir 1984).

[69] 903 F2d 88 (2d Cir 1990).

[70] *Id* 89.

[71] 688 F2d 1297 (9th Cir 1982).

[72] *Id* 1300. The interpretation and use of 28 USC §1292(b) is discussed in detail at **§2.09.**

[73] 688 F2d at 1299, referring to earlier opinion concerning appealability, *In re* Cement Antitrust Litig, 673 F2d 1020 (9th Cir 1981), *affd sub nom* Arizona v Ash Grove Cement Co, 459 US 1190 (1983). The final judgment rule as applied under 28 USC §1291 is discussed in detail at **§2.02.**

As to the first guideline, the court pointed to its prior ruling dismissing the appeal.[74] Although the panel acknowledged that the question of appealability was close, it determined that the disqualification order was not appealable.[75] The correctness of this view is not open to question.[76] However, a party considering filing for mandamus must take a lesson from the Cement Antitrust plaintiffs: when the question of appealability is doubtful, both an appeal and a petition for the writ should be filed.[77] In making this evaluation, the lawyer should study the material on appealability elsewhere in this volume.[78]

Turning to the second guideline, the *Cement Antitrust* court asked whether an erroneous grant of a motion to recuse could ever be reviewed, even on

---

[74] 688 F2d at 1300-02.

[75] *Id* 1301-02. The view that grant or denial of a disqualification motion does not present an appealable order is the general rule. *Id.* However, the mandamus cases are full of reported exceptions to this rule, perhaps because a court of appeals does not want to risk having to reverse a case in which the judge should not have sat, and perhaps because appellate judges become impatient with district judges who ought to have stepped aside.

[76] *See, e.g., In re* United States, 666 F2d 690 (1st Cir 1981). On the use of the extraordinary remedy of mandamus in connection with motions to disqualify a federal district judge, see generally James O. Pearson, Jr, Annotation, *Mandamus as Remedy to Compel Disqualification of Federal Judge,* 56 ALR Fed 494 (1982).

[77] Failure to cover both options may well leave a litigant with no remedy at all. For example, in United States v Helstoski, 442 US 477 (1979), the petitioner filed a petition for writ of mandamus to challenge the trial judge's refusal to grant a motion to dismiss his indictment. The petitioner had been a member of Congress during the time of the alleged offenses. He claimed that the indictment infringed upon his rights under the "speech or debate" clause of the Constitution, US Const art I, §6. *See* Helstoski v Meanor, 442 US 500 (1979). The Court held that speech or debate clause issues are appealable without a final judgment. *See* **§2.05.** Since Helstoski therefore had (in the past) a remedy by appeal, mandamus was not appropriate. However, the Court also noted that his appeal was jurisdictionally out of time so that he was without any remedy at all. The same procedural Catch-22 beset the litigant in Coastal (Bermuda), Ltd v EW Saybolt & Co, 761 F2d 198, 203 (5th Cir 1985). The district judge had stayed an admiralty suit pending arbitration. The court of appeals held (*see* **§2.02**) that the stay order was not appealable. The court then declined to treat the appeal as a petition for writ of mandamus. It noted, however, that the appellant had not asked for such relief, and that mandamus probably would not be proper in any case until the appellant had pursued alternate remedies, such as seeking vacation of the stay on remand to the district court. *But see* Wilk v American Medical Assn, 635 F2d 1295 (7th Cir 1980), discussed below, in which the court on its own motion treated a notice of appeal as a petition for writ of mandamus because the court did not wish to "venture . . . into the quagmire of 'collateral order' lore." *Id* 1298. Compare Judge Goldberg's opinion in Southern Pac Transp Co v San Antonio, 748 F2d 266 (5th Cir 1984), in which the court granted mandamus to compel the district judge to vacate a stay order and permit execution of a judgment the railroad had obtained against the city. The court reaffirmed that mandamus will issue "to correct the grant of a stay which amounts to a clear abuse of discretion." *Id* 270. The case is also significant because the court, at the appellant/petitioner's request, treated a motion for expedited consideration of the appeal as a petition for writ of mandamus. Also granting review of a stay order by mandamus when an appeal was not available is Frederick L. v Thomas, 578 F2d 513 (3d Cir 1978).

[78] **Ch 2,** particularly **§§2.04, 2.09, 2.10.**

appeal from the final judgment. It answered in the negative. True, the erroneous denial of a motion to recuse is always appealable, because a party has been forced to trial before a court that is biased or otherwise unqualified. But "[a] party cannot ordinarily predicate a claim of prejudicial error on the fact that he was required to try his cause before one judge who was duly qualified to preside rather than another."[79] However, the plaintiffs were clearly harmed by the judge's decision, for the entry of a new judge upon the scene would entail "additional cost and unreasonable delay."[80]

The court next considered the fourth guideline and found that the judge's order did not present an "oft repeated error," or "manifest a persistent disregard of the federal rules."[81] However, the last guideline was clearly satisfied because the question was one of first impression and of evident importance to the operation of the district courts. The court noted that the last two guide-

---

[79] *In re* Cement Antitrust Litig, 688 F2d 1297, 1302 (9th Cir 1982), *affd sub nom* Arizona v United States Dist Court, 459 US 1191 (1983), citing authorities. The same analysis can apply to a case in which Congress has forbidden an appeal altogether, such as appeals from remand orders in removed cases. *See* **§2.15.** For discussion of the use of mandamus to challenge remand of a removed case when appeal is barred by statute, see **§2.15.** Mandamus may be denied if the court of appeals concludes that the district judge reached a permissible result, even though the judge purported to act for the wrong reasons. *In re* Wilson Indus, 886 F2d 93 (5th Cir 1989) (district court properly remanded removed case to state court, but gave statutorily impermissible reasons for doing so). As the court of appeals noted, however, the district court's improvidence, when coupled with the improper removal, added months of delay to the lawsuit. The lesson is that parties should provide solid reasons for conclusions they ask the district judge to reach. Had that been done in this case, mandamus might have been denied out of hand.

[80] 688 F2d at 1303. Thus, *In re Cement Antitrust Litigation* is not a case within the matrix of judicial disqualification mandamus authorities that involve the district judge's wrongful refusal to recuse himself or herself, see generally James O. Pearson, Jr, Annotation, *supra* note 76. The case turns, rather, upon the need for mandamus to settle a nonappealable issue early in the course of an extremely complex case in the interest of economy and fairness to the plaintiff. In Unified Sewerage Agency v Jelco, Inc, 646 F2d 1339 (9th Cir 1981), the court held that denial of a motion to disqualify counsel could be reviewed by mandamus both because the defendant might suffer irreparable harm if forced to obtain review on appeal from a final judgment and because the case otherwise met the Ninth Circuit tests for issuance of the writ. See discussion at **§2.04** on appealability of counsel disqualification orders. A nonparty, or one who has intervened for a particular purpose, is in a good position to seek mandamus because such a party would be unduly burdened by waiting to appeal from a final judgment involving matters in which it has no interest and because it may not even have standing to take an appeal. Thus, when such a party presents an important issue—particularly one of constitutional magnitude—mandamus may be an appropriate device. In CBS, Inc v United States Dist Court, 729 F2d 1174 (9th Cir 1984), a television network was able to clarify its rights to broadcast certain material in a highly publicized trial by means of mandamus.

[81] 688 F2d at 1303-04. In the Supreme Court cases, La Buy v Howes Leather Co, 352 US 249 (1957), is an example of repeated error by a district judge, while Schlagenhauf v Holder, 379 US 104 (1964), presents an archetypical instance of a first impression nonrecurring issue reviewable on mandamus.

lines are logically mutually exclusive, because a question of first impression is not likely to have been an occasion of repeated error.[82]

The last guideline restates the teaching of *Schlagenhauf-La Buy* on supervisory and advisory mandamus.[83] A court of appeals will feel justified in considering a mandamus petition on the merits if the question is novel, important, and of such a nature that review by direct appeal is not effective. As the District of Columbia Circuit held, review by mandamus is appropriate "where the decision will serve to clarify a question that is likely to confront a number of lower court judges in a number of suits before appellate review is possible."[84] Thus, even if the matter might eventually be resolved by direct appeal, the court will entertain a mandamus if waiting for appeals will leave district courts without guidance.

The Sixth Circuit, in another class action case, *In re Bendectin Products Liability Litigation,*[85] issued mandamus despite the absence of any indication that the district court had consistently erred, or that the issue in question—certification of a nonopt-out class in a products liability case—was likely to recur often. The court said: "This is clearly not a case where the district judge is persistently disregarding the federal rules. This error is also not an oft-repeated one because, fortunately, mass tort litigation does not frequently occur."[86]

The court generally adopted the Ninth Circuit guidelines, but reaffirmed that they do not all need to point the same way in a particular case for the writ to be a proper remedy.[87] Moreover, the court found the fourth guideline to

---

[82] *In re* Cement Antitrust Litig, 688 F2d 1297, 1304 (9th Cir 1982), *affd sub nom* Arizona v United States Dist Court, 459 US 1191 (1983).

[83] *See* **§§3.02, 3.03.**

[84] National Right to Work Legal Defense & Educ Found, Inc v Richey, 510 F2d 1239, 1243 (DC Cir), *cert denied,* 422 US 1008 (1975), *cited in In re* Cement Antitrust Litig, 688 F2d 1297, 1304 (9th Cir 1982), *affd sub nom* Arizona v United States Dist Court, 459 US 1191 (1983). Eisenberg v United States Dist Court, 910 F2d 374 (7th Cir 1990), in which mandamus was denied, is an unfortunate decision for several reasons. Petitioner is a distinguished civil rights attorney. He sought mandamus to challenge a district court local rule providing that reimbursement for out-of-pocket expenses in indigent cases only be made at the end of the case; he sought an order compelling reimbursement of expenses as incurred. The court took a narrow view of mandamus and denied relief, suggesting that a §1292(b) appeal might be appropriate. Given that the issue is important, that its resolution does not interrupt any ongoing proceeding in the district court, and that the matter is of intense public interest to a large number of lawyers and litigants, the requirements of mandamus would appear to have been satisfied. The weight of recent authority, even in the Seventh Circuit, is against the decision. *See* Wilk v American Medical Assn, 635 F2d 1295 (7th Cir 1980). *See also* Valenzuela-Gonzalez v United States Dist Court, 915 F2d 1276 (9th Cir 1990) (mandamus lies to prevent arraignment of defendant under local rule providing for closed circuit television arraignments rather than in person).

[85] 749 F2d 300 (6th Cir 1984).

[86] *Id* 306.

[87] *Id.* "In fact, the fourth and fifth guidelines can seldom be consistent with each other. A district court decision that presents issues of first impression rarely will also involve an oft-repeated error." *Id* 306 n16. This assertion is not universally true. A recurring problem in the district courts can have escaped the notice of a court of appeals, and

be less important than the others, and certainly less important than the fifth one: "The Supreme Court has approved the use of the writ to review unusual and important procedural questions, . . . and the Fifth Circuit has concluded that the writ can be used as a 'one-time only device to settle new and important problems that might have otherwise evaded expeditious review.' "[88]

The Fifth Circuit case cited in *Bendectin, In re EEOC,*[89] is a well-considered opinion issuing mandamus to restrain a district judge from ordering extensive discovery against an Equal Employment Opportunity Commission employee in a subpoena enforcement proceeding. A key phrase is Judge Randall's reference to the *one-time only* nature of supervisory mandamus.[90] The Supreme Court[91] and the courts of appeals[92] often have made clear in opinions issuing the writ that they intend to settle a new and important question. Thus, the next petition that presents the same issue will not be greeted favorably.[93] For lawyers concerned about having a petition heard on the merits, this counsels emphasizing that the case presented is an opportunity to solve a knotty problem and avoid future litigation.

Returning to the five guidelines discussed above, numbers one, two, four, and five have to do with the court of appeals entertaining the mandamus petition on the merits, rather than dismissing it outright. Guideline three relates more directly to the merits, but is not coextensive with them. *Clearly erroneous as a matter of law*[94] is a chameleon phrase. The district judge's ruling must, to be reviewable by mandamus, be clearly wrong—clear, that is, to the court of appeals. Next, it must be wrong *as a matter of law.* This usually means that the district judge must have made a mistake about a legal rule, rather than about findings of fact[95] Another meaning of *as a matter of law* is that the challenged

---

thus be—for that court—a question of first impression. See, e.g., *In re* Vuitton et Fils, SA, 606 F2d 1 (2d Cir 1979), in which the court granted mandamus directing the district judge to issue a preliminary injunction to protect the petitioner's trademark. The issue of injunctive relief had been presented repeatedly to district judges, yet was of first impression in the court of appeals. See text at note 82, *supra.*

[88] *In re* Bendectin Prods Liab Litig, 749 F2d 300, 306-07 (6th Cir 1984) (quoting *In re* EEOC, 709 F2d 392, 394 (5th Cir 1983)) (other citation omitted).

[89] 709 F2d 392 (5th Cir 1983).

[90] *Id* 394.

[91] *E.g.*, Schlagenhauf v Holder, 379 US 104, 110 (1964) (mandamus to decide "basic, undecided question").

[92] *E.g.*, Wilk v American Medical Assn, 635 F2d 1295, 1298 n6 (7th Cir 1980).

[93] *Id.* However, novelty and importance of a district judge's order concerning opt-out and opt-in provisions of a class certification order were not enough in Bauman v United States Dist Court, 557 F2d 650 (9th Cir 1977), to induce the court of appeals to treat the merits of a mandamus petition. It would, however, require some temerity to conclude that the district judge's actions would be reversed when and if the matter were presented on direct appeal from a final judgment.

[94] *In re* Cement Antitrust Litig, 688 F2d 1297, 1305-07 (9th Cir 1982), *affd sub nom* Arizona v United States Dist Court, 459 US 1191 (1983).

[95] *See* Washington Pub Utils Group v United States Dist Court, 843 F2d 319, 324 (9th Cir 1987).

order must be the kind of order that appellate courts may appropriately review. An order granting a new trial, for example, historically has been within the trial judge's unreviewable power. For that reason, such an order will hardly ever be reviewed on mandamus because it lies within the district judge's discretion, bounded only by the most general legal constraints.[96] Another aspect of the standard is the degree of certainty which the court of appeals must possess with respect to the district court's action: the writ will issue only if "after a full review of the authorities, [the court of appeals is] firmly convinced that the district court's interpretation was incorrect."[97]

Fortunately, the advocate who must file a petition for mandamus is not remitted solely to juggling the five guidelines listed above. There is some guidance on the kinds of questions that are and are not reviewable without waiting for a final judgment, arguing about the collateral order rule, or seeking certification under 18 USC §1292(b). In considering categories of cases in which courts of appeals have considered use of the writ, it must be recalled that no single factor determines whether the writ is an appropriate remedy. If a case falls into or out of a category where writ review is more readily available, that is only one consideration among several.

§3.05 —Complex Cases and Novel Issues

The courts of appeals are more willing to guide the actions of district judges in complex cases because waiting for a final judgment—with the prospect that a reversal may occasion a retrial—seems to be a waste of judicial resources. Complex cases include mass tort or antitrust class actions, multidistrict cases consolidated for pretrial purposes under 28 USC §1407, and civil cases that involve many difficult issues.

Indeed, 28 USC §1407(e) expressly provides for review by extraordinary writ of orders of the judicial panel on multidistrict litigation and orders in a multidistrict action after transfer for consolidated or coordinated pretrial proceedings.[98] This provision does not mean that every order in a multidistrict case will be reviewable on the merits by writ; it means only that review by appeal is not available.

---

[96] Allied Chem Corp v Daiflon, Inc, 449 US 33, 36 (1980) (new trial grant hardly ever appealable). Of course, a new trial order in a criminal case is now appealable, 18 USC §3731, discussed in **§2.11.** The concept of unreviewable trial court discretion does not mean that a trial judge is presumptively free to do anything at all: it means simply that within a carefully defined area he or she can apply certain defined legal principles without interference from the appellate court. *See generally* George Fletcher, *Some Unwise Reflections About Discretion,* 47 Law & Contemp Probs 269 (Autumn 1984).

[97] *In re* Cement Antitrust Litig, 688 F2d 1297, 1306 (9th Cir 1982) (footnote omitted), *affd sub nom* Arizona v United States Dist Court, 459 US 1191 (1983).

[98] 28 USC §1407(e) reads as follows:

> No proceedings for review of any order of the panel may be permitted except by extraordinary writ pursuant to the provisions of title 28, section 1651, United States Code. Petitions for an extraordinary writ to review an order of the panel to set a transfer hearing and other orders of the panel issued prior to the order

In *In re Cement Antitrust Litigation,*[99] the Ninth Circuit was disposed to consider the mandamus petition on the merits because the district judge who had recused himself had "an extensive working knowledge of this complex litigation," and "inevitable cost and delay"[100] would result if a new judge were assigned the case. In a less complex case, a court of appeals might well decide that review on final judgment would be an adequate remedy.

Wilk v American Medical Assn[101] illustrates the use of mandamus to smooth the path of complex litigation. Five chiropractors filed an antitrust class action against the AMA and other medical groups and individuals in the United States District Court for the Northern District of Illinois. By the time the lawsuit was three years old, 100 depositions had been taken and 100,000 pages of documents produced on discovery. As the action progressed, other similar class suits were filed by other plaintiffs in other judicial districts. Because the Illinois action was so far advanced, the multidistrict panel denied transfer and consolidation of these other suits under 28 USC §1407.[102] The panel did make clear in its order denying transfer that it contemplated that discovery in the Illinois action would be available in the other cases.[103]

The state of New York, a plaintiff in one of the other cases, intervened in the Illinois action to move for modification of a protective order precluding its access to discovery in that action. The district judge denied the motion to modify.

The court of appeals first considered whether the order would be appealable under the collateral order exception.[104] It determined that the appealability

---

> either directing or denying transfer shall be filed only in the court of appeals having jurisdiction over the district in which a hearing is to be or has been held. Petitions for an extraordinary writ to review an order to transfer or orders subsequent to transfer shall be filed only in the court of appeals having jurisdiction over the transferee district. There shall be no appeal or review of an order of the panel denying a motion to transfer for consolidated or coordinated proceedings.

[99] 688 F2d 1297 (9th Cir 1982), *affd sub nom* Arizona v United States Dist Court, 459 US 1191 (1983) (per curiam). See also J.H. Cohn & Co v American Appraisal Assoc, 628 F2d 994 (7th Cir 1980), in which the court refused to issue mandamus to compel the district judge to certify a class under Fed R Crim P 23(b). Such orders are generally not appealable (*see* **§2.02**) and the district judge had not observably applied improper factors nor abused his discretion.

[100] 688 F2d at 1301.

[101] 635 F2d 1295 (7th Cir 1980).

[102] *Id* 1297. The order denying transfer is not reviewable by appeal or otherwise. 28 USC §1407(e).

[103] 635 F2d at 1297 n4 and accompanying text.

[104] The court noted, *id* 1298, that in two cases, American Tel & Tel Co v Grady, 594 F2d 594 (7th Cir 1978), *cert denied,* 440 US 971 (1979), and First Wis Mortgage Trust v First Wis Corp, 571 F2d 390 (7th Cir), *adopted en banc on question of appealability,* 584 F2d 201 (7th Cir 1978), the Seventh Circuit had construed the collateral order exception to the final judgment rule in terms that suggested that the order under review was appealable. On this point, see **§2.04.** The difficulty faced by the panel in deciding the appealability question illustrates again the wisdom of seeking relief in the alternative. *See also* **§3.15.**

question was sufficiently knotty that mandamus should be considered, and treated the notice of appeal as an application for writ of mandamus.[105] Mandamus was appropriate because two federal appellate cases had upheld use of the writ to compel disclosure of discovery materials for use in a related case.[106] The case clearly involved an important question of supervisory control over the district court, if only because the district court had misapplied Seventh Circuit precedent in denying the motion to modify.[107]

Wilk contains a caveat: the court's issuance of the writ established only the general principle that a party in the petitioner's position should not be burdened by redoing a massive amount of discovery in a closely similar lawsuit. However, the court warned that:

> Our decision on the merits may require the district court to decide whether certain parts of the Wilk discovery are either irrelevant to the New York litigation or are privileged, and hence not discoverable by New York. Since such decisions require only application of relatively well-settled law to fact, we think it extremely unlikely that the district court's rulings on those details would merit immediate appellate review via collateral order appeal, or mandamus.[108]

Put another way, supervisory mandamus is not only exceptional and one-time only, but the court of appeals will not strip the district judge of power to decide the proper and detailed application of the rule it announces in issuing the writ.[109] Mandamus will be denied in the first instance if a party is complaining about details.[110]

Wilk is also instructive because it involves the application of mandamus to a civil discovery dispute. Generally, such disputes are not reviewable except

---

[105] Wilk v American Medical Assn, 635 F2d 1295, 1298 (7th Cir 1980).

[106] *Ex parte* Uppercu, 239 US 435 (1915); Olympic Ref Co v Carter, 332 F2d 260 (9th Cir), *cert denied,* 379 US 900 (1964), *cited in* 635 F2d at 1298.

[107] The *Wilk* court found the district judge to have misapplied American Tel & Tel Co v Grady, 594 F2d 594 (7th Cir 1978), *cert denied,* 440 US 971 (1979). The case is therefore interesting because it can be cited in opposition to the assertion that an issue must be of first impression for mandamus to be appropriate. The Seventh Circuit had, in *Grady,* already considered the meaning and application of Fed R Civ P 26(c) to modify a protective order entered under closely analogous circumstances. The court in *Wilk* nonetheless found mandamus proper because it was important, under the circumstances, to exercise supervisory authority over the district court.

[108] *Wilk,* 635 F2d at 1298 n6.

[109] *Id* 1298. Cases that illustrate the principle that the issuing court will set the general guidelines and let the district judge work out the details include Platt v Minnesota Mining & Mfg Co, 376 US 240 (1964); Van Dusen v Barrack, 376 US 612, 615 (1964).

[110] See generally Kerr v United States Dist Court, 426 US 394 (1976), in which the petitioner claimed that the district judge's order of disclosure imperiled sensitive governmental information. The Court held that the claimed collision was either fanciful or had not yet occurred. See the discussion at **§3.06.**

by appeal of a final judgment, although some other exceptions are discussed below.[111]

In re Société Nationale Industrielle Aérospatiale[112] is another illustration of mandamus in the setting of a complex case. The court denied the writ, but determined that the issue presented was sufficiently important to warrant review on the merits. The Supreme Court, in reviewing the Eighth Circuit's decision, did not question the propriety of plenary review on mandamus. Aérospatiale, a French corporation owned by the Republic of France, manufactures aircraft. An airplane it manufactured and sold in the United States was involved in an accident in Iowa. Americans involved in the accident sued in federal district court.

The case rapidly turned into a major discovery battle. Aérospatiale contended that the plaintiffs' sole means for taking discovery abroad was through the procedures authorized by the Hague Convention.[113] It also resisted some discovery on the basis that disclosure of information would violate a French statute that carried criminal penalties for disclosure.[114] The magistrate rejected both contentions, holding that plaintiffs could take discovery from a party litigant without compliance with the Hague Convention, and that Aérospatiale had not shown that it was at risk under the French statute.

As a noted commentator observed, judicial officers make discovery rulings every day.[115] Use of mandamus to correct their alleged errors is fraught with peril for the orderly administration of justice. However, the court of appeals decided to consider the matter on the merits for two reasons. First, both the Hague Convention and the French statute presented novel and important questions. This characterization was adopted despite the court's later acknowledgment that the Hague Convention had been construed by several courts of appeals, and that the court was going to adopt "the better rule, which has been

---

[111] See *In re* Attorney Gen, 596 F2d 58, 61 (2d Cir), *cert denied,* 444 US 903 (1979), discussed below. In Evanson v Union Oil Co, 619 F2d 72 (Temp Emer Ct App), *cert denied,* 449 US 832 (1980) the district court, acting under Fed R Civ P 37(b)(2), imposed sanctions on the defendant oil company for giving false answers to interrogatories. The sanctions consisted of deeming certain facts to be established. The defendant appealed and also sought mandamus. The court of appeals held that discovery orders, even those imposing sanctions, are not appealable. It also denied the petition for writ of mandamus, finding no usurpation or abuse of discretion in a fairly routine exercise of discretion under Rule 37. *See also* **§2.04.**

[112] 782 F2d 120 (8th Cir 1986), *vacated & remanded on other grounds sub nom,* Société Nationale Industrielle Aérospatiale v United States Dist Court, 482 US 522 (1987).

[113] Also known as the Multilateral Convention on the Taking of Evidence Abroad in Civil and Commercial Matters, Mar 18, 1970, 23 UST 2555, TIAS No 7444, UKTS 20 (1977).

[114] Code Penal (France) Law 80-538, discussed in *In re* Société Nationale Industrielle Aérospatiale, 782 F2d 120 (8th Cir 1986), *vacated & remanded on other grounds sub nom* Société Nationale Industrielle Aérospatiale v United States Dist Court, 482 US 522 (1987)

[115] Charles A. Wright, *The Doubtful Omniscience of Appellate Courts,* 41 Minn L Rev 751, 775 (1957).

adopted by the vast majority of courts."[116] The French statute raised an issue that also had been the subject of frequent judicial determination.[117] Second, and perhaps more plausibly, the court noted that the construction of these legal provisions was likely to "recur prior to any opportunity to review a final judgment."[118]

In sum, review by writ may be available in a complex case to obtain threshold resolution of problems that are likely to recur, the resolution of which will predictably conserve judicial resources.

The novelty of the issue presented may influence the court of appeals to hear a petition for mandamus or prohibition. Issues can be novel in two ways. First, an issue may be of great and possibly recurring importance, but not yet have been addressed by an appellate court. Resolving this form of novel issue guides the lower courts.[119]

Second, an issue may be novel in the sense that the district judge has so far departed from accepted norms that an essentially equitable corrective discipline must be applied. Many mandamus cases have this air of equitable intervention about them. The writ sometimes can be used when access to justice seems blocked in a frustrating way. *In re Ramu Corp,*[120] shows a wise use of mandamus to remind district courts to listen to arguments made by litigants. Petitioners' homes and places of business were seized in a civil forfeiture action brought by the Drug Enforcement Administration. Over their objection, the district court granted an indefinite stay of the proceedings without hearing, argument, or findings and conclusions, and based upon vague representations by the government. On this record, the court of appeals held that there was a serious legal issue as to application of the forfeiture statute, and that the district court's summary disposition provided it no claim "to greater familiarity with the matter than can be gleaned from the pleadings."[121] Characterizing the issue as novel and important, the court of appeals noted the hardship imposed by the stay and remanded with directions to hold a hearing.[122]

---

[116] *In re* Société Nationale Industrielle Aérospatiale, 782 F2d 120, 124 (8th Cir), *vacated & remanded on other grounds sub nom* Société Nationale Industrielle Aérospatiale v United States Dist Court, 482 US 522 (1987). This case is yet another instance of the practical wisdom that the power of a court of appeals to issue mandamus is so broad that one often will find an opinion that hears a petition on the merits even when the issue lacks the importance and uniqueness that some case law suggests is required.

[117] 782 F2d at 126-27.

[118] *Id* 123.

[119] See, e.g., Schlagenhauf v Holder, 379 US 104 (1964), discussed in **§§3.02, 3.06** (resolving validity and application of Federal Rule of Civil Procedure).

[120] 903 F2d 312 (5th Cir 1990).

[121] *Id* 318 (footnote omitted).

[122] Id 317. *See also In re* Fibreboard Corp, 893 F2d 706 (5th Cir 1990) (mandamus granted to vacate the district court's order establishing a *representative case* mechanism to dispose of common issues in asbestosis litigation; order portended interference with jury trial rights, traditionally a proper subject for mandamus; mandamus issued because of district judge's asserted departure from state product liability law principles and the class certification standards of Fed R Civ P 23); *In re* Bituminous Coal Operators' Assoc,

§3.06 —Discovery Disputes

As noted above, discovery disputes generally are not reviewable on mandamus, although *Schlagenhauf v Holder* is a noted exception.[123] In *Kerr v United States District Court,*[124] inmates of California prisons brought a class suit challenging practices of the California Adult Authority concerning the authority's determinations of length and conditions of confinement. The plaintiffs sought employee and inmate files under Federal Rule of Civil Procedure 34. The district court had overruled claims that disclosure violated the official information privilege.

Defendants sought mandamus, which the court of appeals denied. The Supreme Court affirmed the denial, concluding unanimously that the district judge's challenged orders seemed to contemplate file-by-file review of the documents to make a detailed disclosure determination. The record did not disclose that the district judge was insensitive to, or unaware of, the legal standard to be applied. Thus, mandamus would interfere with the exercise of a function that district judges customarily exercise. Moreover, if the defendants disagreed with the judge's decision about any particular file, they would at that time have other remedies.

The judicial reluctance to review discovery orders other than after a final judgment is well documented. *In re Attorney General,*[125] an exceptional case in which mandamus review eventually was granted, illustrates this principle. The Socialist Workers Party (SWP) and some of its affiliates and members sued the Federal Bureau of Investigation and present and former government officers and employees for allegedly engaging in unlawful investigations of the SWP with the objective of disrupting or destroying its lawful activities. The district

---

949 F2d 1165 (DC Cir 1991) (over defendant's objection, mandamus issued to overturn a district judge order appointing a special master to resolve all issues; excellent discussion; rationale is that district court has no authority to enter such an order, therefore mandamus appropriate).

[123] 379 US 104 (1964). *Schlagenhauf* is discussed in **§3.02.** Illustrating that mandamus is not usually used to intervene in a discovery dispute, in one employment discrimination case an employer was not permitted to assert, by means of mandamus, a claim that it possessed an internal self-evaluation privilege and therefore was entitled to a protective order that the district judge had refused to grant. *In re* Burlington N, Inc, 679 F2d 762 (8th Cir 1982). Also holding that discovery disputes are not ordinarily reviewable by mandamus was NLRB v Interstate Dress Carriers, Inc, 610 F2d 99 (3d Cir 1979). However, in Sanderson v Winner, 507 F2d 477 (10th Cir 1974), *cert denied,* 421 US 914 (1975), and IBM Corp v United States, 471 F2d 507 (2d Cir 1972), *affd on rehg,* 480 F2d 293 (2d Cir 1973), *cert denied,* 416 US 980 (1974), discovery orders in complex antitrust cases were reviewed by mandamus on an abuse of discretion standard. A district judge's order refusing to permit recordation of depositions by other than stenographic means, as a cost-saving device for an impecunious litigant, may be reviewable by mandamus as it presents an important question under the Federal Rules of Civil Procedure and will have significant impact in the ongoing litigation. Colonial Times, Inc v Gasch, 509 F2d 517 (DC Cir 1975).

[124] 426 US 394 (1976).

[125] 596 F2d 58 (2d Cir), *cert denied,* 444 US 903 (1979) (prior appeal); *In re* United States, 565 F2d 19 (2d Cir 1977), *cert denied,* 436 US 962 (1978).

court ordered disclosure of FBI files relating to the activities of confidential informers. The defendants appealed and also sought mandamus. On the first trip to the Second Circuit, the court reaffirmed that discovery orders are not appealable and denied the writ. Executive privilege questions are important, but not extraordinarily so; informer privilege questions have been the subject of many judicial opinions and are not, therefore, of first impression. While denying the writ, however, the court of appeals warned the district court of the perils of unnecessary disclosure.[126]

The district judge persisted. So did the defendants. The Attorney General asserted custody of the files and declined to produce them. The district judge warned of sanctions. The Attorney General was undeterred. The district judge found the Attorney General in contempt, asserting the judge's authority under Fed R Civ P 37(b)(2).[127] The Attorney General appealed and also petitioned for mandamus. The Second Circuit held that a contempt order against a party for violation of a discovery order was not appealable.[128]

The court held mandamus available, however, its touchstones being that this was an exceptional case, warranting supervisory control; it was a case of extraordinary significance, with extreme need for reversal.[129] The Second Circuit noted that its decisions showed more reluctance to issue supervisory or advisory mandamus than other circuits.[130] However, the court did cite the Har-

---

[126] The court spoke at length about the perils to governmental interest that would arise if the district judge persisted, as he seemed poised to do, in making what the court of appeals panel plainly thought was undue disclosure. In this case, the panel opinion on the first appeal was a warning that the district judge arguably disregarded; hence, the second appeal. In *Kerr,* however, the Supreme Court's opinion was laden with guidance for the district judge on how to handle future disclosure matters. *Kerr* is a clear example of the petitioner winning even as the petition was denied, for it would be a temerarious district judge who would disregard the polite suggestions in the opinion upholding denial of the writ. The case under discussion is a somewhat less clear example of the same thing.

[127] Socialist Workers Party v Attorney Gen, 458 F Supp 895 (SDNY 1978) (mandamus granted); *In re* Attorney Gen, 596 F2d 58 (2d Cir), *cert denied,* 444 US 903 (1979). Imposition of Fed R Civ P 37(b)(2) sanctions is ordinarily a matter well within the district judge's discretion. For example, in National Hockey League v Metropolitan Hockey Club, Inc, 427 US 639 (1976), the Supreme Court reversed the Third Circuit's reversal of a dismissal order entered under Rule 37. See also Evanson v Union Oil Co, 619 F2d 72 (Temp Emer Ct App), *cert denied* 449 US 832 (1980), discussed in **§3.05.**

[128] *In re* Attorney Gen, 596 F2d 58, 61-62 (2d Cir), *cert denied,* 444 US 903 (1979). *See* **§2.02.**

[129] 596 F2d at 62-64.

[130] *Id* 63 (citing National Super Spuds, Inc v New York Mercantile Exch, 591 F2d 174, 181 (2d Cir 1979)); Kaufman v Edelstein, 539 F2d 811, 816-19 (2d Cir 1976), and distinguishing Colonial Times, Inc v Gasch, 509 F2d 517 (DC Cir 1975). However, as noted in **§3.03,** the Second Circuit has gone quite far in issuing mandamus on the government's petition in criminal cases. See also *In re* Vuitton et Fils, SA, 606 F2d 1 (2d Cir 1979), discussed at note 87, *supra,* for an adventurous use of mandamus by the Second Circuit. *National Super Spuds* has not been followed by the Eighth Circuit, *In re* Grand Jury Proceedings (Malone), 655 F2d 882 (8th Cir 1981), and Seventh Circuit, *In re* Klein, 776 F2d 628 (7th Cir 1985).

vard Mandamus Comment,[131] and noted that the limiting language of *Will v Calvert Fire Insurance Co*[132] had not commanded a majority of the Supreme Court.

In deciding to issue the writ, the court was, of course, influenced by the fact that the Attorney General of the United States was the person held in contempt.[133] However, other factors that may recur in other contexts also were important. These factors parallel those considered by other circuits and discussed above.

The Attorney General had no appeal from the order.[134] The damage from improper disclosure of sensitive governmental information was apparent, at least to the Second Circuit.[135] The question was one of first impression, and the litigation itself was unique.[136] It could not be said that the district judge had persistently violated the federal rules, but this standard, as noted before, is less important than the others and usually will not be present if the *first impression* test is satisfied.

As to the third factor, *clearly erroneous as a matter of law,* the Second Circuit did not phase the matter in these terms but was at pains to explain its position so as not to open the door to wholesale review of discovery orders by extraordinary writ. In doing so, it demonstrated adherence to this standard. The district judge's order involved, the court held, a fundamental misconception of the structure and nature of the sanctions provided in Fed R Civ P37 for failure to provide discovery. Contempt, the court of appeals said, was a "last resort."[137] The court should have considered lesser sanctions, such as deeming certain facts to be established, or prohibiting the defendants from relying upon claims or defenses related to the withheld discovery. And, of course, the sanction of dismissal would be available for persistent flouting of discovery orders.

This case illustrates the narrow scope of writ review of discovery disputes. Mandamus may be available to review the construction of a rule, but generally

---

[131] Comment, *Supervisory and Advisory Mandamus Under the All Writs Act,* 86 Harv L Rev 595 (1973).

[132] 437 US 655 (1978), discussed at **§3.03.**

[133] *In re* Attorney Gen, 596 F2d at 63, 64. This same consideration did not, however, move the court to expand its collateral order appeal principles. *Id* 61.

[134] *Id. See also* Estate of Domingo v Republic of Philippines, 808 F2d 1349 (9th Cir 1987) (former Philippine President Marcos could not appeal order denying motion to terminate deposition because he had not placed himself in contempt of subpoena).

[135] The revelations ordered by the district judge and the message that would be sent to informants and potential informants by the disclosure "would adversely affect the entire law enforcement and entire law enforcement and intelligence-gathering apparatus of the United States." *Id* 64 & n 11. One wonders how a party faced with such an affidavit would respond; tactically, it seems that one might seek to cross-examine the affiant, to attempt to find a counteraffiant to minimize the seriousness of the problem, and to cite cases (such as Alderman v United States, 394 US 165 (1969)) in which disclosure of sensitive material was ordered. The opponent, after all, has only the burden of showing that this is not an extraordinary case, not necessarily that the district judge was right. See discussion at **§3.17.**

[136] *In re* Attorney Gen, 596 F2d at 63-64.

[137] *Id* 65. However, it is not clear that contempt would be a last resort if the alleged contemptor were not a Cabinet officer.

not the detailed application of a rule. Moreover, the court of appeals will not issue the writ unless and until the petitioner has no prospect of gaining the relief being sought in the district court. This principle explains why in *Kerr* mandamus was not appropriate: the governmental agency still had ample means to protect its interests by shaping the nature of compelled disclosure. It also helps explain why the Second Circuit did not grant relief on the Attorney General's first trip to the court: the case was not yet ripe.

Discovery disputes involving privacy protecting privileges are the most prolific source of mandamus decisions. For example, in *Haines v Liggett Group, Inc,*[138] the district judge in a high visibility cigarette litigation overruled a magistrate's report and held the attorney-client privilege inapplicable to tobacco company documents. The judge also revealed the contents of some of the documents before the court of appeals could review the dispute and made publicly reported statements sharply critical of the tobacco industry. The court of appeals issued the writ, not only to protect the attorney-client privilege,[139] but also to order the judge to recuse himself because his remarks had raised questions as to his perceived partiality. The court stressed the importance of maintaining attorney-client privilege documents confidential until all avenues of review are exhausted.

§3.07 —Transfer Orders

A district court may entertain a transfer under 28 USC §1404(a) "[f]or the convenience of parties and witnesses, in the interest of justice."[140] Under 28 USC §1406(a), the district court may transfer a "case laying venue in the wrong division or district."[141] Under both sections, the case may only be transferred to a district where it might or could have been brought.[142] In several cases,

---

[138] 975 F2d 81 (3d Cir 1992). *See also* Chase Manhattan Bank v Turner & Newall, PLC, 964 F2d 159 (2d Cir 1992) (order overruling claim of attorney-client privilege not appealable despite the importance of the issue; however, review available, and granted, by way of mandamus directing the district court's judge to pay more attention to the privilege); *In re* Weisman, 835 F2d 23 (2d Cir 1987) (mandamus denied to review civil discovery order that allegedly infringed attorney-client privilege). Admiral Ins Co v United States Dist Court, 881 F2d 1486 (9th Cir 1989) (mandamus granted to overturn discovery order invading party's attorney-client privilege; not all of *Bauman* factors need be present to justify mandamus); Westinghouse Elec Corp v Republic of the Phillipines, 951 F2d 1414 (3d Cir 1991) (mandamus appropriate as a means of reviewing a discovery dispute involving attorney-client privilege, work product privilege, and claims of waiver. However, on the merits, the petition is denied). *Compare* Republic of the Phillipines v Westinghouse Elec Corp, 949 F2d 653 (3d Cir 1991) (denying stay pending consideration of appeal and mandamus).

[139] As noted at **§2.04,** attorney-client privilege issues arising during discovery are reviewable by appeal in some circuits.

[140] *See* Charles A. Wright, Federal Courts §44, at 259-67 (4th ed 1983).

[141] *Id* 258-59.

[142] "*Might*" occurs in 28 USC §1404(a); "*could*" in 28 USC §1406(a). For a discussion of the differences between the two sections and the controversies concerning their proper application, see generally Ellis v Great Southwestern Corp, 646 F2d 1099 (5th

the Supreme Court has upheld review by mandamus of orders granting or denying transfer.[143] However, the writ is available only when the district court errs in "interpreting the legal limitations upon and criteria for" transfer.[144] Even then, the courts will limit themselves to correcting the district judge's legal misimpression and sending the case back to permit him or her to apply the proper test to the transfer motion.[145]

In addition to the statutory venue transfer provisions, federal litigants are entitled to move for forum non conveniens dismissal when the proper forum is not within the federal system. Usually, such motions seek dismissal so that the litigation may be recommended in another country. The cases do not speak with a single voice, but there is a decided preference against interfering with the district judge's decision regarding whether to grant or deny the motion.[146]

Thus, mandamus may be available if a district judge refuses to entertain a transfer motion,[147] grants a transfer motion without giving the opponent an opportunity to be heard,[148] transfers the case to a district where it could not have been brought,[149] or applies an improper test in deciding the motion.[150]

Cir 1981). For a discussion of the use of mandamus in connection with transfer under these sections, see generally S.R. Shapiro, Annotation, *Mandamus, Prohibition, or Interlocutory Appeal as Proper Remedy to Seek Review of District Court's Disposition of Motion for Change of Venue Under §1404(a) or §1406(a) of Judicial Code,* 2 ALR Fed 573 (1969). *See also* Louisiana Ice Cream Distribs, Inc v Carvel Corp, 821 F2d 1031 (5th Cir 1987) (denial of motion to dismiss for improper venue not appealable; mandamus denied; insufficient findings by district court to make review possible).

[143] Platt v Minnesota Mining & Mfg Co, 376 US 240 (1964); Van Dusen v Barrack, 376 US 612 (1964); Hoffman v Blaski, 363 US 335 (1960) (in companion case, Sullivan v Behimer, Court transferred action to district where it could not have been brought; mandamus granted).

[144] Van Dusen v Barrack, 376 US 612, 615 n3 (1964). In Platt, the claim was that the district judge had applied an improper factor. Van Dusen presented a complex question concerning the interrelationship between Fed R Civ P 17(b) and 28 USC §1404(a).

[145] 376 at 646; Platt v Minnesota Mining & Mfg Co, 376 US 240, 245 (1964).

[146] *See In re* McClelland Engrs Inc, 742 F2d 837, 839 (5th Cir 1984) (court of appeals refuses mandamus, but "request[s]" the district judge to certify his order denying forum non conveniens dismissal; district judge rested his order on "novel" grounds, declined to make a determination of the substantive law that would apply, and questioned controlling precedent; case was obviously a good candidate for mandamus, but the court of appeals was tactful), *cert denied,* 469 US 1228 (1985); Carlenstolpe v Merck & Co, 819 F2d 33 (2d Cir 1987) (denial of forum non conveniens dismissal not appealable; mandamus refused).

[147] *E.g.,* Northern Acceptance Trust 1065 v Gray, 423 F2d 653 (9th Cir), *cert denied,* 398 US 939 (1970). In Bankers Life & Casualty Co v Holland, 346 US 379, (1953), the Court noted that mandamus would be available to compel a district court to do its duty, while denying mandamus to review the transfer order under consideration.

[148] *E.g., In re* Chatman-Bey, 718 F2d 484 (DC Cir 1983); Fine v McGuire, 433 F2d 499 (DC Cir 1970).

[149] *E.g.,* Relf v Gasch, 511 F2d 804 (DC Cir 1975). Note, however, that courts of appeals differ about the meaning of *might* or *could* have been brought. This is a matter beyond the scope of this work. *See generally* Ellis v Great Southwestern Co, 646 F2d 1099 (5th Cir 1981).

[150] Van Dusen v Barrack, 376 US 612 (1964), and Platt v Minnesota Mining & Mfg

For example, mandamus will be available if the district judge applies state law rather than federal law to a 28 USC §1404(a) transfer motion,[151] disregards a forum selection clause, or misconstrues federal law provisions on venue.[152] However, mandamus probably will not lie to correct an erroneous determination that venue is not wrong under §1406(a), because that is an issue that could be dealt with on appeal from a final judgment.[153] It might be argued, however, that in a particular case early review on mandamus of a novel venue issue would produce a net savings in judicial resources.[154]

For example, in *Washington Public Utilities Group v United States District Court,*[155] the district judge had ordered a §1404(a) transfer of a massive civil securities case from Washington to Arizona. The judge had determined that liability in the case so clearly would affect almost all Washington taxpayers and utility consumers that a fair jury could not be obtained. The court of appeals denied relief, but did entertain the mandamus petition on the merits and render an opinion.

Co, 376 US 240 (1964), recognize this principle. *See also* AJ Indus v United States Dist Court, 503 F2d 384 (9th Cir 1974) (holding that mandamus is available when district judge considered "improper factors" when such factors are "closely intertwined with other contentions" reviewable by mandamus); Ellicott Mach Corp v Modern Welding Co, 502 F2d 178 (4th Cir 1974) (noting that appellate review by mandamus is appropriate when district courts fail to properly consider elements of transfer motion).

[151] A federal court sitting in diversity should apply federal law—28 USC §1404(a)—in deciding a motion to transfer a case to a venue provided in a contractual forum-selection clause. Stewart Org, Inc v Ricoh Corp, 487 US 22, 32 (1988). The reasoning of the case implies that any venue dispute in diversity will henceforth be governed by §1404(a), 487 US at 29-31, although the issue was narrowly stated, *id* at 24.

[152] Sunshine Beauty Supplies, Inc v United States Dist Court, 872 F2d 310 (9th Cir 1989) (mandamus issued to block transfer of a civil suit; district court failed to consider a forum selection clause, as mandated by Stewart Org, Inc v Ricoh Corp, 487 US 22 (1988); venue provisions of the Arbitration Act are mandatory).

[153] Large and duplicative litigation costs, no matter how great, generally will be insufficient to show the requisite prejudice where the parties can seek review of the issue after judgment. *See* Washington Pub Util Group v United States Dist Court, 843 F2d 319, 325 (9th Cir 1987). See also *In re* Dalton, 733 F2d 710 (10th Cir 1984), *cert dismissed,* 469 US 1185 (1985), in which the court held that the collateral order doctrine cannot be invoked to review a transfer order, because review would be available on appeal from a final judgment in the transferee circuit, and that mandamus would not be granted. Dalton contended that the transfer was granted without a hearing and that he therefore had been denied due process. The court of appeals applied the Ninth Circuit five-guideline test, as discussed at **§3.04.** It also acknowledged that a transfer order might be the subject of mandamus if entered without consideration of the proper factors. The court noted that, although no oral hearing had been held, the transfer determination had been made only after extensive briefing and exchange of written contentions, and the district judge had justified his order in a writing that discussed the applicable legal standards.

[154] *See In re* Cement Antitrust Litig, 688 F2d 1297 (9th Cir 1982), *affd sub nom* Arizona v United States Dist Court, 459 US 1191 (1983) (per curiam), discussed at **§3.04.** The only basis for compelling a district judge to grant a forum non conveniens dismissal is by means of mandamus. Castanho v Jackson Marine, Inc, 650 F2d 546 (5th Cir), *rehg denied,* 656 F2d 700 (5th Cir 1981).

[155] 843 F2d 319 (9th Cir 1987).

The court analyzed the case in light of the five elements discussed at **§3.04** and reaffirmed its rejection of the notion that the cost of retrying complex civil cases necessarily means that appeal is an inadequate remedy. However, the court expressly reaffirmed *Varsic v United States District Court,*[156] in which mandamus was granted to redress an improper cross-country venue change of a pension suit by an indigent social security recipient.

In re Regents of the University[157] raises unique issues of reviewability of transfer orders in civil cases. First, the Federal Circuit asserted mandamus jurisdiction, though denying relief on the merits, to review an order of the judicial panel on multidistrict litigation consolidating five pending law suits for coordinate pretrial proceedings. Second, in the ordinary case, where lawsuits are transferred there may be a question of which geographic circuit has jurisdiction. This will depend on when the mandamus petition is filed in relationship to when the actual case records are moved from the transferor to the transferee district. However, the Federal Circuit has nationwide jurisdiction over any action in the district courts, that is, among the types of cases specified by Congress as within Federal Circuit jurisdiction. Therefore, there can be no geographic bar to mandamus review by the Federal Circuit.

Some courts of appeals have permitted review of erroneous transfer orders under the interlocutory appeal provisions of 28 USC §1292(b).[158] Counsel therefore should seek certification under that provision. The petition for writ of mandamus would then be joined with an application for leave to appeal under §1292(b).[159] If a transfer order is wrongly granted to a judicial district in a different circuit, and counsel wants review by writ or appeal, a stay order must be sought in the district court; once the transfer of the case actually has occurred, the court of appeals for the circuit of the transferor court may lack jurisdiction.[160]

---

[156] 607 F2d 245, 251-52 (9th Cir 1979).

[157] 964 F2d 1128 (Fed Cir 1992).

[158] See discussion at **§2.09.** However, if an interlocutory appeal is not available because the district judge does not issue the required certification, review by mandamus may still be granted. Kasey v Molybdenum Corp of Am, 408 F2d 16 (9th Cir 1969). Review of a transfer order by mandamus is proper under extraordinary circumstances. Technitrol, Inc v McManus, 405 F2d 84 (8th Cir 1968), *cert denied,* 394 US 997 (1969). The court of appeals has the power to issue mandamus to redress a district judge's abuse of discretion in handling a transfer motion; §1292(b) relief is not available on particular facts. A. Olinick & Sons v Dempster Bros, 365 F2d 439 (2d Cir 1966).

[159] See discussion at **§3.15.**

[160] The possible future jurisdiction of a potential transferee circuit is not a sufficient basis for mandamus jurisdiction. General Elec Co v Byrne, 611 F2d 670 (7th Cir 1979) (per curiam) (court of appeals lacks authority to issue writ of mandamus to district judge in another circuit and possible future transfer of case to that circuit does not confer such authority); Petersen v Douglas County Bank & Trust Co, 940 F2d 1389 (10th Cir 1991) (§1404(a) transfer, even if erroneous, deprives the transferor appellate court of jurisdiction once the files have been physically transferred).

§3.08 —Disqualification of Judge or Counsel

Two federal statutory provisions govern disqualification of federal judges, 28 USC §§144 and 455.[161] Section 144 deals with bias or prejudice and requires the district judge to determine whether the allegations of bias are legally sufficient. Section 455, on the other hand, sets forth certain objective tests for disqualification, such as financial relationship to a party.[162] As might be expected, courts of appeals are more willing to entertain writ applications when the objective standards of §455 are involved than when it is alleged that the district judge has made a subjective error in assessing his or her own bias under §144.[163]

As noted in *In re Cement Antitrust Litigation,* the allegedly erroneous granting of a disqualification motion generally will not permit mandamus.[164] One argument against mandamus to review wrongful denial of a motion to disqualify is that a disqualification order is reviewable by appeal from a final judgment.[165] However, where the judge's action is clearly wrong, most courts of appeals have at one time or another issued the writ,[166] although the circuits are split on the issues.[167]

---

[161] See also **§3.13** for a discussion of mandamus to disqualify a judge in a criminal case.

[162] Discussion of the precise reach and application of these sections is beyond the scope of this work. *See generally* Liljeberg v Health Serv Acquisition Corp, 486 US 847 (1988); James O. Pearson, Jr, Annotation, *Mandamus as Remedy to Compel Disqualification of Federal Judge,* 56 ALR Fed 494, 496 (1982), and authorities cited there. This annotation also deals in detail with mandamus to compel disqualification.

[163] SCA Servs, Inc v Morgan, 557 F2d 110 (7th Cir 1977), recognizes the principle stated in the text. The Third Circuit granted mandamus in a case involving §455, Rapp v Van Dusen, 350 F2d 806 (3d Cir 1965), distinguishing Green v Murphy, 259 F2d 591 (3d Cir 1958), in which it had refused mandamus in a case involving §144.

[164] 688 F2d 1297, 1302 (9th Cir 1982), *affd sub nom* Arizona v United States Dist Court, 459 US 1191 (1983) (per curiam), discussed at **§3.04.** The Fifth Circuit denied appealability and refused mandamus to review a district judge's refusal to recuse himself in a complex multidistrict antitrust suit, *In re* Corrugated Container Antitrust Litig, 614 F2d 958 (5th Cir), *cert denied,* 449 US 888 (1980). The court did note, however, that courts often reach the merits of disqualification issues in determining whether mandamus will issue and that in "exceptional circumstances the writ will lie." *Id* 961 n 4. Compare the Fifth Circuit's grant of mandamus in a criminal case, discussed at **§3.13.**

[165] *See, e.g.,* Korer v Hoffman, 212 F2d 211 (7th Cir 1954) (criminal case). The matter is discussed, with citation of authorities, in *In re* Cement Antitrust Litig, 688 F2d 1297, 1302 (9th Cir 1982), *affd sub nom* Arizona v United States Dist Court, 459 US 1191 (1983) (per curiam). Some courts have held that review by appeal under 28 USC §1292(b) is available, if the district judge has granted permission. *See* **§2.09.** However, as *In re Cement Antitrust Litigation* holds, unavailability of the appeal remedy will not preclude mandamus.

[166] Disqualification cases holding mandamus appropriate in certain circumstances include Liddell v Board of Educ, 677 F2d 626 (8th Cir), *cert denied,* 459 US 877 (1982); *In re* United States, 666 F2d 690 (1st Cir 1981); *In re* International Business Mach Corp, 618 F2d 923 (2d Cir 1980). However, as noted in Annotation, *supra* note 162, at 494, the Third, Sixth, and Seventh Circuits have expressed greater reluctance to grant interlocutory review of disqualification denials.

[167] The circuit split on whether mandamus may be used to test a judge's refusal to

In summary, here as in other fields the petitioner for mandamus must show that the district judge committed an egregious abuse of discretion, entertained a misconception of the applicable legal standard,[168] or refused to consider a proper application, or that the failure to grant review by writ would entail serious and costly consequences for the judicial system.[169]

In re School Asbestos Litigation[170] provides an instructive and comprehensive review of mandamus law, policy, and tactics in the disqualification arena. The district judge had attended, with his expenses largely reimbursed, a conference characterized by the court of appeals as pro-plaintiff. The conference dealt with the dangers of asbestos in school buildings, which was the very subject of the lawsuit. In addition, the court of appeals held that it was improper for the district judge to refuse consideration of summary judgment motions without having set deadlines by which such motions must be filed. The court of appeal's opinion surveys a number of other defense contentions concerning the district judge's conduct of the case, and largely refuses to interfere in case management decisions made by the district judge; however, the court warns that some case management decisions may be reviewable by way of mandamus. Although the court ordered the district judge disqualified, it did not vacate the judge's earlier orders, reasoning that disqualification was required only by an appearance of partiality. The case reflects a court of appeals willingness to deal broadly with case management of complex litigation. The court noted that a mandamus petition should contain a reasoned statement of why an interlocutory appeal would not be an adequate remedy.

As noted at **§§2.04** and **2.05,** the Supreme Court has held that orders disqualifying counsel are not appealable in civil or criminal cases. This rationale denies appeal to orders refusing to disqualify counsel. However, the supposed rule has been shot through with exceptions, all created by courts of appeals entertaining mandamus petitions. These cases reflect the courts' concern that an otherwise valid judgment will have to be reversed if an error concerning counsel is allowed to stand. The tone of the decisions—at times sharply critical of

---

disqualify himself was noted in Martin v Knox, 112 S Ct 620 (1991) (Stevens, J, dissenting from denial of certiorari) (citing *In re* Beard, 811 F2d 818 (4th Cir 1987)) (refusal to disqualify reviewable on mandamus); Union Carbide Corp v United States Cutting Serv, Inc, 782 F2d 710 (7th Cir 1986) (same); Pittsburgh v Simmons, 729 F2d 953 (3d Cir 1984) (refusal to disqualify reviewable only after final judgment).

[168] In addition to cases cited above, see *In re* Union Leader Corp, 292 F2d 381 (1st Cir), *cert denied,* 368 US 927 (1961); Gladstein v McLaughlin, 230 F2d 762 (9th Cir 1955) (egregious case of judge conducting vendetta against trial lawyer). *See also In re* Cement Antitrust Litig, 688 F2d 1297, 1305-07 (9th Cir 1982), *affd sub nom* Arizona v United States Dist Court, 459 US 1191 (per curiam), *opinion supplemented,* 709 F2d 521 (9th Cir 1983).

[169] See discussion in *In re* Cement Antitrust Litig, 688 F2d 1297, 1301-05 (9th Cir 1982), *affd sub nom* Arizona v United States Dist Court, 459 US 1191 (1983) (per curiam).

[170] 977 F2d 764 (3d Cir 1992). See also Haines v Liggett Group, Inc, 975 F2d 81 (3d Cir 1992), discussed at **§3.06.**

counsel—also suggests impatience with lawyers who do not know when they should step aside. As the Seventh Circuit said, cases involving counsel disqualification can " 'break the mold' " of "the orthodox formula for mandamus."[171]

§3.09 —Constitutional Issues

Where the district judge's action threatens the exercise of a constitutional right, review by mandamus will be available more generally than otherwise. For example, in *In re Halkin,*[172] the district judge had forbidden public disclosure of discovery material obtained from a party to civil litigation. The court of appeals held that the First Amendment interest in public dissemination of this material was an important consideration in exercising its discretionary power to issue the writ. First Amendment issues posed by gag orders also are reviewed routinely on mandamus.[173] In addition, the Supreme Court has repeatedly held mandamus available to review a district judge's order improperly denying a civil litigant a jury trial as guaranteed by the Seventh Amendment.[174]

---

[171] *In re* Sandahl, 980 F2d 1118, 1119 (7th Cir 1992) (quoting Maloney v Plunkett, 854 F2d 152, 155 (7th Cir 1988)); mandamus available to review erroneous disqualification of law firm from representing defendant in commercial litigation; order is plainly wrong, and can impose substantial hardship on litigants; expansive statement of court of appeals power). *See also* Christensen v United States Dist Court, 844 F2d 694 (9th Cir 1988) (mandamus available to correct erroneous order disqualifying counsel in civil case); *In re* American Airlines, 972 F2d 605 (5th Cir 1992) (although orders denying motion to disqualify counsel are not appealable under §1291, *Firestone* itself confirms that mandamus might be available "in . . . exceptional circumstances" (Firestone Tire & Rubber Co v Risjord, 449 US 368, 378 n13 (1981)); participation by attorney in early stages of antitrust litigation on behalf of American Airlines, followed by attorney's entrance of appearance for opponent in antitrust suit is matter of sufficient importance to justify writ of mandamus overturning district judge's order denying motion to disqualify counsel) (Higginbotham, J); *In re* Dresser Indus, 972 F2d 540, 543 (5th Cir 1992) (mandamus granted to order disqualification of counsel, although standard of review is different than it would be on direct appeal; the right to relief must be "clear and undisputable" (citing Allied Chem Corp v Daiflon, Inc, 449 US 33, 35 (1980); opinion is highly critical of disqualified counsel)).

[172] 598 F2d 176 (DC Cir 1979). On the merits, *Halkin* has been questioned as giving too much publicity to discovery materials containing confidential data. *See, e.g.,* Tavoulareas v Washington Post Co, 737 F2d 1170 (DC Cir 1984). *See also* Seattle Times Co v Rhinehart, 467 US 20, 25 (upholding public access to discovery materials), *cert denied,* 467 US 1230 (1984).

[173] *See, e.g.,* CBS, Inc v Young, 522 F2d 234 (6th Cir 1975). *Cf* Sacramento Bee v United States Dist Court, 656 F2d 477 (9th Cir 1981) (mandamus not proper to compel district judge to amend possibly constitutionally erroneous trial closure order when judge had carefully balanced competing interests), *cert denied,* 456 US 983 (1982).

[174] The leading case is Beacon Theatres, Inc v Westover, 359 US 500 (1959). The district judge had set the trial of equitable claims ahead of the legal claims, thus compromising petitioner's right to a jury trial. Another case involving use of the writ to enforce the Seventh Amendment is Dairy Queen, Inc v Wood, 369 US 469 (1962).

A variety of other constitutional questions have also been found appropriate for resolution by mandamus. For example, in *In re Justices of the Supreme Court of Puerto Rico,*[175] bar association members in Puerto Rico sued to challenge the mandatory bar membership and dues requirements. Among the defendants were the Justices of the Supreme Court of Puerto Rico, who have an adjudicative capacity with respect to attorney discipline. The First Circuit held that the justices' claim was the stuff of which classic mandamus petitions are made: it was claimed that the district court lacked jurisdiction over them under the United States Const art III, because the justices were only nominal parties with whom the plaintiffs had no real case or controversy. The court concluded that mandamus was appropriate to resolve so weighty an issue, but then decided the merits on nonconstitutional grounds.[176] However, the other defendants—the bar association and bar foundation—were held not entitled to mandamus to obtain interlocutory review of their nonconstitutional contentions.

§3.10 —Other Issues

Roche,[177] *La Buy,*[178] and *Schlagenhauf*[179] put the law of extraordinary writs into an extraordinary posture. The words courts of appeals use to justify issuance or denial of a writ are vague enough to leave considerable discretion in appellate judges' hands. Some of the cases seem to be results in search of a rationale. The lawyer considering whether to seek a writ should, after reviewing the material in this section, devise a legal research strategy dealing with the substantive issue involved to see whether the law relating to that issue has been developed in part through the use of extraordinary writs. It is obviously beyond the scope of a work on appellate procedure to treat every such field in detail. However, one would find material on the use of extraordinary writs in works dealing with judicial disqualification, the right to jury trial, and so on. If counsel has access to a computer legal research service, the task of searching for precedent is simplified. One can devise a search that describes the legal issue and then add the words *mandamus, extraordinary writ,* and *prohibition* to the search request. Further consideration of the decision whether to seek mandamus appears at **§3.15.**

§3.11 Mandamus and Prohibition in Criminal Cases—General Principles

The general principles that govern issuance of the writ are the same in civil and criminal cases, with an important difference. The Supreme Court and the courts of appeals have stressed time and again that the final judgment rule is of particular importance in criminal cases. The accused's petition will meet the

---

[175] 695 F2d 17 (1st Cir 1982).

[176] *Id* 20-25.

[177] Roche v Evaporated Milk Assn, 319 US 21 (1943).

[178] La Buy v Howes Leather Co, 352 US 249 (1957).

[179] Schlagenhauf v Holder, 379 US 104 (1964).

argument that there is almost always an adequate remedy by appeal and that interlocutory appellate rights are narrowly confined by Supreme Court precedent.[180]

The government as petitioner must look to the standards set out in *Will v United States.*[181] A district judge had ordered the government to provide, by bill of particulars, a list of the witnesses who would testify in the government's case-in-chief. The Seventh Circuit issued the writ, directing the district judge to vacate this portion of his order.[182] The Supreme Court reversed, without dissent.[183]

The Court's opinion, by Chief Justice Warren, reaffirmed that the "policy against piecemeal appeals takes on added weight in criminal cases, where the defendant is entitled to a speedy resolution of the charges against him."[184] Moreover, the government could not use mandamus to circumvent statutory and constitutional limitations upon its right to appeal, nor is the case against permitting the writ to be used as a substitute for interlocutory appeal "made less compelling . . . by the fact that the Government has no later right to appeal."[185] This means that the government cannot plead inadequacy of the appellate remedy as a controlling reason for issuance of the writ. Finally, the Court noted that it had "never approved the use of the writ to review an interlocutory procedural order in a criminal case."[186]

---

[180] See discussion at **§2.04.** *See also* Phillip E. Hassman, Annotation, *Propriety of Issuing Writ of Mandamus in Federal Criminal Proceedings,* 29 ALR Fed 218 (1976).

[181] 389 US 90 (1967).

[182] The court of appeals had initially denied the petition, and then inexplicably entered a minute order granting it. *Id* 94 n2. The court of appeals' terseness no doubt helped influence the Supreme Court to vacate and remand for further proceedings in light of its opinion.

[183] The opinion was not unanimous. Justice Black concurred and Justice Marshall did not participate.

[184] *Will,* 389 US at 96.

[185] *Id* 97. As noted at **§2.11,** the double jeopardy clause of the Fifth Amendment places limits upon the appellate jurisdiction of the courts of appeals. This has been reaffirmed when the government has sought mandamus to challenge a district judge's action in terminating a criminal proceeding after jeopardy has attached. In Fong Foo v United States, 369 US 141 (1962), *revg* 366 US 959 (1961), the Supreme Court reversed a grant of mandamus. The court of appeals had directed the district judge to set aside judgments of acquittal entered after seven days of jury trial and to retry the defendants. The Court held that such action violated the defendants' double jeopardy rights. In United States v Ellison, 684 F2d 664 (10th Cir 1982), a panel of the Tenth Circuit stayed a judge's order of acquittal because it was not clear from the record that the district judge actually had evaluated the government's evidence and found it insufficient. However, in a brief order, the en banc court vacated this opinion the following day, no doubt because it was clearly contrary to *Fong Foo.* 722 F2d 595 (10th Cir 1982). In United States v Ember, 726 F2d 522 (9th Cir 1984), the court denied the government's petition for mandamus to correct an allegedly erroneous grant of acquittal, relying on the double jeopardy clause.

[186] Will v United States, 389 US 90, 98 (1967), with the qualification that review would be available if the interlocutory order "ha[d] the effect of a dismissal." The government, which in most instances has no direct appeal from discovery orders in criminal cases,

Despite entreaties in influential publications for a narrow reading of *Will,*[187] the courts of appeals have been sparing in the use of mandamus in criminal cases.

§3.12 —Government Petitions

In *Will v United States,*[188] the Court noted that mandamus has issued to correct action of a district judge that seriously interfered with the government's right to initiate a prosecution or that threatened to deprive it of the benefits of a conviction. Such cases do not, however, involve interlocutory procedural orders.

The United States Court of Appeals for the Second Circuit has been confronted with several government applications for mandamus that take court of appeals' power to the outer limits suggested in *Will.* In *United States v Lasker,*[189] the district judge dismissed seven indictments, holding that he was required to do so under the court of appeals' rules regarding prompt disposition of criminal cases. Because the cases had arisen prior to the 1970 amendment to 18 USC §3731,[190] the court of appeals had no jurisdiction to review the dismissals by way of appeal. Noting that the case did not involve an interlocutory procedural order, nor implicate the defendants' double jeopardy rights, the court turned to the supervisory mandamus standards of *La Buy* and *Schlagenhauf.*[191] There, it found ample justification for issuing the writ to clarify the meaning and application of rules that the court of appeals had itself promulgated.

In *United States v Dooling,*[192] the Second Circuit issued the writ to prevent a district judge from entering an order dismissing an indictment after a jury ver-

---

obtained review by mandamus in United States v United States Dist Court, 717 F2d 478 (9th Cir 1983). The district judge had ordered the prosecutor to comply with the defendant's Freedom of Information Act requests, without regard to the relevance of many such documents to the pending criminal charge.

[187] Comment, *Supervisory and Advisory Mandamus Under the All Writs Act,* 86 Harv L Rev 595, 624-28 (1973).

[188] 389 US 90, 97-98 (1967), citing authorities.

[189] 481 F2d 229 (2d Cir 1973), *cert denied,* 415 US 975 (1974).

[190] *See* **§2.11.** Because Congress has progressively expanded the government's right to appeal in criminal cases, there are many fewer occasions for mandamus than formerly. It should be noted that in *Will,* the Court cautioned that §3731 is presumptively the sole basis for the government to secure appellate review in criminal cases.

[191] La Buy v Howes Leather Co, 352 US 249 (1957) and Schlagenhauf v Holder, 379 US 104 (1964), discussed at **§3.02.** In United States v Hughes, 413 F2d 1244 (5th Cir 1969), *vacated as moot sub nom* United States v Gifford-Hill-American, Inc, 397 US 93 (1970), the court of appeals held that supervisory mandamus was appropriate to construe a newly amended discovery provision of the Federal Rules of Civil Procedure.

[192] 406 F2d 192 (2d Cir), *cert denied,* 395 US 911 (1969). *In re* United States, 834 F2d 283 (2d Cir), *granting mandamus to overturn* United States v Gallo, 654 F Supp 463 (EDNY 1987), is another misguided appellate effort to curb the discretion of a district judge to assure fairness in a complex criminal case by ordering pretrial disclosure of statements made by defendants and alleged co-conspirators to persons who were not government agents. The court of appeals issued mandamus on the government's petition. *Compare* United States v Santtini, 963 F2d 585 (3d Cir 1992) (parties may proceed alter-

dict of guilty. A number of circumstances had convinced the district judge that the defendants' trials were unfair. The district judge had, however, merely written a memorandum indicating his intention to enter a dismissal, and had not entered any order to that effect. The court of appeals opinion makes clear its utter disagreement, on the merits, with the district judge's proposed course of action. It also notes that no Federal Rule of Criminal Procedure appeared to justify the dismissals.

However, under 18 USC §3731 as it then stood, the government would not have had the right to appeal from a postverdict dismissal. Although the Second Circuit ostensibly acknowledged the limitations imposed by *Will* under such circumstances, and despite the fact there was no actual order to review, it issued the writ and directed the district judge to enter judgment on the verdict. *Dooling* represents the furthest reach of a mandamus on the government's petition. Its result and rationale are, to say the least, controversial.[193]

To the same effect is *United States v Weinstein,*[194] in which the district judge dismissed an indictment "in the interest of justice"[195] after verdict and sentence. However, the district judge had said that he had doubts about his power to enter a dismissal, and had for that reason imposed sentence. The Second Circuit, relying upon *Dooling,* issued the writ.

Dooling and *Weinstein,* despite the breadth of the court's language, may be justified by noting that in neither instance did the district judge have authority under the Federal Rules of Criminal Procedure to take the challenged action. Neither case involved interlocutory review of a type that would directly infringe either double jeopardy or speedy trial rights.[196]

In sum, the government may be entitled to mandamus, if it acts promptly,[197] if the district judge exceeds powers granted by statute or federal rule. Thus, mandamus will lie to prevent a judge from authorizing pretrial depositions of government witnesses under circumstances not contemplated by the Federal

---

natively with application for writ and interlocutory appeal, leaving it to court to choose which avenue is most appropriate; court holds that challenged order of district judge that precluded federal law enforcement agents from arresting the subject did not qualify as an injunction and was not an appealable collateral order, but was reviewable upon writ of prohibition; writ granted).

[193] See discussion at **§2.11.** *See also* Phillip E. Hassman, Annotation, *Propriety of Issuing Writ of Mandamus in Federal Criminal Proceedings,* 29 ALR Fed 218, 253-54 (1976). *Dooling* was distinguished in United States v Sam Goody, Inc, 675 F2d 17 (2d Cir 1982).

[194] 452 F2d 704 (2d Cir 1971), *cert denied,* 406 US 917 (1972).

[195] *Id* 707.

[196] *See* **§2.11.**

[197] In United States v Carter, 270 F2d 521 (9th Cir 1959), the government's mandamus petition, seeking to vacate sentencing orders, was denied in part because the government had delayed filing and the defendants had come to rely upon the challenged orders.

Rules.[198] A district judge may be prevented from accepting, over the government's objection, a guilty plea to a lesser offense than that charged in the indictment or information, because Fed R Crim P 11 confers no such power.[199] Because the Jencks Act, 18 USC §3500, gives a defendant the right to prior statements of a government witness only after he or she testifies, a district judge may be precluded by mandamus from ordering earlier production.[200] When a district judge held, in effect, that he possessed no power to hold a hearing to determine the source of a defendant's bail money, the court of appeals held mandamus was a proper means to tell him that he did have such power;[201] however, the court did not tell the judge how the discretion should be exercised in a particular case.

The court held mandamus available to restrict a district judge's actions in sua sponte ordering discovery of Selective Service files of fugitive draft refusal defendants.[202] The judge had planned to turn the files over to a noted law professor who presumably would use them to make dispositive motions and thus help the judge clear his docket of these cases.[203] The Second Circuit did not absolutely prohibit the judge from seeking to arrange for review of such cases, but laid down rules respecting the proper conduct of such review. And, despite the Supreme Court's warnings concerning the unavailability of mandamus to circumvent the nonappealability of interlocutory orders relating to search and seizure, the Sixth Circuit reviewed by writ a district judge's holding concerning warrantless national security wiretapping. The court termed the issue one of first impression for an appellate court, and of great constitutional significance.[204]

---

[198] *In re* United States, 348 F2d 624 (1st Cir 1965).

[199] United States v Gray, 448 F2d 164 (9th Cir 1971), *cert denied,* 405 US 926 (1972).

[200] United States v McMillen, 489 F2d 229 (7th Cir 1972), *cert denied,* 410 US 955 (1973). However, it is routine for counsel in criminal cases to agree to early Jencks Act production as part of an overall discovery arrangement approved by the trial court. A district judge can evidence displeasure in many ways with prosecutors who refuse to enter into such arrangements, and a wise prosecutor would avoid such a confrontation.

[201] United States v Nebbia, 357 F2d 303 (2d Cir 1966).

[202] United States v Weinstein, 511 F2d 622 (2d Cir), *cert denied,* 422 US 1042 (1975), annotated in 29 ALR Fed 207 (1976). The court of appeals did not, however, forbid all orders with respect to absent defendants. In a later case, Judge Weinstein entertained and granted a motion to dismiss in one of the cases, United States v Salzmann, 417 F Supp 1139 (EDNY), *affd,* 548 F2d 395 (2d Cir 1976). *See also* United States v RMI Co, 599 F2d 1183 (3d Cir 1979) (disagreeing with *Weinstein*).

[203] There were other examples of district judges exercising the power to dismiss the cases of fugitive Selective Service defendants. *See, e.g.,* United States v Daneals, 370 F Supp 1289 (WDNY 1974).

[204] United States v United States Dist Court, 444 F2d 651 (6th Cir 1971), *affd,* 407 US 297 (1972). The holding seems extraordinary. The district judge held the electronic surveillance unlawful. This triggered the government's obligation to disclose it to the defense or suffer a dismissal of its case. *See generally* Alderman v United States, 394 US 165 (1969). At that point, the government would have had a remedy by appeal. There is, therefore, no basis other than the extraordinary, or perhaps very interesting, nature of the issue presented for issuing the writ. The Supreme Court noted the mandamus

The Seventh Circuit granted the government's petition when a district judge had ordered a nonjury trial in a criminal case with the defendant's consent but over the government's objection. This was beyond the court's power under Fed R Crim P 23, the court of appeals held, and therefore mandamus was appropriate.[205]

In *United States v United States District Court,*[206] the Ninth Circuit returned to an extremely broad formulation of its power and discretion in mandamus cases. The defendants were charged with producing pornographic films in which a 16-year-old girl had a starring role. They asserted their good faith belief that she was not a minor and the district judge denied a pretrial government motion in limine to exclude such evidence.

The government sought mandamus. No appeal was possible under 18 USC §3731 because the order did not exclude evidence. The order was clearly interlocutory. The court of appeals reviewed the district judge's order on the merits on the government's petition repeated language from the cases about mandamus as a one-time only device to settle important questions, and referred to *advisory* mandamus.[207]

On the merits, the court found that a scienter requirement was dictated by the First Amendment and that the district judge had been correct. The case had been argued on April 13 and decided on September 29, thus entailing a delay (counting time for briefing and postopinion petitions and suggestions) of almost a year in this criminal trial. Entertaining government mandamus petitions after the trial judge has denied motions in limine in criminal cases has become rather usual in the Ninth Circuit and implicates serious questions about circumvention of the congressional limits on government appeals and the constitutional guaranty of speedy trial.[208]

It would, therefore, be an overstatement to say that the government's right to mandamus is so sharply limited as to be insignificant. Of course, the steady expansion of §3731 since 1970 and the Supreme Court's clarification of the double jeopardy clause have reduced the government's need for mandamus.[209] Only rarely does one find a case in which the government is granted mandamus

---

issue, but passed over it by noting that the defendants below did not object to interlocutory review. In United States v Kane, 646 F2d 4 (1st Cir 1981), the court denied mandamus to compel the district judge to vacate orders directing disclosure of information to the defense. The district judge had said that he might prohibit the introduction of evidence on certain issues if the disclosures were not made. This prospect of future exclusion did not confer appellate jurisdiction under 18 USC §3731, and mandamus was inappropriate.

[205] United States v Igoe, 331 F2d 766 (7th Cir 1964), *cert denied,* 380 US 942 (1965). The government had refused to proceed to trial without a jury and the district judge dismissed for want of prosecution. Today, the dismissal would be reviewable under 18 USC §3731. *See* **§2.11.**

[206] 858 F2d 534 (9th Cir 1988).

[207] *Id* 537.

[208] *See generally* Douglas L. Colbert, *The Motion in Limine in Politically Sensitive Cases: Silencing the Defendant at Trial,* 39 Stan L Rev 1271 (1987).

[209] *See* **§2.11.**

without a clear showing that the district judge acted without, or beyond his or her, power.[210] The Second Circuit has denied a government petition claiming serious abuse of discretion by a district judge in refusing to reinstate an indictment dismissed for want of prosecution.[211] In the days before a motion granting a new trial was appealable under §3731, the government's petition for mandamus to set aside a new trial grant was denied by the District of Columbia Circuit.[212] The court of appeals did note that a juror's failure to disclose important information on voir dire was the proper subject of a timely new trial motion made by a defendant. It therefore distinguished cases in which mandamus was granted to overturn new trial orders entered on the trial judge's own motion or based upon grounds not contemplated by the Federal Rules.[213]

§3.13 —Defendant Petitions

The defendant is also constrained by the strong judicial preference for finality in criminal cases. The Supreme Court has, as noted in Chapter 2, grudgingly and narrowly defined the scope of interlocutory appeal, and the courts of appeals have policed these boundaries by limiting the use of extraordinary writs.[214]

---

[210] Other than the cases cited in the text, mandamus has been issued to correct a district judge's abuse of discretion in *In re* United States, 565 F2d 173 (1st Cir 1977) (mandamus to vacate new trial order based upon allegedly improper factors; it is questionable whether this case is good authority after Allied Chem Corp v Daiflon, Inc, 449 US 33 (1980), discussed at **§3.03**); United States v Werker, 535 F2d 198 (2d Cir), *cert denied,* 429 US 926 (1976) (mandamus to prevent district judge from communicating probable sentence to defendant considering guilty plea). *But see* United States v United States Dist Court, 693 F2d 68 (9th Cir 1982) (refusing to follow *In re United States*).

The government has a high success rate when it can show that the judge has acted without power or beyond his or her power. *See, e.g.,* United States v Denson, 603 F2d 1143 (5th Cir 1979) (mandamus to correct illegal sentence of probation); United States v Busic, 592 F2d 13 (2d Cir 1978), rejected by, Government of VI v Douglas, 812 F2d 822 (3d Cir 1987) (mandamus to correct illegal sentence); *In re* United States, 608 F2d 76 (2d Cir 1979), *cert denied,* 446 US 908 (1980). Also, as discussed at **§3.11,** mandamus may be available at the instance of a third-party media representative to challenge trial closure orders. *See, e.g.,* United States v Chagra, 701 F2d 354 (5th Cir 1983); United States v Sherman, 581 F2d 1358 (9th Cir 1978).

[211] United States v DiStefano, 464 F2d 845 (2d Cir 1972). *See also* United States v Hester, 325 F2d 654 (9th Cir 1963) (mandamus not proper to review dismissal for want of prosecution under the particular facts presented).

[212] *In re* United States, 598 F2d 233 (DC Cir 1979). To the same effect is United States v Sam Goody, Inc, 675 F2d 17 (2d Cir 1982); United States v Dior, 671 F2d 351 (9th Cir 1982); United States v Winner, 666 F2d 447 (10th Cir 1981).

[213] *In re* United States, 598 F2d 233 (DC Cir 1979). The court also distinguished United States v Smith, 331 US 469 (1947), in which the Supreme Court held that mandamus was appropriate to vacate a new trial order entered by the district judge on his own motion after the seven-day period mandated by Fed R Crim P 33 had expired.

[214] *See, e.g.,* United States v Mehrmanesh, 652 F2d 766 (9th Cir 1980).

Thus, in *Roche v Evaporated Milk Assn,*[215] the district court struck defendants' pleas in abatement, in effect denying pretrial motions addressed to the grand jury's power to return an indictment. The Supreme Court held that mandamus was not a proper remedy, even though an error in overruling the motions would require the defendants to go through a lengthy antitrust criminal trial.

In *Platt v Minnesota Mining & Manufacturing Co,*[216] the defendant in a criminal antitrust case petitioned for and obtained mandamus from the Seventh Circuit directing the district judge to transfer the case to another district under Fed R Crim P 21(b). The Supreme Court reversed. The government did not, in the Supreme Court, challenge the availability of mandamus in any case where the district judge used an improper factor in deciding a transfer motion. The Court did, however, admonish the court of appeals that it was improper to issue a writ directing that the district judge grant a transfer. At most, the court of appeals should have "determine[d] the appropriate criteria and then [left] their application to the trial judge on remand."[217]

The change of venue provisions of the Federal Rules of Criminal Procedure, like those of the Judicial Code,[218] may raise difficult questions of law that will be reviewable on mandamus. In *Jones v Gasch,*[219] a criminal defendant moved for transfer under Fed R Crim P 21(b). The district judge denied the motion. The court of appeals, by a divided vote, refused to issue the writ but did hear the case on the merits and wrote a lengthy opinion on the law of transfer under what was then a relatively new amendment to the rules. The court noted, however, that the district judge had not used an improper factor in denying transfer and his evaluation of the motion could not be termed a *plain abuse of discretion.*[220]

Other cases granting mandamus on a defendant's motion involve either clear abdication of a judicial duty imposed by statute or the Federal Rules of Criminal Procedure or interference with a defendant's right that is collateral to the main litigation yet of conceded importance in the administration of justice.[221]

---

[215] 319 US 21 (1943), discussed at **§3.02.**

[216] 376 US 240 (1964).

[217] *Id* 245.

[218] *See* **§3.07.**

[219] 404 F2d 1231 (DC Cir 1967), *cert denied,* 390 US 1029 (1968). *See also* Hoffa v Gray, 323 F2d 178 (6th Cir) (mandamus not available to review denial of motions for change of venue and for dismissal), *cert denied,* 375 US 907 (1963).

[220] 404 F2d at 1241-42.

[221] *See, e.g., In re* Arvedon, 523 F2d 914 (1st Cir 1975) (district judge refused to accord rights to transfer and to plead guilty under Fed R Crim P 20 and 11; writ granted); *In re* Evans, 524 F2d 1004 (5th Cir 1975) (district judge refused to admit defense counsel pro hac vice in federal criminal prosecution; writ granted); Munoz v United States Dist Court, 446 F2d 434 (9th Cir 1971), *cert & prohibition denied,* 404 US 1057, 1059 (1972) (similar case to Evans); Chase v Robson, 435 F2d 1059 (7th Cir 1970) (district judge entered gag order against defendants and counsel in highly publicized case without making specific findings of potential harm from public discussion; writ granted). *Cf* United States v West, 672 F2d 796 (10th Cir) (mandamus issued to compel district judge to vacate order directing production of Justice Department files in connection with new trial hearing in criminal case), *cert denied,* 457 US 1133 (1982). Even if a constitutional

For example, in *In re Faulkner,*[222] the court of appeals granted mandamus on the defendants' petition to compel a district judge to recuse himself from trial of a criminal case in which his impartiality might reasonably be questioned. The judge was related to someone who had been involved in transactions like those alleged in the indictment. The panel did not discuss the basis for its view that mandamus was available. However, the merits turned upon the recent and broad strictures of *Liljeberg v Health Services Acquisition Corp,*[223] and the decision rests upon settled Fifth Circuit mandamus principles.

Occasionally, courts of appeals have interceded by mandamus in grand jury proceedings when no other remedy was available. A grant jury witness who wishes to obtain review of a refusal to answer or to produce documents must generally do so by appeal from an order of contempt.[224] However, clear abuse of discretion by the district judge—particularly involving a protected interest such as the right to counsel—may be reviewed on mandamus,[225] and a nonparty privilege holder (or someone in an analogous position) may be able to obtain the writ.[226] For example, *In re Oswalt,*[227] holds mandamus appropriate to challenge an order upholding a grand jury subpoena because the movant was required by the district court to turn over documents he claimed were protected by the privilege against self-incrimination, without any opportunity to test the validity of his constitutional position in contempt litigation. The message is that even though review by appeal is the ordinary and preferred path, the petition may be granted if an about-to-be-loosed cat cannot be rebagged.[228]

§3.14 Court of Appeals Jurisdiction to Issue Other Writs

Under limited circumstances, the court of appeals can issue a writ that is not a substitute for an appeal. The courts of appeals are not subject to the art III

---

issue is present, mandamus may be denied if the court of appeals concludes that appeal from a final judgment is an adequate remedy. Oswald v McGarr, 620 F2d 1190 (7th Cir 1980).

[222] 856 F2d 716 (5th Cir 1988).

[223] 486 US 847 (1988).

[224] *See* **§2.03.**

[225] *In re* Weiss, 596 F2d 1185 (4th Cir 1979).

[226] Velsicol Chem Corp v Parsons, 561 F2d 671 (7th Cir 1977), *cert denied,* 435 US 942 (1978). *See also In re* Vargas, 723 F2d 1461 (10th Cir 1983).

[227] 607 F2d 645 (5th Cir 1979).

[228] The Second Circuit declined to issue mandamus to review a district court's order denying an injunction against a grand jury proceeding, saying that the district court had the power to decide and that mandamus was, therefore, inappropriate. *In re* Doe, 546 F2d 498 (2d Cir 1976). This case sharply contrasts with those cited at **§3.12,** in which the Second Circuit has reached out to issue mandamus in cases not presenting any question of a district judge's power.

limitation, relied upon in *Marbury v Madison,*[229] upon issuance of extraordinary writs other than in aid of their appellate jurisdiction, because they are inferior courts whose jurisdiction the Congress may constitutionally prescribe.[230] However, jurisdiction to issue such writs is limited by statute, and cases involving extraordinary writs other than as substitutes for appeal are rare.

In *Frazier v Heebe,*[231] an attorney sought a writ of prohibition from the Fifth Circuit restraining application to him of a federal district court rule forbidding lawyers with no office in the state where the court sits from being regular members of the federal court's bar. The Fifth Circuit remanded the case to the district court for decision and then affirmed that court's ruling. The Supreme Court reversed on the merits, but did not question the propriety of using an extraordinary writ to challenge a district court rule or practice that was not case-specific.

The court of appeals can issue a writ to enforce its own mandate.[232] If a district court, administrative agency, or administrator refuses or fails to follow a direction the court of appeals has given, mandamus is a proper remedy.[233] The writ ensures more expeditious relief than would be available by appeal.

Federal Rule of Appellate Procedure 22(a) explicitly recognizes that judges of the courts of appeals have original jurisdiction to issue writs of habeas corpus under 28 USC 2241(a), but that such jurisdiction seldom will be exercised. If a habeas corpus petition is filed with a court of appeals judge, it generally will be transferred to the appropriate federal district court.[234]

---

[229] US (1 Cranch) 137 (1803), discussed at **§3.01.**

[230] US Const art III.

[231] 482 US 641 (1987).

[232] For a complete discussion of the court of appeals' mandate and the *mandate rule,* see **§10.15.**

[233] In Silverman v NLRB, 543 F2d 428 (2d Cir 1976), the court of appeals issued mandamus to the NLRB and its regional director to enforce its own judgment of five years previously. Similarly, the Court of Customs and Patent Appeals (now the Court of Appeals for the Federal Circuit) may direct a mandamus to the Commissioner of Patents & Trademarks. McNally v Mossinghoff, 673 F2d 1253 (CC P 1982). For a discussion of the jurisdiction of the Court of Appeals for the Federal Circuit, see **§4.14.** Even though a litigant has a remedy by appeal, mandamus is available to compel a district judge to comply with the court of appeals' earlier order. Citibank NA v Fullam, 580 F2d 82 (3d Cir 1978). Also holding that mandamus is the proper means to compel compliance with a mandate is Estate of Whitlock v Commissioner, 547 F2d 506 (10th Cir 1976), *cert denied,* 430 US 916 (1977).

[234] As the Advisory Committee Notes to Fed R App P 22(a) state:

> Title 28 USC §2241(a) authorizes circuit judges to issue the writ of habeas corpus. Section 2241(b), however, authorizes a circuit judge to decline to entertain an application and to transfer it to the appropriate district court, and this is the usual practice. . . . Title 28 USC §2253 seems clearly to contemplate that once an application is presented to a district judge and is denied by him, the remedy is an appeal from the order of denial. But the language of 28 USC §2241 seems to authorize a second original application to a circuit judge following a denial by a district judge. In re Gersing, 79 US App DC 245, 145 F2d 481 (DC Cir, 1944) and Chapman v Teets, 241 F2d 186 (9th Cir, 1957) acknowledge the availability of

§3.15 How to Seek or Oppose a Writ—General Principles

Deciding to seek mandamus is, as the conflicting caselaw has already shown, a matter of discretion and judgment and not of strict law. Judge Charles Clark, according to his clerks, bemoaned "procedural particularism," by which he meant the studied misinterpretation of a procedural rule to justify an unstated preference for a substantive result.[235] The landscape of mandamus jurisprudence is littered with evidence of procedural particularism. The court of appeals often will deny the writ in ostensible compliance with restrictive dicta from countless mandamus cases, when it is clear to everyone that the court is really sending a message about the merits. This becomes clear when in another case the writ is granted, or at least considered on the merits, simply because the court finds the substantive issue compelling and wants to express an opinion on it.

The advocate who is considering expending valuable resources in pursuit of mandamus must first consider the justice of his or her cause. Are the merits attractive? Will a palpable injustice be done if the district judge is permitted to continue along a particular course? Does a premature effort at mandamus lable the petitioner as vexatious, and will the label still stick when the time comes to appeal on the merits? Only after debating such questions can one turn to the relatively open-textured and flexible law of mandamus that has been discussed earlier in this chapter.

Because a petition for mandamus can, as shown below, be drafted with relatively little expenditure of time, the investment decision is much simpler than that faced by a party considering a full-fledged appeal, as discussed in Chapter 5. As the discussion below emphasizes, the petition is a summary of position. If the court orders a response and sets a briefing schedule, there will be time for fuller briefing. By then, it will be clear that the issue is being taken seriously and that the expenditure of resources is worth it.

The party seeking mandamus or prohibition must file a petition, in accordance with Fed R App P 21(a)[236] and any applicable local rules. Every circuit has some particular rule on writ petitions, dealing with issues ranging from the proper naming of parties, to where and how the issues presented must be stated, to routing the petition through the court.

Under Fed R App P 21(a), the petition is rather like a civil complaint, with a statement of facts and issues, a summary of why the writ would be properly issued, and the legal rules that govern the merits. The mandamus petition is

---

> such a procedure. But the procedure is ordinarily a waste of time for all involved, and the final sentence [of Fed R App P 22(a)] attempts to discourage it.

A court of appeals, as opposed to an individual circuit judge, has no original habeas jurisdiction. See cases discussed in the Advisory Committee Notes to Fed R App P 22(a).

[235] Recalled by Charles Alan Wright and Harry Reasoner, two of Judge Clark's most distinguished law clerks.

[236] The full text of Fed R App P 21(a) is in **app A.**

not a full brief. Federal Rule of Appellate Procedure 21(b) provides that no response may be filed unless the court directs. Therefore, the petition is a necessarily brief statement to convince a busy judge or judges that the matter is serious enough for plenary consideration. It is, in this sense, like a suggestion of the appropriateness of rehearing en banc or a petition for certiorari.

The petition must be served on one's opponent and on the district judge, who is the nominal respondent though seldom the real party in interest. If the constitutionality of a federal statute is drawn into question, Fed R App P 44 requires notice of this to the clerk, who in turn will notify the Attorney General.

§3.16 —Drafting the Writ

Typically, the petition is screened by the clerk's office and referred to a panel of judges for review. Unless the panel orders a response, the petition is dead. Oral argument is almost never granted at this stage. Docket pressure limits the time that can be given to reviewing the petition. Therefore, it must be concise, persuasive, and complete. It must, without distorting the facts or law, show clearly and in the fewest possible words why a writ should issue. It must include, in easily accessible form, all the relevant portions of the record, so that the reader is not forced to scurry around to obtain a sense of what occurred in the district court. It must cite the relevant law. Because many if not most courts of appeals judges rely upon staff attorneys or law clerks to prepare a summary of writ petitions, the petition must be so arranged that it permits easy summarization.

First, the caption. Many circuits require that the petition be styled simply in re [name of petitioner], without mentioning the district judge. In such a circuit, however, it is wise to name the real parties in interest in the caption. Thus, in *Jones v Smith,* if Jones petitioned for mandamus, the caption would read:

IN THE UNITED STATES COURT OF APPEALS
FOR THE [NAME] CIRCUIT

In re Mary Jones, Petitioner
(Mary Jones, Plaintiff
v
William Smith, Defendant)

No. [court of appeals number]
(No. [district court number])

PETITION FOR WRIT OF MANDAMUS TO THE
UNITED STATES DISTRICT COURT FOR THE
[NAME] DISTRICT OF [NAME]

In a court of appeals that does not follow this rule, the form would be:

IN THE UNITED STATES COURT OF APPEALS
FOR THE [NAME] CIRCUIT

Mary Smith, Petitioner
(Plaintiff)

v

Hon. Cynthia Doe, United States
District Judge for the [Name]
District of [Name], Respondent
William Smith, Defendant

No. [court of appeals number]
(No. [district court number])

PETITION FOR WRIT OF MANDAMUS TO THE
UNITED STATES DISTRICT COURT FOR THE
[NAME] DISTRICT OF [NAME]

The petition should consist of numbered paragraphs, rather like a civil complaint. One difference will be that the paragraphs may be lengthier than in the typical civil complaint and will contain legal argument as well as factual material. The "parts of the record" required to be attached should be subdivided into numbered or lettered appendixes with tabs and referenced in the body of the petition for ease of access. The various parts of the petitions should be identified with subheads in capital letters, again for ease of reference. These subheads would include, in a typical petition: *Jurisdiction, Nature of the Case, Challenged Order, Factual Background, Why the Writ Should Issue.* If the petition is more than 10 pages long, it would be best to put the caption on a separate cover page, and have a table of contents and table of authorities. There must, of course, be a certificate of service as required by Fed R App P 21(a).

The petition should begin with a statement of jurisdiction, just like a civil complaint under Fed R Civ P 8(a)(1). For example, "This court has jurisdiction of this petition because it would have jurisdiction over a final judgment in the action below under 28 USC §1291. *See Roche v Evaporated Milk Association, 319 US 21 (1943).*"

The next paragraph should be like a journalist's summary of an important story, or like a good, short, informative review of a motion picture. This is the single most important paragraph in your petition. It must tell the court what is at stake in this litigation, what occurred in the court below, and why mandamus is appropriate. It is a guide to the detailed discussion that is to follow.

For example, what might petitioners have said regarding the nature of the case in *In re Société Nationale Industrielle Aérospatiale?* [237] They would, of course, have known that discovery disputes seldom are reviewed by extraordinary writ. They might have written:

> This case presents issues of first impression in this Circuit under the Hague Convention (formally the Multilateral Convention on the Taking

[237] 782 F2d 120 (8th Cir 1986), *vacated & remanded on other grounds sub nom* Société Nationale Industrielle Aérospatiale v United States Dist Court, 482 US 522 (1987).

> of Evidence Abroad in Civil and Commercial Matters, Mar 18, 1970, 23 UST 2555, TIAS No 7444[238] and under provisions of foreign law that may very well subject petitioners to criminal liability if they comply with the orders of the district judge. Petitioners are government-owned French corporations that advertise and sell high-quality aircraft in the United States. One of these aircraft was involved in an accident in Iowa, leading to the complex litigation in the court below. Petitioners are now subject to discovery orders that pose serious consequences for them. The issues raised in this petition undoubtedly will recur in this litigation, and unless this petition is heard there can be no review of these issues until a final judgment is entered. This is, as is demonstrated below in detail, an extraordinary case, calling for the exercise of this court's supervisory powers. See, e.g., Schlagenhauf v Holder, 379 US 104, 111-12; La Buy v Howes Leather Co, 352 US 249, 254-55 (1957). See generally Comment, Supervisory and Advisory Mandamus Under the All Writs Act, 86 Harv L. Rev 595 (1973).

The (hypothetical) author of this paragraph has fulfilled the functions of an introduction. The author also has cited as authority the two Supreme Court cases that speak most expansively on the use of mandamus and the Harvard comment that not only supports such use but is widely cited. To this list, one should probably add a case from the circuit in question. The Supreme Court authority is chosen because it is addressed to any reader of the petition. The court of appeals judge obviously will recognize these cases. The law clerk, who may not recognize them and will perhaps read them, will be directed to the basics.

The third section, *The Challenged Order,* must describe the district judge's action in terms that anticipate the discussion of why the writ should issue. The summary must include the salient facts that make it reviewable by mandamus. This discussion should cover all of the five factors discussed at **§3.04** that will be urged in support of the petition. For example, after a summary of the challenged order, the petition might say:

> Petitioners have no adequate remedy, by direct appeal or otherwise. If forced to provide discovery, they will be immediately harmed in ways not correctable on appeal. Further, the district judge's order is clearly erroneous as a matter of law, in that it involves the misconstruction both of Federal Rule of Civil Procedure 26 and of the Hague Convention. Finally, this petition presents a novel and important question of law. [Cite cases embodying this standard.][239] The precise basis for these contentions is set forth below.[240]

---

[238] Mar 18, 1970, 23 UST 2555, TIAS No 7444, UKTS 20 (1977), discussed at **§3.05.**

[239] Cases embodying this standard are collected at **§§3.05-3.06.**

[240] Another form appears in S.R. Shapiro, Annotation, *Mandamus, Prohibition, or Interlocutory Appeal as Proper Remedy to Seek Review of District Court's Disposition of Motion for Change of Venue under §1404(a) or §1406(a) of Judicial Code,* 2 ALR Fed 573, 585 (1969).

The next section, *Factual Background,* will describe the course of the litigation leading up to the matters at issue in the petition. In writing this section, one should refer to the chapter on the appellate brief, and in particular the discussion of the statement of the case. There is one vital difference, however: a mandamus petition must carry with it the portions of the record that are relevant to the matters under discussion. Thus, one can sometimes summarize facts more pithily and refer to "Appendix [X], attached to this petition." The Factual Background cannot simply be a chronological presentation of the facts leading to the lawsuit and the suit itself. The court is not interested in these matters. If the factual presentation sounds run-of-the-mill, the petitioner will be remitted to the run-of-the-mill remedy: an appeal from a final judgment.

The final section, entitled *Why the Writ Should Issue,* should contain a detailed statement of the legal bases for issuing mandamus, invoking the factors discussed above. This section need not and probably should not be as detailed and lengthy as an appellate brief on the same issue would be. The petitioner's purpose at this stage is to have the matter heard on the merits. If the court decides to order a response and consider the merits, further briefing will be possible.

If proceedings in the district court are likely to moot the requested relief, counsel also must ask for a stay. This should be done by a separate pleading, filed at the same time as the petition and referring to the petition for detailed discussion of the merits.

§3.17 —Opposing the Writ

If the court denies the petition outright, the opponent has nothing to do.[241] However, if the court orders a response, the opponent must consider tactical options. The first question is who shall file a response. While many, if not most, federal district judges ostensibly are indifferent to the outcome of writ petitions, some of them do appear by counsel to defend the correctness of their decisions. It is not improper for counsel to inquire of the district judge whether he or she will be making an appearance in the court of appeals. Obviously, the district judge's presence in the action may help the court of appeals to understand the basis of the challenged order and the unwisdom of issuing the writ.

The nonjudicial opponent's response must emphasize the two hurdles facing the petitioner and the court. First, he or she must discount the existence and importance of the factors that permit or encourage a court of appeals to hear a mandamus petition on the merits. Because the matter is essentially one of discretion, the task may seem daunting. As Lord Chief Justice Holt said, "Discretionary is but a softer word for arbitrary." But there are some stars to steer by.

---

[241] The petitioner may seek Supreme Court review by certiorari or by another original petition in that Court. Certiorari is the more usual means. Although detailed discussion of Supreme Court review is beyond the scope of this treatise, see **§11.06** for an introductory discussion of the subject.

The opponent should begin by quoting from the Supreme Court cases discussed at **§§3.02-3.03** the terms such as *extraordinary, abuse of discretion, usurpation,* and *clear and indisputable right to the writ.* These are strong words and not merely precatory. They reflect a deep judicial commitment to the final decision rule. The opponent can then arrange the petition in terms of the various specific tests imposed by the courts of appeals for reaching the merits of a writ petition.

The second task of the opponent is to show that the district judge was right on the merits. This task must in turn be seen from two vantage points. If the district judge's ultimate decision, as embodied in the challenged order, was correct in every respect, then that argument should be made. However, if the opponent of the writ believes that the district judge might have applied an improper standard or that the rule in question may require clarification by the court of appeals, an alternative argument may be used: the court of appeals can then set the standard and define the rules to be applied. The opponent of the writ must make clear, in an alternative argument, that the court of appeals usually should not instruct the district judge to reach a particular conclusion. Rather, if the writ issues, it should simply direct the judge to confine his or her discretion in a particular way, make factual findings, and apply the rules as elaborated by the court of appeals, or to reconsider a prior decision in light of the court of appeals' opinion. By this means, the opponent may preserve yet another opportunity to obtain the ultimate result he or she seeks. Cases are legion in which the court of appeals or the Supreme Court has left matters open in this way.[242]

The form of an opposition to mandamus will be dictated by the nature of the arguments being made. No allegation concerning jurisdiction is necessary, except in the rare case where a jurisdictional issue truly exists. In place of a Nature of the Case paragraph, the opponent will begin with a Summary of Reasons for Opposing the Writ.

In the rare case where an opponent agrees that the petition should be heard on the merits, this should be made clear. However, the parties cannot confer jurisdiction by consent.[243]

If the court determines to take the matter beyond the petition and answer, Fed R App P 21(b) provides for filing of briefs and, in the discretion of the court, oral argument. These subjects are dealt with in Chapters 9 and 10.

---

[242] Van Dusen v Barrack, 376 US 612 (1964), discussed at **§3.07,** is an example. Also, in Will v Calvert Fire Ins Co, 437 US 655 (1978), Justice Blackmun provided the fifth vote to deny mandamus, but would have remanded to permit the district judge to apply the proper legal test. His vote, plus that of the four dissenters, would make five votes for this approach. *See* **§3.03.**

[243] Noted in United States v Hughes, 413 F2d 1244, 1247 (5th Cir 1969), *vacated as moot sub nom* United States v Gifford-Hill-American, Inc, 397 US 93 (1970).

4 Where to Appeal: The Twelve Circuits and the Specialized Courts of Appeals

§4.01 The Courts of Appeals: Establishment, Staffing, Choice among Courts

There are 12 geographical or regional courts of appeals and two specialized courts: the Temporary Emergency Court of Appeals and the Court of Appeals for the Federal Circuit.[1] In most cases, it will be obvious which court of appeals uniquely possesses the jurisdiction to decide an appeal and the notice

[1] This treatise will not discuss the Rail Reorganization Court. *See* Charles A. Wright, Federal Courts 5, 18-19 (4th ed 1983).

of appeal will designate that court.[2] In the following types of matters, a party may have some choice. First, there may be choice on review of certain agency orders, as discussed at **§§2.16** and **6.09.** The choice may be significant if there is an intercircuit conflict on an important legal issue.

Second, there may be a choice on review of Tax Court decisions by virtue of provisions of law permitting election of the place of trial, as discussed at **§§2.13** and **6.07.** In addition, cases arising under the Internal Revenue Code may be reviewable, at the taxpayer's option, in the United States Claims Court, the United States District Court, or the United States Tax Court.[3] This choice of forum will dictate which court of appeals will have jurisdiction; it could make a difference in a case involving a rule of law on which there is an intercircuit conflict.

Third, a choice may arise on review of transfer orders from one district court to another, as discussed at **§3.07.** If the advocate moves quickly before the transfer takes place, he or she may be able to obtain review in the transferor circuit. By waiting, review presumably would be available in the transferee circuit, seeking remand to the transferor court.[4]

The problems facing the advocate who must choose between one of the geographical circuits and one of the specialized courts of appeals are discussed at **§§2.12** and **6.09,** as well as at **§§4.14** and **4.15.** In many instances, choice of the wrong circuit can be remedied by invoking the transfer provisions of 28 USC §1631.[5]

---

[2] 28 USC §1294, the text of which appears in **app E,** allocates judicial business among the geographic courts of appeals, and provides that Canal Zone cases go to the Fifth Circuit, Virgin Islands cases to the Third Circuit, and Guam cases to the Ninth Circuit.

Under 28 USC §1407(b), a transferee district judge in a multidistrict case sits as a district judge in any judicial district where a matter may require his attention. Therefore, in such cases, the court of appeals having review power will be that for the district in which the judge is sitting, regardless of the district for which his or her commission was issued. Where a court in one circuit determines that a case properly belongs in another, that determination becomes the law of the case, although the transferee court may review the decision to transfer when it is clearly wrong. Christianson v Colt Indus Operating Corp, 486 US 800 (9th Cir 1988). However, a §1404(a) transfer, even if clearly erroneous, deprives the transferor appellate court of jurisdiction once the files have been physically transferred. Petersen v Douglas County Bank & Trust Co, 940 F2d 1389 (10th Cir 1991).

[3] *See* **§§2.13, 6.07.**

[4] *See* **§3.07.**

[5] *See* Oliveira v United States, 734 F2d 760, 762 (11th Cir 1984) (discussing §1631 and summarizing case law); Center for Nuclear Responsibility, Inc v NRC, 781 F2d 935, 943-46 (DC Cir 1986) (Ginsburg, J, dissenting in an opinion discussing many cases); FMC Corp v Glouster Engg Co, 830 F2d 770 (7th Cir 1987), (court of appeals with jurisdiction over district where antitrust complaint originally filed lacked jurisdiction over appeal from order entered by Massachusetts district court to whom case had been transferred by the Judicial Panel on Multi-district Litigation; appeal lies to the geographic circuit wherein lies the transferee court; case transferred under 28 USC §1631), *cert dismissed,* 486 US 1063 (1988); Alexander v Commissioner, 825 F2d 499 (DC Cir 1987) (28 USC §1631 did not remove court's inherent power to transfer, rather than dismiss, appeals for lack of proper venue).

The geographical courts of appeals and the Federal Circuit are established and their functions are set forth in 28 USC **§§41-49.** The statutory basis for the Temporary Emergency Court of Appeals is discussed at **§4.15.**

The courts of appeals are art III courts and their judges hold office during good behavior.[6] Judges are selected by the President with the advice and consent of the Senate.[7] Except in the District of Columbia, circuit judges must, at the time of appointment, be residents of the circuit for which they are appointed.[8] After a specified number of years of service, and at no less than 65 years of age, a circuit judge may take senior status.[9] The senior judge becomes ineligible to sit on rehearings en banc unless he or she participated in the panel decision, and the President may name a successor judge.[10]

The Chief Justice of the United States each year names himself and the associate justices as circuit justices, one for each of the courts of appeals. The most important of the circuit justice's duties is to hear applications for stays pending review of civil cases, for stays of execution in capital cases, and for bail in criminal cases.[11]

The Chief Justice of the United States may designate circuit judges to sit temporarily outside their home circuits, and the chief judge of a circuit or the circuit justice may designate district judges to sit on court of appeals panels. However, a district judge may not "hear or determine an appeal from the decision of a case or issue tried by him."[12] The chief judge of the circuit is, generally speaking, the nonsenior judge with the most seniority.[13]

Each of the geographical circuits and the Federal Circuit hold an annual judicial conference, which all district and bankruptcy judges must attend. Most courts of appeals make some provision for selected members of the bar to attend the conference.[14]

Each circuit also has a judicial council, consisting of the chief judge and a group of circuit and district judges. This body is the legislature of the circuit, with authority to issue, amend, and enforce its rules and to administer the circuit's business.[15] The circuit rules supplement the Federal Rules of Appellate Procedure, and must be consulted at every stage of an appeal.

---

[6] US Const art III; 28 USC §44(b).

[7] 28 USC §44(a).

[8] *Id* §44(c).

[9] *Id* §§294(b), 371(b), 372(a).

[10] *Id* §46(c).

[11] *See* Sup Ct R 22 (applications to individual justices) and 23 (stays).

[12] 28 USC §47. *See* Charles A. Wright, *supra* note 1, at 3, 11.

[13] 28 USC §45.

[14] *Id* §333.

[15] *Id* §332.

Courts of appeals usually sit in panels of three judges, except when hearing cases en banc.[16] However, a quorum of a panel—two judges—may decide a case in the event that a panel member is disqualified or unable to serve.[17] Disqualification of court of appeals judges is governed by the same provisions of law applicable to district judges.[18]

Each court of appeals has authority to control membership in its bar, and to determine to what extent, if any, it will permit nonmembers to argue pro hac vice. This subject is regulated by Fed R App P 46 and by a local circuit rule in each court of appeals. Several circuits, for example the District of Columbia, Second, and Ninth, permit law students to appear as counsel and to brief and argue cases. Such rules are under consideration in other circuits as well. Usually, these student practice rules are administered in conjunction with law school appellate practice clinics under the supervision of law professors who are members of the circuit bar.

§4.02 District of Columbia Circuit

The District of Columbia Circuit covers only the District of Columbia and has 12 authorized judges in regular active service.[19] It sits, and its judges have chambers, only in the United States Courthouse in the District of Columbia.[20] Its clerk's office is at:

5409 Federal Courthouse
3rd & Constitution Avenue, N.W.
Washington, D.C. 20001
(202) 535-3308[21]

---

[16] However, the Federal Circuit, as authorized by 28 USC §46(c), may provide that its judges will sit in panels of more than three. *See* Fed Cir R 3.

[17] 28 USC §46(d). A majority of the panel in any circuit must consist of "judges of that court" under 28 USC §46(b). However, this requirement may be dispensed with if "the chief judge of that court certifies that there is an emergency including, but not limited to, the unavailability of a judge of the court because of illness." 28 USC §46(b). When a court of appeals is unduly pressed by the volume of pending cases or when there are vacancies on the court, chief judges declare an emergency under this provision to permit visiting judges from other circuits and district judges to comprise a majority on panels. On the meaning of "judges of the court," see Cone Corp v Hillsborough County, 995 F2d 185 (11th Cir 1993) (requirement that two of three panel members be judges of 11th Circuit is met even when one of the two is a senior judge).

[18] 18 USC §§144, 455. Many courts of appeals require counsel to state the names of interested parties in their briefs, so that judges may evaluate the need for recusal. Counsel must make inquiry, however, to determine whether a basis for recusal exists.

[19] 28 USC §§41, 44(a).

[20] *Id* §48(a).

[21] An important reference source for this information is Want's Federal-State Court Directory, published annually by Want Publishing Co, 1511 K Street, NW, Washington, DC, 20005, (202) 783-1887, Fax (202) 393-5106.

§4.03 First Circuit

The First Circuit covers Maine, Massachusetts, New Hampshire, Puerto Rico, and Rhode Island, and has six authorized judges in regular active service.[22] It sits in regular session in Boston.[23] Its judges have chambers in cities throughout the circuit; for a list, consult a current volume of Federal Reporter, 2d series. Its clerk's office is at:

1606 John W. McCormack Post Office and Courthouse Building
Boston, MA 02109
(617) 223-9057

§4.04 Second Circuit

The Second Circuit covers Connecticut, New York, and Vermont, and has 13 authorized judges in regular active service.[24] It sits in regular session in New York.[25] Its judges have chambers in cities throughout the circuit; for a list, consult a current volume of Federal Reporter, 2d series. Its clerk's office is at:

United States Courthouse
40 Foley Square
New York, NY 10007
(221) 791-0103

§4.05 Third Circuit

The Third Circuit covers Delaware, New Jersey, Pennsylvania, and the United States Virgin Islands, and has 14 authorized judges in regular active service.[26] It sits in regular session in Philadelphia.[27] Its judges have chambers in cities throughout the circuit; for a list, consult a current volume of Federal Reporter, 2d series. Its clerk's office is at:

21400 United States Courthouse
Independence Mall West
601 Market Street
Philadelphia, PA 19106
(215) 597-2995

---

[22] 28 USC §§41, 44(a).
[23] *Id* §48(a).
[24] 28 USC §§41, 44(a).
[25] *Id* §48(a).
[26] 28 USC §§41, 44(a).
[27] *Id* §48(a).

§4.06 Fourth Circuit

The Fourth Circuit covers Maryland, North Carolina, South Carolina, Virginia, and West Virginia, and has 15 authorized judges in regular active service.[28] It sits in regular session in Richmond, Virginia, and Asheville, North Carolina.[29] The court also sits regularly in special session in Baltimore and Greensboro. Its judges have chambers in cities throughout the circuit; for a list, consult a current volume of Federal Reporter, 2d series. Its clerk's office is at:

United States Courthouse
Tenth & Main Streets
Richmond, VA 23119
(804) 771-2213

§4.07 Fifth Circuit

The Fifth Circuit covers the District of the Canal Zone, Louisiana, Mississippi, and Texas,[30] and has 17 authorized judges in regular active service.[31] It sits in regular session in New Orleans, Fort Worth, and Jackson.[32] However, almost all oral arguments are heard in New Orleans, and panels of the court occasionally sit in each of the major cities of the circuit, giving preference to cities where law schools are located. Its judges have chambers in cities throughout the circuit; for a list, consult a current volume of Federal Reporter, 2d series. Its clerk's office is at:

102 U.S. Courthouse
600 Camp Street
New Orleans, LA 70130
(504) 589-6514

§4.08 Sixth Circuit

The Sixth Circuit covers Kentucky, Michigan, Ohio, and Tennessee, and has 16 authorized judges in regular active service.[33] It sits in regular session in

---

[28] 28 USC §§41, 44(a).

[29] *Id* §48(a).

[30] 28 USC §41. Prior to October 1, 1981, the Fifth Circuit covered its present territory, plus the states that now comprise the Eleventh Circuit. *See* Pub L No 96-452, 94 Stat 1994 (1980) (the transition provisions). The precedent of the old Fifth Circuit is binding in the Eleventh Circuit unless overruled by that court sitting en banc. However, even prior to 1981, the Fifth Circuit sat in administrative units pursuant to Pub L No 95-486, §6, 92 Stat 1633 (1978).

[31] 28 USC §44(a).

[32] *Id* §48(a).

[33] 28 USC §§41, 44(a).

Cincinnati.[34] Its judges have chambers in cities throughout the circuit; for a list, consult a current volume of Federal Reporter, 2d series. Its clerk's office is at:

538 United States Post Office and Courthouse
5th and Walnut Streets
Cincinnati, OH 45202-3988
(513) 684-2953
Fax (513) 684-2775

§4.09 Seventh Circuit

The Seventh Circuit covers Illinois, Indiana, and Wisconsin, and has 11 authorized judges in regular active service.[35] It sits in regular session in Chicago.[36] Its judges have chambers in cities throughout the circuit; for a list, consult a current volume of Federal Reporter, 2d series. Its clerk's office is at:

United States Courthouse &
Federal Office Building
219 South Dearborn Street
Chicago, IL 60604
(312) 435-5850

§4.10 Eighth Circuit

The Eighth Circuit covers Arkansas, Iowa, Minnesota, Missouri, Nebraska, North Dakota, and South Dakota, and has 11 authorized judges in regular active service.[37] It sits in regular session in St. Louis, Kansas City, Omaha, and St. Paul.[38] Its judges have chambers in cities throughout the circuit; for a list, consult a current volume of Federal Reporter, 2d series. Its clerk's office is at:

1114 Market Street
St. Louis, MO 63101-2077
(314) 539-3609

---

[34] *Id* §48(a).
[35] 28 USC §§41, 44(a).
[36] *Id* §48(a).
[37] 28 USC §§41, 44(a).
[38] *Id* §48(a).

§4.11 Ninth Circuit

The Ninth Circuit covers Alaska, Arizona, California, Idaho, Montana, Nevada, Oregon, Washington, Guam, and Hawaii, and has 28 authorized judges in regular active service.[39] It sits in regular session in San Francisco, Los Angeles, Portland, and Seattle, although it holds special sessions in cities around the circuit.[40]

The Ninth Circuit has resisted proposals to split into two separate geographic courts of appeals; one objection has been that cases from California comprise about half the circuit's caseload, and the notion of a geographic circuit that includes only one state has appeared unseemly, mostly for reasons of history. The Ninth Circuit has revised its en banc procedures as authorized by a 1978 statute that is not codified in title 28 USC. This statute permits a court of appeals with more than 15 active judges to "constitute itself into administrative units . . . and may perform its en banc function by such number of members of its en banc courts as may be prescribed by rule of the court of appeals."[41]

Ninth Circuit judges have chambers in cities throughout the circuit; for a list, consult a current volume of Federal Reporter, 2d series. The Ninth Circuit's clerk's office is at:

121 Spear Street, 2d Floor, Room 205
San Francisco, CA 94105
(415) 744-9800

For emergency or overnight deliveries, the clerk's office street address is:

Clerk of Court
U.S. Court of Appeals for the Ninth Circuit
50 United Nations Plaza
San Francisco, CA 94102-4909

§4.12 Tenth Circuit

The Tenth Circuit covers Colorado, Kansas, New Mexico, Oklahoma, Utah, and Wyoming, and has 12 authorized judges in regular active service.[42] It sits in regular session in Denver, Wichita, and Oklahoma City, although almost

---

[39] 28 USC §§41, 44(a). The Northern Mariana Islands are considered part of Guam for this purpose. Pub L No 95-157, §1(a), 91 Stat 1265 (1977). *See generally* Cruz v Abbate, 812 F2d 571 (9th Cir 1987) (appeal from district court appellate division under 48 USC §1424-3(b)).

[40] 28 USC §48(a).

[41] Pub L No 95-486, §6, 92 Stat 1633 (1978).

[42] 28 USC §§41, 44(a).

all arguments are heard in Denver.[43] Its judges have chambers in cities throughout the circuit; for a list, consult a current volume of Federal Reporter, 2d series. Its clerk's office is at:

1929 Stout Street
Room C-404
Denver, CO 80294
(303) 844-3157

§4.13 Eleventh Circuit

The Eleventh Circuit covers Alabama, Florida, and Georgia, having been split off from the "old" Fifth Circuit in 1981.[44] It has 12 authorized judges in regular active service.[45] It sits in regular session in Atlanta, Jacksonville, and Montgomery.[46] Its judges have chambers in cities throughout the circuit; for a list, consult a current volume of Federal Reporter, 2d series. Its clerk's office is at:

56 Forsyth Street, N.W.
Atlanta, GA 30303
(404) 331-6187

§4.14 The Court of Appeals for the Federal Circuit

The United States Court of Appeals for the Federal Circuit was established by the Federal Courts Improvement Act of 1982.[47] It took over appellate matters from the Claims Court and the Court of International Trade, Patents and Trademarks, adopting its predecessors' precedents.[48] It has 12 authorized

---

[43] *Id* §48(a).

[44] 28 USC §41. *See* **§4.07.**

[45] 28 USC §44(a).

[46] *Id* §48(a).

[47] Pub L No 97-164, 96 Stat 25. The Federal Circuit Bar Association and the Appellate Practice Committee of the Section of Litigation, American Bar Association, issue a regular Federal Circuit Newsletter that anyone handling a matter within the Federal Circuit's appellate jurisdiction will find invaluable. For information on how to join the Section of Litigation and its Appellate Practice Committee, write Section of Litigation, ABA, 750 North Lake Shore Drive, Chicago, IL 60611.

[48] *See generally* 17 Charles A. Wright, Arthur R. Miller, & Edward H. Cooper, Federal Practice & Procedure: Jurisdiction 2d §4104 (1988 & Supp 1993); 13 *id* §3508, at 33-35 (1984). South Corp v United States, 690 F2d 1368, 1369 (Fed Cir 1982) (court adopts as precedent case law of predecessor courts). The legislative history of the Federal Courts Improvement Act is recorded in S Rep No 275, 97th Cong, 2d Sess, *reprinted in* 1982 USCCAN 11, 11-50. *See generally* Arthur D. Gray, *The Impact on the New Court of Appeals for the Federal Circuit on Patent Holdings of the Federal Courts,* 100 FRD 499, 681-86

judges in regular active service.[49] It is headquartered in Washington, D.C., although it is directed to schedule its sittings "with a view to securing reasonable opportunity to citizens to appear before the court with as little inconvenience and expense to citizens as is practicable."[50]

The Federal Circuit is unique in that it is authorized to sit in panels of more than three judges, and its rules provide that any "odd number of judges not fewer than three" may constitute a panel.[51]

The jurisdiction of the Federal Circuit is determined in one of two basic ways: by the origin of the case or by its subject matter. The latter basis of jurisdiction has proven the more fecund progenitor of controversy. In addition, statutes confer interlocutory jurisdiction on the Federal Circuit somewhat more broadly than on the geographic courts of appeals.

The Federal Circuit's origin of the case jurisdiction is set out in 28 USC §1295(a)(3)-(a)(10), (b), and (c).[52] In summary, these subsections confer jurisdiction in the following situations: (1) appeals from final decisions of the United States Claims Court;[53] (2) appeals from decisions of (a) the Board of Patent Appeals and Interferences of the Patent and Trademark Office with respect to patent applications and interferences, (b) the Commissioner of Patents and Trademarks or the Trademark Trial and Appeal Board with respect to applications for registration of marks and related proceedings, and (c) a district court to which a case was directed under 35 USC §145 (civil action to obtain patent) or §146 (civil action in case of patent interference);[54] (3) appeals from final decisions of the United States Court of International Trade;[55] (4) review of the final determinations of the United States International Trade Commission relating to certain unfair practices in import trade;[56] (5) appeals (on questions of law only) reviewing the findings of the Secretary of Commerce relating to certain import issues;[57] (6) appeals under the Plant Variety Protection Act;[58] (7) review of Merit Systems Protection Board decisions; and[59] (8) appeals from

---

(1983); George M. Schwab, *Defending a Patent Case Under the Watchful Eye of the Federal Circuit,* 70 J Pat & Trademark Off Socy 100 (1988).

[49] 28 USC §44(a).

[50] *Id* §48(d).

[51] Fed Cir R 47.2(a); 28 USC §46(b).

[52] The full text of 28 USC §1295 is in **app E.**

[53] 28 USC §1295(a)(3).

[54] *Id* §1295(a)(4).

[55] *Id* §1295(a)(5).

[56] *Id* §1295(a)(6).

[57] *Id* §1295(a)(7).

[58] *Id* §1295(a)(8).

[59] *Id* §1295(a)(9). *See* Lindahl v OPM, 470 US 768 (1985) (Federal Circuit has jurisdiction over MSPB decisions concerning retirement disability claims; Tucker Act suit not prerequisite to review), noted in *Lindahl v Bronger: The Federal Circuit's Jurisdiction over the MSPB's Civil Service Retirement Decisions,* 34 Am U L Rev 695 (1985).

certain agency contract determinations.[60] Subsections 1295(b) and (c) confer jurisdiction to review certain decisions by an agency board of contract appeals.[61] The Federal Circuit has interlocutory appellate jurisdiction over orders refusing transfer of district court cases to the United States Court of Claims.[62]

The Federal Circuit's jurisdiction over district court orders and judgments is based upon the district court's subject matter jurisdiction. The Federal Circuit is designed as a specialized court with expertise to handle certain intellectual property and claims litigation.[63] Its grant of exclusive jurisdiction was designed to reduce forum shopping.[64]

The legislative history of the act establishing the Federal Circuit contains a suggestion that its jurisdiction is to be tested by an *arising under* test similar

---

[60] 28 USC §1295(a)(10). However, the entity whose decision is being reviewed must render its decision pursuant to the Contract Disputes Act of 1978, 41 USC §601 *et seq.* *See* Tatelbaum v United States, 749 F2d 729, 730 (Fed Cir 1984). *See also* United States v General Dynamics Corp, 828 F2d 1356, 1360-62 (9th Cir 1987) (Federal Circuit jurisdiction to review orders of Armed Services Board of Contract Appeals).

[61] *See* Robert D. Wallick & Neil R. Ellis, *The United States Court of Appeals for the Federal Circuit: At the Leading Edge of High Technology Issues,* 36 Am U L Rev 801 (1987).

The rationale and extent of Federal Circuit jurisdiction was clarified in United States v Hohri, 482 US 64 (1987) (Federal Circuit, rather than regional court of appeals, has appellate jurisdiction to review district court decision of a mixed case involving both a nontax Little Tucker Act claim and a Federal Tort Claims Act action; therefore, the Court of Appeals for the District of Columbia Circuit lacked jurisdiction over an appeal from a district court decision holding that claims arising from the internment of Japanese-Americans during World War II were barred; proper remedy is, therefore, to vacate court of appeals' decision and remand with instructions to transfer the case to the United States Court of Appeals for the Federal Circuit under 28 USC §1631), *vacating* 782 F2d 227 (DC Cir 1986).

[62] 28 USC §1292(d), as amended by the Judicial Improvements and Access to Justice Act, Pub L No 100-702, 1988 USCCAN (102 Stat) 4642, 4652. The legislative history of this amendment notes the litigative confusion over whether Tucker Act cases fall within the jurisdiction of the district court or the Claims Court. *See* 28 USC §§1346, 1491. The courts of appeals have been divided over whether there can be immediate appellate review of a district court decision on transfer. Congress has continued to strengthen the hand of the Federal Circuit within its sphere of statutory competence by providing not only for interlocutory appeal and stay, but for Federal Circuit exclusive jurisdiction of appeals. *See* HR Rep No 889, 100th Cong, 2d Sess pt 1, at 51-54, *reprinted in* 1988 USCCAN 5982, 6011-15.

[63] *See* discussion of legislative history earlier in this section. *See also* Atasi Corp v Seagate Technology, 847 F2d 826 (Fed Cir 1988).

[64] *See* Cable Elec Prods, Inc v Genmark, Inc, 770 F2d 1015, 1032 (Fed Cir 1985) (§1295(a)(1) does not limit appellate court jurisdiction solely to review of patent claims; when patent and nonpatent claims are joined, the nonpatent claims accompany the appeal of the patent claims to the court of appeals, avoiding bifurcation of appeals between the Federal Circuit and the appropriate regional circuit); Smith v Orr, 855 F2d 1544 (Fed Cir 1988) (although Federal Circuit has exclusive jurisdiction over the merits of appeals from federal district courts if the jurisdiction of those courts was based on subject matter falling under §1295, it does not have exclusive appellate jurisdiction to determine whether a district court's jurisdiction was based on subject matter under that section).

to that used in measuring federal question jurisdiction in the district courts.[65] The Federal Circuit has acquiesced in a Seventh Circuit decision holding that a district court final judgment in a case originally filed as a patent matter must be appealed to the Federal Circuit even if the judgment does not involve any issue of patent law.[66]

In *Christianson v Colt Industries Operating Corp*,[67] the Supreme Court upheld the Federal Circuit's refusal to take jurisdiction of a case in which patent law claims were pleaded as a defense to an antitrust suit. The Court held that jurisdiction in the Federal Circuit extends only to those cases "in which a well-pleaded complaint establishes either that federal patent law creates the cause of action or that the plaintiff's right to relief necessarily depends on resolution of a substantial question of federal patent law, in that patent law is a necessary element of one of the well-pleaded claims."[68]

The Federal Circuit distinguished *Christianson* in *Aerojet-General Corp v Machine Tool Works*,[69] and held that it had jurisdiction over an appeal when patent law claims were advanced in well-pleaded counterclaims with an independent federal jurisdictional basis. In such a case, patent law issues are involved in the same way they would be if asserted in the complaint. The Circuit noted that the counterclaim was compulsory under Fed R Civ P 13, but the rationale of its opinion would extend to any counterclaim over which the district court has jurisdiction under 28 USC §1338.

In assessing the district court's subject matter jurisdiction to determine if the Federal Circuit is the court to which appeal lies, the entire case is to be judged as a unit, rather than the individual claims as they may be appealed.[70] The jurisdictional test is applied as of the time the complaint is filed; severance of claims after filing will not affect jurisdiction.[71] However, an amendment of

---

[65] Handgards, Inc v Ethicon, Inc, 743 F2d 1282 (9th Cir 1984) (even though 28 USC §1295(a)(1) confers exclusive appellate jurisdiction to the Federal Circuit regarding patent matters, court of appeals nonetheless had jurisdiction to hear appeal in antitrust action alleging bad faith prosecution of patent infringement suits, since such action did not arise under 28 USC §1338), *cert denied*, 469 US 1190 (1985) discussing legislative history; Ballard Medical Prods v Wright, 823 F2d 527 (Fed Cir 1987) (contract dispute between patent owner and licensee, where scope of patent may control scope of licensing agreement, does not arise under patent laws so as to give appellate jurisdiction to Federal Circuit; appeal dismissed).

[66] Kennedy v Wright, 851 F2d 963 (7th Cir 1988), *affd*, 867 F2d 616 (Fed Cir 1989).

[67] 486 US 800 (1988).

[68] *Id* 809.

[69] 895 F2d 736 (Fed Cir 1990) (en banc). The Federal Circuit has proven much more hospitable to the rights of patent and trademark holders than the federal courts of general jurisdiction. Therefore, advocates asserting such rights are well-advised to bring their cases from within its jurisdiction.

[70] Bandag, Inc v Al Bolser's Tire Stores, Inc, 750 F2d 903, 908 (Fed Cir 1984).

[71] Atari, Inc v JS&A Group, Inc, 747 F2d 1422, 1431 (Fed Cir 1984).

the complaint may relate back to the beginning of the action and defeat or confer Federal Circuit jurisdiction.[72]

The cases and commentators sometimes speak uncertainly on these difficult issues.[73] Fortunately, choosing the wrong circuit is not fatal. Title 28 USC §1631 permits transfer to the proper court.[74]

The last aspect of Federal Circuit jurisdiction that requires discussion is finality. Title 28 USC §1292(c) defines the orders that the Federal Circuit may review within the ambit of its subject matter jurisdiction.[75] It may review: (1) any decision that would meet the finality test of 28 USC §1291; (2) any interlocutory decision that would be reviewable by a geographic circuit under §1292(a) or §1292(b); (3) any patent infringement judgment that is final except for an accounting; and, (4) any interlocutory order of the Court of International Trade or Claims Court that meets the standards of §1292(d)(1) or (2).

The Federal Circuit has taken a narrow view of its jurisdiction to review interlocutory orders in cases involving both patent and nonpatent claims. In *Johannsen v Pay Less Drug Stores Northwest, Inc,*[76] the plaintiff sought damages and an injunction on both patent infringement and unfair competition theories. The district court entered a judgment finding liability for unfair competition

---

[72] *See* Van Drasek v Lehman, 762 F2d 1065, 1069 (DC Cir 1985) (if an amendment to complaint significantly changes action, jurisdiction is determined at date of amendment).

[73] *See generally* 15A Charles A. Wright, Arthur R. Miller, & Edward H. Cooper, Federal Practice and Procedure: Jurisdiction 2d §3903.1 (1992). The statutory language *in whole or in part* has caused the most difficulty. *See* Christianson v Colt Indus Operating Corp, 798 F2d 1051 (7th Cir 1986) (encyclopedic discussion), *disagreed with,* 822 F2d 1544 (Fed Cir 1987), *vacated in part,* 486 US 800 (1988); Sharp v Weinberger, 798 F2d 1521, 1522 (DC Cir 1986).

Federal Circuit jurisdiction extends to collateral matters such as the right of attorneys to practice before the Patent and Trademark Office. Jaskiewicz v Mossinghoff, 802 F2d 532 (DC Cir 1986) (dismissing petition for review filed in DC Circuit).

Nonpatent claims may be heard under the pendent jurisdiction doctrine. Christianson v Colt Indus Operating Corp, 798 F2d 1051, 1058 (7th Cir 1986); Hohri v United States, 782 F2d 227, 259 (DC Cir 1986) (Markey, J, dissenting), *vacated,* 482 US 64 (1987).

When the Federal Circuit considers pendent or procedural claims, it will apply the law of the regional circuit that would otherwise hear the case. Atari, Inc v JS&A Group, Inc, 747 F2d 1422, 1439 (Fed Cir 1984); Heat & Control, Inc v Hester Indus, 785 F2d 1017, 1021 (Fed Cir 1986).

[74] United States v Hohri, 482 US 64, 76 (1987) (remanding to DC Circuit with instructions to transfer to Federal Circuit).

[75] In addition to these statutory provisions, which will be interpreted in harmony with their counterparts in the geographic circuit jurisdictional statutes, the Federal Circuit has applied the *Cohen* collateral order test. Heat & Control, Inc v Heater Indus, 785 F2d 1017, 1021 (Fed Cir 1986). Moreover, there is some indication that the Federal Circuit will take an expanded view of finality. Electro-Methods, Inc v United States, 728 F2d 1471, 1474-75 (Fed Cir 1984).

The Federal Circuit has the power to issue an extraordinary writ if it would have appellate jurisdiction over the case. Baker Perkins, Inc v Werner & Pfleiderer Corp, 710 F2d 1561, 1563 (Fed Cir 1983).

[76] 918 F2d 160 (Fed Cir 1990).

but not infringement, and pronounced the judgment "final except for an accounting of damages."[77] Defendant appealed to the Federal Circuit, invoking §1292(c)(2)'s grant of jurisdiction "of an appeal from a judgment in a civil action for patent infringement which . . . is final except for an accounting."[78] The court held that the grant of appellate jurisdiction is limited to cases in which the district court has found liability for patent infringement. Because an interlocutory judgment of no infringement would not be appealable in the absence of an unfair competition claim, the court reasoned that the judgment before it should not be reviewable.[79]

The Federal Circuit clerk's office is located at:

717 Madison Place, N.W., #401
Washington, D.C. 20439
(202) 633-6550

§4.15 The Temporary Emergency Court of Appeals

The Temporary Emergency Court of Appeals (TECA) was created by a 1971 amendment[80] to the Economic Stabilization Act (ESA) of 1970[81] as a specialized court of appeals to review cases arising under the act's wage, price, and rent control provisions. As noted below, it was abolished, effective in 1993. In 1973, the Emergency Petroleum Allocation Act (EPAA) added petroleum price, classification, certification, and allocation matters to TECA's jurisdictional grant.[82]

---

[77] *Id* 161 (quoting judgment below).

[78] 28 USC §1292(c)(2).

[79] This decision will create controversy. The statute does not base the grant of appellate jurisdiction on the subject matter of the district court's judgment, but on that of the civil action in which the judgment is entered. An approach to the jurisdictional issue more in keeping with the statutory language is Unique Concepts, Inc v Manuel, 930 F2d 573 (7th Cir) (if plaintiff's complaint is based on patent law, and there is a permissive counterclaim under state law, Federal Circuit has exclusive jurisdiction to review judgment: (1) on jury verdict on bifurcated counterclaims and (2) granting plaintiff's motion to dismiss its patent claims without prejudice; dismissal does not take away Federal Circuit reviewability, which depends on the initial case being based in whole or in part on patent law; decision focuses on nature of action and not nature of relief actually granted), *affd,* 937 F2d 622 (Fed Cir 1991).

[80] Pub L No 92-210, §211(b)(2), 85 Stat 743, 749 (1971) (expired 1974), *discussed in* 12 USCA §1904 note (West Supp 1993). *See generally* 17 Charles A. Wright, Arthur R. Miller & Edward H. Cooper, Federal Practice & Procedure: Jurisdiction 2d §4105, at 430-40 (1988 & Supp 1993); Note, *The Appellate Jurisdiction of the Temporary Emergency Court of Appeals,* 64 Minn L Rev 1247 (1980).

[81] Act of August 15, 1970, Pub L No 91-379, tit II, 84 Stat 799, *as amended,* 12 USCA §1904 n (West Supp 1993).

[82] *See* Pub L No 93-159, 87 Stat 628 (1973); *see* notes to 15 USCA §751, now omitted (West Supp 1993), and, for legislative history, see 1973 USCCAN at 2582. *See also* Amber Ref, Inc v Occidental Oil & Gas Co, 961 F2d 225, 230 (Temp Emer Ct App 1992) (discussing TECA's jurisdiction).

Finally, TECA had exclusive jurisdiction over appeals arising under the Emergency Natural Gas Act (ENGA) of 1977, as well as certain original jurisdiction under ENGA.[83]

TECA consisted of a number of district judges selected by the Chief Justice of the United States, who also appointed TECA's Chief Judge.[84] Congress abolished TECA and transferred its existing caseload to the United States Court of Appeals for the Federal Circuit, effective April 29, 1993. Section 102(d) and (e) of Pub L No 102-572, 106 Stat 4506 (1992) provided:

> (d) Abolition of Court.—The Temporary Emergency Court of Appeals created by section 211(b) of the Economic Stabilization Act of 1970 is abolished, effective 6 months after the date of the enactment of this Act [Oct. 29, 1992].
> (e) Pending cases.—(1) Any appeal which, before the effective date of abolition described in subsection (d), is pending in the Temporary Emergency Court of Appeals but has not been submitted to a panel of such court as of that date shall be assigned to the United States Court of Appeals for the Federal Circuit as though the appeal had originally been filed in that court; (2) Any case which, before the effective date of abolition described in subseciton (d), has been submitted to a panel of the Temporary Emergency Court of Appeals and as to which the mandate has not been issued as of that date shall remain with that panel for all purposes and, notwithstanding the provisions of sections 291 and 292 of title 28, United States Code [sections 291 and 292 of this title], that panel shall be assigned to the United States Court of Appeals for the Federal Circuit for the purpose of deciding such case.

§4.16 Proposals to Create New Specialized Courts

In every session of Congress, legislation is proposed to create a national court of appeals as an intermediary between the courts of appeals and the Supreme Court. Other perennial proposals include forming a pool of circuit judges to resolve legal issues on which the courts of appeals are divided. These proposals have been opposed by influential bar groups, including the American Bar Association, and the likelihood of any of them being adopted is small. However, former Chief Justice Burger was an enthusiastic supporter of this legislation and some present members of the Supreme Court have spoken approvingly of it.

---

[83] Act of February 2, 1977, Pub L No 95-2, §10(b), 91 Stat 4, 9.

[84] ESA, §211(b)(1). *See* Note, *supra* note 80, at 1259.

5 Whether to Appeal, Fees for Appeal, Preparing for Appeal

§5.01 How to Decide Whether to Seek Appellate Review—The Investment Decision

The decision to seek appellate review is an investment decision, just as the decision to file a lawsuit, conduct discovery, file dispositive motions, and take a case to trial should be. The investment factors are not, however, only financial, or all to be found in the particular lawsuit.

When faced with a loss in the agency or lower court, the lawyer and client may be disappointed and angry. This is not the best frame of mind in which to make a complicated decision as to whether it is better to take an appeal or to accept the judgment.

It would be soothing—but very misleading—to say that the decision to appeal could be reduced to a formula. For example, one might try to quantify the chance of reversal, and then multiply that factor by the judgment.[1] Such an approach is wrong because the chance of reversal cannot be determined with precision. The lawyer, still smarting from defeat, may tend to overstate it.

Nonetheless, statistical analysis of reversal rates provides useful perspective for a multifaceted decision. For calendar year 1985, the reversal rate figures were as follows:

Percentage

Circuit	Average	Criminal	U.S. Civil	Private Civil	Administrative Appeals
All Circuits	15.2	5.5	19.0	16.9	10.0
D.C.	15.1	9.1	13.5	22.8	13.3
1st	22.9	13.1	37.2	20.1	13.0
2nd	12.3	4.5	13.7	16.3	12.0
3rd	17.7	7.2	21.4	20.3	9.1
4th	11.0	9.0	14.6	10.1	10.6
5th	17.2	11.2	21.6	19.2	8.7
6th	18.4	9.7	10.0	20.6	17.1
7th	11.9	5.0	10.6	16.0	3.7
8th	13.3	8.6	18.8	12.4	9.9
9th	15.9	11.3	18.7	20.2	8.5
10th	13.4	13.1	15.7	14.0	3.4
11th	16.2	5.6	23.9	17.7	8.4

Source: Federal Court Management Statistics-1985

More detailed figures illuminate this chart. For example, in the 12-month period ending June 30, 1987, the Fifth Circuit affirmed 69.1 per cent of all cases decided, up from 67.8 per cent in the prior year. It reversed 16.6 percent of all cases. The remaining cases consist of 9.1 percent listed as "affirmed/reversed in part" and 5.2 per cent listed as "dismissed/other." Thus, the relatively low reversal rates in the chart include only those cases counted as complete reversals. Obviously, a reversal in part may at times give a party everything it reasonably expected.

---

[1] But cf as an example of questionable use of quantification to classify the unquantifiable, the Seventh Circuit formula for issuance of a preliminary injunction set out in American Hosp Supp Corp v Hospital Prods, Ltd, 780 F2d 589, 593-94 (7th Cir 1986).

For the 12-month period ending June 30, 1991, the reversal figures were:

Percentage

Circuit	Total	Criminal	U.S. Prisoner Petitions	Other U.S. Civil	Private Prisoner Petitions	Other Private Civil	Bankruptcy	Administrative Appeals
All Circuits	11.1	7.4	5.6	17.5	9.3	14.5	17.2	10.9
D.C.	16.8	16.9	6.3	21.0	7.7	21.3	—	14.2
1st	14.0	6.9	8.8	18.0	22.7	17.0	27.3	6.9
2nd	4.5	3.4	—	5.4	5.7	5.6	11.4	2.7
3rd	9.7	7.5	4.9	12.7	9.5	11.5	11.1	5.5
4th	11.1	7.1	6.1	18.5	9.1	14.1	17.1	18.3
5th	12.8	8.2	7.3	19.3	13.3	15.0	11.7	20.6
6th	10.7	6.7	3.4	15.9	5.9	16.6	22.9	12.4
7th	13.3	9.7	5.6	15.0	10.2	18.7	36.8	15.3
8th	10.3	8.7	5.5	19.5	7.4	11.6	13.9	16.0
9th	10.3	7.4	5.3	16.8	7.7	14.9	13.9	1.3
10th	11.5	9.7	9.5	18.8	6.7	14.5	14.9	9.3
11th	12.9	6.1	6.3	24.1	17.5	17.8	31.6	7.4

Source: Annual Report of the Director of the Administrative Office of the United States Courts, 1991.

In addition, the gross figures do not purport to say how a particular district judge has fared in particular kinds of cases—jury v nonjury, civil rights v federal tort claims, and so on. Some publications purport to give reversal rates for certain judges or judicial districts, but such figures are highly suspect, if only because most federal cases are not appealed and most appeals are disposed of without published opinion.[2]

The main purpose of reversal rate charts is to provide the lawyer and client with graphic evidence that the odds are against the appellant. This evidence alone should provoke exploration of alternatives to appeal, but in a criminal case, or a civil case with much at stake, an appeal may be practically inevitable because one wants to take every possible step to head off an unacceptable result.

Since the decision to appeal may involve extensive discussion, and in the case of a corporate or institutional client, several levels of approval, trial counsel must keep in mind the deadlines for filing post-trial motions to improve appellate prospects or simply to keep appellate issues alive.[3] Counsel must also make sure that a notice of appeal is timely filed, if only as a protective measure.[4]

---

[2] For example, in Brian L. Weakland, *Judging the Judges,* 75 ABAJ 58 (July 1987), the author pulls together figures that suggest a much higher reversal rate than are shown in the table in the text. The figures used in the journal article are subject to serious methodological criticism, but the study is nonetheless an interesting profile of lawyer behavior, citizen perception of the courts, and the investment decisions that arise in a lawsuit.

[3] *See* **§5.15.**

[4] *See* **§§6.03-6.04.**

Out of the many considerations that have guided such decisions over many years, what follows is a suggested analysis of whether an appeal is warranted. This analysis can be performed when considering whether to take an interlocutory appeal or seek a writ, as well as when faced with an adverse final judgment.[5] It can also be used to evaluate the prospect of a cross-appeal. Below is a checklist of investment considerations. The balance of this chapter discusses ways to determine whether the odds on any particular case are better or worse than average and ways to estimate the costs of going forward.

1. Does the appeals court have jurisdiction to review the order or judgment in question?

2. What are the statistical chances of success? Can I get more information about the reversal rate of the judge or agency?[6]

3. How much will it cost to appeal, counting appeal bond, fees, and out-of pocket expenses? In **§5.14,** there is a detailed guide to fee-setting on appeal that can be used to answer this question with precision.

4. What are the strong appellate issues? For guidance, see **§§5.03-5.13.** In addition to abstract legal analysis, one should try to spot trends in the court of appeals' treatment of the issues involved in one's case. For example, the court may have rendered a series of opinions on an issue of evidence law, or procedure, that point a certain direction. Broader-gauge trends, based on changes in the personnel of the court, may be at work.[7]

5. What is the preclusive effect of the adverse judgment on the present claim between these parties and on issues necessary to decision, as to other parties who will try to take advantage of it? An adverse judgment bars suit against one's opponents in the litigation.[8] Often overlooked, however, is the nonmutual collateral estoppel effect of a judgment that may be used offensively or defensively by those who are not parties. For example, a criminal conviction may be the basis of civil tax liability.[9] An unsuccessful challenge to an SEC action may pre-

---

[5] A group of researchers under the leadership of Professor David Trubek studied civil litigation in a metropolitan area and noted the relationship between the lawyers' investment of time, and both the perceived financial stakes and the amount actually recovered. David M. Trubek, Austin Serat, William L.F. Felstiner, Herbert M. Kritzer, & Joel B. Grossman, *The Costs of Ordinary Litigation,* 31 UCLA L Rev 72 (1983). Unfortunately, no similarly detailed study exists of the appellate process, but Trubek's work suggests a method for analyzing a case when one is considering taking an appeal.

[6] *See* charts above, and note 2. Experienced counsel may have valuable anecdotal evidence to offer on this score. Westlaw or LEXIS searches may reveal that a particular district judge has been reversed often on particular issues or types of cases.

[7] Eric Schnapper has argued in a persuasive article that federal appeals courts are increasingly willing to overturn or reduce judgments based on jury verdicts. Eric Schnapper, *Judges Against Juries—Appellate Review of Federal Civil Jury Verdicts,* 1989 Wis L Rev 237.

[8] Fleming James, Jr, Geoffrey Hazard, & John Leubsdorf, Civil Procedure §§11.7-11.22 (4th ed 1992).

[9] Considine v United States, 645 F2d 925, 929 (Ct Cl 1981), *cert denied,* 459 US 835 (1982), and Armstrong v United States, 354 F2d 274, 289-91 (Ct Cl 1965), *as noted in* 2 Darrell McGowan, Daniel G. O'Day, & Kenneth E. North, Criminal and Civil Tax Fraud §25.12 (1986).

clude a party in a later shareholder suit.[10] A judgment in favor of one individual may be the basis of a class suit on behalf of those who claim to be similarly situated. Thus, the amount at stake may be much more than the dollars represented by the judgment itself.

6. Other than collateral estoppel and res judicata, what effect will an adverse judgment have on other cases involving the same party? A party must think of the stare decisis or persuasive authority effect of an adverse decision as to issues likely to recur in its ongoing activities. For example, a newspaper faced with an adverse libel judgment must weigh the effect of the district court decision, and opinion if any, the prospect of reversal, and the effect of an adverse decision by an appellate court whose opinion will have even greater precedential effect. Beyond the formal effect of precedent, a judgment may affect the behavior of others toward the losing party. Letting a judgment stand may be interpreted as a sign of vulnerability.

Any litigant who is a repeat player will face a similar analysis. The point may be illustrated by example. An insurance company, a civil rights organization, a legal services office, or a public agency will see the same legal issue in many cases. When one considers the cost of obtaining appellate review, such an entity hypothetically should spread that cost over the entire set of similar cases that will be affected by the ruling. Such an analysis may lead the entity to take an appeal in a case where the stakes are small.

The litigant evaluating future and present related litigation will be able to spread the cost of appeal over the related litigation. For example, a public interest law firm, public agency, or corporation—or even a law firm that frequently handles cases of a particular type—should consider that the cost of vindicating a particular legal position on appeal is attributable to all the cases that will be benefitted by a favorable decision. As one considers future litigation, the cost analysis is necessarily speculative, but no more so than any other investment decision that looks to long-term return.

In making these assessments, keep in mind that a district court decision has limited precedential effect and far less than an adverse court of appeals decision. One can take a lesson from the most assiduous repeat player in the federal system, the Solicitor General of the United States who supervises all government appeals.[11] The Solicitor General will often decline to appeal a district court decision adverse to the government, because the factual situation, or the form in which the legal issues are presented, is not sufficiently compelling to make reversal likely.

7. Are personal rights at stake that cannot be quantified, but are worthy of protection? A criminal defendant may have been sentenced to a term of probation, yet the collateral consequences of conviction remain. Some of these, such as impact on future employment or a professional license, are measurable. Others, such as loss of the right to vote, are not. A lawyer given a private reprimand for alleged misconduct may not be able to point to any specific anticipated

---

[10] *See* Parklane Hosiery Corp v Shore, 439 US 322 (1979). *See generally* Fleming James, Jr, Geoffrey Hazard, & John Leubsdorf, *supra* note 8, §11.25, at 622-24.

[11] *See* **§5.17.**

financial consequence, but the sanction harms professional self-image and may deter zealous advocacy in the future.[12] The lawyer must carefully distinguish among the nonfinancial reasons a client may offer in support of taking an appeal.

Some clients want to pursue their adversaries to the end of their time and the adversary's resources. Extreme cases of such litigiousness result in sanctions.[13] Arguable cases may require the lawyer to say frankly that the issue is not worth pursuing.[14]

8. Does the adverse decision set a precedent that should be challenged in the public interest or on behalf of a group of which the client is a member?

9. How much time will the appellate process take? Does the uncertainty over legal relations during that time counsel an attempt to settle the case now rather than taking an appeal? The time from notice of appeal to final action in the court of appeals is approximately one year, less if the case is on interlocutory appeal or petition for a writ, and more if the case is complicated or if the court of appeals has developed a large backlog of cases. This estimate can be way off if there are delays in assembling or transmitting the record or if the opinion falls to a judge whose pace of work is slower than the norm, or for any number of other reasons.

10. Can the lawyer say with conviction, based upon a thorough review of the record and adequate legal research, that the case merits appellate review? This is in great measure a restatement of the questions above, with an added consideration: the lawyer as well as the client may be liable for sanctions if the appeal is found frivolous. This point is considered in more detail in **§5.02.** An investment decision is implicated because sanctions represent a financial burden as well as a professional embarrassment.

§5.02 The Rules and Risk of Sanctions

Sanctions against lawyers, law firms, and clients for violating appellate rules and procedures, pursuing frivolous appeals, engaging in dilatory and unfair tactics, and even outright fraud have dramatically increased since 1983. In that year, Fed R Civ P 11 was amended to require a sanction when an attorney

---

[12] This is the reason a young lawyer named Dominic Gentile was willing to make his case a test of the power of courts and bar associations to punish truthful speech related to pending cases. *See* Gentile v State Bar, 111 S Ct 2720 (1991).

[13] *See* **§5.02.**

[14] Sir Thomas More's biographer tells a story of how More counselled his successor as Chancellor to be cautious in advising Henry VIII:

> Master Cromwell, you are now entered into the service of a most noble, wise and liberal prince; if you will follow my poor advice, in your counsel-giving unto his Grace, ever tell him what he ought to do, but never what he is able to do. . . . For if a lion knew his own strength, hard were it for any man to rule him.

signed a pleading not well-grounded in fact or law.[15] The 1983 amendment led to a flurry of caselaw, including cases holding the rule applicable to attorney conduct in the courts of appeals.

In *Cooter & Gell v Hartmarx Corp,*[16] however, the Supreme Court changed the sanctions landscape. It held that Fed R Civ P 11 does not authorize a court of appeals to impose a Rule 11 sanction of attorney fees incurred in defending a district court sanction award. Federal Rule of Civil Procedure 11 is applicable only in federal district courts. On appeal, sanctions may only be imposed under other provisions of law, discussed below.[17]

The Rule 11 wave had, however, left the appellate landscape dramatically altered. The courts of appeals moved quickly to reassert their sanctioning power on other bases: federal rules,[18] statute,[19] and inherent power.[20]

This section first discusses the legal basis for sanctioning attorneys and parties in the courts of appeals, as well as the sanctions that typically are imposed. Then, it describes the kinds of conduct that led to such sanctions. This section seeks to present a unitary view of sanctions law, describing what an advocate may encounter at different stages of the appellate process. The risk of sanctions for a frivolous appeal is one element of the calculation of whether an appeal should be taken, and what issues one should raise. The risk continues throughout the process if one does not scrupulously follow the rules.

Sanctions may be imposed on counsel and parties under Fed R App P 38[21] for a frivolous appeal. The term *frivolous* does not mean simply that the appeal itself is brought in bad faith. Counsel may be sanctioned for presenting meritless claims on an otherwise proper appeal.[22] 28 USC §1927 provides for sanctions against an attorney who vexatiously and needlessly multiplies the proceedings. And, in *Chambers v NASCO, Inc,*[23] the Court held that federal courts have inherent power[24] to award attorney fees as discipline for meritless or vexatious litigation. The Court noted that several federal rules and 28 USC §1927 provide trial and appellate courts with great power to discipline attorneys and parties. However, it said that the inherent sanction power arises outside of and

---

[15] For a thorough and well-documented treatment of sanctions, see Section of Litigation, American Bar Association Sanctions: Rule 11 and Other Powers (2d ed 1988); Gregory P. Joseph, Sanctions: The Federal Law of Litigation Abuse (1989) (covering trial and appellate sanctions law; supplemented annually).

[16] 496 US 384 (1990).

[17] In light of *Cooter & Gell,* the courts of appeals retreated from their reliance on Fed R Civ P 11 as the basis for sanctioning appellate counsel. *See, e.g.,* Partington v Gedan, 923 F2d 686 (9th Cir 1991) (en banc) (Ninth Circuit overrules prior sanctions cases based upon Fed R Civ P 11 and incorporation of Rule 11 into Circuit Rules).

[18] *E.g.,* Fed R App P 38.

[19] *E.g.,* 28 USC §1927.

[20] Chambers v NASCO, Inc, 111 S Ct 2123 (1991).

[21] The full text of Fed R App P 38 is in **app A.** For discussion of Fed R App P 38 issues involving assessment of costs on appeal, see **§10.16.**

[22] Coghlan v Starkey, 852 F2d 806, 815 (5th Cir 1988).

[23] 111 S Ct 2123 (1991).

[24] *Id* 2133, 2135.

goes beyond these express provisions. Sanctions imposed as a matter of inherent power are reviewable, like Rule 11 sanctions, under an abuse of discretion standard.[25] The Court reaffirmed older cases that confer broad powers on courts of appeals as well as district courts to investigate and punish all manner of wrongful conduct, including fraud on the court.[26] Chief Justice Rehnquist and Justices Scalia, Kennedy, and Souter dissented, noting the constitutional concept of limited judicial power and the roster of expressly authorized sanctions available to judges.[27]

Attorneys must be members of their own state bar and of the bar of the court of appeals to appear in a case, or be admitted pro hac vice under the circuit rules.[28] They are therefore subject to discipline for professional impropriety, limited of course by constitutional provisions such as the First Amendment.[29]

In addition to sanctions—usually of costs, attorney fees, other monetary impositions, or suspension from practice before the court—the courts of appeals can and do redress improper conduct by deciding the merits of the case against the offending advocate. For example, a failure to include required and relevant matter in the record on appeal, or in the excerpts of record, will prompt the court to reject an argument as unsupported.[30] A cursory mention of a point on appeal, without citation of authority, will prompt the court to disregard the point.[31]

Although the clear trend of caselaw authority is in favor of giving an attorney or party notice and hearing before sanctions are imposed, there are cases holding that no hearing is required.[32]

---

[25] *Id* 2138 (citing *Cooter & Gell*). *Cooter & Gell* established rules for appellate review of sanctions imposed by the trial court, principally under Fed R Civ P 11, and held that abuse of discretion is the applicable standard. For a perceptive discussion of the sanctioning process in the trial court, see Judge Sam Johnson's opinion for the en banc Fifth Circuit in Thomas v Capital Sec Servs, 836 F2d 866 (5th Cir 1988), disagreed with by Kale v Combined Ins Co of Am, 861 F2d 746 (1st Cir 1988).

[26] Citing Hazel-Atlas Glass Co v Hartford-Empire Co, 322 US 238 (1944). On the use of a fraud on the court theory to obtain collateral review of a judgment, see **§11.07.**

[27] The dissenters might also have considered the historic limitations upon the also inherent contempt power. Anderson v Dunn, 19 US (6 Wheat) 204, 227-28 (1821). *See also In re* Dellinger, 461 F2d 389, 397-401 (7th Cir 1972), *affd,* 502 F2d 813 (7th Cir 1974), *cert denied,* 420 US 990 (1975); *Ex parte* Robinson, 19 US (Wall) 505, 512 (1874); and Eash v Riggins Trucking, Inc, 757 F2d 557, 577-79 (3d Cir 1985) (Sloviter, J dissenting) (providing historical perspective). It is one thing for the court to rely on inherent power to protect its processes by vacating a judgment, and quite another to use such power to punish a private individual absent express legislative authorization for doing so.

[28] Fed R App P 46, the full text of which is in **app A.**

[29] Gentile v State Bar, 111 S Ct 2720 (1991).

[30] *See* **ch 7.**

[31] See **§1.01** for an introduction to this problem. The entire subject of preparing the brief on appeal is discussed in **ch 9.**

[32] Braley v Campbell, 832 F2d 1504 (10th Cir 1987) (en banc) (attorney must be given notice and an opportunity to be heard before a sanction is imposed); *In re* Gubbins, 890 F2d 30 (7th Cir 1989) (attorney suspended for practice, but only after adversary hearing on alleged violations of rules); Hagerty v Succession of Clement, 749 F2d 217 (5th Cir 1984) (imposing sanction without notice to offending attorney) *cert denied,* 474

The court of appeals' sanctioning authority extends to lawyers who sign briefs and pleadings, whether or not a member of the court's bar,[33] and to clients who participate in sanctionable behavior,[34] as by directing or acquiescing in improper conduct. Obviously, the due process requirements of notice and hearing are most important when determining the respective roles of the attorney, the law firm, and the client.

The most troubling use of sanctions power is against lawyers and clients whose claims are deemed frivolous, for sanctions can chill the zealous advocacy to which every litigant is entitled.[35] To be sure, there are cases in which the motive to bring a meritless claim is clear.[36] There are others in which intemperate judicial approval is troubling.[37] Careful evaluation of proposed points on appeal, and of the standard of review, will almost always suffice to prevent sanctions for a frivolous appeal or presentation of a frivolous point on appeal. It is not necessary to label every innovative argument as novel, but candor and good sense require the advocate to tell the court if one is making an argument that the court has rejected in a prior case.[38]

US 968 (1985); United States v Nesglo, Inc, 744 F2d 887, 890 (1st Cir 1984) (notice generally required); Knorr Brake Corp v Harbil, Inc, 738 F2d 223, 227 (7th Cir 1984) (hearing generally required); Toepfer v DOT, 792 F2d 1102 (Fed Cir 1986) (attorneys not entitled to hearing prior to imposition of damages and costs under Fed R App P 38).

[33] United States v Song, 902 F2d 609 (7th Cir 1990) (court of appeals has authority to fine lawyer who appears before it, but is not a member of its bar, and who abuses procedural rules by unexplained indolence and inattention to client's interests).

[34] Hilmon Co (VI) v Hyatt Intl, 899 F2d 250 (3d Cir 1990) (attorney may be liable personally for Fed R App P 38 just damages and multiple costs for pursuing frivolous appeal and deliberately disregarding procedural rules; extensive discussion of basis for holding attorney personally liable or liable jointly and severally with client).

[35] Golden Eagle Distrib Corp v Burroughs Corp, 809 F2d 584 (9th Cir 1987) (Noonan, J, dissenting from denial of sua sponte request for en banc hearing) (in Fed R Civ P 11 case, held that overzealous use of sanctions power could deter advocates who wish to make innovative arguments).

[36] Tax protester cases are often the target of merited sanctions. *See, e.g.*, Mathes v Commissioner, 788 F2d 33 (DC Cir) (double costs and reasonable attorneys' fees as sanction for filing frivolous appeal in tax case), *cert denied*, 479 US 972 (1986).

[37] *See, e.g.*, *In re* Solerwitz, 848 F2d 1573 (Fed Cir 1988) (imposing one-year sanction on attorney who filed over 100 frivolous appeals), *cert denied*, 488 US 1004 (1989); Atwood v Union Carbide Corp, 847 F2d 278 (5th Cir 1988) (attorney and client liable for double costs as sanction for frivolous appeal), *cert denied*, 489 US 1079 (1989). *See also* Michael E. Tigar, *Judges, Lawyers and the Penalty of Death*, 23 Loy LA L Rev 147 (Nov 1989). Sometimes appellate judges mistake vigorous advocacy for disrespect. In Olympia Equip Leasing Co v Western Union Tel Co, 802 F2d 217 (7th Cir 1986), *cert denied*, 480 US 934 (1987), two judges gratuitously attacked a lawyer who had strenuously, but with solid support in the record and the decided cases, argued in a petition for rehearing that the judge who authored the panel opinion was wrong. The prospect of such judicial pique should not deter the lawyer. The opinion is rightly criticized in Howard W. Gutman, *Advance Sheet: A Posnerian Trilogy*, 13 Litig 51, 52 (Winter 1987), as "horrendous."

[38] *See* United States v Merit Petroleum, Inc, 731 F2d 901 (Temp Emer Ct App 1984)

Appointed counsel in criminal cases are subject to special obligations. If one believes the appeal to be frivolous, one must write a brief explaining that view and raising any issues that "might arguably support the appeal."[39] Counsel must furnish a copy of this brief to the client, who may then urge any additional points pro se. The court of appeals will review the brief and the client's submission and determine whether or not counsel will be relieved.[40]

The most common use of sanctions is against lawyers who persistently violate procedural rules relating to timing and form of briefs and motions,[41] misstate facts or misrepresent the record,[42] resort to personal attack,[43] or are grossly inattentive to their client's interests.[44] Such cases do not present difficult factual issues—the misconduct is almost always easily documented from the court's records. The sole issue is whether the court will impose a sanction and, if so, what it should be.

Government lawyers are as liable for sanctions as are private attorneys,[45] although reported instances of sanctions being imposed on government coun-

---

(sanctions imposed because the same law firm had repeatedly advanced the same arguments in crude oil cases, without noting that TECA had rejected these arguments).

[39] Anders v California, 386 US 738, 744 (1967).

[40] *Id;* Jones v Barnes, 463 US 745 (1983); Penson v Ohio, 488 US 75 (1988) (elaborating on the *Anders* requirements); United States v Castello, 830 F2d 99 (7th Cir 1987) (defense attorney permitted to withdraw on filing of *Anders* brief; appeal dismissed). *See generally* Wayne R. LaFave & Jerold Israel, Criminal Procedure §26.1 (Hornbook ed 1985). See also **§6.15** on representation of indigents in civil and criminal cases.

[41] *See, e.g., In re* Gubbins, 890 F2d 30 (7th Cir 1989) (attorney suspended from practice before the court of appeals for three months, after an adversary proceeding, for repeatedly moving for unwarranted extensions of time for filing briefs, despite having been rebuked by the court for doing so).

[42] *See, e.g., In re* Kelly, 808 F2d 549, 552 (7th Cir 1986) (reprimanding an attorney for an error in an affidavit, but not imposing formal discipline); *In re* Disciplinary Action (Boucher), 837 F2d 869 (9th Cir) (attorney suspended from court of appeals practice for six months for material misrepresentations of record on appeal), *order modified by,* 850 F2d 597 (9th Cir 1988); Braley v Campbell, 832 F2d 1504 (10th Cir 1987) (en banc) (under Fed R App P 38, attorney may be personally liable for costs, expenses, and counsel fees through conduct that manifests either intentional or reckless disregard of duties to the court).

[43] *See, e.g.,* David v United States, 820 F2d 1038, 1044 (9th Cir 1987) (attorneys narrowly escape sanction, even though both sides' briefs lacked citations to record and contained "vindictive falsehoods," because counsel apologized at oral argument; "[i]f attorneys insist upon approaching this court through the woods of obfuscation, they should beware of the sanction wolf").

[44] *See, e.g.,* United States v Song, 902 F2d 609 (7th Cir 1990) (court of appeals has authority to fine lawyer who appears before it, but is not a member of its bar, and who abuses procedural rules by unexplained indolence and inattention to client's interests).

[45] *See, e.g.,* United States v Williams, 952 F2d 418 (DC Cir 1991) (conviction affirmed, but court of appeals issued a public reprimand of the government because the brief on appeal contained material misstatements of the record; court held it would not impose sanctions on this occasion, but said it would do so in the future if the problem arose again), *cert denied,* 113 S Ct 148 (1992); Derechin v State Univ, 963 F2d 513 (2d Cir 1992) (court affirms a sanction imposed on a government lawyer by the district court

sel are harder to find. Because judicial attitudes towards lawyer sloth or error vary, and because busy courts do not notice every advocate misstep, there is some risk of sanctions law being applied unevenly.

§5.03 Grounds for Appeal and Standards of Review—Generally

The issues for appellate review will sometimes be obvious because the case seems to turn on a factual or legal question that has been briefed extensively and argued in the lower court or agency. If the advocate on appeal is new to the case, talking with trial counsel and with the client can provide perspective on the case. Even though the client, or for an institutional party, the client's representative, is not a lawyer, there are valuable perceptions to be gained.

When making the final selection, however, rules on preserving issues for appeal will be of decisive importance. Even the most exciting and powerful appellate issue may evaporate unless the record shows that it was raised and preserved.

This section deals with preserving claims of error by timely objection, and waiver and forfeiture of claims by affirmative conduct or failure to object. It then takes up exceptions to the requirement of contemporaneous objection, such as the plain error rule. Finally, this section addresses-in a general way-standards of appellate review for many kinds of alleged error, as well as the concept of harmless error. In the sections that follow, the standards of review for many kinds of alleged error are discussed and categorized according to the type of issue and proceeding. The differing applications of harmless error doctrine are also discussed. In the section describing administrative agency review (**§5.11**), there is a discussion of the exhaustion of administrative remedies doctrine, supplementing the treatment at **§2.16.**

A requirement of timely objection is the norm in civil and criminal cases. In criminal cases, Fed R Crim P 51[46] states that a clear objection suffices to preserve a contention. Federal Rules of Civil Procedure 46[47] is virtually identical. The requirement of contemporaneous objection to improper jury instructions is set out, again in virtually identical language, in Fed R Crim P 30[48] and Fed R Civ P 51.[49]

Under these rules, the federal courts have developed a set of rules regarding when the failure to object will be excused, and a party permitted to raise on appeal a contention not presented in the lower court. The most complete state-

---

and upholds the district court's direction that the lawyer not obtain reimbursement from any source, including a state hold harmless statute for its employees).

[46] The full text of Fed R Crim P 51 is in **app C.**

[47] The full text of Fed R Civ P 46 is in **app B.**

[48] The full text of Fed R Crim P 30 is in **app C.**

[49] The full text of Fed R Civ P 51 is in **app B.**

ment of these principles occurred in a criminal case, *United States v Olano.*[50] In that case, alternate jurors were permitted to deliberate with other jurors, in violation of Fed R Crim P 24(c), which requires that the alternate jurors be discharged after the jury retires to consider its verdict. The defense did not object. The defense argued on appeal that the error was "plain error . . . affecting substantial rights" under Fed R Crim P 52(b), and as such "may be noticed although . . . not brought to the attention of the court."[51] The Supreme Court, reversing the Ninth Circuit, held that Rule 52(b) did not avail the defendants, and that the contention was forfeited by failure to object.

The Court used its opinion to restate the principles that govern the contemporaneous objection requirement in federal cases reviewed on direct appeal. Federal Rules of Criminal Procedure 52 has no exact counterpart in the civil rules, but the principle that plain error may be noticed even though not raised in the trial court is applicable in civil cases as well.

The Court analyzed *plain error* as a text. First, there must be an *error,* that is, a violation of some rule of law or procedure. The error must not have been waived by the defendant. A waiver, the intentional relinquishment of a known right, extinguishes a potential error and forecloses any objection. For example, all defendants are entitled to a trial, but if a defendant voluntarily and validly pleads guilty, the right is waived and he cannot thereafter say his conviction was obtained improperly. A right validly waived is extinguished, although one may continue to litigate the validity of the asserted waiver.[52]

A failure to object, the Court said, conditionally forfeits a right to claim error. The failure need not represent a voluntary or considered act—it is an omission to act that may or may not have been deliberate. Rule 52(b), and the equivalent rule that obtains in civil and tax court litigation, imposes on counsel the duty to make a seasonable objection.

The error thus forfeited may, however, be addressed by the court of appeals or the Supreme Court if it is "plain error . . . affecting substantial rights."[53] This language, the Court held in *Olano,* requires a two-step inquiry. First, the

---

[50] 113 S Ct 1770 (1993).

[51] The full text of Fed R Crim P 52 is in **app C.**

[52] *Olano,* 113 S Ct at 1777. This discussion in the Court's opinion is a bit artificial, because a guilty plea only moves the inquiry to a different level. There are plenty of cases challenging convictions obtained by guilty pleas, based on departures from the rules that surround the taking of such a plea. The *waiver-forfeiture* distinction insisted upon in the Court's opinion is taken from Peter Westen's article, *Away from Waiver: A Rationale for the Forfeiture of Constitutional Rights in Criminal Procedure,* 75 Mich L Rev 1214, 1214-15 (1977). *See also* Freytag v Commissioner, 111 S Ct 2631, 2635 n2 (1991) (Scalia, J, concurring in the judgment) (Supreme Court will consider validity of Tax Court special trial judge assignment procedure, despite taxpayers' having consented to procedure in Tax Court; case makes clear that plain error/contemporaneous objection analysis is applicable to cases coming from Tax Court as well as to civil and criminal cases from the district courts).

[53] Fed R Crim P 52(b).

error must be *plain,* in the sense of *obvious.*[54] Under the law as it stands at the time of trial, the error must be one that a prudent trial judge wold notice.

Second, the error must also *affect substantial rights,* under Rule 52(b), in the sense of being prejudicial.[55] Of course, almost all error must be prejudicial, that is, harmful to the claimant, to be a basis for reversal. Error not objected to, however, must be shown by the appellant to be prejudicial. That is, the failure to object shifts the "burden of persuasion with respect to prejudice."[56] The Court recognized that some errors, such as violation of a basic guarantee of procedural fairness, will always be regarded as harmful and reversible even if no specific prejudice can be shown; this analysis will apply to error that is not objected to as well as to error to which objection is made.[57]

The Court's analysis in *Olano* seems straightforward, but it leaves much discretion in the hands of appellate judges to consider issues not raised and preserved below. In civil cases, there may be more leeway.[58] In *Olano,* the Court reaffirmed a principle established in a tax case that " '[a] rigid and undeviating judicially declared practice under which courts of review would invariably and under all circumstances decline to consider all questions which had not previously been specifically urged would be out of harmony with . . . the rules of fundamental justice.' "[59]

Another path to waiving or forfeiting error is to invite it. A party may not assign as error conduct in the trial court, such as improper argument by the adversary, that the party *invited.* This principle is akin to estoppel.[60]

The government has had some notable successes in obtaining appellate review of issues on which it did not make objection in the lower court. For example, in *United States v Williams,*[61] the Supreme Court held that the government has no duty to present exculpatory evidence to a federal grand jury. The government had not preserved this point in the court of appeals and, indeed, argued that it had such a duty. It asserted only that the duty had not been breached in this case. Having lost in the court of appeals, the government obtained certiorari based on its no duty position. The Court held, over three

---

[54] United States v Olano, 113 S Ct 1770, 1777 (1993).

[55] *Id* 1778.

[56] *Id.*

[57] *Id* (citing Arizona v Fulminante, 499 US 279 (1991)).

[58] See the witty and trenchant comments of Professor Robert J. Martineau in *Considering New Issues on Appeal: The General Rule and the Gorilla Rule,* 40 Vand L Rev 1023 (1987), discussing the circumstances under which an appellate court will consider an issue not raised below and focusing upon United States v Krynicki, 689 F2d 289 (1st Cir 1982) (four criteria for review of issue not raised below: if issue is purely legal, not doubtful, certain to arise in other cases, and if failure to consider it would result in miscarriage of justice).

[59] *Olano,* 113 S Ct at 1776 (citing Hormel v Helvering, 312 US 552, 557 (1941)).

[60] Fleming James, Jr, Geoffrey Hazard, & John Leubsdorf, Civil Procedure §12.9 (4th ed 1992).

[61] 112 S Ct 1735 (1992).

dissents, that the issue was preserved by objections made by government lawyers in another case. There are, however, many cases holding that the government has forfeited a contention by not making a proper objection.[62]

The principle that claims of error must be raised or they will be treated as forfeited also applies to raising claims on appeal. Claims not made on a first appeal will be lost in subsequent appeals.[63]

The standards for raising and preserving objections may well be different on collateral attack than on direct review.[64] The United States Supreme Court has established more stringent standards for habeas corpus petitioners who are challenging their state court convictions and whose claims are first presented in the federal court. However, these are rules first applied by the federal district court in deciding the habeas corpus petition, rather than principles of federal appeals law.[65] An appellate law issue does arise if a state prisoner raises a contention for the first time on appeal from the district judge's denial of the petition and has not exhausted state remedies as to that contention. In *Granberry v Greer*,[66] the Supreme Court held that if the state raises a claim of nonexhaustion of state remedies for the first time on appeal in a federal habeas proceeding, the court of appeals has the option of addressing the merits forthwith or remanding to the district court for determination of the exhaustion issue.[67]

Once the advocate has determined that the legal issue to be presented on appeal was either raised below or subject to a plain error exception, the next step is to determine what standard of review and harmless error standard will be applied. Federal Rule of Criminal Procedure 52(a) directs that "error . . . which does not affect substantial rights shall be disregarded."[68] In civil cases, the same principle applies, under Fed R Civ P 61, which contains similar lan-

---

[62] See, e.g., cases on sentencing appeals cited at **§2.11.**

[63] *See, e.g.*, Northwestern Ind Tel Co v FCC, 872 F2d 465, 470 (DC Cir 1989) ("[i]t is elementary that where an argument could have been raised on an initial appeal, it is inappropriate to consider that argument on a second appeal following remand" (citing Laffey v Northwest Airlines, 740 F2d 1071, 1089-90 (DC Cir 1984), *cert denied*, 469 US 1181 (1985)); court would not consider issue even though of constitutional proportions), *cert denied*, 493 US 1035 (1990).

[64] *See, e.g.*, Weisman v Charles E. Smith Management Co, 829 F2d 511 (4th Cir 1987) (allegation of fraud in obtaining judgment should first be raised in district court; court of appeals would not order new trial when plaintiff did not file appeal from denial of relief from judgment).

[65] For a thorough discussion of all such issues, see generally James S. Liebman, Federal Habeas Corpus Practice and Procedure (1988), and annual supplements. *See also* Ira P. Robbins, Habeas Corpus Checklists (1993) (an invaluable short guide).

[66] 481 US 129 (1987).

[67] *See also* Weaver v Foltz, 888 F2d 1097 (6th Cir 1989) (court of appeals exercises its discretion under *Granberry*, reverses dismissal of a state prisoner's habeas petition and directs the district court to hear the merits).

[68] The full text of Fed R Crim P 52 is in **app C.**

guage.[69] Federal Rule of Evidence 103(a) contains a harmless error standard for evidentiary rulings.[70] These rule provisions echo the command of 28 USC §2111:

> On the hearing of any appeal or writ of certiorari in any case, the court shall give judgment after an examination of the record without regard to errors or defect which do not affect the substantial rights of the parties.[71]

The precise contours of the harmless error standard vary according to the type of case and issue. Where no standard of review has been established by statute or otherwise, the Supreme Court will make a "determination that, as a matter of the sound administration of justice, one judicial actor is better positioned than another to decide the issue in question."[72] Thus, where the district court is particularly qualified to decide the issue, reviewing courts may reverse only on a showing of abuse of discretion. In *Underwood,* the Court applied the abuse of discretion standard to the award of attorneys' fees under the Equal Access to Justice Act, finding that the district court was best qualified to determine whether the United States's position in the underlying lawsuit had been "substantially justified."[73]

The notion of harmless error is intertwined with the standard of review, which will be, for example, *abuse of discretion, de novo,* or *clearly erroneous.* The various standards of review are discussed in the sections immediately following, according to the type of case and issue being appealed. The standard of review is among the most important factors influencing the decision about whether to take an appeal. Where the appellate court has considerable latitude to change the result below, an appeal is more attractive, all else being equal; a more deferential standard diminishes the appellant's chances.

The detailed and complex principles of standard of review and harmless error law are well-treated in *Federal Standards of Review,*[74] co-authored by Professors Steven Childress & Martha Davis. This book is a valuable companion to this Treatise.

---

[69] The text of Fed R Civ P 61 is in **app B.** *See* Steven A. Childress & Martha S. Davis, Federal Standards of Review §§6.05-6.06 (2d ed 1992).

[70] *See* 1 Stephen A. Saltzburg & Michael M. Martin, Federal Rules of Evidence Manual 15-38 (5th ed 1990).

[71] 28 USC §2111.

[72] Pierce v Underwood, 487 US 552, 559-60 (1988) (quoting Miller v Fenton, 474 US 104, 114 (1985)).

[73] *Id* 559-60.

[74] Steven A. Childress & Martha S. Davis, *supra* note 69. *See also* Steven A. Childress, *A Standards of Review Primer: Federal Civil Appeals,* 125 FRD 319 (1989).

§5.04 —Civil Case Fact Issues

Federal Rule of Civil Procedure 52(a) has governed the reviewability of district court factfinding since the rules were adopted. It was amended in 1985 to read, in relevant part: "Findings of fact, whether based on oral or documentary evidence, shall not be set aside unless clearly erroneous, and due regard shall be given to the opportunity of the trial court to judge of the credibility of the witnesses."[75] The amendment makes clear that deference must be accorded the trial judge's findings even when they rest "solely on documentary evidence."[76] The rule is based upon

> the public interest in the stability and judicial economy that would be promoted by recognizing that the trial court, not the appellate tribunal, should be the finder of the facts. To permit courts of appeals to share more actively in the fact-finding function would tend to undermine the legitimacy of the district courts in the eyes of litigants, multiply appeals by encouraging appellate retrial of some factual issues, and needlessly reallocate judicial authority.[77]

Rule 52(a) removes much of the uncertainty that had existed in the case law. Even when the trial judge adopts a party's proposed findings verbatim, and even when the findings are based on nontestimonial evidence, the *clearly erroneous* standard will apply.[78] This is despite some judicial criticism of the practice of adopting party findings.[79]

In bankruptcy cases, the court of appeals treats the district court or bankruptcy appellate panel factfindings like those of a district judge in a nonjury case.[80] This standard is a deferential one; if "the district court's account of the

---

[75] The full text of Fed R Civ P 52 is in **app B.** *See* Icicle Seafoods, Inc v Worthington, 475 US 709 (1986) (applying Fed R Civ P 52(a) standard); Anderson v City of Bessemer City, 470 US 564 (1985).

[76] Advisory Committee Notes, 1985 amendment to Fed R Civ P 52(a).

[77] *Id* (citing many cases and assessing importance of Rule).

[78] Anderson v City of Bessemer City, 470 US 564, 571-576 (1985).

[79] *Id* 572 (noting potential for overreaching by attorneys preparing factfindings) (citing J. Wright, The Nonjury Trial—Preparing Findings of Fact, Conclusions of Law, and Opinions, Seminars for Newly Appointed United States District Judges 159, 166 (1962)).

[80] *See* **§2.14.** There is some confusion in the Ninth Circuit's approach to party-drafted findings, at least in bankruptcy cases. Compare *In re* T.H. Richards Processing Co, 910 F2d 639, 643 n2 (9th Cir 1990) (court criticizes "regrettable practice" of bankruptcy court adopting party-drafted findings "wholesale," and reviews such findings with "special scrutiny") (quoting Sealy, Inc v Easy Living, Inc, 743 F2d 1378, 1385 n3 (9th Cir 1984) *with In re* Wolverton Assocs, 909 F2d 1286 (9th Cir 1990) (trial court, including bankruptcy court, findings reviewed under clearly erroneous standard even when adopted from proposed findings of winning party). A court of appeals reviewing district court affirmance of bankruptcy court will apply the *two-court rule,* whereby factual findings approved by two lower courts will not be reviewed absent obvious error. Judge v Production Credit Assn, 969 F2d 699, 700 (8th Cir 1992).

evidence is plausible in light of the record viewed in its entirety, the court of appeals may not reverse it even though convinced that had it been sitting as the trier of fact, it would have weighed the evidence differently."[81] Even where the district court is imprecise about the bases for its factual conclusions, the appellate court may not "engage in impermissible appellate factfinding."[82]

A finding is " 'clearly erroneous' when although there is evidence to support it, the reviewing court on the entire evidence is left with the definite and firm conviction that a mistake has been committed."[83]

Review of civil jury determinations is limited by the Seventh Amendment command that "no fact tried by a jury shall be otherwise re-examined in any Court of the United States, than according to the rules of the common law."[84] The sufficiency of the evidence to create a jury issue is therefore one of federal law in cases tried in federal court.[85] The question is whether there is evidence on which a rational jury could find for the party in whose favor the verdict was given under the applicable burden of persuasion.[86]

The reference to the burden of persuasion must be kept in mind in any analysis of factfinding by the trial judge or the jury. If a party, in order to prevail, must establish its claim by clear and convincing evidence, a jury verdict may not stand unless a rational juror could make a finding by that standard.[87]

Similarly, if the trial judge is making a determination on a claim that must be established by clear and convincing evidence, he or she must be seen to have applied that standard and not a lesser one. To take an example from the summary judgment field, a district judge must assess under Fed R Civ P 56 whether there is a genuine issue for trial.[88] The Supreme Court has stated that "the injury involved in a ruling on a motion for summary judgment or for a directed verdict necessarily implicates the substantive evidentiary standard of proof that would apply at the trial on the merits."[89]

The Court has applied this rule in a libel case involving a public figure plain-

---

[81] Amadeo v Zant, 486 US 214, 223 (1988) (quoting Anderson v City of Bessemer City, 470 US 564, 573-74 (1985)).

[82] *Id* 228.

[83] Anderson v City of Bessemer City, 470 US 564, 573 (1985) (quoting United States v United States Gypsum Co, 333 US 364, 395 (1948).

[84] US Const amend VII.

[85] Byrd v Blue Ridge Rural Elec Coop, Inc, 356 US 525 (1958).

[86] *See* 9 Charles A. Wright & Arthur R. Miller, Federal Practice & Procedure: Civil §2524, at 541-47 (1971); Steven A. Childress, *Summary and Sources of Standards of Review: Fifth Circuit Appeals,* 4 Fifth Circuit Rep 97 (1986).

[87] Anderson v Liberty Lobby, Inc, 477 US 242, 252 (1986) (noting that summary judgment and directed verdict standards are the same).

[88] *Id.* Other important questions on standard of review in this context are Matsushita Elec Indus v Zenith Radio Corp, 475 US 574 (1986) (when claims are implausible, claimant must advance more evidence than otherwise would be necessary to avoid summary judgment); Celotex Corp v Catrett, 477 US 317 (1986).

[89] 477 US at 252.

tiffs, requiring that plaintiff show actual malice by clear and convincing evidence under *New York Times Co v Sullivan*[90] and its progeny:

> Just as the "convincing clarity" requirement is relevant in ruling on a motion for directed verdict, it is relevant in ruling on a motion for summary judgment. When determining if a genuine factual issue as to actual malice exists in a libel suit brought by a public figure, a trial judge must bear in mind the actual quantum and quality of proof necessary to support liability under *New York Times.* For example, there is no genuine issue if the evidence presented in the opposing affidavits is of insufficient caliber or quantity to allow a rational finder of fact to find actual malice by clear and convincing evidence.[91]

In sum, a trier of fact will find deference at the hands of the appellate court when it has made a factual determination on a record that reflects that the proper standard was applied in its factfinding role.

There is at least one avenue of escape from the clearly erroneous standard. If the trial judge's findings are incomplete or ambiguous, so that meaningful appellate review is impossible, the court of appeals may remand for further findings or even decide the matter itself and render judgment.[92]

Another vexing problem in appellate review involves summary judgment. Grant or denial of summary judgment is, by the weight of authority, reviewed "de novo, applying the same standard as did the district court."[93] Yet, a district judge can draft factual findings in support of granting a motion for summary judgment, and even in denying one. The standard for summary judgment speaks as much to fact as to law: "viewing the facts in the light most favorable to the opposing party, there is no genuine issue of material fact in dispute and the moving party should prevail as a matter of law."[94] One could well argue that at least some summary judgment dispositions, where fact-findings are central to the determination, should be reviewed under a *clearly erroneous* standard.

§5.05 —Civil Case Legal Issues

The court of appeals reviews questions of law de novo. This seemingly simple

---

[90] 376 US 254 (1964).

[91] 477 US at 254 (quoting 376 US at 285-86).

[92] Steven A. Childress & Martha S. Davis, Federal Standards of Review §§2.11-2.12 (2d ed 1992). *But see* Icicle Seafoods, Inc v Worthington, 475 US 709 (1986) (limiting power of appellate court to find facts on its own).

[93] Raymond v Mobil Oil Corp, 983 F2d 1528, 1534 (10th Cir) (citing Miller v Coastal Corp, 978 F2d 622 (10th Cir 1992), *cert denied,* 113 S Ct 1586 (1993)), *cert denied,* 114 S Ct 81 (1993).

[94] *Id* 1534 (quoting Woolsey v Marion Lab, Inc, 934 F2d 1452, 1456 (10th Cir 1991), *cited by* Millensifer v Retirement Plan for Salaried Employees of Cotter Corp, 968 F2d 1005, 1007 (10th Cir 1992).

standard has proven complicated in application.[95] When a factual determination involves an important principle, such as the First Amendment, the appeals court may redesignate the issue as one of law and review the trial court's decision by a more exacting standard.[96] On the other hand, a trial court's legal determination, for example, in crafting a jury instruction, may be given more deference than the de novo review standard would imply; the trial judge has discretion as to the form of instructions, provided the legal principles are conveyed adequately.[97] These conceptual difficulties do not, however, destroy the general principle.[98]

Questions of law arise in several ways during a trial. On the pleadings, a judge decides an issue of law in assessing the sufficiency of a pleading in point of substance: does the pleading set forth a claim or defense that is properly in the case?[99] In ruling on admissibility of evidence, a judge must necessarily determine whether the proffered evidence tends to prove "any fact that is of consequence to the determination of the action."[100] This necessarily implicates the substantive law of claims and defenses.

A trial judge decides issues of law in fashioning jury instructions on the elements of the parties' cases. In a judge-tried case, issues of law are decided in the conclusions of law that usually must be filed by the court.

Issues of law also may be involved in deciding dispositive motions, such as those addressed to the court's jurisdiction, for summary judgment,[101] or for judgment on the pleadings. Motions for directed verdict, new trial, and judgment notwithstanding the verdict—now collectively called judgment as a matter of law[102]—may rest upon legal as well as factual premises.

---

[95] *See* Fleming James, Jr, Geoffrey Hazard, & John Leubsdorf, Civil Procedure §12.9 (4th ed 1992).

[96] Bose Corp v Consumer Union of United States, Inc, 466 US 485 (1984) (Supreme Court reaffirms independent appellate review on the whole record for First Amendment claims), discussed at **§5.13.**

[97] *See generally* 9 Charles A. Wright & Arthur R. Miller, Federal Practice & Procedure: Civil §2556 (1971).

[98] *See generally* Steven A. Childress & Martha S. Davis, Federal Standards of Review §§2.14 (issues of law), 4.23 (jury instructions) (2d ed 1992).

[99] *See generally id* §3.09. The advocate obviously will find helpful authorities in annotated or textual discussions of Fed R Civ P 8 and 9.

[100] Fed R Evid 401. This is the test of Fed R Evid 401, which must be read together with Fed R Evid 402 (relevant evidence generally admissible) and 403 (exclusion of relevant evidence on various grounds). The formulation of Fed R Evid 401 collapses the traditional distinction between materiality—whether the fact the evidence is offered to prove is properly in the action—and relevance—whether the evidence does in fact tend to prove the fact it is offered to prove. *See* 1 Stephan A. Saltzburg & Michael M. Martin, Federal Rules of Evidence Manual 123-54 (5th ed 1990).

[101] *See* **§5.04.**

[102] Despite the new collective name under Fed R Civ P 50, motions for judgment as a matter of law made at different times have different procedural effects corresponding to their prior names. This fact, and the inevitable inertia of lawyers, will no doubt cause the old names to continue to be used.

Legal errors at the pleading stage may well have been mooted by later events, because the theory of the case may have changed in the course of trial so that the judgment rests upon a different and better foundation than that provided in the complaint and answer.[103] Moreover, a judgment will be sustained if clearly based upon several grounds, any of which will support it.[104] This rule is qualified in jury cases: a general verdict may mask the true basis for the verdict and the court of appeals may be unable to say with confidence that the jury chose the right ground for its decision.[105]

Errors of law that formed the basis for wrongly admitting or excluding evidence may be weak reeds on which to rest a claim of error unless the trial judge excluded an entire line of claim or defense.[106]

Finally, all claims of legal error must be tested against the applicable harmless error standard. While a court of appeals reviews the law de novo, its finding that the trial court erred is the beginning and not the end of inquiry. The error must, in general, have contributed to a wrong result in some identifiable way.[107] The lawyer must be able to articulate this causal nexus between error and harm, and point to some part of the judgment that would have been different if the error had not been committed.

§5.06 —Civil Case Procedural Issues

The record of every trial can be dissected for procedural error, but—to pursue the metaphor—seldom will such an error prove to have been the efficient cause of death. In the course of a trial, district judges are called upon to make myriad rulings respecting pleading, joinder, timing, and kindred matters. Errors in making such rulings often are reviewed only under an abuse of discretion standard that almost always will insulate the judgment for reversal.[108] This

---

[103] *See* Charles A. Wright, Federal Courts §68, at 442-43, §76, at 513, §98, at 658 (4th ed 1983).

[104] *See, e.g.*, SEC v Chenery Corp, 318 US 80, 88 (1943) (would be wasteful to send back a case that reached the right result, even if for the wrong reasons); Griffin v United States, 112 S Ct 466 (1991) (general verdict stands if any proper ground is supportable on the record). *See* 5 Am Jur 2d *Appeal & Error* §785 (1962).

[105] *See* Charles A. Wright, *supra* note 103, §94, at 631-32 (on use of special verdicts to minimize reversal risk).

[106] Fed R Evid 103. The cases construing this provision, and stating the rule set out in the text, are collected in 1 Stephan A. Saltzburg & Michael M. Martin, *supra* note 100, at 15-38.

[107] **§5.03.** *See generally* Steven A. Childress & Martha S. Davis, Federal Standards of Review §§6.05, 6.06 (2d ed 1992).

[108] *See generally* Herring v New York, 422 US 853, 862 (1975); Fleming James, Geoffrey Hazard, & John Leubsdorf, Civil Procedure §12.9 (4th ed 1992); Maurice Rosenberg, *Appellate Review of Trial Court Discretion*, 79 FRD 173 (1979).

standard has been characterized as requiring appellate acceptance of the trial judge's "guess unless it is too wild."[109]

Some discovery matters may provide a fruitful ground for appeal, particularly if an entire claim or defense was declared off-limits, a claim of privilege was overruled improperly, or a party engaged in misconduct such as improperly withholding discovery materials.

A good beginning checklist of procedural error is the Federal Rules of Civil Procedure, which enumerate the basic rights of every party as a case progresses. For example, many of the defenses listed in Rule 12(b) would, if overruled, provide a basis for appeal.[110] Improper rulings on motions raising the amendment of pleadings and relation back rules of Rule 15 may create reversible error.[111] Other fecund sources of appellate litigation include Rules 17 (capacity, real party in interest),[112] 19 (necessary and indispensable parties),[113] 23 (class actions),[114] 38 (jury trial),[115] and 51 (jury instruction procedure).[116] The treatise by Professors Childress and Davis, cited numerous times in this chapter, will be a valuable resource.

---

[109] Ford Motor Co v Ryan, 182 F2d 329, 332 (2d Cir), *cert denied,* 340 US 851 (1950). The standard is discussed in David W. Robertson, *Forum Non Conveniens in America and England: "A Rather Fantastic Fiction,"* 103 Law Q Rev 398, 415-16 (1987).

[110] These defenses are: "(1) lack of jurisdiction over the subject matter, (2) lack of jurisdiction over the person, (3) improper venue, (4) insufficiency of process, (5) insufficiency of service of process, (6) failure to state a claim upon which relief can be granted, (7) failure to join a party under Rule 19." Fed R Civ P 12(b). The discussion in this treatise cannot be compendious. The purpose is only to help the advocate create a checklist and to suggest avenues of research.

[111] See Schiavone v Fortune, 477 US 21 (1986), which upholds dismissal of a complaint and denial of a motion to amend.

[112] *See generally,* Charles A. Wright, Federal Courts §70 (4th ed 1983).

[113] *Id* 457-64 (discussing development of rule and noting 1966 amendment to Fed R Civ P 19 that clarified the law of necessary and indispensable parties).

[114] For a discussion of appellate issues that may arise in the interpretation of Fed R Civ P 23, see **§§2.04** and **3.05.** Among the issues are certification and decertification of the class; problems of notice to class members, Eisen v Carlisle & Jacquelin, 417 US 156 (1974) (subject matter jurisdiction of aggregated claims); Zahn v International Paper Co, 414 US 291 (1973) (judicial supervision of settlement, and, of course, allocation of attorneys' fees); *see* Boeing Co v Van Gemert, 444 US 472 (1980). *See generally* Charles A. Wright, *supra* note 112, at §72. Richard L. Marcus & Edward F. Sherman, Complex Litigation (2d ed 1992) (this is a casebook for law school use, but is a valuable reference tool as well). *See also* Manual for Complex Litigation, Second (1985) (a revision compiled under the capable direction of Chief Judge Sam Pointer).

[115] The right to jury trial in civil cases is guaranteed by the Seventh Amendment. The right may be imperiled by trial of equitable claims before legal ones or by judicial determination that a case is too complex for a jury. These issues are canvassed in Charles A. Wright, *supra* note 112, at 605. Of course, as pointed out at **§3.04,** denial of jury trial is reviewable by extraordinary writ. *See also* Parklane Hosiery Co v Shore, 439 US 322 (1979), holding that a declaratory judgment in a case brought by the SEC and tried to a judge had collateral estoppel effect in a shareholder derivative suit that had been filed before the SEC action, but which had not come to trial by the time the SEC judgment was final. The Court majority rejected the argument that denial of collateral estoppel effect was mandated by the Seventh Amendment. Compare Lytle v Household Mfg, Inc, 494 US 545 (1990), denying preclusive effect to a judgment obtained in a nonjury proceeding, where petitioner had sought jury resolution of his contentions.

If a procedural error is found to be an abuse of direction, or is reviewed and found under a stricter standard, the appellant must show that the error was not harmless.[117]

The days when a slip of the sergeant's quill could doom the client's action fortunately are gone. The modern rules of civil procedure are flexible and are meant to be flexibly applied. To win on appeal, a party must show how the error was unfair and harmful in a practical way. A good example of practical reasoning is *Bufford v Rowan Companie.*[118] The Buffords sued for workplace injury. At trial, defense counsel attacked plaintiffs' counsel's integrity, and the trial judge shut off the opportunity to respond. In the heat of trial, many intemperate things are said, and it is difficult to gain a reversal based on such conduct.

In *Bufford,* however, the court of appeals reversed. It acknowledged that the standard of review was that the offensive comments from counsel or the court "so permeate the proceedings that they impair substantial rights and cast doubt on the jury's verdict."[119] However, the court noted that defense counsel's conduct apparently was planned and certainly repeated, and that the trial judge "inadvertently exacerbated the situation."[120] The court's opinion, by Judge Politz, is a study in how a record of procedural error may be put in a context that makes reversal and a new trial seem the only fair outcome.

§5.07 —Criminal Case Fact Issues

When a court of appeals reviews the evidence in support of a judgment of conviction, it first asks whether the claim of insufficiency was preserved by a motion for acquittal at the close of all the evidence under Fed R Crim P 29.[121] If not, the insufficiency claim will be reviewed on a manifest injustice standard.[122]

If a proper Fed R Crim P 29 motion has been made, and indulging all the inferences in favor of the government, the question is whether a rational juror could have found beyond a reasonable doubt for the government on every element of the offense.[123] This is the standard set out in the often cited case of *Glasser v United States.*[124] Few verdicts fail under such a standard.

---

[116] The right of counsel to know in advance what instructions the judge will give, and to make timely objection, is fundamental. *See, e.g.,* Delano v Kitch, 663 F2d 990 (10th Cir 1981), *cert denied,* 456 US 946 (1982).

[117] *See* **§5.03.**

[118] 994 F2d 155 (5th Cir 1993).

[119] *Id* 157 n1.

[120] *Id* 158.

[121] On standards of review for criminal appeals, see generally Lissa Griffin, Federal Criminal Appeals (1991).

[122] **§5.03.** *See, e.g.,* United States v Osgood, 794 F2d 1087 (5th Cir), *cert denied,* 479 US 994 (1986).

[123] *See generally* 2 Charles A. Wright, Federal Practice & Procedure: Criminal 2d §§461-470 (1982).

[124] 315 US 60 (1942).

Rays of hope for the appellant sometimes shine through. Judge Rubin has cautioned that even when viewing the evidence through "Glasser glasses," the court of appeals should not blind itself to blemishes in the government's evidence.[125] Further, the government's burden must be met on every element of the offense and the evidence with regard to each must be analyzed separately.[126] For example, in a multidefendant case in which the evidence of a scheme is clear, a given participant may not have been shown to have the requisite knowledge of the conspiracy and intent to further its unlawful objects.[127]

The difficulty of obtaining reversal based on insufficiency of the evidence must be measured against the negative impact of conceding guilt on appeal and relying only upon legal issues. Thus, as noted elsewhere in this treatise at greater length, a marginal argument on sufficiency may well buttress other arguments, if only to preclude a finding of harmless error on the legal issues.[128]

Moreover, a reversal for insufficiency of the evidence bars retrial under the double jeopardy clause. Under *Burks v United States*[129] and *Greene v Massey*,[130] the court of appeals is obliged to rule upon an appellant's claim that the evidence was insufficient to convict. If the court of appeals reverses for insufficient evidence, there can be no retrial, regardless of "whether any failure of proof is the fault of the government or the result of an erroneous ruling by the trial court."[131]

Criminal appeals present factual issues other than those presented by general verdicts of guilty. With regard to such issues, the cases are in some disarray on the standard of review. Materiality is an element of the offense of perjury, but is most often held to be for the judge and not the jury to decide.[132] Some offenses based upon disobedience of administrative agency orders make validity of the order an element of the offense, but to be determined by the judge.[133] In either case, the court of appeals may either defer to the district judge on

---

[125] United States v Goss, 650 F2d 1336, 1341 n3 (5th Cir 1981) (Rubin, J).

[126] *See* United States v Brim, 630 F2d 1307 (8th Cir 1980) (sufficiency of each element of the offense); United States v Gjurashaj, 706 F2d 395 (2d Cir 1983) (failure of proof on one element of offense), *cert denied,* 452 US 966 (1981).

[127] *See, e.g.,* Direct Sales Co v United States, 319 US 703 (1943); United States v Falcone, 311 US 205 (1940); United States v Spock, 416 F2d 165 (1st Cir 1969) (First Amendment implications of conspiracy law); Milam v United States, 322 F2d 104 (5th Cir 1963) (mail fraud scheme), *cert denied,* 377 US 911 (1964).

[128] *See* **§9.08.**

[129] 437 US 1 (1978).

[130] 437 US 19 (1978).

[131] United States v Ustica, 847 F2d 42, 47 (2d Cir 1988).

[132] United States v Slawik, 548 F2d 75, 79 n8 (3d Cir 1977). While *Slawik* has been criticized in the Fifth Circuit, United States v Crippen, 579 F2d 340 (5th Cir), *on rehg from* 570 F2d 535 (1978), *cert denied,* 439 US 1069 (1979), the criticism did not extend to the point under discussion here. The consequence of this rule is that materiality determinations will be given plenary, de novo review in the court of appeals.

[133] Cox v United States, 332 US 442 (1947).

the theory that a fact is involved, or review de novo because the issue is classified as one of law.[134]

Similarly, in reviewing orders granting or denying suppression of evidence, or dispositive motions such as those attacking prosecutorial misconduct, the courts of appeals have spoken neither clearly nor unanimously about the standard of review.[135] Thus, the advocate in each case must identify the factual dispute that underlies the legal issue, then turn to the decisional law for the particular court of appeals to find the standard that will be applied.

In most criminal cases, the jury returns a general verdict of guilty or not guilty,[136] although a special verdict may be obtained on such matters as forfeiture.[137] If the general verdict can be sustained on any ground supported by the evidence, the conviction will be affirmed even if one cannot tell whether the jury in fact relied upon a basis that the evidence did not support. If, however, the jury was given two legal theories on which conviction might be based, and one of these was legally erroneous, the general verdict must be set aside.[138]

§5.08 —Criminal Case Legal Issues

The checklist of legal issues in criminal cases is similar to that in civil cases.[139] As in civil cases, appellate attacks on the pleadings—in a criminal case, the indictment and bill of particulars—have found less and less favor in recent years.[140] The courts still occasionally reverse a conviction for failure of the indictment to state the elements of the offense.[141] Error in granting or denying a bill of particulars rarely will be a basis for reversal;[142] failure to grant a bill is probably better classified as a procedural matter.[143]

In criminal cases, legal and procedural issues may involve constitutional rights. Review of such issues is discussed at **§5.13.**

---

[134] *See generally* United States v McConney, 728 F2d 1195 (9th Cir) (en banc) (discussing when de novo review versus abuse of discretion review is appropriate in criminal appeals), *cert denied,* 469 US 824 (1984).

[135] *Id.*

[136] Fed R Crim P 31. It is error to take a special verdict on guilt over the defendant's objection. United States v Spock, 416 F2d 165, 183 (1st Cir 1969).

[137] Fed R Crim P 31(e).

[138] Griffin v United States, 112 S Ct 466 (1991). *See* **§5.08.**

[139] **§5.05.**

[140] Cases are collected and analyzed in 1 Charles A. Wright, Federal Practice & Procedure: Criminal 2d §§121-131 (1982) (discussing the leading case of Russell v United States, 369 US 749 (1962)).

[141] *See id* §§125-126; United States v Berlin, 472 F2d 1002, 1007 (2d Cir), *cert denied,* 412 US 949 (1973).

[142] 1 Charles A. Wright, *supra* note 140, at §§129-131. But in United States v Bortnovsky, 820 F2d 572 (2d Cir 1987), and again in United States v Davidoff, 845 F2d 1151 (2d Cir 1988), the court reversed convictions because the government failed to provide a bill of particulars that would have clarified vague charges.

[143] **§5.09.**

The most fruitful source of legal error in a criminal case will center upon the statutory definition of the offense. Did the trial judge adequately instruct the jury on each element?[144] Jury instructions obviously are crucial to the process of determining innocence or guilt, for they represent the only way a lay jury hears about what the government must prove. Despite the importance of proper jury instructions, appellate courts' reluctance to reverse is manifested in a number of ways. First, failure to object specifically and timely waives any objection, unless there has been plain error.[145] Second, the appellate court will caution against singling out a particular part of the instructions for attack, and will affirm if the instructions, taken as a whole, adequately convey the required elements of the offense.[146] Thus, a failure to instruct in detail on so crucial an element as specific intent may be excused or held to be harmless if the general portions of the jury charge refer adequately to the mental element.[147]

In *Griffin v United States,*[148] the Supreme Court clarified the circumstances under which reversal will be available in a conspiracy case involving two or more object offenses, and in the process reaffirmed that errors of law in jury instructions are subject to plenary review. When the jury returns a general verdict of guilty, and the evidence is inadequate to support conviction as to one of the objects, the conviction will be affirmed nevertheless. The court reaffirmed, however, that illegal error in one of the multiple objects will require reversal, calling this a *clear line* that

> happens to be a line that makes good sense. Jurors are not generally equipped to determine whether a particular theory of conviction submitted to them is contrary to law—whether, for example, the action in question is protected by the Constitution, is time barred, or fails to come within the statutory definition of the crime. When, therefore, jurors have been left the option of relying upon a legally inadequate theory, there is no reason to think that their own intelligence and expertise will save them from that error. Quite the opposite is true, however, when they have

---

[144] Basic sources for research on jury instructions are 2 Charles A. Wright, Federal Practice & Procedure: Criminal 2d, at §§481-502 (1982); Edward J. Devitt, Charles B. Blackmar, Michael A. Wolff, & Kevin F. O'Malley, Federal Jury Practice & Instructions (4th ed 1992). In addition, many circuits have published pattern jury instructions that are issued by West Publishing as supplements to the Devitt & Blackmar treatise and also available independently.

[145] 2 Charles A. Wright, *supra* note 144, at §484, commenting upon Fed R Crim P 30.

[146] *See* Cupp v Naughten, 414 US 141, 146-47 (1973); Henderson v Kibbe, 431 US 145 (1977).

[147] The general rule is that failure to instruct on the intent element, or an instruction that shifts the burden on this issue, is plain error and grounds for reversal even if no objection is made. *See* 2 Charles A. Wright, *supra* note 144, at §497.1. *But see* Henderson v Kibbe, 431 US 145 (1977) (on collateral attack, party bears heavy burden of showing prejudice from wrong instruction).

[148] 112 S Ct 466 (1991).

> been left the option of relying upon a factually inadequate theory, since jurors *are* well equipped to analyze the evidence.[149]

Given these caveats, a defendant is entitled to have the court instruct on every element, and under certain circumstances, to have his or her theory of the case embodied in an appropriate instruction.[150] Since the right of trial by jury is fundamental to constitutional criminal procedure, neither the trial judge nor the court of appeals may substitute its judgment for that of the jury. Seldom indeed will a court of appeals be able to save a verdict rendered by a jury that was not instructed on an element of the offense.

Legal theories also may be implicated in rulings on evidence. The trial judge may have excluded evidence on the theory that it did not relate to a legally cognizable defense. The premise of the trial judge's ruling will be reviewed as a question of law.[151]

Questions of law are reviewed de novo by the court of appeals, although the harmless error standard usually is applied.[152] If the legal error deprived the defendant of a constitutional right, however, a more stringent standard of review will be applied.[153]

§5.09 —Criminal Case Procedural Issues

The procedural matrix within which a criminal case is tried is established by the Federal Rules of Criminal Procedure, the Federal Rules of Evidence, the procedural provisions found in statutes (principally title 18, United States Code), and the Constitution. Constitutional error is discussed in more detail at **§5.13.**

As noted above, objections to the sufficiency of the charging papers are seldom the basis for reversal.[154] However, a claim of error may be founded upon an indictment that does not give fair notice of what the defendant must meet.[155]

---

[149] *Id* 474 (citation omitted).

[150] *See, e.g.,* United States v Vole, 435 F2d 774 (7th Cir 1970). For example, in an appropriate case, a mail fraud defendant is entitled to have the jury instructed that evidence of good faith may raise a reasonable doubt. *See, e.g.,* United States v Goss, 650 F2d 1336 (5th Cir 1981).

[151] *See, e.g.,* United States v Staggs, 553 F2d 1073 (7th Cir 1977) (error to exclude defense evidence negating intent).

[152] *See, e.g.,* Steven A. Childress & Martha S. Davis, Federal Standards of Review §7.06 (2d ed 1992).

[153] *See* **§5.13.** For example, in United States v McClain, 545 F2d 988 (5th Cir 1977), the court said that improperly denying the defendant a jury determination of a disputed factual issue could not be cured by a harmless error analysis because the defendant has a right to jury trial on all such issues.

[154] **§5.07.**

[155] *See, e.g.,* United States v Pazsint, 703 F2d 420 (9th Cir 1983) (forbidden amendment of indictment to add additional crime).

Variance between indictment and proof may, if prejudicial, constitute reversible error.[156]

The best checklist of error based upon violations of the Federal Rules of Criminal Procedure is Charles Alan Wright's Criminal 2d volumes in the set, *Federal Practice and Procedure.*[157] The errors that count most in the calculus of reversal are those that can be said to have disabled the defendant's ability to defend himself or herself. Withholding vital evidence,[158] denying the right of cross-examination,[159] failing to sanitize the jury against improper influence[160]—this sort of error is so fundamental that it is sometimes held to implicate the constitutional guarantees of fair adversary procedure embodied in the Fifth and Sixth Amendments.[161]

When courts of appeals evaluate claims of error based on the Federal Rules of Criminal Procedure, they often begin or end the discussion by saying that the defendant is entitled to a fair trial but not a perfect one.[162] This is another way of phrasing the *harmless error* standard.[163] The advocate must, in this as in all quests for error, be able to articulate the nexus between error and a wrong result.

---

[156] United States v Sutherland, 656 F2d 1181 (5th Cir 1981) (summarizing doctrines of variance and misjoinder), *cert denied,* 455 US 949, 991 (1982).

[157] See also Wayne R. LaFave & Jerold Israel, Criminal Procedure (Hornbook ed 1985), and—for fuller treatment—the multivolume edition by the same authors. *See also* Joel Androphy, White Collar Crime (Shepard's/McGraw-Hill 1992).

[158] *See generally* W. LaFave & J. Israel, *supra* note 157, at §19.5.

[159] Davis v Alaska, 415 US 308 (1974), Smith v Illinois, 390 US 129 (1968). *See generally* Peter Westen, *The Compulsory Process Clause,* 73 Mich L Rev 71 (1974); Peter Westen, *Compulsory Process II,* 74 Mich L Rev 191 (1975) (brilliant synthesis of defendant's right to confrontation and compulsory process).

[160] *See, e.g.,* United States v Williams, 809 F2d 1072 (5th Cir 1987) (reversing conviction because jury not sufficiently interrogated about adverse midtrial publicity).

[161] See **§5.13** for discussion of standards of review of constitutional error. In addition to the Peter Westen article cited above, see, e.g., Wayne R. LaFave & Jerold Israel, *supra* note 157, at chs 19, 21, 23.

[162] *See, for example,* Fontaine v United States, 411 US 213, 215 (1973); Lutwak v United States, 344 US 604, 619 (1953).

[163] In addition to authorities cited above concerning the harmless error rule, see Rose v Clark, 478 US 570 (1986) (conviction stands if court can say that constitutional error was harmless beyond a reasonable doubt); Darden v Wainwright, 477 US 168 (1986) (prosecutor's improper closing argument and degrading comments about the defendant were harmless error given inviting nature of defendant's closing argument and the heavy evidence against him); Delaware v Van Arsdall, 475 US 673, 684 (1986) (confrontation clause error is subject to harmless error analysis; "correct inquiry is whether, assuming that the damaging potential of the cross-examination were fully realized, a reviewing court might nonetheless say that the error was harmless beyond a reasonable doubt"; whether error is harmless depends upon things such as: importance of witness's testimony; whether it was cumulative, corroborated, or contradicted; extent of permitted cross-examination; and strength of prosecution's case in general). Some errors are so fundamental that they cannot be excused as harmless, including admission of a coerced confession, trial before a biased tribunal, and complete denial of the right to counsel. *See* **§5.13.**

The cases speak of three different standards of review, *abuse of discretion,*[164] *clearly erroneous,*[165] and *de novo.*[166] *Clearly erroneous* applies most logically to factual determinations that underlie procedural rulings and *de novo* to conclusions of law.

Most procedural rulings that do not have constitutional overtones will be reviewed for abuse of discretion. Prominent among these is denial of a motion for severance under Fed R Crim P 14 for prejudicial joinder. Indeed, some trial lawyers and trial judges mistakenly call a Rule 14 motion one for discretionary severance. Such characterization obscures the crucial distinction between the trial judge's duty in passing on the motion and the appellate court's deference to a denial. If the trial judge exercises purported discretion based upon a manifestly improper standard, then review should be as with any other error of law. Were it not so, Lord Chief Justice Holt's dictum that "discretionary is but a softer word for arbitrary" would seem truer than ever.

By contrast with Fed R Crim P 14 decisions, the question of which offenses may properly be joined under Fed R Crim P 8 presents a question of law that is reviewed de novo. However, as with almost every other error of law, misjoinder will not result in reversal if the error is deemed harmless.[167]

Some questions of procedure affect the fairness of a defendant's trial in a fundamental way, yet are not clearly classifiable as constitutional in nature. For example, suppose the prosecutor withholds vital evidence from the defense. The error may simply be a violation of a discovery obligation,[168] or it may constitute a violation of due process or of the right of confrontation.[169]

Federal appellate caselaw is rife with defense motions for new trial, claiming that a government witness committed perjury during trial.[170] It is sometimes difficult to determine whether the decisions in such cases are based upon due process grounds or a construction of Fed R Crim P 33. Some of the federal cases are habeas corpus challenges to state criminal convictions, as to which the court has power under the constitution or not at all.

---

[164] *See, e.g.,* 1 Charles A. Wright, Federal Practice & Procedure: Criminal 2d §227 (1982) (collecting abuse of discretion cases concerning Fed R Crim P 14).

[165] *See* United States v Gann, 732 F2d 714 (9th Cir) (collecting cases that use the abuse of discretion and clearly erroneous standards), *cert denied,* 469 US 1034 (1984).

[166] *See* United States v McConney, 728 F2d 1195, 1201 (9th Cir) (en banc) ("[q]uestions of law are reviewed under the non-deferential, de novo standard," reflecting the policy that appellate courts are in a better position than trial courts to decide questions of law because: (1) appellate judges can concentrate solely on legal issues rather than both legal and factual issues, and (2) at least three panel members hear and pass judgment on the case), *cert denied,* 469 US 824 (1984).

[167] United States v Lane, 474 US 438 (1986) (harmless error standard applied to misjoinder issue).

[168] *See, e.g.,* Gelbard v United States, 408 US 41 (government has statutory obligation to disclose electronic surveillance), *cert denied,* 408 US 922 (1972).

[169] *See* Wayne R. LaFave & Jerold Israel, *supra* note at §§19.3, 19.5.

[170] *See* 3 Charles A. Wright, Federal Practice & Procedure: Criminal 2d, §§557.1, 557.2 (1982).

In reviewing a federal conviction obtained by use of perjured testimony of which the prosecution was aware or should have been aware, the court of appeals will set aside the verdict "if there is any reasonable likelihood that the false testimony could have affected the judgment of the jury."[171] If the government was unaware of the perjury, a new trial will be granted only if the testimony was material and "the court [is left] with a firm belief that but for the perjured testimony, the defendant would most likely not have been convicted."[172]

With criminal case procedural issues, as with those in civil cases, the defense should first attempt to classify the issue as one of law, or even of constitutional law.

The government may, as noted elsewhere in this treatise, appeal from some trial court orders concerning questions of procedures, including pretrial rulings that exclude evidence and dismissals before jeopardy has attached.[173]

§5.10 —Civil and Criminal Case Evidence Issues

Rulings on evidence to which proper objection was made will provide a basis for appeal under some circumstances. As noted at **§5.03,** Fed R Evid 103 contains a harmless error and a plain error provision. Most rulings on admission or exclusion of evidence are reviewed under an abuse of discretion standard.[174]

To assess potential evidence issues, the advocate can use an evidence treatise based upon the Federal Rules of Evidence.[175] The longer the trial, the less an error in admitting or excluding evidence will seem to matter to the court of appeals. However, prejudicial admission or exclusion of evidence, in clear contravention of the Federal Rules of Evidence, has often been the basis for reversal.[176]

---

[171] United States v Wallach, 935 F2d 445, 456-58 (2d Cir 1991) (quoting United States v Agurs, 427 US 97, 103 (1976), *cited by* Perkins v LeFevre, 691 F2d 616, 619 (2d Cir 1982)).

[172] *Id* 456 (quoting Sanders v Sullivan, 863 F2d 218, 226 (2d Cir 1988)) (a habeas corpus case).

[173] *See* **§2.11.**

[174] *See, e.g.,* 2 Stephan A. Saltzburg & Michael M. Martin, Federal Rules of Evidence Manual 27-30 (5th ed 1990) (admission or exclusion of expert testimony); 1 *id* at 172-74 (Fed R Evid 403 balance of probative value against prejudice).

[175] Stephan A. Saltzburg & Michael M. Martin, Federal Rules of Evidence Manual (5th ed 1990), is probably the best resource for this purpose, because it is compact and its authors have collected the most significant federal cases and recited them in some detail.

[176] *See, e.g.,* United States v Check, 582 F2d 668 (2d Cir 1978) (failure to exclude hearsay evidence was prejudicial error requiring reversal; reversed and remanded for new trial). Josephs v Harris Corp, 677 F2d 985 (3d Cir 1982) is illustrative. The court found that the trial judge erred in excluding evidence bearing upon the standard of care in a defective products case. Other cases are collected by Stephan A. Saltzburg & Michael M. Martin, *supra* note 174, in their discussion of Fed R Evid 403.

Given the abuse of discretion standard, however, the advocate should attempt to recast the contention as one of law. For example, Fed R Evid 702 permits introduction of expert testimony by one who is "qualified as an expert by knowledge, skill, experience, training, or education."[177] If a trial court admits expert testimony after considering these factors, and concludes that the testimony will assist the trier of fact, that judgment will not be disturbed on appeal unless the court abused its discretion.[178] However, if the trial judge applies the wrong legal standard and excludes expert testimony by insisting on too strict a test of qualification, that judgment will be reviewed as an error of law.[179]

Often, an appellate court will fault a trial judge for not having made a clear record in deciding to admit or exclude evidence. When the court of appeals cannot say with conviction that the trial judge applied the correct standard, it will reverse more readily.[180] For example, a trial judge asked to admit evidence of other crimes, wrongs, or acts under Fed R Evid 404(b) first must determine that the evidence is offered for a proper purpose. Then, the court must perform the balancing test mandated by Fed R Evid 403.[181]

Federal Rule of Evidence 104 provides the procedure for making admissibility decisions. The trial judge must not only follow Rule 104, but must have been seen to have done so.[182] Often, a question of admissibility consists of both factual and legal elements. For example, a district judge acts under Fed R Evid 104 to determine facts justifying admission in evidence of coconspirator hearsay. The rule is that a clearly erroneous standard will be applied to the factual determination and an abuse of discretion standard to the admissibility decision generally.[183]

Because the rules of evidence are fundamental to the adversary system, their application may raise constitutional issues.[184] For example, hearsay evidence may violate the confrontation clause.[185] A defendant's right to introduce evidence, even when the rules seem to require exclusion, may implicate the due process or compulsory process clauses.[186] Some evidence may offend other constitutional guarantees. In *Dawson v Delaware,*[187] for example, the Supreme Court held that evidence of a murder defendant's membership in a white supremacist gang implicated "nothing more than [the defendant's] abstract

---

[177] Fed R Evid 702.

[178] 2 Stephan A. Saltzburg & Michael M. Martin, supra note 174, at 27-30.

[179] *See generally* Daubert v Merrell Dow Pharmaceuticals, Inc, 113 S Ct 2786 (1993).

[180] *See, e.g.,* cases collected in 1 Stephan A. Saltzburg & Michael M. Martin, *supra* note 175, at 172-74.

[181] *Id* 198-99 (collecting cases).

[182] *See id* 217-19.

[183] *See, e.g.,* United States v Gessa, 971 F2d 1257 (6th Cir 1992) (en banc).

[184] *See* **§5.13.**

[185] *See, e.g.,* Ohio v Roberts, 448 US 56 (1980).

[186] *See, e.g.,* Chambers v Mississippi, 410 US 284 (1973); Peter Westen, *The Compulsory Process Clause,* 73 Mich L Rev 71 (1974).

[187] 112 S Ct 1093 (1992).

beliefs" and that admitting the evidence violated the defendant's First Amendment rights.[188]

§5.11 —Administrative Agency Cases

The basic standard of review for agency adjudicative determinations is provided by 5 USC §706:

> Scope of Review
>
> To the extent necessary to decision and when presented, the reviewing court shall decide all relevant questions of law, interpret constitutional and statutory provisions, and determine the meaning or applicability of the terms of an agency action. The reviewing court shall—
>
> (1) compel agency action unlawfully withheld or unreasonably delayed; and
>
> (2) hold unlawful and set aside agency action, findings, and conclusions found to be—
>
> (A) arbitrary, capricious, an abuse of discretion, or otherwise not in accordance with law;
>
> (B) contrary to constitutional right, power, privilege, or immunity;
>
> (C) in excess of statutory jurisdiction, authority, or limitations, or short of statutory right;
>
> (D) without observance of procedure required by law;
>
> (E) unsupported by substantial evidence in a case subject to sections 556 and 557 of this title or otherwise reviewed on the record of an agency hearing provided by statute; or
>
> (F) unwarranted by the facts to the extent that the facts are subject to trial de novo by the reviewing court.
>
> In making the foregoing determinations, the court shall review the whole record or those parts of it cited by a party, and due account shall be taken of the rule of prejudicial error.[189]

The provisions of §706 establish a presumptive floor under court of appeals review of agency action. Particular statutes governing agency review, and case law construing them, may provide for a different standard of review or for additional bases for review.[190]

---

188 *Id* 1098.

189 5 USC §706.

190 *See generally* Robert L. Rabin, *Federal Regulation in Historical Perspective,* 38 Stan L Rev 1189 (1986). This article is an indispensable guide to judicial review trends.

For example, in *INS v Abudu,*[191] the Court held that the court of appeals should apply an abuse of discretion standard in determining whether the Board of Immigration Appeals (BIA) erred in denying a motion to reopen a deportation proceeding on the basis of the alien's failure to justify not having asserted an asylum claim at the outset of proceedings. The Court expressly declined to decide what constitutes a prima facie case for asylum or what standard of review would be applied to a Board decision on the merits of such a claim.[192]

The term *abuse of discretion* has a chameleon quality. Many decisions are committed to agency discretion, but it is fundamental to the rule of law that the discretion bestowed by statute be confined precisely and narrowly enough to escape invalidation as an improper delegation.[193] Further, no claim of discretion will insulate agency action undertaken by procedural devices that deny or endanger basic rights, or based upon impermissible line drawing.[194] For example, in *Edward J. DeBartolo Corp v Florida Gulf Coast Building & Construction Trades Council,*[195] the Supreme Court held that although the NLRB's construction of the National Labor Relations Act is normally entitled to great deference, the Court will reject the NLRB's position when it raises serious First Amendment problems that an alternative construction would avoid.

In *Gutknecht v United States,*[196] the Selective Service System had adopted regulations that stripped a registrant of his deferment or exemption and accelerated him for induction if the local board found he had committed a violation of Selective Service rules and procedures. This power endangered First Amendment rights and was exercised in a way that raised due process concerns. The Court struck down the regulations, however, by finding that Congress had not authorized the System to make them. The Court held that regulations that endanger constitutional liberty will require a clearer basis of delegated legislative authority than other kinds of regulations.

If the agency is establishing or interpreting rules within its statutory grant of authority, its holdings are entitled to deference because it has been entrusted with developing a coherent body of specialized law.[197] However, questions of the scope of agency power, and especially those involving claims of constitu-

---

[191] 485 US 94 (1988).

[192] For a discussion of the standards applicable to review of BIA decisions and a thoughtful analysis in the context of refugee asylum claims, see Judge Noonan's opinion in Lazo-Majano v INS, 813 F2d 1432 (9th Cir 1987).

[193] Louis L. Jaffe, Judicial Control of Administrative Action 359-63 (1965).

[194] *See generally* See v City of Seattle, 387 US 541 (1967) (search and seizure rights); Camara v Municipal Court, 387 US 523 (1967); National Student Assn v Hershey, 412 F2d 1103 (DC Cir 1969) (First Amendment rights); Wolff v Selective Serv Local Bd No 16, 372 F2d 817 (2d Cir 1967) (same).

[195] 485 US 568 (1988).

[196] 396 US 295 (1970).

[197] Robert L. Rabin, *supra* note 190, at 1295-1326, discusses the Court's changing attitude toward review of agency decisions, in light of such cases as Citizens to Preserve Overton Park, Inc v Volpe, 401 US 402 (1971) (Secretary of Transportation decision not based upon adequate record).

tional right, probably will be reviewed de novo.[198] In any case, an agency claiming the right to deference must have made a record that shows how and upon what factual basis it reached its specialized conclusion.[199]

The general topic of agency review is the subject of many specialized treatises.[200]

§5.12 —Tax Court Cases

The appropriate court of appeals has exclusive jurisdiction to review Tax Court decisions "in the same manner and to the same extent as decisions of the district courts in civil actions tried without a jury."[201]

The court of appeals therefore will review de novo the Tax Court's decisions on questions of law and will decline to accord the Tax Court any special deference, even on interpretation of the Internal Revenue Code.[202]

An abuse of discretion or harmless error standard applies to review of the Tax Court's procedural and evidentiary rulings.[203] Tax Court factfindings are subject to the clearly erroneous standard, although presumably a finding implicating the First Amendment would be accorded independent review on the whole record.[204] It has been held that review of a Tax Court determination on a question of value is particularly grudging to the party seeking reversal.[205]

---

[198] *See generally* Louis L. Jaffe, *supra* note 193, at chs 14, 16. The scope of agency power may interact with questions of constitutional right. Agency action that threatens constitutional values will be scrutinized closely to determine whether the agency's power extends far enough to make the challenged rule or determination. *See, e.g.,* Gutknecht v United States, 396 US 295 (1970) (Selective Service System had no authority to issue regulations stripping registrants of deferments without hearing); Greene v McElroy, 360 US 474 (1959) (Department of Defense not authorized to make regulations denying rights of confrontation and cross-examination); Kent v Dulles, 357 US 116 (1958) (Secretary of State had no power to deny passports based upon political affiliation).

[199] *See* Citizens to Preserve Overton Park, Inc v Volpe, 401 US 402 (1971); Robert L. Rabin, *supra* note 190, at 1296-98.

[200] Kenneth C. Davis, Administrative Law Treatise (2d ed 1978), and Professor Jaffe's classic book, *supra* note 193, are the standard works. In addition, Commerce Clearing House and Bureau of National Affairs, among other publishers, have an extensive catalog of looseleaf services.

[201] 26 USC §7482(a)(1). *See* **§2.13.**

[202] Kreider v Commissioner, 762 F2d 580 (7th Cir 1985).

[203] Estate of Shafer v Commissioner, 749 F2d 1216 (6th Cir 1984).

[204] Metallics Recycling Co v Commissioner, 732 F2d 523 (6th Cir 1984); Dreicer v Commissioner, 665 F2d 1292 (DC Cir 1981). First Amendment issues can arise in tax cases. *See* United States v Sun Myung Moon, 718 F2d 1210 (2d Cir 1983), *cert denied,* 466 US 971 (1984).

[205] Estate of Brown v Commissioner, 425 F2d 1406 (5th Cir 1970).

§5.13 —Constitutional Issues

As noted above, factual, legal, procedural, and evidence issues may at times raise constitutional concerns. When a constitutional question is present, the appellate court should be particularly vigilant, and much less deferential to the factual and legal rulings of the agency or lower court whose action is being reviewed. The advocate on appeal benefits from casting issues in constitutional terms, if this can be done persuasively.[206]

Many decided cases have addressed the special position of constitutional issues in appellate review, and their common teaching is that appellate courts often will make an independent review not only of the constitutional claim but also of the factual basis upon which it is said to rest.[207]

For example, in *Bose Corp v Consumers Union of the United States, Inc,*[208] the defendant had published an article highly critical of Bose's high-fidelity stereo speakers. The district court held that Bose was a public figure, but that it had sustained its burden under *New York Times Co v Sullivan*[209] of proving by clear and convincing evidence that Consumers Union acted with actual malice, that is, with knowledge of the article's falsity or with reckless disregard of whether it was true or false.

On appellate review, *Bose* relied upon the command of Fed R Civ P 52(a) that the district judge's factual findings must be sustained unless they were clearly erroneous.[210] A majority of the Supreme Court held that the clearly erroneous standard does not apply to review of malice findings in public figure libel cases. In such a case, the First Amendment is always in the balance and fidelity to its command requires that appellate judges " 'make an independent examination of the whole record' in order to make sure 'that the judgment does not constitute a forbidden intrusion on the field of free expression.' "[211] The Court cited a number of cases, civil and criminal, upholding this independent factfinding function in First Amendment cases.[212]

---

[206] Counsel representing petitioners for federal habeas corpus have a special responsibility to raise every conceivable issue because successive petitions for habeas corpus are disfavored. *See* **§6.08.**

[207] The cases do not speak with a single voice, as the Supreme Court recognized in Pullman-Standard v Swint, 456 US 273, 289-90 n19 (1982). However, it is fair to say that the factual predicate for a trial court determination against a constitutional claim will very likely be considered to present a "mixed question[ ] of law and fact" and therefore be reviewable de novo or, as the rule is sometimes phrased, "independently." *Id.* However, the Court stressed in *Pullman-Standard* that it was not deciding this issue. *See also* United States v McConney, 728 F2d 1195, 1203 (9th Cir), *cert denied,* 469 US 824 (1984); Rose v Clark, 478 US 570 (1986).

[208] 466 US 485 (1984).

[209] 376 US 254 (1964).

[210] *See* **§5.03.**

[211] 466 US at 499 (quoting New York Times Co v Sullivan, 376 US 254, 284-86 (1964)).

[212] *Id* 498-511. The teaching of *Bose* was applied in Hartke-Hanks Communications, Inc v Connaughton, 491 US 657 (1989) (court of appeals reviewing a libel judgment in favor of a public official or public figure must exercise independent judgment and determine whether the record establishes actual malice with convincing clarity).

The same obligation of independent review of the whole record is not imposed on appellate courts with respect to every constitutional claim.[213] The claim itself—the formulation of a legal rule—will be reviewed de novo; the court of appeals is as qualified to make such a determination as the district court.[214] The district judge's factual determinations in accepting or rejecting the constitutional claim may be judged by the independent review, de novo review, or clearly erroneous standard, depending upon the claim and the court of appeals.[215]

The presence of a constitutional claim may influence the decision of a nonconstitutional issue. For example, if exclusion of defense evidence might raise a claim under the compulsory process clause, a court will be more inclined to avoid the constitutional issue and find for admissibility on another standard.[216]

While constitutional claims are reviewed de novo, a finding of constitutional error does not automatically spell reversal. Some claims in criminal cases involve fundamental rights, such as the reasonable doubt standard; violation of that standard will always mandate reversal without any showing of prejudice.[217] In other cases, the constitutional error will trigger reversal unless it was harmless beyond a reasonable doubt.[218] On federal habeas corpus, constitutional error in state criminal convictions is judged by a *substantial and injurious effect* standard, although there is some doubt about the way in which such a standard will be applied.[219]

In civil cases, the harmless error standard is less well developed. *Bose* holds that constitutional facts are reviewed de novo, out of deference to the First Amendment issues that lurk in every public figure/public official defamation case. If the district court has erred in an unconstitutional way on a legal issue, for example, by giving a constitutionally defective jury instruction in a libel case, it will difficult for the appellee to show that there is no possible prejudice

---

[213] *See* United States v McConney, 728 F2d 1195, 1203 (9th Cir), *cert denied,* 469 US 824 (1984). The Supreme Court declined to determine whether the *Bose* standard of review applies to trial courts' findings of fact in cases striking down governmental restrictions on speech as contrary to the First Amendment by denying certiorari in Don's Porta Signs, Inc v City of Clearwater, 485 US 981 (1988). Justice White, dissenting, would have granted certiorari to resolve the split between circuits over whether de novo review is required whenever a court has considered a First Amendment claim or only when that claim has been rejected.

[214] In Pullman-Standard v Swint, 456 US 273 (1982), the Court rejected the de novo review standard for findings of discriminatory intent under the Civil Rights Act.

[215] *See id;* United States v McConney, 728 F2d 1195, 1203 (9th Cir), *cert denied,* 469 US 824 (1984).

[216] *See* United States v Salerno, 937 F2d 797 (2d Cir 1991), *revd,* 112 S Ct 2503 (1992).

[217] Sullivan v Louisiana, 113 S Ct 2078, 2083 (1993).

[218] Chapman v California, 386 US 18 (1967).

[219] Brecht v Abrahamson, 113 S Ct 1710, 1714 (1993) (quoting Kotteakos v United States, 328 US 750, 776 (1946). Compare Justice Stevens' concurring opinion, discussing de novo review of the record when a constitutional claim is raised. *Id* 1723-25.

from the error. In sum, it is hard to imagine a civil case in which reversal will not follow a finding of constitutional violation.

§5.14 Retainer Agreement and Fee-Setting for a Federal Appeal

This section first outlines the elements of time and expense that must be considered in setting a fee. Next, it discusses office procedures for time and expense accounting. Finally, it sets out the elements of an engagement letter for a federal appeal. For reasons discussed more fully below, every appellate matter should be covered by an engagement letter.[220]

The fees and costs in a federal appeal will consist of:

1. Lawyer time
2. Paralegal time, if billed
3. Cost of transcript and record preparation
4. Docketing fees
5. Copying charges
6. Cost of reproducing brief and appendix or record excerpts
7. Travel for oral argument
8. Mailing and overnight delivery charges
9. Long distance telephone charges, including fax; and
10. Computer legal research, including cite checking through use of Shepard's, Insta-Cite, Auto-Cite, or WestCheck

If the case is to be accepted for a fixed figure that is to cover fees and expenses, the estimate is all-important. However, even clients who will pay an hourly fee insist upon an estimate before the work begins. In some jurisdictions, an estimate of overall costs may be required or strongly suggested by the rules of professional responsibility.

Every law firm, lawyer, and legal services office and agency should make an estimate in every case, regardless of whether the client wants it or whether there is a paying client in the usual sense of that term. An estimate of quantifiable items is a means of managing litigation efficiently, equalizing workloads among lawyers and other staff members, and evaluating lawyer performance.

Lawyer time[221] can be estimated for the various phases of the appeal and in a multilawyer office should be based upon the lawyers who will be performing different roles in the appellate process. The first item is review of the transcript and record to spot issues on appeal. This estimate will vary based upon the reviewing lawyer's familiarity with the record. The task should include tak-

---

[220] In some jurisdictions, such a written engagement is mandatory in some circumstances. *See* DC Bar Rule 1.5(b).

[221] The calculation should include law clerk time.

ing notes and outlining the record for later digesting. One should calculate how many pages of transcript or record a lawyer can review in one hour; there obviously will be variations based upon the complexity of the record, the experience of the lawyer, and the completeness of the proposed review. A lawyer may review from 100 to 500 pages of transcript per hour, depending upon the complexity of the case. Using the docket entries to skip unnecessary items, the same rate can be applied to the pleadings record.

The next phase will include supervising preparation of the digest and index, researching the legal and factual issues, and making an outline of the proposed brief.[222] The best way to estimate the time required for these tasks is to ask how quickly the lawyer who will perform them can complete the tasks if he or she were to work full-time. If the answer is "one week," then the number of hours will be that lawyer's anticipated weekly workload, which obviously varies from law office to law office. The number of hours calculated for this phase should be increased by 10 per cent to cover the time that should be spent in brainstorming about the case among the lawyers in a multilawyer office. A multilawyer office should have a policy that such discussions are encouraged and should be noted on the billable time record of each lawyer participating.

The next phase will include drafting the brief, a task that may be divided among several lawyers in a multilawyer office. Again, the best way to set a number is to ask how long it would take to do the task if the lawyer or lawyers worked at it full-time. The time of law clerks may be estimated here as well.

Then, the estimate must take into account time for editing the final product and checking the citations. The same calculation must be applied to the reply brief, if one is to be filed. Calculating the time required to prepare for oral argument, and the travel time to the court of appeals, is relatively easy. In addition to the above, the time spent supervising the assembly of the joint appendix or record excerpts must be included.

Finally, a figure of about 5 per cent should be added to the total to cover the time spent making and responding to procedural motions. In a relatively simple case, such motions may consume a disproportionately large amount of time and 10 percent is a better figure.

Paralegal time is charged by many if not most law firms.[223] The digesting, indexing, and other paraprofessional functions performed by nonlawyers should surely be accounted for in assessing the cost of doing an appeal. If the firm does not bill for these separately, they must be reflected in the hourly charges of the lawyers.

Most law firms have some experience with using paraprofessionals to digest depositions and other discovery materials. Preparing a digest of the transcript and record for appeal may take about 25 per cent less time because the parale-

---

[222] *See* **ch 7.**

[223] Many law offices have discovered that legal secretaries with some experience in a litigation setting will be better at digesting transcripts—and indeed, at a whole range of paralegal functions—than someone with no prior legal training and fresh out of a paralegal certificate program. If secretarial personnel perform these functions, they should keep time records for that part of their duties.

gal may be instructed to summarize briefly and focus upon the matters that are the subject of appeal. The method of estimating time is the same as that for lawyers: imagine that the digester would be working on the project full-time and estimate the number of days that would be required.

The cost of transcript and record preparation will be known as soon as the court reporter makes an estimate. Prior to that time, one should simply multiply an estimated number of pages by the reporter's page rate and add 10 per cent to deal with miscellaneous record preparation expenses. The cost may be less if a number of parties appeal and if each orders a copy of the transcript.

Docketing fees are set by the Judicial Conference of the United States under 28 USC §1914 and periodically are revised.

Copying charges can be a major source of expense, particularly if the advocates working on the case routinely make copies of the major cases and other authorities. These copies can then be used to prepare for oral argument. In addition, other copies of important documents will be necessary, including the digest and index of the record. Most law offices estimate copy charges by including not only the cost of the copying itself, but that reflected by the lawyer, secretary, law clerk, or paralegal standing at the copy machine.[224] The cost of reproducing brief and appendix or record excerpts must be estimated from (1) the firm's internal practice, if the firm has reproduction and binding equipment; (2) a commercial copying service, which will have separate and fixed fees for copying, collating, punching, and binding; or (3) a commercial printer. It is unwise to use a commercial printer who is not experienced in doing legal briefs, in part because cost estimates from such a printer can be unreliable.[225] The law office will be uncertain about the number of pages in the brief and appendix or record excerpts, but the estimate can allow for this uncertainty.

Travel for oral argument, mailing and overnight delivery charges, and long distance telephone charges obviously will vary based upon distance and the estimated length and complexity of the case. If drafts of the brief must be exchanged, overnight delivery or fax charges will be incurred and can represent a substantial amount.[226]

Computer legal research has become a mainstay of appellate lawyers in federal cases.[227] However, many lawyers use this tool inefficiently and therefore

---

[224] This rate billed is usually about five times the net per page cost: that is, if the copying supplies and machine average 5 cents per copy, the client will be billed 25 cents. Time spent in indexing cases will be repaid later, when copies are assembled for use in doing a reply brief or oral argument.

[225] *See* **§9.04.**

[226] Some firms have intercity networks that permit easier and more cost effective transmission of information. In other instances, it will be possible to transfer files by modem, which also will produce savings when compared with the costs of overnight delivery and fax.

[227] *See* **§1.07.** Westcheck, an invaluable resource developed by West Publishing, has developed citechecking software that can be integrated with your word processing program to run citation verifications at the various levels of detail.

expensively. The final review of the brief must include Insta-Cite and Shepardization.[228] The estimate should assume one connect minute per citation.[229]

For the basic legal research, the responsible lawyer should be asked to estimate the amount of computer research time that will be necessary, and should not exceed that estimate without a revaluation of the entire cost picture of the appeal. For example, the use of more computer time may turn out to save lawyer time and therefore be cost-effective.[230]

Once all of these fee and cost elements are assembled and added up, it may be possible to revise them downward or upward. A revision downward might be achieved by assigning some lawyer tasks to paralegals or law clerks or by substituting associate time for partner time. The client may be given an option of who will be the principal lawyer on the brief and who will argue it. If new counsel is being retained for appeal, perhaps (with the client's consent) time will be saved by using trial counsel's work product. On the other hand, clients often want a new lawyer to have somebody take a new look at the case.

The firm may be able to quote a fee for stages of the appeal, anticipating a possible settlement, a pending dispositive case that may resolve an important legal issue, or perhaps filing a dispositive motion. These downward revision tactics are useful even on a pro bono case or in a public agency: the estimate may serve to provoke a more efficient use of resources.

Upward revision of a fee will be justified by the difficulty of the case, the need to jettison other work to take it on, and the perceived importance of victory.[231] In many instances, an upfront agreement for a bonus in the event of victory will be wise.

For nongovernmental parties, a written agreement concerning the terms on which the appeal will be handled, and the precise responsibility of the lawyers who will be doing the work, is an absolute necessity. Even for government lawyers, the pitfalls of missed deadlines make it wise to have a written under-

---

[228] *See* **§9.05.**

[229] To determine the amount to bill for computer legal research, take the bills for such service for a representative three-month period and divide the total dollar amount by the number of minutes of connect time used. This will provide an average figure, since connect time may cost different amounts based upon usage, time of day, specialized databases, and search surcharges. To this per minute figure should be added an amount that represents amortization of hardware and software and the cost of computer supplies and maintenance. Each use of the computer research database should be concluded by the user obtaining a printout of the minutes used. This printout should be identified with a client name or number and routed to whoever keeps billing records. In this way, this very valuable but very expensive resource can pay its own way.

[230] For example, time can be saved by not having to go to a law library for something that can be accessed at the computer. However, the trade-off is not one-to-one. The law firm generally makes a profit on associate and paralegal time; it usually only breaks even at best by billing computer time as an out-of-pocket disbursement.

[231] Venegas v Mitchell, 495 US 82 (1990). Any bonus or surcharge must be evaluated carefully to determine that it complies with the ethical standards applicable in a particular jurisdiction.

standing of the particular agency, entity, or lawyer responsibility.[232] Some jurisdictions require written engagement agreements, and they are preferable everywhere for any matter as complex as a federal appeal.

The retainer letter should specify who is responsible for filing a notice of appeal, ordering the transcript, and the other chores that are necessary to get the appeal underway. Often it is a good idea for trial counsel to have these responsibilities, given the ways in which ongoing trial court proceedings can affect the timing and content of what must be filed.[233]

The letter should identify the duties that appellate counsel will and will not perform, possibly identifying the lawyers who will work on the case, and set out the fee arrangements. If the appeal involves multiple clients, the letter should address the issue of multiple representation.

What follows is a sample letter:

> Re: United States v. John Smith, et al.
> No. 93-2154 (U.S. District Court for the Northern District of Shepard)
>
> Dear Mr. Smith:
>
> The purpose of this letter is to set out the terms and conditions under which Richard Roe and the law firm of Roe & Doe have agreed to provide legal services in an appeal of your criminal conviction to the U.S. Court of Appeals for the 13th Circuit.
>
> Our representation will include prosecution of an appeal of your criminal conviction to the Court of Appeals. It is understood, however, that your current attorney, William Wilson, will be responsible for filing a timely Notice of Appeal on your behalf. It also is agreed that you will make arrangements to order the trial transcript and to pay the court reporter directly for the transcript.
>
> We will prepare a certification of the record, prepare and file an opening brief and reply brief, and participate in oral argument if the court grants oral argument. In the event of an adverse determination from the Court of Appeals on the merits of your appeal, we will determine, in our sole discretion, whether a Petition for Rehearing or a Suggestion of Rehearing *en banc* is appropriate and permissible under the court's rules. If so, we will prepare and file such petition and suggestion on your behalf. Our obligation specifically excludes any representation before or further appeal to the U.S. Supreme Court.
>
> Our representation also will include assisting William Wilson in preparing and filing a motion for bail pending appeal, should such a motion

---

[232] For example, the government may have lost a case in a way that generates an appealable order, and want the appeal handled by a regional office or by agency attorneys in Washington, D.C. While responsibility for handling the appeal is being assigned, the date for filing a notice of appeal or ordering the record may pass. This difficulty can be obviated by consulting the checklist at **§1.02** when the appeal first comes into the office and making clear in writing who has what responsibility.

[233] *See* **§§5.15, 6.01-6.04, 6.13-6.14.**

be necessary. In the event that you are sentenced to a term of incarceration and the court refuses to grant bail pending appeal, we will seek bail pending appeal on your behalf from the U.S. Court of Appeals for the 13th Circuit.

We will raise all meritorious issues on appeal, including any issues that could result in reversal of your conviction or remand for a new trial. We will determine, in consultation with you, those issues that hold the greatest prospect for success and should ultimately be included in any presentation to the court. Our representation will not extend to any civil law suits, any collateral matters, or other forms of representation not encompassed within the above scope of work. Representation of this case will be provided by the law firm of Roe & Doe. Richard Roe will be the partner in charge of the matter at Roe & Doe. Mr. Roe will present oral argument, should the court grant oral argument.

Our agreement is for a flat fee of $[ ]. This fee includes attorneys' fees associated with the above-referenced scope of work. You will be charged separately for out-of-pocket expenses on a monthly basis. This will include items such as phone charges, duplication, travel, and similar expenses.

If the foregoing meets with your approval, please execute a copy of this agreement and return a signed copy to us. Upon payment of the fee in this matter, and receipt of the executed retainer letter, we will begin our representation, but will undertake no representation until that point.

We look forward to the opportunity to represent you and hope that we will be able to accomplish the result that we both desire.

The fee might be due in installments, such as:

> Our agreement is for a flat fee of $[ ], payable $[ ] on the signing of this letter, and the balance on the date the opening brief on appeal is filed. However, the entire sum of $[ ] will be paid on signing of this letter by a check to the firm of Roe & Doe, the initial payment of $[ ] to be regarded as earned when paid, and the balance to be held in our client trust account until the opening brief is filed.

Or, the fee might be hourly, in which case the fee paragraph might read:

> Our fee for this appeal will be our standard hourly rates for cases of this kind, as those rates may be adjusted by our firm from time to time. At the present time, the hourly rates of the lawyers expected to work on the case are [list rates]. You will be separately charged for out-of-pocket expenses on a monthly basis. This will include items such as phone charges, duplication, travel, and similar expenses.
>
> We will bill you monthly for fees and expenses, and you agree to pay each statement within twenty-one days after receiving it.

In such an arrangement, a retainer might be charged against which time would be billed.

The problem of multiple representation can arise on appeal, but the potential conflicts of interest should be much easier to judge than in the pretrial setting. Here are two forms that deal with multiple representation issues. First, a form that would add language concerning the hypothetical Smith case:

> We have further agreed that, in the event that Alice Jones wishes us to represent her, we will include representation of her appeal to the U.S. Court of Appeals for the 13th Circuit of her criminal conviction for an additional flat fee of $[ ]. The scope of representation of Ms. Jones would be governed by a separate retention agreement with her that will only cover representation in the Court of Appeals and not extend to matters in the U.S. District Court. Any representation of Ms. Jones is conditioned on our judgment that such representation would not raise a conflict of interest, and on the execution of appropriate conflict of interest waivers by you and Ms. Jones.

Here is a form that might be used in a civil case involving multiple appellants:

> While each of you acknowledges that the interests of the clients who are parties to this agreement are substantially similar, it is understood by all such clients that their interests are not completely identical and that we have a potential conflict of interest in simultaneously representing all of the clients. By signing this agreement, each client waives any objection to our potential conflict of interest in undertaking this joint representation. If, in this course of our representation, we receive conflicting instructions from different clients, we will endeavor to reconcile the conflicting instructions to the mutual agreement of the clients involved. If the conflicting instructions cannot be reconciled, we will proceed with the course of action that we reasonably determined to be in the overall best interest of the group of clients. If these conflicts cannot be resolved, we reserve the right to terminate representation. All of the clients signing this agreement acknowledge that they have been provided with an opportunity to discuss this conflict of interest waiver with independent counsel of their own choosing.

§5.15 Positioning the Case for Appeal

When considering whether and when to seek appellate review, the advocate should review the steps that may be taken in the agency or lower court that will enhance the chances of success on the merits and help to ensure that the appellate court has jurisdiction to decide.

Some of the steps that may be taken to prepare for a trip to the court of appeals are discussed in Chapter 2: for example, **§2.09** deals with seeking certification of an order to permit appeal under 28 USC §1292(b) and **§2.10** discusses the certification procedure under Fed R Civ P 54(b). Chapter 3 discusses the possibility of seeking a writ, perhaps as alternative relief to an interlocutory appeal. If one is to appeal from a final judgment, the judgment must have been entered, as discussed at **§2.02** (civil cases) and **§2.03** (criminal cases). If the case is being appealed from the district court, the notice of appeal must be filed with the clerk of that court, as noted at **§6.02.**

This section discusses the steps that may and in some cases must be taken to clarify legal and factual issues for appellate review. In a civil case, a party may, after judgment is entered, renew a motion for judgment as a matter of law under Fed R Civ P 50, move for additional findings of fact and conclusions of law under Fed R Civ P 52(b), and move to amend the judgment or for a new trial under Fed R Civ P 59. Each of these motions, as discussed elsewhere in this treatise, affects the time for filing notice of appeal.[234] The *JNOV* type Rule 50 motion is, under one view of the caselaw, required in order to confer jurisdiction on the court of appeals to reverse and render judgment for the verdict loser, as opposed to merely granting a new trial.[235]

The advocate contemplating an appeal in a civil case, and especially one newly retained, should consider using one or more of these procedural devices to put the case in a better position for appeal in addition to whatever merit these motions may have on their own account. Motions for additional findings and conclusions, and to amend the judgment, can be used to make clear the factual and legal basis upon which the judgment rests. It may be that a small favorable concession can thus be wrought. On the other hand, if an advocate can imagine the court of appeals asking "did the district judge really decide such-and-such," it can be vitally important to seek a clear indication that the district judge did precisely that.

Moreover, at trial an argument may have been made hurriedly and without full support in the briefs, due to the pressure of moving the case toward judgment. This is the nature of trial advocacy. The posttrial setting provides an opportunity to flesh out arguments for which a basis exists in the record and to seek more thorough review. The trial lawyer will have made a checklist of such motions in any case in the effort to minimize or overturn an unfavorable ruling. With an eye on the court of appeals, he or she must go over the list again to refine the points upon which an appeal may be based. Making posttrial motions on such points can obviate an argument on appeal that the issues were not presented to the trial court.

If the case has been disposed of on motion, the loser must consider whether to try to keep it alive in the district court or seek appellate review immediately.[236] For example, a party whose complaint is dismissed with leave to amend usually must try to draft a complaint that will meet the district court's standards. If the party refuses to amend and appeals, the court of appeals may say that it has consented to the judgment.[237] There are exceptions to this principle, however, where it is clear that amendment would be futile or foolhardy given the district court's order of dismissal. For example, in *Bastian v Petren Resources*

---

[234] *See* **§6.03.**

[235] The strands of caselaw authority on the need for a JNOV type motion are gathered in **§10.15.**

[236] Some of the considerations involved have jurisdictional aspects. *See* **§2.02.**

[237] *See* **§2.02.**

Corp,[238] plaintiffs sued under several theories, including RICO and SEC Rule 10b-5. The district judge dismissed the complaint with leave to amend, but warned that the 10b-5 claims were so thin that realleging them would be fraught with the peril of Fed R Civ P 11 sanctions if plaintiffs did not eventually prevail. Plaintiffs amended their complaint, but omitted any 10b-5 allegations. The district judge again dismissed, this time with prejudice. The court of appeals held that plaintiffs had adequately preserved their 10b-5 contentions and were to be commended for not wasting the district court's time.

The prevailing party also can use the posttrial period to solidify the basis on which the judgment rests. For example, the findings and conclusions may not adequately reflect alternative bases that the record supports. Such alternative factual findings and legal theories provide additional support for the judgment and help insulate it from reversal.[239]

In a criminal case, there is no argument that posttrial motions are necessary to preserve for appeal a claim that the evidence was insufficient. However, such motions can still serve the purpose of clarifying trial rulings and ensuring that legal and procedural claims are reflected in the record.[240]

The Supreme Court has clearly held that moving for new trial does not waive the defendant's claim on appeal that the evidence is insufficient to convict. Formerly, it was held that a defendant who moved for a new trial, and particularly one who pursued the denial of a new trial on appeal, waived the right to have the appellate court consider and rule upon his or her claim that the evidence was insufficient to convict. However, in *Burks v United States,*[241] the Supreme Court overruled its earlier decision in *Bryan v United States*[242] and held that an appellate court must consider the sufficiency of the evidence if the defendant raises the issue and must bar a new trial if the government's proof was inadequate.[243]

§5.16 Settlement as an Alternative to Appeal

Settlement discussions need not be suspended while an appeal is being considered or is pending. The judgment winner should calculate the loser's reasonable prospects of success on appeal and formulate an offer based upon immediate cessation of all hostilities. Obviously, a prevailing party should not threaten to interpose meritless objections on appeal, just as an appellant ought not pursue an appeal solely for delay. Such tactics invite the profession's censure and the court's imposition of sanctions.[244]

---

[238] 892 F2d 680 (7th Cir), *cert denied,* 496 US 906 (1990).

[239] See **§5.04,** discussing the problem of incomplete findings triggering a remand, while complete findings are reviewed for clear error.

[240] Of course, a motion for new trial on newly discovered evidence is a prerequisite to presenting such evidence to the court of appeals.

[241] 437 US 1 (1978).

[242] 338 US 552 (1950), *overruled by* Burks v United States, 437 US 1 (1978).

[243] *See* **§§5.07, 10.15.**

[244] *See* **§5.02.**

However, there is surely some discount that a prevailing plaintiff could accept in exchange for immediate satisfaction of the judgment. Therefore, despite the prospect of postjudgment interest and the security provided by whatever supersedeas bond or equivalent has been posted, immediate payment has a present value that the parties may be able to agree upon.

A plaintiff who has encountered a take-nothing verdict or whose entire claim has been dismissed may have less room to maneuver. The defendant in such a case may well have decided that settlement on almost any terms is impossible because it cannot concede claims of the type being sued upon. For example, media defendants often have a policy against settlement of libel actions, and corporate directors may be unable to settle cases of alleged intentional wrongdoing because their errors and omissions policies do not cover such claims.

Some institutional litigants will appeal to obtain a favorable rule of law that can be used in many cases. For them, the costs connected with a particular case may not be as important. For example, a corporation or government agency may be willing to invest resources in a case out of proportion to perceived return, as measured by that case, because the prospect of savings spread across an entire litigation docket will absorb the cost.[245] In such a case, settlement strategy must focus upon why the present case is not the best vehicle for vindicating an issue of principle.[246] As noted below, it may be possible to eliminate the prospect of unfavorable precedent by a settlement that includes vacating the judgment.

Absent some such all or nothing attitude, the room for negotiation is fairly large. In addition to discounts for present payment, the parties must consider the odds of success on appeal. The global reversal percentages set forth above can help in this evaluation,[247] but each side must conduct its own evaluation of the merits. This process will involve the tentative examination of the record discussed above.[248]

In addition, the appeal process imposes both quantifiable and nonquantifiable costs. The former are those discussed in the fee-setting discussion at **§5.14.** The latter include the limitations that continuing contingent liabilities may place upon a party's business and personal decision making.[249]

In an effort to induce settlement, the victorious party should consider the possibility of cross-appealing. For example, if a civil plaintiff in a products liability suit has obtained a money judgment, and the defendant threatens an

---

[245] *See* **§5.01.**

[246] There are several significant excerpts from provocative articles on valuing litigation in Robert M. Cover & Owen M. Fiss, The Structure of Procedure 2-46 (1979), including an extract from a significant work of Professor (now Judge) Posner on enterprise evaluation of litigation positions.

[247] **§5.01.**

[248] **§§5.03-5.13.**

[249] Many companies, particularly those subject to federal or state securities laws, must file regular reports of financial condition. In that connection, public accountants routinely send to counsel form letters seeking counsel's frank evaluation of contingent liabilities arising from litigation. The pendency of litigation with substantial potential liability can have an adverse impact upon a company's access to debt and capital markets

appeal, the plaintiff can file a protective cross-appeal directed to issues that may arise on a retrial and that would enhance the potential damages if the suit were tried again. The prospect of cross-appealing becomes a bargaining counter in the effort to reach agreement.[250]

When should settlement discussions begin? In a jury-tried case, the time between verdict and judgment may be propitious to avoid entry of a final judgment. If judgment has been entered, there is a premium upon prompt resolution because the transcript preparation usually constitutes the single largest item of costs on appeal.

Suppose settlement looms after the appeal is underway. There is a judgment in the district court that, if allowed to remain, will pose collateral estoppel problems for the losing party. Yet, the winner may be convinced by the strength of the appellant's position that settlement is wise, accepting a discount from the victory won in the district court. Settlement discussions in such a case should perhaps await service of the appellant's opening brief or, at least, completion of the brief so that an advance copy can be furnished to the other side.

The question will then arise regarding whether a settlement may include agreement that the judgment of the district court will be vacated, removing its precedential and collateral estoppel effects. Arguably, this result should always obtain in the federal courts. If the parties agree that the controversy is no longer alive, the mootness doctrine discussed at **§2.18** would require the court of appeals to vacate the judgment below as moot.

The matter has not proven so simple, however. The parties can always move for voluntary dismissal of the appeal, as noted in **§8.09;** they cannot, however, always obtain an order vacating the district court's judgment. One must begin with *United States v Munsingwear, Inc,*[251] which held that when a case in the federal system becomes moot during the appellate process, the court of appeals (or Supreme Court) normally will vacate the judgment below and remand with directions to dismiss. The *Munsingwear* rule is subject to the same limitations as the mootness doctrine generally, such as "capable of repetition, yet evading review."[252]

In addition, appeals courts have been wary of vacating the judgment below as moot when the parties have settled their dispute or the losing party obeyed the judgment and then sought vacatur. The rationales for such exceptions are variously stated. The D.C. Circuit said in *Clarke v United States,*[253] that a party should not be able to "manipulat[e] the judicial process by voluntarily ceasing the complained of activity, and then seeking a dismissal of the case, thus securing freedom to 'return to his old ways.' " This concern with manipulating the judicial process has led to decisions that deny vacatur, even at the parties' request, when a case settles on appeal.[254]

---

[250] See **§6.10** for discussion of when a party may and must cross-appeal.

[251] 340 US 36, 39 (1950).

[252] *See* **§2.18.** *See also* Air Line Pilots Assn Intl v UAL Corp, 897 F2d 1394 (7th Cir 1990) (expressing reservations about *Munsingwear* doctrine).

[253] 915 F2d 699, 705 (DC Cir 1990) (en banc).

[254] See cases collected *id* at 711 (dissenting opinion).

In *In re United States,*[255] the court further explained its view that a motion by all parties to vacate a judgment on the grounds that settlement had been reached should be denied. The court accepted that there could be no unfairness to the parties, all of whom requested vacatur. However, it followed the Seventh Circuit's opinion in *In re Memorial Hospital of Iowa County, Inc,*[256] reasoning that:

> [w]hen a clash between genuine adversaries produces a precedent, . . . the judicial system ought not allow the social value of that precedent, created at cost to the public and other litigants, to be a bargaining chip in the process of settlement. The precedent, a public act of a public official, is not the parties' property.[257]

The Ninth Circuit applied the same reasoning in *Bates v Union Oil Co,*[258] but at so late a procedural hour that Union Oil had thought the issue had been put to sleep. A Union Oil franchisee sued and won. While appeal was pending, Unocal settled, on condition that the adverse district court judgment be vacated, which was done. A different group of franchisees then brought suit. The district court held that the earlier, vacated judgement had preculsive effect against Unocol. The Ninth Circuit affirmed,[259] holding that the district court is not required to vacate a judgment when the appellant causes the dismissal of an appeal by settling. When a case is settled and the parties ask the district court to vacate, the court must—preferably on the record—balance "the competing values of finality of judgment and right to relitigation of unreviewed disputes."[260] The district judge who vacated the earlier judgment had not applied the balancing test mandated by Ninth Circuit law. Thus, the district judge presiding over the *Bates* case was free to disregard the order vacating the earlier judgment. The Ninth Circuit held that the *Munsingwear* holding requires the court to vacate a judgment only when circumstances beyond the parties' control deprive the judgment of appellate review.

Bates unsettles potential settlements, because it raises the spectre that an ostensibly final order vacating a judgment may be undone at the behest of other parties who sue later.

§5.17 Special Problems When the United States Is a Party

When one's opponent is the United States, there are certain procedural variations concerning notice of appeal and jurisdiction of the court of appeals

---

[255] 927 F2d 626 (DC Cir 1991).

[256] 862 F2d 1299 (7th Cir 1988).

[257] *Id* 1302.

[258] 944 F2d 647 (9th Cir 1991), *cert denied,* 112 S Ct 1761 (1992).

[259] *Id* 650 (citing Ringsby Truck Lines v Western Conference of Teamsters, 686 F2d 720, 722 (9th Cir 1982)).

[260] *Id* (quoting 686 F2d at 722).

which are dealt with in other chapters. This section discusses why the United States is an opponent with a different agenda than the usual litigant. Many of the suggestions at **§5.16** will also be relevant to a case in which the United States is a party.

This section deals with the cases in which the United States is not wholly satisfied with the judgment or order, and is considering appealing. The government trial attorney often will routinely file a notice of appeal, even when his or her superiors have not finally decided that an appeal is warranted. The process by which government agencies decide whether to pursue an appeal usually permits intervention by the opposing advocate in an effort to persuade them not to.

In all federal criminal cases, and in most civil cases, the government will not pursue an appeal without approval of the Solicitor General of the United States.[261] The approval mechanism works as follows: the trial attorney, whether a Department of Justice trial attorney or an Assistant United States Attorney, will write a memorandum on the need for and desirability of appealing. A Deputy Solicitor General will solicit the aid of someone in the Appellate Section of the Criminal Division to study the case and make a recommendation. The final decision lies with the Solicitor General or the designee Deputy.

The government does not appeal every criminal judgment or order that it loses and has the right to appeal. The review process is designed to ensure not only that the appeal would have merit, but also to try and shape the development of law in areas in which the Solicitor General (and often the Attorney General) are interested. For example, if the district court has granted a motion to suppress the fruits of an unconstitutional search, the Solicitor General will not approve an appeal if he or she perceives a risk that the case will result in a precedent unacceptable to the government.

On the other hand, the Solicitor General will sometimes seek out series of cases raising a particular issue to force a series of appellate court confrontations that he or she believes will ultimately result in a rule of law favorable to the government. For example, for a number of years the Solicitor General favored appealing cases in which the warrant clause of the Fourth Amendment was in issue, all in a conscious effort to develop a body of pro-police law that eventually would be reviewed by the Supreme Court.[262]

The advocate who wishes to have some influence on the decision to appeal should first seek to persuade the government trial attorney not to seek permission to take an appeal. If this effort is unsuccessful, or if it would obviously be futile, the next step is to write a letter to the Solicitor General of the United

---

[261] There are some expections in cases involving regulatory crimes. For example, the Justice Department Tax Division evaluates appeals in criminal tax cases. However, the conference procedure discussed in the text can be initiated with the responsible officials in that division.

[262] See, e.g., United States v Chadwick, 433 US 1, 17 (1977), in which Justice Blackmun, joined by Justice Rehnquist, noted in dissent: "I think it somewhat unfortunate that the Government sought a reversal in this case primarily to vindicate an extreme view of the Fourth Amendment that would restrict the protection of the Warrant Clause to private dwellings and a few other 'high privacy' areas."

States. The letter should set out the basic information about the case, in addition to some discussion of the advocate's reasons for thinking the case is not an appropriate vehicle for appeal. The advocate should stress not only the merits, but also the considerations that make the case an inappropriate vehicle for appellate review from the government's point of view.

The government is, as the Supreme Court has reminded us, not an ordinary party to litigation.[263] It has an obligation to govern fairly and to be seen to do so. It should not evaluate every case from the perspective of "can this be won," but rather with some sense of whether the government deserves to win.

The advocate should also request that the letter be given to the attorney in the Department of Justice who is preparing the recommendation to the Solicitor General. The advocate may ask for the name of this attorney, so that he or she can seek to press the position by telephone. When major policy issues are at stake, the Department of Justice has granted personal audiences to advocates seeking to dissuade the government from an appeal.

The scenario above may vary slightly depending upon the nature of the case. For example, if there are criminal tax charges, the Solicitor General will routinely seek the advice of the Appellate Section of the Justice Department Tax Division. The advocate's task is to find out exactly how the review process will occur, in order to have the best opportunity to influence it.

If the importance of the issue justifies it, the advocate may consider retaining specialized counsel who are experienced both in federal appellate practice and dealing with the Department of Justice.[264]

In routine civil cases, the review process may not be as formal. The United States Attorney's office may have authority to appeal. If so, the advocate should initiate discussions at that level.

In complex civil cases and in much agency litigation, the Department of Justice or agency general counsel's office will review any proposal to take an appeal. Similar considerations to those that govern criminal cases will apply. The government is an institutional litigant, and when behaving in rational conformity with that posture will judge the impact of an appeal not only upon the case at hand but also upon its entire enforcement or litigation effort in particular area of law. For example, the government may decide not to appeal an unreporeted adverse district court decision in a claims case, if by doing so it risks an unfavorable court of appeals precedent. The advocate seeking to persuade government lawyers not to take an appeal must do legal research that will support an argument that the overall costs of losing on a legal issue of consequence far outweigh the potential benefits of winning a specific case.

Once the advocate has determined who is in charge of the review process, he or she should send a letter to the responsible government lawyer. If the case warrants it, the advocate should see a personal audience.

---

[263] Berger v United States, 295 US 78, 88 (1935).

[264] In selecting such specialized counsel, there are many sources of information. Many specialized practitioners are involved in the leadership of the Committee on Complex Crimes Litigation of the Litigation Section of the ABA.

For example, in a civil rights case involving a federal law enforcement agency, a district judge has sustained the plaintiffs' charge that the agency had discriminated in hiring and promotion practices. The government had the right of appeal. In a matter of such importance, it was logical that the Solicitor General and the Director of the agency would confer about a potential appeal. Counsel for plaintiffs therefore wrote to the Solicitor General, with an outline of reasons why an appeal would not be in the government's best interest, and asked permission to contact the Director, who was a lawyer but was the client in this setting. This letter triggered negotiations that led the government not to appeal the judgment.

6 Notice of Appeal and Other Postjudgment Proceedings in the District Court, Tax Court, or Agency

§6.01 Introduction: Managing the Appellate Timetable

Throughout this chapter, stress is laid upon various duties that must be fulfilled in a timely manner. Some of these, such as filing a notice of appeal, are jurisdictional in the sense that the statutes and rules provide that beyond a certain point failure to perform them must invariably lead to dismissal of the appeal.[1] One cannot always tell from reading the rules whether a relatively minor departure will lead to dismissal of the appeal. A well-organized law office must be prepared to meet the obligations imposed by the rules. This section will focus upon some methods for ensuring that duties are not overlooked, while the remainder of this chapter provides a detailed guide to those duties. It always will be necessary to have the rules themselves close at hand—both the rules reprinted in the Appendices to this treatise and the rules of the circuit to which one is taking an appeal. Some of the duties outlined in this chapter also will require consulting the rules of the district court. Federal Rule of Appellate Procedure 1(a) expressly provides that when the Federal Rules of Appellate Procedure call for an action to be done in the district court, "the procedure for making such motion or application shall be in accordance with the practice of the district court."[2]

The best way to oversee appellate litigation is to establish a master calendar and tickler system. Many attorney malpractice insurance carriers insist that the insured attorney or law office have such a system. It is designed to pinpoint, for every matter and every lawyer in a law firm or section of a law firm, the dates on which particular tasks must be done and to remind the responsible attorney far enough in advance of those dates. Regardless of the calendar system established, and regardless of whether the task of maintaining it falls to a secretary or paralegal, the attorney of record bears complete responsibility to the court and the client for seeing that dates are met.

There are several basic systems for maintaining the master calendar. One is an index card file, with tabs for each month and a card for each day of the coming year. Another is a large wall or desk blotter calendar, displaying the current month and perhaps also the month ahead. A third system is a computer calendar system, from which a lawyer, paralegal, or secretary prints a daily or weekly hard copy for a distribution list.

Many computer software providers have developed calendar programs that will serve all the functions outlined in this section. Some of these programs are designed specifically for law offices and are advertised in legal publications such as the ABA Journal. Less expensive programs for general business use fulfill the same function, however. Some programs have a "memory-resident" or "pop-up" feature that permits items to be added, deleted, consulted, and retrieved while the user is running another program.

In a multilawyer office, the master calendar method should be supplemented with a notebook maintained by the senior partner, section chief, or supervising

---

[1] The courts of appeals' insistence upon, and occasional delight in, rigid application of rules about timing and form often seems unnecessary. See the critique in Mark A. Hall, *The Jurisdictional Nature of the Time to Appeal,* 21 Ga L Rev 399, 399 (1986): "The appellate courts have made a fetish of their own authority by characterizing timing defects in notices of appeal as 'jurisdictional' and dismissing untimely appeals late in the appellate process even though the parties entirely overlook the error." Hall argues that appeal periods, like statutes of limitations, primarily affect the interests of the parties and should be waivable expressly or by failure to object. His analysis makes sense, but faces a formidable body of adverse precedent.

[2] The text of Fed R App P 1 is in **app A.**

lawyer. In this notebook, there should be a copy of the basic information on every case in the office or section, including due dates, clerk's office address, opposing counsel, and so on. The basic data in the notebook will be taken from the cover sheet or case origination sheet on the matter. Each lawyer should be responsible for sending the supervising lawyer update pages with current due dates and case status. The notebook, together with the lawyer's weekly agendas, permit the supervising lawyer to monitor timeliness and workloads. It also serves as a handy basis for office meetings to discuss cases and share ideas. Such meetings enhance the quality of appellate work.

The next question is how information is entered on the calendar and notebook. When the law office is retained, appointed, or designated to handle an appeal, the lawyer to whom the case is assigned must sit down with the Federal Rules of Appellate Procedure, the circuit rules, the district court rules, any relevant statutes, and a calendar in hand to compute the dates on which various duties must be performed. Having noted those dates—ordering transcript, notice of appeal, designation of record, transmission of record, and so on—the lawyer should backtrack a week from each date and note a tickler or reminder date that the due date for each given task is approaching.

There are several reasons for this seemingly compulsive insistence on precision. Even the memory of an experienced appellate lawyer can play tricks, and a misremembered time period for fulfilling some task can be fatal to the case. Second, some time periods in the rules and statutes are cast in terms of 30 or 60 days. The lore of law practice—or malpractice—is rife with stories of lawyers who did not count out the days on a calendar and who carelessly assumed that 30 days equals one month or that 60 days equals two months; neither equation is accurate. Third, no court, client, or malpractice carrier will be impressed by hearing that the task of computing jurisdictional dates was done from memory or delegated to a nonlawyer.

Once the dates are entered, a paralegal, clerk, secretary, or lawyer must be designated to maintain the calendar and remind everyone as relevant dates approach. Each office will adopt its own system for disseminating such information and designate a backup when the main calendar keeper is ill or on vacation.

The lawyer responsible for a given matter must also see that revised dates are entered on the calendar when continuances are obtained or time is shortened by agreement or order.

§6.02 Contents of Notice of Appeal in Appeals as of Right

Federal Rule of Appellate Procedure 3[3] tells the advocate how to take an appeal as of right and what to expect from the district court clerk's office. This section might have been entitled, "What is a notice of appeal?" The succeeding sections in this Chapter tell when a notice of appeal or similar document must be filed and how to perfect the appeal.

---

[3] The text of Fed R App P 3 is in **app A.**

Federal Rule of Appellate Procedure 3(a) provides that the notice of appeal from the district court to the court of appeals shall be filed in the district court clerk's office. "Failure of an appellant to take any step other than the timely filing of a notice of appeal does not affect the validity of the appeal, but is ground only for such action as the court of appeals deems appropriate, which may include dismissal of the appeal."[4] The provisions of Fed R App P 3 are not applicable to agency review,[5] certain bankruptcy proceedings,[6] nor to §1292(b) appeals.[7] The district court clerk's office will serve the notice of appeal on all parties.[8]

Federal Rule of Appellate Procedure 3 is straightforward. As amended in 1993, it contains few pitfalls for the unwary.

The notice is a written document. The caption will contain the name of the district court whose judgment or order is being appealed and the caption of the case. It will generally follow the form suggested in Form 1 to the Federal Rules of Appellate Procedure.[9]

The caption should contain the name of every party who wishes to appeal. Federal Rule of Appellate Procedure 3(a) was amended in 1993 to permit use of terms such as *et al.* to describe groups of appellants and to state that informality in the notice will not invalidate the appeal. Under the former rule, the Supreme Court had held, in *Torres v Oakland Scavenger Co,*[10] that failure to specify a party to the appeal was a jurisdictional bar to considering that party's claim. The present rule makes good the appeal of any "party whose intent to appeal is otherwise clear from the notice."[11] Although the *Torres* principle has been undone by rule amendment, the case law on names in notices of appeal is instructive as to how far the courts of appeals were or were not willing to go to preserve an appeal that began with a procedural misstep.[12]

---

[4] Fed R App P 3(a).

[5] *See* **§6.09.**

[6] *See* **§6.06.**

[7] *See* **§6.05.**

[8] Fed R App P 3(d).

[9] The text of Form 1 is in **app A.**

[10] 487 US 312 (1988).

[11] Fed R App P 3(c).

[12] The harsh result under the former rule obtained even where, as in *Torres,* the omission of a party's name from the notice of appeal resulted from a clerical error. The Supreme Court specifically disapproved of the phrase *et al,* which "utterly fails to provide" notice of intention of appeal to either the court or the opponent. *Torres,* 487 US at 318. The Fifth Circuit distinguished *Torres* in Pope v Mississippi Real Estate Commn, 872 F2d 127 (5th Cir 1989), when the court held that where James and Mary Pope had been the only two plaintiffs in the district court, styling the notice of appeal "James William Pope, et al." could not lead to confusion. *Id* 129. Hence, the notice was effective.

As one might expect, *Torres* issues spawned extensive litigation, with the courts of appeals in some disagreement. *See* Mikeska v Collins, 928 F2d 126 (5th Cir 1991) (a multiparty pro se notice of appeal, if timely and validly filed as to any appellant, will be deemed valid as to any nonsigner who affirms the intention to join the appeal within 10 days of the posting of an inquiry by the clerk of the court of appeals); Minority Employees v Tennessee Dept of Employee Sec, 901 F2d 1327 (6th Cir) (notice of appeal

The notice should describe the order or judgment appealed from with sufficient particularity that neither the court nor other parties are misled.[13] Errors in designating the judgment are not necessarily fatal, but may lead other parties to file motions to dismiss the appeal.[14]

The Supreme Court has said, in *Foman v Davis,*[15] that harmless error in the notice of appeal is insufficient to justify dismissal. Noncompliance with Fed R App P 3(c)'s command that notice specify "the judgment, order, or part

---

must name all appellants in caption or elsewhere on the face of the notice; neither *et al* nor generic terms such as *plaintiffs* will suffice; discussion of prior circuit precedent; case influential in other circuits), *cert denied,* 498 US 878 (1990) (en banc); Pratt v Petroleum Prod Management, Inc Employee Sav Plan & Trust, 920 F2d 651 (10th Cir 1990) (Tenth Circuit follows Sixth Circuit interpretation of *Torres* and requires naming of parties in notice of appeal); Morales v Pan Am Life Ins Co, 914 F2d 83 (5th Cir 1990) (four exceptions to *Torres* rule: (1) when there are two appellants, "et al" includes the second one; (2) in class action, listing only the named plaintiff is sufficient; (3) when parties sue in their own right and on behalf of their children, "et al" preserves the children's appeal; (4) when notice is defective due to use of "et al," and plaintiffs filed within 30 days a pleading listing all plaintiffs to original action, the original defect is cured; note, however, that this list applies only in Fifth Circuit); Albedyll v Wisconsin Porcelain Co Revised Retirement Plan, 947 F2d 246 (7th Cir 1991) (literal compliance with *Torres* can be excused where notice taken as a whole reveals who is taking the appeal; here, it is clear that the missing party had to be an appellant because the other parties were not proper subjects of a judgment; missing party was the alter ego of the named parties; however, excusable neglect can never be failure to comply with unambiguous rules, such as the provisions on who should be named on a notice of appeal); Gilbreath v Cutter Biological, Inc, 931 F2d 1320, 1323 (9th Cir 1991) (liberal construction of *Torres* doctrine; notice of appeal that recited "plaintiffs, as consolidated into this cause" was sufficient, as the opponent could look in the court records to see who was included).

In *Torres,* the Court noted that the specificity requirement "is met only by some designation that gives fair notice of the specific individual or entity seeking to appeal." 487 US at 318. *Compare also* Collier v Marshall, Dennehey, Warner, Coleman & Goggin, 977 F2d 93 (3d Cir 1992) (notice of appeal from sanctions against attorney that lists only client's name does not confer jurisdiction on court of appeals to review sanctions awards; appeal dismissed); Aetna Life Ins Co v Alla Medical Servs, 855 F2d 1470, 1473 (9th Cir 1988) (since only one party had the right to appeal, appearance of another party on the notice of appeal could not have been confusing or prejudicial); *with* Finch v City of Vernon, 845 F2d 256 (11th Cir 1988) (pro se litigant who filed brief within time for filing notice of appeal deemed to have complied with requirement that notice be filed); Cotton v United States Pipe & Foundry Co, 856 F2d 158 (11th Cir 1988) (notice of appeal in class action employment discrimination case that specified only *named plaintiffs* conferred jurisdiction on court of appeals only as to claims of class representatives in their individual capacities; appeals of other class members dismissed).

[13] Brookens v White, 795 F2d 178 (DC Cir 1986); Gates v Central States Teamsters Pension Fund, 788 F2d 1341 (8th Cir 1986).

[14] *See, e.g.,* Foman v Davis, 371 US 178 (1962) (harmless error in notice of appeal); State Farm Mut Auto Ins Co v Palmer, 350 US 944 (1956) (per curiam); McLaurin v Fischer, 768 F2d 98, 102 (6th Cir 1985); Duran v Elrod, 713 F2d 292, 295 (7th Cir 1983) (no prejudice; parties argued all issues despite defects in notice), *cert denied,* 465 US 1108 (1984).

[15] 371 US 178 (1962).

thereof appealed from"[16] will be forgiven provided that the notice makes fairly clear the appellant's intent to appeal a particular order and that the opponent is not misled. For example, in *Brookens v White,*[17] the appellant had sued a savings and loan association and an individual for breach of contract. A bank intervened. The district court granted the savings and loan associations' and individual parties' motions for summary judgment. After further proceedings that consumed nearly a year, the district court entered judgment for the intervenor bank. The plaintiff-appellant filed a notice of appeal specifying only the judgment in favor of the bank. After the appeal had been pending for some time, the savings and loan and the individual moved in the court of appeals to dismiss. The court granted their motion, holding that the grant of summary judgment as to movants was not a final order that could or should have been appealed when rendered.[18] However, the court held that the notice of appeal failed to inform the movants that the earlier summary judgment orders were being challenged, and that this want of notice prejudiced the movants. The court did not identify any specific harm movants had suffered other than their expectation, based on having read the notice of appeal, that they had nothing more to worry about.[19]

Discussion of *Brookens* is not intended to suggest that courts of appeals routinely nitpick notices of appeal. The message is rather that clarity will save anxiety and expense. For every *Brookens*-type result there are a dozen cases holding vague notices of appeal adequate.[20] For example, in *Smith v Barry,* petitioner filed a premature and therefore invalid notice of appeal. However, he did file an informal brief within the deadline for filing a notice of appeal. The Supreme Court held this the equivalent of a notice of appeal because it provides the information required by Fed R App P 3. The Court said that judges should "liberally construe" the designation requirements of Fed R App P 3.[21]

---

[16] Fed R App P 3(c).

[17] 795 F2d 178 (DC Cir 1986).

[18] *Id* 179-80. For such an order to have been appealable, a Fed R Civ P 54(b) certification would be required. *See* **§2.15.**

[19] The court referred only to "[t]he repose that is due" the movants. 795 F2d at 181.

[20] *See* 795 F2d at 180 for citations.

[21] 112 S Ct 678, 681 (1992) (citing Foman v Davis, 371 US 178, 181-82 (1962)). *See also* Meehan v County of Los Angeles, 856 F2d 102, 105 (9th Cir 1988) (mistake in designating judgment appealed from does not bar appeal if intent to appeal can be fairly inferred and the appellee is not prejudiced or misled by the mistake).

The liberality of *Foman v Davis,* is limited, however. A good illustration is Lusardi v Xerox Corp, 975 F2d 964 (3d Cir 1992), in which appellant's notice of appeal specified two district court orders with great specificity. The court of appeals rejected the effort to expand the scope of review to include other, broader orders of the district court. The Third Circuit test for application of the *Foman v Davis* authority to consider orders not specified in the notice of appeal is that "there is a connection between the specified and unspecified order, the intention to appeal the unspecified order is apparent and the opposing party is not prejudiced and has a full opportunity to brief the issues," 975 F2d at 972 (citing Williams v Guzzardi, 875 F2d 46, 49 (3d Cir 1989)). In *Lusardi,* appellant's error was to have been very specific in their designation of the orders

The notice of appeal should state the date of the judgment or order appealed from. Noting the date and describing the judgment or order help the advocate focus upon the proper timing of the notice, as discussed at **§§6.03** and **6.04.**

The notice of appeal also must specify the court of appeals to which the appeal is taken.[22] Generally, this will be the court of appeals for the geographical circuit in which the district court is located. However, as noted at **§§2.12, 2.13, 4.14** and **4.15,** some orders must be appealed to a specialized court of appeals. If, as is often true in cases arguably within the jurisdiction of the the Federal Circuit, counsel is unsure about which court will have jurisdiction, two notices should be filed: one to the Federal Circuit and the other to the proper geographic circuit.[23]

Some judicial districts have a standard form that counsel is encouraged to use for the notice of appeal. The typical form contains space for the date and a description of the judgment or order appealed from in addition to a checklist for certification that counsel has made arrangements with the court reporter for the transcript. Use of this form is not required, but is certainly encouraged, for it assists both counsel and the clerk in getting the appeal under way.[24]

The notice of appeal, in whatever form, should be filed in the clerk's office by counsel or a member of his or her staff, and a file-stamped copy obtained for the file. This copy will obviate any disputes if the clerk's office fails through oversight to process the appeal.

Once the notice of appeal is filed, counsel should not dismiss the appeal to continue litigating in the district court or to try to solve some technical problem with the notice. By the time the appeal is back on track, the time for challenging the initial or underlying action of the district court may have run or the challenge may be held to have been waived. In *Barrow v Falck,*[25] for example, the defendants' appeal in a civil rights action triggered a letter from the court of appeals legal staff asking defendants to explain why the appeal should not be

---

appealed from. Such specificity is more likely to mislead the opposing party than generality or vagueness.

But see Mosley v Cozby, 813 F2d 659 (5th Cir 1987) (pleading entitled Motion to Reconsider or in the Alternative for Leave to Take Interlocutory Appeal In Forma Pauperis, which does not clearly evince intent to appeal, is not equivalent of notice of appeal). The court may have the power to amend the notice of appeal to correct a harmless error, unless the error can be corrected outside of court. *See* Chathas v Smith, 848 F2d 93 (7th Cir 1988) (failure to include name of one respondent where all respondents represented by same counsel, correctable by letter to opposing counsel), and cases cited therein.

[22] In United States v Musa, 946 F2d 1297 (7th Cir 1991), the court held that a notice of appeal that improperly stated appeal was being taken to the United States Court of Appeals for the Eighth Circuit complied with Fed R App P 3(c). No one was misled. It is not known whether the same result would obtain when the parties had a choice as to the circuit that could hear the appeal.

[23] It may be possible to transfer a case from an improper court of appeals to the one with jurisdiction, invoking 28 USC §1631. *See* **§§2.13, 4.14.**

[24] The form will be available in the district court clerk's office.

[25] 977 F2d 1100 (7th Cir 1992).

dismissed for lack of jurisdiction. The problem was that the defendants had, in their notice of appeal, specified the wrong order as that from which an appeal was taken. Rather than clarify the mistake in their notice of appeal, as they were entitled to do,[26] they voluntarily dismissed their appeal. When they sought to reinstate the appeal, claiming that the court of appeals had erred in sending them the notice, the court of appeals held that this effort was doomed. The appeal on the merits therefore was dismissed.

When the court of appeals receives its copy of the notice of appeal, the clerk of that court will docket the appeal and send counsel information on transmission of the record and the briefing schedule.

§6.03 —Civil Cases

Federal Rule of Appellate Procedure 4(a)[27] tells the advocate *when* a notice of appeal must be filed when seeking to appeal a judgment or order in a civil case, except for an order certified under §1292(b), discussed at **§6.05.** Bankruptcy appeals are discussed at **§6.06,** Tax Court appeals at **§6.07,** habeas corpus cases at **§6.08,** and agency review at **§6.09.**

Basically, the notice must be filed with the district court clerk within 30 days of entry[28] of the order appealed from, or 60 days in a case to which the United States is a party.[29] A cross-appellant has at least 14 days from the date of the first-filed timely notice of appeal.[30] Complications arise, however, when the order is challenged by various substantive motions. There also may be difficulty in determining whether certain matters that relate to the main action, such as attorney fees, should be resolved before trying to appeal.

Counsel must determine whether, in an appeal as of right, the case is civil and ruled by Fed R App P 4(a) or criminal and ruled by Fed R App P 4(b). Here, the only difficulty arises in certain postconviction proceedings to which the United States is a party, but is not prosecuting. The question is not free from doubt, but several cases hold that the 10-day defendant's appeal period in Fed R App P 4(b) applies in ancillary criminal matters and some writ proceedings;[31] prudence, therefore, dictates filing the notice within that period.

---

[26] Under Foman v Davis, 371 US 178 (1962).

[27] The text of Fed R App P 4 is in **app A.** The timing provisions of the rule echo 28 USC §2107.

[28] Fed R App P 4(a)(7) defines entry as entry in compliance with Fed R Civ P 58 and 79(a). *See* **§2.02.**

[29] A prisoner's notice is timely if filed with the prison mail system within the time provided in Fed R App P 4. See the discussion at **§6.04.** *See also* Houston v Lack, 487 US 266 (1988). At least one circuit has held that the 60-day period begins to run from the date final judgment is docketed, not the date on which the judgment is filed. United States v Doyle, 854 F2d 771 (5th Cir 1988).

[30] Fed R App P 4(a)(3) *See* **§6.10.**

[31] *See* Yasui v United States, 772 F2d 1496 (9th Cir 1985) (coram nobis motion is step in criminal process; notice of appeal must be filed within 10 days). *Yasui* and an Eighth Circuit case, United States v Mills, 430 F2d 526, 528 (8th Cir 1970) (same hold-

If the case is civil, all parties have 30 days to appeal unless the United States is a party. Reasoning that "it would be unjust to allow the United States . . . extra time and yet deny it to other parties in the case,"[32] the Advisory Committee drafted the rule so that a final judgment in a case to which the United States is a party "fire[s] the starting gun for all appeals." The 60-day period applies even if, in the particular case, the United States will not be party to the appeal and has no interest in it.

There may, however, be two situations in which the presence of the United States in a civil case will not extend the 60-day period to all parties. If the appeal is taken by a nongovernmental party from an interlocutory order "with which the United States had no concern"[33] and the United States will not be a party to the interlocutory appeal, the 30-day private party period may be applicable.[34] The same rule may apply if the appeal is taken under Fed R Civ P 54(b) from a final judgment to which the United States is not a party and with which it has no concern.[35] Such judicial constructions of Fed R App P 4(a) seem strained and confusing, but prudence will dictate filing within the 30-day period in such a case.

In a civil case, a party who had not intended to appeal but whose opponent decides to do so will have at least 14 days to cross-appeal.[36] A cross-appeal

---

ing), *cert denied,* 400 US 1023 (1971), construe a footnote in a 1954 Supreme Court decision, United States v Morgan, 346 US 502, 505-06 n4 (1954), about the nature of coram nobis. There is a split in the circuits. Compare United States v Cooper, 876 F2d 1192, 1194 (5th Cir 1989), *abrogated on other grounds,* Smith v Barry, 112 S Ct 678 (1992) (coram nobis petitions essentially a civil proceeding, like a motion to vacate sentence under 28 USC §2255; thus, time for appeal governed by civil appeal provisions of Fed R App P 4(a)(1)); United States v Keogh, 391 F2d 138, 140 (2d Cir 1968) (holding appeal from denial of coram nobis provisions governed by Fed R App P 4(a)(1)). *See also* Lopez-Nieves v United States, 917 F2d 645 (1st Cir 1990) (60-day time limit for civil appeals involving the government applies to appeals from denial of motions to vacate sentence under 28 USC §2255); United States v Buitrago, 919 F2d 348 (5th Cir 1990) (defendant's appeal from denial of Fed R Crim P 35 motion to correct illegal sentence treated as appeal from denial of motion under 28 USC §2255 and, therefore, subject to 60-day time for filing notice of appeal in civil cases to which the government is a party). See also **§6.04** for discussion of grand jury proceedings.

[32] Quoted in Montelongo v Meese, 777 F2d 1097, 1099 (5th Cir 1985) (cross-appeal by plaintiffs after appeal by nongovernment defendants in suit in which United States was a defendant, on issue in which United States had no interest, was timely because filed within 60 days from order appealed from).

[33] Virginia Land Co v Miami Shipbuilding Corp, 201 F2d 506, 508 (5th Cir 1953).

[34] *Id. Virginia Land Co* was distinguished in *Montelongo.*

[35] This result is suggested by language in *Montelongo,* 777 F2d at 1099, to the effect that its holding was limited to cases in which appeal is taken from a final judgment that "was also final against the United States." *See also In re* Combined Metals Reduction Co, 557 F2d 179 (9th Cir 1977) (United States not a party for purposes of a bankruptcy appeal from an order in which the United States had no interest). The similarity between such a case, and one in which the United States is left in the case while on appeal is taken under Fed R Civ P 54(b) on some other part of the case, should be obvious.

[36] Fed R App P 4(a)(3). The 14-day provision is contingent on the first notice having been timely filed.

must be filed if the party wishes to challenge any aspect of the judgment in the court of appeals.[37]

The principal difficulty in applying Fed R App P 4(a) has been with Fed R App P 4(a)(4). The rule was amended in 1993 to soften the difficulties that had appeared under the earlier rule. As Fed R App P 4(a)(4) now stands, when the district court enters final judgment in a civil case, all parties may then appeal. However, if any party timely files any of the enumerated motions,[38] the time for appeal as to all parties does not begin to run until "entry of the order disposing of the last such motion outstanding."[39]

In a change from the pre-1993 rule, Fed R App P 4(a)(4) provides that a notice of appeal filed "after announcement or entry of the judgment but before disposition of any of the [enumerated] motions" is ineffective, but becomes effective once all the motions have been ruled upon. The party filing the notice must, however, file an amended notice if the party wishes to challenge the rulings on any of the motions.

It remains the case that a party may file a notice of appeal after a judgment or order is announced, but before the judgment or order is entered. Under Fed R App P 4(a)(2), the notice is "treated as filed on the date of and after the entry." This provision remains unchanged in the rule.

The Supreme Court clarified the application of Fed R App P 4(a)(2) in *FirsTier Mortgage Co v Investors Mortgage Insurance Co,*[40] holding that the rule "permits a notice of appeal from a nonfinal decision to operate as a notice of appeal from a final judgment only when a district court announces a decision that *would be* appealable if followed by the entry of judgment."[41] A ruling on a discovery dispute, an evidentiary objection or even sanctions would not, if thereafter embodied in a Fed R Civ P 58[42] judgment, be appealable.

In *FirsTier,* the district court announced on January 26 an intention to grant summary judgment and asked for findings and conclusions, stating that the ruling extinguished FirsTier's claims. Judgment was not formally entered until March 3, but FirsTier had filed a notice of appeal on February 8. The Court held that the notice should have been treated as effective when the judgment was entered and as commencing an appeal from the later judgment. *FirsTier* makes sense. A notice of appeal need not specify the challenged order with

---

[37] *E.g.,* SEC v Youmans, 729 F2d 413 (6th Cir), *cert denied,* 469 US 1034 (1984).

[38] The motions are those under Fed R Civ P 50(b) to amend the judgment; under Fed R Civ P 52(b) to amend or make additional findings; under Fed R Civ P 59 to alter or amend the judgment or for a new trial; under Fed R Civ P 54 for attorney fees, but only if the district court extends the time for appeal under Fed R Civ P 58; or under Fed R Civ P 60 for relief, but only if the motion is served within 10 days after entry of the judgment.

[39] Fed R App P 4(a)(4).

[40] 498 US 269 (1991).

[41] *Id* 653.

[42] On Fed R Civ P 58, see the discussion at **§2.02.**

the same specificity required under *Torres*[43] in enumerating the *parties* taking the appeal. The appellate rules have been, and should be, construed with only enough rigor to prevent unfair surprise to an opponent and to give the court of appeals and district court fair notice of what is being appealed.[44]

Under the pre-1993 rule, notices of appeal were held to be nullified by the filing of any of the enumerated motions.[45] There were problems determining which motions would trigger nullity of an already filed notice and other problems with counsel not receiving notice when motions were filed or disposed of.[46] Moreover, a notice of appeal filed after the district judge announced a

---

[43] Torres v Oakland Scavenger Co, 487 US 312 (1988) discussed at **§6.02.**

[44] *See also* Warfield v Fidelity Deposit Co, 904 F2d 322 (5th Cir 1990) (notice of appeal under Fed R App P 4(a)(2) is effective even if filed before announcement of judgment, contradicting Seventh Circuit position that such a notice is valid only if filed after judgment is announced but before it is entered, United States v Hansen, 795 F2d 35, 37-38 (7th Cir 1986)).

[45] Griggs v Provident Consumer Discount Co, 459 US 56 (1982). The Court held that Fed R App P 2's permission to suspend the rules for good cause could not be applied.

[46] A party may file a motion in the district court without labelling it, or even under the wrong label. Therein was a principal difficulty under the old rule. The Supreme Court decided that a motion for prejudgment interest constitutes a motion to alter or amend the judgment under Rule 59(e). Osterneck v Ernst & Whinney, 489 US 169 (1989). Osterneck had filed an antitrust suit against numerous defendants, including Ernst & Whinney. Osterneck prevailed against some defendants, but lost to Ernst & Whinney and one other defendant. Osterneck first filed a motion for prejudgment interest, then a notice of appeal against the two successful defendants. After judgment had been amended to reflect the award of interest, Osterneck filed another notice of appeal, but neglected to name the Ernst firm in that notice. Held, the first notice was ineffective because it was filed while a Rule 59(e) motion was pending; the second notice failed to confer jurisdiction over Ernst & Whinney. In the footnotes, the Court foresees the same result where prejudgment interest is available as a matter of right. *Id* 176 n3. The circuits were in disarray over which motions are in effect under Fed R Civ P 59. An excellent summary of the law is Elizabeth A. Phelan & Theresa J. Collier, *The Elusive Appeal,* 18 Litig No 3, at 27 (Spring 1992). Representative leading cases include Faysound, Ltd v Falcon Jet Corp, 940 F2d 339 (8th Cir 1991) (one party's notice of appeal voided by other party's filing of Fed R Civ P 9(e) motion to amend judgment; appeal dismissed, even though it had been pending for many months and all parties had assumed that it was validly before the court of appeals; needlessly technical judgment), *cert denied,* 112 S Ct 1175 (1992); New Castle Co v Hartford Accident & Indem Co, 933 F2d 1162, 1176 (3d Cir 1991) (Third Circuit has not "gone as far as the Fifth and Seventh Circuit," and will not treat any motion to amend adjudgment served within 10 days after entry of judgment as a Rule 59(e) motion; however, it will generally so construe a motion filed within the 10 days that "questions the correctness of the judgment"), *revd on the merits after remand,* 970 F2d 1267 (3d Cir 1992). In Wright v Preferred Research, Inc, 891 F2d 886 (11th Cir 1990), the court summarized the principles to be applied when a postjudgment motion in the district court arguably suspends the finality of the judgment, tolls the time for appeal, and nullifies any previously filed notice of appeal. The root principle is that "[w]hether a motion for post-judgment relief can be categorized as a motion under Rule 59 is not determined by whether the movant so labels it. Rather, the court must determine independently what type of motion was before the district court, depending upon the type of relief requested." *Id* 889 (citing Livernois v Medical Disposables, Inc, 837 F2d 1018, 1020 (11th Cir 1988)). The proper

decision on posttrial motions, but before entry of the order, was not valid.[47] Federal Rule of Appellate Procedure 4(a)(4) as amended in 1993 changes that, as noted above.

Federal Rule of Appellate Procedure 4(a)(4) now counsels the advocate to err on the side of filing notice of appeal as soon as the judgment is announced or entered. Later events may require that the notice be amended, but one valid notice will have been filed.[48]

What happens if the district court grants a preliminary injunction, then grants summary judgment and dismissal during the pendency of the appeal? The court of appeals retains jurisdiction over the interlocutory appeal, even if the injunction itself does not survive the grant of partial summary judgment.[49]

Filing the notice of appeal means actually depositing it with the clerk; mailing will not suffice, except in the case of an incarcerated prisoner filing pro se.[50]

A vexing problem under Fed R App P 4(a) that seems likely to persist even though the rule is amended, is presented by cases in which a number of potentially appealable issues are bundled together in one case, but decided separately and at different times. As noted in chapter 2, counsel can sometimes unbundle discrete issues by using Fed R Civ P 54(b) or an interlocutory appeal.

The example of counsel fees is discussed at length at **§2.02** as it relates to finality of a judgment on the merits when counsel fees remain to be determined. The question is also one of timing, however, for the counsel fee decision may be made after the time for appeal of the merits judgment has ended.

---

name of a posttrial motion may not be determined until the case reaches the court of appeals. *See* Herzog Contracting Corp v McGowen Corp, 976 F2d 1062 (7th Cir 1992) (district court entered summary judgment for holder of promisory notes, but did not state the dollar amount to which holder was entitled; one month later, on holder's motion, district judge "clarified" earlier order and stated a dollar amount; district judge characterized this action as "nunc pro tunc"; held earlier order was not a final judgment and time for appeal did not begin to run until the district judge's "clarification" was entered, specifying a dollar amount; district judge's characterization of its order is not inclusive; "Latin is a wonderful language, but it is not properly used to destroy people's legal rights").

[47] Acosta v Louisiana Dept of Health & Human Resources, 478 US 251 (1986).

[48] There is a caveat, however. Filing a notice of appeal may divest the district court of jurisdiction as to matters not specifically listed in Fed R App P 4(a) or some other provision of law. *See* Henry v Independent Am Sav Assn, 857 F2d 995 (5th Cir 1988) (district judge dismissed complaint; notice of appeal filed and judge vacated orders of dismissal; held, because notice of appeal divests district court of jurisdiction, court of appeals had jurisdiction to review dismissals; query whether the order vacating the dismissal should be held to moot the appeal). *See also In re* Colley, 818 F2d 443 (5th Cir) (moving for reconsideration and appealing the denial of reconsideration waives right to review of underlying order), *cert denied,* 484 US 898 (1987).

[49] *See* Alabama v EPA, 871 F2d 1548, 1553-54 (11th Cir) (consolidating the appeals from the preliminary injunction, the grant of summary judgment, and the grant of a permanent injunction), *cert denied,* 493 US 991 (1989).

[50] *See, e.g.,* Vogelsang v Patterson Dental Co, 904 F2d 427 (8th Cir 1990) (notice of appeal is filed when received by court clerk, except for pro se prisoners). As to prisoners, see discussion above and at **§6.04.**

Again, counsel's best course is to file a notice of appeal when the first adverse decision that is arguably final is entered, then to file later notices as other orders are entered. A motion to consolidate can be filed in the court of appeals and one may have to litigate which of the notices of appeal are valid.[51]

If the starting gun for taking an appeal fires but the advocate does not hear it, time still may be running. A number of cases hold that a litigant is not excused from filing a timely notice of appeal because he or she did not receive notice that the challenged judgment or order was entered on the docket,[52] but these cases mostly antedate the 1991 amendment to Fed R App P 4(a)(6), which provides the possibility of escape when "a party entitled to notice of the entry of a judgment or order did not receive such notice from the clerk or any party within 21 days of its entry." If the party moves within 7 days of receiving notice, or within 180 days, whichever comes first, and if the district court finds that no party is prejudiced, the time for appeal may be reopened for 14 days.[53]

This provision is in addition to that for excusable neglect in Fed R App P 4(a)(5), which allows the district court, on motion, to extend the time of filing for up to 30 days—before or after the time has run. The courts of appeals have not been liberal in construing *excusable neglect.*[54] Beyond the extension permitted

---

[51] Beyond the general principles discussed at **§2.02,** the question can best be studied by example. For instance, where a party files several successive motions for the same kind of relief, such as a preliminary injunction, the time for appeal begins to run after disposition of the first. A contrary rule would permit extension of the time for appeal by the filing of duplicative motions. Consistent with this rationale, the rule does not apply where there are changes in fact, law, or circumstance since the previous ruling. *See* Gill v Monroe County Dept of Social Servs, 873 F2d 647 (2d Cir 1989). *See also* Albert v Maine Cent RR, 898 F2d 5 (1st Cir) (time for appeal in one of several consolidated actions runs from grant of summary judgment, not from final disposition of all consolidated cases; appeal dismissed as untimely), *cert dismissed,* 498 US 87 (1990).

[52] Ashby Enters v Weitzman, Dym & Assocs, 780 F2d 1043 (DC Cir 1986) (failure of district court to send notice of judgment to plaintiff did not entitle plaintiff to have district court vacate its judgment and re-enter it to restart appeal period because defendant did receive notice, citing cases in which this device has been approved; result compelled, however, by Fed R Civ P 77(d)). The result would be different if neither party had received notice. Expeditions Unlimited Aquatic Enters v Smithsonian Inst, 500 F2d 808 (DC Cir 1974) (per curiam). *See also* Beaudry Motor Co v Abko Properties, Inc, 780 F2d 751 (9th Cir) (minute order was a judgment, triggering time for filing appeal; appeal dismissed as untimely), *cert denied,* 479 US 825 (1986); Fiester v Turner, 783 F2d 1474 (9th Cir 1986) (untimely motion for reconsideration does not suspend time for filing notice of appeal; however, court will review denial of reconsideration motion on abuse of discretion standard); Muhammad v DeRobertis, 788 F2d 1268 (7th Cir 1986) (plaintiff's counsel, without notice to plaintiff, filed a timely Fed R Civ P 59(b) motion after plaintiff had, pro se, filed a notice of appeal; appeal dismissed).

[53] 28 USC §2107, the text of which is in **app E,** was amended to make it consistent with Fed R App P 4(a)(6).

[54] For example, the Ninth Circuit has construed *excusable neglect* harshly. In Pratt v D.J. McCarthy, 850 F2d 590 (9th Cir 1988), the Court refused to allow an extension of time for a habeas corpus appeal where each of appellant's pro bono counsel mistakenly thought the other would file a notice of appeal and counsel filed a notice as soon as the mistake was discovered. *See also* Allied Steel v City of Abilene, 909 F2d 139 (5th Cir 1990) (reversing district court Fed R App P 4(a) extension of time for filing

by the rule, the court of appeals is powerless to entertain the appeal.[55]

§6.04 —Criminal Cases

Federal Rule of Appellate Procedure 4(b) provides that the notice of appeal in a criminal case shall be filed within 10 days after judgment. If the notice is filed after the decision, sentence, or order is announced, but before the judgment or order is entered, then the notice is treated as filed "on the date of and after the entry."[56]

The time for appeal is extended by timely filing certain enumerated posttrial motions listed in Fed R App P 4(b)[57] and will run for 10 days after disposition of those motions, or 10 days after judgment of conviction, whichever is later. A notice of appeal filed after decision on one of the enumerated motions is

---

notice of appeal granted after time for appeal had run; abuse of discretion standard more stringently applied, as compared with extensions granted before appeal time has run; appeal dismissed; note that appellees challenged the extension by noticing an appeal and then moved to consolidate with the appeal on the merits); Reinsurance Co of Am v Administratia Asigurarilor de Stat, 808 F2d 1249 (7th Cir 1987) (failure to file a timely notice of appeal was the result of sloth and not excusable; held, district judge's refusal to extend the time affirmed); Osterneck v Ernst & Whinney, 489 US 169 (1989) (discussed in detail earlier this section); *In re* Air Crash at Dallas/Fort Worth Airport on Aug 22, 1985, 852 F2d 842 (5th Cir 1988) (Fed R Civ P 60(b) motion insufficient to extend time for appeal and does not excuse the requirement of Fed R App P 4(a)).

[55] This is the rule of Griggs v Provident Consumer Discount Co, 459 US 56 (1982), discussed above. However, there may be devices to save an appeal from dismissal as untimely. For example, in Sine v Local No 992, Intl Bhd of Teamsters, 790 F2d 1095 (4th Cir 1986), the district court entered default judgment against plaintiffs, and later denied their postjudgment motions as moot because plaintiffs already had filed a notice of appeal from the default. The court of appeals held that the notice of appeal from the default was premature, having been filed during the pendency of motions to alter or amend the default judgment. However, a second notice of appeal, attacking the denial of their motions as moot, was valid, and, therefore, the judgment below would be vacated and remanded for consideration of the motions that were pending at the time the plaintiff filed its first notice of appeal. In Butler v Coral Volkswagen, Inc, 804 F2d 612 (11th Cir 1986), the losing party relied on the district court's erroneous granting of an extension of time within which to file a new trial motion. The court held that the time for appeal would run from the denial of the motion, relying upon the unique circumstances exception to the strict requirements of Fed R App P 4(a). *But see* Fine v Paramount Pictures, 181 F2d 300 (7th Cir 1950), disallowing the appeal; however, the 11th Circuit in Butler held that the reasoning of Fine was implicitly rejected by the Supreme Court in Wolfsohn v Hankin, 376 US 203 (1964) (memorandum), revg 321 F2d 393 (DC Cir 1963); Thompson v INS, 375 US 384 (1964). *See also* Harris Truck Lines v Cherry Meat Packers, Inc, 371 US 215 (1962). The reasoning of these cases is that a litigant may be lulled by the district court into not filing a timely notice.

[56] Fed R App P 4(b). The text of Fed R App P 4 is in **app A.**

[57] The motions are those for judgment of acquittal, in arrest of judgment, for a new trial on any ground other than newly discovered evidence, or for a new trial based on newly discovered evidence if the motion is made before or within 10 days after entry of the judgment.

announced, but before the motion is disposed of becomes fully effective when the last of the pending motions is decided, or when the judgment of conviction is entered, whichever is later. That is, the defendant need not file a new notice of appeal after timely posttrial motions are decided or amend a prior timely notice of appeal to include a challenge to the posttrial motions ruling. The earlier notice of appeal will be treated as sufficient to challenge such a ruling.[58]

The government has 30 days to appeal an order when it is permitted by law to appeal, the time being computed from the date of the order appealed or the date on which the defendant notices an appeal. The latter provision is designed for the situation, such as sentencing review, in which the government has the right to cross-appeal. This disparity in time to appeal has been sustained against a due process challenge.[59]

The district court may extend the time for appeal by as much as 30 days upon a showing of excusable neglect.[60]

An incarcerated inmate's notice of appeal in a civil or criminal case is timely if deposited in the prison's internal mailing system within the time allowed by Fed R App P 4.[61] The appellate process in criminal cases is simpler, though less symmetrical, than that in civil cases. The asymmetry results from the government's inability to appeal a final judgment in favor of the accused rendered after jeopardy has attached. When a motion to suppress evidence is granted in part and denied in part, the government may appeal the grant but the accused has no right of cross-appeal; he or she has only the limited interlocutory appeal rights discussed at **§2.11.**

Federal Rule of Appellate Procedure 4(b)'s relatively stringent time limitations apply not only to criminal convictions, but also to matters that may be characterized as criminal, such as grand jury proceedings.[62] Moreover, the appeal period for some collateral orders entered in a criminal case may begin

---

[58] Fed R App P 4(a) specifically provides for such an interpretation of a notice of appeal, "notwithstanding the provisions of Rule 3(c)." *See* **§6.02.**

[59] United States v Avendano-Camacho, 786 F2d 1392 (9th Cir 1986).

[60] As the rule says, the 10-day filing period may be extended for up to 30 days upon a showing of *excusable neglect.* Where the defendant files a notice within the 30-day period and the district court accepts it, the court of appeals may construe the district court's acceptance as a finding of excusable neglect and a granting of additional time. The practice is discretionary, however, and ordinarily the district court must specify any such finding. United States v Anna, 843 F2d 1146 (8th Cir), *appeal decided by,* 863 F2d 31 (8th Cir 1988). See cases on excusable neglect under Fed R App P 4(a)(5), discussed at **§6.03.**

[61] Fed R App P 4(c), which provides a mechanism for proving timely filing in the event of dispute.

[62] *See, e.g., In re* Grand Jury Proceedings (Co X), 835 F2d 237 (10th Cir 1987) (notice of appeal from denial of motion to quash grand jury subpoena must be filed within 10 days of order; 60-day period for civil actions to which government is a party, not applicable), *cert denied,* 492 US 905 (1989).

to run from the date of the order, not from when a judgment of conviction is eventually entered.[63]

Federal Rule of Appellate Procedure 4(b) is like Fed R App P 4(a) in that failure to observe the time limits for filing a notice of appeal is fatal to an appeal: the court of appeals will be without jurisdiction.[64]

For a defendant appealing a final judgment, the timing rules usually present no difficulty. When the jury's verdict is rendered, counsel prepares and files posttrial motions within the time permitted by the Federal Rules of Criminal Procedure[65] or as enlarged by timely motion to the district court. Meanwhile, the probation officer prepares a presentence report. The trial judge usually disposes of the post-trial motions before or at the time of imposing sentence and entering a judgment. In such a case, it will be clear when the 10-day appeal period begins.

In *United States v Corey,*[66] the Tenth Circuit discussed the effect of the defendant's motion to reopen sentencing, filed 5 days after final judgment was entered: "It is well established that a motion for rehearing or reconsideration of an order in a criminal case that is filed within the permissible time period for appeal renders an otherwise final order of the district court nonfinal until disposition of the motion."

After the defendant's motion was denied, he filed a notice of appeal of his sentence within 10 days of the denial. The court agreed that this notice was timely as to the original final judgment entered against him 20 days earlier.

Once a notice of appeal is filed, the district court loses jurisdiction of the case, except for its power under Fed R App P 4(b) to correct a sentence under Fed R Crim P 35(c), to rule on certain procedural matters such as the content of the record, and to decide the defendant's bail status and any stays of fines or forfeitures. An accused whose appeal is pending who wishes to make a new trial motion must file the motion with a request that the district court ask the court of appeals to remand the case.[67] If the district judge determines that the new trial motion may have merit, he or she will have jurisdiction to grant it

---

[63] *See* United States v Estevez, 852 F2d 239 (7th Cir 1988) (district court ruled that defendant's attorney could exempt only $40,000 in attorneys' fees from a forfeiture order; attorney appealed this order within 10 days of entry of judgment against the defendant, but months after entry of the fee order; held, court of appeals lacked jurisdiction), *cert denied,* 492 US 908 (1989).

[64] *E.g.*, United States v Schuchardt, 685 F2d 901 (4th Cir 1982) (court of appeals without jurisdiction to hear untimely appeal, despite defendant's claim that he did not receive notice of entry of judgment). In the typical case, the defendant will be well aware that judgment is entered, because he must be present at the sentencing.

[65] Fed R Crim P 29(c) (postverdict motion for judgment of acquittal); 33 (new trial); 34 (arrest of judgment). These motions must be made within seven days after verdict, or within such longer period as the judge may direct by an order entered within the seven-day period. For a detailed discussion of the function and timing of these motions, see the relevant portions of Charles A. Wright, Federal Practice and Procedure, Criminal 2d (1982).

[66] 999 F2d 493, 494-95 (10th Cir 1993).

[67] United States v Cronic, 466 US 648, 667 n42 (1984). *See* 3 Charles A. Wright, *supra* note 65, §557, at 338-40.

only if the case has been remanded to the district judge for that purpose. If the motion is denied, the accused should file a new notice of appeal. If the motion is granted, the government will appeal.[68] The defendant should never abandon an appeal once commenced in order to litigate some newly arisen issue in the district court. Doing so risks losing the right to appeal. The proper course is to litigate in the district court, appeal any unfavorable result and seek to consolidate with the pending appeal.[69]

Because entry of an order on the criminal docket fires the notice of appeal starting gun, counsel must check the docket regularly when motions are pending.

§6.05 Petition for Permission to Appeal under 28 USC §1292(b)

The court of appeals' power to hear interlocutory appeals under §1292(b) is discussed at **§2.09.** That section also discusses the legal standard applied by the court of appeals in deciding whether to grant a petition for leave to appeal under §1292(b) and provides guidance on fashioning a persuasive application to the district court to certify a question.

Once a party obtains the required certification, a Petition for Permission to Appeal must be filed in the court of appeals within ten days. Federal Rule of Appellate Procedure 5 sets out the procedure for filing of and decision on the petition. If the district judge first enters an order and later decides to permit an appeal, Fed R App P 5(a) allows the judge to amend the earlier order at any time to add the required certification.

Federal Rule of Appellate Procedure 5(b) requires that the petition contain a statement of facts, a statement of the question, and an explanation of why the question meets the §1292(b) standards. The petition must include, or have annexed to it, a copy of the order. When the petition is filed and served, the clerk of the court of appeals usually will notify the opposing parties and tell them of their obligation to file a response within seven days. The clerk's notice is not essential, however; any answer must be filed timely. Oral argument usually is not allowed on Fed R App P 5 petitions.

If the court grants the petition, the appellant must pay the docketing fee and ensure the transmission of the record.[70] The court will set a briefing schedule.

Although Fed R App P 5(b) requires that the petition enumerate how the §1292(b) conditions are met, this does not dispense with the need for a state-

---

[68] *See* **§2.11.**

[69] *See, e.g.*, United States v Mendes, 912 F2d 434 (10th Cir 1990) (defendant was sentenced and filed timely appeal; government sought mandamus to challenge claimed illegal sentence, and court of appeals granted writ and remanded for resentencing; during mandamus proceedings, defendant withdrew notice of appeal, apparently believing conviction would be reviewable after remand; after resentencing, defendant filed new notice of appeal; held, neither petition for mandamus nor grant of writ disturbed judgment of conviction, and withdrawal of earlier notice of appeal was fatal to review of it; court of appeals would review only the sentence newly imposed on remand).

[70] Fed R App P 5(d).

ment by the district court to justify its order granting leave to appeal. The court of appeals will be as interested in the district court's reasoning as in the advocates'.[71] The advocate should set out the question of law presented for review and summarize the precedents that create the substantial basis. This portion of the petition should focus upon the differences of opinion or uncertainties that make the case appropriate for court of appeals review.

In discussing whether interlocutory review will advance the termination of the litigation, the advocate should compute the costs and benefits of immediate review. If the district court's order is wrong, what time and money costs must the parties and the court incur in litigating fruitlessly? Taking an example from the discussion at **§2.09,** assume that the district court has ruled that a prior judgment does not collaterally estop a party on an important issue. How many days of depositions, of whom, and what other discovery must be taken to make a new record on the disputed fact?

About half of the §1292(b) petitions are granted. To maximize chances of success, the petition must be lively and informative. The advocate should imagine speaking to the judge and saying in effect, "I know you are busy and I know you don't have to hear this question, but it is an important, interesting question on which the district judge has asked for your help. It is a discrete question that does not involve a great deal of sifting through a complex record. If you take the time to decide the question now, it will save a great deal of judicial time in the future—in this case and others." To make these points, one must write like a journalist and make these points in the petition's introductory paragraphs.

Federal Rule of Appellate Procedure 5 is the exclusive means to bring a §1292(b) appeal to the court of appeals. Filing a notice of appeal will not take the place of the required petition.[72] The 10-day period is jurisdictional, and a later filing also is fatal to the appeal.[73] There are two escape routes from this problem. The first is in Fed R App P 5(a) itself, which provides that the district court may amend its order to include the required statement at any time, triggering a new 10-day period. Second, the district court may reexamine its prior order and statement, and recertify—giving the party a new 10-day period in which to petition.[74]

---

[71] See Isra Fruit, Ltd v Agrexco Agri Export Co, 804 F2d 24 (2d Cir 1986), discussed at **§2.09.**

[72] *See, e.g.*, Aucoin v Matador Servs, 749 F2d 1180, 1181 (5th Cir 1985) (where petitioner filed notice of appeal but did not file timely request for permissive appeal as required by Fed R App P 5(a), the appeal must be dismissed "for lack of appellate jurisdiction").

[73] *See, e.g.*, Aparicio v Swan Lake, 643 F2d 1109, 1111 (5th Cir 1981) (failure to file the petition within the proscribed 10-day period deprives the appellate court of jurisdiction; the period for filing cannot be extended by the appellate or the district court).

[74] *See* **§2.09.**

§6.06 Bankruptcy Appeals

As discussed at **§2.14,** appeals in bankruptcy cases fall into two broad categories: (1) appeals from orders of the district court sitting as a bankruptcy court in the first instance; and (2) appeals under 28 USC §1589(d) from bankruptcy appeal panels or from district judges sitting to review orders of bankruptcy judges.

For the first category, Fed R App P 6(a)[75] provides that the appeal from a final judgment "shall be taken in identical fashion as appeals from other judgments, orders or decrees of district courts in civil actions." Appeals under provisions of law other than 28 USC §1291 would be taken as outlined in the parts of Chapter 2 and this chapter discussing those appealability provisions.

For the second category, Fed R App P 6(b) provides the procedure for appeals from bankruptcy panels and district judges sitting in review of bankruptcy judges. The procedures are substantially the same as for any appeal from a final judgment, except that the notice of appeal is prescribed by Form 5 and some of the Rules of Appellate Procedure will be inapplicable. The Form 5 notice of appeal must be filed within the same time and in the same manner as a notice of appeal from the judgment in a civil case.[76]

If the district court or bankruptcy panel renders its decision and a party files a timely motion for rehearing under Bankruptcy Rule 8015, the time for appeal runs from the disposition of the motion. A notice of appeal filed after the initial decision, but before the rehearing motion is decided, is of no effect until the rehearing motion is decided. At that point, the notice of appeal springs to life and is fully effective to trigger review, but only of the initial order. A party wishing to challenge the disposition of the rehearing motion should amend any previously filed notice of appeal or file a notice if that has not yet been done.[77]

This procedure is somewhat complex, but it at least avoids the problem of notices of appeal becoming completely ineffective, which had been the situation under prior versions of the rules governing appeals in civil cases.[78]

Federal Rule of Appellate Procedure 6(b)(2)(ii) provides designation of the record on appeal. The appellant must file a designation of record and of the issues to be presented on appeal, and serve these on all other parties. This represents a difference from the procedure in ordinary civil cases, in which a designation of issues is not required unless one is ordering less than the entire transcript or unless a circuit rule so provides.

The clerk's transmission of the record, as provided in Fed R App P 6(b)(2)(iii), is by a procedure similar to that described at **§6.14.**

---

[75] The text of Fed R App P 6 is in **app A.**

[76] *See* **§§6.02-6.03.**

[77] Fed R App P 6(b)(i).

[78] *See* **§6.03.**

§6.07 Tax Court Appeals

The court of appeals' jurisdiction over appeals from the United States Tax Court, including the question of which court of appeals will have jurisdiction over the appeal, is discussed in Chapter 2.[79]

In cases from the Tax Court, Fed R App P 13(a)[80] provides that a notice of appeal shall be filed within 90 days after "the decision of the Tax Court is entered." However, if any party files a timely motion to vacate or revise under the Tax Court rules, that motion suspends the time for appeal until it is decided.[81] The full time for appeal then begins to run again when the motion is decided. If any party files a notice of appeal within the 90 days, any other party may file one within 120 days from the entry of decision.[82] There is no provision for an untimely notice of appeal and the court of appeals has no power to extend the time limits provided in the rule.[83]

If a party files a timely notice of appeal, and a motion to vacate or revise is filed, that earlier notice probably becomes a nullity,[84] although there is little authority on the point. It will be necessary to file a new notice once the motion is decided.

Under the Tax Court Rules, it may be difficult to determine when a decision is entered. Tax Ct R 155(a) provides that "[w]here the Court has filed or stated its opinion . . . in a case, it may withhold entry of its decision" while the parties determine the exact amount of the deficiency, liability, or overpayment. Thus, the court may decide the case, and its decision will not constitute an appealable order until the calculations envisaged by Tax Ct R 155 are completed, and the results put into the court's decision. This process may be lengthy and may even result in additional matters being presented to the court for decision. The decision will then be "entered," and the time for appeal will begin.

The Fed R App P 13 notice of appeal is similar to that in a civil case. Federal Rule of Appellate Procedure Form 2 is a good guide.[85] For guidance on the contents of the notice of appeal, see **§6.02.**[86] The notice of appeal must specify

---

[79] **§2.13.**

[80] The full text of Fed R App P 13 and 14, dealing with cases from the Tax Court, is in **app A.**

[81] *See* Robert Louis Stevenson Apartments, Inc v Commissioner, 337 F2d 681 (8th Cir 1964) (timely post-trial motions going to heart of case delay time for appeal).

[82] Fed R App P 13(a).

[83] Fed R App P 13; 26 USC §7483. The courts of appeals are divided on the applicability of the 120-day period when there have been separate opinions on different aspects of a consolidated case. *Compare* Davies v Commissioner, 715 F2d 435 (9th Cir 1983) (taxpayer may not rely upon a timely notice of appeal from one of separate opinions in a consolidated case to support filing after 90 but within 120 days) *with* Dowell v Commissioner, 738 F2d 354 (10th Cir 1984) (notice of appeal is timely if filed within 120 days in such a case).

[84] Feistman v Commissioner, 587 F2d 941 (9th Cir 1978). *See* **§6.03.**

[85] Form 2 is reprinted in **app A.**

[86] Failure to comply precisely with rules as to the form of a notice of appeal may be excused under some circumstances. *See* Pasternack v Commissioner, 478 F2d 588 (DC

the court of appeals to which the appeal is being taken, in accordance with the statutory provisions uniquely applicable to Tax Court proceedings.[87]

On appeal from the Tax Court, all the Rules of Appellate Procedure are applicable except those dealing specifically with other kinds of appeals.[88]

§6.08 Habeas Corpus Cases

As noted in Chapter 3[89] and Fed R App P 22(a), although judges of courts of appeals have jurisdiction to issue the writ of habeas corpus, application for the writ is almost always made first in the district court for the district where the prisoner is confined.[90] Issues raised by writ reach the court of appeals on appeal from the district court.

If the habeas corpus case involves other than a state prisoner in custody, the appeal will be treated like that in a normal civil case. When the petitioner is in custody resulting from an order of a state court, Fed R App P 22(b)[91] requires that the petitioner obtain a certificate of probable cause from the district judge or from a circuit judge. If the petitioner fails to seek such a certificate the notice of appeal may be treated as a request for one. Similarly, a motion for certificate of probable cause may be treated as a notice of appeal.[92]

Rule 22(b) requires a certificate of probable cause only when the "detention complained of arises out of process issued by a state court."[93] In all other cases, appeals are governed by the same procedures as in other civil matters.

Cir 1973) (a letter to the Tax Court requesting reconsideration and advice on rights of appeal was an adequate substitute for a notice of appeal from the judgment).

[87] 26 USC §7482(b)(1) (venue proper in principal place of business of entity seeking review, determined as of the time the Tax Court petition was filed; District of Columbia is the forum if no other forum is proper). *See also* 26 USC §7482(b)(2) (Secretary and taxpayer may stipulate in writing for a particular court of appeals). *See also* Becker v Commissioner, 716 F2d 285 (5th Cir 1983) (no transfer under 28 USC §2112, but transfer might be available to proper court of appeals under 28 USC §1631); Alexander v Commissioner, 825 F2d 499 (DC Cir 1987) (28 USC §1631 construed not to limit court of appeals' inherent power to transfer case filed in wrong circuit).

[88] As noted in Fed R App P 14, Fed R App P 4-9, 15-20, 22, and 23 are inapplicable.

[89] *See* **§3.14.**

[90] This is a specialized field, particularly given the use of federal habeas review for capital cases. The best specialized resource is James F. Liebman, Federal Habeas Corpus Practice & Procedure (1988), *reviewed in* Michael E. Tigar, *Book Review, Habeas Corpus and the Penalty of Death,* 90 Colum L Rev 255 (1990). In addition, Ronald Sokol's classic, Federal Habeas Corpus 17-17.4 (2d ed 1968), is still useful.

[91] The text of Fed R App P 22 is in **app A.**

[92] *See* Thames v Dugger, 848 F2d 149 (11th Cir 1988) (motion for certificate of probable cause filed in the district court within 30 days of judgment satisfied requirement).

[93] Fed R App P 22(b).

In discussing state court custody cases, Fed R App P 22(b) must be read together with Fed R App P 8[94] and 23,[95] dealing, respectively, with stays and custody of habeas petitioners. Discussion of how these rules interact is best divided into two parts, non-capital cases and capital cases.

In non-capital cases, federal habeas is most often used to collaterally attack a state criminal conviction.[96] If the district judge grants relief, the state or its representative may appeal without obtaining a certificate of probable cause. However, if the prisoner wishes to appeal, he or she must obtain such a certificate from either the district judge or the court of appeals. This certificate is not a substitute for a notice of appeal, which also must be timely filed.[97]

The certificate of probable cause will be issued upon a finding that the prisoner's claims merit appellate review. The finding of probable cause is based on a higher standard than the grant of leave to appeal in forma pauperis.[98] If the district judge denies the certificate, counsel must move for it in the court of appeals. The motion should contain a discussion of why the issues presented are substantial as a matter of law and are supported by evidence in the district court record.[99] The requirement of a certificate of probable cause should alert counsel to the importance of pleading a habeas petition with specificity and of attaching copies of relevant parts of the state court record to the petition. In this way, if the petition is dismissed without a hearing, and a certificate of probable cause denied by the district judge, counsel will have a basis upon which to present contentions to the court of appeals.

Rule 23(a) provides that prisoners may not be transferred in ways that would defeat jurisdiction over the writ.[100]

Federal Rule of Appellate Procedure 23(b) and (c) provide for bail pending decision on a petition for habeas corpus. Experience teaches that bail in habeas

---

[94] Stays are discussed at **§6.11.**

[95] These rules are reprinted in full in **app A.**

[96] *See generally* Wayne R. LaFave & Jerold H. Israel, Criminal Procedure ch 27 (Hornbook ed 1985). The federal law of habeas corpus to review state criminal convictions continues to develop. The cited source is the best initial guide to research.

[97] Fitzsimmons v Yeager, 391 F2d 849 (3d Cir), *cert denied,* 393 US 868 (1968).

[98] *See, e.g.,* Clements v Wainwright, 648 F2d 979 (5th Cir 1981). If the district court grants a certificate of probable cause, the court of appeals must hear the appeal on the merits. Carafas v LaVallee, 391 US 234 (1968).

[99] The court of appeals will not make an initial determination of probable cause to appeal. McKibben v Hopper, 565 F2d 1316 (5th Cir 1978). The standards used by courts of appeals in determining whether to issue a certificate of probable cause when one has been denied by the district court are variable. *See generally* Ronald Sokol, *supra* note 90. It is fair to say that in death penalty cases, the court of appeals will usually review the district court's denial of habeas corpus on the merits.

[100] Custody of the petitioner within the territorial jurisdiction of the court is the usual measure of habeas jurisdiction. Ronald Sokol, *supra* note 90, at 85. *See* Hammer v Meachum, 691 F2d 958 (10th Cir 1982) (violation of rule against transfer did not require order of retransfer where petitioner had not been prejudiced), *cert denied,* 460 US 1042 (1983).

appeals seldom is granted when the petition has been denied in the district court.[101] An order denying bail pending appeal is, however, appealable.[102]

Even if the petition has been granted, the most common form of the order requires the prisoner to be retried within a certain time. The Fed R App P 23(c) determination concerning release will be made in the first instance by the district court. If that court orders release, the state or its representative must then seek a stay of that order in accordance with Fed R App P 8.[103]

If the district judge grants relief on some claims in the habeas petition and denies it on others, and the state or its representative appeals, the prisoner must nonetheless obtain a certificate of probable cause to cross-appeal.[104] The circuits are in conflict as to whether the district judge may cut off appeal of some issues by issuing a certificate limited to less than all the issues the petitioner wants to appeal. The Second Circuit approves of limited certificates, whether they be granted by the district judge or the court of appeals itself. The Third, Sixth, Seventh, and Ninth Circuits hold that limited certificates do not affect the court of appeals' power to hear all issues raised on appeal.[105]

Death penalty cases pose special problems on habeas corpus; some courts of appeals have adopted special procedures to deal with stays of execution and last minute petitions.[106] If the petition is granted in a death case, the state's appellate rights are the same as in any other habeas case.

If the district judge denies the petition, and the death date has been set, counsel faces a difficult procedural maze if the prisoner's life is to be spared.[107] Counsel must first seek a certificate of probable cause from the district judge and file a notice of appeal. Counsel also should seek a stay of execution from the district judge. If the certificate and stay are denied, counsel should immediately seek a stay under Fed R App P 8 and a certificate of probable cause under

---

[101] *See, e.g.*, Smith v Caldwell, 339 F Supp 215 (SD Ga), *affd*, 458 F2d 160 (5th Cir 1972) (although district court has more leeway to grant bail pending appeal from denial of habeas corpus than on appeal from a federal conviction, bail would be denied).

[102] Grune v Coughlin, 913 F2d 41 (2d Cir 1990) (court of appeals has collateral order jurisdiction over appeal from denial of bail to habeas corpus petitioner, provided district court has ruled on application for certificate of probable cause).

[103] *See, e.g.*, Hill v Rose, 579 F Supp 1080 (MD Tenn 1983), which sets forth the standards to be applied to the state's motion to overcome the presumption in favor of release. On stays, see **§6.11.**

[104] Roman v Abrams, 790 F2d 244 (2d Cir 1986) (while court of appeals has power to limit a certificate of probable cause to one or more specified issues on the prisoner's appeal, the prisoner may not, without obtaining a certificate of probable cause, cross-appeal the denial of some habeas claims when the state appeals the granting of the writ on other grounds), *revd on the merits*, 822 F2d 214 (2d Cir 1987), *cert denied*, 489 US 1052 (1989).

[105] *See* Smith v Chrans, 836 F2d 1076 (7th Cir 1988).

[106] Counsel may obtain a copy of the current local circuit procedures by telephoning or writing the court of appeals clerk's office. The addresses and telephone numbers are provided in **ch 4.**

[107] The two-volume James F. Liebman treatise, cited *supra* note 90, is a reliable guide. Counsel also can obtain assistance from one of the federally funded capital punishment resource centers, or from the ABA death penalty project, whose address is given at **§6.15.**

Fed R App P 22(b) from the court of appeals. Telephone contact with the court of appeals clerk's office usually will provide assistance in assembling the necessary papers and making sure that these applications are in proper form. If the hour of execution impends, the clerk's office may be asked to communicate by telephone with the judge assigned to rule on such applications. Once a stay and certificate have been obtained, the court of appeals will set a schedule for filing the record, briefing, and argument. A justice of the Supreme Court also has the power to stay an execution if relief is not obtained in the court of appeals.[108]

The law of federal habeas corpus is dealt with in a number of specialized works that detail the procedural and substantive law of the writ.[109] While procedures on federal habeas corpus in capital cases vary depending on circuit rules, some general principles have emerged. *Barefoot v Estelle,*[110] generally has been interpreted as giving almost every inmate under sentence of death one opportunity for federal post-conviction review of claims with arguable merit. While *Barefoot* stresses that issuance of a certificate of probable cause is not automatic and must rest upon something more than the nonfrivolous nature of the appeal, the courts of appeals have been fairly liberal in granting such certificates to first-time habeas applicants. The courts of appeals have, however, taken *Barefoot's* approval of expedited procedures for death cases seriously and some provide for telephone argument to a panel of the court and for other time-compressing devices.

If the court of appeals denies relief, counsel faces the holding in *Barefoot* that stays pending application for certiorari are not automatic.[111] The law relating to stays of execution after denial of relief by the court of appeals can only be described as chaotic. If the court of appeals, to whom the application for stay must first be presented according to *Barefoot,* grants relief, then Justices of the Supreme Court usually have denied applications by the state to vacate the stay.[112] Since it takes only four votes to grant certiorari, one faces the realistic prospect that a stay will be denied or a motion to vacate granted when there is a numerical possibility that the case could be heard on the merits if the prisoner's life was spared.

The standards for granting a stay of execution are those familiar in other contexts: (1) likelihood of success on the merits; (2) showing of irreparable injury if the stay is not granted; (3) whether granting the stay would substan-

---

[108] Sup Ct R 43, 44. Counsel also may invoke the aid of specialized defender groups for assistance. The local or regional chapter of the American Civil Liberties Union will be able to provide current telephone numbers and addresses. On proceedings in the Supreme Court (a subject beyond the scope of this book), see generally Robert L. Stern, Eugene Gressman, & Stephan M. Shapiro, Supreme Court Practice (6th ed 1986).

[109] *See* Ronald Sokol, *supra* note 90; Wayne R. LaFave & Jerold H. Israel, *supra* note 96.

[110] 463 US 880 (1983).

[111] *See* Autry v Estelle, 464 US 1 (1983) (per curiam).

[112] *Compare* Dugger v Johnson, 485 US 945 (1988) (motion to vacate stay denied, two Justices dissenting) *with* Wainwright v Booker, 473 US 935 (1985) (motion to vacate stay granted, four Justices dissenting).

tially harm other parties; and (4) whether granting the stay would serve the public interest.[113] Petitions for habeas corpus, after the first one, are subject to an even more expedited procedure.[114]

On appeal in a capital habeas case, counsel may face the problem of seeking a stay of execution to petition for certiorari on an issue that the Supreme Court may be considering, but that is foreclosed by controlling law of the court of appeals where the case is pending. The Fifth Circuit has held that even a grant of certiorari on such an issue will not necessarily entitle a prisoner to a stay of execution.[115]

§6.09 Petition for Review of Administrative Agency Orders

The procedure for seeking review is set out in Fed R App P 15.[116] Federal Rule of Appellate Procedure 15(a) provides for filing a petition to review agency action which is subject to review in the court of appeals. The rules provide a form for petitioning,[117] which is a good guide to follow. Federal Rule of Appellate Procedure 15(b) provides for filing an application for enforcement of an agency order, such as from the National Labor Relations Board, which the court of appeals has jurisdiction to enforce. The agency itself is almost invariably the party applying for enforcement. Under Fed R App P 15(b), if the party subject to the order fails to respond within 20 days, the agency order shall be enforced by default.[118]

All parties seeking review of the agency order must be named in the notice or petition. This is an application to obtain agency review of the rule in appeals from the district courts, as discussed at **§6.02.**[119] The petition must adequately specify the matter on which review is sought. Again, the rule applicable in ordinary civil cases obtains in agency review proceedings, including the rule that non-prejudicial omissions in the notice will not prejudice the petitioner's

---

[113] O'Bryan v McKaskle, 729 F2d 991, 993 (5th Cir 1984).

[114] *See, e.g.*, Moore v Butler, 819 F2d 517 (5th Cir) (application to stay execution and for certificate of probable cause denied; fourth successive petition criticized as abuse of the writ), *cert denied*, 482 US 920 (1987).

[115] Selvage v Lynaugh, 842 F2d 89 (5th Cir), *stay granted*, 485 US 983 (1988) (three Justices dissenting), *vacated on other grounds*, 494 US 113 (1990). In *Selvage*, the Supreme Court clerk's office told counsel that a fourth justice had opposed the stay but had asked that his vote not be recorded. The grant of a stay in *Selvage* without reasons does not clarify the issue decided by the court of appeals, however.

[116] The text of Fed R App P 15 is in **app A.**

[117] The text of Form 3 is in **app A.**

[118] Fed R App P 15(b). NLRB v Johnson Elec Co, 472 F2d 161 (6th Cir 1973) (NLRB's order was enforced by default where respondent failed to either file answer within 20 days or file for extension).

[119] Goos v ICC, 911 F2d 1283 (8th Cir 1990) (petition for review of ICC order confers jurisdiction only over claims of parties named in petition and not of those referred to as "et al"; applying *Torres* rule discussed at **§6.02** to Fed R App P 15).

case.[120] Potential intervenors are directed by Fed R App P 15(d) to file a motion to intervene, unless a statute provides for a different procedure.

The petition, application, or motion takes the place of the notice of appeal that would be filed in the ordinary civil case. Indeed, under Fed R App P 20, Fed R App P 3-14, and 22 and 23 are not applicable to agency review proceedings. Of course, these procedures are applicable only to agency orders that are reviewable in the first instance in the court of appeals. The statutory grant of power to each agency will specify the path of review. Some petitions for review of agency orders must be brought in the district court in the first instance, not in the court of appeals.[121]

Other specific Fed R App P provisions govern review of agency final decisions.[122] Rules 16 and 17 provide for assembling, transmitting, and filing the record; these rules conform to the requirements of 28 USC §2112, which deals with the record in agency review proceedings.[123]

Stays pending review are governed by Fed R App P 18,[124] which provides procedures quite similar to Fed R App P 8, discussed at **§6.11.** Application for a stay must first be made to the agency. Review is by motion in the court of appeals.[125] Whether seeking court of appeals review suspends the agency's order probably will be regulated by specific provisions in the agency's authorizing legislation, although the court of appeals has jurisdiction under the All Writs Act to control agency action pending review.[126]

Federal Rule of Appellate Procedure 19 directs that the agency file a proposed judgment after the court of appeals issues its opinion. This rule bespeaks deference to agency expertise. If the respondent objects to the proposed judgment, it must file its own proposed judgment in response, within seven days.[127]

---

[120] *See* Castillo-Rodriguez v INS, 929 F2d 181 (5th Cir 1991) (court of appeals applies the rule of *Foman v Davis,* 371 US 178, 181 (1962), discussed at **§6.02,** to a petition under Fed R App P 15(a); petitioner designated as the subject of his appeal the immigration judge order of deportation, rather than the final order of the BIA; since this error did not affect substantial rights and it was clear which judgment petitioner intended to appeal, he did not forfeit right of appeal).

[121] *See, e.g.,* Five Flags Pipe Line Co v Department of Transp, 854 F2d 1438 (DC Cir 1988) (concerning orders of the Department's Research and Special Programs Administration governing natural gas pipeline user fees).

[122] The text of these rules is in **app A.**

[123] The statute defines the contents of the record and sets out what it is to comprise; it is almost identical to Fed R App P 16(a).

[124] The text of Fed R App P 18 is in **app B.**

[125] In addition, stays and interlocutory orders in many of the most commonly occurring review proceedings are governed by 28 USC §§2341-2350.

[126] *See* Texas v United States, 837 F2d 184 (5th Cir) (court of appeals denies ICC request for an injunction against a Texas state court proceeding pending the court of appeals disposition of an appeal from an ICC decision, but notes that "the All Writs Act, 28 USC §1651, gives this court limited authority "to preserve the court's jurisdiction or status quo by injunction pending review of an agency's action through the prescribed statutory channels' " (quoting FTC v Dean Foods Co, 384 US 597 (1966)), *cert denied,* 488 US 821 (1988).

[127] The text of Fed R App P 19 is in **app A.**

Agency review is, as noted at **§2.16,** interwoven with complex doctrines of administrative law and specific substantive rules governing particular areas of agency expertise.[128] One of the most challenging aspects of agency review is the *first filed* rule for cases in which review is sought by more than one party. It is often the case that a party may seek review in more than one court of appeals, and still more often, that different parties may have access to different courts based upon their respective residences or places of business. The rule is generally that the notice of appeal filed first takes precedence,[129] although there have been legislative proposals to curtail the resultant races to the courthouse and to provide a uniform rule.[130] Some courts of appeals have special rules on this subject.[131]

The court of appeals' jurisdiction to affirm, modify, enforce, or set aside the agency order, in whole or in part, attaches when the application or petition is filed.[132] The court of appeals' jurisdiction usually becomes exclusive when the record is filed.[133] If any party wishes to adduce additional evidence, it must move the court of appeals for a remand to the agency. The agency will enter new findings and conclusions based upon the additional proceedings.[134]

The proliferation of federal administrative agencies has created problems of management and control far beyond the scope of this treatise. However, thoughtful writers have noted that the race to the courthouse is partly a reflection of the agencies' determination to behave as they wish, despite what courts may say. For example, many agencies follow the practice of *nonacquiescence,* by which they mean to maintain their positions in all circuits other than the one

---

[128] *See generally* 16 Charles A. Wright, Arthur R. Miller, Edward H. Cooper, & Eugene Gressman, Federal Practice and Procedure §§3940-44, 3961-66 (1977 & Supp 1993).

[129] 28 USC §2112(a). *See however* Charles A. Wright, *supra* note 128, at §3944.

[130] Charles A. Wright, *supra* note 128, at §3944. Some courts of appeals have local rules on this subject which must be consulted.

[131] For example, the Fifth Circuit has found that many lawyers, anticipating that an administrative order (particularly from the Federal Energy Regulatory Commission (FERC)) may soon be posted, file for review in the forum of their choice. As a result, the courts of appeals docket many proceedings to review nonexistent orders. The Fifth Circuit insists, in 5th Cir R 15.3.1, that a party filing for review represent, by counsel's certificate, that the order sought to be reviewed has been "posted, filed or entered" by the agency. With respect to the FERC, the DC and 10th Circuits have deemed orders posted just before or just after the regular times of 10:00 a.m. or 3:00 p.m. to have been filed at the scheduled posting time for purposes of judicial review. When there have been multiple filings, a panel of the court will determine which is the proper forum. *See e.g.,* Mobil Oil Exploration v FERC, 814 F2d 998 (5th Cir 1987), in which the Fifth Circuit accepted venue as a result of a coin toss conducted by the DC Circuit based on a one-second difference in filing times of petitions for review of the same order.

[132] 28 USC §2349 applies to many administrative agency review proceedings and is the model for most others.

[133] 28 USC §2349 is a typical provision.

[134] The court of appeals does, however, have broad latitude to supplement the record before it. *See* Charles A. Wright, *supra* note 128, at §3962.

issuing an adverse ruling and to refuse application of the ruling to all except the parties to it.[135]

This general description will vary, depending upon the agency whose action is being reviewed. Review beyond the court of appeals is available in the Supreme Court by certiorari or by the court of appeals certifying a disputed question to the Supreme Court.[136]

§6.10 Cross-Appeals and Protective Cross-Appeals

The rules regarding cross-appeals and protective cross-appeals flow from the same considerations that dictate the content of a notice of appeal. The notice of appeal must identify the judgment or order appealed from to inform the other parties and the court of appeals of what to expect. If a party is wholly satisfied with the judgment or order appealed from, and wants only to see it affirmed or the appeal dismissed, it need do nothing except await the opportunity to file a brief or a dispositive motion in the court of appeals.

A cross-appeal will be appropriate if a party is not wholly satisfied with the judgment and wants relief from the unsatisfactory portions. The cross-appellant's notice of appeal in that instance will challenge the judgment unconditionally. For example, if the district court enters a judgment that A is liable to B for $100,000, and B appeals on the grounds that the damages are inadequate, A may cross-appeal and claim that there is no liability at all.

A protective cross-appeal will be necessary to preserve an issue that will arise, if at all, only if the judgment or order appealed from is reversed or modified. For example, if the defendant has prevailed on the merits, but had interposed a procedural defense such as improper venue, lack of personal jurisdiction, or disqualification of the trial judge, and the plaintiff appeals, the defendant should file a protective cross-appeal.[137] The notice of appeal would read: "The defendant, A.B., appeals from the orders of the district court dated July 30, 1986, denying its motion to dismiss for want of personal jurisdiction, and seeks

---

[135] For a thoughtful treatment of these problems, see Peter L. Strauss, *One Hundred Fifty Cases Per Year: Some Implications of the Supreme Court's Limited Resources for Judicial Review of Agency Action,* 87 Colum L Rev 1093 (1987).

[136] 28 USC §2350.

[137] *See generally* Robert L. Stern, *When to Cross-Appeal or Cross-Petition—Certainty or Confusion?,* 87 Harv L Rev 763 (1974) (collecting cases); Peoria & PU Ry v United States, 263 US 528, 536 (1924) (defense of improper venue must be raised by cross-appeal when plaintiff appeals from dismissal on the merits). The party in such a case is exercising his or her right to "accept benefits of the separate features of the judgment and challenge the features adverse to him." United States v Newton Livestock Auction Mkt, Inc, 336 F2d 673, 676 (10th Cir 1964). However, as noted at **§2.02,** a prevailing party who has been ordered to accept a remittitur, or in the alternative a new trial, may not accede to the remittitur and then cross-appeal to gain back the amount remitted. The only remedy in such a case is to accept the new trial, and then appeal any adverse judgment and claim that the entire original award must be sustained. Also, if the court of appeals is without jurisdiction of the appeal, the proper means to raise such a questior is by motion to dismiss and not by cross-appeal.

review of this order only if the court of appeals reverses the judgment in defendant's favor on the merits." The term protective cross-appeal is not a term of art, but simply a convenient way to describe what the appellant in such a case is seeking to do.[138]

The wisdom of cross-appealing is illustrated by *Memorial Hospital System v Northbrook Life Insurance Co.*[139] In a case removed to federal court, the district judge granted summary judgment on two state law claims, holding them preempted by ERISA, and remanded two other claims to state court. On plaintiff's appeal, the court of appeals held that it did not have jurisdiction to review the remand order because the appellees had not noticed a cross-appeal. The same lesson is taught by *Rollins v Metropolitan Life Insurance Co,*[140] in which the court of appeals held that a cross-appeal is not necessary to urge all grounds in support of judgment, but is necessary if the appellee wishes to claim that the judgment was flawed even more fatally than appellants contend. For example, when the district court grants relief on a constructive trust theory, and plaintiff appeals the award as inadequate, the defendant must file a cross-appeal in order to urge that imposition of the constructive trust was improper.

In theory, one might simply let the other side's appeal run its course, await a final judgment on remand, and then raise all remaining issues on appeal from that judgment. That course has risks, for the district court on remand, or the court of appeals on a later appeal, might hold that the prior decision was meant to resolve the issue a party is seeking to raise.[141] A party may be genuinely uncertain about whether to file a cross-appeal on an issue that may or may not recur. For example, suppose that in a lengthy trial the trial judge made a number of evidentiary rulings to which a defendant objected, but that there was a defense verdict on which judgment was entered. Should the defendant cross-appeal on the evidentiary issues to seek guidance from the court of appeals in the event of an eventual retrial?

Prudence clearly dictates yes. While the court of appeals may decline to reach the evidentiary issues, on the basis that they might not recur in quite the same setting on retrial, the interests of judicial economy often will lead the court to discuss them. Thus, entirely aside from the risks of waiver by failing to cross-appeal, the opportunity for clarification should not be lost. Often, the court of appeals' ruling on these subsidiary issues will put the case in a more favorable settlement posture on remand by limiting a party's evidence or the scope of its claims.[142]

---

[138] *See* Robert L. Stern, *supra* note 137; Langnes v Green, 282 US 531 (1931).

[139] 904 F2d 236 (5th Cir 1990).

[140] 912 F2d 911, 917 (7th Cir 1990).

[141] This is a matter of construing the mandate on the first appeal. *See* **§10.15.**

[142] If the cross-appeal raises an issue going to the heart of the case, the court of appeals may be duty-bound to consider that issue. *See* Falkirk Mining Co v Japan Steel Works, Ltd, 906 F2d 369 (8th Cir 1990) (district court granted defendant's motion to dismiss complaint for failure to state claim, denied defendant's motion to dismiss for want of personal jurisdiction; parties cross-appealed; held, (1) personal jurisdiction issue must be resolved first, despite parties' desire for decision on whether complaint states claim;

A cross-appeal in a civil case is governed by Fed R App P 4(a)(3),[143] which gives the cross-appellant 14 days from the date of the first-filed timely notice of appeal or until the expiration of the time set in Fed R App P 4(a)(1), whichever is later.[144] A cross-appeal in a Tax Court case is governed by Fed R App P 14(a).[145] Cross-petitions for enforcement, review, or modification of agency orders are dealt with in Fed R App P 15(b).[146]

In a criminal case, the right of cross-appeal does not enlarge any rights of appeal that a party ordinarily would have; that is, if the portions of an order or judgment that are unsatisfactory to a party would not be appealable in the absence of the opponent's appeal, a cross-appeal will not lie.[147]

§6.11 Bond, Supersedeas, and Stay

This section deals with what a party must do to ensure that a judgment against it not be enforced pending appeal. Almost invariably, the first step will be to seek a stay in the district court under Fed R Civ P 62. Only the evident futility of doing so will excuse one from taking this step. Applications in the district court are made in accordance with that court's rules and procedures.[148] Stay procedure is primarily a matter of trial court law, and as such is outside the scope of this treatise.[149]

If a party is appealing from a money judgment, and posts a supersedeas bond that fully secures the judgment creditor, Fed R Civ P 62(d) has been held to provide that it is entitled to stay of execution on the judgment pending appeal. However, the district judge possesses discretion to grant a stay without requiring a supersedeas bond under the better reasoned cases.[150] Waiving the bond may be appropriate when the judgment debtor's ability to pay cannot reasonably be doubted or when the judgment is so large that the bond may prejudice the debtor's other creditors.[151] The district judge also has discretion to require alternative security short of a supersedeas bond.[152]

---

and (2) due process precludes personal jurisdiction, therefore appeal on sufficiency of complaint dismissed).

[143] The text of Fed R App P 4 is in **app A.**

[144] *See* **§§6.02-6.03.**

[145] The text of Fed R App P 14 is in **app A.**

[146] *See* **§§2.16, 6.09.**

[147] *See* **§§2.03, 2.05, 2.11.** In habeas cases, the cross-appealing petitioner is not excused from obtaining a certificate of probable cause, as discussed at **§6.07.**

[148] Fed R App P 1(a), the text of which is in **app A.**

[149] The multi-volume Federal Practice and Procedure, by Charles A. Wright (and a host of others that varies by volume), is the best source.

[150] *See* Olympia Equip Leasing Co v Western Union Tel Co, 786 F2d 794, 796 (7th Cir 1986) (posting a bond entitles appellant to a stay; by not posting one, it risks the district judge denying a stay).

[151] *Id.*

[152] *Id.*

If the judgment creditor is dissatisfied with the district judge's solution to the supersedeas and stay problem, it may appeal that order as a collateral order under the *Cohen* doctrine.[153]

If the judgment debtor is dissatisfied with the terms imposed by the district court on its right to appeal, it may seek review in the court of appeals under Fed R App P 8(a),[154] which provides the method and procedure for seeking review.[155] Review is by motion, to which affidavits and relevant portions of the record may be attached. A party also may use the provisions of Fed R App P 11(g) to bring up portions of the record.[156]

The court of appeals' power to regulate stay and supersedeas under these circumstances is an outgrowth of the All Writs Act.[157] There are constitutional

---

[153] *Id. See* **§2.04.**

[154] The text of Fed R App P 8 is in **app A.**

[155] See Fed R App P 8(a), which provides for a motion in the court of appeals:

> (a) Stay Must Ordinarily Be Sought in the First Instance in District Court; Motion for Stay in Court of Appeals. Application for a stay of the judgment or order of a district court pending appeal, or for approval of a supersedeas bond, or for an order suspending, modifying, restoring or granting an injunction during the pendency of an appeal must ordinarily be made in the first instance in the district court. A motion for such relief may be made to the court of appeals or to a judge thereof, but the motion shall show that application to the district court for the relief sought is not practicable, or that the district court has denied an application, or has failed to afford the relief which the applicant requested, with the reasons given by the district court for its action. The motion shall also show the reasons for the relief requested and the facts relied upon, and if the facts are subject to dispute the motion shall be supported by affidavits or other sworn statements or copies thereof. With the motion shall be filed such parts of the record as are relevant. Reasonable notice of the motion shall be given to all parties. The motion shall be filed with the clerk and normally will be considered by a panel or division of the court, but in exceptional cases where such procedure would be impracticable due to the requirements of time, the application may be made to and considered by a single judge of the court.

See also Shiley, Inc v Bentley Labs, Inc, 782 F2d 992 (Fed Cir), *affd,* 794 F2d 1561 (Fed Cir 1986), *cert denied,* 479 US 1087 (1987) (Fed R App P 8(a) is exclusive remedy for reviewing denial of stay of permanent injunction pending appeal).

[156] *See* **§6.14.**

[157] Advisory Committee Notes to Fed R App P 8(a) (citing cases). *See also In re* First S Sav Assn, 820 F2d 700 (5th Cir 1987) (district judge abused discretion in denying stay pending appeal; mandamus issued); Sckolnick v Harlow, 820 F2d 13 (1st Cir 1987) (district court did not abuse discretion in ordering appeal bond of $5,000); Elaine A. Carlson, *Mandatory Supersedeas Bond Requirements—A Denial of Due Process Rights,* 39 Baylor L Rev 29 (1987); Congregation Lubavitch v City of Cincinnati, 923 F2d 458 (6th Cir 1991) (extensive discussion of standards granting a stay pending appeal, noting four factors mentioned in Hilton v Braunskill, 481 US 770, 776 (1987); stay denied); Republic of Philippines v Westinghouse Elec Corp, 949 F2d 653 (3d Cir 1991) (party not entitled to stay pending appeal of a district court decision to conceal documents, because they failed to show they were likely to prevail in their argument that the district court was wrong; note that the disclosure of the documents effectively moots the appeal; court of appeals ably discussed the various factors bearing upon issuance of a stay; in Westinghouse Elec Corp v Republic of Philippines, 951 F2d 1414 (3d Cir 1991), court denies mandamus relief from order). *See* Stone v City & County of San Francisco, 145 FRD

limitations upon a court's power to impose a ruinous supersedeas bond requirement on a litigant as a condition of staying execution of a judgment during appeal.[158] As the District of Columbia Circuit has said, while reversing an order imposing a $10,000 bond requirement:

> We sympathize fully with the District Court's desire to protect [the appellee] from further expense in this phase of the legal battle which [appellant] has waged unremittingly. . . . Excessive bond, however, is not an acceptable control. While, in the federal system, appeals found to be frivolous cannot command judicial respect, those possessing merit are normally a matter of right. Courts accordingly must be wary of orders, even those well-meaning, that might impermissibly encumber that right.[159]

If a party ordered to post a supersedeas bond does not do so, its appeal still may proceed, but it lacks protection against execution on the judgment pending appeal.[160] It may be possible to agree with the judgment creditor on an acceptable alternative to posting a bond.

It is true that any appellant, except one proceeding in forma pauperis, may be required under Fed R App P 7[161] to give security for costs on appeal. Federal Rule of Appellate Procedure 7 provides only for prepayment, by bond or otherwise, of costs that would be taxable under Fed R App P 39.[162] It is not authority to condition an appeal upon posting a sizeable amount. The district court also may not decide the appeal is frivolous and anticipate that the appellant will be liable for double costs and damages under Fed R App P 38.[163] If the appeal is frivolous, the remedy is not for the district court to impose a greater burden upon the appellant. The appellee may move to dismiss or may ask the court of appeals to act under Fed R App P 38.[164]

A party seeking an injunction pending appeal, or a stay of such an injunction, must satisfy the traditional test for grant or denial of interlocutory equitable relief.[165] Again, the application must be filed in the district court in the first

---

553 (ND Cal 1993) (contempt fines do not continue to accrue while matter is on appeal, provided that district court has stayed contempt order).

[158] The existence of such limits, although not their extent, is suggested in *In re* American President Lines, 779 F2d 714, 718-19 (DC Cir 1985). Olympia Equip Leasing Co v Western Union Tel Co, 786 F2d 794, 798 (7th Cir 1986), contains an excellent discussion of the standard for review of the district court's orders concerning a bond on appeal.

[159] *In re* American President Lines, 779 F2d 714 (DC Cir 1985).

[160] Olympia Equip Leasing Co v Western Union Tel Co, 786 F2d 794 (7th Cir 1986).

[161] The text of Fed R App P 7 is in **app A.**

[162] The text of Fed R App P 39 is in **app A.** See **§10.16** on costs generally.

[163] *In re* American President Lines, 779 F2d 714 (DC Cir 1985).

[164] *See* **§§5.02, 10.16.**

[165] United States v Baylor Univ Medical Ctr, 711 F2d 38 (5th Cir 1983), *affd, modified & vacated in part,* 736 F2d 1039 (5th Cir 1984), *cert denied,* 469 US 1189 (1985); Ambulance Servs v Nevada Ambulance Servs, 819 F2d 910 (9th Cir 1987) (on appeal from grant of summary judgment to defendant in antitrust case, appellant sought injunction pending appeal; injunction denied).

instance, and filing the notice of appeal does not deprive that court of jurisdiction to act.[166]

The test for granting injunctive relief pending appeal is the likelihood of success on the merits, whether irreparable injury otherwise will result, whether granting the relief would substantially harm other parties, and whether the public interest is served.[167] The test for granting or denying a stay of injunctive relief entered in the district court is the same as that used in assessing the grant or denial on the merits; obviously, at the threshold the district judge's determination is entitled to deference.[168]

In criminal cases, stays are of three basic types. The stay of execution is of practical concern in federal habeas corpus review of state convictions, although it may become relevant on direct appeal of convictions under federal death penalty law. Stays of execution in capital cases are discussed at **§6.08.** The stay of execution of a sentence of incarceration is in reality a bail determination, discussed at **§6.12.** The stay of execution of a fine or forfeiture is dealt with in Fed R Crim P 32(b)(2) and 38(a)(3). Orders of the district courts in such instances are reviewable under Fed R App P 8(a) by filing a motion in the court of appeals.[169]

§6.12 Bail Pending Appeal in Criminal Cases

Bail pending appeal[170] is governed by Fed R App P 9(b) and (c),[171] which refer to the statutory standards in 18 USC §3143.[172] The defendant has the burden of showing that "the defendant will not flee or pose a danger to any other person or to the community and that the appeal is not for purpose of delay and raises a substantial question of law or fact likely to result in reversal or in an order for a new trial."[173]

As noted at **§2.05,** the court of appeals' power to review district court bail determinations pending appeal is an incident of its power over the entire

---

[166] Deering Milliken, Inc v FTC, 647 F2d 1124 (DC Cir), *cert denied,* 439 US 958 (1978). *See also* Shiley, Inc v Bentley Labs, Inc, 782 F2d 992 (Fed Cir), *affd,* 794 F2d 1561 (Fed Cir 1986), *cert denied,* 479 US 1087 (1987).

[167] United States v Baylor Univ Medical Ctr, 711 F2d 38, 39 (5th Cir 1983), *affd, modified & vacated in part,* 736 F2d 1039 (5th Cir 1984), *cert denied,* 469 US 1189 (1985).

[168] The deference to the district court is a function of whether its order is considered to be one based on fact or law. See **ch 5** on standards of review, **§§5.03–5.13.**

[169] *See* 3 Charles A. Wright, Federal Practice & Procedure, Criminal 2d §§631-35 (1982 & Supp 1993). The RICO, 18 USC §1963(f), and Continuing Criminal Enterprise, 21 USC §853, statutes prescribe in personam forfeitures for those convicted. These statutes and Fed R Crim P 32(b)(2) permit the district judge to make orders relating to the manner in which the forfeiture is to occur. This would include the posting of security to avoid forfeiture pending appeal of the underlying conviction.

[170] Review of bail orders entered prior to conviction is discussed at **§2.15.**

[171] The text of Fed R App P 9 is in **app A.**

[172] Release pending trial is governed by 18 USC §3142, and appeals from pretrial detention orders are discussed at **§2.05.** *See also* Fed R Crim P 38 in **app C.**

[173] Fed R App P 9(c).

appeal. Therefore, a new notice of appeal is not necessary to obtain review of a bail determination, provided that the defendant has already filed a notice of appeal from the conviction itself. It is certainly the better practice to file a notice of appeal instantly if the defendant is ordered confined pending appeal.

Defense counsel must make application in the district court and, if unsuccessful there, file a motion in the court of appeals.[174] The practice in such cases is the same as with any other motion, except that most courts of appeals have established detailed circuit rules governing what must be included in the Fed R App P 9(b) application.[175] Federal Rule of Appellate Procedure 9(b) requires that relevant record materials be attached to the moving papers.

The 18 USC §3143 standards referred to in Fed R App P 9(c) are those introduced in the 1984 recodification of federal bail law.[176] The court of appeals should, on the better view, apply those standards de novo rather than deferring to the district court's judgment.[177] The "substantial question . . . likely to result

---

[174] Fed R App P 9(b). *See* **ch 8.**

[175] For example, the Fifth Circuit requires the appealing defendant to file in the court of appeals a copy of the entire transcript of the district court bail proceedings. United States v Crabtree, 754 F2d 1200 (5th Cir), *cert denied,* 473 US 905 (1985). On transmission of a partial record, see **§6.14.**

[176] 18 USC §3143, as amended in 1984, reads:

> (a) Release or detention pending sentence.—The judicial officer shall order that a person who has been found guilty of an offense and who is waiting imposition or execution of sentence, be detained, unless the judicial officer finds by clear and convincing evidence that the person is not likely to flee or pose a danger to the safety of any other person or the community if released under section 3142(b) or (c). If the judicial officer makes such a finding, such judicial officer shall order the release of the person in accordance with section 3142(b) or (c).
> (b) Release of detention pending appeal by the defendant.—The judicial officer shall order that a person who has been found guilty of an offense and sentenced to a term of imprisonment, and who has filed an appeal or a petition for a writ of certiorari, be detained, unless the judicial officer finds—
> (1) by clear and convincing evidence that the person is not likely to flee or pose a danger to the safety of any other person or other community if released under section 3142(b) or (c) of this title; and
> (2) that the appeal is not for purpose of delay and raises a substantial question of law or fact likely to result in reversal, an order for a new trial, or a sentence that does not include a term of imprisonment.
> If the judicial officer makes such findings, he shall order the release of the person in accordance with the provision of section 3142(b) or (c).
> If the judicial officer makes such findings, such judicial officer shall order the release of the person in accordance with the provision of section 3142(b) or (c) of this title.
> (c) Release or detention pending appeal by the government.—The judicial officer shall treat a defendant in a case in which an appeal has been taken by the United States under section 3731 of this title, in accordance with section 3142 of this title, unless the defendant is otherwise subject to a release or detention order.

[177] *See* United States v Valenzuela-Verdigo, 815 F2d 1011, 1013 (5th Cir 1987) (district court's order will be sustained if "it is supported by the proceedings below" (citations omitted)); United States v Delker, 757 F2d 1390, 1399-400 (3d Cir 1985). *But see* United States v Fortna, 769 F2d 243, 250 (5th Cir 1985). The court of appeals, when acting

in reversal" standard does not mean that the defendant must persuade the district court that it was probably in error, or that he or she must hurdle a pre-appeal barrier of convincing the court of appeals that reversal is inevitable.[178] Rather, the defendant must show that there is a substantial issue that, in the event of success, will result in a reversal of the whole case or some segregable part of it;[179] that is, the defendant does not meet the burden by pointing to error that goes to one count on which a concurrent sentence has been imposed, by raising specious issues, or by claims of error that probably are harmless. The error must infect the entire case or some portion of it on which the defendant received a consecutive sentence.[180]

On appeal from revocation of probation, a defendant will not be entitled to bail absent a showing of exceptional circumstances.[181]

§6.13 Ordering the Transcript

Federal Rules of Appellate Procedure 10 and 11[182] govern the assembly and content of the record on appeal. The appellant's first duty is to consult with the court reporter to order the transcript. Federal Rule of Appellate Procedure 10(b)(1) allows 10 days for taking this step, counted from the time the notice of appeal is filed. A copy of the order must be filed with the clerk. Then, as discussed at **§6.14,** one should meet with the deputy clerk to see about the other parts of the record. The rules provisions, as supplemented by district and circuit rules, are straightforward.

If counsel is not ordering the entire transcript, Fed R App P 10(b)(3) requires the appellant to notify all other parties of the issues it intends to raise on appeal. The other parties can then determine if additional parts of the transcript should be ordered. The rule provides for a 10-day period within which they may order those additional parts.

Failure to follow the rules may result in dismissal of the appeal. The rules formerly provided a set period within which the record was to be transmitted and also placed upon the appellant the duty of obtaining extensions of time if the transcript was not timely completed or the record not ready to transmit.

---

under Fed R App P 9(b), is not reviewing the judgment of the district court, but performing a function incident to its appellate jurisdiction. Therefore, independent review seems the better practice. *See also* Justice Brennan's opinion in chambers in Truong Dinh Hung v United States, 439 US 1326 (1978) (Brennan, J, Circuit Justice). Compare the treatment of this issue in Lissa Griffin, Federal Criminal Appeals §6.10 (1991).

[178] *See, e.g.,* United States v Handy, 761 F2d 1279 (9th Cir 1985) (discussing many cases and adopting test set forth in text).

[179] United States v Miller, 753 F2d 19, 24 (3d Cir 1985).

[180] *Id.* On appeal, the court of appeals may deny bail, order the defendant released, or remand for further proceedings. United States v Wheeler, 795 F2d 839 (9th Cir 1986). *See generally* 3A Charles A. Wright, Federal Practice & Procedure, Criminal 2d §772 (1982 & Supp 1993).

[181] United States v Bell, 820 F2d 980 (9th Cir 1987).

[182] The text of Fed R App P 10 and 11 is in **app A.**

This state of affairs was a bit unwieldy, because the appellant had no real control over either the court reporter or the clerk. Federal Rule of Appellate Procedure 11(b) now puts initial responsibility upon the court reporter to estimate the time required to complete the transcript and to obtain the necessary extensions. When the transcript is finished, the clerk assembles the record and transmits it forthwith.[183]

In most circuits, as noted elsewhere, there is a printed form notice of appeal available in the district court clerk's office that includes a transcript order form. By using this form, the appellant's timely notice of appeal will include verification that the transcript is ordered, the court reporter's required statement, and notice to the other parties of what has and has not been ordered so that they can order additional portions if they wish.

Even in circuits with such a form, there may be a requirement that each appellant file a docketing statement in the court of appeals shortly after the notice of appeals is filed. Such a statement serves various functions in different courts of appeals, such as identifying the issues to be briefed and signalling that the record may be lengthy or the issues complex and difficult. In some instances, however, the docketing statement serves as further required verification that the appellant has indeed ordered the transcript and given the required notice.

The first paragraph of Fed R App P 11(b) requires the reporter to acknowledge receipt of the order and note the date on which he or she expects to have the transcript finished. This paragraph also establishes a mechanism for the district court and court of appeals, and their respective clerks, to enforce promptness on the court reporter's part.

Counsel in a multiparty nonindigent case in which several copies of the transcript are being ordered for the parties, in addition to that filed with the court will find it easier to negotiate prompt completion of the transcript, for it is very much in the court reporter's financial interest to prepare such a record.

Counsel should make every effort to agree with other parties on the transcript order. In any trial of any length, it is unrealistic to assume that any court of appeals judge, or even a law clerk, will sit and read the entire transcript to get the feel of the case. The transcript is used as a resource to write an opinion, the outlines of which are fairly well decided by the briefs, oral argument, and a joint appendix or excerpts of record.

Overdesignating is a common and wasteful practice, particularly by advocates insecure about leaving something out. A transcript of the opening statement is rarely necessary unless some alleged error then occurred. Voir dire usually can be left out. Of course, when an appellate advocate picks up a transcript, the closing argument or opening statement may provide some quick cues as to what the case is "about," but the court of appeals will not be viewing the transcript in that way.

---

[183] *See* **§7.01.**

§6.14 Assembling the Record in District Court, Tax Court, or Agency

The court reporter's transcript is only one part of the record on appeal. Federal Rule of Appellate Procedure 10(a)[184] provides that the appellant must see that the docket entries and papers and exhibits are assembled. The docket entries are an essential part of the record in every case; every circuit requires that sufficient copies of them be reproduced for the use of the judges and their clerks.

Papers and exhibits need not be assembled and transmitted to the court of appeal in their entirety. Federal Rule of Appellate Procedure 11(b)[185] provides that documents of unusual bulk or weight and physical exhibits other than documents need not be transmitted to the court of appeals. Local district court and circuit rules also will provide guidance on this subject. Federal Rule of Appellate Procedure 11(f) provides that parts of the record may, by agreement of the parties, be retained in the district court. The court of appeal may thereafter order the retained material to be forwarded to it. In addition, Fed R App P 11(c) provides that the record may be retained in the district court for use by the parties in preparing their appeal and transmitted when the briefs are filed, or when the parties agree.

Taken together, these rules permit counsel to keep the record on appeal to a manageable size and to have access to it while preparing the briefs on appeal. To make best use of the rules, and to ensure compliance with district and circuit rules, counsel taking an appeal should personally visit the clerk's office and discuss the proper procedures with a deputy clerk. In this way, counsel also can be sure that an exhibit which would otherwise not be transmitted, but which is important to counsel's case, finds its way to the court of appeals to begin with. This will obviate the need for a motion under Fed R App P 10(e).[186]

If there is to be an emergency or preliminary hearing in the court of appeals, for example on a motion,[187] Fed R App P 11(g) provides a mechanism for transmitting a partial record.

The record transmitted under Fed R App P 11 will not necessarily be reviewed in its entirety by the court of appeals. That court is justified in limiting its review to the material presented to the district court in support of the legal issue being appealed. For example, appellants' summary judgment motion to the district court had stated that it was supported "by the entire record on file in this action" in *Harkins Amusement Enterprises v General Cinema Corp.*[188] Appellant therefore suggested that the entire record below was *presented* to the trial court and subject to de novo review. The court of appeals sensibly rejected this sug-

---

[184] The text of Fed R App P 10 is in **app A.**

[185] The text of Fed R App P 11 is in **app A.**

[186] *See* **§6.17.**

[187] *See* **ch 8.**

[188] 850 F2d 477, 482 (9th Cir 1988), *cert denied,* 488 US 1019 (1989).

gestion and limited its consideration to the items referred to in the parties' summary judgment memoranda.

In appeals from the Tax Court, Fed R App P 10, 11, and 12 on assembling and transmitting the record are made applicable by Fed R App P 13(d).[189]

In cases from federal agencies, assembly and transmission of the record will vary from agency to agency. Federal Rule of Appellate Procedure 17[190] provides a general procedure.

§6.15 Special Problems in Indigent Cases

28 USC §1915[191] provides that an indigent person may appear in any federal court without prepayment of costs, upon the filing of an affidavit of indigency. Representation of indigents raises two procedural issues: leave to proceed in forma pauperis and appointment of counsel.

In forma pauperis proceedings in the court of appeals are governed on appeal by Fed R App P 24[192] as well as §1915. One should distinguish four kinds of cases for the purposes of Fed R App P 24: civil appeals, agency and Tax Court appeals, federal criminal direct appeals, and post-conviction criminal appeals.

In civil cases, the application for leave to proceed without paying fees and costs on appeal must first be made in the district court, on a form affidavit set out in the rules as Form 4.[193] The court will grant the motion where the appeal "presents legal points which have arguable merit and are, therefore, not frivolous."[194] The district court has broad discretion in making this determination.[195] The Seventh Circuit has held, however, that the district court may not grant leave to proceed on one claim but not another of a suit; the entire suit, not the individual claim, forms the basis for decision.[196]

If a party has proceeded in forma pauperis in the district court, Fed R App P 24(a) provides that that status will continue unless the district judge determines that "the appeal is not taken in good faith or . . . that the party is otherwise not entitled so to proceed." Section 1915(a) provides that "an appeal may not be taken in forma pauperis if the trial court certifies in writing that it is not taken in good faith."[197]

If the district judge does deny in forma pauperis status for the appeal, the aggrieved party will be notified of that action and then has 30 days in which

---

[189] The text of Fed R App P 13 is in **app A.**

[190] The text of Fed R App P 17 is in **app A.**

[191] The full text of 28 USC §1915 is in **app E.**

[192] The full text of Fed R App P 24 is in **app A.**

[193] Form 4 is reprinted in **app A.**

[194] Payne v Lynaugh, 843 F2d 177, 178 (5th Cir 1988).

[195] *Id.*

[196] Dixon v Pitchford, 843 F2d 268, 270 (7th Cir 1988).

[197] 28 USC §1915(a).

to file an application in the court of appeals under Fed R App P 24(a).[198] The application must be accompanied by the form affidavit, which must include the grounds of proposed appeal to prevent the application's likely denial.[199] The proper course is for an indigent party to file a notice of appeal on the merits of the claim and also seek leave under Fed R App P 24 to proceed in forma pauperis. However, on occasion courts of appeals have treated the application as equivalent to a notice of appeal.[200]

The in forma pauperis application is not to be judged by the same standards that will be applied on the merits.[201]

The Supreme Court limited the reach of §1915, however, in *Rowland v California Men's Colony, Unit II Men's Advisory Council.*[202] It held that only a natural person may qualify for treatment *in forma pauperis.* An inmate organization suing to redress prison conditions is not a *person* within the meaning of the statute. The four dissenting Justices noted that 1 USC §1 states a general rule that *person* includes *associations.* The decision seems wrong, if only because permitting associations to sue can promote judicial efficiency in the resolution of important issues.

In addition, the constitutional right to proceed in forma pauperis is of uncertain dimension. Many cases echo the theme, particularly in the wake of the Supreme Court's controversial decision in *United States v Kras,*[203] that an allegedly bankrupt indigent has no right to waiver of bankruptcy court filing fees and that indigent status is a privilege rather than a right.

In forma pauperis status relieves a party from paying docketing fees and costs. If one wishes other services, such as a free copy of the transcript, the court has discretion to grant, restrict, or deny. The party should make a motion showing a need for the transcript or other service. It may be possible to obtain an order permitting an indigent party to photocopy a transcript ordered by

---

[198] *See, e.g.,* Oatess v Sobolevitch, 914 F2d 428 (3d Cir 1990) (when district court dismisses under 28 USC §1915(d) as frivolous, litigant must reapply to court of appeals for in forma pauperis status). Johnson v United States, 352 US 565 (1957), holds that a district judge's denial of leave to proceed in forma pauperis is reviewable by the court of appeals. The review should be sought by a motion under Fed R App P 24, although an appeal also may be lodged. *See* 16 Charles A. Wright, Arthur R. Miller, Edward H. Cooper, & Eugene Gressman, Federal Practice and Procedure §3970 (1977 & Supp 1993). The motion must be timely filed. Borning v Hymel, 764 F2d 1041 (5th Cir 1985).

[199] *E.g.,* United States v Ramey, 559 F Supp 60, 67 (ED Tenn 1981) (petitioner's failure to include a statement of issues to be presented on appeal in the form affidavit is fatal to his motion to appeal in forma pauperis, even where the required statement of issues was included in petitioner's motion).

[200] Hatchell v Heckler, 708 F2d 578 (11th Cir 1983).

[201] *See, e.g.,* Coppedge v United States, 369 US 438, 445 (1962) (nonfrivolous appeal should be allowed); Kitchens v Alderman, 376 F2d 262 (5th Cir 1967); United States v Slater, 96 FRD 53 (D Del 1982).

[202] 113 S Ct 716 (1993).

[203] 409 US 434 (1973) (bankruptcy applicant has no right to waiver of filing fees; one can be too poor to go broke).

another party and to obtain other portions of the record without payment.[204]

When one is proceeding in forma pauperis in the district court, one's legal position is subject to greater scrutiny. Section 1915(d) provides for dismissal of a frivolous claim. The Supreme Court defined the circumstances under which a claim may be dismissed as frivolous in *Denton v Hernandez.*[205] Such dismissals are reviewable for abuse of discretion and the court of appeals must consider whether the plaintiff was proceeding pro se, whether the court inappropriately resolved genuine issues of disputed fact, whether it applied erroneous legal conclusions, and whether the district court provided a statement explaining the basis of its decision.

A major focus of dispute has been whether federal courts have the power to compel counsel to represent indigent civil litigants, even though no funds are available to pay counsel. In *Mallard v United States District Court,*[206] the Supreme Court held that §1915(d) confers no such authority, but left open whether a court's inherent power would permit appointing counsel. Given the reaffirmation of inherent power in other contexts, the answer would seem to be yes.[207] Certainly, poor litigants have inadequate access to counsel, and the bench and bar have a duty to remedy that situation. The court clearly has authority to appoint counsel who is willing to serve.

If counsel is appointed in the district court, the appointment will not automatically carry over to the court of appeals.[208] The court of appeals may itself seek to appoint counsel, however. Appointment of counsel is made sparingly and typically only after a preliminary screening on the merits of the claim.[209] There is no general statutory authority to pay appointed lawyers in such cases, although fee-shifting statutes such as the Equal Access to Justice Act provide assistance in some types of cases.[210] If counsel is helping a party prepare papers

---

[204] Statutory authority for such action will vary depending upon whether the United States is a party. *See* 28 USC §1915(b). *See also* Thomas v Computax Corp, 631 F2d 139 (9th Cir 1980) (right to transcript at government expense; dictum); Toliver v Community Action Commn to Help the Economy, Inc, 613 F Supp 1070 (SDNY 1985), *affd,* 800 F2d 1128 (2d Cir), *cert denied,* 479 US 863 (1986); Maloney v El DuPont de Nemours & Co, 396 F2d 939 (DC Cir 1967), *cert denied,* 396 US 1030 (1970). The court surely will have authority to waive fees for copies of court documents.

[205] 112 S Ct 1728 (1992).

[206] 490 US 296 (1989).

[207] *See* **§5.02.**

[208] *See, e.g.,* DiAngelo v Illinois Dept of Pub Aid, 891 F2d 1260 (7th Cir 1989) (counsel need not file *Anders* brief in court of appeals seeking to withdraw). On *Anders* briefs, see below. *See also* **§5.02.**

[209] In collateral attack cases, appointment of counsel is governed by the rules applicable to habeas corpus petitions and motions to vacate sentence. For civil rights actions, see generally Slaughter v City of Maplewood, 731 F2d 587 (8th Cir 1984). In other cases, the due process limits on a right to appointed counsel have been traced in, e.g., Lassiter v Department of Social Servs, 452 US 18 (1981) (no right to appointed counsel in parental rights termination case); Note, *Denial of a Pro Se Litigant's Motion to Appoint Counsel,* 50 Fordham L Rev 1399 (1982).

[210] 28 USC §2412. This is but one of many federal statutes that provide for legal fees to a prevailing party.

for leave to proceed in forma pauperis, counsel should describe any fee arrangements that have been made.[211]

Litigants seeking review of agency proceedings or appealing from the tax court pleadings are governed by Fed R App P 24(c), which provides that an indigent person seeking review should make application for in forma pauperis status directly in the court of appeals on Form 4. If that status is granted, the party is relieved from the payment of costs and fees. In agency cases, the court will have discretion to grant a free transcript.[212] As for counsel, appointment rarely will be granted, although counsel may be more willing to serve given fee-shifting statutes that provide for payment of counsel fees if the appeal is successful.[213]

In criminal cases on direct appeal, there is a constitutional right to counsel. Federal Rule of Appellate Procedure 24 works in conjunction with the Criminal Justice Act[214] to provide for appointment in the district court and in the court of appeals.[215] There is a Criminal Justice Act form for appointment, which certifies the appointment and starts the paperwork to ensure that counsel is paid.[216] Usually, appeals appointments are made in the district court, where the notice of appeal is to be filed. The appointment forms also contain information on ordering a transcript of proceedings for use on appeal.

Appointed counsel on appeal must be an active advocate for the client and not simply a friend of the court.[217] This means that appellate counsel, while exercising independent judgment that may at times conflict with the accused's sense of which issues ought to be raised, must present every claim that can be argued persuasively. Under *Anders,* appointed counsel who finds the appeal

---

[211] *See* Evensky v Wright, 45 FRD 506, 507 (ND Miss 1968) (where attorney files complaint for pauper, he must also file affidavit describing any fee arrangements).

[212] *See* SEC v Samuel H. Sloan & Co, 369 F Supp 994 (SDNY 1973) (recognizing power to order transcript, but declining to exercise it).

[213] 26 USC §7430. *See* Note, *Examining Unreasonable IRS Behavior and the Award of Attorney's Fees In Tax Cases: Underlying Action v Litigation Position,* 37 U Fla L Rev 1013 (1985).

[214] 18 USC §3006A.

[215] Criminal defendants' access to retained counsel on appeal, as at trial, will be affected by the Supreme Court's decision in Caplin & Drysdale, Chartered v United States, 491 US 617 (1989), and United States v Monsanto, 491 US 600 (1989), upholding application of criminal forfeiture laws to attorney fees. The decision may mean that a defendant will be compelled to file an affidavit of indigency to obtain appointed counsel. Counsel may be compelled to demonstrate that fees came from an untainted source. *Compare* United States v Friedman, 849 F2d 1488 (DC Cir) (defendant who suffered forfeiture of assets under RICO not entitled to partial remission of forfeiture to pay retained counsel on appeal), *cert denied,* 498 US 1110 (1988).

[216] Appointed counsel in federal courts may not seek or accept compensation other than that provided under court auspices. This is contrary to the practice in some state systems, but most compensation forms in federal appeals (including CJA Form 24) require a certification that counsel has complied with this standard.

[217] Anders v California, 386 US 738 (1967); Jones v Barnes, 463 US 745 (1983); Penson v Ohio, 488 US 75 (1988) (elaborating on the *Anders* requirements). *See also* **§5.02.**

meritless must file a brief to that effect and furnish a copy of the brief to the client, who may raise whatever points he or she wishes.[218] The court will then determine if the appeal is indeed frivolous.[219]

In capital cases, of course, the duties of counsel may well be greater and raising every conceivable issue is a counsel of prudence even if not an absolute duty. Speaking of the appellate court's duty to review carefully "any colorable claim of error," the Court suggested as much in *Zant v Stephens*,[220]

An appellant in a postconviction case has the same rights as any other litigant to proceed in forma pauperis under §1915 and Fed R App P 24. The Supreme Court has, however, decided that the Sixth Amendment does not guarantee counsel on postconviction review, even in death cases. In *Pennsylvania v Finley*,[221] a divided Court held that denial of counsel to indigents on direct appeal is forbidden as a matter of equal protection under the law and that *Anders* is a device for enforcing the right to counsel under those circumstances. Because the Court refused to recognize a right to counsel in postconviction proceedings, a prisoner in such proceedings is not entitled to *Anders* procedures if counsel is appointed and then wishes to withdraw.

Congress has provided for postconviction representation in capital cases, and has even allocated funds to pay appointed counsel, as well as for defender-type centers to provide such representation. In addition, the American Bar Association and many state bar groups recruit volunteer counsel for such cases.[222]

§6.16 Appeals on Agreed Statement or When Record Is Unavailable

Federal Rule of Appellate Procedure 10(c)[223] provides for a statement of evidence or proceedings when there is no transcript or other available record of

---

[218] A narrow majority of the Supreme Court has upheld a Wisconsin statute which goes even further by imposing a "discussion requirement." McCoy v Court of Appeals, 486 US 429 (1988). The statute requires the lawyer who believes his or her client's appeal is frivolous to file a *no merit* brief which identifies anything in the record which might arguably support the appeal and a discussion of why the issue lacks merit. Justice Brennan's dissent eloquently argues that the Wisconsin requirement "reneges on these longstanding assurances [of equal justice before the law] by permitting a State to force its appointed defender of the indigent to advocate against his client upon unilaterally concluding that the client's appeal lacks merit." *Id* 445.

[219] *See, e.g.*, United States v Castello, 830 F2d 99 (7th Cir 1987) (defense attorney permitted to withdraw on filing of *Anders* brief; appeal dismissed); Comment, *The Right to Counsel in "Frivolous" Criminal Appeals: A Reevaluation of the Guarantees of Anders v California*, 67 Tex L Rev 181 (1988). See also **§5.02** for additional authorities.

[220] 462 US 862, 885 (1983).

[221] 481 US 551 (1987).

[222] The ABA's Postconviction Death Penalty Representation Project has up-to-date information on the status of such programs. The project is located at 1800 M Street, N.W., Washington, DC, 20036, (202) 331-2273.

[223] The full text of Fed R App P 10 is in **app A.**

the proceedings. Almost every court proceeding is recorded in some fashion. District court proceedings routinely are covered by a court reporter. Magistrate hearings are tape recorded if a reporter is not present. Sometimes, however, the recording or transcript is lost. Sometimes a conference with the judge or magistrate is held without a court reporter present; only later does it occur to the advocate that something significant happened that ought to be part of the record on appeal. Rule 10(c) is designed for such a situation.[224]

Rule 10(c) is not available to a litigant for whom the transcript is unavailable due to lack of funds to pay for it. That person must seek in forma pauperis status.[225]

Rule 10(c) must be observed literally. Unless the district court certifies the record, or portion of the record, in the manner provided, the court of appeals cannot use the party's statement as the basis for review.[226] If the district court's approval cannot be obtained, the advocate must resort to the correction or modification procedures of Fed R App P 10(e), or seek to persuade the court of appeals to take judicial notice of the additional material.[227]

Rule 10(d) provides for an "agreed statement as to the record on appeal;" that is, the parties, with the district court's approval, may send up a record consisting only of a "statement of the case showing how the issues presented by the appeal arose and were decided in the district court and setting forth only so many of the facts averred and proved or sought to be proved as are essential to a decision of the issues presented."[228] The rule provides a convenient means to avoid the expense of preparing a transcript in cases involving straightforward issues that are not essentially fact-bound. Party agreement on the statement generally will ensure that the court acts favorably on the submission.

The advocate thinking of using Fed R App P 10(d) should remember that the record agreed upon, and the questions it illuminates, can be enlarged only with great difficulty. The court of appeals will, absent compelling circum-

---

[224] *See* United States v Chesapeake & Ohio Ry, 281 F2d 698 (4th Cir 1960); Bailey v United States, 270 F2d 86 (9th Cir 1959).

[225] Richardson v Henry, 902 F2d 414 (5th Cir), *cert denied,* 498 US 901 (1990) (inability to pay for a transcript does not make the transcript "unavailable" within the meaning of Fed R App P 10(c); without a transcript, court will not review sufficiency of evidence; appeal dismissed as to that issue); Thomas v Computax Corp, 631 F2d 139, 143 (9th Cir 1980) (Fed R App P 10(c) applies only where the transcript is "physically unobtainable").

[226] United States v Chesapeake & Ohio Ry, 281 F2d 698 (4th Cir 1960).

[227] The appeals courts disagree on the propriety of and procedure for taking judicial notice on appeal of matters not in the record. *See* Minnesota Fedn of Teachers v Randall, 891 F2d 1354, 1359 n9 (8th Cir 1989), for a collection of relevant authorities. In Colonial Penn Ins Co v Coil, 887 F2d 1236, 1239-40 (4th Cir 1989), the court of appeals took judicial notice that plaintiffs suing on an arson insurance policy had pleaded guilty to arson. *See also* **§7.01.**

[228] Fed R App P 10(d).

stances, hold the parties to their bargain and refuse to reach questions outside the record as submitted.[229]

§6.17 Correction or Modification of Record

Federal Rule of Appellate Procedure 10(e)[230] provides for correction or modification of the record on appeal, to be certain that the record "truly discloses what occurred in the district court."[231] It does not permit a district court to modify any of its orders under the guise of correcting the record.[232] Authority for such modification must be sought in the Federal Rules of Civil Procedure.[233]

Rule 10(e) also permits the court of appeals to order amendments to and supplementation of the record. This power usually is exercised solely to correct errors or to send up additional matter reflecting what was before the district court or agency.[234] The rule is not a license to build a new record, although the court of appeals does have a very limited and rarely exercised power to order the record supplemented with evidence not reviewed by the district court.[235]

The district court's power to correct or modify the record should be invoked by a motion in that court. If the modification is agreed to by all parties, a stipulation to that effect must be filed and the district court clerk will proceed to assemble and certify the omitted or corrected matter.

---

[229] Discretion to consider matters outside the record as submitted has been upheld in, e.g., Ross v Kemp, 785 F2d 1467 (11th Cir 1986); Dickerson v Alabama, 667 F2d 1364 (11th Cir), *cert denied,* 459 US 878 (1982). *See also In re* GHR Energy Corp, 791 F2d 1200 (5th Cir 1986) (court of appeals can invoke Fed R App P 10(e) on its own motion).

[230] The full text of Fed R App P 10 is in **app A.**

[231] Fed R App P 10(e). *See* United States v Page, 661 F2d 1080 (5th Cir 1981), *cert denied,* 455 US 1018 (1982) (Fed R App P 10(e) was properly used to supplement the record where pretrial conference, at which defendant waived right to jury trial, had been omitted from record).

[232] *See* Studiengesellschaft Kohle MBH v Eastman Kodak Co, 713 F2d 128 (5th Cir 1983) (where notice of appeal has deprived district court of jurisdiction, Fed R App P 10(e) cannot be used to amend award); Kennedy v United States, 115 F2d 624 (9th Cir 1940) (pre-Rules decision) (Fed R Civ P 75(h) allows appellate court to correct record only to accurately reflect district court proceedings, and not to add findings not clearly made by district court).

[233] By means of posttrial motions, the effect of which on the appeal is discussed at **§§ 5.05** and **6.03.** Authority to correct clerical errors is found in Fed R Civ P 60(a).

[234] *In re* GHR Energy Corp, 791 F2d 1200 (5th Cir 1986).

[235] Anthony v United States, 667 F2d 870 (10th Cir 1981) (not licensed to build new record), *cert denied,* 457 US 1133 (1982); Turk v United States, 429 F2d 1327 (8th Cir 1970) (supplementing district court's record with proceedings before magistrate); National Nutritional Foods Assn v FDA, 491 F2d 1141 (2d Cir) (supplementing record with additional evidence about alleged FDA failure to give proper consideration to certain objections), *cert denied,* 419 US 874 (1974). *But see* Borden, Inc v FTC, 495 F2d 785 (7th Cir 1974) (court of appeals without power to supplement record with FTC administrative manual).

Suppose, however, that the parties do not agree. For example, a crucial exhibit may have been omitted from the record. The proponent of the exhibit insists it was offered and received in evidence. The opponent denies this. The courtroom deputy clerk's notes and the court reporter's transcript are ambiguous. The district judge will hear and decide the motion to include such an item in the record on appeal. At the hearing, the proponent should make sure that the disputed matter is placed in the record of the hearing.

If the district judge denies the motion, what is the proper means to obtain review of the order? There is no clear answer, and the author has discussed this question with court of appeals deputy clerks. The safest way to obtain review is to file a timely notice of appeal from the district court's order. This new appeal can be consolidated in the court of appeals with that on the merits. The record for this new appeal will include the disputed item of evidence or the disputed portion of the record. As an alternative, review of the district court's order might be sought by filing a motion in connection with the main appeal and attaching the disputed item and a copy of the relevant Fed R App P 10(e) proceedings in the district court.

A party should not seek to enlarge the record by simply including an item as an appendix to the briefs. While the court of appeals may have power to take judicial notice of such material, there is no assurance it will do so.[236] Indeed, the effort may lead the court to think that the advocate is trying to sneak something past it. If an advocate wants the court to consider something that cannot be added under Fed R App P 10(e), the proper procedure is to move in the court of appeals that judicial notice be taken. The court of appeals can, for example, judicially notice proceedings in related cases, although the record of such a case cannot be certified under Fed R App P 10(e).[237]

---

[236] Authorities on the court of appeals taking judicial notice are collected at **§7.01.** *See also* **§6.16.** *In re* GHR Energy Corp, 791 F2d 1200, 1201-02 (5th Cir 1986), notes that attachments to the briefs are not a substitute for invoking Fed R App P 10(e).

[237] *See* **§7.01;** United States v Lowell, 649 F2d 950, 966 (3d Cir 1981) (court of appeals takes judicial notice of testimony before grand jury in a related case, but rejects motion to supplement record, finding it "inappropriate to weigh the probative value of [the witness's] testimony in deciding the appeal").

7 Handling the Record in the Court of Appeals

§7.01 The Importance of Assembling and Transmitting the Record

To decide the case in an advocate's favor, the court of appeals must have before it the evidence on which the advocate relies. That evidence must, with few narrow exceptions,[1] be contained in the record brought up from the court below or from the agency whose action is being reviewed.

Counsel's tasks in assembling the record in the district court are discussed in Chapter 6. Federal Rules of Appellate Procedure 16 and 17 deal with assembling and transmitting the record on review of an administrative agency decision. Federal Rule of Appellate Procedure 13(d) deals with the record in Tax Court cases. The record in bankruptcy cases is handled under Fed R App P 6(b)(2)(iii) and (iv). The limited record presented for bail review is discussed at **§6.12.** For court of appeals review that is sought by mandamus or other original writ, assembling the relevant record is discussed at **§3.15.**

Federal Rule of Appellate Procedure 11(b) provides that "[w]hen the record is complete for purposes of the appeal, the clerk of the district court shall trans-

---

[1] The court of appeals may take judicial notice of facts. *See, e.g.*, St Louis Baptist Temple, Inc v FDIC, 605 F2d 1169, 1172 (10th Cir 1979) ("federal courts . . . may take notice of proceedings in other courts, both within and without the federal judicial system, if those proceedings have a direct relation to matters at issue"). In addition, it may consider legislative facts such as social science data presented by the parties in their briefs. *See* 1 Stephen A. Saltzburg & Michael M. Martin, Federal Rules of Evidence Manual 70-76 (5th ed 1990). See also authorities collected at **§6.16.**

mit it forthwith to the clerk of the court of appeals."[2] Under Fed R App P 12(b), the court of appeals clerk will give notice to all parties that the record has been filed.[3] In the usual case, the Fed R App P 12(b) clerk's notice will signal that the advocate has 40 days within which to file an opening brief. However, the clerk's office may issue a scheduling order that provides for more or less time.

In addition to preparing a brief, the advocate must comply with the Fed R App P 30 provisions on joint appendix or record excerpts. Each circuit has adopted its own procedures within the general guidelines of Fed R App P 30, and the advocate should have a copy of the circuit rules at hand. The advocate will always have some discretion about how much of the record to reproduce for the court's use. This discretion must be exercised wisely to single out and emphasize those portions of the record, and only those, that bear critically upon the issues being briefed. The court will have neither time nor patience to sift through a voluminous and unfamiliar stack of paper to find the scrap of evidence that supports a party's position.

Although the case comes from a joint appendix circuit, *United States v Friedman*[4] illustrates this point for all cases. In *Friedman,* the defendant challenged the prosecutors' summations as improper and prejudicial. Counsel had not reproduced the offensive summation in the joint appendix, however. The entire record below was, of course, in the clerk's office. But the joint appendix (or in some circuits the record excerpts) are sent to each judge's chambers. The court criticized counsel for putting an undue burden on the court:

> The bar has come to expect that the judges of this court will attend argument fully informed about the appeal. The joint appendix, available to all members of the panel at their resident chambers, provides the basis for thorough . . . preparation. . . ."[5]

The court stressed that the parties must include in the appendix "those portions of the record essential to consideration of the issues raised on appeal."[6] It underscores the importance of the appendix or record excerpts to point out that on the merits, the court reversed the convictions based on the improper summations.

The discussion below classifies the methods used by the courts of appeals to tame the unwieldy record and make its contents accessible to judges and their law clerks.

---

[2] Fed R App P 11(b).

[3] The text of these rules is in **app A.** In addition, many of the courts of appeals have local rules and operating procedures that elaborate on the Federal Rules of Appellate Procedure.

[4] 909 F2d 705 (2d Cir 1990).

[5] *Id* 708.

[6] *Id* 708-09.

§7.02 Variations among Circuits in Record Handling—Joint Appendix

Federal Rule of Appellate Procedure 30[7] provides three options for the court of appeals and for lawyers as to reproducing portions of the record for the court's use on appeal. The first is the joint appendix method, which is discussed in this section. The second is the deferred joint appendix, provided for by Fed R App P 30(c), and discussed at **§7.03.** The third method, provided for by Fed R App P 30(f) and discussed at **§7.04,** calls for transmitting the full record to the court of appeals and for preparation of record excerpts for the court's use.

Federal Rule of Appellate Procedure 30 is quite detailed, setting out provisions on timing and presentation of the joint appendix. Rule 30(a) envisions that appellant's counsel will serve a designation of matters to be included in the joint appendix and of issues presented for review within 10 days after the record is filed in the court of appeals. The appellee cross-designates within 10 days. The rule deals with cost-sharing and the mandatory items for inclusion in the appendix.

The advocate's first task is to consult the circuit rules to see if the joint appendix has been dispensed with for some or all cases. If no joint appendix is required, the advocate may file whatever record excerpts are called for at the time the opening brief is filed.[8] However, if a joint appendix is required in the circuit where the appeal is pending, the advocate must decide whether to seek deferral of the appendix under Fed R App P 30(c). Deferral gives the lawyer a chance to write the brief on appeal, and choose relevant record portions in that process. Often, counsel is better able to choose the material for inclusion in the appendix. The advantages may, however, be illusory. Many courts of appeals require a docketing statement within a few days after the record on appeal is filed, that lists the issues to be presented on appeal. To identify those issues, counsel must be familiar with the record, and probably familiar enough that designating the appendix does not take a great deal more effort.

Some circuits permit a party to dispense with the joint appendix with the court's approval. In a circuit that otherwise requires a joint appendix, it seldom will be wise to seek such relief. If the cost of reproducing the appendix seems prohibitive, counsel should recall that Fed R App P 32 is quite liberal in permitting the use of photocopy as a substitute for printing. The party can scissor and paste the relevant record portions and produce a quite respectable and legible product at fairly minimal cost. Most commercial copying services have relatively inexpensive plastic spiral bindings that permit the finished product to lie flat when opened.[9] An indigent litigant may seek government funds to pay the costs of reproduction.[10]

---

[7] Text reproduced in **app A.**

[8] *See* **§7.04.**

[9] An office that does an extensive appellate practice may find it worthwhile to invest in spiral binding equipment. See discussion of computer use at **§§1.07, 9.04.**

[10] *See* **§6.15.**

It is to a party's advantage, as the discussion above indicates, to have relevant record material easily available to the judge while he or she is reading the brief. If for any reason the advocate decides to seek relief from the joint appendix requirements, the motion under Fed R App P 30(f) should at least recite that the advocate will prepare an appendix to the briefs consisting of the docket entries, the judgment or order appealed from, and other matters that are indispensable to understanding the appeal.

The greatest faults of joint appendixes are unclear indexing and overdesignation. The joint appendix is not the place to give the court the flavor of the case below. That is the function of a persuasive brief. An appellate judge and his or her law clerks will not thank the advocate who compels them to wade through irrelevancy. Indeed, Fed R App P 30(b) was amended in 1991 to provide that "[e]ach circuit shall provide by local rule for the imposition of sanctions against attorneys who unreasonably and vexatiously increase the costs of litigation through the inclusion of unnecessary material in the appendix."[11] On the other hand, counsel must be careful to include any of the trial judge's rulings or comments on which review is sought, and record materials that show counsel made the proper and seasonable objection.[12]

The index or table of contents should identify each record item that is included with a brief neutral description. Thus, an entry might include not only the title of the document but an explanatory parenthetical note, for example, "Motion to Dismiss for Want of Personal Jurisdiction, filed January 3, 1991 (motion of defendant James Johnson, resident of Oklahoma)." A transcript excerpt might state "Transcript, July 15, 1991 (testimony of plaintiff Mary Smith concerning accident)."

The temptation to overdesignate is discouraged by the second paragraph of Fed R App P 30(b), which permits cost shifting to the overdesignator at the instance of the opponent or the court. Rule 30(a) provides a starting point for deciding what to include. The terms *judgment, order,* and *decision* should be read in the plural. The advocate should include every order to which objection is being made. If a particular order was made orally in the course of the trial, the party should include so much of the transcript as will show the order, the dispute that led to the order, and the objection or other statement that preserves the matter for appeal.

In reproducing motions in the appendix, it is neither necessary nor wise to include the legal memoranda filed in the district court. The only exception will be if the advocate wishes to emphasize that a particular legal theory was urged upon, and rejected by, the court below.

The decision of how much of the transcript to reproduce is the most difficult. Generally, if the advocate intends to claim that the judgment is not supported by the record, enough of the transcript and exhibits must be included to let

---

[11] Fed R App P 30(b).

[12] *See, e.g.,* Mortell v Mortell Co, 887 F2d 1322 (7th Cir 1989) (appellant's failure to follow a circuit rule requiring the appendix to contain any trial court statement supporting the judgment is sufficient ground to refuse review of the judgment and, therefore, to affirm).

the court of appeals fairly evaluate this contention. If no such claim is being made, and the facts are mostly not in dispute, the appellant should be far more sparing in designation. In every case, the transcript should be as tightly edited as possible. It may be possible to reach agreement with the opponent on a relatively limited designation based upon mutual assurances that the facts are mostly undisputed. If the advocate feels that the adversary's assurances cannot be trusted in this regard, then he or she should seek leave of court to defer the appendix so that both sides can designate precisely the materials that bear upon the disputed areas.

§7.03 —Deferred Joint Appendix

If the court of appeals defers the joint appendix in all cases, or in a class of cases of which the advocate's appeal is a part, Fed R App P 30(c) will govern the procedure to be followed. There are, however, cases in which the advocate will seek leave to defer the appendix. The first step in such a case is to seek agreement of all parties. Of course, a motion will be required to obtain the court's approval whether or not there is agreement.

Deferral may be needed if the 10-day provisions of Fed R App P 30(b) are onerous, because the case is large and complex and the advocate has not yet honed the selection of issues. In such a case, deferral is the only means to prevent overdesignation.

The second paragraph of Fed R App P 30(c) permits the advocates a choice: they can file their briefs in final, printed form with references to the original record, or they can file typewritten briefs with such references and then replace these with printed briefs containing citations to the deferred joint appendix. The advocate should opt for the latter course. The joint appendix is robbed of utility if the judge and law clerks cannot use it easily while reading through the briefs.

§7.04 —Record Excerpts

Many courts of appeals have exercised their power under Fed R App P 30(f) to dispense with the joint appendix entirely. Prior to the adoption of the Federal Rules of Appellate Procedure in 1969, some circuits had required that the entire record be reproduced.[13] The joint appendix provisions of Fed R App P 30 were a step forward. With the increasing complexity and length of much federal litigation, courts of appeals are attempting to reduce the judges' and law clerks' paperwork load still further by taking advantage of the Fed R App P 30(f) option.

In such cases, the circuit rules will provide that the appellant must file "Record Excerpts" or "Excerpts of Record" that contain the docket entries and certain other basic documentation, as well as any other brief extracts on which a party wishes to rely. This document usually must be filed together with

---

[13] *See* Advisory Committee Notes to Fed R App P 30(a).

the appellant's opening brief. If the respondent or cross-appellant wishes to bring additional matters to the court's attention, it may file an additional set of excerpts along with its brief.

The court of appeals decision to dispense with the joint appendix reflects the decisional reality that reversals for insufficient evidence are rare, given the deference accorded to lower court or agency factfinding. All the court feels it really needs in most cases are the portions of the record that show the rulings appealed from and, of course, the indication that the point was preserved.

Circuits that have dispensed with the joint appendix rely upon the briefs to sharpen the factual issues and to identify places in the record that support or cast doubt upon the arguments. In the adversary process, the court assumes that each advocate will catch and comment on an opponent's errors. Thus, the statement of the facts, and factual recitals in support of arguments, assume greater importance.[14] Of course, the advocate must be sure to include the appropriate cite to the full record for every factual assertion. The judge will read the briefs and direct the law clerks to go into the record and resolve disputes, usually prior to argument. Then, after argument, the writing judge will have access to the full record.

In no appendix circuits, the record excerpts should usually not exceed 50 pages. Even where the circuit rules do not mandate a limit, experience counsels self-limitation. Some courts of appeals impose page limits by circuit rule.[15] The form of the record excerpts will be dictated by circuit rule. As with the joint appendix, the advocate should provide a readable, well-bound, and well-indexed document. Counsel must ask himself or herself what the judges who read the brief would find essential as a handy reference while reading the brief.

In such circuits, however, the circuit rules usually identify items that must be in the record excerpts. Violation of these rules can spell defeat on appeal.[16]

§7.05 Digesting and Indexing the Record

Regardless of whether a joint appendix is filed, counsel should prepare a digest and index of the record in every case, with citations to the original record and to the joint appendix or record excerpts. If the appellate advocate was also trial counsel, the trial notebook digest may be updated for this purpose.

---

[14] *See* **§9.10.**

[15] For example, the Fifth Circuit limited the length of optional materials in the record excerpts to 40 pages without leave of court, which may be granted by the clerk. 5th Cir R 30.1.6.

[16] *See* McGinnis v Gustafson, 978 F2d 1199 (10th Cir 1992) (appellant's failure to provide transcript of hearing at which district judge gave reasons for granting summary judgment violates Tenth Circuit rule that appellant furnish not only copies of the judgment or order appealed from, but all written and oral findings and transcripts; court has "no alternative but to affirm the affected ruling"); SEC v Thomas, 965 F2d 825 (10th Cir 1992) (where appealing defendant fails to provide essential references to record, to aid the court in identifying alleged errors, court is empowered to affirm the judgment; however, court did review arguments and determine that reversal was not warranted).

The digest summarizes briefly all the important court filings, exhibits, and testimony. In most cases, it should be no larger than will fit in a notebook that can be taken to the lectern for oral argument. The index is a cross-reference to the digest, broken down by topic.

While some digesting can be done by a legal secretary, law clerk, or paralegal, the advocate must do the initial work himself or herself. When beginning work on the case, the first task should be to page through the entire record with a yellow pad, a dictating machine, a typewriter, or a word processor and begin to identify the potential issues, noting in each instance the relevant page and a few words that describe the way in which the issue arose, how it was resolved by the district court or agency, and whether a claim of error was preserved by a proper objection.

In addition, this first read-through must focus on the strength of the evidence in support of the judgment or order being appealed. This focus is necessary for two reasons, even if the advocate is sure that there will be no challenge to the sufficiency of the evidence. First, the harmless error rule may be applicable to claims of legal error, and the relative strength or weakness of the evidence is the most vital element of that determination.[17] Second, whether acknowledged or not, a court is more reluctant to reverse a judgment based on evidence it regards as overwhelming. The advocate's opponent will know both of these things, and it therefore is wise to anticipate arguments based upon them by noting the most important bits of evidence.

The first read-through should result in a skeleton digest and outline. The task of following through with a more detailed document can then be assigned to a capable nonlawyer with specific instructions about what to highlight. If the digester is instructed to use the same descriptive words for each occurrence of a particular point in the record, a first draft of the index can be generated using the search function on a word processor. For example, if the digester is told that every time an evidence point is dealt with, the word evidence or admissible should be used in the digest entry, instances of the word chosen can be located by the word processor for purposes of compiling a topic index.[18]

The digest and index can be circulated to other lawyers in the office or section as the basis for discussion of the proposed brief. They are accessible and useful for preparation of the brief itself and are a good reference for an initial check of the accuracy of factual assertions in the opponent's brief.

The digest and index will travel to oral argument. If the arguing advocate was not the author of the brief—which often happens, particularly in large firms—he or she can use it for preparation. At argument, the digest and index help counsel answer the court's questions about the record quickly and pinpoint citations to the record. The opponent's misstatements can be identified quickly and corrected. And when the opinion comes down, the digest and index are the documents of first resort in considering or opposing rehearing on the basis of claimed factual inaccuracies.

---

[17] See generally **§5.09.**

[18] See **§9.04** for a discussion of the use of the word processor for appellate briefing.

Any advocate who has read a record and not digested it, and then has had to search thousands of pages for the dimly remembered and yet elusive bit of transcript, knows how much the initial investment in a good digest and index will be repaid.

8 Motions Practice in the Court of Appeals

§8.01 How to Use Motions Practice

Federal Rule of Appellate Procedure 27(a) provides that "Unless another form is elsewhere prescribed by these rules, an application for an order or other relief shall be made by filing a motion for such order or relief with proof of service on all other parties."[1] Although Rule 27 provides for the form of motions and supporting briefs, each circuit has its own supplementary rules and internal procedures about form and content, and many circuits even require a special form of cover sheet for motions.

A motion may be filed for almost anything, from a routine continuance to dismissal or summary affirmance. Federal Rule of Appellate Procedure 27(b) recognizes the distinction between procedural motions, which may be acted upon without a response from the other party, and those that affect the substance of the case, as to which there is a right of reply before the court decides.

Motions steer your case through the court of appeals. Within the court's premises, motions determine timing and procedure, and permit your client maximum flexibility and freedom pending appeal. Some motions, which may

[1] The full text of Fed R App P 27(a) is in **app A.**

be termed *dispositive,* steer the case through the court and out the door, with a dismissal or summary decision. The advocate must, therefore, be adept at motions practice.

Most of the law and lore of motions practice is not codified. Federal Rule of Appellate Procedure 27 gives only the bare outlines, and the caselaw under it is scant, but the local rules also provide guidance. This chapter attempts to introduce the advocate not only to the rules and the caselaw, but also to describe in practical terms how and when to use motions practice to smooth the path through the court and help ensure that the case goes out the proper door.

First, one must have in mind a taxonomy of motions. Procedural motions include continuances,[2] authorization to file an overlength brief, and leave to file an amicus brief. The advocate who wants relief of this sort should consult **§8.02** for advice on seeking the opponent's consent to the motion. If the opponent will not consent, the advocate should next determine whether the motion can be acted upon by the clerk of court. The circuit rules probably will list the types of motions that fall into this category, discussed further at **§8.03.** As mentioned above, the court, or the clerk with delegated power, can grant many procedural motions without waiting for a reply.[3]

The next step up is the motion that a single judge of the court can decide, as authorized by Fed R App P 27(c). The list of such motions is determined by each court of appeals and can be found in its local rules. The clerk's office will tell the advocate whether the relief being requested is within the power of a single judge. For more details, see **§8.04.**

Finally, as discussed at **§8.05,** there are motions on which a panel of three judges will decide. Such motions, as one might expect, include those that will dispose of the case entirely; for example a motion to dismiss for want of appellate jurisdiction.

Sometimes a motion must be filed quickly and a speedy ruling obtained. Examples include motions for a stay under Fed R App P 8,[4] for bail under Fed R App P 9,[5] for stay of an agency order under Fed R App P 18,[6] and for stay of the mandate under Fed R App P 41.[7] Federal Rule of Appellate Procedure 27(a) expressly permits the court to shorten response time for such motions. Under Fed R App P 25(a), the courts of appeals may establish by local rule a procedure for filing motions by facsimile. When permitted by local rule, this procedure makes it easier to file emergency motions.

Most occasions for filing a motion will be apparent. The advocate will face a procedural problem or the need to seek relief from a time deadline or procedural rule. However, the advocate should also consider at the beginning of

---

[2] Extensions of time are expressly dealt with in Fed R App P 26(b).

[3] Fed R App P 27(b).

[4] *See* **§6.11.**

[5] *See* **§6.12.**

[6] *See* **§6.09.**

[7] *See* **§§10.15, 11.02.**

an appeal how well-timed and well-reasoned motions can shape the context in which the case is heard. This point is best illustrated by example.

In one criminal case, information became available after verdict that the trial judge and the bailiffs might have had unauthorized ex parte communications with the jury. The information was reliable and detailed enough to permit trial counsel to file a motion for new trial before sentencing, seeking a hearing at which the entire matter would be explored. The motion also sought recusal of the trial judge.

The trial judge denied relief and sentenced the defendants, who filed a timely notice of appeal. It was in the defendants' interest to obtain a prompt hearing on the allegations of misconduct, before juror memories faded. Most district courts have strict limits on attorney and party posttrial contact with jurors; thus, a hearing was the only means of perpetuating the testimony.

As soon as the notice of appeal had been transmitted to the court of appeals,[8] appellants' counsel moved to bifurcate the appeal and to set an expedited briefing and argument schedule on the jury issue. The court granted the motion, a partial record was transmitted on that one issue,[9] briefs filed, and argument held within two months of the notice of appeal. The court's decision, remanding to a different judge for a hearing, followed within five weeks.

In a civil case example, the district court remanded a removed case to the state court. The plaintiffs filed a notice of appeal and a petition for writ of mandamus, for they recognized the limited appealability of remand orders.[10] In any case where the appealability of an order is in doubt, and mandamus is used as a backstop, there is a risk that neither route to review will be available.[11] The risk can be minimized by moving to consolidate the petition and the appeal, and to postpone the question of jurisdiction to the hearing on the merits.

In another criminal case, there was postjudgment evidence that a principal witness had perjured himself and that government attorneys knew or should have known of the perjury. The notice of appeal from the conviction was timely filed. A motion for new trial was filed in the district court. Counsel then filed a motion in the court of appeals to remand the case for taking of evidence on the new trial motion, to permit a renewed appeal on a fuller record. The court of appeals granted the motion.

---

[8] *See* Fed R App P 3(d); **§7.01.**

[9] *See* **§§6.14, 7.02.**

[10] *See* **§2.15.**

[11] For example, suppose the district judge certifies an order under 28 USC §1292(b), discussed in **§2.09.** The court of appeals may not grant the petition for leave to appeal. If the order is arguably appealable under §1291, a notice of appeal should be filed. *See* **§2.02.** Mandamus might then be sought as a third alternative. It is almost imperative that counsel file a motion to consolidate these three proceedings, and make clear that the entire effort is designed only to protect the right to review and not to frustrate it. Counsel might cite Helstoski v Meanor, 442 US 500 (1979), in which the Supreme Court held that mandamus was not available to a criminal litigant whose speech or debate clause claim was rejected by the district court, but that an appeal would lie. Unfortunately, the litigant had not taken an appeal, and the time had run.

If counsel had not moved to remand, or if the motion had been denied, a different motions strategy would have been in order. If counsel wanted to have the appeal heard on a record that included the new trial proceedings, these options were available: If the district judge indicated that he would grant a new trial, a renewed motion for remand could be made in the court of appeals, which almost would certainly remand.[12]

If the district judge denied a new trial, the defendant has a right of appeal from that order. The defense could then move in the court of appeals to consolidate the new trial appeal with the main case. While the new trial motion is pending in district court, counsel can move in the court of appeals to postpone the filing of the brief in the pending appeal. The reason for postponing is to permit a single brief to be filed with all the issues and a single response by the government. If the court of appeals denies such a postponement, it may nonetheless defer oral argument until all briefs are filed in the various appeals. Deferral may be sought by motion, noting that judicial economy is served by having all the issues arising from a single trial resolved by one panel at one time. These illustrations show how motions practice can be used to shape the case in ways that present its most persuasive aspects and maximize a party's procedural options.

Beyond procedural aspects, motions practice is used to challenge the court of appeals' jurisdiction over the appeal and seek summary reversal or affirmance. The latter type of motion is seldom used; rather, counsel usually should seek an expedited briefing schedule. Summary disposition of an appeal, by affirmance or reversal, requires the advocate to demonstrate that "the merits . . . are so clear as to justify expedited action."[13] If one's opponent persists in violating procedural rules on appeal, the court may impose the sanction of dismissal or affirmance.[14]

---

[12] This example is from criminal litigation. In a civil case, the rules are the same. When a party in a civil case wishes to move for a new trial while appeal is pending, the proper procedure is to file a motion in the district court. If that court indicates that it will grant the motion, the movant may then move the court of appeals for a remand. Smith v Pollin, 194 F2d 349 (DC Cir 1952).

[13] Walker v Washington, 627 F2d 541, 545 (DC Cir) (citing United States v Allen, 408 F2d 1287, 1288 (DC Cir 1969), *cert denied,* 449 US 994 (1980)). *See also* Parker v Lewis, 670 F2d 249 (DC Cir 1981) (summarily affirming part of attorney fee award and expediting remainder of appeal; expeditious treatment fulfills purpose of Title VII of Civil Rights Act).

[14] It is a rare decision dismissing an appeal for failure to comply with the time limitations for filing a brief. *See, e.g.,* Marcaida v Rascoe, 569 F2d 828 (5th Cir 1978) (dismissal not warranted); Community Coalition for Media Change v FCC, 646 F2d 613 (DC Cir 1980) (strong warning). However, violation of other procedural rules can and has led to dismissal or other merits-based sanctions. *See, e.g.,* McGinnis v Gustafson, 978 F2d 1199, 1201 (10th Cir 1992) (appellant's failure to provide transcript of hearing at which district judge gave reasons for granting summary judgment violates Tenth Circuit rule that appellant furnish not only copies of the judgment or order appealed from, but all written and oral findings and transcripts; court has "no alternative but to affirm the affected ruling"); SEC v Thomas, 965 F2d 825 (10th Cir 1992) (where appealing defendant fails to provide essential references to record to aid the court in identifying alleged

Jurisdictional issues are, however, a fertile source of motions practice. Sources of such challenges will be found in Chapter 2's many sections on appellate jurisdiction, in Chapter 4's discussion of geographic and subject matter competence of the courts of appeals,[15] and in Chapter 6's many sections on timing and content of the notice of appeal. Fully one-fourth of federal appeals are disposed of on procedural grounds, including jurisdiction.

If counsel has a dispositive[16] jurisdictional claim, should it be raised by motion or in the brief on the merits? Economy of effort says that earlier is generally better. Counsel can attach to the motion copies of the relevant docket entries and record excerpts without the necessity of bringing up the entire record.[17] If the motion is denied, the merits panel can reconsider the issue.[18]

Oral argument is almost never granted on motions. Therefore, if counsel believes that argument materially aids in understanding the issues, that belief suggests adding the issue to the merits brief rather than raising it by motion.[19]

The advocate's staunchest allies in motions practice are the circuit rules, the telephone, and the right attitude. The circuit rules tell which motions may be granted by the clerk and provide vital information about the proper form for motions in the particular court of appeals. The telephone can be used to conduct the informal motions practice discussed at **§8.02;** it also should be used to resolve any doubts about the form of a motion and even the chances of obtaining relief.

The right attitude is not difficult to attain. Almost without exception, court of appeals clerk's office personnel know their jobs and will go out of their way

---

errors, court is empowered to affirm the judgment; however, court did review arguments and determine that reversal was not warranted); Mortell v Mortell Co, 887 F2d 1322 (7th Cir 1989) (appellant's failure to follow a Circuit Rule requiring the appendix to contain any trial court statement supporting the judgment is sufficient ground to refuse review and, therefore, to affirm). Other relevant cases are found in this treatise under the section dealing with each particular procedural requirement.

[15] Of course, even if the appeal is taken to the wrong court of appeals, dismissal will not follow if transfer is possible under 28 USC §1631 or §2112. *See* **§4.01.**

[16] Some jurisdictional errors are not "dispositive," but can be cured. For example, the court of appeals has the authority to remedy a want of jurisdiction in the district court under limited circumstances. If the allegations of jurisdiction are defective, 28 USC §1653 permits amendment in the trial or appellate court. If, however, jurisdiction is lacking because a nondiverse party is present, the court of appeals has the authority to dismiss the nondiverse party. It need not remand to the district court for this purpose. Newman-Green, Inc v Alfonzo-Larrain, 490 US 826 (1989). *See* **§2.01.**

[17] Fed R App P 27(a).

[18] *See, e.g.,* Duran v City of Douglas, 904 F2d 1372 (9th Cir 1990) (panel that hears the merits will consider jurisdiction anew and not apply the law of the case doctrine to the motions panel decision finding jurisdiction); Pioneer Properties, Inc v Martin, 776 F2d 888 (10th Cir 1985) (denial of motion to dismiss appeal was interlocutory order that placed appeal on calendar for briefing, and did not preclude plenary review of issues raised on motion).

[19] It is, however, the practice in some circuits to have motions and other procedural matters reviewed by a staff attorney who makes a recommendation to a panel of the court. In such a case, counsel may be able to appear before the staff attorney. *See* 9th Cir R 22.

to assist the advocate who is courteous, who has evidently tried to master the procedural rules, and who wants to do the job in a way that serves both the client and the reasonable demands of the clerk's office. There are clerks who do not meet these standards, but since they have the power to make an advocate's life miserable, one should maintain good humor and tact.

§8.02 Informal Motions Practice

The first objective of motions practice is to simplify it. If there is any prospect that one's opponent will agree to the motion, the advocate should telephone him or her and seek consent. This consent will almost invariably make granting of the requested relief a matter of routine. The motion as filed need simply recite the consent. If one lacks entire confidence in the opponent's integrity, the telephone call should be followed up with a letter. If the opponent is a notorious double-dealer, one should obtain his or her signature on the motion papers as consenting to the grant of relief. An otherwise routine motion is no place to stage an unnecessary credibility contest. When consent is forthcoming, however manifested, the motion papers discussed at **§8.07** need not make extensive legal argument.

The most informal—and easiest—motions practice is conducted entirely on the telephone. As noted at **§8.03,** the clerk of the court of appeals may have been given authority to grant many types of motions. Some courts of appeals have adopted a case expediter system that puts a deputy clerk in charge of a given group of cases.[20] Other courts have delegated motion duties in other ways. Counsel's first task is to check the local rules to determine the practice of the particular court of appeals.

Second, any Fed R App P 27(b) motion may be granted without allowing the opponent any time to object. Of course, the wise advocate will have called the opponent to obviate objection. This combination of circumstances may permit the advocate to obtain an extension of time, a continuance of an oral argument date, or any of a number of other forms of relief by telephone.

The procedure would be as follows: first, determine what relief is required; second, seek agreement from the opponent; third, check the circuit rules to see if the relief can be granted by the clerk and be aware of the provisions of Fed R App P 27(b); fourth, determine which deputy clerk is responsible for the case at hand or for the granting of routine motions. This determination can sometimes be made from the information first sent out by the court of appeals after the appeal is docketed. Otherwise, a telephone call to the clerk's office is in order.

Finally, the advocate should call the proper deputy clerk and announce his or her name and the fact that he or she is counsel for, for example, "Appellant

---

[20] The Fifth Circuit has adopted this system. The Ninth Circuit, in complex cases, may put a staff attorney in charge of a given appeal to play the same role. The court of appeals' first notice to counsel after docketing will contain information about whether such a system obtains.

John Jones in Smith and Jones versus Widget Company, court of appeals docket number 87-4563." A sample oral request might then be:

> I see by Fifth Circuit Rule 27.1.1 that you have authority to grant me an extension of time for filing my opening brief. My opponent does not object to a continuance of 30 days, to and including February 20, 1987, and I wonder if I should file a formal motion or if you can grant this request. Of course, I would send a follow-up letter to you confirming the new date.

This statement identifies the speaker and the case, the source of the clerk's authority, and the relief requested. It also tells the clerk that counsel knows what he or she is doing. Informal motions practice is entirely discretionary with the deputy clerk; he or she can require a written motion to be filed. Courtesy and an air of competent confidence are essential.

Developing the rapport with the clerk that permits routine business to be done on the telephone will save hours of lawyer time for more interesting tasks. Of course, a follow-up letter must be sent as protection, with copies to all counsel and a notation to that effect on the letter.

§8.03 Motions Decided by the Clerk of the Court of Appeals

As noted at **§8.02,** the clerk of court may have authority to decide certain motions. When a matter within the clerk's jurisdiction cannot be resolved by telephone,[21] a written motion must be filed. The motion must comply with Fed R App P 27(d), and the last paragraph of Fed R App P 32(b).[22] The circuit rules also may contain a provision concerning proper form and number of copies of motions addressed to the clerk.

Even when a written motion is required, a telephone call to the clerk's office can alert the deputy clerk that the motion will be on its way and, in some cases, can determine whether it is even worthwhile to present a motion. For example, if counsel wants a continuance of an oral argument date, the clerk may know something about the court's calendar that makes it highly unlikely the motion would be granted. Another example: if the advocate believes that his or her brief will be over the allowed length, the clerk's office may be able to give informal advice on the odds of getting permission to exceed the page limit. Such advice will not invariably be dispositive of the decision to file a motion, but may—in the example given—lead counsel to spend the time that would be used to draft a motion in reediting the brief. In addition, the clerk's office may let counsel know the sorts of reasons why particular relief would be granted; for example, "We never yield to conflicts with trial court appearances, but continuances are granted when counsel has a longstanding commitment to a family vacation."

---

[21] *See* **§8.02.**

[22] The full text of these rules is in **app A.** *See also* **§8.07.**

Rule 27(b) provides that a party aggrieved by the clerk's decision on a procedural motion may apply to the court. Such a request, in the absence of contrary circuit rule or practice, should be entitled Motion to Vacate Clerk's Order, followed by a description of the challenged order.

§8.04 Motions Heard by a Single Judge

Each court of appeals has developed its own procedures for determining which motions will be decided by a single judge and which must be referred to a panel of three. The circuit rules will provide the answer, supplemented by a call to the clerk's office if necessary. One reason to make sure is that the circuit may require more copies of the moving papers if the motion is to be heard by a panel.

The Advisory Committee Notes to Fed R App P 27(c) provide useful guidance on the scope of the rule:

> Within the general consideration of procedure on motions is the problem of the power of a single circuit judge. Certain powers are granted to a single judge of a court of appeals by statute. Thus, under 28 USC §2101(f) a single judge may stay execution and enforcement of a judgment to enable a party aggrieved to obtain certiorari; under 28 USC §2251 a judge before whom a habeas corpus proceeding involving a person detained by state authority is pending may stay any proceeding against the person; under 28 USC §2253 a single judge may issue a certificate of probable cause. In addition, certain of these rules expressly grant power to a single judge. See Rules 8, 9 and 18.
>
> This subdivision empowers a single circuit judge to act upon virtually all requests for intermediate relief which may be made during the course of an appeal or other proceeding. By its terms he may entertain and act upon any motion other than a motion to dismiss or otherwise determine an appeal or other proceeding. But the relief sought must be "relief which under these rules may properly be sought by motion."
>
> Examples of the power conferred on a single judge by this subdivision are: to extend the time for transmitting the record or docketing the appeal (Rules 11 and 12); to permit intervention in agency cases (Rule 15), or substitution in any case (Rule 43); to permit an appeal in forma pauperis (Rule 24); to enlarge any time period fixed by the rules other than that for initiating a proceeding in the court of appeals (Rule 26(b)); to permit the filing of a brief by amicus curiae (Rule 29); to authorize the filing of a deferred appendix (Rule 30(c)), or dispense with the requirement of an appendix in a specific case (Rule 30(f)), or permit carbon copies of briefs or appendices to be used (Rule 32(a)); to permit the filing of additional briefs (Rule 28(c)), or the filing of briefs of extraordinary length (Rule 28(g)); to postpone oral argument (Rule 34(a)), or grant additional time therefor (Rule 34(b)).
>
> Certain rules require that application for the relief or orders which they authorize be made by petition. Since relief under those rules may not

properly be sought by motion, a single judge may not entertain requests for such relief. Thus a single judge may not act upon requests for permission to appeal (see Rules 5 and 6); or for mandamus or other extraordinary writs (see Rule 21), other than for stays or injunctions *pendente lite,* authority to grant which is "expressly conferred by these rules" on a single judge under certain circumstances (see Rules 8 and 18); or upon petitions for rehearing (see Rule 40).

A court of appeals may by order or rule abridge the power of a single judge if it is of the view that a motion or a class of motions should be disposed of by a panel. Exercise of any power granted a single judge is discretionary with the judge. The final sentence in this subdivision makes the disposition of any matter by a single judge subject to review by the court.

No matter how many judges will rule on the motion, counsel may wish to know whether the decision will be made by the panel, or a member of the panel, that will hear and decide the appeal. Again, the practice varies from court to court. At some point in processing the appeal, a panel of the court generally acquires plenary control, with the authority to decide all questions related to that case unless and until rehearing en banc is granted. In many cases, this control attaches at the time the appellant's brief is filed, and after the clerk's office or staff attorney has determined the level of complexity of the case so that the workload is evenly divided among panels of the court. Sometimes, the panel is not assigned a case until a determination is made whether to grant oral argument.

Knowing whether the judge that decides the motion also will hear the case is important mostly for the insight that the ruling on the motion may give to the hearing panel's attitude about the case. To take the clearest example, a judge's denial of a motion for bail or for a stay often will give the advocate some indication regarding whether he or she faces an uphill fight on the merits.

The rules of most courts of appeals will tell the advocate whether a particular motion will be referred to a single judge and how many copies of the moving papers must be filed in that event. Review of a single judge's determinations under Fed R App P 28(c) may be triggered by filing a motion for panel review, as the rule expressly provides.

§8.05 Motions Heard by a Panel of the Court

Federal Rules of Appellate Procedure 27(c) provides that dispositive motions must be decided by a panel of the court rather than by a single judge; the various courts of appeals have each determined by rule and practice which other matters must be heard by a panel. The Advisory Committee Notes to Fed R App P 27(c), quoted at **§8.04,** set out various rule and statutory provisions under which a single judge may not act and a panel decision is required.

One question that has vexed advocates is what, if any, review may be obtained from an adverse decision by a panel of the court. If the decision disposes of the appeal or is the practical equivalent of a final judgment, then the rehearing provisions of Fed R App P 40[23] and the rehearing en banc provisions of Fed R App P 35[24] are triggered. Suppose, however, that the panel's action lacks this finality. If a panel denies a stay of execution of a civil judgment and a party is seriously compromised by this action, can it invoke Fed R App P 35 and 40? Or, if a criminal defendant is denied bail pending appeal, are Fed R App P 35 and 40 available?

Rule 40 requires entry of judgment as a precondition to seeking panel rehearing, which seems to require finality in the same sense discussed at **§§2.02-2.08.** Rule 35 permits rehearing en banc of an appeal or other proceeding. A textual argument could be made that en banc review of a significant preliminary order is, in principle, available. Such review rarely would be warranted, but cases with significant issues might well be tendered that would meet the Fed R App P 35 standards. Despite the language of Fed R App P 35, however, some courts of appeals routinely refuse to file en banc suggestions concerning preliminary orders. Of course, a party might be able to obtain review by filing a separate proceeding directed to the issue. For example, the party denied a stay or bail on motion could file an original petition for writ of mandamus[25] and a bail applicant would have review by habeas corpus.[26] Since neither of these proceedings involves a motion, the normal Fed R App P 35 and 40 will apply if the court of appeals denies relief.

§8.06 Prehearing Conference

Federal Rules of Appellate Procedure 33[27] provides for an optional prehearing conference to be attended by the attorneys for the discussion of procedural and substantive matters on appeal. Some courts hold such conferences in complex civil, criminal, tax, and agency matters. Others limit the use of the prehearing conference largely to agency cases, which tend to involve many parties. Despite the language of Fed R App P 33, the court may delegate the conduct of the conference to a staff attorney, deputy clerk, or conference director.[28] In such a case, the conference results in a recommended order that must be approved by the court and to which any party will have an opportunity to object.[29]

The prehearing conference, if held, generally is scheduled after the time for appeal and cross-appeal has passed, and as soon as it becomes apparent that the case is complex due to the legal issues, the length of the record, or the number of parties. In a complex or multiparty case, the conference provides a forum in which to discuss briefing responsibilities, timing, and handling the

---

[23] *See* **§11.01.**

[24] *Id.*

[25] *See* **§3.11.**

[26] *See* **§3.14.**

[27] The full text of Fed R App P 33 is in **app A.**

[28] *See* 10th Cir R 33.1.

[29] *Id. See also* 9th Cir R 33-1.

record and joint appendix. There may be some discussion of the amount of oral argument the parties desire and how that argument will be divided, though this issue may be premature. The court of appeals' jurisdiction of the appeal will always be a proper topic. The advocates may be asked to state the issues they intend to present in their briefs; if these statements of issues become part of the prehearing conference order, a later modification may be difficult to obtain.

By holding a prehearing conference, the court, or its designee, is looking for help from the parties in moving the case. The advocate who attends must have full authority to make agreement and to take a position on any issue. He or she must have prepared alternative proposals that will help serve his or her client. In a multiparty case, the advocate should have held a preconference discussion with counsel representing allied interests to the end of coordinating efforts. For example, several counsel may decide that they will divide various issues among themselves and adopt one another's arguments. The conference order should recite this division thereby making a formal motion to adopt unnecessary.[30] If the advocate wants an unusual amount of time for filing an opening brief, he or she should be prepared to argue that point. For example, the advocate might say that the coordination among counsel will take longer than the 40 days allowed by Fed R App P 31 for filing the opening brief, but that the time will be used to ensure that the briefs are not repetitive.

In keeping with the goal of simplifying and settling cases, statements made by counsel at a prehearing conference conducted by a court officer—not a judge—should be regarded as confidential and not disclosable to the court. The Tenth Circuit rules, for example, so provide.[31]

Some courts also use Fed R App P 33 as authority to compel the parties to seek settlement. For example, 10th Cir R 33.2 requires all parties to civil cases to hold a settlement conference and to report the results to the clerk.

§8.07 How to Write a Persuasive Motion

As noted above, some courts of appeals have a motion form or cover sheet that must be used. The advocate must consult the circuit rules and the clerk's office. Paper size, form, and number of copies of motions also are governed by circuit rule and practice and Fed R App P 32(b),[32] and will depend upon who is to decide the motion; the clerk, a single judge, or a panel.

---

[30] Absent a motion to adopt, or an order dispensing with the need for doing so, a party may be deemed to have waived an issue even if it is presented in a co-appellant's brief. United States v Williams, 809 F2d 1072, 1083 (5th Cir 1987).

[31] 10th Cir R 33.1. *See* Clark v Stapleton Corp, 957 F2d 745 (10th Cir 1992) (remarks made during a settlement conference under circuit rules are confidential and may not disclosed to the court by counsel). Counsel doubting whether confidentiality will obtain should write a letter clarifying the matter and analogizing the conference to a settlement discussion under Fed R Evid 408.

[32] The full text of Fed R App P 32(b) is in **app A.**

Unless the court of appeals' rules or practice forbid it, a cover sheet is preferable to a caption, and should have the same large docket number used on a brief. The cover sheet should look like that used for a typewritten brief, with the descriptive title of the motion occupying the space ordinarily used for the words "Appellant's Opening Brief" or other description. This preference is to a large extent personal: a motion in this form is easier to link up with the case file in the clerk's office and with any portions of the record to which the deciding judge(s) or clerk may refer. If the motion is written using a word processor, this suggested format will be the same as that used for briefs.[33]

The title of the motion should tell the court who the movant is and exactly what it wants: for example, "MOTION OF APPELLANT MICRO-ENGINEERING, INC. TO DISMISS THE CROSS-APPEAL OF SOFTWARE MART FOR UNTIMELY FILING OF NOTICE OF APPEAL." This title tells the clerk to route this motion to a panel of judges and tells the judges what issue they must decide.

If the motion is lengthy, a table of contents and table of authorities may be a good idea. The circuit rules and the clerk's office will tell the advocate if these are required.

The body of the motion must begin with a clear statement of who the movant is and what it wants, citing the appropriate statute, provision of Federal Rules of Civil, Criminal, or Appellate Procedure, circuit rule, or other authority that is the basis for the application. For example,

> The appellant Micro-Engineering, Inc. moves this Court pursuant to Federal Rule of Appellate Procedure 4(a)(3) to dismiss the cross-appeal of Software Mart. The grounds for this motion, as more fully set forth in the following memorandum of law, are that Software Mart's notice of appeal was filed 15 days after the first-filed notice of appeal, and 72 days after the district court entered judgment.

The next section of the motion probably will be a concise Statement of Facts, including references to the record if it is available. If the relevant portions of the record are not yet in the court of appeals, counsel can invoke Fed R App P 11(g)[34] or, more often, simply attach copies of the relevant portions of the record to the motion. If this latter method is chosen, and in any case in which counsel is bringing facts to the court's attention, the advocate's affidavit should be attached to the motion attesting to the verity of the assertions and authenticity of any papers filed. An Argument should follow, in accordance with the general principles set out in Chapter 9.[35]

Most procedural motions will not require a separate argument section. There is no body of reporter authority on when courts will grant continuances or permit extra-long briefs: the advocate will seek to persuade by setting out relevant facts and showing how these facts bear upon the request for relief. Most circuits

---

[33] *See* **§9.04.**

[34] *See* **§6.17, 7.01.**

[35] **§§9.06-9.13.**

require, and in any event prudence dictates that a proposed order be attached to the motion.

The motion must, of course, be served on all parties. If the advocate wants prompt consideration of the motion, then he or she should recite in the moving papers that other counsel have been informed by telephone of the filing, while also noting in the body of the motion that service will be made by overnight delivery. Rule 26(c) automatically grants the opponent an additional three days for response if service is made by mail. Service is governed by Fed R App P 25, but Fed R App P 25(d) permits the clerk to accept papers for filing that do not show proof of service subject to later addition of the required proof.

When a motion raises an issue of importance, counsel should request oral argument. Such requests seldom result in a scheduled court appearance, but counsel may be able to obtain argument by telephone conference call with a panel of judges. The clerk's office will be helpful in letting counsel know the exact method for communicating the request to the panel.

§8.08 When and How to Oppose a Motion

There are two kinds of motions made by one's adversary, as to which it is easy to know the proper response. Consent should be given to a routine scheduling motion, in which your adversary seeks the kind of accommodation lawyers usually should grant one another. A dispositive motion that terminates the case in your adversary's favor should be opposed. This section tells the advocate how to respond to the majority of motions that fall in between these two poles.

When one's adversary calls and seeks consent to a motion, one must first consider whether the motion is likely to be granted regardless of the position taken. If it is likely to be granted, then opposition wastes time and squanders credibility with the clerk's office. Examples include motions to extend time, file an overlength brief, or schedule oral argument in a certain way. The proper course is to seize this opportunity to gain reciprocal concessions and obviate the need for repetitive motions practice.

For example, suppose appellant's counsel calls and requests an extension of time to file the opening brief, and—because the case is very complex—leave to file a brief that is overlength. This telephone call is the time to reach agreement on a briefing schedule that allows extra time for the appellee's brief and for any page concessions that may be necessary. Perhaps one also would try to agree that oral argument should be set in the case, if the circuit rations argument. Then, the two sides can file a joint motion for the entire package of schedule changes. In some circuits, as noted at **§8.02,** matters such as timing can be dealt with by the clerk in a telephone call, and the consent obviates the need to do more than send a letter.

If the adversary's proposed motion may run into difficulty if not consented to, one faces a dilemma. There are no hard-and-fast rules, but rather a set of considerations that influence a decision. First, do not lightly consent to things that trouble the court. For example, wholesale extensions of page limits are not favored because judges have enough to read and rightly believe that most overlength briefs could be made shorter by careful editing.

Second, it probably is best to withhold consent when the opponent seeks to circumvent rules that concern the nature of the appellate process. For example, the record on appeal defines the issues decided by the lower court and presented to the court of appeals. One should presumptively resist efforts to expand the record under Fed R App P 10 or by judicial notice. Such expansion may in the end be permitted, but the party seeking it usually is deploying a procedural request in support of a substantive goal of improving the chances of success on appeal.

If the circuit rules require lawyers to consult with their adversaries before filing a motion—and many do—the potential for agreement always will be present. Even where no such requirement exists, the clerk's office may encourage consultation.

If, however, a motion is filed and served without prior notice, the advocate must move swiftly. As noted at **§§8.01** and **8.04,** many motions can be granted by the clerk or a single judge without waiting for a reply. If one wishes to respond to such a motion, whether to oppose or to suggest a modification, call the clerk's office and say so. Ask the clerk if a follow-up letter by mail, overnight delivery, or fax is appropriate. Then, respond quickly and concisely.

If the motion is acted upon before a reply can be filed, Fed R App P 27(b) permits one to ask the court for reconsideration. However, the weight of inertia is firmly behind a procedural order that has been granted and one should request reconsideration only where the order really hurts. If seeking reconsideration, try to identify a compelling reason that would not have appeared in the moving papers. For example, in one case a party moved for an extension of time, citing counsel's scheduling problems. The clerk routinely granted the motion. In fact, the extension was sought to hold the appeal while further proceedings were taking place in the district court, the outcome of which might improve the movant's position on appeal. There is nothing untoward about filing a request for reconsideration that supplies facts and circumstances omitted by one's opponent, provided that the matters are significant to the court and the alternative relief requested is significant to the loser's case (as opposed to the loser's ego).

The response to a motion should be labelled clearly, for example: "OPPOSITION TO MOTION FOR EXTENSION OF TIME, AND PROPOSED BRIEFING SCHEDULE," or "OPPOSITION TO MOTION TO DISMISS FOR WANT OF JURISDICTION." It should begin with a short statement of position that identifies the key issues. The motion will be read by a staff attorney or law clerk before it is read by a judge. That person will draft a decision memo for the judge. The advocate is most effective by trying to write a sentence, or a short paragraph, that will be the introduction to the staff attorney or clerk memorandum to the judge. Recall that court of appeals judges may make a half-dozen motions decisions per day.

Faced with a difficult dispositive motion, one should consider seeking deferral of the decision pending the briefs on the merits.

Such deferral sometimes is not possible: the clerk's office and staff attorneys in most circuits screen cases for jurisdictional issues and their review may trigger briefing on a motion to dismiss by inquiry to the parties.

§8.09 Moving for Voluntary Dismissal

Federal Rules of Appellate Procedure 42 provides for voluntary dismissal of appeals. If the appeal has not been docketed, Fed R App P 42(a) governs: the dismissal takes place in district court. If the appeal has been docketed, Fed R App P 42(b) sets out the procedure for filing a stipulation covering such matters as costs.

In either case, the court retains control of the case and need not accept the parties' submissions. Even a voluntary dismissal consented to by all parties and providing for payment of fees and costs may be reviewed by the district court or court of appeals, as the case may be.[36] Dismissal on agreed terms also is subject to review by the court of appeals, although such a motion almost certainly will be granted.[37]

The appellant's motion to dismiss on terms fixed by the court will generally be granted if the movant offers to pay costs and if the motion is made before the appeal is substantially under way.[38] If the nonmoving parties have been put to substantial expenditure of lawyer time, they may well seek to have dismissal conditioned on payment of attorneys' fees. The authority, if any, for the court of appeals to impose such a condition must be found either in Fed R App P 38[39] or in some provision of law relating to awards of attorneys' fees by the court of appeals.[40]

The court of appeals may balk at granting dismissal after the case is submitted, and a motion to dismiss after decision is almost certainly untimely.[41] In addition, if the appellant represents a class or presents a matter of public interest, the court of appeals may refuse to dismiss.[42]

Parties often seek to discontinue an appeal to avoid an adverse final judgment or even to undo a judgment that has already been entered. Courts of appeals are hesitant to endorse such bargains. The caselaw on this point is collected at **§5.16.**

---

[36] Once an appeal has been docketed in the court of appeals, only that court can dismiss it. United States v Ramey, Puckett 559 F Supp 60 (ED Tenn 1981).

[37] *See, e.g.,* Creaton v Heckler, 781 F2d 1430 (9th Cir 1986) (consenting to dismissal of appeal; Sneed, J, dissenting); Brookhaven Landscape & Grading Co v JF Barton Contracting Co, 681 F2d 734 (11th Cir 1982).

[38] *See In re* Penn Cent Transp Co, 630 F2d 183 (3d Cir 1980).

[39] The full text of Fed R App P 38 is in **app A.**

[40] *See, e.g.,* Waldrop v United States Dept of Air Force, 688 F2d 36 (7th Cir 1982) (government's motion to dismiss appeal could not be conditioned on award of attorneys' fees to plaintiff; however, court could remand to district court for limited purpose of determining fees).

[41] Brookhaven Landscape & Grading Co, Inc v JF Barton Contracting Co, 681 F2d 734 (11th Cir 1982).

[42] *See, e.g.,* United States v Washington Dept of Fisheries, 573 F2d 1117 (9th Cir 1978) (dismissal not appropriate when appeal presents substantial question of law that was likely to recur); Shellman v United States Lines, 528 F2d 675 (9th Cir 1975) (terms for dismissal; discussion of dismissal in public interest case), *cert denied,* 425 US 936 (1976).

9 The Brief on Appeal: Timing and Content

§9.01 Function of the Brief on Appeal

The appellate brief is the single most important element of success on appeal. It is a win-or-lose document. Even when oral argument is granted, each judge on the court will make an initial decision based on the briefs. And, in circuits where the record is distilled into a joint appendix or further truncated into excerpts of record, the judge and law clerk will initially dip selectively into the record, if at all. Only after seeking to understand the case by reading the briefs will they be likely to venture into the murky and cumbersome collection of transcript and pleadings generated in the court below.

This chapter deals with three different aspects of appellate briefing. First, it discusses the form of the brief, including both the items that are required to be included and the process of producing the brief. Second, it discusses the timing of appellate briefs. Third, it discusses how to write a persuasive brief. The material on choosing and ordering issues on appeal should be read in connection with Chapter 5. The material on citing and discussing the record below should be read in connection with Chapter 7. Background information on the lawyer's library, the use of computers in brief-writing, and the work habits of appellate judges is contained in Chapter 1. Jurisdictional matters are treated in Chapters 2 and 3.

The appellate brief must demonstrate not only that a lawyer is right, but that the lawyer knows and cares about the standards that govern appellate review and the responsibilities of appellate lawyers. A brief that asks for review of a factual finding without recognizing the deference due the district court will seem unpersuasive because the lawyer demonstrates ignorance of standards. A brief that fails to state issues clearly and concisely invites impatience. And woe betide the lawyer who through sloth or zeal misstates the record. Credibility is important; lawyers forfeit it by playing fast and loose with the facts. A brief that is repetitious, turgid, or boring will dissuade the judge, the law clerk, and the staff attorney[1]—all of whom must wade through hundreds of pages of written material every day.

On the positive side, the brief makes a first impression for the appellant and the appellee. It organizes the appellate litigation and the record. If the brief is well written, concise, honest, and well prepared, it may earn the author added consideration. Not that any judge would change a decision based upon the superficial allure of a snazzy brief, but rather that a good brief may benefit its author because it will liven up the judges' and clerks' task of reading literally hundreds of appellate briefs every year. Does anyone doubt that the will to finish a well-written book is easier to summon, and that one tends to retain and to savor the plot and characters of such a book?

Every circuit has specialized rules for the form and content of briefs to supplement the principles set out in the Federal Rules of Appellate Procedure and in this chapter. In addition, many commercial legal printers publish summaries of the circuit rules on the form of briefs.

---

[1] For a discussion of staff attorneys and their functions, see **§10.02**

§9.02 Time Limits for Filing Briefs

The briefing schedule is governed by Fed R App P 31(a).[2] Appellant's opening brief is due 40 days after the date on which the record is filed, and appellee's brief 30 days after service of appellant's brief. The appellant may file a reply brief 14 days thereafter, but no later than three days before oral argument.

These are the dates to follow absent contrary direction from the clerk's office. Usually, the clerk will send a scheduling order with the dates on which briefs are due. In addition, the parties may have been required to meet other deadlines, such as a docketing statement or statement of issues, required by circuit rules.

In addition, as noted in Chapter 8, a party may file a motion to shorten or extend the time for briefing.

Timing issues can be tricky, however, due to the interplay of three rules: Fed R App P 31(b), on filing and service of briefs; Fed R App P 25, on filing and service generally; and Fed R Civ P 26, on computation of time. All three rules must be read together, along with any relevant circuit rule and clerk's office directive.

To see how the rules work, take a hypothetical typical case. The record is filed on April 30, 1993, which is a Friday. Under Fed R App P 31(a), appellant has 40 days to file a brief. Fed R App P 26(a) provides that the 40 days starts the day after April 30, 1993, or May 1, 1993. The brief is due June 9, 1993. However, if the due date falls on a Saturday, Sunday, holiday, or day the clerk's office is closed, the brief is due the next day not among the foregoing.[3]

What does it mean that the brief is *due*? For all papers except briefs and appendices, *due* means received by the *clerk*. For briefs and appendices, it is sufficient if the party mails the item on the due date.[4] However, *mail* means mail by the Postal Service and not some form of private overnight delivery.[5]

The appellant's brief, when filed, must be served on all parties and a certificate of service included in the brief. The appellee's 30 days to file a responsive brief runs from the date of service, except that if the appellant serves by mail, the appellee will have an additional three days to file and serve its brief.[6] Service by mail is notoriously unreliable. It is a good idea to get an agreement that the parties will, in addition to complying with the rules, serve one another by a reliable form of overnight delivery or even by fax. Sometimes a clerk's office will order such service when entering an order for expedited briefing.

---

[2] The text of Fed R App P 31 is in **app A.**

[3] Fed R App P 26(a).

[4] Fed R App P 25(a).

[5] Prince v Poulos, 876 F2d 30 (5th Cir 1989) (Federal Express shipment is not "mailing," and will not give the filer the additional time that he or she would get by simply using first class mail; Postal Service Express Mail is the only overnight service that will qualify under this holding). However, some circuits have local rules designed to simplify the computation of time. For example, the Tenth Circuit adds three days to most brief due dates, to avoid having the clerk's office figure out who mailed their brief and who did not. *See* 10th Cir Statement of Internal Operating Procedures, VI, B.

[6] Fed R App P 26(c).

§9.03 The Mechanics of Brief Writing—The Notebook Theory of Brief Writing

Organizing the drafting and production of an appellate brief is difficult. The most enervating and frustrating part of the task is assembling all the sections and producing a final product that is legally and technically correct in every detail. At the last minute there always is some detail that seems to have been overlooked, and as the deadline looms, relatively minor omissions can create a crisis that can be resolved only by staying up until midnight or by a last-minute desperate effort to get a continuance.

The most common fault of appellate brief-writing efforts is leaving organizational details of the project to the last minute. The resulting crunch makes the brief more costly because it consumes hourly employee overtime. It also puts undue pressure on everyone connected with the case.

These pitfalls can be avoided by rigid attention to deadlines and by adherence to a form. Lawyer, paralegal, and secretarial time is wasted in prodigious amounts because appellate lawyers fail to adopt simple devices to organize the work of preparing an appellate brief.

A notebook can be of great assistance. The notebook should be a standard three-ring binder with a tab for every element of the brief, as required by the Federal Rules of Appellate Procedure,[7] the local rules of the relevant court of appeals,[8] and the outline of facts and law as developed in the lawyer's office. On its cover or as the first page, the notebook should contain (on a standard form developed for this purpose in the lawyer's office):

1. The style (name) of the case
2. The case number in the district court
3. The case number in the court of appeals
4. The due dates for record, briefs, and argument
5. A set of internal deadlines for production
6. The name, address, and telephone number of the deputy clerk in the court of appeals who must be contacted for any information or assistance[9]
7. The name(s) of the lawyer(s) working on the case
8. The name and address of opposing counsel and all others who must be served with any papers
9. The name, address, and telephone number of the printer (if used)

---

[7] Fed R App P 28(a).

[8] For example, a court of appeals may require a certificate of interested persons to be placed before the table of contents. By establishing a separate tab for each such item, and integrating these tabs with those for the parts required by Fed R App P 28(a), the risk of errors of form is minimized.

[9] On informal clerk's office practice, see **§8.02**.

The tabs in the notebook will usually be as follows, remembering that variations in requirements in particular circuits will require additional tabs or reordering of the tabs:[10]

1. Cover
2. Table of Contents
3. Table of Authorities (in a large case, divided into subcategories: Cases, Statutes and Rules, Other Authorities)
4. Statement of Subject Matter and Appellate Jurisdiction[11]
5. Statement of the Issues Presented[12]
6. Statement of the Case (in a large case, divided into Nature of the Case, Course of Proceedings Below, Disposition Below, and Statement of Facts)[13]
7. Argument (divided into the various numbered sections according to issue and perhaps preceded by a summary of argument)[14]
8. Conclusion
9. Certificate of Service

The appellee's notebook will have a similar set of tabs, except that the statement of jurisdiction, issues, and of the case may be omitted unless the appellee is dissatisfied with the statement of the appellant.[15]

Armed with this notebook, the lawyer can direct an associate, paralegal, or secretary to keep periodic track of progress on the brief, enter changes in due dates, and monitor the process of production.

On the question of production, it is acceptable to print briefs, many lawyers prefer to do so. However, it also is acceptable to reproduce them more quickly and cheaply by a photocopy process, which produces quality that is as good or better.[16] Almost every commercial copying firm, especially franchise outlets, will have the facilities to reproduce the brief cover on heavy stock of the proper color and bind the brief with a spiral binding so that it lies flat when opened. Such binding is recommended in the rules of at least one court of appeals[17] and will be welcomed by every judge and law clerk. The large, clear type of such a brief is preferred by many appellate judges to the printed product.

---

[10] For example, some circuits require a statement of interested parties, and Fed R App P 26.1 requires a corporate disclosure statement by a corporate party.

[11] *See* **§9.09.**

[12] *See* **§9.10.**

[13] *See* **§9.11.** The statement of facts may be further subdivided, as discussed at **§9.11.**

[14] *See* **§§9.12** and **9.13.**

[15] Fed R App P 28(b). *See* **§§9.14-9.16.**

[16] See **§1.07** on computer-related research tools, and **§9.04** for a discussion of type-sizes for word processor briefs.

[17] *See* 5th Cir R 32.3.

Most of what follows is based upon the assumption that the brief will be produced by a photocopy process. If the brief will be printed, counsel should set up a schedule with the printer as far in advance as possible. Most legal printers set the brief into type from a diskette, which minimizes typographical errors. However, when a printer receives the copy at the last minute, there will likely be heavy overtime charges to get the brief finished on time.

Returning to the notebook tabs, it is obvious that the cover, the conclusion, the certificate of service, and some of the table of contents can be set up as soon as the record is docketed in the court of appeals.[18] The cover stock (blue for the appellant's brief, red for the appellee's brief, white for a reply brief) may have to be ordered; reproducing the cover need not await the completion of the entire brief.[19] The routine jobs of compiling the certificate of service also can be done early.

Blank, or partially blank, pages can be put in the notebook after the Statement of the Case and Argument tabs for notes and outlines of arguments. As portions of the brief are completed, they are placed in the binder at the appropriate tab. In this way, progress on the brief can be monitored instantaneously at any time. It would be wise to adopt an office rule that until the lawyer in charge has read and initialled each section, it cannot be regarded as in final form.

When a draft of the brief, or some portion of it, is finished, it is placed in the notebook. When this portion is edited, the edited version can be returned for retyping of changes. All word processing programs allow for a header or footer on the draft, which prints out the date, time, and page number, perhaps with the word *DRAFT*. Such a header or footer helps to ensure that the most recent version of the brief is in the notebook. The three-hole format also facilitates editing because it allows the editor to cut, paste, or staple, and reassemble with minimal risk of getting the pages mixed up and out of their intended order. Using the notebook helps to ensure that the editing process is done with the entire brief in hand, rather than in a series of nibbles. This avoids repetition and helps the brief tell a coherent story.

§9.04 —Using Word Processing and Other Computer Programs in Appellate Practice

At **§1.07**, there is an extensive discussion of computer assistance in legal research and writing. Computers with word processing and spreadsheet capability are nearly essential to efficient brief-writing. The computer permits easier editing and it can reduce the amount of paper involved in creating drafts. With a local area network (LAN), a modem, or just plain disk-swapping, it can permit several lawyers to collaborate more easily.

---

[18] The court of appeals will promptly inform counsel that the appeal has been docketed and this communication will contain the docket number.

[19] Cover colors are regulated by Fed R App P 32, as supplemented by the local circuit rules.

With a notebook computer and a portable printer, the lawyer can take case files and indices to the site of a meeting or the oral argument. Even without a printer, a notebook computer with a fax modem can be used to print documents—just fax them to the hotel desk from the hotel room or set up the fax modem in the office one is using for preparation.

Most lawyers have at least some knowledge about how word processing programs function. Many lawyers also know how spreadsheet programs work. With these programs and compatible legal research software, a brief can be produced and checked much more efficiently that was the case even 10 years ago.

For example, a word processing program can set up a matrix for the elements of the brief, listed at **§9.03.** If the case is complicated, a spreadsheet program can be used to summarize key facts and issues. For example, in a complex criminal appeal, the spreadsheet program can be used to list the counts of the indictment, the statutory sections, the defendants charged, a brief summary of each count, and the verdict. This tabular presentation can be put into the brief, either as part of the Statement of the Case or as an appendix bound at the end of the brief.

Most word processing programs have an outline function that can be used to organize the brief. Some programs permit one to code case and other citations in the body of the brief; the coded citations are then extracted for the Table of Authorities. WestCheck, a Westlaw program, can extract citations from some word processing formats and perform cite-checking automatically. The software is being updated constantly to work more closely with Westlaw.

As soon as the record on appeal is on its way to the court of appeals, or even as soon as the appeal is in the office, the notebook discussed at **§9.03** should be created. Not only should there be a tab for each element of the brief, but the word processor also should be used to create the cover sheet form, a form for the cover of the brief, and a series of pro forma pages containing the proper headings for use in the brief, such as Table of Contents, Table of Authorities (with proper subheadings), Statement of Issues Presented, and so forth. This matrix can be a master document, used in every appellate case in any given circuit. If the law firm handles appeals in different courts of appeals, variations based upon local circuit rules can be programmed in. Then, as portions of the brief are completed, they can be inserted at the proper place.

Some lawyers believe that the production of a brief is a matter for the secretary and the ordering of equipment for the office manager. They are mistaken. If a lawyer becomes involved in production of a single brief in order to set up the procedures discussed in this section, then future briefs will be produced at great savings in time and overhead. It is essential to the theory of this book, and to its teaching, that appellate practice involve investment decisions as well as legal and factual research, and that all aspects of the process be analyzed, understood, and organized for efficient production of a quality product.

Word processing programs vary, and some are far more sophisticated than others. However, the following discussion shows how a typical word processing program will assist the lawyer and others who work in the office to produce an appellate brief.

Move. Using the notebook, one often finds that the text can be rearranged to make the presentation more persuasive. This involves anything from a paragraph or footnote to rearrangement of the order of all the arguments. The move function on a word processing program is essential to this task.

Copy. When the brief is drafted, the Table of Contents must be prepared. By copying headings and subheadings from the brief to the Table of Contents, one saves time and ensures that the Table is accurate. The copy function can be used in conjunction with the code mentioned above to create the Table of Authorities.

Search and Replace. Almost every word processing program has the ability to find a given string of letters and numbers and to replace them with others or not, at the typist's option. This function has importance in several settings. For example, after the Table of Authorities is assembled, there should be a final cite-check for accuracy of form and content, using such tools as Shepard's, Insta-Cite, Auto-Cite, and perhaps with WestCheck. For example, suppose an error is found: a "certiorari denied" citation has been omitted. The Table of Authorities citation can be changed and the citation corrected in the text using the search and replace function. If a volume number has been misstated, every instance of the citation of the case in question can be found using the search function. Search and replace can also be used to be certain that footnotes are in chronological order by searching for the superscript command. Misspellings of names or erroneous citations also can be corrected.

Pagination. Unless leave of court is obtained to file a longer brief, the page limitations of Fed R App P 28(g) must be observed. The pagination function can keep regular track of how long the brief is becoming as successive sections are drafted and edited. The pagination function can be used to insert mandatory page breaks to keep a block of text together. If, on the other hand, the brief is at the limit of permissible length, a page or two can be saved with pagination. For example, Fed R App P 32 permits printed matter on a photocopied brief to be 6-½ by 9-½ inches. This will permit 28 lines of text per page, although a 27-line page looks less crowded. Repaginating from 27 to 28 lines saves nearly two pages in a 50-page brief.

The Lawyer Who Types Drafts. Many lawyers type their own drafts. A law office should encourage this practice and capitalize on it by making sure that the lawyer and the secretarial work stations have compatible equipment. This will permit the data from the lawyer work station to be transmitted directly to the secretarial work station. Drafts can be sent from one workstation by several means, as discussed earlier.

The lawyer who types drafts can be provided with a matrix for the brief, as discussed at **§9.03** above. If the lawyer is not an excellent typist, there are time-saving strategies. Often, when legal research is completed on a brief, the lawyer will make photocopies of the cases and other authorities on which principal reliance will be placed. The secretary can type out a list of the full, correct citation of each case, statute, and other authority, and the lawyer typing the draft need only refer to them with an apt abbreviation. The secretary can insert the full citations by using the copy function.[20]

Other Computer Aids. These aids include spell-checking and alphabetizing of data. There are even programs that analyze writing style and syntax. They are, however, adapted to standard expository writing and may therefore be of marginal use to the brief writer.[21]

A majority of briefs filed with the courts of appeals are created on word processors, printed on laser printers, copied, and bound. As a result, the page limit distinctions between standard printed briefs and those reproduced by other means have been abolished. Federal Rule of Appellate Procedure 28(g)[22] allows 50 pages for principal briefs and 25 pages for reply briefs.

Most courts of appeals have adopted rules to deal with the proportionally spaced fonts available on most word processing programs. Desktop publishing and laser printer technology make it possible to pack about 20 per cent more text into the same number of pages. Judges complain that the page limitations are being abused by this device. One possible solution is for the court to require that all briefs not printed be filed with 10 pitch (or 11 point) Courier type. Most courts have opted to permit use of proportional fonts, but decrease the permitted number of pages by 20 per cent.[23] Because the judges are sensitive to increases in their reading workload, the clerk's office will likely check every brief for compliance. If the brief is rejected, you will be compelled to refile a revised version very quickly and may face sanctions. Egregious or repeated rule violations may result in dismissal of an appeal.[24]

The numbers and descriptions used by these rules and by word processing and printer manuals can be confusing. Here is a brief glossary.

> *Pitch* refers to the number of characters per inch in a line of typewritten text. The term has been carried over to some word processing applications. *12 pitch* typewriter text has 12 characters per inch, *10 pitch* has 10 per inch. Some electric typewriters permitted use of proportional spacing

---

[20] Alternatively, if the lawyer uses the same code each time he or she means to refer to a given case, then the global search and replace function may be used.

[21] Not only must briefs at times be more turgid than ordinary prose, but the intermixing of citations and text will no doubt cause the editing program to think there are too many dependent clauses.

[22] The full text of Fed R App P 28 is in **app A.**

[23] *See, e.g.*, 5th Cir Rule 32.1 which provides an Option A (Courier type) and Option B (12 point proportional font).

[24] *See* EDC, Inc v Navistar Intl Transp Corp, 915 F2d 1082 (7th Cir 1990) (warning of sanctions for squeezing in more text than the rule allows); TK-7 Corp v Estate of Barbouti, 966 F2d 578, 579 (10th Cir 1992) (Tenth Circuit rule 32.1(a) requires that briefs not exceed 50 pages and that typewritten text "must be no smaller than pica with no less than 10-pitch spacing"; defendants, whose motion to file a 60-page brief had been denied, filed a 51-page brief with 102 footnotes; "[u]sing a favorite undergraduate gambit, defendants have visibly shrunk the type face and spacing of the footnotes and re-started the numbering several times"; court says that the technology of word processing should not cause lawyers to yield to the "temptation . . . to the wordy to compress, rather than edit"; held, defendant's brief stricken).

(e.g., an "i" would take less space than an "m"), but these are now obsolete.

Point is a measure of type size drawn from traditional letterpress printing. There are 72 points to an inch. There are 12 points to a *pica.* Thus, there are 6 picas to an inch. 12 point type is typically set six lines per inch, which is the same number of lines per inch as on a standard typewriter. However, letterpress letters are of varying widths, hence the name *proportional fonts.* A *font* simply means a style of type.

Serif: Many courts prohibit the use of *sans serif type. Serif* is another printer's term, referring to a fine cross stroke on a letter, particularly at its bottom or top. The bold headings in this book are in a sans serif type.

In a world now populated with word processors and the paraphernalia of desktop publishing, the question of what constitutes taxable costs has become complex. In *Martin v United States,*[25] Judge Easterbrook attempted to adapt the world of modern desktop publishing to the old language of Fed R App P 39(c). He concluded that the marginal cost of converting a word processing document to a brief in form to be filed is recoverable as cost, but not the fully distributed and allocated costs of producing the document, which would include some element of amortization for the equipment itself.

§9.05 —Assembling and Printing the Brief

Assume that the brief (appellant's opening, appellee's, reply, or even the record excerpts) is in draft form. The various elements of it are assembled in the notebook, as suggested at **§9.03.** Counsel is certain that every element of the brief is in the form required by the circuit's rules.

Now is the time to do the following:

1. Check the Federal Rules of Appellate Procedure and the circuit rules and internal operating procedures to be sure that every element of the brief is present and in the proper order.
2. Monitor the creation of the Table of Contents and Table of Authorities to make sure that they accurately reflect what is in the brief itself.
3. Read the brief from beginning to end to make sure it tells a coherent, unified, and persuasive story. The earlier edits of portions of the brief are no substitute for this step.
4. Subject every case in the brief to Shepard's check or to one of the equivalent electronic searches, as discussed at **§9.04.**
5. Let someone not connected with the case read the brief for errors of spelling, grammar, and punctuation.
6. When the brief arrives back at the office in finished form, one of the lawyers whose name is on the cover should take the copies to be filed and give each one a cursory inspection. Are all the pages there, in the proper order? Is the

---

[25] 931 F2d 453 (7th Cir 1991).

brief properly bound? Is the case number correct? Are the elements required in the particular circuit all present?

7. Finally, one of the lawyers whose name is on the brief should make sure that the brief is filed properly. If the brief is not to be physically carried to the court of appeals, it must be sent by some means that provides proof of mailing.[26]

§9.06 How to Persuade Judges—Rule-Oriented versus Party-Oriented Writing

The decision about issues on appeal will dictate the structure and content of the Statement of the Case and provide a unifying theme for the entire brief. This is little different from the unifying theme that every trial lawyer brings to opening statement and final argument.

As the author has described in more detail in a book on the theory and practice of persuasion, *Examining Witnesses,* "deciders perceive whole stories."[27] Practical experience, theories of language, and the insights of Gestalt theory teach us that someone who must make a decision arranges the available data wholistically and then uses that entire perception as the basis for a decision.

These insights are obviously relevant in jury trials, where story-telling seems most clearly appropriate. They are often overlooked in the appellate setting. Consider, however, that appellate judges ask "How should this case be decided?" That decision relies upon evaluations of individual legal arguments, but in the ultimate judgment—reversed or affirmed—these evaluations are mediated by rules about the significance of perceived errors and the overall justice of a result. Those who doubt this formulation should examine evidence of the impact of ideology on appellate decision-making.[28]

The brief should, therefore, tell a story. But what kind of story? Almost any litigated event can take on an entirely different complexion, depending on the facts that one chooses to emphasize in the telling of it. Here is an example from *Examining Witnesses:*

> Here is Professor Jack Balkin, talking about a torts case that we probably all studied in law school.
>
> Every torts professor has a favorite hypothetical about causal responsbility—some wildly improbable and outrageous chain of events triggered by the defendant that somehow leads inexorably to the plaintiff's

[26] On timing of filing by mail, see **§§9.01, 9.02.**

[27] Michael E. Tigar, Examining Witnesses 5 (1993). This book can be ordered through the American Bar Association, 750 North Lake Shore Drive, Chicago, IL 60611. The long excerpt from *Examining Witnesses,* later in this section, is from pages 14-18. The incendiary rat case is United Novelty Co v Daniels, 42 So 2d 395 (Miss 1949), the discussion of which owes much to Jack Balkin, *The Rhetoric of Responsibility*, 76 Va L Rev 197 (1990).

[28] Eric Schnapper, *Judges Against Juries—Appellate Review of Federal Civil Jury Verdicts,* 1989 Wis L Rev 237.

injury. I have always been partial to the facts of United Novelty Co. v. Daniels. In Daniels the defendant negligently set the nineteen-year-old decedent to work cleaning a coin-operated machine with gasoline; the decedent worked in a small room warmed by a gas heater with an open flame. The gasoline vapors surrounding the machine ignited when a rat ran from the machine into the flame, caught fire, and then ran back toward the machine, causing an explosion that killed the decedent. Naturally, the defendant company argued that it was not causally responsbile for the freak accident. Nevertheless, the court upheld a jury verdict against the company because it could have foreseen that setting the decedent to work in the room under these conditions was unduly dangerous.

The opinion in Daniels takes up barely a page in the reporters, but within this miniature one can find many of the most common structures of argument about human moral responsibility that occur in legal discourse. Consider, for example, the arguments that the defendant company might make (and probably did make) on its behalf:

(1) The explosion was caused by the unpredictable movement of a rat, not by the defendant's negligence.

(2) When the decedent began cleaning the machine with gasoline, it was completely unforeseeable that a rat would jump out of the machine, run headlong toward an open flame, catch fire, and then run back precisely where it could do the most damage.

(3) Decedent was at fault for cleaning the machine with gasoline in the first place. The decedent must have known of the danger when the decedent voluntarily began to work.

Next consider the plaintiff's likely responses:

(1) Although the rat was the immediate cause of the explosion, the real cause was the defendant's ordering the decedent to work under unsafe conditions.

(2) It is completely foreseeable that if you set someone to work in a small room filled with gas vapors and an open flame, there is an unacceptable risk of an explosion.

(3) The decedent cannot be held responsible for the explosion, because the decedent was following the orders of the defendant employer and was a minor.

As one would expect, the defendant's arguments are designed to minimize the defendant's causal, legal, and moral responsiblity, while the plaintiff's arguments are designed to enhance them. More importantly, however, each side recharacterizes the facts to support its position, emphasizing some details, minimizing or even omitting others—creating a coherent portrait of the situation from the raw materials of experience. Like all pictures, these characterizations are selective, for to record experience is always also to re-order and even to suppress it. In the second argument presented above, for example, the defendant describes the situation in minute detail, while the plaintiff speaks in more general, abstract terms. In this way each side can make plausible its claim about the foreseeability or unforeseeability of the decedents's injuries.

Balkin uses the terms "picture" and "portrait" instead of "story," but he is talking about lawyers and the trial process in the same way that we have been. "Story" is more descriptive of the rhetorician/dramatist/troubadour. "Picture" is metaphorical, but also helpful. Manuals on photography tell you to decide what will be the main subject of your picture and tell you to choose a point of view that will emphasize that subject.

When a witness describes a scene, you want to use enough detail to make the jurors have a mental picture. When proving how the accident happened, plaintiff's counsel will ask the witnesses to start by talking about the workplace and the boss's control of people's schedules and duties. By the time the decedent gets into that room, the plaintiff wants the jury to picture acts being directed and controlled by others.

There are two aspects of "how you tell it." The first is the rhetorical exercise of structuring the argument to lay the facts in a certain order and pattern. The second is understanding how principles of proof serve or disserve the advocate's effort to present the pattern.

STRUCTURE AND ORDER

In the incendiary rat case, both sides begin with accepted principles of personal injury litigation. The defense stresses that we are all responsible for our own actions. We all ought to feel good about having such a sense of responsibility and about expecting others to have it. Therefore, we will not hesitate to treat the plaintiff's decedent as we would want to be treated—as someone who freely chose a certain course of action—even when the consequences are uncompensated injury.

The plaintiff will stress the employers' superior knowledge and control of the situation—its power to affect events, including the power to put the decedent in a place of danger. We should, as community representatives, want to have and enforce rules about the exercise of such power.

Professor Balkin's article, however, is not about rat and gasoline cases. He shows how the basic positions I have just described, which he calls "individualist" versus "communalist," take a very similar form throughout the law of torts. Similar sets of ideologically based pairings can be found in contracts, property, or criminal law—indeed, every field of law that is shaped by the adversary system.

A litigator faced with two persuasive ways to describe the same facts may have a sense of insecurity or unease. If either formulation may be validated by the verdict of a jury, how will the jurors choose? The answer will lie in the ability of the lawyers on both sides and on the choices made by judges who preside at trials and review the results of trials.

Being able to render issues in these opposing, mutually exclusive pairings does not mean that legal rules are indeterminate or without principle. The statement of issues is paradigmatic, simply a structure to be filled

> in each case with particular factual content. When the content has been added, then juries and judges must exercise judgments based on their perceptions and, inevitably, their own sense of rightness.
>
> In our daily lives, we often say, "that's just a value judgment," or "that's just your opinion," meaning that all such judgments or opinions are unverifiable and therefore arbitrary. Yet, as lawyers, we must constantly embrace value judgments about such things as responsibility, "just deserts," and rights. We must exhibit evidence to jurors and make arguments to build images of reality and validate the opinions and judgments that we want the jury to use in deciding.
>
> Nor, as we shall see, will there always be a bright line between appeals to principle and arguments about facts. The line that Aristotle tried to draw, separating ethical, logical, and emotional arguments from one another, has long since proven impossible to maintain. Similarly, the Aristotelian distinction between matters merely probable and those demonstrable has evaporated, at least in litigation, and probably in the sciences as well.
>
> Whether we like or not, jurors bring all their faculties to bear in making sense of a case: intuition, feeling, and attitude, as well as the ostensibly rational processes of inductive and deductive reasoning. Therefore, persuasion through evidence must reach all of these faculties.

As another way to see the choice of approach, consider that some legal cases are party-oriented and some are law (or rule)-oriented. The appellate advocate must choose. In turn, the appellee may wish to meet these arguments on their own terms or recast them to impose a different orientation.

A party-oriented argument asserts that the appellant deserves to win because it is worthy or is a victim of injustice. Such an argument seeks to brush away or minimize technicalities in the interest of doing substantial justice. Many appellate judges will go quite far to overlook procedural defaults and to find a favorable rule applicable for a party who seems to be in the right.

A rule-oriented (or law-oriented) argument emphasizes the importance of procedural and substantive rules that at times require a court to deny relief to an ostensibly deserving party or to reach a result that seems harsh or even foolish. The advocate is stressing the importance of consistency and of adherence to rules until the rules are changed in the proper manner.

An excellent example of a party-oriented argument is provided by Judge, later Justice, Cardozo's opinion in a celebrated contract case, *Jacob & Youngs, Inc v Kent*:[29]

> The plaintiff built a country residence for the defendant at a cost of upwards of $77,000, and now sues to recover a balance of $3,483.46, remaining unpaid. The work of construction ceased in June, 1914, and the defendant then began to occupy the dwelling. There was no complaint of defective performance until March 1915. One of the specifications for the plumbing work provides that "All wrought-iron pipe must be well

[29] 230 NY 239, 240-41, 129 NE 889, 890 (1921).

galvanized, lap welded pipe of the grade known as 'standard pipe' of Reading manufacture."

The defendant learned in March, 1915, that some of the pipe, instead of being made in Reading, was the product of other factories. The plaintiff was accordingly directed by the architect to do the work anew. The plumbing was then encased within the walls except in a few places where it had to be exposed. Obedience to the order meant more than the substitution of other pipe. It meant the demolition at great expense of substantial parts of the completed structure. The plaintiff left the work untouched, and asked for a certificate that the final payment was due. Refusal of the certificate was followed by this suit.

The issue on appeal was whether the trial court erred in excluding plaintiff's evidence that the pipe used was as good quality as that called for in the contract. As should be obvious from the way Judge Cardozo stated the facts, the plaintiff/appellant won. Strict principles of contract yielded to a judgment that the wealthy defendant was seeking an unfair advantage.

The case is an example of party-oriented advocacy triumphing over rule orientation. Judge Cardozo is an advocate, as are most authors of appellate opinions. He crafts the statements of facts as an advocate must, and engages the reader at the level on which the case will be decided. The defendant can afford a country residence costing $77,000 in 1914 dollars.[30] The complaint about the pipe seems to be an afterthought. The defendant's claim would require ripping out walls. Therefore, the strict rules of contract would yield and the plaintiff would be denied recovery.

By contrast, a rule-oriented argument prevailed in the Supreme Court's well-known snail darter case, *TVA v Hill.*[31] A provision of the Endangered Species Act, if literally applied, would have required shutting down an entire Tennessee Valley Authority dam project that might destroy the only habitat of a small fish, the snail darter. The Supreme Court held that the Act applied, despite the heavy financial and other consequences of terminating the dam project. Chief Justice Burger quoted from the Robert Bolt play, A Man for All Seasons, in stressing the importance that the law be applied as Congress had plainly written it.[32] This rule-oriented approach stresses systemic consequences of departing from a rule to meet the asserted hardship or necessity of the individual case.

Rule orientation may be seen in many opinions in the criminal law and procedure area. When a defendant on appeal contends that the right to counsel or the right to be free from unlawful search and seizure has been violated, there is usually little question that a crime has been committed. Often, the crime will be particularly brutal. The successful advocate will stress the importance of upholding the constitutional principles that underpin the various rights of a person charged with crime. The government will, while resisting such argu-

---

[30] I owe this perception of Cardozo's opinion to my colleague, Ed Sherman.

[31] 437 US 153 (1978).

[32] *Id* 195.

ments on their own terms, make sure to tell the court about the defendant's conduct.[33] This tension between party orientation and rule orientation can be seen in appellate opinions in which there is a dissent. The two sides often take positions that echo the parties' tactical choices.

An instructive Supreme Court decision is *Federated Department Stores, Inc v Moitie.*[34] The Supreme Court majority rejected a claimed exception to the doctrine of res judicata.[35] The respondent had convinced the court of appeals that a party who did not appeal an adverse judgment, and let that judgment become final, could benefit from the victory won by a coparty who did appeal and prevailed. The court of appeals had reasoned that the nonappealing party presumptively suffered the same legal wrong as did the party who did appeal and that "simple justice" required the court to extend the benefits of a victory won by others.

The Supreme Court's response well illustrates the point under discussion:

> [W]e do not see the grave injustice which would be done by the application of accepted principles of res judicata. "Simple justice" is achieved when a complex body of law developed over a period of years is evenhandedly applied. The doctrine of res judicata serves vital public interests beyond any individual judge's ad hoc determination of the equities in a particular case.[36]

The majority opinion was saying, in effect, that the evaluation of harms and benefits from the application of res judicata was made as the rule was being developed. The rule itself thus represents an accommodation of interests such as that asserted by the plaintiff and there is, therefore, no reason to discuss the asserted hardship to the plaintiff of applying the rule in this case. The judicial task is simply to see whether the plaintiff is precluded by the rule as it exists.

Two justices, while concurring in the judgment, could not join the majority opinion. They argued that the rules of res judicata must at times give way to "overriding concerns of public policy and simple justice,"[37] that is, the rule should be flexible enough to accommodate party-oriented advocacy.

There is nothing novel about the tension between rule orientation and party orientation. The distinction is similar to that conventionally drawn between law and equity.[38] In addition, the distinction may not be absolute: a court may

---

[33] This is an example of seeking to shift the court's focus away from the orientation urged by one's opponent. It is familiar ground to a reader of opinions by divided courts on issues of criminal procedure. For a similar analysis, see Alan D. Hornstein, Appellate Advocacy in a Nutshell 6-1 to -6 (1984).

[34] 452 US 394 (1981).

[35] *Id* 395, 398.

[36] *Id* 401.

[37] *Id* 403 (quoting 611 F2d at 1269).

[38] *See, e.g.*, Guaranty Trust Co v York, 326 US 99, 112-19 (1945) (Rutledge, J, dissenting, and insisting upon the equitable character of the relief requested as crucial to the matter in controversy).

strain to reinterpret a rule to avoid a harsh result for a party, while professing perfect obedience to the rule. The advocate must, however, make a choice. That choice will permit the brief to make a single coherent statement rather than being a disconnected jumble of arguments.

To be sure, a given case may find both sides opting for a party orientation or a rule orientation. These sides are not mutually exclusive: a choice by the appellant does not thrust the opponent into the opposite mode of argument. For example, in a contract case, both sides may face hardship if their interpretation of the law is not upheld. In a criminal case, the defendant on appeal may stress the favorable aspects of his or her conduct, while the prosecution dwells upon the social harm caused and upon the consequences to the victims.

Examples of this duality occur often in criminal procedure and civil rights cases. In both areas, the last decade has found judges less willing than formerly to protect constitutional rights.[39] The lawyer must understand this development to make arguments that will reach judges at a level at which they are willing to be persuaded. Arguments in such cases often contain elements of party orientation: the criminal defendant on appeal may stress the lack of evidence of guilt; the civil rights plaintiff on appeal will discuss the governmental wrongdoing that led to the lawsuit. However, both kinds of cases inescapably involve both sides in rule-oriented arguments that are counterposed to one another.

The civil rights plaintiff, who may or may not be sympathetic, stresses the formal legal guarantees of rights and the jurisdictional, procedural rules that have (at least since the post-Civil War period) been fashioned to enforce these guarantees. The criminal defendant also stresses the importance of protecting the rights of those who are the subject of police attention. The opponent in both cases makes a rule-oriented argument that has underlain much of the restrictive judicial interpretation of constitutional rights in both types of cases. He or she points to the institutional constraints upon federal courts[40] and to the consequences of broadly construing the asserted rights.

The opponent says, in short, that an open door to civil rights litigation threatens to overburden already crowded dockets. He or she may seek narrow interpretations of federal jurisdiction and justify those in terms of the limited jurisdiction of federal courts. This sort of rule orientation thus proceeds from assumptions about the powers and duties of federal courts that are quite different from those invoked by the plaintiff, but are nonetheless grounded in rule-based considerations that are independent of the merits of the particular dispute.

The civil rights defendant on appeal also will invoke various rule-oriented defenses, such as absolute or qualified immunity, that rest upon the institutional position of the defendant and not upon the character of his or her conduct upon a particular occasion.[41]

---

[39] *See generally* Michael E. Tigar, *Whose Rights? What Danger?*, 94 Yale LJ 970 (1985).

[40] For example, to concerns about federalism, see *id.*

[41] *See* Judge Higginbothan's analysis of immunity in Wyatt v Cole, 994 F2d 1113 1118-21 (5th Cir 1993), *on remand from* 112 S Ct 1827 (1992).

The prosecutor-appellee in a criminal procedure case may invoke similar considerations by arguing that a pro-defendant decision will promote post-conviction litigation. Such litigation is already the source of considerable judicial impatience[42] and many decisions of the past decade have narrowed the availability of such relief. These door-closing[43] decisions rest in large measure upon the asserted narrow base of federal jurisdiction and upon a decided rule-oriented preference for finality.

§9.07 —Good Writing Is Persuasive Writing

Good writing requires effort at two levels: (1) overall structure and (2) sentences and paragraphs. A brief has a formal structure dictated by the rules of appellate procedure and its nature as a persuasive document. Structure is discussed in each section of this chapter as it applies to each part of the brief.

This section deals with sentences and paragraphs. All too often, legal writing is to writing as legal reasoning is to reasoning: artificial, strained, and impenetrable to the uninitiated. All lawyers would benefit from reading any one, or more, of a dozen good books on writing.[44] Opinions by careful prose stylists also are worthy of study.[45] These works provide more complete guidance than can be given here.

There are some rules, however. First, get away from the dictated draft and from the pleadings file. Too many briefs appear to have been dictated from a combination of recalled testimony and the indexes of the pleadings and witness files. "The defendant then filed and brought on for hearing on the appointed day a motion in limine to preclude the prejudicial and irrelevant testimony concerning the plaintiff's surgical complications." And so on, with event after event strung out in relentless procession. In a common variation on this theme, the advocate states the facts in a series of paragraphs, each of which begins, "The next witness called by the government was. . . . " Outlining the record and the transcript is essential. Drafting a brief is a literary endeavor that requires translating that outline—or even a mental picture of events—into

---

[42] *See, e.g.,* Stone v Powell, 428 US 465 (1976).

[43] Remarks of Associate Justice Brennan, Fifth Circuit Judicial Conference, May 1984, cited in Micheal E. Tigar, *supra* note 39.

[44] *See, e.g.,* William Strunk, Jr & Elwynn B. White, The Elements of Style (3d ed 1979); Herbert E. Read, English Prose Style (1980); Richard C. Wydick, Plain English for Lawyers (2d ed 1985).

[45] Among noteworthy stylists are Carolyn King and Patrick Higginbotham of the Fifth Circuit, Stephen Reinhardt and Alex Kozinksi of the Ninth Circuit, and Richard Posner of the Seventh Circuit.

Other good works on brief writing include Albert Tate, Jr, *The Art of Brief-Writing: What a Judge Wants to Read,* ABA Section of Litigation, The Litigation Manual 229 (1983); Christopher H. Hoving, *The Art of the Appellate Brief,* 72 ABAJ 52 (Jan 1986); Eugene Gressman, *Winning on Appeal: The Shalls and Shall Nots of Effective Criminal Advocacy,* 1 Crim Just 10 (Winter 1987); Harry Pregerson, *The Seven Sins of Appellate Brief Writing and Other Transgressions,* 34 UCLA L Rev 431 (1986) (excellent advice on brief-writing and valuable guide to appellate practice in the Ninth Circuit).

prose designed to encapsulate past events for a reader and hold that reader's interest.

Second, to quote the best advice in an excellent book on writing, "Omit needless words."[46] Use simple declarative sentences. Experts on language tell us that when meaning is embedded in complex phrasing, the reader or hearer is quickly lost.[47] Consider this sentence: "The officer testified *that* he took a sample *of* the breath *of* the defendant to test for *the presence* of traces *of* fumes of alcohol." Every italicized word identifies a connective word or words that embed, or mask, communication. When a modifier is used with a preposition, instead of being placed with the word modified, the sentence is weakened: "alcohol fumes" instead of "fumes of alcohol." Whenever a connective must be used, strike out its excess baggage: "the presence of," in the example, but also "in terms of," "the fact that," and other offenders. Go through the draft looking for remnants of tautological lawyerspeak: "The learned trial judge ordered and decreed . . . " One verb is enough to power that sentence, particularly if the baggage-word *learned* is jettisoned.

Third, speak as directly to the audience as style and custom permit. Like the style manual of this publisher, custom does not permit the advocate, in writing a brief, to say "you" and "your" in referring to the intended audience. It is "this court's teaching" in a prior case and not "your teaching." But get as close as good manners will allow. "This court's holding in . . . " is much better than "It was held in. . . . "

Fourth, speak of real people, not of categories. The plaintiff, defendant, and witnesses have names. Use them. A busy judge or law clerk might forget whether a witness was called by one side or the other, or might even get the plaintiff and defendant confused in the midst of a densely written argument. One may include an occasional subtle reminder by repeating a phrase such as "the plaintiff Mr. Smith." By the way, all people in judicial proceedings have titles, such as Mr., Ms., and so on; they are not simply surnames. This is particularly important in personifying a criminal defendant.

Fifth, avoid the passive voice. Write sentences in which people are doing things. This is a more general statement of rule 3. "It was testified that Mr. Smith failed to inspect the coupling before the day shift reported for work" is twice weakened by "It was testified that." First, the passive phrase does not tell us who testified, which may be important. Second, the sentence may be a missed opportunity to tell the reader something important about Mr. Smith's error. If a governmental agency investigated and concluded that Mr. Smith erred, the sentence should reflect that. If Mr. Smith is the plaintiff-appellant, if contributory negligence is an issue, and if the advocate is the appellee, then the sentence might read, "Several witnesses testified, and the jury could well conclude, that Mr. Smith failed to inspect the coupling before the day shift reported for work."

---

[46] William Strunk & Elwyn B. White, *supra* note 44, at 23.

[47] The same issue is raised by police-citizen confrontations. *See* Michael E. Tigar, *Crime on Camera,* Litig 24 (Fall 1982).

Sixth, get rid of jargon. Most lawyers have cars. They drive to meet people or to keep appointments. Yet when required to write a brief about government agents making an arrest, they insist that the police responded to the scene, exited their vehicles, and effected arrests. Would it be better to write: "On January 14, 1987, John Doe opened his front door. On the steps stood five government agents, armed with everything except a search warrant." By careful editing, every stilted lawyer word can be purged. It sometimes helps to read the draft out loud because most lawyers use less jargon in ordinary speech.

Seventh, put away the sugar bowl, the saccharine pills, the purple crayon, the cliché mill, and the metaphor gun. Sickly sweet, sophomoric, cliché-ridden writing, studded with inapt metaphors, is unpersuasive. The quiet force of facts, arrayed in active declarative sentences, will bear the argument along.

Eighth, watch out for humor and sarcasm. The only people entitled to be funny are the judges, and everyone will laugh at their jokes. The advocates' attempt at humor may come off as churlish or forced. Be eliquent, but dignified.

Finally, although it has been said before, be accurate. This canon is only partly one of style. The deadliest retort, from opponent or judge, is that a fact is misstated or exaggerated,[48] or that an authority is miscredited or—worse yet—has been overruled. Credibility lost by such carelessness is not easily regained, if at all.

§9.08 Appellant's or Petitioner's Opening Brief— Selecting Issues and Order of Presentation

The decision to appeal has been made, as discussed in Chapter 5. Usually, however, the final selection of issues on appeal is not made until after the record has been combed and digested. Why should this case be one of the less than 20 per cent of federal appeals to result in reversal? If the advocate can answer that question in one or two brief, cogent paragraphs, he or she is well on the way to identifying and ordering the issues in the opening brief.

Unless the lawyer is "soloing" on the appeal, an open-ended discussion is the best means to make these decisions. And even the solo lawyer should search out someone with whom to rehearse the issues, perhaps a law clerk or another lawyer.

A brief memorandum should be prepared for the meeting, outlining the facts and possible legal theories. The theories should be broken down as indicated in Chapter 5: legal errors, factual errors, and procedural errors. The memorandum should note whether any proposed claims of error were not raised and preserved in the trial court or agency.

Lawyers are afraid of cutting down the number of issues presented on an appeal. They are afraid of missing something. This is a valid fear, but lawyers

---

[48] Another reason for being careful in stating facts is illustrated by City Natl Bank v United States, 907 F2d 536 (5th Cir 1990) (court of appeals may, in its discretion, treat statements in briefs as binding judicial admissions).

are trained and paid to make judgments. It cannot be repeated too often: this appellate brief may win or lose the case. An advocate does not enhance the chances of winning by throwing in marginal issues.

If the lawyers discussing the appeal are those who tried the case, it will be more difficult to gain the needed distance from the trial process and evaluate the merits and importance of issues on appeal. Being in trial is exhilarating and enervating. The courtroom battles that loom largest in memory are those that filled one with a particular sense of triumph or defeat at the time. These will not be the battles that necessarily produce the best issues for appeal, or the ones that replay well—or even interestingly—on the cold record. Too, trial lawyers cannot survive without huge egos. Wounds to the trial lawyer's ego are not the stuff of which appeals are made. Theoretically, only unjustified wounds to the client's liberty or pocketbook are fair game in the court of appeals.

One is not free to compromise by raising issues in a kind of laundry list in the brief, without discussion. As noted in **§1.01,** an issue tersely and uninformatively mentioned is not preserved, and the court is free to disregard it.[49] Another major theme of discussion must be the increased judicial reliance upon the harmless error rule in civil and criminal cases.[50] Deference is the watchword of appellate judges with busy dockets. Appellate judges look for a way to find the district judge fundamentally right. They strain to disregard errors that did not deprive a party of a fundamentally fair trial and would not if corrected on remand or retrial reshape the outcome. As noted elsewhere in this book,[51] this rule of deference yields at times in compelling cases. But it must dominate the discussion of issues for the brief.

The rule of deference looks to the merits. For this reason, one should pay close attention to any issue of fact worthy of appellate consideration. For example, suppose the issues are sufficiency of the evidence, an error of law in the jury charge, and a procedural point concerning voir dire. While the general rule is that jury charges are read as a whole,[52] every appellate court knows the importance of properly instructing the jury on the elements of the claims and defenses involved in the lawsuit.[53] An instruction error, if preserved by proper objection, is therefore a good candidate for top billing in the appellate brief.

However, even with such an issue, the sufficiency point should have pride of place if the lawyer can, without exaggeration and after careful review of the record, argue persuasively that the judgment below is not supported by the

---

[49] Judge Posner's remark in United States v Dunkel, 927 F2d 955, 956 (7th Cir 1991), *affd,* 986 F2d 1425 (7th Cir 1993), that "[j]udges are not like pigs, hunting for truffles buried in briefs" (as quoted in **§1.01**) is worth remembering—for more than one reason.

[50] *See* **§§5.01-5.13.**

[51] **§§5.13, 2.18.**

[52] *See* **§§5.04, 5.07.**

[53] *Id.*

evidence.[54] If the sufficiency point is marginal or doubtful, then the legal argument should go first and counsel should, in the summary of argument and in introducing the sufficiency point, note that the error of law misdirected the trier of fact. The evidence may not be insufficient to support the judgment, but counsel must argue that the legal error could have made a difference in a factual dispute that was fairly debatable.

A final canon of choice is: give preference to issues that decide the whole case rather than pieces of it. While there is no jurisdictional bar to the court considering an issue that does not result in reversal of the entire judgment, there are strong prudential reasons for leading with the larger issues. First, courts of appeals have discretion to refuse review of nondispositive issues under certain circumstances. Second, the attention span of judges and law clerks is no different, on the average, from that of ordinary mortals. To hold the reader's attention, a brief must start strong.

§9.09 —Statement of Subject Matter and Appellate Jurisdiction

Under Fed R App P 28(a), as amended in 1993, a statement of of subject matter and appellate jurisdiction is mandatory in every appellant's opening brief. Some circuits had routinely required such a statement before the amendment, and it was always a counsel of prudence to show the court why it had jurisdiction. This was usually done in the Statement of the Case, when describing the proceedings below. The rule provision simply underscores the importance of jurisdictional issues.[55]

The proper form of the statement should be short and informative, containing all the elements required by the rule. In a civil case, the first part can track the language of the complaint in the court below.[56] The second part tells the court what statute authorizes it to act. For example:

> The district court had jurisdiction of this civil action under 28 USC §1331 because of the parties' diverse citizenship. This appeal is from a final judgment for defendant, entered April 14, 1993. The judgment disposed of the entire case as to all issues and all parties. A timely notice of appeal was filed May 5, 1993. This court has jurisdiction under 28 USC §1291.

---

[54] For discussion of the related question of choosing points for oral argument, see **§10.05.**

[55] See **ch 2** on appellate jurisdiction generally, and **ch 5** on how jurisdictional issues are raised and decided at the threshold of the appeal.

[56] Fed R Civ P 8(a) requires that the complaint begin with a "short and plain statement" of the court's jurisdiction.

Modify the statement to provide complete information. If post-trial motions complicated the issue of time to appeal, briefly describe that process.[57] If the judgment disposed of less than the entire case, tell the court and explain under what statutory provisions it has jurisdiction. Using the provisions of Chapters 2 and 3, let the court know that the issue of jurisdiction has been thoroughly thought out.

This jurisdictional statement will be scrutinized closely by the clerk's office, with the help of staff attorneys. It will be on their agenda after routine questions such as timeliness, proper color cover, organization of the brief, and page limitations have been answered.

§9.10 —Statement of Issues Presented

Federal Rule of Appellate Procedure 28(a)(2) requires "[a] statement of the issues presented for review." Far too many brief writers fall into one of two errors: (1) they reproduce the headings from the body of the brief; or (2) they state the issue in terms so general as to be useless. Both errors are annoying to the reader and both represent missed opportunities for effective advocacy.

The headings in the brief already appear there and in the table of contents. There is no reason to repeat them; Rule 28 does not, one should assume, ask an advocate to do an idle act. The statement of issues is there for a purpose.

Generalized issue statements give the reader no guide as to what follows. Consider, for example, a typical statement: "Whether there was probable cause for the defendant's arrest." Contrast a more effective statement: "Whether there was probable cause for a warrantless arrest, in a public restaurant, based upon the largely uncorroborated tip of an anonymous informant, when the tip had been contradicted by other information obtained by the arresting officers."

Some other examples:

GOOD	NOT GOOD
"Whether Santobello v New York, [cite], requires specific performance of [appellant]'s plea bargain, and dismissal of the indictment.	Whether the defendant's plea bargain was breached.

The preferred form sets forth an issue that is specific to this case. It alerts the court to a Supreme Court decision that is well known and that the advocate asserts controls this case. It identifies the precise remedy sought—specific performance and dismissal. It personalizes the argument by including the appellant's name.

Here is an example from a civil case:

---

[57] *See* **§6.03.**

GOOD	NOT GOOD
Whether the district court abused its authority in imposing a receivership on a limited partnership when the moving party presented no evidence of dissipation of assets or of the inability of the general partner to manage the affairs of the limited partnership under an injunction that had already been entered.	Whether the district court erred in appointing a receiver to manage the affairs of the partnership.

In the preferred form, the advocate is signalling the argument that will be made: an objection to the appointment of a receiver. Such an order is within the equitable discretion of a federal district judge under certain circumstances. However, here the claim is that the judge failed to balance the equities. The advocate is saying that the injunction adequately protects the movant, and that there is no evidence to the contrary that would justify the (arguably) extreme step of removing the general partner from the management of the business.

Of course, the issues presented should not be so unwieldy or laden with detail as to be impenetrable. The discussion at **§9.07** of levels of meaning in advocates' prose applies here as well. The example given just above is probably about as long as an issue should be.

An advocate is free to make a statement of issue that is more than a single sentence, if breaking it down will add clarity. Here is an example from the Fifth Circuit's helpful guide:[58]

GOOD	NOT GOOD
The defendant was charged with conspiracy to import cocaine. The judge was requested to charge the jury that the prosecution must prove that the defendant had the intent to join a conspiracy and did so knowingly. The court refused to do so. Was this error?	Did the district court err in failing to give a requested jury charge concerning specific intent?

A somewhat different view is expressed by Chief Judge John C. Godbold, in his article, Twenty Pages and Twenty Minutes—Effective Advocacy on Appeal. The advocate is well advised to heed the views of appellate judges on the rules for effective advocacy: as the aphorism has it, to know how best to catch fish, one should ask fish and not fishermen. Judge Godbold writes:

---

[58] Fifth Circuit Rep, July 1985.

> Compare these two statements of an issue:
>
> (1) The plaintiff was not contributorily negligent when, as plaintiff was on his way to church, defendant's 6-ton Mack truck thundered through the red light and upon plaintiff's Pinto automobile at the intersection of 8th and North streets in Savannah, Georgia, on February 2, 1974.
>
> (2) The trial judge was plainly erroneous in entering a finding of fact that the plaintiff was guilty of contributory negligence.
>
> There is everything wrong with (1). Whether the truck ran the light and struck the plaintiff's automobile, or plaintiff ran the light and drove in front of the truck, was a disputed question of fact on which the entire contributory negligence question turned. The references to defendant's six-ton truck, to plaintiff's Pinto automobile, and to plaintiff's being on the way to church, were sophomoric appeals to prejudice and sympathy. These matters had already been set out in the statement of facts and none had any relevance to the contributory negligence issue. There was only one accident, so the names of the city and of the streets and the date were of no significance except to designate the state in a diversity case.
>
> The greatest fault, however, in the first statement is that the reader cannot discern the message that the writer is attempting to communicate. Does he mean that the trial judge found contributory negligence and that this finding was plainly erroneous? Or, does he mean that there was a jury finding of contributory negligence not supported by sufficient evidence? Or, does he mean that there was no evidence of contributory negligence, so that as a matter or law the plaintiff was not guilty of it? Or, is he attempting to say that there was some evidence of contributory negligence but not enough to submit to a jury? Compare example (2) where in a short and simple statement the court is told everything it needs to know without more.[59]

Judge Godbold is certainly right in castigating example (1), which goes on at length without clarifying the message the advocate wants to send. As the tone of his criticism suggests, such verbosity is not merely unnecessary; it has a negative impact on the tribunal.

However, example (2) could—in this author's view—be improved. It does not comply with the Fifth Circuit's suggestions, for it does not clearly identify which formulation of the contributory negligence issue counsel is presenting. If the case was jury-waived, and the trial judge found contributory negligence, the issue might better be framed:

> Whether in a nonjury trial, the trial judge was clearly erroneous in finding the plaintiff guilty of contributory negligence.

If the facts warrant, a further explanation might be added: "when it was undisputed that plaintiff's failure to keep a proper lookout was not a contribut-

---

[59] 30 Sw LJ 801, 813-14 (1976) (Copyright 1976 by Southern Methodist University. Reprinted with permission from Southwestern Law Journal).

ing cause of the accident." This suggested formulation lets the court know that it is to review the findings in a nonjury case, it identifies the finding, and it acknowledges that the proper standard of review, derived from Fed R Civ P 52(a),[60] is clearly erroneous. The added detail, if the facts warrant, is neither otiose nor sophomoric: it keys the court to something that may separate this review of the factual findings case from many another.

§9.11 —Statement of the Case

Federal Rule of Appellate Procedure P 28(a)(4)[61] requires a "statement of the case," consisting of three elements: "the nature of the case," "the course of proceedings and its disposition in the court below," and a "statement of the facts" with record references. The appellant's statement of the case is the most difficult part of the brief to craft, particularly in a long or complex case. In some measure, this difficulty is the inevitable product of the rules respecting review of factual determinations. The appellant, by definition, was the loser in the court or agency below. The statement of the case presents facts. The factual determinations of the court or agency, with few exceptions, are given great deference by the court of appeals. Therefore, the appellant is presenting his or her view of the facts to judges who are institutionally committed to being skeptical about the appellant's version.

This institutional bias can be overcome only if one acknowledges the verdict-loser's burden and shoulders it honestly.[62] The present question is one simply of organization. The statement of the case, as suggested by Fed R App P 28, should be divided into subheadings reflecting the elements that the rule requires, plus any special requirements of the circuit rules. These subheadings would usually be: "Nature of the Case, Course of Proceedings and Disposition Below," and "Statement of Facts." In addition, the statement of facts should be broken down into subheadings. These subheadings break the narrative into manageable segments, like the internal headings used in good journalistic writing. To appreciate the use of this sort of subheading, the advocate should study a well-written newspaper such as the Wall Street Journal.[63]

---

[60] *See* **§5.04.**

[61] The full text of Fed R App P 28 is in **app A.**

[62] This is a question of standard of review. *See* **§§5.01-5.13.**

[63] For example, here are the subheadings from the brief on appeal for appellant London in United States v Wallach, 935 F2d 445 (2d Cir 1991):

A. Cast of Characters
B. London's Background and Introduction to Wedtech
C. Meetings and Agreements Between Wedtech and London
D. London's Services for Wedtech
E. Payment of the $1 Million and London's Invoice
F. Wedtech "Restructures the Transaction": Guariglia Again
G. London's Dealings with Chinn During 1985 and 1986
H. $99,999.98 to IFCI
I. Trial Events, Trial Results
J. Guariglia Unmasked, Besmirched, Whitewashed

A second use of subheadings is to identify the portions of the statement of facts that relate to particular issues on appeal. On appeal from a criminal conviction, if the appellant is claiming that the indictment fails to state an offense, that there was variance between indictment and proof, that there was an unlawful search, and that the evidence is insufficient to sustain the conviction, separate subheadings should mark off the facts relative to these arguments. Subheadings would include "The Allegations of the Indictment," "The Unlawful Search of Defendant's Home and Office," and "The Evidence at Trial."

If the argument will be party-oriented, the appellant should also include a brief description of the defendant. This can appear either as the first subheading in the statement of facts or in the discussion of the nature of the case. Here are examples of sentences introducing a client:

Criminal case: "The appellant, Jane Doe, is a 69-year-old woman of previously unblemished reputation, having made a success in oil, cattle, cutting horse, and other business endeavors." Or, for a less affluent client: "The appellant, Richard Roe, is a 25-year-old borderline mentally retarded man who, as the evidence showed, is unduly susceptible to the dominance of others."

Civil case: "Alice Poe, who was seriously injured in an industrial accident at the factory where she had worked for ten years, appeals from a judgment entered on a verdict in favor of her employer; she argues that the jury was improperly instructed and that the verdict is against the overwhelming weight of the evidence." Or, for the other side, "Multinational, Inc., appeals from a judgment entered upon a jury verdict for $5 million in a case involving an injury to plaintiff's hand from which he had, by the time of trial, completely recovered."

These brief introductions can help to identify the people in the case. One point to recall is that the appeal is not being brought by the lawyer, but by a person—the appellant—who is seeking justice.

The next step, after identifying the elements of the statement, is to determine the order in which these elements will be arranged. The statement must be coherent, in the sense that the narrative flows from beginning to end.[64] It must also be tied to the points to be made in the argument section of the brief. For example, the disposition of a pretrial motion generally will be discussed early in the statement of facts. However, if the argument section claims that the disposition was error, and if the advocate has decided to make that claim subordinate to a claim concerning sufficiency of the evidence, then a subheading on "Pretrial Motions" may logically follow the discussion of evidence at trial. By breaking the statement of facts with subheadings, the advocate can use the word processor to rearrange the order in editing the brief.[65]

Lawyers who know how to present a statement of facts in opening to a jury often forget their craft when writing a brief. The tasks of opening and fact stating are similar; they are defined by the nature of the litigation process. A lawsuit

---

[64] *See* **§9.06.**

[65] *See* **§9.04.**

is about facts that occurred at a past time in the external world. Those past facts do not recreate themselves. The trier finds the facts by making inferences from the testimony of witnesses and from documents and objects.[66]

The lawyer's summary of facts is both (1) a reference to the real time past events that brought about the case, and (2) a commentary upon the reliability and meaning of the direct and circumstantial evidence that is assembled for trial. How much of each aspect the advocate stresses depends upon how contested the facts are. Put another way, the advocate must discuss the facts, considered as external events, and the evidence, considered as the fallible recollection of witnesses and the arguable significance of documents and other tangible objects.

Consider, for example, a tax fraud criminal case in which the sole defense is "advice of counsel," that is, the defendant claimed that he reported his income and tax incorrectly because, having made full disclosure to an attorney, he was (wrongly) advised to report that way.[67] In such a case, the overstatement of deductions or understatement of income is conceded, as is the deficiency in tax.[68] Part of the statement of facts will, therefore, be a narrative of real time events about which there is no dispute. This portion of the statement may carry the subheading "The Conceded Underreporting," and begin with "Mr. __________ does not dispute that he underpaid his 1980 income tax."

In discussing the disputed question of intent, however, the advocate will focus on the evidence that bears upon intent, and assess its reliability. The contours of this discussion will depend on the way in which the disputed issue of advice of counsel is presented. If the trial judge refused a proposed jury instruction, the advocate need only show that the evidence raised a fair question on the issue.[69] If the defense was presented to the jury, the advocate must demonstrate that a reasonable juror could not have found guilt beyond a reasonable doubt;[70] the advocate's discussion must not only assess the evidence, but must also evince awareness of the proper standard of review.

Whether a particular part of the discussion is of facts or of evidence, the advocate must seek the thematic unity and clarity that characterize a good opening statement. To be sure, a written statement of facts is more formal than an oral opening. The differences are obvious: in a brief, one expects more precision of expression, avoidance of dramatic flourishes, and detailed citations to the record. But if the idea of narrative, of telling a story, is grasped early, it will not be difficult to edit for these qualities. A draft that begins by making the errors highlighted in this section is probably unsalvageable.

Some factual discussions should be deferred to the section of the brief that deals with the legal issue to which the facts relate. A complex search and sei-

---

[66] *See* Michael E. Tigar, Examining Witnesses 18-22 (1993).

[67] The defendant would therefore be defending on the basis of "advice of counsel" negating specific intent. *See* Edward J. Devitt, Charles B. Blackmar, Michael A. Wolff, & Kevin F. O'Malley, Federal Jury Practice & Instructions §19.08 (4th ed 1992).

[68] On elements of tax evasion, see generally *id* §56.03.

[69] *See* **§5.08.**

[70] *See* **§5.07.**

zure, administrative procedure, or statutory construction issue may be incomprehensible unless the facts and the legal discussion are united.

Deferral courts risks, however. When judges, preparing for oral argument or for decisions on the summary (nonargument) calendar, sit down with the briefs, they often look first at the statements of facts in the appellant's and appellee's briefs.[71] They may get a feel for the case based on these statements. In a case involving factual disputes, where the standard of review is *clearly erroneous,* the respective statements of facts carry strong initial weight. The reviewing judge is alert for reasons to find the district judge correct. It is, in such cases, risky to defer a crucial factual discussion to the body of the brief.

When deciding whether to defer a factual discussion, the advocate should ask self-critically whether the preference for deferral arises from the difficulty of editing the statement of facts into a coherent whole or from a genuine tactical choice.

A final and related point: the statement of facts must be both accurate and filled with helpful citations to the record. In circuits that use a joint appendix or record excerpts system, the advocate must make sure that the statement of facts meshes with the appendix or excerpts.[72] The judges will have these easily accessible along with the briefs. In any circuit, every factual assertion must be backed up with a record reference.

Detailed citation of the record serves also the subliminal purpose of demonstrating that the advocate knows his or her case and is not afraid of the facts. It is a challenge to the opponent to unearth an error. If the challenge is not accepted, the failure may not go unnoticed.[73]

---

[71] *See generally* Talk Given by Judges Rubin and Higginbotham at the Appellate Advocacy Seminar Sponsored by the Bar Association of the Fifth Federal Circuit on October 16, 1984, 2 Fifth Cir Rep 143, 147-48 (1985).

[72] This means that the statement of facts must contain proper and detailed citations to the appendix, the record excerpts, and/or the record—depending on the record-handling method in the particular circuit. Absent such citations, the court may disregard challenges to the evidence. *See, e.g.,* Holmberg v Baxter Healthcare Corp, 901 F2d 1387 (7th Cir 1990) (references in brief to non-record matters stricken; Fed R App P 10 not appropriate means to add matters to appellate record that were not considered by the district court); Lemelson v United States, 752 F2d 1538 (Fed Cir 1985) (court will not review admissibility of evidence where brief does not cite offers of proof and arguments on admissibility from the record); United States v Gleason, 726 F2d 385, 388 (8th Cir 1984) (attorney's argument that was too general and did not point to "specific testimony that was improperly excluded" violated Fed R App P 28(e). *Compare* Balistreri v Pacifica Police Dept, 901 F2d 696 (9th Cir 1990), *disagreed with on other grounds sub nom* DeShaney v Winnebago County Dept of Social Servs, 489 US 189 (1989) (failure of pro se litigant to comply with technical requirements of Fed R App P 28 concerning form of brief excused; discussion of rationale).

[73] *See* United States v Williams, 952 F2d 418, 421-22 (DC Cir) (reprimanding Government for material misstatements of record), *cert denied,* 113 S Ct 148 (1992); Holcomb v Colony Bay Coal Co, 852 F2d 792, 797 (4th Cir 1988) (charging double costs to attorney for misstating the record in his brief and oral agreement).

The full record is, of course, available to the judges and their law clerks. Few judges take the time to read it, however, and most do not even have their law clerks do so unless and until that judge is assigned the task of writing an opinion.[74] By that time, of course, the case is decided.

§9.12 —Summary of Argument

Federal Rule of Appellate Procedure 28(a)(5) states: "The argument may be preceded by a summary"; the rules of many circuits require a summary of the argument.[75]

This will be the last substantive part of the brief the advocate writes. If the headings on sections of the brief, which are reproduced in the Table of Contents, are informative, and if the issues presented are well drawn, then one may query the necessity of a summary of argument. In circuits that do not require one, the advocate may choose not to bother.

However, if the brief contains one or more long and complex arguments, a summary can be useful and should be included. Of course, if the circuit's rules require it, there is no choice. The summary should be no more than 5 to 7 per cent of the length of the argument, that is, if the argument portion of the brief consumes 20 pages, the summary should be no more than two or three. This is a challenge, not to be avoided by simply repeating the issues presented or the headings in the brief.

The summary of argument represents a unique opportunity to give an overview of the entire case and of some or all of the issues. Here is a sample introductory paragraph from a case challenging some Selective Service regulations on many constitutional and administrative law grounds:

> In a multifaceted attack upon the delinquency power which the Selective Service System has arrogated to itself, the argument below contends that the delinquency regulations are invalid on their face and as applied to the petitioner.

Another opening might be:

> The appellant Mary Doe argues that the jury's verdict in this case was based upon insufficient evidence; she was entitled to recover. Not only that: the trial judge wrongly admitted evidence of offers in compromise, failed to give a requested instruction on negligence per se, and misapplied Georgia law in allocating the burden of persuasion.

This sort of introduction to the summary lets the court know that the issues are interrelated, a function fulfilled by no other part of the brief.[76]

---

[74] *See* **§10.13.**

[75] For the full text of Fed R App P 28(a)(5), which was amended in 1993, see **app A.**

[76] The summary picks up the thematic note that one has sounded in the "Nature of the Case" part of the "Statement of the Case." *See* **§9.11.**

In what follows, each argument in the brief must be encapsulated in a paragraph. This is the advocate's chance to single out the most important aspect of each argument and telegraph it to the judge. The best illustration of how to approach this task is to examine how the reader—the judge—will probably use the summary.[77]

In 1985, two court of appeals judges of different political persuasions and different backgrounds held an informal seminar on how they read through a stack of briefs that comes in about once a month. They described an argument calendar of 20 cases. This would mean a minimum of 60 briefs—appellants', appellees', and reply briefs. This would represent about 2500 pages of briefs; record excerpts would add to the total.

One judge described his method: "I take the 20 [sets of briefs] and give them a cursory reading; to get a feel for them. . . . I start reading the briefs and making notes to myself so at the end I have a little bench memorandum to myself. I will read the lead cases. . . . " The other judge's method was similar, except he uses a dictating machine while reading and asks his clerk to photocopy the leading cases.

These stories suggest that the summary must contain citations to the most important cases (and perhaps statutes and, rarely, other authorities) supporting the advocate's position. For example, in a criminal case, rather than simply saying that the district judge improperly amended the indictment, the summary should say that he or she did so contrary to the holding in a particular case.

The citation of these leading cases cannot take the place of a summary, for one cannot assume that the judges remember the facts and holding of every case ever decided. Usually, the citation must be followed by a short parenthetical that summarizes the key holding of the case, like the parentheticals used throughout this book.

The summary must set out the argument in capsule form. The cases should be cited illustratively. The choice of cases is dictated by answering the question: "What 'leading cases' would I want the judges to single out and read on their first trip through this brief?"

§9.13 —Argument on Issues Presented

The previous sections have described the preparation to write an argument, suggested some ways to organize a law office to maximize efficient brief production, provided guidance on selecting issues on appeal, and discussed writing style in general terms. This section discusses the strategy and tactics of making a winning argument.

The first canon of appellate advocacy is that advocacy is not memorandum writing. It is designed to persuade, to grasp the claimed error rather than lead through the thickets of doctrine to a promised insight. General principles doubtless belong in some arguments, for sometimes a result is more conge-

---

[77] The DC Circuit requires counsel to mark authorities principally relied on with an asterisk (*) in the Table of Authorities. This identifies the lead cases.

nial—or less uncongenial—if it can be seen to fit with an established body of doctrine. But generalization from the principle that rules the case at hand usually should follow, rather than precede, the main body of the argument.[78]

Thus, each point on appeal will be in a separate section, identified with a roman numeral. Each section will have a descriptive heading. Subheadings will mark off the segregable portions of the argument to guide the reader. Subheadings also let the reader find a particular point more quickly by reference to the table of contents. For the author, subheadings make the editing process easier and permit the author to cross-reference from one part of the brief to another with reasonable precision and without using page numbers.

There is no talismanic guide for organizing the argument section of the brief. The pecularities of a given case, along with the advocate's informed discretion, are the ultimate arbiters. What follows is a basic guideline that will meet the lawyer's needs 90 per cent of the time.

Each point should begin with a paragraph or two that summarize the claim of error and the facts that underpin it. For example:

> Mr. Johnson's counsel requested a burden-shifting res ipsa loquitor jury instruction. Defense counsel objected and the trial judge refused the instruction. The trial judge was thus led into reversible error, for Connecticut law has long required such an instruction in defective food cases.[79] This error of law is reviewed de novo.

It may seem unnecessary to say *reversible error,* or to tell the court that the issue is to be reviewed de novo. It is not. Some courts of appeals, such as the Ninth Circuit,[80] require that each argument be preceded by stating the standard of review. Even in the absence of such a requirement, the advocate should acknowledge the appropriate standard. For example, for an insufficiency of evidence point, the standard of deference to the trier of fact would be mentioned.[81]

Logically, the first subheading—unless circuit rules dictate that one begin with standard of review—should state the underlying facts in enough additional detail to provide all the information the court will need to decide the point. This recital can refer back to the appropriate subheading in the statement of the case. As with the statement of facts itself, this discussion can focus upon either the facts that give rise to the point being made, or upon the evidence of those facts, or both. In any case, this discussion must be spare, accurate, and adversarial.

In the next subheading, the advocate should discuss the legal principles that specifically support the position being taken. This discussion must include:

---

[78] The advocate must bear the page limits in mind when mapping the brief. Courts of appeals are increasingly reluctant to grant waivers of the limits, except in the case of consolidated briefs.

[79] *See* Prosser & Keeton on the Law of Torts §39, at 245 n40 (W. Page Keeton 5th ed 1984).

[80] 9th Cir R 28-2.5.

[81] *See* §§**5.04** (civil cases), **5.07** (criminal cases).

(1) the legal principle the advocate asserts; (2) the authorities that support that principle, with enough discussion to identify the important passages; (3) an identification and appreciation of the relevant standard of review; and (4) a candid assessment of whether the issue was properly preserved in the trial court. Each of these elements deserves discussion.

The legal principle should be put in the words the advocate hopes the court will use in deciding the case his or her way. It may be presented in several parts that build to a conclusion. For example, in a search and seizure case, the affidavit in support of the application for a search warrant may be based on stale information, may not establish probable cause, and may contain false information. The discussion of legal principle will set out each of these infirmities, accompanied by citations.

The authorities on which the advocate relies will, one should presume, not be familiar to the reviewing court. Most court of appeals judges do not carry around in memory all the significant cases on every issue. And, the court should not have to guess on which passage or holding the advocate relies. The advocate must provide specific identification. Two good rules are: no string citations and no lengthy quotations. String citations do not tell the court anything about why the particular case is important. The only possible reason to use them is to illustrate an assertion that a given principle has been repeatedly applied without criticism, perhaps in a number of jurisdictions whose cases are cited or in a number of learned treatises that are listed. At a minimum, citations should contain "jump page" citations to the relevant language. Lengthy quotations are a signal to many readers to skip over the quoted material. A few words, or a sentence or two, are enough to convey the thought. Often, a better way to explain a citation is to borrow from a standard law review technique and put a few explanatory words in parentheses after the citation.

Sometimes one case will be on "all fours." That case should be highlighted by "stating it" and drawing a comparison to the case at hand. A typical form would be, "This case is controlled by this court's decision in A v B. In that case, [here state the pertinent facts of A v B in a sentence or two at the most]. This court held [here state the holding, including a quoted phrase if possible]."

In choosing authorities, the first source will always be Supreme Court cases, followed by decisions in the same circuit. As the Fifth Circuit guide puts it:

> Cite authority for each legal proposition. This will not only support your statement but will enable the panel members to authenticate it. The most helpful citations are decisions by the Supreme Court, the Fifth Circuit Court of Appeals, and, in diversity cases, decisions of the appropriate state courts. In addition, it is helpful to give citations to the decisions of other federal courts of appeals, authoritative texts (e.g. Wigmore on Evidence Moore's Federal Practice, Wright & Miller, Federal Practice), and law review articles. If other circuits have decided a question, but this circuit has not, you must cite the other decisions whether or not they support

> your position. Chain citations are never helpful and should be avoided. Lengthy footnotes should also be avoided.[82]

The reason for citing direct authority from other circuits is that most courts of appeal have a formal or informal policy of avoiding intercircuit conflicts, if possible. If a decision will conflict with that of another circuit, the judges may take an informal en banc poll before issuing a panel decision.

To what extent may the advocate rely upon dicta in reported cases, or observations made in explaining holdings? *United States v Oshatz,*[83] provides some guidance. Judge Jon Newman, writing for the court, acknowledged that:

> not every observation contained in an opinion of this Court deserves to be regarded as the law of the Circuit. Opinion authors frequently express thoughts peripheral to the holding of a case, and these thoughts do not bind the Circuit, nor even the concurring judges on the panel. If every phrase in an opinion were accorded binding effect, there would be a tendency either to refine language with such meticulous care as to imperil the prompt disposition of the Court's work or to reduce opinions to bare pronouncements of holdings.[84]

Judge Newman's eloquence and candor tell the advocate that even panel members who join an opinion are not necessarily endorsing its every word. Judge Newman went on to say that expressions of views in opinions are not automatically to be disregarded. Often a court will express concern over an issue, yet find insufficient basis to reverse. For example, when the court makes "a clear statement of an approved or disapproved aspect of trial court procedure,"[85] it expects its views to be heeded, because "harmless error rules are not a license to disregard procedural constraints announced by an appellate court." On the merits, the court cautioned prosecutors to obey warnings in appellate opinions about their behavior, but found harmless error.

Treatises can be helpful because they encapsulate a number of decisions in few words. Law review articles are particularly helpful if the question being argued is novel, difficult, or the subject of current debate and reexamination. Many judges like to refer to law review articles, or have their clerks do so, to keep track of current debates in the law. Law clerks, it must be recalled, are mostly law review editors, and they are likely to read a good, relevant law review article cited in a brief, because they will feel it helps the research they must do in order to write a bench memorandum on the case for their judge.

In the section of the argument under discussion, however, lengthy treatments of legal theory probably should be avoided. These can be deferred to a more general treatment under a different subheading.

---

[82] Preparing Your Appeal to the Fifth Circuit, *reprinted in* 2 Fifth Cir Rep 431, 433 (1985) (copy available from Clerk, United States Court of Appeals for the Fifth Circuit, 600 Camp Street, New Orleans, Louisiana 70130).

[83] 912 F2d 534 (2d Cir 1990), *cert denied,* 111 S Ct 1695 (1991) (Newman, J).

[84] *Id* 540.

[85] *Id.*

The standard of review will vary depending upon whether the issue is factual or legal, and in the latter case, whether some variant of the harmless error rule insulates error from reversal.[86] If it will require more than one paragraph to say why the error is reversible—clearly erroneous, not harmless, or some other standard—the discussion should be placed under its own subheading. It is, however, essential that the advocate brief the standard of review issue.

Sometimes, standard of review questions seem more in the nature of a defense, and the temptation is to defer them to the reply brief after one sees what one's opponent has to say. It is rarely, if ever, wise to underestimate one's opponent. Court of appeals judges prefer to see the standard of review acknowledged and intelligently addressed. If an issue of, for example, harmless error seems more a matter of defense, the opening brief can mention it without its own subheading.

Preservation of issues in the trial court presents a vexing problem to the appellate lawyer. If the issue has been preserved by an appropriate objection, the advocate can cite (and perhaps quote from) the relevant portion of the record. Sometimes the flavor of an exchange between judge and counsel will illuminate both the objection and the rightness of the appellant's position.

If the record shows that the point was not directly raised and preserved in the trial court, the advocate must say so candidly and directly. True, there may be some means to excuse the failure: lack of opportunity to object, some objection that served the purpose of alerting the trial judge to the appellant's position, and so on. Or, in criminal cases, one may have a rare instance in which counsel's failure to object does not waive a point.[87]

It is, however, foolish and counterproductive to evade the issue. The resultant loss of credibility will only further undermine the advocate's position.

After the advocate has introduced the issue, set out the facts in support, and made the argument, the task may well be done. However, there are some special problems that may remain to be addressed.

The issue may rest upon empirical data and require a "Brandeis brief" approach. The conclusions of social scientists, natural scientists, and other learned authorities may support the appellant's position. These authorities deserve to be set off in a separate subheading.[88]

The issue may have been the subject of debate in professional journals, appellate opinions, or other scholarly publications. If this context is relevant, and often it is, it should be explored in a separate subsection. For example, one might use a subheading, "Strict Liability in Exploding Widget Cases Reflects the Dominant Trend in American Law." This subsection would be the appropriate place to discuss authorities from other jurisdictions, law review and treatise discussions, and other relevant developments. This is also the place to put contrary precedent from other jurisdictions into context. Contrary authority from the Supreme Court and one's own circuit will have been cited

---

[86] *See generally* **ch 5.**

[87] See **§5.03** for a discussion of plain error.

[88] The court of appeals has authority to take judicial notice of such materials. *See* **§§6.17, 7.01.**

in the preceding subsection. Citation of contrary authority in a discussion that purports to be compendious is ethically correct and tactically sound. An egregious failure to cite such authority may lead the court to conclude that the advocate has tried to mislead; loss of the case may be accompanied by sanctions.[89]

Sometimes an issue may be resolved favorably to the appellant on more than one ground or with different procedural consequences. For example, an appeal may attack the validity and application of an administrative regulation. It may be argued that the regulation, as properly applied, does not reach the appellant's conduct. Alternatively, the regulation may have been beyond the agency's power to enact. Or, if both of these hurdles are crossed, the regulation may be facially invalid as violating one or more provisions of the Constitution.

In preparing to make these arguments, the advocate must make a chart or graph, noting the relationship of the issues to one another and setting out the order in which they should be addressed. The form of the argument is:

> X position is correct.
> However, even if X position is not correct, Y position entitles the appellant to prevail.
> However, even if neither of these is accepted, Z position requires reversal.

These alternatives should be reflected in a series of subheadings.

In what order should these arguments be made? The canon of decision is that a court does not decide a constitutional issue unless it must.[90] This is a corollary to the principle that the court generally will seek the narrowest possible ground for decision. Usually, therefore, the arguments will proceed from the narrowest to the broadest ground of decision.

However, these principles are but guidelines, and they are not unfailingly applied. If decision of a broader issue than strictly necessary to decide a given case will provide guidance to trial judges and litigants and avoid further litigation, the court may well reach out and decide.[91] If the appellant is seeking such a declaration—as where a narrow ground provokes a retrial and a broader one averts it—the broader ground should be placed first. In such a case, the advocate must persuade the court of the wisdom, if not the necessity, of reaching the larger issue.

A corollary: one device for avoiding a constitutional issue is to interpret a statute or decisional rule as not in conflict with the constitutional principle. Examples abound: when a defendant offers reliable evidence that is arguably excludable as hearsay, a court will invoke the compulsory process and due pro-

---

[89] *See generally* **§5.02.** For an example of imprudent recycling of rejected arguments, see United States v Merit Petroleum, Inc, 731 F2d 901, 907-08 (Temp Emer Ct App 1984) (law firm, without announcing that it was doing so, filed same arguments in more than one case and gave misleading citation to prior authority; sanctions imposed).

[90] *See* Justice Rutledge's statement in Rescue Army v Municipal Court, 331 US 549, 569 (1947) (Court will not decide constitutional issues unless such decisions are unavoidable).

[91] This is an aspect of mootness. *See* **§2.18.**

cess clauses of the constitution as counselling latitude in admissibility.[92] When a statute or regulation is challenged as violating the First Amendment guarantee of free speech, the court will seek an interpretation that honors rather than dishonors the First Amendment interest.[93] When an administrative regulation or statutory grant of administrative authority raises a serious constitutional issue, it may be interpreted to avoid the constitutional conflict.[94] In such cases, the advocate will begin by making an interpretive argument. Then, probably in a separate subsection, the advocate will show that the interpretation contended for promotes harmony with a constitutional principle.

Related to the concern with ordering issues is that of telling the court what relief is sought. As one court's guidelines say, "Tell us exactly what relief you think we should order. It is helpful if, in your summary, you frame the court's mandate as you would like to have it."[95]

The relief sought must be stated clearly in a conclusion that is a separate section in a single-issue case or a separate subsection of each major heading in a multi-issue case.

The ideal result is to end the case for good. In criminal appeals, this means a reversal with direction to enter a judgment of acquittal. An order suppressing the government's evidence may have the same effect. In a civil case, the equivalent result is a direction to enter judgment for the appellant, or an opinion that the appellee's crucial evidence must be excluded on retrial. A remand for a new trial is still a victory, but not nearly as desirable. A remand for further hearings on some collateral issue, with the trial judge empowered to enter a new judgment, is perhaps the least desirable sort of victory.

Appellate courts are reluctant to decide more than they have to, so a reversal with directions to enter judgment for the appellant will be rare except in cases involving a successful challenge to the evidence received below.[96] However, if in the absence of the error below the appellant would have been entitled to judgment, this point should be urged. For example, if the trial court erroneously admitted an item of evidence or wrongly instructed the jury, and if without these errors the appellant clearly would have prevailed, the court should be urged to order judgment for the appellant to obviate further litigation.

Then, as an alternative to that request for relief, the advocate should seek a remand that directs the trial judge to examine the case in light of the appellate

---

[92] *See* Chambers v Mississippi, 410 US 284 (1973).

[93] *See* Arnett v Kennedy, 416 US 134, 162 (1974) ("the language 'such cause as will promote efficiency of service' in the Act excludes constitutionally protected speech, and . . . the statute is therefore not overbroad"). As the dissenters point out, the narrowing construction rationale can be used to authorize punishment of speech as well as to protect it. *Id* 204.

[94] *See* **§5.13.**

[95] Preparing Your Appeal to the Fifth Circuit, *supra* note 82.

[96] That is, the court of appeals will order judgment of acquittal entered if the evidence is insufficient to support the conviction and that issue is properly preserved. *See generally* 2 Charles A. Wright, Federal Practice & Procedure, Criminal 2d §466 (1982 & Supp 1993).

court's opinion and enter an appropriate judgment. The alternative of remanding for a new trial should be listed last.

A related point: if the court reverses for a new trial on, for example, an erroneous jury instruction, there is no need to decide other issues, such as claimed errors in admitting or excluding evidence. However, courts of appeals can and often do decide such questions if they are likely to recur on retrial.[97] The "Conclusion: relief sought" subsection must identify these potentially recurring issues and specifically request that the court address them.

The request for relief, and alternative requests, should then be repeated in summary form in the Conclusion, just before the signature. The court of appeals' power to fashion relief is nearly plenary, limited only by constitutional constraints in criminal cases, principally those imposed by the double jeopardy clause. The question of power to grant relief is dealt with in detail at **§10.15.** Jurisdictional limits on criminal appeals are discussed at **§2.11.**

§9.14 Appellee's or Respondent's Brief—Counterstatement of Issues

Federal Rule of Appellate Procedure 28(b) states: "The brief of the appellee shall conform to the requirements of subdivisions (a)(1)-(5), except that a statement of jurisdiction, of the issues, or of the case need not be made unless the appellee is dissatisfied with the statement of the appellant."[98]

It usually is foolish to counterstate the issues or organize the appellee's brief, in an order different from that adopted by the appellant. Doing so risks confusing the reader to no good purpose. If the appellant's ordering of issues seems inapt, for example, because it leaves the important issues to the end, the summary of argument can set the matter straight in an introductory paragraph.

However, the appellee often will want to counterstate the issues. The appellee is defending the rightness of the judgment below. He or she has the benefit of rules that insulate that judgment from reversal unless—according to the issue—it was clearly, or harmfully, wrong. The appellee will, therefore, cast issues in terms of deference.

An appellant's statement of an issue might be: "Whether the government's proof, which was at best ambiguous, was insufficient to sustain a verdict of guilty." The appellee would say, "Whether, indulging all inferences favorable to the verdict, a jury's guilty verdict in this drug manufacturing case should be affirmed, given the evidence that the defendant participated in the purchase of narcotics paraphernalia and was associated with the principals in the manufacturing ring."[99]

---

[97] Such issues are not moot. **§2.18.**

[98] The full text of Fed R App P 28, with annotations, is in **app A.**

[99] For an interesting illustration, see United States v Cook, 783 F2d 1207 (5th Cir), *affd on reconsideration,* 793 F2d 734 (5th Cir 1986), in which the court of appeals first reversed then changed its mind on rehearing and affirmed a conviction, basing the change upon a very different total view of the evidence.

The appellee should, of course, recall that the statement of issues is designed to inform. One cannot expect to put an entire argument into each statement, nor should one cavil about a word or two out of place in the appellant's issues.

§9.15 —Counterstatement of the Case

A distinguished circuit judge, describing how he approached a set of briefs, said, "I frequently dictate a note to my law clerk and myself that may read something like this: 'There is a good statement of facts in the appellee's brief. The district judge's opinion looks correct. Please read the briefs and see if you agree with me that this looks like an affirmance.' "[100]

Advocates should heed that message. The appellee should not shirk the duty of counterstating the case unless the case involves no factual disputes. All the advice at **§9.11** should, of course, inform the style, organization, and content of the appellee's statement.

There are so many instances of appellee-style versus appellant-style that one could not list them all. However, appellee-style is driven by the need to put the trial court's action in the best possible light. This often will require providing context. Context can move an issue into the realm of trial court discretion, and thus trigger appellate court deference. For example, suppose the appellant claims the trial judge erred by restricting cross-examination of a key witness. In a criminal case, such restriction may violate the Sixth Amendment right of confrontation.[101] In a civil case, such an error also is taken seriously. The appellant will no doubt describe the judge's action in terms that evoke the common law preference for full cross-examination.

The appellee must acknowledge the importance of cross-examination, but must justify the trial judge's action. He or she can seek some rule of law that holds the subject of inquiry that was cut off to be off limits, such as an evidentiary privilege,[102] the prohibition against exploring offers in compromise,[103] or the bar on evidence of subsequent remedial measures.[104]

If none of these counterrules avails, the appellee must turn to the general area of trial judge discretion to control the presentation of evidence. Relevant evidence, even on cross-examination, may be excluded if it is cumulative,

---

[100] Talk Given by Judges Rubin and Higginbotham at the Appellate Advocacy Seminar Sponsored by the Bar Association of the Fifth Federal Circuit on October 16, 1984, 2 Fifth Cir Rep 143, 147 (1985).

[101] *See* Davis v Alaska, 415 US 308 (1974).

[102] Fed R Evid 501, *discussed in* Stephen A. Saltzburg & Michael M. Martin, Federal Rules of Evidence Manual 403-515 (5th ed 1990).

[103] Fed R Evid 408, discussed in Stephen A. Saltzburg & Michael M. Martin, *supra* note 102, at 348-66.

[104] Fed R Evid 407, discussed in Stephen A. Saltzburg & Michael M. Martin, *supra* note 102, at 326-47.

unduly prejudicial, misleading, or confusing.[105] The trial judge's discretion to make this sort of decision is saluted in a number of appellate opinions. The appellee's statement of facts, therefore, will focus upon matters in the record that suggest the discretion was properly exercised.

In sum, the appellee's statement of facts seeks to shelter the judgment from reversal by covering it with the prestige and authority of the trial judge.

Truth to tell, there will be some issues on which the trial judge may have been right for the wrong reasons, or for no stated reason at all. In such a case, the appellee should say candidly that the record may not reflect the precise basis for the trial judge's action, but that there is ample support to be found. Then the appellee must find it.

§9.16 —Arguing in Defense of the Judgment or Order Below

A wise advocate never assumes an unnecessary burden. While the appellant speaks of justice denied, the appellee engages him or her on that terrain with caution. The appellee speaks of justice, to be sure, but laces the argument with considerations of deference to the trier of fact, of deference to the lower court (or agency), of decided issues, and of an end to litigation.

The appellee is, in short, restrained and enlightened. As an example of what appellees are tempted to write, but should not, consider this paragraph from an appellee's brief filed in a major civil case:

> In its attempt to reverse the judgment below, [appellant] has argumentatively distorted the extensive trial record. [Appellant]'s effort is understandable, for what the record reveals is a clear case of arrogant interference with legal rights and an orchestrated deceit which stripped [appellee] of the uniquely valuable [property in dispute]. That the jury unanimously found in [appellee's] favor was no surprise to those who saw and heard the evidence unfold.

Here is an unfortunately typical piece of unpersuasive overstatement. It bears every sign of having been written by a committee, with perhaps a subcommittee on modifiers having the final word. It may be that a metaphor mixer was used to blend several early versions. Would not the same point be better made by saying:

> A unanimous jury awarded [the appellee] substantial damages for [the appellant]'s deceit and interference with contract rights. The trial judge correctly entered judgment on the verdict. [The appellant] has misrepresented to this court the evidence the judge and jury heard.

Turning to the question of organization, the sections of the appellee's brief track the appellant's. Each point in the argument should begin with a carefully

---

105 *See* **§5.10.**

crafted one or two sentence rebuttal that underscores the correctness of the decision below. The main portion of the argument should show how any authority relied upon by the trial court supports its action. Citation and discussion of such authority does not, however, complete the appellee's task.

In the heat of trial, many decisions are made that are quickly argued and cursorily justified, if at all. The trial judge's reasoning will not in such instances fully have found its way into the record. The appellee must take what is there and build it into a coherent defense.

Moreover, since the trial there may well have arisen appellate opinions, journal articles, or other authorities that bear upon the rightness of what occurred below. The lawyer must be assiduous to find these.

Context is important. The casebooks are full of rules designed to insulate trial court decisions from review because the judge's conduct, taken as a whole, did not prejudice a party's rights.[106] A jury charge that is not quite right will be upheld if the charge taken as a whole was fair. A ruling excluding evidence will survive review if the party was permitted a fair opportunity to explore the matter in some other way. A prejudicial jury argument may not overturn a decision if the argument as a whole was not unduly inflammatory.

The following checklist[107] is designed to identify the most common bases upon which a decision under review may be supported:

Deference to factual findings. Appellate courts give great deference to factual findings of courts and agencies. This rule is based upon the trier having seen the witnesses and evaluated their credibility, upon institutional concerns about the respective roles of trial and appellate courts, and in civil cases upon the Seventh Amendment command that jury verdicts are not to be reviewed except under common law standards.

Harmless error. An error may not have significantly impaired a party's rights. This is a consideration related to, though different from, the question of whether error occurred at all.[108]

Failure to object. An alleged error not challenged in the court below will be reviewed, if at all, only to see whether it occasioned a miscarriage of justice. There are few exceptions to this general rule of waiver. Counsel's failure to object usually will bind the client.

Alternate paths to the same result. If the trial court's action can be sustained on grounds in addition to those discussed in the record, it is wise and proper to discuss those additional grounds.

§9.17 Reply Brief: When and What to File

The appellant typically has 14 days from service of the appellee's brief in

---

[106] *See generally* **ch 5.**

[107] *See also* **§§5.03-5.13.**

[108] See Darden v Wainwright, 477 US 168 (1986).

which to file a reply brief.[109] The time may be shortened by court order or in certain classes of cases by circuit rule. In addition, because oral argument may be scheduled soon after the appellee's brief is due, a prudent advocate will want or need to file a reply brief, if any, in less than 14 days. Federal Rule of Appellate Procedure 31(a) requires that the reply brief be filed no less than three days before oral argument.

A reply brief is not inevitable. It is useful only if the opponent (1) has misstated the facts or law in a way that is not obvious from reading the appellant's opening brief, (2) has introduced a new issue or basis for upholding the decisions below, or (3) has discussed an authority or legal principle that has arisen since the appellant's brief was filed which requires discussion.

Given the paperwork that judges must wade through preparing for argument or decision, failure to file a reply brief is not regarded as unusual or requiring justification. The advocate should, however, memorialize the decision not to file with a letter to the clerk of the court of appeals announcing and explaining the decision. If the decision not to file a reply brief is reached after consultation in the law office and with the client, that should be reflected in a memorandum to the file. This procedure shows that the decision reflected informed judgment and was not a result of sloth or negligence.

The advocate must remember: the reply brief is not the place for arguments that were overlooked in the opening brief. Some courts have overlooked belated presentation of matters that should have been in the opening brief, but the risk should not be courted willingly. Many court of appeals cases hold that an issue first raised in a reply brief is waived.[110]

This discussion suggests the details that should be included in a reply brief if one is filed. The following checklist should be helpful, although it is not exhaustive.

1. The appellee misstates the record. Briefly, in "headline" style, identify the significant misstatements and direct the court to the exact place in the record, record excerpts, or appendix that supports the appellant's view

2. The appellee claims deference for the decision below to which it is not entitled. For example, an appellee might claim that the decision was factual and therefore entitled to deference under the Fed R Civ P 52(a) standard.[111] If the rule is that the particular matter should be reviewed by a different standard, this should be stated.

3. A point allegedly waived was in fact preserved by some appropriate objection. Since failure to object is fatal in most cases, the appellee's allegations on this score must be rebutted as well as the record permits.

---

[109] See **§9.02** for discussion of variations on the timing rule when the brief is served by mail and when oral argument is imminent.

[110] Ordinarily, issues cannot first be raised in reply brief. Mississippi River Corp v FTC, 454 F2d 1083, 1093 (8th Cir 1972); Greyhound Corp v Blakely, 262 F2d 401 (9th Cir 1958) (failure to raise issue until reply brief excused when no prejudice to opponent); Finsky v Union Carbide & Carbon Corp, 249 F2d 449 (7th Cir 1957) (issue first raised in reply brief would not be considered), *cert denied,* 356 US 957 (1958).

[111] *See* **§5.04.**

4. The appellee invites an intercircuit conflict, that is, the appellee invites the court to take a position adopted by another circuit that is contrary to the law in the circuit where the case is pending. Most courts of appeals have a formal or informal policy of avoiding intercircuit conflict whenever possible, and, of course, such conflicts may trigger Supreme Court review.[112]

5. The appellee cites a case, discusses it in a way that seems persuasive, but misstates the facts of the case, distorts the holding, chooses a quotation out of context, or commits some other blunder. The wise advocate follows football rules: no piling on. However, he or she briefly describes the error committed by the opponent. This discussion is not necessary if the appellee's argument has been anticipated in the appellant's opening brief.

§9.18 Special Problems—Cross-Appeals

Federal Rule of Appellate Procedure 28(h)[113] provides that when cross-appeals are taken, the party who first files a notice of appeal is deemed the appellant for purposes of briefing.[114] If notices of appeal are filed the same day, the party who was plaintiff below is treated as the appellant. This order can be varied by agreement of the parties or order of the court on motion of any party. In an NLRB enforcement action in the court of appeals, however, each party adverse to the Board shall proceed first in briefing and oral argument.

The order of proceeding that the Fed R App P 28 establishes as the norm is usually satisfactory. However, the defendant in the court below should be regarded as the appellant whenever he or she is clearly the one principally aggrieved by the judgment, that is, the party designated as appellant should be the one with the greatest stake in overturning the decision below.

For example, if the defendant is appealing a judgment imposing substantial damages in tort, and the plaintiff's cross-appeal raises issues of attorneys' fees or prejudgment interest, the logic of the matter dictates that the defendant below become the appellant and file a brief attacking the underlying judgment.

Counsel should attempt to achieve agreement on this issue and, failing that, a motion is in order to set a briefing schedule. The motion[115] should set out the practical reasons for establishing the desired order of briefing and argument. In most cases, it makes no practical difference which side goes first, and most lawyers would like to see the opponent's case before committing their own work to paper. However, where the normal procedure is clearly illogical, counsel should seek to exercise control.

---

[112] *See* **§§11.05, 11.06.**

[113] The full text of Fed R App P 28 is in **app A.**

[114] On oral argument of cross-appeals, see **§10.12.**

[115] *See* **ch 8.**

§9.19 —Multiple Parties

Federal Rule of Appellate Procedure 28(i)(1)[116] provides that in cases involving multiple appellants or appellees, parties may join in one another's briefs or adopt all or part of one another's briefs by reference. Because appellate judges often lament the quantity of printed paper that burdens their work, the suggestions in this rule should be followed whenever possible to avoid duplication of argument.

In a multi-appellant case, where the interests of parties are identical, counsel's first effort should be to coordinate with counsel for other parties to file a consolidated brief on common issues. This saves the court's time and, as will be seen below, makes the paperwork easier.

A consolidated brief may be unwise, however. If the arguments are party-oriented, and each appellant has a separate story to tell, a combined statement of facts will dilute the force of everyone's presentation. In such a case, cross-references to the briefs of other parties on particular legal issues, or a later motion to adopt portions of a coparty's brief, will be preferable.

Adoption of issues, or a consolidated brief, generally are not appropriate when several parties are challenging the sufficiency of the evidence to support the judgment. In such cases, each party should be striving to present factual and legal arguments that not only are persuasive but may also be unique to it, that is, a sufficiency point almost never will be equally strong for all appellants. Similarly, if the issue is, for example, failure of the trial judge to grant a severance of defendants in a criminal case, the evidence as to each defendant must be examined separately, and it may even be counterproductive to file a consolidated brief. To do so may suggest that the appellants have the very commonality of interest that they were at pains to disprove in their motions for severance.

Experienced trial lawyers know that, in a multiparty case, it is often important for each advocate to keep a fair distance from other advocates and their clients. One does not want to give a subliminal impression of conspiratorial unity. The same considerations operate in the appellate setting and the same instinct will guide the lawyer toward a correct decision on consolidation or adoption of issues. On the other hand, it almost never is wise for parties on the same side of a case—at trial or on appeal—to attack one another gratuitously; doing so plays the opponent's game.

There is little point in filing a consolidated brief if each party must file a supplemental individual brief that is so substantial that the entire effort appears fragmented. In such a case, the parties should agree on who will give principal treatment to which issue and which motions to adopt issues should be filed by the other parties.

Such coordination will be easier in circuits that require a preliminary statement of issues on appeal filed soon after the notice of appeal. In other circuits, the advocate will often be hard pressed to coordinate the activities of all the

---

[116] The full text of Fed R App P 28 is in **app A.**

lawyers in a multi-appellant case. The effort should be made, however. The court will appreciate efforts to ease its work and the resulting presentation will be more effective.[117]

Motions to adopt filed after the opening briefs are routinely granted, but are unlikely to find their way into the to-read pile of the judges deciding the case. They are random pieces of paper that may interfere with the coparties presenting a coherent overall picture of the litigation. If a party seeks or will seek formal leave to adopt the issues briefed by a coparty, it is best to include a reference to this in the opening brief—appellant's or appellee's, as the case may be—so that the court is aware when reading the briefs that more than one party is concerned with a particular point. Failure to adopt a coparty's brief or issues may cause the court of appeals to hold that the issue is waived by the delinquent party.[118]

Some courts of appeals mandate by rule or order that co-parties to an appeal file a single brief. Usually this presents no difficulty. However, counsel should move for leave to file separate briefs where the interests of co-appellants are antagonistic.

§9.20 Informing the Court about Supplemental Authorities

Federal Rule of Appellate Procedure 28(j)[119] provides that a party may inform the court about pertinent and significant authorities' that come to [its] attention after the briefs are filed or after oral argument but before decision. The device for informing the court is the Rule 28(j) letter,

> with a copy to all counsel, setting forth the citations. There shall be a reference either to the page of the brief or to a point argued orally to which the citations pertain, but the letter shall without argument state the reasons for the supplemental citations. Any response shall be made promptly and shall be similarly limited.

This procedure is straightforward. The usual times for sending in new authorities are (a) shortly before argument, when renewed research uncovers something; (b) after a reply brief is filed, when new research provides an answer to a question not theretofore asked; (c) after argument, when the argument suggests another look at the law; and (d) when regular reading of the advance sheets or browsing on Westlaw or LEXIS turns up something.

---

[117] As noted elsewhere, see **§8.06,** some courts of appeals are using prehearing conferences to facilitate coordination in complex cases.

[118] *See* United States v Williams, 809 F2d 1072, 1093 (5th Cir) (court cannot reverse for prejudicial publicity where appellant fails to argue those grounds or adopt co-appellant's arguments pursuant to Fed R App P 28(i)), *corrected on rehg*, 828 F2d 1 (5th Cir) (record corrected to reflect that appellant did in fact argue or adopt co-appellant's arguments for reversal on grounds of prejudicial publicity), *cert denied,* 484 US 896 (1987).

[119] The full text of Fed R App P 28 is in **app A.**

The rule does not require that the authorities be newly decided, only that they be newly discovered by counsel.[120]

The 28(j) letter should not be an excuse to reargue a point, but, as the Rule requires, should be strictly limited to citing the authorities and referring to the parts of the brief or oral argument to which they pertain.[121]

Rule 28(j) is designed for the diligent: counsel should have a system for spotting late-breaking decisions from the Supreme Court, the circuit in question, and other circuits. It may be possible to monitor law journals and publications dealing with state court decisions. If a law office specializes in certain types of cases, specialized publications will alert the advocate to new decisions. The law office should be open enough that lawyers other than those whose names are on the brief are watching out for important new decisions that could be relevant.[122] If a law office has enough federal business to justify it, a publication such as West Publishing Company's Federal Case News, a weekly summary of federal decisions received by West, should be scanned as it comes in. Perhaps this task can be delegated to one or more lawyers who are generally familiar with issues in pending cases. An advocate with a practice based in one circuit should read the opinions of that circuit on a regular basis.[123]

---

[120] *See* Cunico v Pueblo Sch Dist No 60, 917 F2d 431, 434 n1 (10th Cir 1990) (Fed R App P 28(j) may be used to cite additional authority even if not newly decided; however, counsel must obey rule and direct court's attention to portions of brief to which new authority applies).

[121] *See* United States v Ianniello, 824 F2d 203 (2d Cir 1987) (rejecting counsel's postargument letter because not limited as required by Rule 28(j)).

[122] Diligence—in this case reading the advance sheets—pays off. In Gulden v Crown Zellerbach Corp, 890 F2d 195, 197 n2 (9th Cir 1989), the court held for the plaintiff-appellants in a diversity action based in part on a state court case decided and cited to the court of appeals by Fed R App P 28(j) after the briefs had been filed.

[123] It is possible to set a legal research computer program such as LEXIS or Westlaw to retrieve new cases that respond to certain defined search parameters.

10 Oral Argument, Decision, Judgment, and Mandate

§10.01 Benefits of Oral Argument

Oral argument is always important and should never be waived.[1] Court of appeals judges vary greatly in the degree to which oral argument may influence

---

[1] Advocates should never decline a chance to speak, if only to practice a principal element of their art. Alan D. Hornstein, Appellate Advocacy §8-1, at 239 (1984) (citing E. Barrett Prettyman, *Some Observations Concerning Appellate Advocacy*, 39 Va L Rev 285 (1953)). Oral advocacy, particularly the interchange with an opponent and a group of interrogators, is a skill that improves with practice.

them, but almost all judges who have written or spoken on the issue acknowledge that argument changes their minds in a significant number of cases.

Some years ago, the author represented the appellee on the government's appeal from a dismissal in the district court. The court of appeals set the case for 10 minutes argument per side in a distant city. Given that the district court is entitled to deference, and given that the legal issues seemed fairly straightforward, the temptation to waive argument was strong. Also, the 10 minutes per side looked like a hint that the court was on its way to a noncontroversial, perhaps nonpublished, affirmance.

Fortunately, the temptation was not yielded to. The panel had indeed set the case for only 10 minutes, apparently believing that the district judge was just plain wrong on the law and that he had made findings that showed he did not appreciate the correct legal standard. The 10-minute argument, driven along by the court's questions, went on for 30 minutes. The panel members genuinely struggled to reconsider their tentative view of the case.

Two Eighth Circuit judges, Myron H. Bright and Richard Sheppard Arnold, kept track for 10 months of all cases argued before them.[2] They asked themselves three questions in each case: "(1) Was oral argument necessary? (2) Was oral argument helpful? (3) Did it change the judge's mind?[3] The results of their survey are striking: Judge Bright thought oral argument necessary in 85 per cent of the cases, Judge Arnold in 75 per cent of the cases. Judge Bright thought argument helpful in 82 per cent of the cases, Judge Arnold in 80 per cent of the cases. This is not a misprint: Judge Arnold found argument helpful in a few cases where he did not find it necessary. Did oral argument change the judge's mind? For Judge Bright, it was "yes" in 24 per cent of the cases and "maybe" in 7 per cent. Judge Arnold reported "yes" in 15 per cent of the cases and "maybe" in 2 per cent.[4]

In seeming contrast, the late Alvin B. Rubin of the Fifth Circuit once noted: "My own experience is that less than one-in-ten, perhaps one-in-twenty, cases, do I change my tentative opinion at oral argument."[5] Fifth Circuit Judge Patrick E. Higginbotham acknowledges being influenced by oral argument to a somewhat greater degree.[6]

A Federal Judicial Center study of all United States courts of appeals reported that judges acknowledge changing their minds on oral argument in

---

[2] Myron H. Bright & Richard S. Arnold, *Oral Argument? It May Be Crucial!*, 70 ABAJ 68 (Sept 1984). Shortly after the article was published, the author argued to the Eighth Circuit en banc. Judge Bright later told the author that the argument had indeed changed his vote from the tentative conclusion that he had reached before taking the bench.

[3] *Id.*

[4] *Id* 70.

[5] Transcript of Talk Given by Judges Rubin and Higginbotham at the Appellate Advocacy Seminar Sponsored by the Bar Association of the Fifth Federal Circuit on October 16, 1984, 2 Fifth Cir Rep 143, 144-45 (1985).

[6] *Id.*

somewhat less than 10 per cent of the cases they hear.[7] These figures are significant, though not dispositive. As Judge Rubin remarked, "That doesn't mean that oral argument isn't important because even if it is 1 case in 100 the problem is you are never sure which case it will be that will change your mind."[8]

There are lawyers, such as Milton Gould of New York, who have concluded that oral argument is a luxury that judges "grudgingly allowed to the lawyers."[9]

Informal talks with judges yield a contrariety of opinion similar to that reflected in the examples given above. Most courts of appeals ration oral argument, adopting a system to choose the cases to be argued. Judges who believe that the opportunity to argue, however briefly, should be given in every case, will cite anecdotal evidence similar to that of the scheduled 10-minute argument that turned into a much longer discussion.

Some judges are tacitly or openly suspicious of, even condescending to, advocates. Such judges see oral argument as a waste of their time and they seek to ration it in the interest of the court's time. Increasing docket pressure leads many judges to vote for some limitation on argument in the interest of being able to focus more time on cases identified as posing more difficult issues.

The evidence does not point all one way, but the following may be offered in support of the categorical statement with which this section began:

1. In a circuit that rations oral argument, obtaining argument separates your case from the bunch and guarantees that it will get more attention. As discussed below,[10] nonargued cases are often sent to a staff attorney or pool clerk for an initial draft opinion. While these attorneys are well-qualified, the draft is unlikely to receive the judicial attention in chambers that will be given to the opinion in an argued case that is to be reported.

2. Even a judge with a fixed opinion probably will listen to argument, if only to detect some false note or weak spot in his or her proposed disposition of the case. Even the judges who say that oral argument rarely changes their minds will admit that cases are more often won than lost in argument. The advocate who shows up the opponent in oral argument may undermine the confidence of judges who were prepared to vote for the opponent's position.

3. Argument is a last clear chance. Sometimes the issues do not come together clearly until the advocate revisits the case to present it orally. Argument may provide an opportunity to move beyond the relatively detached and formal tone of the briefs into a persuasive and short summary statement of the justice of one's case. Edward Bennett Williams always prepared for oral

---

[7] *Id* 145.

[8] *Id.*

[9] Quoted in Myron H. Bright & Richard S. Arnold, *supra* note 2.

[10] For discussion of the ways in which the courts of appeals decide cases that are not orally argued, see **§10.14.**

argument on the *last clear chance* theory, immersing himself in the record and the authorities and continually looking for ways to reshape the case.[11]

4. Argument teaches lawyers, even if it does not teach judges, in two distinct ways. Most lawyers give more than one oral argument in their careers. Even if the appeal being argued is not the end point of the case, it is not the end point of the advocate's concern with the issues being argued. The thrust-and-parry of oral argument can illuminate strong and weak points in a continuing case, instructing the advocate who must continue to make tactical and strategic decisions. At a minimum, succinctly presenting the heart of the case in limited time, and then responding to the nearly inevitable questions from a well-prepared panel of judges, freshens a different and uniquely valuable set of advocacy skills. Briefing a case gives latitude for fairly lengthy analysis. One restates one's view of the case. Oral argument forces concentration on, and engagement with, other views of the case.

5. One can view the value of argument by hypothesizing a worst case. Suppose the case is straightforward, with one or two issues at most. The advocate is confident that her position will prevail, and the briefs and record are strong. Surely, one would argue, there is no reason to hazard a loss by seeking oral argument. The opponent will no doubt want argument, hoping that the advocate will somehow lose the case by ineptitude or solecism. Even in such a case, oral argument should be sought, because a long career will teach that judges or their clerks may have detected a flaw in the argument that requires explanation. Without argument, there would be no opportunity to confront the point. Even if the argument proves that there was a winning case all along, it is an opportunity to try and shape the way in which the case is stated in the opinion.

6. By contrast, the advocate with a very difficult position will want oral argument to dispel misimpressions and to state the issues clearly. Suppose, as is often the case, that the advocate is defending a judgment below and must acknowledge that there was error. The way in which one responds to the opponent's argument, and to the court's questions, can provide vital reassurance that the error did not affect substantial rights. In other cases, one may be able to point out that the error was not preserved for appeal in the proper way, while at the same time minimizing its impact on the proceedings.

7. Most persuasively, the argument to a panel of judges steeped in the briefs and record excerpts—which describes the overwhelming majority of cases in the federal courts of appeals—gives new insight into the judges' view of the case. A brief is the advocates' best judgment about which facts and which legal theories are most likely to be persuasive. But one is not doing an appeal in the abstract; one is doing this appeal, on these facts, on this law, to these judges,

---

[11] For a concrete example, read the briefs in Alderman v United States, 394 US 165 (1968) and its companion cases, *Ivanov v United States* and *Butenko v United States*, and then Williams's brilliant oral argument in these consolidated cases. The argument pulls together the broad themes of the lengthy briefs. The briefs are microformed on US Sup Ct Records, Briefs 1968, 1967 term, No 133, Cards 4-7 (NCR Microcard Editions, Inc) and the argument is microformed on Oral Arguments of the Supreme Court of the United States: The Warren Court, 1953 Term-1968 Term, Case 133, Reargument 1967 term, Fiche 1 (Univ Pubs of Am).

who are assisted by these law clerks and staff attorneys. The argument brings the specific decisional process into the open. After hundreds of arguments, one continues to be surprised at the insights into one's case, and the judge's view of it, that argument provides. Usually the insight dawns early enough in the argument that the advocate has a chance to make use of it in answering the judge's concerns.

All of these reasons for seeking argument suggest, indeed, assume, two canons of conduct: Argument must be done by an advocate thoroughly prepared on the record and the law; and argument must not be a repetition of the briefs.

§10.02 Obtaining Oral Argument When the Court of Appeals Rations It

All courts of appeals dispense with oral argument in some cases.[12] For example, the Fifth Circuit hears oral argument in fewer than 45 per cent of the cases it decides.[13] Other circuits that ration argument report similar results. When a court of appeals has fewer judges than its Congressionally authorized number, because the appointment and confirmation process has failed to fill vacancies, the percentage of nonargued cases will increase. Also, it seems that circuits in which the judges must travel from their chambers to one or more headquarters cities to sit in panels and hear argument are more likely to ration argument because geography makes argument even more time-intensive than usual.

Judges of courts of appeals that ration oral argument are staunch defenders of their practice. The late Judge Alvin B. Rubin has said, referring to the Fifth Circuit, that "every one of the cases we decide without oral argument is, I think, of the kind Justice Cardozo called cases that should not have been appealed, for perhaps 90% of all appealed cases, he said, were destined to be decided one way."[14]

Most of this chapter deals with obtaining and delivering oral argument. However, **§10.14** describes the court of appeals' decisional process when oral argument is not granted.

In 1986, Fed R App P 34(a)[15] was amended to set minimum standards for deciding which cases merit argument. The rule permits the court of appeals to dispense with argument in defined classes of cases after giving parties a chance to state why they believe argument should be heard. Rule 34(a) sets a minimum standard by providing that:

> Oral Argument will be allowed unless (1) the appeal is frivolous; or (2) the dispositive issue or set of issues has been recently authoritatively

---

[12] This section deals with rationing argument on the merits. Oral argument on motions is even more restricted. *See* **§8.05.**

[13] 3 Fifth Cir Rep 47 (1986). However, as Judge Rubin pointed out in the remarks cited above, in many cases (17% in a recent year in the Fifth Circuit) neither side requested oral argument.

[14] Alvin B. Rubin, *Does Law Matter? A Judge's Response to the Critical Legal Studies Movement*, 37 J Legal Educ 307, 310 (1987).

[15] The full text of Fed R App P 34(a) is in **app A.**

decided; or (3) the facts and legal arguments are adequately presented in the briefs and record and the decisional process would not be significantly aided by oral argument.

Rule 34(a) provides much leeway and there is virtually no opportunity to challenge a denial of oral argument as not within the rule's broad terms.[16] The decision to dispense with argument must be made unanimously by a panel of judges acting under local rule.[17] That is, any judge may decide that the case would benefit from oral argument.

In practice, the judicial decision to deny oral argument takes place only after the case is screened by staff attorneys in the Clerk's office. The circuits vary greatly in the amount of judicial involvement in the screening process, and even within circuits, different judges pay greater or lesser attention to reviewing the initial screening decisions.

For example, the Tenth Circuit has adopted a system whereby a judge reviews appellants' opening briefs to flag cases that can be disposed of without oral argument and perhaps on an expedited basis. In the Fifth Circuit, by contrast, initial review is performed by staff attorneys. These procedures are, of course, subject to revision, and are not codified in formal rules.[18]

The staff attorney's office consists of lawyers who assist the court in doing its administrative business, and in many instances in researching and briefing procedural motions, indigent collateral attack proceedings, and nonargued appeals.[19] Given increasing caseloads, the staff attorney's office has become more important in recent years. In the Fifth Circuit, the staff attorney roster more than doubled to about 50 between 1990 and 1992. There are now more staff attorneys than judicial law clerks. Some 80% of Fifth Circuit opinions have drafting input from staff attorneys.

Based on the factors outlined in Rule 34(a), and on the local rule and practice, the Clerk's office rates cases based on complexity, merit, and novelty of issues. The rating system not only helps to determine which cases will be argued orally; it also helps to equalize the workload among the judges of the circuit, so that one judge or panel of judges is not overwhelmed with the more difficult cases. Whenever and in whatever form oral argument is sought, counsel must present a clear, articulate, and persuasive statement of the reasons for granting it. It is never enough to quote one or more of the three standards set out in Fed R App P 34(a).

Many circuits obtain the unanimous panel consent as the Fifth Circuit does. The initial staff attorney recommendation is sent to a single judge for review.

---

[16] If oral argument is denied, and the decision is adverse, the petition for rehearing and suggestion of the appropriateness of rehearing en banc can stress the need for argument. *See* **ch 11.** Cases reheard en banc almost always are argued.

[17] Fed R App P 34(a), the full text of which is in **app A.**

[18] The Clerk's office will be able to discuss the current system with counsel. In circuits with active bar associations, membership and participation in the association will keep one current on changes in the procedure and perhaps give a voice in its operation.

[19] See **§1.04** on judicial decisional techniques, and **§10.14** on decisions without oral argument.

If that judge decides that no argument is warranted, he or she sends the briefs to the two other panel judges along with a draft opinion. This opinion may well have been prepared initially by the staff attorney's office.[20]

Under two of the three Rule 34(a) standards, the court is not supposed to ask, "What are the merits?" but rather, "Is this case important?" The advocate seeking argument will have the same vocabulary as the petitioner for a discretionary writ.[21] First impression, recurring, difficult, of constitutional dimension—these are the sorts of words that convey the importance of the issue the court must decide.

But courts of appeals do not have a discretionary jurisdiction, as does the Supreme Court on certiorari. They are supposed to decide, on the merits, every case over which they have jurisdiction. It should matter to the court that the case is very important to the parties. And while there is no reported jurisprudence of argument granting, judges profess to be concerned that their judgments be rendered by a process that enhances the perceived fairness of the system. For this reason, party-oriented advocacy can be effective in requesting oral argument.

Examples teach better than description. Dick DeGuerin, of Houston, Texas, made this request in a criminal case involving nine appellants:

> If for no other reason than to expand upon the shoddy treatment all defendants and their counsel received from the District Court, this case needs to be presented live and in color. This Court has never been reticent to ask questions in oral argument. In a trial spread out over several months, and over thirty volumes of transcript, the lawyers can better bring life to the cold transcript by a live presentation. . . .

This bold statement committed DeGuerin to arguing persuasively that the district judge behaved improperly. DeGuerin's experience and reputation, coupled with his having made this assertion at the beginning of the brief, permitting the reader to evaluate it, made this seemingly audacious approach good advocacy. The request was based upon claimed injustice to the defendant and his counsel.

DeGuerin's second statement was an invitation that the court surely would be tempted to accept, especially in a full record circuit like the Fifth. Counsel proposed, quite reasonably, that oral argument could help guide the court through a lengthy and complex record.[22]

Another approach, this time from Samuel J. Buffone of Washington, D.C., "This is a case of first impression, which brings before the court the issues

---

[20] This procedure is discussed in Transcript of Talk Given by Judges Rubin and Higginbotham at the Appellate Advocacy Seminar Sponsored by the Bar Association of the Fifth Federal Circuit on October 18, 1984, 2 Fifth Cir Rep 143 (1985). See also Judge Sam Johnson's discussion of this issue, 2 Fifth Cir Rep 345 (1985). The Fifth Circuit has, however, changed the initiating judge procedure in at least some cases. *See* **§10.14.**

[21] *See* **§3.15.**

[22] DeGuerin was granted argument and won his case. United States v Williams, 809 F2d 1072 (5th Cir 1987).

of nonliable third-party interests in a RICO forfeiture." The request for oral argument must descend from generalities. Note that Mr. Buffone did not simply say "This is an issue of first impression," and leave it to the court to figure out if he was right and what that issue might be. He made a concise statement of the issue.

There are pitfalls to avoid in the statement seeking oral argument. A complex case presenting many issues may be a good candidate for argument, but not because counsel can argue every issue. A laundry list of contentions that should be argued tells the court that the advocate does not understand the practical limits on the 20 or so minutes of allotted argument time, and may waste the court's time by trying to argue too many points. The court may find such an offer easy to refuse.

If one can foresee that the opponent will seek denial of oral argument by claiming that the issues are settled or that argument will not be valid, then the argument for denial should be anticipated and met. For example:

> Although the issue of proximate cause is discussed in many opinions of this Circuit, most recently in *Quackenbush v Chicken Little, Inc,* this case presents such an issue in a challenging and novel context. In this case, the defendant claimed that his negligence was not the proximate cause because its faulty light pole had been erected and not repaired or inspected during the eighteen months from installation until the accident that killed the plaintiff's decedent.

This example is hypothetical, but the point is real. Counsel must pick out the facts and law that make this case challenging and interesting, one that anybody—including three judges—would enjoy hearing about for 40 minutes.

Self-test: Counsel should answer in 25 words or less, to himself, herself, or a willing listener, the question: "You know what is really fascinating about this case?" The answer provides a basis for requesting oral argument.

The referral to staff attorneys may occur as early as the filing of appellant's brief and will in many cases take place before the appellant files a reply brief. It therefore would be a mistake for an appellant to make only a pro forma request for oral argument in the opening brief in the hope that the opponent's objections can be treated more fully in the reply brief.

With the considerations listed above in mind, the following checklist outlines some reasons for oral argument:

- Question of first impression.
- Question on which courts of appeals are divided.
- Question on which there arguably are two lines of authority in the circuit.
- Complex record that argument may illuminate.
- Difficult issues of statutory construction of a statute or rule that often is considered by the court.
- Jury instruction issue that can be resolved so as to guide litigants and district judges in future cases.

- More generally, any issue the resolution of which can be said to provide guidance to lower court, agency, or litigants in ways that will foreclose future appellate litigation.
- Allegations of misconduct by lower court, counsel, or litigant that should not be resolved without giving an opportunity for the court to hear from and question advocates.
- Substantial constitutional issues.
- Any substantial and arguable reason for reversing judgment below; the court is much less likely to reverse than to affirm without argument.
- Recurring or significant questions of appellate jurisdiction or practice, the resolution of which may guide litigants.
- Indications that the agency or court below has embarked on a course that threatens identifiable interests beyond the particular case.

Rule 34(a) does permit denial of argument in frivolous appeals. Lawyers rarely pursue frivolous appeals. If, however, an opponent claims oral argument should be denied on this ground, the advocate should always reply. The reply constitutes not only a rebuttal to the claim that no argument should be allowed, but permits an attorney to defend against possible sanctions.[23]

In emergency matters, such as applications for stays of execution in capital cases, some courts of appeals hold oral argument by telephone conference call. When filing an application for emergency relief, one should ask the clerk's office for the means of scheduling such an argument.

§10.03 How the Court of Appeals Schedules Oral Argument

The process by which counsel is notified that oral argument may be set is sometimes confusing. Often, the first scheduling order from the clerk's office will set due dates for briefs and contain a boilerplate statement that the case is set, or may be set, for argument during a certain week or month. Most courts of appeals hear oral argument during fixed terms. In the Fifth Circuit, for example, oral arguments usually are set for mornings during the first week of the month. In other circuits, argument calendars are established well in advance, although not with such predictable regularity.

The initial notification does not guarantee that oral argument will be granted in a circuit that rations it. The schedule is also subject to change if time for filing briefs is extended or if the court must rearrange arguments because an urgent matter requires attention.

When a notice arrives that even tentatively predicts oral argument, lead counsel on the case must see and respond to the notice quickly. In a large office

---

[23] The frivolous appeals standards and sanctions are discussed at **§5.02.** *See also* Glick v Koenig, 766 F2d 265 (7th Cir 1985) (oral argument not required in case of alleged constitutional violation arising from issuance of traffic citation; review of Fed R App P 34(a) standards).

or firm, there is a temptation to treat scheduling matters as routine and not for consideration by the senior lawyer. When argument is involved, this temptation must be overcome.

If the proposed date is inconvenient, or if the court seems to be rushing the case unduly, the time for action is short. This point is best illustrated by examples.

In the Tenth Circuit, counsel are usually notified of an approximate oral argument date when the briefing schedule is set. The advocate who does not wish oral argument should promptly inform the clerk by letter, stating the reasons why argument is unnecessary. The letter should contain a suggestion that the court can decide the case as soon as the briefs are filed. If the proposed week in which oral argument is tentatively set poses serious scheduling problems for arguing counsel, the clerk should be informed. Relief from a proposed argument date should be sought sparingly. It is, however, possible to ask that the argument be set on a particular day of the week during the argument calendar.

In the Second Circuit, the clerk often sends a letter giving a tentative argument date and asking counsel to tell the court if the proposed date poses an irreconcilable scheduling conflict. Ignoring this letter leads to a specific argument setting that is nearly impossible to move.

If the court grants oral argument, but the scheduled date is impossible for counsel, the best first step is to call the clerk's office and inquire about the proper procedure for seeking a continuance. This step is advisable even though the clerk may suggest only that counsel should file a motion. It may be that the argument has been set for a particular week, and before a particular panel, for some compelling administrative reason. The clerk usually will know if this is so. For example, a case may have been grouped with other cases involving the same issue. In a circuit such as the Fourth, Fifth, Eighth, or Ninth that hears argument in several different cities, the case may have been set before a panel that is hearing argument only on one or two days, so that a continuance is not, or nearly not, possible. If the clerk's office suggests that argument has been set on some such basis, a continuance motion may be fruitless or counterproductive. Not only may the motion be denied, but the consideration of it might provoke a panel decision that oral argument is not necessary after all.

An early telephone call to the clerk may, however, obviate the need for a motion. If counsel simply wants argument set on one day of an argument session rather than another, the clerk can sometimes grant this relief by telephone, subject to a follow-up letter.

Federal Rule of Appellate Procedure 34(b) cautions that any motion for postponement or for additional argument time "must be made by motion filed reasonably in advance of the date fixed for hearing."[24]

In responding to the argument notice, the advocate also can seek to arrange the argument in the most effective way. Requests for additional argument are discussed in **§10.15.** Suppose, however, that there are multiple appellants or

---

[24] Fed R App P 34(b), the full text of which is in **app A.**

multiple appeals. Cross-appeals are usually argued with the main appeal, the order of argument being determined by the order in which the notices of appeal were filed.[25] There is no fixed rule for allocating time when there are multiple appellants or consolidated appeals, except the caution in Fed R App P 34(d) to "avoid duplication of argument."[26]

Order of argument can, however, make a difference. Counsel can propose to the court how the argument time should be divided, as discussed in **§10.12.**

Each court of appeals has its own rules on informing lawyers of the panel who will hear the case. *See* **§10.06.** When the clerk's office definitively sets argument, counsel will receive a printed calendar for the entire day or week of argument, with a courtroom assignment and a list of cases to be argued that day or week. The time at which each day's session of argument—which usually consists of four or five cases—will begin also is listed. Counsel will be asked to return a card stating who will present argument. Although the calendar lists the cases in a particular order, the panel may change the order, even as late as the morning of argument. Thus, counsel must be at court well in advance of the argument session, in plenty of time to sign in with the clerk and become familiar with the physical arrangement of the courtroom and lectern.

For most circuits, arguments are held in the court's headquarters city. For large circuits such as the Ninth, argument is scheduled on a rotating basis around the circuit, with preference being given to the larger cities. Other circuits travel at least once a year, usually to cities where law school moot courtrooms may be available or cities in which one or more circuit judges have chambers. If a circuit judge is physically unable to travel, arguments may regularly be set in his or her home city.

§10.04 Obtaining Additional Argument Time

In almost every circuit, a staff attorney or deputy clerk rates each argued case and determines how much time to allocate for oral argument. Each circuit has a typical time allowed. When the Federal Rules of Appellate Procedure were adopted in 1968, 30 minutes per side was the norm, and the Advisory Committee encouraged courts to extend this time if the case so warranted.[27]

Today, 20 minutes has become the norm in most circuits. Some circuits—for example, the Second, Eighth, and Ninth—have adopted 10-minute per side arguments as a routine matter in single issue or noncomplex cases. The Second Circuit seldom allots more than 15 minutes per side.

---

[25] Fed R App P 34(d). If the notices were filed simultaneously, the party who was plaintiff below is treated as appellant in determining the order of argument. The appellant opens and closes the argument. Fed R App P 34(c).

[26] *Id.*

[27] Advisory Committee Notes, Fed R App P 34. However, Judges Bright & Arnold, in Myron H. Bright & Richard S. Arnold, *Oral Argument? It May Be Crucial!*, 70 ABAJ 68 (Sept 1984), speak of the advisability of mini-arguments of only a few minutes in many cases, to at least give the panel a chance to put questions to the advocates and help ensure that nothing is missed.

The amount of time allocated will be printed on the argument calendar that definitively sets the argument date. However, the clerk's office may state a tentative argument allocation in the initial scheduling order. Or, as in the Fifth Circuit, the court may have a heavy presumption in favor of 20-minute arguments.

Once the argument calendar is printed, it is difficult to obtain more than another 10 minutes or so of additional argument time. If counsel cannot foresee wanting more than that amount of extra time, the motion for additional time may be deferred until the argument is definitely scheduled.

In most cases, however, one can have two chances to seek additional argument time. First, when requesting oral argument in the initial briefs, counsel should not only say why argument is necessary but also propose a certain amount of time and how it should be divided. This request will be considered by the panel in deciding whether any argument should be allowed, and by the clerk and staff attorney in determining the amount of time for argument.

The next opportunity arises when the calendar arrives. At that point, a specific panel has been assigned to hear argument and the panel can consider how it will best be served by argument in each case. Seeking more time from the panel requires a motion.[28] Sometimes the order setting argument will invite such a motion; the invitation should be accepted.

Good reasons for additional argument include presence of multiple parties; issues of first impression; complex and interrelated issues that cannot adequately be addressed in 15 or 20 minutes; issues on which the court is at odds with another circuit; and issues on which there is genuine and demonstrable concern among the district judges in the circuit.

Bad reasons for additional argument include the desire to split the argument for a single appellant among multiple counsel[29] or generalized assertions that the case is important. Complexity of the facts may not be a good reason for additional time. Most circuits read the briefs and enough of the record or record excerpts to have a fairly firm grasp of the facts. Indeed, some circuits routinely advise counsel, as does the Fifth Circuit with each notice of argument: "You should not start with a recitation of the background facts, but should go immediately to the key issues upon which the case turns." However, if the case presents significant legal issues in a complex factual pattern, additional time for oral argument may have merit on this basis.

A motion for additional argument should spell out exactly how counsel intends to use the additional time, even if the only reason is to give a coherent picture of complex and disputed facts. If multiple issues or multiple counsel are involved, for example in a consolidated or multiparty appeal, the motion should recite just how many lawyers will be arguing and the time and issues each will discuss. In such a case, a motion is much more likely to be granted if counsel have clearly identified important issues, rather than simply seeking time to argue everything.

---

[28] This is a procedural motion under Fed R App P 34(b) that can be decided without waiting for a reply. *See* **ch 8.**

[29] *See* **§10.12.**

One should consider innovative approaches to argument. For example, in a consolidated case with one or two common issues and a number of individual ones, the motion might seek 45 minutes per side, with a statement that:

> If the motion is granted, Michael E. Tigar will argue for twenty-five minutes on issues common to all appellants. Counsel for appellants Jones and Smith will each argue for five minutes on an issue unique to their clients. Mr. Tigar will reserve ten minutes for rebuttal.

In a complex and multiparty appeal from a 14-month criminal trial, the Second Circuit responded to counsel's request for additional time by setting aside an entire morning of argument. As the Court described the process:

> This megatrial resulted in a mega-appeal, in which the eight appealing defendants filed separate briefs, raising collectively at least sixteen distinct issues. . . .
>
> Oral argument was a similar ordeal, in which we departed from our usual practices in two ways. First, we alloted for oral argument two hours (and ended up using three), where we normally allow no more than fifteen minutes per side. Second, in view of the unusual number of significant issues raised, we allowed each advocate for each defendant to make his argument, followed immediately by the government's rebuttal argument. We heard six different advocates for the appellants, while two assistant United States Attorneys divided the chores for the government. Our task was informed by fine briefing and extraordinary oral advocacy on all sides. Their extensive efforts to cope with a case of this magnitude were commendable.[30]

§10.05 Preparing for Oral Argument—Research and Study

The sections that follow track oral argument from the initial, most general preparation through research about the panel that is to hear argument,[31] to the details of an argument notebook and its accompanying file,[32] through the argument itself.[33] This section describes an initial approach to argument, on the theory that oral argument is a fundamentally different form of communication than the written brief.

In many law firms and government agencies, oral argument is done by a senior lawyer who receives a series of briefing memos and some coaching from relatively junior lawyers. This process results, more often than not, in a wooden argument that does not add significantly to the briefs. Even worse, this method

---

[30] United States v Salerno, 937 F2d 797, 803-04 (2d Cir 1991), *subsequent history retold in* United States v DiNapoli, 1993 WL 440282 (2d Cir Nov 1, 1993).

[31] *See* **§10.06.**

[32] *See* **§10.07.**

[33] *See* **§§10.09-10.12.**

of preparation often leaves the arguing attorney unfamiliar with large parts of the record in a complex case. Such an attorney may well harm the cause by misstatement or exaggeration or, worse yet, make damaging concessions in the thrust and parry of questioning from the court.[34]

The great appellate advocates[35] prepare for oral argument as they would for a jury trial. They seek mastery of the record through careful study. As an exercise, they put aside the briefs and try to frame the issues anew, with a view to the special constraints and opportunities of oral advocacy. They seek new insights. They ponder the opponent's position and ask how its weaknesses can be demonstrated in the face-to-face clash of oral advocacy. They rehearse portions of the argument informally with associates, seeking to find weak spots and refine statements of issues.

At the same time, a great appellate advocate never forgets that argument, like a jury trial, is a dynamic process. Indeed, its dynamism is enhanced because the deciders—the judges—are free to ask questions and argue back to the lawyers. The other side may choose to focus on a different mix of issues. The advocate must be prepared, and not simply briefed, on the whole of the case and upon legal theories that may be injected by the panel.

Regardless of one's theory of argument, the advocate's most valuable asset is a thoughtful, probing question from the judges. Answering the question takes precedence over everything. When the question is answered, however, time will likely remain in the argument, so structure and planning are always important.

The first step in preparation is mastery of the record. If counsel has followed the suggestions in Chapter 7, the record will have been digested. Thus, counsel will be able to make an index, if one has not already been made. The index should be organized by topic, with a list of transcript and record references under each topic heading. In a case with a lengthy record, the index should key to a summary or digest of the entire transcript. In a joint appendix circuit, the index should be keyed both to the joint appendix and to the original record.

---

[34] Most courts of appeals tape record arguments for the court's convenience. The tape and any transcript usually are not available to counsel. Most courts of appeals will entertain a motion to have a court reporter take down and transcribe the argument on condition that the transcript be made available to the panel. One's opponent also can order a copy. However, courts of appeals have granted motions to have the argument tape transcribed, or even to have it loaned out to a court reporter to be transcribed. Such a request would be made only in extraordinary circumstances, as where one's opponent had made a significant concession or misstatement. Even if there is no transcription, concessions and misstatements made during argument can be recaptured and quoted back at counsel by the court. This happens more frequently than many lawyers realize and is an additional reason for not confiding the argument to someone based on anything other than thorough knowledge of the record and the law.

[35] Edward Bennett Williams is a sterling example. His Supreme Court arguments can be studied in any major law library, first by finding his name as arguing counsel in Westlaw, then by locating Oral Arguments of the Supreme Court of the United States, microformed by Court Terms by University Publications of America. For other examples of great argument, see the sources cited at **§1.08.**

In a record excerpts circuit, dual references are also important to help counsel and the court best access a disputed point of fact.

The index is designed to help the arguing lawyer prepare by identifying relevant material in the record. It should be easy enough to use, and the advocate familiar enough with it, that two other tasks can be accomplished. First, the arguing lawyer should be able to answer a judge's questions about the facts quickly and easily with an appropriate citation to the record if necessary; the citation can be to the joint appendix, the record excerpts, or the original record. Second, the arguing lawyer (and anyone at the table helping) should be able to catch the opponent's misstatements of the record and answer them at the appropriate time.

Mastery of the issues and the law is the next step in preparation. All cases in all briefs should be Shepardized again in preparation for argument.[36] This process guards against missing an overruling or a case from another circuit that conflicts with circuit law. Equally important, it also helps alert the arguing lawyer to potential questions from the panel or arguments by the opponent. The judges' law clerks will be doing research to prepare bench memoranda. Judges may pursue some issues on their own and many enjoy querying counsel about recently decided relevant cases that are not in the briefs.

In addition, counsel should develop search queries for relevant recent cases that may not have cited the ones contained in the tables of authorities of the briefs. Finally, one must scan the most recent slip opinions from the circuit for any relevant authorities that may not yet appear in Westlaw or LEXIS.

The appellate advocate must then select the issues on which the argument will focus. Generally, these will be the lead issues in the brief. This selection process does not obviate the need to prepare on all issues[37] both to answer questions from the court and to reply to an opponent. However, selecting issues will ensure that the short time allotted to argument is wisely used and not fractured into so many pieces that it resembles a rapid reading of the headings in the brief.

In the initial parts of this process, counsel may well identify more issues for argument than possibly can be addressed. By contrast, one may see that two or more issues can be combined and discussed under a common heading.

For each issue, try to phrase each individual point of argument persuasively, in 25 or so words. Support this formulation in no more than two paragraphs of oral expression. Invite associates, clerks, and partners to attack this formulation. This process should continue until the arguer is confident that he or she has framed the issue as persuasively as possible and is prepared to meet every possible objection.

---

[36] The WestCheck program provides a quick mechanism for performing this task. Assuming one has used the program to check citations in the brief, WestCheck will create a citations list in the format that it reads. One simply adjusts the request to take account of the earlier search, starts the program, and evaluates the results.

[37] Some courts make it a practice to require that all counsel who are to argue be prepared to answer questions on any aspect of the case. Being unprepared is not only embarrassing, but can be lethal to one's position.

Often, this process will point to the need for additional research. If research turns up other significant authorities, notify the court in accordance with Fed R App P 28(j), which permits counsel to notify the court by letter of supplemental citations. The rule provides a limited right of reply to such a letter.[38]

Usually, this process will yield a formulation of the issues at least slightly different from that in the briefs. This is a boon. Oral argument is an opportunity for a new synthesis, based on the parties' respective positions and the range of choices open to the court. The reformulation of party positions should be a natural part of this process and will necessarily include additional research.

For example, the author argued an appointed criminal appeal involving several search and seizure issues. The briefs dealt minutely with the facts of each search and the arguments uniquely applicable to each. The author decided that the most useful way to argue these questions was to pose a "search issue" that united all the disputed contentions under two headings: the warrant clause of the Fourth Amendment and standing to challenge a search. This broad-gauge reformulation provided a matrix within which to examine each of the searches, and to distinguish—or challenge the authority of—all the cases on which the government relied.

In another case, there might be a question of appealability, but the merits will be addressed if the court determines it has jurisdiction. This duality arises often in appeals from remand orders in federal removal cases.[39] The appellee faces a genuine dilemma, because he or she cannot seem to concede appealability by too willingly arguing the merits. The proper approach might be to stress the statutory bar to appeal and then stress how the bar makes sense in the present case. For example:

> The Congress has provided in 28 United States Code section 1447, as construed by this Court in the *Shell Oil* case,[40] that these remand orders are not appealable. Ordinarily, that would put an end to the matter. But the appellant cites a vaguely defined Congressional intent that he says cuts against the clear words of the statute. He seems to have a machine that detects intent, and it works best the farther away from the statute you hold it.
>
> But this case shows why Congress was right. The district judge held he had no jurisdiction because he saw through the appellant's effort at collusively creating the illusion of federal court power over this lawsuit.

Following this transition, one would argue that the district judge was right in remanding. Thus, one has argued both appealability and the merits without one argument weakening the other.

In the quoted example, one might return to the theme in conclusion:

---

[38] *See* **§9.19.**

[39] *See* **§2.15.**

[40] Cited at **§2.15.**

> The statutes that say there is no jurisdiction on appeal are sometimes frustrating, because there is a temptation to peek behind the curtain that they draw over events in the district court and see what happened down there. In this case, however, if you do look behind the curtain, all you'll see is a district judge doing his job as the law requires and provides.

Or, counsel may choose to begin by emphasizing the specific facts that are claimed to spell victory, rather than starting from a general principle. Of course, even a general approach requires detailed mastery of the facts. The point is that argument provides an opportunity, always worth evaluating, often worth accepting, to frame the issues anew.

When one has identified the most important issues, one should strive to find a common thread or theme that unites them, beyond the obvious one that they arise in the same case. The thread or theme should introduce the argument.

If the evidence was insufficient to sustain the verdict, this probably should be the theme. One can do more in a short argument than to cite one or two illustrations of an insufficiency of evidence point. That point can then be used to make a transition that explains how the jury came to its inadequate verdict. Perhaps the instructions were wrong, or prejudicial evidence wrongly admitted, or the rules on expert testimony wrongly applied—or some combination of these.

In another case, the theme might be the misapplication of an important legal principle, leading the district judge to deny summary judgment and directed verdict, and to give erroneous jury instructions.

The theme does three things. It introduces the argument, it unites the separate points being argued, and it is a short and powerful statement of why the advocate's client should win. The process of reinventing the case yields argument that is more likely to address the concerns that the court brings to argument. By treating the case as new, the advocate brings to it a cast of mind similar to that of the judges who will decide it.

§10.06 —Focusing on the Panel That Will Hear the Case

In most circuits, counsel may know the identity of the panel who will hear argument a week or so in advance. This information is usually available by calling the clerk's office. In some circuits, the panel members' names are posted in the clerk's office.[41] Other circuits announce the names by a recorded message on an answering machine.

---

[41] The Ninth Circuit posts the names of judges for the coming week's arguments on a public bulletin board and instructs counsel to submit a self-addressed envelope with a card listing the name and number of the case. The clerk's office will then send the names of the judges to counsel. Counsel, fearful of delays in the mail, should ask a friend or associate in the city where the clerk's office is located to scan the bulletin board and telephone.

Knowing the panel members' identities is of vital help to the advocate, because it enables him or her to focus on their prior opinions and backgrounds. It is almost never possible to control who will be on the panel that decides a case. If the case relates to one previously decided, one should so inform the clerk's office, which will perhaps inquire of the court whether the same panel should be assembled. A panel that has retained jurisdiction and remanded may reassemble to hear an appeal after remand, although this is not invariably done. Negative control of the panel can only be achieved by recusal of one or more judges; the certificate of interested persons in the brief[42] identifies potential conflicts for the court. Alternatively, a motion to recuse can be filed under 28 USC §455.[43]

To probe the judges' backgrounds, consult the Almanac of the Federal Judiciary,[44] a valuable publication that contains capsule biographies, lawyer evaluations of judicial performance, and brief extracts from the judge's most significant opinions. Talk to those who have appeared before the panel judges or who know them in other contexts. A judge's former law clerks may be valuable sources, though their judgment may be biased by their professional association with the judge.

One may find it worthwhile to look up the judge's confirmation hearing record if there is likely to be valuable data there. Most federal appellate judges are routinely confirmed. However, some appointments are controversial enough to have attracted the attention of Senate Judiciary Committee members and provoked a lengthy hearing. In that case, the hearing may provide information on the character and judicial philosophy of the judge.

One is looking for two principal clues to the possible behavior of panel members. One is the judge's outlook on legal issues, which can be a valuable predictor of position, particularly when the judge has not written anything on the subject matter of your case.

An equally important issue is the judge's behavior at oral argument. Does he or she ask a lot of questions? Are the questions designed to trap the lawyer or are they genuine clues to issues that trouble the judge? Does the judge sometimes ask devil's advocate questions to explore an issue in a way that is designed to influence other panel members? Does the judge write his or her own questions or are they taken from a bench memorandum authored by law clerks? (Law clerks are the most reliable sources of information on this issue, but observant lawyers who have appeared before the judge may well have formed a cogent opinion.)

It is important to ask whether the judge's behavior at argument changes depending on the issue. Some judges ask hard questions, but are civil and cor-

---

[42] Fed R App P 26.1 (corporate disclosure statement). The certificate, which enables judges to evaluate recusal obligations, is in most circuit rules. *E.g.*, 5th Cir R 28.2.1.

[43] *See* Liljeberg v Health Servs Acquisition Corp, 486 US 847 (1988).

[44] Almanac of the Federal Judiciary (Barnabas D. Johnson ed 1984 & Supp 1993). The Almanac's evaluation of judges is not to be taken as gospel. This is to be expected since the polling of lawyers for their opinions is necessarily selective, and some lawyers will hesitate to express a candidly unflattering view of a judge, even under the assurance of anonymity.

dial to all advocates under all circumstances. Others may be courteous unless the issue strikes a particular ideological chord, at which time they turn aggressive and even rude. This sort of behavior is fortunately rare, but the advocate who is unprepared for it can be struck speechless—a distinct occupational handicap.

Knowing the judge's background, writings, and prior opinions can provide valuable clues in replying to the judge's questions. A judge with substantial trial experience, as a lawyer and on the bench, may be looking for a different answer than a judge whose interest in issues is more theoretical.

For example, in one case a district judge sitting by designation asked the author whether the jury's knowing that a witness perjured himself in their presence was any more significant than knowing that the witness had lied on other occasions. The judge had been a trial lawyer for many years before taking the bench. Such a question is never abstract. It is that judge's question, in a particular case, as part of a specific panel. The questioner may be searching for his or her own reasons, or for some theme that will command the assent of the other judges.

The author answered in effect, "I have not tried so many cases as your honor, but I think we share a tradition that says this: 'If the witness kisses the Book, and thereafter looks the jury in the eye and lies, that is always decisively important in the tournament of trial. Some might say this faith of ours is based partly on myth, but if so it is a myth so deeply ingrained in our legal system that none of us—on either side of the bench—is free to doubt it. Perjury in the jury's presence, when exposed, is always decisive.' "

In another case, a question might reflect a judge's persistent concern with a legal issue. One would not know this except by reading what the judge had written before.

The importance of learning insights into a judge's manner of questioning cannot be overstated. To illustrate the kind of evidence to be sought, some examples from the United States Supreme Court may be helpful, as they are not confined to a particular circuit. Justice Sandra Day O'Connor typically asks only one or two questions during an oral argument. However, those questions almost invariably focus on an issue or issues that she regards as dispositive and troublesome, for herself and for at least several other members of the Court.

Justice Anthony Kennedy asks pointed, intense, practical questions that are also keys to his views.

Justice Souter's questions are quiet and probing. He is unfailingly courteous to counsel, but he demands thoughtful and considered answers. He will not be easily deterred from a line of questioning on which he has embarked.

Justice Ruth Bader Ginsburg's questioning style, while on the DC Circuit, was sharp and incisive. She becomes visibly impatient when lawyers are ill-prepared, do not know the record, or try to evade her questions. She wants short, definitive answers.

The next main line of research is a computer search for opinions authored by panel members. Depending on how long the judge has served, one may be able to scan all the opinions or only those selected by a broad-based computer search.

The first search parameter is the court or courts, in addition to other sources, that you will search. Many federal appeals judges served as district judges, and a few on state courts of record. Opinions written in earlier judicial service can be valuable clues to present views. Some judges have written law journal articles. While on the federal district court, a present day court of appeals judge may have sat by designation on the court of appeals. Search parameters must be broad enough to cover all these possibilities.

Assuming one cannot read everything the judge has written, how does one formulate a search? One begins by taking the list of cases from the table of authorities and searching them for any that were authored or participated in by the panel members.

Next, one develops search questions that sweep more broadly than the issues in the case. For example, in a case involving a search and seizure issue to be argued in the Fifth Circuit, the Westlaw request would be made to database CTA5, and the query would be "search arrest warrant & topic (110) & A B C," where 110 is the topic number (to restrict the search to criminal and criminal-related cases), and A, B, and C are the last names of the panel members.

Note that a Westlaw field search to "Judge (A)" would retrieve only opinions authored by that judge, to the exclusion of opinions in which he or she was merely on the panel. If the judge has a common name, such as Smith, the proposed search must be constructed to retrieve only instances of the name within the same sentence as the word *circuit.*[45]

It is much less significant that a judge was on the panel than that he or she authored the majority or a concurring or dissenting opinion. How much less significant is a matter of debate. When court of appeals workloads were less, opinions for the court were given much more attention by the nonwriting panel members than is the case today; there was more time.

As noted at **§10.13,** the majority opinion is assigned immediately after the panel hears argument in an argued case, and by a fairly random process for nonargued cases. Once the assignment is made, the other judges may have little to do with the case except to read and initial the draft prepared by the author. Some judges pay a great deal less attention than others to opinions in which they concur but do not author. The upshot is that nonwriting panel members may not have, and do not feel, any sense of authorship in the language, as opposed to the bare holding of such opinions.[46]

---

[45] The same restrictive search would use the word *district* if a district judge is sitting by designation. However, since the identification of a district judge sitting by designation on the court of appeals is usually in a footnote at the beginning of the opinion, a different search must be constructed.

[46] United States v Oshatz, 912 F2d 534 (2d Cir 1990) (Newman, J), *cert denied,* 111 S Ct 1695 (1991), provides guidance to the appellate lawyer reading judicial opinions for all they might say or for the least they might have held. The search will depend on which side the lawyer has been retained to represent. The court acknowledged that: "not every observation contained in an opinion of this Court deserves to be regarded

As a final check, the advocate must at least scan all opinions by the particular court for a period of one month to six weeks before the scheduled argument, just to be certain that there is nothing relevant in any recent decision that escapes notice.

In researching for oral argument, counsel should also be aware of nonpublished opinions by the court and particularly by members of the panel. All courts of appeals issue some opinions that are not published and, in some circuits, most are not. For example, in the 12-month period ending June 30, 1987, the Fifth Circuit issued a published opinion in only 45.4 percent of decided cases.

Circuit rules limit, to varying extents, the instances in which such *nonpubs* may be cited. However, the nonpubs can provide insight into the views of panel members and may be ammunition to answer an opponent's argument. They will be particularly useful in defense of the judgment below because most nonpubs are affirmances. To find nonpublished opinions, one can use word-based search strategy in either LEXIS or Westlaw, or track prior citations through these services. Until 1987, Westlaw carried fewer nonpubs than LEXIS, but West has now decided to put them on line with a notation as to the circuit rules concerning citation in briefs or argument.

Knowing something about the panel is not an exercise in preparing for flattery. The insights gained should never be used to suggest in argument that a panel of the court, or a given judge, would not follow the law as set out in other panel opinions. The astute reader may detect that a particular panel, composed of judges of a given philosophical bent, is more likely to rule a given way than a panel constituted differently. Good manners require that the advocate not suggest that cases in general, or this case in particular, can turn on the luck of the draw.

It is, however, proper to save time and drive home a reference with an argument in the following form:

> As for the government's contention that a motion to suppress can be closed to the public, and the defendant and his counsel excluded, this court has disposed of that issue. In *United States v Norris,* in an opinion by Judge Davis [who is on the panel being addressed], the court cited *Waller v Georgia* and said that the motion to suppress is really part of the trial for public trial purposes. On the related issue of the district judge basing his decision on evidence the defendant had no opportunity to con-

---

as the law of the Circuit. Opinion authors frequently express thoughts peripheral to the holding of a case, and these thoughts do not bind the Circuit, nor even the concurring judges on the panel. If every phrase in an opinion were accorded binding effect, there would be a tendency either to refine language with such meticulous care as to imperil the prompt disposition of the Court's work or to reduce opinions to bare pronouncements of holdings." *Id* 540.

front, Judge Davis was on the panel that decided in *United States v Glass* that confrontation was an essential right.[47]

This form of argument telescopes information by identifying the cited case only briefly. It involves a member or members of the panel in the argument process. It invites questions or distinctions from the judge whose opinion is cited.

A judge whose opinion is cited to him or her may not recall the opinion, and may even say so.[48] A typical judge authors more than 100 opinions per year and participates in decisions on at least three times that many. Therefore, the reference to an opinion by a panel member must be complete enough to make recall likely.

Some court of appeals judges formulate questions to counsel that are mailed out shortly before the argument. Sometimes the questions are to be answered briefly in writing and sometimes the court requests that the advocate answer them at oral argument. Usually, the identity of the particular judge or judges who formulated the questions is not disclosed, but the content and tenor of the questions can provide valuable insight into the court's perception of the case. Counsel should not, however, regard the questions as discouraging argument on issues not inquired about.

The preargument questions may provoke legal research into points already in the brief in addition to other issues that the questions suggest. There is nothing wrong with preparing a Fed R App P 28(j) letter with any additional citations that research may uncover.[49] Indeed, sometimes the clerk's office will accept a short list of additional citations the morning of argument, provided it is given with the assurance that one's opponent has received a copy. One can make polite inquiry whether the panel will receive such a communication, as there is no rule on the subject and the practice varies among judges even on the same court of appeals.

§10.07 —Making an Oral Argument Notebook

This section spells out how to make an oral argument notebook and accompanying file. It should be read together with **§§10.05** and **10.06,** on the structure of argument and adapting the argument to the panel that is to hear the case.

---

[47] In arguing Gelbard v United States, 408 US 41, *cert denied,* 408 US 922 (1972), the author prepared by collecting opinions by six justices that would be called into doubt were the Court to rule against the author's client. This is not a form of judge-shopping, but a mark of respect to the tribunal and its members, and to the canon that consistency of interpretation is one element of stare decisis.

[48] It is easy to overdo these references to judges' prior opinions. The author once cited to Judge John R. Brown, the longtime Chief of the Fifth Circuit, an opinion that Judge Brown had written many years before, and made the mistake of saying, "As the court will remember, in that case Chief Judge Brown said. . . ." Judge Brown interrupted with the cheerful rebuke, "Oh, yes, Mr. Tigar, we have written thousands of opinions, and you can be sure we remember every single one."

[49] *See* **§9.19.**

The oral argument notebook does not contain a text of the argument, to be read to the court. Some advocates, and even some authors on advocacy, suggest writing out one's argument. Experience and the emphatic opinions of judges counsel in the strongest terms that one should never write out one's argument and never read a prepared argument to the court. This rule even forbids delivering a memorized rendition of a written argument. This is because such techniques throw away the most valuable benefit of oral argument—the opportunity to be face-to-face with the deciders, to look them in the eye, to try to fathom their true views and concerns, and to respond to their questions.[50]

More often than not, the panel's questions dictate that the argument one planned to make must be changed. This does not mean that themes one came prepared to stress must or should be abandoned. Quite the contrary: the careful planning for oral argument should not lightly be cast aside, any more than one would throw out an entire trial plan because one witness or exhibit did not perform as expected.[51] The oral argument notebook helps the lawyer respond to a question and then return to themes planned in advance. The lawyer with a set speech cannot easily take up the challenge of questions, work in a theme that had been planned for later development, then return to the uncompleted thought that the question interrupted.

Example: A distinguished advocate was making an argument in the court of appeals in a celebrated case. He had written out a powerful and cogent argument, focusing principally on one main theme. Because of the advocate's reputation, the panel of judges was perhaps more than usually courteous, even deferential. Halfway through the advocate's presentation, the presiding judge interrupted to say that he hoped to hear something from the advocate on another important issue in the case. The advocate interrupted his set speech, made a short rather offhand remark about the issue on which the judge made inquiry, and continued reading his prepared argument. The judge was plainly taken aback. From the advocate's perspective, it was a significant opportunity wasted.

In another celebrated case, a government lawyer was reading out a prepared argument. A panel member interrupted with a question. The lawyer responded, "I'll be getting to that later in my argument." Here, of course, was more than a missed opportunity. The advocate had crossed over into overt rudeness and the presiding judge rebuked him.

The prepared argument is wrong for the same reason that writing out one's cross-examination of a key trial witness is wrong. One gives up one's place in

---

[50] The first edition of this treatise decried the written-out oral argument in milder terms. Since then, the author has participated in many programs on appellate advocacy and procedure, and has heard from dozens of United States court of appeals judges on this issue. Their unanimous opinion is that it is a mistake to deliver a written or memorized argument. This admittedly anecdotal evidence supplements personal observation.

[51] *See generally* Michael E. Tigar, Examining Witnesses ch 1 (1993). In the first chapter of Examining Witnesses, the author sets out a theory of trial persuasion and organization that is largely applicable to appellate argument.

the dynamic of litigation. One stops listening to the process. One stands to miss gifts in the form of spontaneous statements by the person to whom one is speaking; in a trial, that person is the witness, in an appellate argument it is the judges collectively.[52]

After working out potential themes of argument, making the oral argument notebook is the next step. One could organize the material in a file folder, or on the sheets of a legal pad, but the notebook format makes it easy to use the material during argument, and to change its content and order during preparation.

Here are some suggestions on the materials to use in making a notebook. Use a good three-ring binder with sheet protectors to prevent the pages from tearing. Use good quality tabbed dividers, preferably those that permit label changes when the order and naming of the subjects to be included in the notebook should be changed. The tabs should be labelled and organized so that they are easily visible—after all, one must be able to find material quickly in the notebook. For sheets within the notebook, one can use either three-hole punched legal pad paper or letter-size paper that has been punched; the choice depends on whether one writes out one's notes or uses a word processor.[53]

The appellant's notebook should have tabs corresponding to the themes of argument, the issues that may arise in questioning, the potential rebuttal issues, and the index to the record. The appellee's notebook should also have tabs on the appellant's potential themes that appellee's counsel does not intend to raise unless the appellant does.

Any notebook should also contain briefs of the most important cases and excerpts from other significant authorities. Finally, one must include an index to the record, edited down to make it useful in answering any factual question that might arise.

At the argument, the advocate will have the notebook, along with other files—preferably red ropes—containing the full text of very important cases, the briefs and record excerpts or joint appendix, and perhaps copies of more important parts of the record itself. One's objective is to make the notebook an adequate single source for the entire argument and for every question that one can anticipate being asked. The other files are simply there in case something unanticipated happens. Having a file with the full texts of significant cases and excerpts from the record permits one to respond to precise questions with precision, showing command of the case and respect for the court.

Given the canon that the notebook be a self-contained reference, one can see that it forces the advocate to prepare thoroughly and then to distill that preparation in a way that respects the oral argument process and the limited time the court allots to it. One must anticipate that no more than one-third to one-half the allotted time will be spent in delivering the argument one planned to make. The remainder will be devoted to answering questions,

---

[52] Michael E. Tigar, *supra* note 51, at ch 8.

[53] A laptop computer with a portable printer can be invaluable if argument preparation is to take place away from the advocate's home city. *See* **§9.04.**

addressing issues suggested by questions, and responding to arguments framed by the opponent.

Every advocate comes to know that much if not most of the time during argument will be taken by questions, but no doubt fears what might happen if there are no questions. What does one do to fill the entire time if few questions are asked? There are two responses: First, in addition to the must do points, the argument notebook should contain tabs with optional points to be made in case there is time. These optional points should not involve entirely separate and distinct intellectual constructions, otherwise the entire argument becomes cluttered and diffuse. They should rather be additional *reasons* in support of the main theme already chosen for argument.

The second, though perhaps heretical, way to deal with extra time left by the panel's lack of questions is to be quiet and sit down. There is nothing wrong with saying, "That is our argument. If the panel has no questions"—looking at each member to be sure—"I would like to yield the balance of my time." If only a couple of minutes remain, this is the proper response, certainly preferable to dithering, or seeming to.[54]

The notebook must also contain tabs for issues that the advocate does not plan to argue, but that may be raised by the opponent or by the panel. Examples would include issues of harmless error, waiver, failure to object, and other troublesome procedural arguments.

To see how these anticipatory tabs would be used imagine the following colloquy at oral argument:

> Counsel for appellant [in mid-argument]: The failure to focus the jury's attention on the powerful exculpatory content of this evidence. . . .
>
> Judge [interrupting]: But was there an objection made at the time the trial judge charged the jury?
>
> Counsel: No, there was not, but . . . .
>
> Judge: Then isn't the contention waived, or defaulted?
>
> Counsel [turning to the notebook tab marked "Waiver"]: No, for three reasons. First, the Texas courts have squarely held that no contemporaneous objection is necessary to preserve an objection of this kind. That is Black v. State, which is cited in our brief. Second, as the Texas courts hold, objection would be futile given the position of the Court of Criminal Appeals. Third, counsel for the state failed to claim waiver or procedural default in the district court, and so the waiver issue has been waived.
>
> Another Judge: But as a practical matter, why wouldn't the lawyer object?
>
> Counsel: Because given the state of Texas law at that point, the lawyer might have gotten a jury instruction that was even worse than the one that was given and lost any chance at all to win the case in front of the jury.

---

[54] On the choice of a theme, see **§§10.05, 10.09, 10.10.**

A contention that one's claim has been waived, or the appeal forgone because of a procedural gaffe, or that the court lacks jurisdiction for some reason is potentially lethal, as discussed often in this treatise. As in the example, the issue may not be one that counsel will choose to argue, unless questioned by the panel or unless the appellee's argument requires dealing with it in rebuttal.

To have a response ready to a question from the bench or to use in rebuttal argument, the advocate would have a tab labelled *Waiver* in the argument notebook. Behind that tab, a page of notes might look like this:

> NO WAIVER, NO DEFAULT
> THREE REASONS
>
> 1. Texas courts hold no objection necessary. Black v. State (AOB [Appellant's Opening Brief] 21.
> 2. Futile, given Texas courts position.
> 3. State did not raise issue in district court.
>
> PRACTICAL REASON
>
> Could get worse instruction by making an issue at trial. Counsel rationally chose.

Having the notes organized in this way keeps the argument on track, saves valuable time by permitting an organized answer, and shows that the advocate has considered the issue.

There is one reason to add to the notebook theory—when one wishes to bring in an exhibit, or a book, or some other object that represents an important point, to the argument. The power of symbols can be great. Although this lesson avails the advocate mainly in trials, it can sometimes be used to effect in appellate argument.[55] Suppose, for example, that a portion of transcript contains a key exchange, one that can be quoted or paraphrased quickly, so as not to waste time. Or suppose there is a key case, from which a few words will illustrate a point. One might copy the relevant passage into the notebook for ease of reference, but having the actual transcript volume or the volume of official reports in hand adds the visual symbol to the verbal message. The device should not be overused, but can sometimes be helpful.

One might even use an exhibit from the trial as a symbol. Court security, and the advocate's good sense, would preclude brandishing a weapon or a controlled substance. Some exhibits or photographs of them that are part of the appellate record and have been transmitted to the appeals court[56] can effectively be present during oral argument.

Some advocates bring charts, diagrams, or other visual aids to argument. Sometimes these props set out important points to be argued. Other times,

---

[55] On the power of symbols, see Michael E. Tigar, *supra* note 51, at ch 6.

[56] Fed R App P 11(b) provides that the district court clerk should not transmit bulky items and exhibits to the court of appeals. Fed R App P 34(g) regulates use of exhibits at argument.

they depict exhibits in the case. This sort of material invariably detracts from argument. The advocate must step away from the lectern to use them, making it difficult to hear. More to the point, the court usually tape records arguments for its own convenience, for reference in writing the opinion. Counsel defeats the recording system by moving around. The court has the briefs in front of it, along with bench memos prepared by its law clerks. There is no need for additional visual material and using it creates a distraction.

The best way to illustrate this process of outlining the argument is to take a hypothetical case and discuss the tactical choices that must be faced and made. Suppose 20 minutes per side has been allotted in an appeal from the judgment in a civil case that was tried to a jury. The issues briefed are: error in a crucial jury instruction; plaintiff's lack of standing to sue on one of the two claims presented; the trial judge's erroneous admission of evidence and failure to exclude evidence; and insufficiency of the evidence.

Errors in admitting or excluding evidence are seldom the basis for reversal; the error must be significant, going to some important element of the case, and the harm probably substantial. So such a point is doubly suspect as a candidate for argument: first, because the judges know that such points are unlikely to require reversal; and second, because explaining why this case is an exception to the general rule usually takes more time than the point is worth.[57]

A strong claim that the evidence is insufficient is a compelling point on appeal,[58] but may take too long to argue in convincing detail. However, the court is much more likely to reverse on a legal issue if convinced that, on the facts, the appellant was wrongly found liable. Some mention of the insufficiency point therefore is probably in order.[59]

Standing can be a good argument issue because it focuses the court on its duty to enforce limits on the judicial power, whether those limits are set by statutory definitions of who can bring suit or by caselaw.[60]

Jury instruction issues are also good candidates for argument both because significant error in instructions is a solid basis for reversal and because the panel's questions can help the advocate make the point even more persuasive that it was in the briefs. A jury instruction issue invites questions about whether the charge as a whole conveyed the law correctly, an objection was timely made,

---

[57] When excluded evidence goes to the heart of the case, particularly in criminal cases where such limitations have constitutional overtones, the point may be worth arguing. An evidence issue that is central is more easily explained in the limited time allowed for argument. *See, e.g.,* United States v Salerno, 937 F2d 797, 803-04 (2d Cir 1991), *subsequent history retold in* United States v DiNapoli, 1993 WL 440282 (2d Cir Nov 1, 1993). (exclusion of exculpatory hearsay).

[58] *See* **§5.07.**

[59] See discussion of arguing insufficiency at **§10.05.**

[60] *See, e.g.,* Raymond v Mobil Oil Corp, 983 F2d 1528 (10th Cir), *cert denied,* 62 USLW (1993) (no ERISA standing for former employees who have received all their pension benefits as a lump sum). *See generally* Robert A. Sedler, *Standing to Assert Constitutional Jus Tertii in the Supreme Court,* 71 Yale LJ 599 (1962) and Robert A. Sedler, *The Assertion of Constitutional Jus Tertii: A Substantive Approach,* 70 Cal L Rev 1308 (1982). On standing to appeal, see **§2.19.**

and the nature of a proper instruction. These questions give the advocate insight into the court's attitude towards the case.

In our hypothetical case, a rational choice might be this: Begin with a strong statement that evokes the claim of insufficiency, without planning to discuss the point at length. Follow immediately with a discussion of the jury instruction issue. Save a couple of minutes for the standing point. Conclude with a few words that again evoke the injustice of the verdict.

Why this order of argument? A strong statement in the beginning shows confidence in one's position. If one or more of the judges is poised to consider the sufficiency argument, the initial statement may well draw a question. The advocate can then respond to the question and shore up that argument. Also, by making the sufficiency claim strongly but briefly, one presents the opponent with the dilemma of pointedly ignoring the issue to save time or taking valuable argument time to recite a version of the evidence.

For example:

> Patterson Products amended its pension plan in 1987. The appellee claims that the choice he faced from that amendment forced him to retire and violated the Age Discrimination in Employment Act. The evidence showed that he made a voluntary and not a forced choice. It showed that Patterson acted for rational, lawful—indeed compelling—business reasons in making the change.

Then, one does what stand-up comedians and disk jockeys call a segue into the first substantive point to be argued.

> But the jury could not make these decisions properly because the trial judge did not properly guide their decision in the jury charge.

The jury instruction point comes after the introduction because it logically follows therefrom. This leaves the standing issue for last. Trying to shoehorn the evidence issue into a 20-minute argument slot would be a mistake.

Assuming these choices, the argument notebook would have tabs labelled:

Introduction
Jury Charge
Standing
Conclusion

Behind each of these tabs would be a single page, or at most two pages, each with notes and key words to guide the argument and any brief quotes that one planned to use in the argument.

There would follow tabs to cover material on which one can expect questions:

Sufficiency
Request

Harmless Error
Evidence

Behind the *Sufficiency* tab, one would have a note on the standard of review and a short, point-by-point attack on the evidence that could be given in a minute or so if there is a question, or perhaps could be used on rebuttal. The other tabs cover issues that may arise in the same ways. Additional tabs could cover matter in the record and the key authorities.

As one prepares for argument, one may find that this proposed order of topics is not best. The tabs can easily be relabelled and the notes reorganized. For example, one might find that the sufficiency point—or at least an element of it—can be stated simply enough that it should form a part of the argument. That decision will probably require dropping one of the other points because a cluttered argument is to be avoided at all costs.

§10.08 —Practicing the Argument

There are honest and reasonable differences of opinion on how best to prepare for an oral argument. The choice of method will depend greatly on the advocate's informed preference.

Necessary first steps include decisions on structure and focus[61] and preparation of an argument notebook.[62] Arguing counsel should, if possible, take these steps in conversation with other lawyers working on the case, even if these lawyers are drafted only to help prepare the argument. Then, one must practice the argument in any of several ways.

One method is to conduct a moot court. Some lawyers never argue without undergoing such a procedure. Other lawyers, including Charles Alan Wright, never use it.

One advantage of a moot court is that it can help the lawyer prepare to confront the panel that will decide the case. Ideally, the moot court members have read the briefs and enough of the decided cases that they can anticipate the kinds of questions that will concern the panel members. An opponent can be recruited from one's own team to make the drill more realistic. The moot court can be of particular help to a relatively inexperienced advocate, for it permits evaluation—and self-evaluation—of technique, posture, gesture, and nuance as well as of the strengths and weaknesses of points being argued and responses to questions.

A moot court can, however, give the advocate a false sense of confidence. This is especially true if the mock judges have not thoroughly prepared, and many cases do not have the kind of budget that permits a large time investment for them; the advocate may falsely conclude that all the possible avenues of inquiry have been explored. The mooting panel may focus too much on technique and not enough on substance.

The author prefers not to do a formal moot. The reasons are no doubt personal, but perhaps worth sharing. A formal moot risks doing what boxers call

---

[61] *See* **§10.05.**

[62] *See* **§10.07.**

"leaving the fight in the gym." Because advocates tend to be combative, one concentrates on winning the moot and not on listening to the give and take of ideas and suggestions.

It is of course impossible to anticipate the exact circumstances of argument. One will always end by arguing the case at a particular and unique moment in time. At that moment, the confluence of study, thought, and experience will determine how one argues.

The challenge of preparation, therefore, is to distill learning about the case and about technique, and to focus that learning on the argument at hand. The learning has taken place through experience, through reading works on appellate practice, and through working on the briefs. To achieve focus, it is easier to act yourself into right thinking than to think yourself into right action. Only a very experienced and very—perhaps too—confident advocate would prepare for argument only by solitary thought.

What kind of action is the best preparation? The author begins to outline argument themes during the preparation of the briefs, in conversation with colleagues working on the case. The order of issues in the brief, the questions presented, and the statement of the case are most influenced by these discussions.

When the argument date is set, preparation continues by debating possible themes and argument issues in a series of small meetings of no more than a half-dozen people. These meetings can take place by telephone conference call. The meeting participants divide up responsibility for doing last-minute research. Their activity redoubles as soon as the panel members are known.

For example, in a complex case with a record that is familiar to the author, final preparation would begin one week before argument. Two days will be spent with one or two associate lawyers or law clerks to put the argument file and tentative argument notebook together. These colleagues are those most familiar with the legal and factual issues in the case. The work consists of a free-ranging discussion, punctuated by the group members going their separate ways to research a point or perform other work. During these breaks, arguing counsel can revise the notebook and consolidate notes on the proposed argument outline.

Four days or so before the argument, the preparation group can expand for a day or two. The expanded group will include the other lawyers who have worked on the case, perhaps the client, and at least one or two lawyers who are relatively unfamiliar with the case. These preparation sessions involve going over the outline of the argument and testing ways of expressing themes. Argument notes, and even the argument structure, are revised.

In this time, it is important to think of transitions or segues from one argument point to another, and from potential responses to questions back into the main argument points. All participants are encouraged to throw questions, comments, and challenges for arguing counsel to field. Then, all are welcome to evaluate arguing counsel's proposed responses. This process differs decisively from a moot court by its open-textured character. Arguing counsel should not be afraid to guide the discussion and to close off avenues of talk that have been explored and exhausted. It is surprising, however, how this sort of debate can lead to new insights.

Once this phase is over, the advocate must retreat back into a much smaller group to do final polishing. Plenty of time must be allowed for solitary thought at this stage, to let the advocate's unclouded judgment be exercised. Some ideas that appear attractive when first raised lose luster when placed into perspective.

Advocates who let the hurly burly of preparation continue to the last hour before argument do themselves and their clients a disservice. Throughout the process, the advocate should take plenty of time for relaxation and exercise. Litigation is as much a physical as a mental and emotional travail.

§10.09 Effective Argument Strategy—Appellant's or Petitioner's Opening Argument

This section discusses argument strategy in terms that will be useful to appellants and appellees, but with principal emphasis on the appellant.

Courthouse preparation steps are important. If one is unfamiliar with the courtroom where arguments are to be held, one should visit it, preferably while the court is in session. Where do the advocates sit before the case is called? Where does one arrange one's notes and papers during argument? Does the lectern have a height adjustment, and if so how does it work? Does the lectern have a light? And so on.

The advocate who is unfamiliar with the panel members should attend arguments before the judges that will hear his or her case. At the least, unless one is set as first case on the first day of an argument session, the advocate should observe the cases to be heard earlier in the week before his or her argument.

There are many theories on dress and demeanor in oral argument. The admonition to "be yourself" may not tell the whole story. Men should dress relatively conservatively, with a dark suit, modest tie, and white shirt. Loud ties offend some judges, and this is no time to assert one's sartorial independence at the client's expense. Some women advocates believe that a conservative suit is the best choice; this certainly is true if the advocate feels most comfortable dressed that way. Judge Deanell Tacha of the 10th Circuit tells women advocates not to be afraid of being stylish and colorful. So long as one's outfit is well-tailored and neat, there is much leeway.

On the morning set for argument, the clerk's office will be open for check-in at the time noted on the calendar. The advocate must make three inquiries. First, how does one reserve rebuttal time? In some circuits, the appellant reserves rebuttal at check-in in the clerk's office. In others, rebuttal must be requested at the beginning of the argument itself. For a 20-minute argument, five or six minutes should be reserved for rebuttal.[63]

Second, what is the system of lights or other warnings that one is about to run out of time? Some courts automatically give a two-minute or five-minute

---

[63] *See* **§10.11.**

warning on the principal argument. Find out whether the warning means that that many minutes are left in the total argument or only in the portion that the advocate has set aside for principal argument. In some circuits, the clerk permits counsel to ask for a warning at a certain number of minutes. Take time to become familiar with the warning system, preferably by watching it operate during someone else's argument.

Finally, where will the panel members be sitting? The judge with the most seniority who has not taken senior status presides; the others sit as custom dictates. The advocate should make a small seating chart if the clerk's office does not routinely provide one.

Articles on the techniques of argument abound. Judge Myron Bright of the Eighth Circuit has distilled excellent advice into *ten commandments.*

1. Know your customer, the court.
2. A.B.P.—Always Be Prepared.
3. Go for the jugular.
4. Questions, questions, good and bad. Answer directly, then return to your main theme.
5. Be flexible and innovative.
6. One lawyer is better than two.
7. Look up, speak up.
8. Don't snatch defeat from the jaws of victory.
9. Believe in your case and be natural.
10. Above all, don't kid yourself. Oral argument is important; indeed, it may be crucial.[64]

The case is called. Counsel moves to the proper counsel table, then to the lectern. The presiding judge says something like, "Ms. Smith, you may begin when you are ready."

The opening argument begins with an introduction of the advocate, the client, and any co-counsel who will argue. This is preceded either by the ritual, "May it please the court," or by acknowledgment of the presiding judge with "Chief Judge Politz and may it please the court."

If counsel is excused from stating the facts because the court has read the briefs, then he or she should go immediately to the main point on appeal. If a statement of the case is expected, it should be short, adversarial, and tailored precisely to the issues counsel will argue.

The Fifth Circuit, among others, expressly counsels lawyers not to waste time

---

[64] Myron H. Bright, *The Ten Commandments of Oral Argument,* 67 ABAJ 1136 (Sept 1981). *See also* Judge Roger Miner's views, in *From the Bench: The Dont's of Oral Argument,* 14 Litig 3 (Summer 1988). Among Judge Miner's fervent pleas is that the advocate not write out the oral argument and read it to the court. This treatise endorses that view; see **§10.07.**

by reciting the facts, but to get right to the points to be argued. Federal Rule of Appellate Procedure 34(c) cautions that "[c]ounsel will not be permitted to read at length from briefs, records or authorities."[65]

The opening statement should be an assertion about the case that is arresting and even somewhat challenging:

> Chief Judge Smith, and may it please the court. This case turned on whether the defendants conducted their activity as part of an *enterprise,* as defined in the RICO statute. This court has said that an enterprise must have an ascertainable structure, must operate as a continuing unit, and must have a goal common to its members. The trial judge denied a defense request to instruct the jury to this effect. Instead the jury was invited to convict these defendants upon a finding of loose and discontinuous association.

If one will argue more than one point, the opening must weave the points together in a single thematic statement:

> Judge Wilson and may it please the court. I am going to show that these several convictions are without support in the evidence, and were obtained under an unprecedented and improper jury instruction on conspiracy and accessory liability. That instruction, sought by the government, was unfairly and repeatedly emphasized to the jury. I also would like to show the court that the jury was led to convict despite the want of evidence by misuse of lethally prejudicial other crimes evidence and by perjury from the government's star witness.

This multi-issue thematic statement is based upon an argument of a complex case with 25 minutes to argue per side. It promises a lot of issues for a single argument, more than one usually would use. But in keeping with the principles discussed in the preceding sections, counsel moved quickly through the sufficiency issue and was indeed able to offer useful discussion on all the issues. The multi-issue approach worked only because it was united by a common theme.

Having opened with a promise, the advocate should begin the discussion of each issue with a brief illustrative comment—a case citation or two, a reference to the record, and invocation of any relevant pattern jury instruction.[66] This introduction sets the stage for counsel to illustrate why this argument sur-

---

[65] Fed R App P 34(c). The full text of this rule is in **app A.**

[66] Several circuits—including the Fifth (for which the author was consultant), Ninth, and Seventh—have their own volumes of pattern jury charges, and there are collections such as the redoubtable multivolume work, Edward J. Devitt, Charles B. Blackmar, Michael A. Wolff, & Kevin F. O'Malley, Federal Jury Practice and Instructions (4th ed 1992). Appellate judges like to approve pattern charges because doing so helps guide the district courts. Also, a pattern charge helps to prevent the often unwise practice of fashioning jury instructions from the language of appellate opinions. *See* 1 *id* §8.02, at 246.

vives the attacks the opponent has made upon it as well as any attacks that the panel might suggest. In argument, you are trying to help these judges write an opinion that decides the case your way. Look for verbal clues to their thought processes because it is important to watch the court's reaction to see how the argument is being received. It is also important to provoke questions.

There is no need to state a decided case in argument if it has been cited and discussed in the briefs in a way that makes obvious its importance. It is enough to refer to the case and mention the page of the brief on which it is cited. If, however, on rereading the case in preparation for argument counsel finds some new insight or newly helpful language, he or she can dwell on it in more length. For example:

> In our brief, we cite *Sutherland.* In light of the government's brief, *Sutherland* becomes of vital importance here, because it represents this circuit's emphatic rejection of the position the government takes. The government rests upon its reading of the *Elliott* case, even though this court said in *Sutherland* that such a reading had been justifiably and almost universally condemned.[67]

The opening sentences of oral argument are a signal: they tell the panel what the advocate thinks is the most important issue; they give a hint of how far the advocate is willing to concede factual or legal positions consistent with eventual victory; and they tend to direct the court's questions.

For example, in a case involving constitutional questions of due process and free speech, the author became convinced that the most likely favorable outcome would rest on an administrative law principle that the court would adopt to avoid deciding the constitutional issue. To make clear that the due process and administrative law issues were bound together, the argument began:

> Mr. Chief Justice and may it please the Court: This case presents a serious question, here and in *Oestereich* against the Selective Service Board, but not decided in that case, of whether the Selective Service System is being used to punish or sanction dissentient behavior without due process, without Congressional authorization and under standards so vague and broad as to offend the First Amendment.[68]

One might, for example, argue:

> Turning to the exclusion of the grand jury testimony, the Supreme Court has taught in *Chambers v Mississippi* that a constitutional issue lurks wherever reliable exculpatory hearsay is kept out of evidence. But the Court

---

[67] The reference is to United States v Sutherland, 656 F2d 1181, 1192 (5th Cir 1981), *cert denied,* 455 US 949 (1982).

[68] Oral argument, Gutknecht v United States, 396 US 295 (1970), microformed on Oral Arguments of the Supreme Court of the United States: The Warren Court, 1953 Term-1968 Term, Case 69-71, 1969 term, Fiche 41, at 2 (Univ Publs of Am).

> need not resolve this constitutional issue, for the Federal Rules of Evidence answer the question more narrowly and precisely.

Forthright argument invites questions. Judge Godbold has written:

> The panels of the Fifth Circuit ask questions, lots of questions, for several reasons. The most likely reason is that the judge wants to know the answer to his particular question. The argument is the place where the court can learn what it does not know. Other possible reasons are: (1) The question is designed to clarify or advance the argument, to get the speaker down to the brass tacks he is not getting to on his own. (2) The questioner is seeking to enliven a dull monologue and stay awake. (3) The question is intended to advance the questioner's own point of view. (At times this is done by the judge's challenging counsel who has a view different from his own, at other times by the judge's serving up "home-run balls" to the counsel with whom the judge agrees. I suppose this is a valid practice but it is overdone.) (4) The judge is engaged in ego play of his own, demonstrating how much he knows about the case and how well he understands it. But at least this may advance the argument and even assist his colleagues.
>
> In an assemblage where the purpose is to inform and persuade, it is like manna from heaven for the potential persuadee to say to the persuader: "Here is what troubles me about the subject on which you are trying to convince me." This opening into the mind of the listener is the most valuable piece of information the persuader can get. Most advocates understand this principle and welcome questions from the bench and know how to capitalize on them. Other counsel feel that the advocate is responsible for his own case and should be permitted to present it in his own way. These attorneys resent questions as intrusions into a carefully prepared and organized presentation. But the court has its own responsibility to reach the correct decision, and only the judge knows what problems still trouble him.
>
> This subject of questioning from the bench came up for discussion in a seminar at the 1975 Fifth Circuit Judicial Conference at Orlando. It surfaced again in some of the state roundtables at the 1976 Judicial Conference in Houston. I was surprised at the number of experienced advocates who believe that they are over-questioned. Perhaps questioning is overdone in the Fifth Circuit. I am certain that often the judge asks for help too soon. Judges enjoy lively dialogue, but they too can, and do, impede the communicative process. The solution lies, I believe, in moderation on both sides of the bench. Counsel can recognize and accept the value of questions to the court and to them. The court can exercise restraint

through fewer and better thought-out questions, and it can be a little slower on the trigger.[69]

Some judges try to drown an advocate in questions, and some do so from a malign motive to overpower a position with which they disagree. Other oral argument questioning is designed to make the advocate concede a point. The advocate must be emotionally prepared to resist conceding, even when the questioning has gone very badly. More often, questions are vital signs of where the court thinks the live issues are. While the lawyer can seldom win a case on oral argument, he or she stands a good chance of losing it. The panel may be predisposed to the advocate's position, using questions to test weaknesses. If the advocate whose position the court tentatively favors falters in oral argument, the tide may turn.

In any event, it is imperative that questions be answered courteously and immediately, giving control of the flow of discussion to the panel. As the following example illustrates, it is unwise to sidestep a question from a Justice:

Q: Do you mean sanction or punishment?
A: Well, I will get to that, Mr. Justice Marshall, and I will address myself—
Q: I would appreciate it now, if you care to.[70]

As noted above, the judges on the panel will come to the bench with a bench memo written by their law clerks. In some courts, a law clerk for one judge will have prepared a memorandum for the entire panel. Some judges prefer that their own clerks write the memorandum in every case. The memorandum may include suggested questions for the judge to ask.

If the advocate senses that the judge who asked a question is not really interested in, or does not know what to do with, the answer, it may simply be that the question was asked from the bench memorandum without the judge having thought much about the importance of the matter or the wisdom of the inquiry. The advocate may, however, be sure that the law clerk who wrote the memorandum probably designed the question to resolve some gap or ambiguity in the record briefs.

Experience teaches that sometimes judges misread the bench memo and ask a question of the wrong side or simply ask the question in order to have something to say. However, the advocate is never in a position to assume this is so.

If one judge on the panel has reached a tentative decision at odds with the

---

[69] John C. Godbold, *Twenty Pages and Twenty Minutes—Effective Advocacy on Appeal,* 30 Sw LJ 801, 818-19 (1976) (footnote omitted). Judge Godbold was later a judge of the 11th Circuit. *See* **§4.13.**

[70] Oral argument, Breen v Selective Service Local Board No 16, 396 US 460 (1970), microformed on Oral Argument of the Supreme Court of the United States: The Warren Court, 1953 Term-1968 Term, Case 69-65, 1969 term, Fiche 39, at 20 (Univ Pubs of Am).

others, oral argument can be crucial in winning over the crucial second vote. Judges use their questioning to position themselves for the decision conference that will, in most instances, immediately follow the day's argument calendar.[71]

Whatever the questioners' motives, the advocate faced with a barrage of questions must remember and follow several simple rules. First, begin by answering the question. "Yes, Judge Randall." "No, Judge Johnson, that is not our position." If the question cannot be answered yes or no, say why: "Judge Williams, we believe the position suggested by your question is tenable and is supported by the law of this circuit. But we also emphasize that the court need not go that far to reverse this case." If the question requires an explanatory answer, say so: "The short answer is 'yes,' but that requires some explanation." This latter device of answering and then explaining is particularly useful if time is running out and the advocate would otherwise risk a misleading answer. Where the question can be answered with a reference to the briefs or the record, include that reference: "Yes, Judge Randall. At pages 31 through 35 of our brief, we answer that question in some detail and the colloquy at transcript page 2524 shows that trial counsel preserved the issue." A more detailed answer can follow, if necessary.

Second, some questions invite concessions of fact or law. Such questions put fear into an advocate's heart, because he or she is afraid that a good answer is out there somewhere in the ether and would come to mind if only his or her knees would stop shaking. If a concession is honestly required, because the advocate finds a position mistaken, it should be made honestly and with an explanation of why it is not fatal. If the advocate is genuinely stumped, he should not be afraid to say, "Quite frankly, I don't have a quick answer to that question. May I respond with a letter or supplemental brief to be filed tomorrow?" The request for a supplemental brief also can be used to head off questions that will involve the advocate in a time-consuming litany of facts: "Judge Hill, there are at least 14 more instances of the trial judge's misconduct that would preclude any argument that the error is harmless or that the conduct was unintentional. May I file a supplemental brief or letter within five days setting out the record references that prove my point?"

Third, if experience or intuition tells the advocate that the panel will be unusually active with questions, he or she should consider an introduction that sets out all the points he or she intends (or hopes) to cover in argument. This communicates the importance of those issues, even though no time may remain to treat them all in detail. Fourth, while flexibility is important, do not lightly abandon the agreed plan of argument in response to the court's questions. Preparation for argument, like that for a jury trial, is designed to ensure that important issues are not thrown away in the heat of battle. The game plan is important.

---

[71] Judges Bright and Arnold discuss this in Myron H. Bright & Richard S. Arnold, *Oral Argument? It May Be Crucial!*, 70 ABAJ 68 (Sept 1984). The decision conference is also discussed in the Fifth Circuit Internal Operating Procedure under Fed R App P 34.

Turning at last to some general rules about the opening argument, the following points should be kept in mind: Humor can be deadly, though it is good medicine if properly administered in appropriate doses. Ridicule of one's opponent can backfire. The judges' jokes are always funny, but if the joke seems to explode the advocate's position, he or she must make some response. The response should not be petulant or angry. Take a deep breath and in a sentence reassert the position taken. With experience of arguing, and with the judges one confronts, counsel will gain a sense of when humor is appropriate, that is, when it does not unfairly deprecate the opponent, seem to take the case too lightly, or show disrespect for the court.

The advocate must have fire in the belly and then control that fire. G.K. Chesterton said of the English judges that they are not cruel, they just get used to things. Busy judges looking for a way to decide a case may tend to trivialize the human consequences of decisions. The advocate's brief will have discussed the real world impact of the decision sought. The argument also must be driven by a communicated sense that the advocate seeks justice. Stump speeches are, however, out of order because they do not focus upon the interrelationship of legal issues and the specific claim for justice being made. For example, error in instructing the jury may present a fairly dry legal issue, but the advocate will be careful to say: "In this case, the trial judge's instruction on 'last clear chance' misstated the law and misguided the jury. This error denied this plaintiff the verdict to which she was entitled."

Oral argument is adversarial. It should not consist of two lawyers making unconnected prepared statements. The wise advocate will consider leaving some questions for the opponent to answer, setting out challenges that appear to require a response. For example:

> The government claims that all it told the district judge during the secret hearing was information about the informer's identity—information that can properly be communicated ex parte. The problem is that they made the same claim in the court below and the district judge found that this is simply not the fact. Now they don't answer that finding in their brief. Maybe they have an answer today and if so we look forward to hearing it.

The precise form of the challenge is not important. It is important to seize control of a portion of the opponent's time by directing attention to an issue that the advocate feels has not been adequately addressed and on which the opponent has a weak case.

Finally, the advocate should prepare, in summary form, a 15-second peroration that summarizes his or her position and asks for judgment. When the warning light goes on, the advocate should be considering how to finish the point being made and then move on to this closing. The closing should not be elaborate. It must not introduce a new issue. It must not be technical. It should be the strongest single overriding reason why the advocate is entitled to prevail:

> The jury was out for four days deliberating. The evidence was thin and hotly-contested. The trial judge's exclusion of this evidence was therefore

wrong in a real, harmful, and verifiable sense. These convictions should be reversed.

This short example focuses on the harm done by the alleged error. It puts out a concrete fact—the length of jury deliberation—as evidence that the evidentiary issues are not abstract.

Needless to say, the peroration should not be read. Nothing kills a good argument more surely than the sight of the advocate evidently reading it from a prepared text. Of all the times to have eye contact with the panel, this is the most important.

If, contrary to expectations, the panel asks no questions and time remains in the argument, one can turn to one of these reserve tabs and fill in. The sufficiency point is the most logical choice for that purpose. Again, there is no harm in sitting down a minute or so early, particularly when the extra time will be added to the allotted rebuttal.

§10.10 —Appellee's or Respondent's Argument

Statistics favor the respondent. The odds against reversal are heavy.[72] Therefore, Judge Bright's warning not to snatch defeat from the jaws of victory[73] is addressed most strongly to respondents.

The respondent should study the general principles in the preceding sections. Moreover, the same considerations that influence the respondent's choice of briefing strategy will dominate oral argument. The first question to ask in preparation is: what is the standard of review? Put another way, why was the district judge right?

With respect to factual findings, the district judge is usually entitled to deference, although a de novo review standard occasionally is applied. On legal questions, no such deference is given, but the judge was in a better position to apply the law to the facts as he or she observed them. Regardless of the standard, if the decision below was on the merits and both sides had a chance to present a case, there is an observable judicial bias against letting the loser relitigate.

All of these considerations will shape the argument, because one elementary rule of advocacy is never to assume a burden that belongs to the other side. Therefore, the advocate's notes for argument should properly begin, at least in the first draft, with: "The district judge was right because . . ." or "The jury's verdict, viewed in the light most favorable to the prevailing party, was right because. . . ."

In a multi-issue case, the respondent faces a difficult task, because he or she cannot know with certainty which points will be stressed by the appellant. The respondent must, therefore, be prepared on every issue. Even if the main issue is clear, the court may have a question about some issue not argued by either side.

---

72 *See* **§5.01.**

73 Cited at **§10.09.**

If the appellant has discussed an issue that the respondent did not plan to treat, the best course is to at least mention the issue and refer the panel to the briefs. If there is a quick answer, give it.

The respondent should be particularly alert to questions asked of the appellant. These questions tell the lawyer something about the panel's concerns. So, if the advocate has a better answer, it is a good idea to give it. In answering, the advocate should not be arrogant, overbearing, or imbued with the evident desire to score a point; he or she should speak matter of factly, in an earnest effort to respond to the inquiring judge's concerns. For example, "Judge Thompson, you had asked whether circumstantial evidence of state of mind would be admissible. This court held in the *Smith* case, which is cited in our brief at page 32, that it could."

The respondent will be unsure how much his or her argument should respond to or be based upon the appellant's presentation. This question is as much one of style as of substance. The answer is clear: the advocate should make his or her own argument in his or her own style. The choice of issues to be argued reflects a considered judgment. Like all strategic game plan decisions, the choice should not be cast aside lightly. As noted above, answering questions from the panel and briefly responding to significant concerns raised by the appellant are exceptions to this general principle. It is therefore true that respondents will alter game plans more often than appellants.

The advocate should make clear his or her choice of issues at the outset, however. For example: "I will focus principally upon the trial judge's charge to the jury on the issue of contributory negligence. However, I do intend to respond to appellant counsel's assertions about the hearsay rule." And while the advocate should not lightly abandon his or her sense of what issues deserve argument, the advocate may more readily rearrange the order in which to present them to make a more coherent reply to the appellant.

As for style, effulgent tub-thumping arguments have largely gone out of fashion, at least in federal appellate courts. They retain some vitality in some jury cases. It is, however, permissible for an advocate to diffract an emotion. The respondent must choose: the preferred attitude is competent, confident, matter-of-fact refutation of the appellant's points.

At times, however, the advocate will be entitled to some carefully controlled indignation. Just as party-oriented advocacy may be useful in a brief,[74] it may belong in an oral argument. The respondent who has been compelled to litigate at length and expensively obtain a judgment, the party who is faced with arguably technical arguments, the party whose recovery is stalled by the appellate process—these are real people who can be hurt. The advocate ought to express their plight. For example:

> This case was filed in 1976. The defendants moved unsuccessfully to dismiss for failure to state a claim and for want of personal jurisdiction. They then moved for change of venue on grounds of forum non conveniens, which also was denied. After an acrimonious and much-litigated spate

[74] *See* **§9.06.**

of discovery, they moved for summary judgment. Denied. Last year, the jury awarded Mrs. Johnson $1,254,322 because the defendants' negligence killed her husband. The defendants have appealed.

§10.11 —Rebuttal Argument

Any lawyer who has argued appellate cases has observed the panel's impatience with rebuttal argument. If, as is usually the case in federal court, the panel has read the briefs, its members will have mentally evaluated each argument as it is presented and noted the points that might be made on the other side. To judges in such a frame of mind, rebuttal seems unnecessary—a waste of time.

One might also attribute this judicial impatience to a more generalized skepticism about the value of oral argument. In any case, the rebuttal argument should be waived unless it would serve a purpose and unless the advocate intends to see that purpose served. Waived? Yes. The advocate should not be afraid to stand and say, "I see nothing that is not answered by our briefs. Unless there are questions, I yield the balance of my time."

On the other hand, sometimes the respondent raises a novel issue that requires more extended treatment than is possible during the time reserved for rebuttal. The advocate can ask the panel for a couple of minutes of additional time. This sometimes will be granted. If it is not, and the respondent's argument is truly novel, counsel should ask for leave to file a supplemental brief.

Rebuttal should not be waived, however, in the majority of cases. The presumption against rebuttal serves mainly as a reminder that rebuttal must be confined to its proper purposes; it is a form of internalized self-discipline.

Rebuttal argument is necessarily abbreviated, pointed. It is not the time to trot out a new grand theory. Its purpose is to reply quickly and decisively to the respondent.

Most rebuttal points can be anticipated and put into the oral argument notebook. One cannot, in the principal argument, answer all of the opponent's contentions. Beyond taking too much time, doing so also would make the argument ineffective.

The advocate therefore should map out one or two points that the opponent is sure to make and devise quick responses for rebuttal. These should be items that can be used if necessary, but are not indispensable. At the argument, more compelling matters may push the prepared rebuttal items aside.

When listening to the opponent's argument, take notes, though not so copiously that they are worthless as a reference for rebuttal. Leave a space on the paper to star or highlight points that require rebuttal. Select one or two (rarely more) items from this list and the prepared list to use on rebuttal. Some good candidates for rebuttal are listed below.

First, has the respondent misstated the record? If so, the advocate with his or her index[75] will have spotted the errors and will have the transcript or record page ready. If the misstatements are many and cannot be addressed by referring the panel to the briefs, counsel should focus on a couple of them and ask leave to file a supplemental brief. Judges usually take notes when counsel points to specific record references to refute an opponent; their law clerks almost always do. And, as noted previously, most courts of appeals tape record arguments for the court's use in drafting the opinion.

Second, has the respondent made an argument that was not anticipated by the appellant's argument and is addressed in the briefs? If so, the advocate will refer the court to the briefs.

Third, can the appellant answer a question asked of the respondent in a way that is advantageous to his or her case? If so, the appellant should do so. For example:

> Judge Smith, you asked appellee's counsel whether this court's decisions on the right to counsel of choice are still good law. The answer is yes. This court constitutionalized the choice of counsel, as a Sixth Amendment matter, just as the choice of religious practices is constitutionalized by the First Amendment. The Supreme Court has expressly recognized this constitutional dimension.

Fourth, are there other brief and decisive replies to particular points?

And fifth, the last word is important. If rebuttal is otherwise advisable, it should end strong. The advocate should have prepared a 10-second closing that focuses upon a strong point of his or her position or, better yet, that unites disparate elements of the case. Sometimes time will run out before this closing can be delivered, but it is best to have something ready.

§10.12 Special Problems in Multiparty and Multilawyer Cases

There are two kinds of special problems in multiparty and multilawyer cases—those created by the court and the case, and those created by the lawyers. Court-created problems can be solved by consulting the rules and working with the clerk's office. Lawyer-created problems may be more intractable.

When multiple appeals are consolidated, a single slice of argument may be allotted to the consolidated case. Federal Rule of Appellate Procedure 34(d) expressly provides that "[a] cross or separate appeal shall be argued with the initial appeal at a single argument, unless the court otherwise directs."[76] In an NLRB enforcement action, Fed R App P 15.1 provides that each party adverse to the Board shall proceed first in briefing and oral argument.

---

[75] *See* **§7.05.**

[76] The text of Rule 34 is in **app A.** Determining who is the appellant when a cross-appeal is filed is discussed in **§9.18.**

When all cross-appeals, separate appeals, and consolidated cases involve the same parties and the same lawyers, the most common problem will be inadequate time to argue, as to which a motion can be filed.[77]

When there are multiple parties or multiple counsel, problems of timing and organization mount. The court may be willing to grant additional argument time, but the principal issue is allocation of whatever time is available in the most effective way. When that subject is broached, lawyer difference of opinion is likely to be sharp. Some of this difference can be dismissed as ego—a favorite way to characterize somebody else's position but seldom one's own. Such dismissal persuades no one.

The following views are born of experience. Counsel for one appellant should almost never split argument. The disparate presentations waste time and lack cohesion. In a case involving multiple parties on the same side, counsel should strive to agree on an allocation of time that permits argument to be coherent. For example, one might identify one or more issues that are dominant and affect all or almost all parties, and choose one of the advocates to present those issues. Obviously, that advocate should be allotted a larger than proportional share of the argument time.

Alternatively, effective argument strategy might dictate that each appellant argue separately, to lay stress on issues that each one determines, requiring the appellee to respond separately to each argument. This technique was used in *United States v Salerno,*[78] discussed at **§10.04.**

A proposal to divide appellants' argument in either fashion does not end the agenda. One must also decide whether it is better to have the appellee argument segmented so as to respond to each of appellants' advocates in turn. The appellee can also initiate discussion of divided argument with a similar agenda.

Division of argument by appellant's or appellee's counsel in a single consolidated case can be accomplished by simply informing the clerk of the appellants' wishes, unless the circuit has a local rule or practice that requires leave of court to divide argument among counsel for the same party.[79] Even with the clerk's blessing, an advocate agreement to divide argument among counsel on the same side may not be enforceable against one's colleagues. That is, the clerk may well agree to give each advocate a red light when the portion of the total time has expired. But if the advocate keeps talking, and the court does not intervene, the time taken may be subtracted from the total. In some circuits, the clerk will not be able to police argument even in so minimal a way. It is not wise to trust one's colleagues to sit down when they should.

Having separately allotted times for appellants or appellees requires an order of the court. Counsel wishing to divide argument in this way should seek agreement from the opponent, but be prepared to file the motion immediately if no agreement is forthcoming; this heads off the possibility of the other side moving first to get its schedule imposed.

---

[77] *See* **§10.04.**

[78] 937 F2d 797 (2d Cir 1991), *subsequent history retold in* United States v DiNapoli, 1993 WL 440282 (2d Cir Nov 1, 1993).

[79] Fed R App P 34(d) cautions against duplicating another advocate's argument.

A motion to set argument procedures should provide concrete reasons why the proposed order will be most helpful to the court. In almost every case, counsel must assure the court that every arguing lawyer will be prepared to answer any of the court's questions.

§10.13 How the Court Decides After Argument

Typically, the panel of judges will hear argument in five or six cases, lasting a long morning and into the afternoon. They will then meet in conference and reach tentative decisions on the cases argued. Sometimes, this conference may take place a day or several days later, but the format is the same. The panel reaches its tentative decision after discussing the briefs, record, and arguments.

The presiding judge, who is the senior active judge on the panel, will then assign the opinion unless he or she is dissenting, in which case the next senior judge will make the assignment. The writing judge will receive the full record and will circulate a draft opinion for approval. Any dissents or concurrences also will be circulated. In this process, a dissenting or concurring position may come to command a majority. In most cases, however, the vote taken at the initial conference soon after oral argument will control the outcome. The decisional process underscores the importance of oral argument. In the overwhelming majority of cases, the decision is made within hours. The most tantalizing part of the process is knowing that by the time the advocate's bags are packed and in the airport bus, the case is usually decided—but the decision will remain concealed for months.

When the opinion is ready, having been concurred in by a majority of the panel, the writing judge usually transmits it to the clerk of the court, where the judgment and opinion are entered of record.[80] Counsel often can elect to be notified by collect telephone call that the case has been decided, and this is a wise investment to make. The election is often made on the entry of appearance form sent out by the clerk's office. Counsel should inquire about the practice in the circuit. Telephone notification helps to ensure that the client knows about the decision from counsel (not the press or the opponent) and that consideration of possible rehearing begins quickly. In most circuits, rehearing petitions are due 14 days after the judgment is entered.[81] If the clerk's office waits a day or so to drop the opinion in the mail, and the mails are as slow as usual, counsel will wind up with insufficient time to prepare a decent rehearing petition.

The court's opinion deciding the case will be marked "Publish" or "Not for Publication." Published opinions will appear in Federal Reporter. Nonpublished opinions will be available only on Westlaw and LEXIS, and may be cited only under the restrictive terms provided by each court of appeals in its rules.

---

[80] *See* **§10.15.**

[81] *See* **ch 11.**

The circuit rules will state whether the opinion is to have precedential value, or only res judicata effect as between the parties.[82]

There is substantial controversy over nonpublished opinions, but their use is increasingly frequent given rising appellate caseloads. Any party may move to have published an opinion labelled not for publication on a showing that the case does have precedential value and should be available to the bar generally.[83] Although nonpublished opinions are designed for use when the case poses no great factual or legal dispute, there is a danger that a panel will use them to bury difficult questions.

Some advocates, including this author, have criticized the nonpub trend as contributing to the bureaucratization of courts and limiting the effect of scholarship and advocacy in criticizing judicial performance. Nonpublished opinions also tend to be known to judges and to regular practitioners, thereby creating a special law for the cognoscenti. It would be far better for the courts of appeals to shorten the average length of their opinions and to publish all of them.

Counsel also should be aware that a nonpub designation reduces the chance that the case will be a good candidate for rehearing en banc or certiorari. There is no inherent logic to this observable fact, because a nonpub is typically an affirmance and may involve an issue of great moment which the court of appeals should reconsider.

§10.14 How the Court Decides Nonargued Cases

Cases not orally argued typically are decided at one of two stages—in an initial screening process or after full briefing. The screening process is used in all circuits. Summary disposition after full briefing is used extensively in most circuits. Circuits that permit argument in almost all cases use it more sparingly.

At both stages, the staff attorney's office of the court of appeals plays a major role. When an appeal is first filed, the clerk's office and staff attorneys seek to determine whether appellate jurisdiction is properly invoked and appellate procedures properly followed. This screening for jurisdictional and procedural error continues throughout the case. Some errors, such as an overlength brief, will prompt a letter demanding that the problem be corrected. That sort of problem is not, however, dispositive of the appeal.

The more significant screening asks questions such as timeliness of the notice of appeal, finality of the order being appealed from, and all the other questions dealt with in Chapters 2 and 6 of this treatise. In most circuits, the clerk has a checklist of jurisdictional issues developed by the staff attorney's

---

[82] See, e.g., 9th Cir R 36-3 and 10th Cir R 36.3 which state that nonpublished dispositions have no precedential value nor should they be cited by any courts within the respective circuits except as necessary under the doctrines of law of the case, res judicata, or collateral estoppel.

[83] *But see* Seligson v OPM, 878 F2d 369, 370 (Fed Cir 1989) (court declines to publish an opinion because publication would infringe upon a litigant's privacy interests: "the OPM could itself copy and circulate our unpublished opinion, and if it does, at least the judges are not doing it").

office. This list is used as a basis for identifying matters that should be referred to a staff attorney.[84]

Once a jurisdictional problem is identified, the procedure will vary from circuit to circuit. In some circuits, counsel will receive a letter inviting briefing on the issue. In other circuits, or where the matter appears clear on the record, counsel will receive an order dismissing the appeal with an explanation of rehearing procedures. The order will be issued by a panel of the court,[85] but will have been drafted by the staff attorney's office.

If the problem is knotty or significant enough to warrant a formal opinion of the court, the staff attorney may draft such an opinion and send it to a panel of judges. The panel will determine whether to (a) hold the jurisdictional issue pending full briefing of the case, (b) notify the parties and ask for briefs on the issue, or (c) decide the issue. A significant number of dispositive opinions on jurisdictional issues are issued by the court on its own motion and without the parties having briefed the issue. Being alert to potential jurisdictional problems ensures that one will have an advocate's voice in their resolution.

If a case makes it through the screening process, the next summary decision point is after briefs are filed. Formerly, one could say with confidence that appeals were never decided until all the briefs were in and the court had decided not to grant oral argument. Today, however, at least one circuit does not always wait that long. The Tenth Circuit has gained control of its docket through a number of innovative procedures. For example, when an appellant's brief is filed, it is promptly sent to the panel of judges who will decide the case or to a screening judge. If the brief is truly unpersuasive, and a panel of judges so decides, then the decision below will be summarily affirmed, usually in a nonpublished opinion. Even when the decisional process is not thus abbreviated, a staff attorney will begin to review the case from the time appellant's brief is filed, to fashion a recommendation to the panel on whether oral argument should be granted.

A typical procedure in the courts of appeals is this: Once the briefs are in, if the staff attorney concludes the case does not merit oral argument, he or she will draft a proposed opinion and send it to an initiating judge on the panel. The selection of initiating judge is by a means that equalizes the judicial workload. If that judge concurs that oral argument is unnecessary, he or she will work from the staff attorney draft to prepare an opinion. That opinion is then circulated to the other two judges on the panel.

In the Fifth Circuit, a more collegial approach to decision has been adopted for at least part of the summary disposition cases. In an effort to ensure more judicial supervision of staff attorney work product, the Fifth Circuit now provides that in most such cases all three judges who are to decide the case must meet together and approve at least the result reached in the case. However, the typical workload is 24 cases in a morning.

---

[84] An excellent example is Connie Hanes, *Staff Attorneys' Instructions to Case Managers Re: Checking for Jurisdictional Defects,* 10 Fifth Cir Rep No 7, at 609 (May 1993).

[85] Fed R App P 27(c), discussed at **§8.05.**

§10.15 Opinion, Judgment, and Mandate

The *opinion* of the court is the statement of its reasons for deciding the case in a certain way. The opinion can be consulted to resolve ambiguities in the court's judgment, but does not of its own force require anyone to do anything.[86] The court may incorporate its opinion into its mandate, however, in which case the opinion's language acquires directive force.[87]

The *judgment* of the court is entered in accordance with Fed R App P 36[88] as a separate document. The judgment is usually prepared, signed, and entered by the clerk based on the opinion. However, Fed R App P 36 envisions cases in which the court of appeals directs that the parties agree on a form of judgment that reflects the decision contained in the opinion. If the case is decided without opinion, the court will instruct the clerk what judgment to prepare.

The Advisory Committee notes explain that delay in entry of judgment when the precise terms are to be settled is in harmony with the principle of finality. The practical consequence is that further review will await determination of the entire controversy.[89]

The opinion is filed. The judgment is entered. Time for rehearing runs from entry.[90]

The next step is the *mandate,* as provided by Fed R App P 41. The mandate consists only of the judgment and opinion, unless the court by order or rule provides that something additional be included. Typically, the mandate arrives as a form letter to the clerk of the district court, tax court, or agency, which states: "Enclosed is the opinion and judgment of the court, issued as and for the mandate in the above-captioned case."

---

[86] See United States v Oshatz, 912 F2d 534 (2d Cir 1990), *cert denied,* 111 S Ct 1695 (1991), discussed at **§10.06.**

[87] Jones v Lewis, 957 F2d 260 (6th Cir) (court of appeals mandate provision that district court shall proceed in accordance with opinion incorporates the opinion into the mandate), *cert denied,* 113 S Ct 125 (1992).

[88] The text of all rules is in **app A.**

[89] *See* 16 Charles A. Wright, Arthur R. Miller, Edward H. Cooper, & Eugene Gressman, Federal Practice & Procedure §3982 (1977 & Supp 1993). The court of appeals mandate must be complied with; the district court has no discretion to vary it. Clements v Steele, 786 F2d 673 (5th Cir 1986). Other than deciding the case, the court of appeals does have the option, if a state statute permits, of certifying a question to the appropriate state supreme court. This is not a disposition of the case and no judgment would be entered. Once the certified question is answered, the court decides the case and issues a judgment and mandate. *See, e.g.,* Gulf Life Ins Co v Folsom, 794 F2d 1487 (11th Cir 1986) (certifying to Georgia Supreme Court). Whether to certify a question of state law is within the federal court's discretion. Armijo v Ex Cam, Inc, 843 F2d 406, 407 (10th Cir 1988) ("Certification is not to be routinely invoked whenever a federal court is faced with an unsettled question of state law.") *See also* Barrington Press, Inc v Morey, 816 F2d 341, 342 (7th Cir), *cert denied,* 484 US 906 (1987), discussed in detail at **§2.02.** *See also* Nemours Found v Manganaro Corp, 878 F2d 98 (3d Cir 1989) (district court order certifying state law question to state supreme court is not appealable as a form of "abstention" (citing Van Cauwenberghe v Baird, 486 US 517 (1988)).

[90] Fed R App P 40(a), discussed in **ch 11.**

The mandate is a formal direction to the court below or the agency to do what the court of appeals has commanded in its judgment. The mandate is usually issued 21 days after judgment.[91] This time can be shortened or enlarged by order. Issuance of the mandate is stayed automatically by filing a timely petition for rehearing,[92] and until seven days after disposition of the petition. Stay of the mandate to seek certiorari is dealt with in Fed R App P 41(b), discussed in Chapter 11.

Issuance of the mandate does not preclude seeking or grant of certiorari or even rehearing en banc; it simply means that the proceedings will not be halted while this further review takes place. In exceptional cases, the mandate may be recalled to permit further review or reconsider whether its terms are just.[93]

When it decides a case, the court's power is plenary. 28 USC §2106 provides:

> The Supreme Court or any other court of appellate jurisdiction may affirm, modify, vacate, set aside or reverse any judgment, decree, or order of a court lawfully brought before it for review, and may remand the cause and direct the entry of such appropriate judgment, decree, or order, or require such further proceedings to be had as may be just under the circumstances.[94]

This language has been much-construed.

In criminal cases, the matter is now relatively straightforward. A defendant who has timely moved for judgment of acquittal before verdict need not renew the motion after verdict. If the appeal argues that the evidence was insufficient to sustain a conviction,[95] and the court of appeals agrees, the court must reverse and remand with directions to enter a judgment of acquittal. If the evidence is insufficient, retrial is barred by the double jeopardy clause.[96]

The defendant does not waive the right to a judgment of acquittal based on evidentiary insufficiency by moving for a new trial. Nor does §2106 give a court of appeals power to abrogate the double jeopardy clause by permitting a retrial when the evidence has been found wanting.[97]

In other words, in criminal cases, the double jeopardy clause limits the court

---

[91] Fed R App P 41(a).

[92] *See* **ch 11.**

[93] *See In re* Incident Aboard the D/B Ocean King on Aug 30, 1980, 877 F2d 322 (5th Cir 1989) (exceptional case in which the Court of Appeals recalled a two-year old mandate which had failed to provide for the calculation of interest; dissent noted the claimant's delay and would have denied relief).

[94] 28 USC §2106.

[95] *See* **§5.07.**

[96] *See, e.g.*, United States v Mason, 902 F2d 1434, 1441 (9th Cir 1990).

[97] Burks v United States, 437 US 1 (1978), *overruling* Bryan v United States, 338 US 552 (1950) and its progeny only as to their suggestion that a reviewing court could order a new trial in the face of evidentiary insufficiency in the first trial.

of appeals' power to fashion a mandate. Under *Burks v United States,*[98] and *Greene v Massey,*[99] the court of appeals is obliged to rule upon an appellant's claim that the evidence was insufficient to convict. If the court of appeals reverses for insufficient evidence, there can be no retrial, regardless of "whether any failure of proof is the fault of the government or the result of an erroneous ruling by the trial court."[100]

However, subject only to double jeopardy constraints and to the ordinary requirement that a defendant have raised below all issues presented on appeal, §2106 provides the court of appeals great latitude in fashioning a judgment. Under the plain error doctrine, the court may even notice errors not raised below. Counsel must heed these lessons by noting that the sufficiency of the evidence is being drawn into question, lest the right to foreclose a retrial be lost through inadvertence.

In civil cases, there are complexities and doubts. Section 2106 would seem to be straightforward, and its legislative history shows that its language, which derives from the Judiciary Act of 1789, should be read literally.[101]

A trilogy of Supreme Court cases has been cited to becloud the issue, however. In Cone v West Virginia Pulp & Paper Co,[102] and again in *Globe Liquor Co v San Roman*[103] and *Johnson v New York, NH & HR Co,*[104] the Court held that when a civil verdict loser fails to renew its motion for directed verdict by a timely motion for judgment notwithstanding the verdict, the court of appeals is powerless to order entry of judgment for the verdict loser. If the court is convinced that the jury verdict is based upon insufficient evidence, its sole remedy in such a case is to remand for a new trial.

The *Cone-Globe-Johnson* trilogy continues to be cited, but has been undermined by later Supreme Court precedent that has paid more attention to §2106 and less attention to the verdict-challenge provisions of Fed R Civ P 50. The latter provisions, it should be said, do not mandate the *Cone-Globe-Johnson* result. The trilogy rests on the idea that a trial judge presented with a JNOV motion has the option of granting a new trial instead of entering judgment on or notwithstanding the verdict.

In *Neely v Martin K. Eby Construction Co,*[105] the Supreme Court said that there is no ironclad rule forbidding direction of a judgment for the verdict loser, provided the other party has a chance to argue that a new trial should be awarded as an alternative. Justice Black dissented, claiming that the Court was undermining the *Cone-Globe-Johnson* trilogy. When Fed R Civ P 50 was amended

---

[98] 437 US 1 (1978).

[99] 437 US 19 (1978).

[100] United States v Ustica, 847 F2d 42, 47 (2d Cir 1988).

[101] *See* Revision Notes to 28 USC §2106, at 28 USCA §2106.

[102] 330 US 212 (1947).

[103] 332 US 571 (1948).

[104] 344 US 48 (1952).

[105] 386 US 317, 326, 328-29 (1967).

in 1963 to clarify the practice in district courts and to give some comfort to the *Neely* rationale, Justices Black and Douglas again argued in dissent that the trilogy was being undermined.[106]

The Supreme Court's emphatic statement in *Bryan v United States,*[107] that courts of appeals have broad latitude under §2106 in fashioning a judgment, is not eroded by decision in *Burks,* which overruled *Bryan* only as to its double jeopardy holding.

An appellant wishing to obtain reversal and outright entry of judgment in its favor should carefully weigh the wisdom of moving for judgment notwithstanding the verdict. Sometimes, doing so clearly will be futile given the district court's announced views. There is no principled reason why a party who has moved for directed verdict in a civil case should have to do more than it would in a criminal case and burden the record with a further motion. 28 USC §2106 speaks indifferently to criminal and civil cases, and the goal of orderly judicial review is met if a party has made its position clear once in the district court. Logic aside, courts of appeals continue to refuse review of factual sufficiency when a JNOV motion was not made.[108]

When the court of appeals' mandate is issued, it must be obeyed. The mandate not only tells who wins, but may tell the district court or agency exactly what to do on remand. That body is then limited by the remand order and may not take the occasion to reach out and decide issues not embraced within its scope.[109]

---

[106] 374 US 861, 865 (1963) (Black and Douglass, JJ, dissenting to Amendments to Rules of Civil Procedure).

[107] 338 US 552 (1950).

[108] *See, e g,* Walker v AT&T Technologies, 995 F2d 846, (8th Cir 1993) (employer contention that evidence insufficient to support discrimination verdict could be considered only as to whether a new trial should be granted; reversal with direction to enter judgment foreclosed by defendant's failure to move for JNOV; new trial granted, however).

[109] *See* United States v Davis, 714 F2d 896 (9th Cir 1983) (on remand district court not authorized to decide issue not the subject of remand order). *Compare* Mirchandani v United States, 836 F2d 1223 (9th Cir 1988) (district court did not exceed scope of limited remand in considering new evidence bearing upon extradition of alien); Alter Fin Corp v Citizens & S Intl Bank, 817 F2d 349 (5th Cir 1987) (district court did not exceed remand order by imposing sanctions on attorney and party for multiplying proceedings); Johnson v Uncle Ben's, Inc, 965 F2d 1363, 1369 (5th Cir 1992) ("mandate rule", requiring district court to follow appeals court mandate is part of law of the case doctrine; rule can be overridden in light of developments in law, such as intervening Supreme Court decision that shows court of appeals' earlier holding to have been erroneous), *cert pending;* United States v MCC, Inc, 967 F2d 1559 (11th Cir 1992) (higher court vacatur of lower court judgment, with instructions to reconsider in light of certain principles, permits lower court to reinstate such parts of its earlier judgment as it finds consistent with the upper court's directions, without violating the mandate rule); Sierra Club v Penfold, 857 F2d 1307 (9th Cir 1988) (court of appeals remanded case on limited issue; while on remand, plaintiff amended its complaint and district court addressed issues raised by amended complaint and other matters outside the scope of remand; held, (1) district court was empowered to address additional issues since mandate did not forbid it to do so; (2) court of appeals had jurisdiction over all issues addressed

The court's mandate is also enforced by the law of the case doctrine, which teaches that "a decision of the court in a prior appeal must be followed in all subsequent proceedings in the same case," at least "unless the first decision is clearly erroneous and would result in manifest injustice, an intervening change in the law has occurred, or the evidence on remand is substantially different."[110]

District judges often point out that the remand order either does not adequately instruct them about what to do or it so limits their discretion that the court of appeals might as well have directed the entry of a particular judgment. If the remand order, as issued, is imprecise or does not go far enough, counsel should consider petitioning for rehearing as described at **§11.03.** To obviate such difficulties, counsel should include in the brief suggested language for the mandate.[111]

When remanding, the court of appeals will sometimes specify that the case go to a different district judge. If it does not so specify, the principles of reassignment on remand are set out in several cases. If there is a district court rule providing for reassignment, it should be followed, although some judges will say that such a rule is for judicial convenience and confers no standing on a litigant to ask that a case be sent to a different judge or randomly reassigned. In *United States v Robin,*[112] the en banc court of appeals considered the principles to be applied on remand. It noted that in the Southern District of New York, a judge may request that the assignment committee reassign a remanded case.[113] The en banc court held that

> the principal factors considered by us in determining whether further proceedings should be conducted before another judge are (1) whether the original judge would reasonably be expected to have substantial difficulty

---

on remand); *In re* Wella, AG, 858 F2d 725, 728 (Fed Cir 1988) (Patent Office appeal board impermissibly exceeded scope of court of appeals' remand order by considering issue raised by concurring judge in separate opinion; "inferior court has no power or authority to deviate from the mandate" (quoting Briggs v Pennsylvania RR, 334 US 304 (1948)).

[110] Eichman v Fotomat Corp, 880 F2d 149, 157 (9th Cir 1989). The doctrine also applies when a federal court considers matters resolved by a state court between the same parties. *Id.* For a thorough review of law of the case, see the en banc opinion in Litman v Massachusetts Mut Life Ins Co, 825 F2d 1506 (11th Cir 1987), *cert denied,* 484 US 1006 (1988). This opinion is a coherent outline of the power of federal courts, particularly the United States courts of appeals. The court began with the Evarts Act. It noted that the district court, under the law of the case doctrine, is obliged to follow the mandate of the court of appeals. The law of the case doctrine may not be an "inexorable command," (quoting White v Murtha, 377 F2d 428, 431 (5th Cir 1967)), but "adherence to it helps to ensure that the essential elements are maintained in the process;" the court noted that due process "may be the cornerstone, but finality and stability, as institutional values, may be of equal importance." *See id* 1511. The court reaffirmed that the district judge may address issues not disposed of on the appeal.

[111] *See* **§9.13.**

[112] 553 F2d 8 (2d Cir 1977).

[113] *Id* 9 n1.

> in putting out of his or her mind previously-expressed views or findings determined to be erroneous or based on evidence that must be rejected, (2) whether reassignment is advisable to preserve the appearance of justice, and (3) whether reassignment would entail waste and duplication out of proportion to any gain in preserving the appearance of fairness.[114]

Robin clarified and restated accepted Second Circuit doctrine. In the earlier case of *United States v Stein,*[115] the district judge had sentenced the defendant based on misinformation and misunderstandings of a number of issues, and for procedural errors connected with the sentencing process. The court of appeals held that a different judge must preside on remand, citing the recognized difficulty that an originally sentencing judge may have in rejecting or modifying prior conclusions and the necessity of maintaining the appearance of justice.[116]

In light of this authority, counsel has the opportunity to request that the court of appeals direct assignment to a different judge on remand.

§10.16 Interest, Costs, and Sanctions

Interest on money judgments is regulated by Fed R App P 37.[117] This rule is important in money cases when the appeal is from an order granting a judgment notwithstanding the verdict and directs entry of judgment on the verdict. In such a case, the court of appeals has the power to determine in its mandate whether interest will be paid for a longer period than from the date of its judgment.

The burden of requesting this is on counsel seeking pre-court of appeals judgment interest. Unless the court of appeals includes a provision for interest in its judgment, the district court is powerless to award it.[118] If the mandate

---

[114] *Id* 10.

[115] 544 F2d 96 (2d Cir 1976).

[116] *Id* 104. *Robin* was followed in United States v Ramos, 572 F2d 360 (2d Cir 1978), and explained in United States v Mendel, 746 F2d 155 (2d Cir 1984) (firmness of trial judge's repeatedly expressed views made remand to another judge appropriate), *cert denied,* 469 US 1213 (1985). The *Robin* opinion is consistent with the Congressional reformulation of 28 USC §455, which deals with disqualification of judges and magistrates. §455(a) requires recusal "in any proceeding in which his impartiality might reasonably be questioned." This language covers not only all cases of personal bias and interest, but much more in addition.

[117] The full text of Fed R App P 37 is in **app A.**

[118] *See* Advisory Committee Notes to Fed R App P 37. *See also* Canal Ins Co v First Gen Ins Co, 901 F2d 45 (5th Cir 1990) (if court of appeals does not exercise Fed R App P 37 power to award prejudgment interest, district court is powerless to do so; court of appeals will, on proper application, recall mandate to provide for interest); Leroy v City of Houston, 906 F2d 1068 (5th Cir 1990) (Fed R App P 37 forbids district court award of interest on judgment unless court of appeals' mandate provides for it; party seeking interest must seek recall of mandate).

is issued without providing for interest, the proper remedy is to seek recall of the mandate.[119]

If the court of appeals affirms a money judgment, the payment of interest is governed by 28 USC §1961, which sets out the general rules on awards and computation of interest on district court judgments.[120]

Costs on appeal generally are limited to relatively minor items such as the cost of docketing and reproducing the brief and appendices.[121] Costs under Fed R App P 39 do not include attorney fees. A party who wishes to obtain costs should include a prayer for them in his or her brief. If the judgment does not provide for costs and the case is not one covered by the rule, rehearing may be sought to clarify the entitlement to costs.

A party seeking costs must file an itemized statement within 14 days after judgment is entered.[122] Federal Rule of Appellate Procedure 39(d) contemplates that costs shall be included in the mandate, but they may be added later if the mandate issues before costs are fixed. The United States is now subject to costs in many civil cases under 28 USC §2412.

Sanctions are provided for by Fed R App P 38,[123] which echoes the words of 28 USC §1912. The rule provides for single or double costs or *just damages* as a sanction when a judgment is affirmed. Fed R App P 38 is not the exclusive means for assessing penalties against parties and advocates who abuse the appellate process. 28 USC §1927's authorization for imposing costs and fees against attorneys who vexatiously multiply proceedings is also a basis for action, as is the court's inherent power. The entire subject of sanctions on appeal is canvassed in detail at **§5.02.** This section provides only citations to the relevant rules and statutes.[124]

Federal Rule of Appellate Procedure 38 does supplant state rules. In Burlington Northern Railroad Co v Woods,[125] the defendant removed an Alabama state court tort suit to federal court. Plaintiffs won a judgment for $300,000 and defendant appealed. When the 11th Circuit affirmed, it imposed a sanction on the defendant of 10 per cent of the judgment under an Alabama statute

---

[119] Briggs v Pennsylvania RR, 334 US 304 (1948).

[120] *See* Turner v Japan Lines, 702 F2d 752, 754 (9th Cir 1983).

[121] *See* Fed R App P 39, *reproduced in* **app A.** *See also In re* American President Lines, 779 F2d 714 (DC Cir 1985) (per curiam) (applying Fed R App P 37, district court may require appellant to post bond or other security to ensure payment of appellate costs in civil cases; such costs include, however, only "those that may be taxed against an unsuccessful litigant under Federal Appellate Rule 39;" attorneys' fees therefore are not included). The items of permissible costs are listed in 28 USC §1920.

[122] Fed R App P 39(d).

[123] The full text of Fed R App B 38 is in **app A.**

[124] *See also* Becker v Adams Drug Co, 819 F2d 32 (2d Cir 1987) (double costs and $500 assessed against plaintiff for filing frivolous appeal from dismissal), *cert denied,* 484 US 1015 (1988); Clark v Maurer, 824 F2d 565 (7th Cir 1987) (sanctions imposed on municipal employees for appealing dismissal of civil rights suit, but dissent queried whether sanctions were appropriate when another district court in the same district had refused to dismiss a similar claim).

[125] 480 US 1 (1987).

requiring such a penalty—as a deterrent to frivolous appeals. The Supreme Court held that Rule 38 is valid under the Rules Enabling Act[126] and the federal constitution, and that it conflicted with the Alabama statute. Therefore, Rule 38 must govern. As noted at **§5.02,** Fed R Civ P 11 may not be applied on appeal.

---

[126] 28 USC §2072.

11 Rehearing and Rehearing En Banc

§11.01 Difference between Rehearing and Rehearing En Banc

The party dissatisfied with the court of appeals' opinion has three possible courses of action in the short term: petition for rehearing under Fed R App P 40,[1] suggest rehearing en banc under Fed R App P 35,[2] or petition the Supreme Court of the United States for certiorari.[3] One, two, or three of these courses may be pursued. If the opinion was issued so long ago that time has run out for pursuing these remedies, there are two possible courses of action, both of which have little statistical chance of success: first, one can move to recall the mandate under the general equitable power recognized by the Fifth Circuit and discussed at **§10.15;** second, one can collaterally attack the court of appeals' opinion and judgment, either in the court of appeals or in the district court, as discussed at **§11.07.**

---

[1] The full text of Fed R App P 40 is in **app A.**

[2] The full text of Fed R App P 35 is in **app A.**

[3] Rarely, an appeal will lie to the Supreme Court. *See* **§2.01.** *See generally* Robert L. Stern, Eugene Gressman, & Stephan M. Shapiro Supreme Court Practice (6th ed 1986).

The Fed R App P 40 rehearing petition is directed to the three judges on the panel. The petition must be filed within 14 days unless the time is extended by an order granted on the party's motion or by local rule.[4] No answer may be filed to a petition for rehearing unless the court asks for one. The petition must state clearly the issues of fact or law on which the panel is mistaken.

Rehearing en banc, by all the active judges of the circuit, is governed by Fed R App P 35(a), which provides in part that:

> Such a hearing or rehearing is not favored and ordinarily will not be ordered except
>
> (1) when consideration by the full court is necessary to secure or maintain uniformity of its decisions, or
>
> (2) when the proceeding involves a question of exceptional importance.[5]

Rehearing en banc may be sought by a party, or by any active member of the court, who believes that the issue is important or that the panel is very wrong. For example, in *League of United Latin American Citizens v Clements*,[6] a panel of the Fifth Circuit upheld a voting rights challenge brought by Hispanic plaintiffs. One judge on the panel not only dissented and suggested that the case be reheard en banc, but wrote a proposed en banc decision.[7]

The essential difference between the two forms of review, as discussed in more detail at **§11.03** (rehearing) and **§11.04** (rehearing en banc), is that the Rule 40 rehearing seeks to persuade the panel to correct errors of fact or law in its opinion and is disposed of by the panel members. The latter device, the Rule 35 suggestion, seeks to command a majority vote of all the active judges in the circuit that the issues are worthy of the extraordinary step of all of them congregating to decide the case.

In addition to this functional difference, there is a timing and procedural distinction. The Rule 35 suggestion can be filed at any time, and an advocate with a sufficiently important issue can seek en banc review at the time the initial brief is filed. The Rule 40 petition for panel rehearing is filed only after the panel opinion is issued. The Rule 40 petition also has an effect on further review: if it is timely filed, the time for seeking review in the Supreme Court

---

[4] For example, in the DC Circuit, the period has been extended to 30 days by local rule and to 45 days when the United States or one of its officers or agencies is a party. DC Cir R 14(a).

[5] The full text of Fed R App P 35 is in **app A.**

[6] 986 F2d 728 (5th Cir 1993).

[7] *Id* 819. The majority found evidence to support finding of vote dilutions in eight counties, holding that the state's interest in its electoral methods did not outweigh such dilution and that this dilution was not dispelled by partisan voting evidence.

does not begin to run until it has disposed of.[8] Filing a suggestion under Rule 35 does not have this effect. However, it is not necessary to file either the petition under Rule 40 or the suggestion under Rule 35 to seek review in the Supreme Court. Unless otherwise ordered by the court, the petition for rehearing will suspend the going down of the mandate to the lower court under Fed R App P 41.[9]

For example, in *Missouri v Jenkins*,[10] the distinction between a Fed R App P 40 petition for panel rehearing and a Fed R App P 35 suggestion for rehearing en banc was crucial to the timeliness of a petition for writ of certiorari.[11] In *Jenkins,* the court of appeals issued denials of rehearing en banc on Oct 14, 1988. Because pendency of a rehearing en banc does not toll the time for petitioning for certiorari, the petitions thereafter filed were out of time. On January 10, 1989, the court of appeals recalled the earlier order and "as of October 14, 1988," entered an order denying "petitions for rehearing with suggestions for rehearing en banc."[12] The Supreme Court held this was a valid action, since it arguably reflected the fact that the documents filed could be considered Rule 40 petitions as well as Rule 35 suggestions. The Court made clear that it would not permit the court of appeals to recharacterize its actions without some basis in the record and its prior practice.

In *United States v Buljubasic*,[13] the court construed a document incorrectly labeled "petition for rehearing en banc" as being only a suggestion under Fed R App P 35, not as a request for panel rehearing. The court's action almost certainly meant that a petition for certiorari would be out of time, since the time for petitioning would be counted from the date of the court's opinion and not from the date on which the mislabelled petition was denied.

Even though a petition for rehearing is not prerequisite to seeking Supreme Court review, it probably is advisable to prepare and file one if the advocate intends to seek such review by certiorari.[14] The odds of the writ of certiorari

---

[8] Sup Ct R 13.4. *See generally* Robert L. Stern, Eugene Gressman, & Stephan M. Shapiro, *supra* note 3.

[9] On the mandate, see **§10.15.**

[10] 495 US 33 (1990).

[11] On time for petitioning for certiorari, see Sup Ct R 13. This problem would arise less often in circuits, such as the Fifth, that insist that the two requests be filed in separate instruments.

[12] 495 US at 34 (quoting the amended order).

[13] 828 F2d 426 (7th Cir), *cert denied,* 484 US 815 (1987).

[14] Robert L. Stern, Eugene Grossman, & Stephan M. Shapiro, *supra* note 3, is the best guide to this subject. Supreme Court jurisdiction is divided into original, 28 USC §1251; appeal of right, 28 USC §1253; certiorari, 28 USC §§1254(1), 1257, 1258, 1259; and by certification from a court of appeals, 28 USC §1254(2). Review of federal court of appeals decisions, except for decisions invalidating an Act of Congress, is governed by 28 USC §1254. *See generally* Charles A. Wright, Federal Courts §§4, 105-110 (4th ed 1983). As noted at **§2.01,** the Supreme Court's mandatory jurisdiction is almost gone. *See* Robert L. Stern, Eugene Gressman, & Stephan M. Shapiro, *Epitaph for Mandatory Jurisdiction,* 74 ABA J 66 (Dec 1988). On seeking certiorari, see the excellent discussion in Charles G. Cole, *Petitioning for Certiorari in the Big Case,* No 3, at 12 Litig 33 (Spring 1986).

being granted are about 125 out of 5,000 petitions filed with the Supreme Court. A petition for rehearing therefore is not only a last stand effort in most cases, but it also can, perhaps, sharpen a cloudy issue discussion or make the case more of a candidate for the grant of certiorari. If the case has been decided without a written opinion, or with a brief nonsubstantive memorandum, a rehearing petition may provoke a longer explanation of the court's reasoning that will clarify the issues on which certiorari will be sought.

It must, however, be emphasized that the odds against the advocate faced with an adverse panel opinion are considerable. No procedural step should be taken without searching inquiry into whether it would waste the client's money and—in an extreme case—subject the lawyer to sanctions for dilatory tactics.[15]

§11.02 Procedural Steps Before Seeking Rehearing: Stay of Mandate, Motion to Recall Mandate

As discussed at **§10.15,** the court of appeals' mandate is a crucial document in the rehearing process. The mandate embodies or refers to the judgment, and is sent to the court or agency whose action the court of appeals has reviewed.

The courts of appeals generally follow Fed R App P 41 and, as a matter of course, issue the mandate 21 days after the decision is filed and the judgment entered. However, the advocate must consult the circuit rules on this point. In addition, the panel deciding the case can, on its own motion, order the mandate issued immediately.[16] This procedural step will be reflected in the opinion or judgment, and tells the advocate two important things.

First, the panel regards its decision as so noncontroversial and definitive that neither the panel nor the entire court would be likely to change a single comma. Such a conclusion is rare, and occurs most often when the panel feels the appeal was taken for delay or without adequate foundation. If such a conclusion appears to be the basis for the panel's action, the winning side may consider seeking double costs or some other sanction.

Second, the issuance of the mandate signals an end to the court of appeals' jurisdiction over the case. When the mandate reaches the reviewed court or

---

[15] *See, e.g.,* Westcot Corp v Edo Corp, 857 F2d 1387 (10th Cir 1988) (rehearing petitions restating arguments in principal briefs or going beyond the record are *without merit,* justifying sanction of attorney without show cause order and formal opportunity to respond).

[16] See Johnson v Bechtel Assocs Professional Corp, 801 F2d 412 (DC Cir 1986), holding that when the court of appeals orders the mandate issued within a shorter time than its local rule provides for filing a rehearing petition, the time for petitioning for rehearing is shortened accordingly. The court also held that a mandate may issue immediately when the court is satisfied that it will not change its decision, nor rehear the case en banc, and there is no reasonable likelihood that the Supreme Court would grant review. However, upon a suitable showing the mandate can be recalled to permit filing of a petition for rehearing.

agency, and is formally placed on the latter's record, the reviewed judgment is fully effective and can be executed upon.[17] In a criminal case in which the defendant is on bail pending appeal, his or her bail status will terminate when the mandate is entered of record in the district court. Therefore, the advocate who wants to file a petition under Rule 40 or a suggestion under Rule 35 must move to recall the mandate.[18] Such a motion will be similar in form and content to the motion to stay the mandate, which is discussed later in this section.

Nothing prevents a party from seeking further review—by rehearing, rehearing en banc, certiorari, recall of the mandate or collateral attack—of a court of appeals decision as to which the mandate has been issued. The only danger is that the mandate may cause something to happen that will moot the case.[19] Issuance of the mandate is not usually fatal to further review, but staying the mandate is certainly preferable.

In addition to the reasons stated above, the circuit clerk may on rare occasions omit to send notice of the decision to the advocates. In such an instance, the mandate may be issued before counsel has an opportunity to seek rehearing.

The advocate who wants a continuance of the date for filing a petition for rehearing should consult the clerk's office to ensure that the continuance will operate to stay the mandate until disposition of the rehearing petition. If such a stay is not automatic, the continuance motion must request a stay.[20]

Whatever the occasion for seeking relief, the motion to stay or recall the mandate must contain the same basic analysis and argument. Following the form recommended in Chapter 8,[21] these elements must be present:

Request for relief: this consists of a brief statement of the relief desired—stay of mandate, recall of mandate, continuance—and a citation to the applicable rules. For example:

> John Jones, the appellant, by his undersigned counsel and pursuant to Federal Rule of Appellate Procedure 41 and Fifth Circuit Rule 41, moves for an order continuing the due date for his petition from December 1, 1986, to and including December 22, 1986, a period of twenty-one days,

---

[17] *See id* 415 n16 (mandate returns case to tribunal to which directed for such proceedings as may be appropriate).

[18] The court of appeals has inherent power to recall its own mandate. Sparks v Duval County Ranch Co, 604 F2d 976 (5th Cir 1979), *cert denied,* 445 US 943, *affd sub nom* Dennis v Sparks, 449 US 24 (1980). *See* **§10.15.** If counsel is unable to secure recall of the mandate, he or she may move in the district court for a stay pending further review.

[19] *See* **§2.18.**

[20] Stay of the mandate to petition for certiorari is governed by Fed R App P 41(b). The stay is sought by motion and is to last no more than 30 days unless enlarged by order. This 30-day limit dates from the time when most certiorari petitions were due 30 days after judgment. The time is now generally 90 days. Sup Ct R 13.

[21] **§8.07.** In emergency situations, it may be possible to file the stay motion by facsimile. *See* **§§8.01, 9.02.**

and for a stay of issuance of the mandate to and including the disposition of the petition.

In some circuits, the clerk has the authority to grant brief continuances of this sort, and counsel may be able to obtain relief by telephone, with a follow-up letter confirming the conversation.[22] Obtaining consent from the opponent is sometimes necessary to obtain a telephone order, and is always helpful in any event.

The next section should be headed, I. *Facts Giving Rise to This Motion;* it should let the court know the status of the case and the relevant dates—decision, date rehearing petition otherwise would be due, and so on.

The following section should be headed, *II. Reasons for Granting This Motion,* and should tell the court what issues the advocate will raise if permitted the opportunity to file a petition for rehearing. This discussion need not be lengthy, but it must reflect counsel's considered judgment that the ordinary rules of finality should yield to the opportunity for further review. The advocate must remember that, in most circuits, the motion will be considered by a member of the panel that issued the opinion.[23] The discussion of issues should be a very condensed version of what will appear in the rehearing petition and suggestion. In a criminal appeal, the advocate should also note the defendant's bond status.

Of course, the most persuasive words are: "Counsel represents that he has conferred with opposing counsel and that granting of this motion is not opposed."

§11.03 When and How to Write a Petition for Rehearing

The petition for rehearing, Fed R App P 40 states, must follow the form provided for briefs in Fed R App P 32. Some circuits also provide additional requirements. In setting up the petition for rehearing notebook, the sections to provide for[24] are:

Cover
Table of Contents
Table of Authorities
Questions Presented on Rehearing
Course of Proceedings and Disposition
Statement of Facts
Argument
Conclusion
Certificate of Service

---

[22] This will depend upon the motions power delegated to the clerk. *See* **§8.03.**

[23] This is the same practice as followed with respect to many procedural motions, as discussed in **ch 8.** *See* **§8.04.**

[24] See **§9.03** on the notebook theory of brief writing.

The following discussion assumes that counsel will file a separate petition for rehearing and suggestion of the appropriateness of a rehearing en banc. This is required by the rules of many circuits,[25] in part because—as discussed below—the reasons for seeking panel rehearing are so different from those governing rehearing en banc. However, if the two documents are to be combined into a "Petition for Rehearing and, in the Alternative, Suggestion of the Appropriateness of a Rehearing En Banc," some minor format changes will be necessary based upon individual circuit rules. The "Issues" heading will read "Issues on Rehearing and/or Rehearing En Banc." Right after the Table of Authorities, and under the "Issues" heading, the rehearing petition will state:

> [Name of party], [appellant or appellee] in this court, by undersigned counsel and pursuant to Federal Rule of Appellate Procedure 40, petitions the panel for rehearing of its decision of [date], and presents the following issues: [set out issues].

The combined petition/suggestion would add a citation to Federal Rule of Appellate Procedure 35 and the words, "and in the alternative suggests the appropriateness of a rehearing en banc."

The discussion, of course, of proceedings and the facts will be truncated in a Rule 40 rehearing petition. The advocate is speaking to the judges who decided the case. Although months will have passed since the argument, they will have retained a general sense of what the case is about. In a combined petition/suggestion, the factual discussion should be limited to those elements that present rehearing or en banc issues. Precision and conciseness are watchwords. Detail is necessary only if one is challenging the panel's treatment of the factual record, and in that instance careful citation to the record is a must.

With the technical and preliminary matters under control, one may consider the issues to be presented for rehearing and the style of argument appropriate to a petition. To make this decision, one must know something about the way petitions for rehearing are handled. As discussed in a previous chapter, an argued case is tentatively decided the day of argument. Thereafter, the judges on the panel are unlikely to meet again and discuss the case among themselves. Drafts will be exchanged and there may be some telephone consultation, but the judge who authors the panel opinion usually will be given considerable leeway and deference. Nonargued case opinions originate in one judge's chambers and the same principles apply. These facts about the decisional process underscore the relative lack of collegiality in most courts of appeals and help to explain the considerable inertia behind upholding a panel decision once made. In the case of a nonpublished memorandum or order without opinion, and to a lesser degree with a brief per curiam opinion, one has the additional problem of not knowing which judge is the primary audience for one's efforts.

---

[25] *See, e.g.*, 5th Cir R 35.2.

The petition for rehearing remains under the control of the deciding panel. In most courts of appeals, the writing judge will pay the most attention to the petition, although copies of it will be circulated to the chambers of each judge on the panel. There is little likelihood of collegial discussion of a rehearing petition, even by telephone, unless the petition raises on its face an issue that seems troubling to one or more members of the panel. Such issues may be discussed in three categories: factual, legal, and court of appeals procedural.

Factual disputes are a great deal less important to most court of appeals judges than most lawyers would like to think. There sits the advocate with an unfavorable opinion, perhaps in a case the advocate tried and appealed. "How could they have gotten these facts so twisted?" is a common lament. One reason for this perceived factual bias may be that the judges have applied the settled rule that in reviewing facts, deference is usually due the version that supports the judgment. Second, the author of the opinion may have made a factual error based on the relative difficulty of a busy judge winnowing every grain of relevant fact from a heavy and chaff-laden record. Finally, the judge may have overlooked a relevant fact in haste to write an opinion embodying a conclusion agreed upon at conference among three judges who had not each plowed through the entire record.

In each such instance, there is a basis for making just complaint on rehearing. *Just complaint* does not necessarily translate into victory, for the judges will most likely disregard any error in the opinion that would not change the result: they are principally concerned with deciding cases and settling the legal points presented by the parties. A judge sometimes will candidly admit to the human failing, perhaps intensified in judges appointed for life, of resenting criticism of his or her work. There are, however, solutions.

The answer to the first claim—deference—is that even deference is not surrendered to principle, and an able judge has warned that the record should not be read without regard to its blemishes. Also, the particular case may call for more exacting scrutiny.

The second problem—the overlooked or downplayed fact—is more complex. For example, in *United States v Cook,*[26] the panel on rehearing reversed itself and found sufficient evidence to support the verdict where in its initial opinion it had ruled the evidence insufficient. The crucial changes were two. The panel gave greater weight to an item of evidence that it had noted in its initial opinion, but found not entitled, under the rules of evidence, to be counted in support of the government. Second, the panel found a new reason to consider bits and pieces of evidence in a more coherent whole, rather than as isolated items. A petition for rehearing must, in such a case, note the factual error into which the court has fallen and in measured tones point out the evidence that contradicts the panel opinion.

The final basis for panel factual error—the concurring judges' relative unfamiliarity with the facts—is rather like the second. There may be a vital difference, however. The author of the panel opinion is probably more aware of

---

[26] 783 F2d 1207 (5th Cir), *affd on reconsideration,* 793 F2d 734 (5th Cir 1986).

the intractability of the facts. The other members will not have dug so deeply. The advocate seeking rehearing must understand, even while protesting, that rehearing petitions are many, the nonauthor judges may not have easy access to the record, and the press of judicial business often means that rehearings get low priority. Some judges may rely even more heavily than usual on their clerks to screen rehearings. The Rule 40 petition in such a case may call for a bold presentation of the issue if the record warrants it:

> Counsel represents that the panel opinion rests upon a recital of the evidence that is so far contradicted by the record that the panel's legal conclusion cannot be supported. This assertion is made with full knowledge of the consequences for counsel of misstatement and is fully supported below with detailed citations to the record.

From what had been said so far, it should be obvious that nitpicking objections to the panel's factual statement are not worth pursuing, and will diminish and discredit the remainder of the petition. However, despite the oft-repeated admonition that the rehearing petition is no place to reargue contentions considered and rejected by the panel, pinpoint identification of significant factual errors is always appropriate.

The rehearing petition also presents an opportunity to point out errors in the panel's treatment of the law. Here, the canon that rearguing old and rejected points is improper is of special relevance. The advocate must read and understand the panel opinion on its own terms. He or she must ask, "What are these judges trying to do to the law? Do they understand the consequences of the rule they have adopted? Are there some clues to a limiting principle that might, on rehearing, go far enough to change the result?" The opinion is the first definitive statement from the panel. At argument, the judges may have put questions that more or less embodied their tentative attitudes towards the case. Now they are committed. The advocate must accept that commitment as virtually—though not invariably—final for the present case, and seek a way through that rationalizes the opinion with the result he or she seeks.

Seeking to limit the potential reach of the legal rule announced by the panel is of particular importance to two kinds of litigants: those who face further proceedings on remand and those who have an institutional position.

If the case is remanded, the loser in the court of appeals will want to preserve maximum maneuvering room for the district court. The advocate may use the rehearing petition to suggest that the panel excise or tone down aspects of its decision. For example, in *Wehling v CBS, Inc,*[27] the panel's initial opinion upheld the plaintiff's right to maintain his libel suit and stay discovery so that he would preserve his right against compelled self-incrimination with respect to the alleged conduct that was the basis of the alleged libel. The defendant obtained a vital clarification on rehearing. The panel stated that the defendant could push the case to trial without the plaintiff's deposition, call the plaintiff as a witness, and argue an adverse inference if the plaintiff invoked the Fifth

---

[27] 608 F2d 1084 (5th Cir 1979), *on rehg* 611 F2d 1026 (5th Cir 1980).

Amendment. The rehearing did not take away the plaintiff's right with respect to the discovery phase, but it affirmed that the defendant had significant leverage on remand.

The position of institutional litigants is more obviously benefited by a rehearing petition that seeks and obtains clarification. The archetypical such litigant is the United States government. An example of its use of a Rule 35 rehearing petition is *United States v Ballard.*[28] The court of appeals reversed a conviction for mail fraud and took the occasion to level strong criticism of expansive prosecutorial readings of the mail fraud statute. Responding to the government's rehearing petition, the court withdrew some of its strong language and disavowed the intention to restrict prosecutorial initiative.

An institutional litigant—governmental, corporate, public interest, or other—has the certain knowledge that it will face the same or a similar legal issue in future litigation. It therefore has a strong interest in seeking to shape legal rules in ways that may not benefit it in the present case, but surely will come in handy later.

§11.04 When and How to Write a Suggestion of the Appropriateness of Rehearing En Banc

The rules of many circuits warn the advocate against filing unnecessary suggestions for rehearing en banc. The committee comment to Eighth Circuit Rule 35A cautions that the suggestion "requires substantial processing and the expenditure of time by judges who have not participated in the case, as well as by the hearing panel. The procedure must be reserved for cases necessary to secure or maintain uniformity of decisions or that raise a question of exceptional importance."[29] Eighth Circuit Rule 35A itself warns:

> Counsel who files a frivolous suggestion for rehearing en banc shall be deemed to have multiplied the proceedings in the case and to have increased costs unreasonably and vexatiously in the sum of $250. At the court's order, counsel personally may be required to pay those costs to the opposing party. *See* 18 USC §1927.[30]

The Fifth Circuit Internal Operating Procedure for its 5th Cir R 35 states:

> Suggestions for rehearing en banc are the most abused prerogative of appellate advocates in the Fifth Circuit. While such suggestions are filed in about 15% of the cases decided, less than 1% of the cases decided by the Court are reheard en banc; and frequently rehearings granted result from a request for en banc reconsideration by a judge of the Court initiated independent of any petition.[31]

---

[28] 663 F2d 534 (5th Cir 1981), *rehg denied, opinion modified,* 680 F2d 352 (5th Cir 1982).

[29] Committee comment to 8th Cir R 35A.

[30] 8th Cir R 35A(c)(3).

[31] Internal Operating Procedure under 5th Cir R 35.

To make the point even more sharply, 5th Cir R 35.1 warns lawyers that the court feels "fully justified" in imposing sanctions on the lawyer who signs a meritless suggestion of rehearing en banc, the represented party, or both.[32]

Because the Rule 35 suggestion is not necessary to preserve the right to further review, these cautionary words bear heeding. Many lawyers throw in an en banc suggestion on the basis that it can be made part of the Rule 40 rehearing petition in most circuits, or else can be virtually a duplicate of that document with a different title on the cover. Avoiding unnecessary en banc suggestions is not simply a matter of minimizing the risk of sanctions. A meritorious rehearing petition under Rule 40 risks being trivialized when it is yoked to a somewhat fanciful Rule 35 suggestion.

As discussed at **§11.01,** the en banc suggestion is reserved for extraordinary situations. Rule 35(a) says simply that the suggestion will not be granted unless full court consideration is necessary to "secure or maintain uniformity of its decisions" or the case "involves a question of exceptional importance."[33] These rather cryptic words have come to have a rather settled meaning.

Uniformity refers to the rule that a panel of the court of appeals may not depart from rules laid down by another panel.[34] Departure from this rule is a basis for rehearing. Only the en banc court can overrule a prior panel or en banc decision.[35] There are, of course, ideological differences among judges, and one judge's artful distinction may be another's temerarious nonuniformity. So a panel's uncharitable reading of prior precedent does not guarantee en banc treatment.[36]

The advocate claiming nonuniformity should be able to point to one or more prior decisions of the same court of appeals and state clearly and precisely how the panel decision is at odds with those decisions. This task should be performed in the Statement of Issues on Rehearing En Banc, and in somewhat more detail in the first explanatory paragraph dealing with that issue.

Questions of exceptional importance are harder to classify. A clear candidate for inclusion in such a category would be a decision at odds with the rule in another circuit. This would be so particularly when the panel has expressly declined to follow precedent from the other circuit. Even stronger would be

---

[32] 5th Cir R 35.1. The cited bases for sanctions are Fed R App P 38 and 28 USC §1927. *See generally* **§5.02.**

[33] The full text of Fed R App P 35 is in **app A.**

[34] *See, e.g.,* North Carolina Utils Commn v FCC, 552 F2d 1036 (4th Cir), *cert denied,* 434 US 874 (1977). Because the courts of appeals sit in panels of three, it sometimes happens that a panel will issue an opinion conflicting with an earlier opinion by a different panel. The loser of the later case probably will seek rehearing and rehearing en banc, but if that is unsuccessful, the two conflicting opinions will puzzle counsel in a later case. The Federal Circuit has held, following the general rule, that a court coming upon such a contradiction should endeavor to harmonize the two earlier opinions. If it cannot, it should follow the earlier one or seek en banc consideration of the case. Johnston v IVAC Corp, 885 F2d 1574, 1579 (Fed Cir 1989).

[35] Van Gemert v Boeing Co, 590 F2d 433 (2d Cir 1978), *affd,* 444 US 472 (1980).

[36] One must identify with precision the ways in which the panel has misread a prior circuit case and frame the questions on rehearing to flag this issue.

such a case when the issue is one of first impression in the court of appeals where en banc consideration is being sought. Most courts of appeals take seriously the problems that are created by intercircuit conflicts, and many of them have an informal practice of circulating panel opinions raising such conflicts to all the active judges before the panel decides the case. On the basis of such informal polling, active judges sometimes trigger the en banc process without counsel's intervention.

The significance of intercircuit conflict is enhanced because it is one clear basis for invoking the certiorari jurisdiction of the Supreme Court.[37] When relying upon intercircuit conflict, counsel should be able to identify the conflict with clarity and precision. A difference of approach or theory will not be enough to found a credible claim.

Beyond intercircuit conflict, exceptional importance raises the following questions: does the panel decision conflict with a decision of the Supreme Court? Only that Court can overrule its own precedents; a court of appeals is not free to regard Supreme Court authority as "eroded" by passage of time.[38] Does the panel decide (1) a significant federal question (2) of first impression (3) that is likely to recur? A state law issue is generally not grist for the en banc mill.[39]

The advocate will have a better chance of gaining en banc consideration if he or she can demonstrate that the issue is likely to bedevil the district courts and, therefore, the court of appeals in a number of cases unless resolved authoritatively. This form of argument is a bit like that in a petition for certiorari to the Supreme Court: the advocate is saying not only that the panel was very wrong, but that the issue is so important that it merits consideration quite apart from the advocate's sincere belief that the panel result was wrong.[40] In addressing this question, one might also refer to the bases for extraordinary writ jurisdiction listed at **§3.01**, for the standards are similar in practice. A hearing en banc will more likely be granted if an en banc decision will solve a recurring problem or prevent litigation-engendering confusion.

Only rarely will all three parts of the question asked in the preceding paragraph be satisfied. With every unmet condition the odds of obtaining en banc rehearing move against the advocate.

The paucity of en banc rehearings reflects basic facts about contemporary federal appellate practice. The docket pressure on courts of appeals today creates a powerful inertia not to rehear cases en banc. Busy judges are inclined to let apparent conflicts and unresolved questions "bubble" for awhile before concluding that en banc review is a wise investment of resources.

A rehearing en banc will almost never be granted unless a group of judges, upon reading the suggestion, is willing to lobby for it among their colleagues.

---

[37] *See* Robert L. Stern, Supreme Court Practice, (6th ed 1986).

[38] *See* Hicks v Miranda, 422 US 332, 344-45 (1975) (lower courts must follow Supreme Court authority until that Court says it is no longer binding).

[39] *See, e.g.*, Internal Operating Procedure 5th Cir R 35.

[40] This concern with the importance of the issue rather than the particular injustice being suffered by one's client is the same detachment one employs in seeking certiorari.

A judge who is convinced that en banc review is appropriate must bestir himself or herself not only to request a poll in accordance with Rule 40(b) but also to make sure that like-minded judges are ready to vote for en banc consideration. The advocate will be unaware that this process is going on, although if the suggestion is pending more than 60 days it is likely that serious consideration is being given. Even with this lobbying effort, the judges concerned with the issue may succeed only in convincing the panel to modify its earlier opinion to eliminate the troublesome problem that might justify en banc review, for example, by narrowing the holding or eliminating troublesome dicta.[41]

Rehearing en banc will be very difficult to obtain if the panel members included judges with different judicial philosophies on the issue presented and if the panel opinion was unanimous. Surprising as it may seem, some judges will not press their every concern in every case.

True, some court of appeals judges have the habit of noting a dissent on every appropriate occasion. However, pressures put on judges by the decisional process,[42] coupled with the increased docket load, has meant that most judges will hesitate before dissenting. A judge may feel that the case does not pose a significant threat to his or her deeply held view, and that the panel decision can be distinguished when the appropriate occasion arises. A dissent might lead the opinion writer to a clarification that would cut more deeply into territory the judge wants to protect, and therefore simply joining the panel opinion provides an opportunity to insist on moderation. Or, the judge may feel that dissent is fruitless because the en banc court would not adopt the dissenter's position.

These are several reasons why a unanimous panel opinion joined by judges with different views will usually spell doom for an en banc suggestion. As noted above,[43] the suggestion of the appropriateness of a rehearing en banc may, in most circuits, be combined with the rehearing petition, but Rule 35 envisions a suggestion separate from the Rule 40 rehearing petition and some circuits require a separate document. Whether required or permitted, the Rule 35 suggestion should almost always be separate from the Rule 40 petition. The suggestion will be circulated to the judges of the court, while the petition only goes to those who are relatively familiar with the case from having recently considered it.

The suggestion should not, and in some circuits may not,[44] incorporate by reference any other pleadings or parts of the record. In most circuits, the judges' chambers are widely separated from each other; there is no practical way for each judge to have access to the volume of materials previously filed in the court of appeals, let alone the often voluminous district court record.

Nor is it safe to assume that the judge, and the judge's law clerks, possess an encyclopedic knowledge of every relevant federal judicial decision. The

---

[41] See the discussion at **§11.03** of *Wehling* and *Ballard*.

[42] *See* **§§10.13, 10.14.**

[43] **§11.01.**

[44] *See, e.g.*, 8th Cir R 35A(c).

advocate must therefore write for an audience that has no knowledge of the law or the facts about the case at hand beyond having read the panel opinion. The members of this audience, as noted above,[45] are quite reluctant to regard the case as important enough to do anything about it. The factual statement must usually agree with the facts as stated in the panel opinion; en banc hearings are not granted to resolve quibbles about the record. This means that, even if the advocate has concluded that the panel distorted the facts, and even if that concern is expressed in a petition for panel rehearing, he or she must argue that en banc consideration is appropriate regardless of one's view of the record. It is reasonable to note disagreement with the panel's view of the facts, perhaps in a footnote, but an en banc suggestion that seems to require viewing the record through the loser's spectacles is doomed to denial.

Before sitting down to write, the advocate must ask, "Why should a dozen or so busy judges take time from their other duties to gather and decide my issue the way I want it decided, and why is this issue so important to their concerns that they would do that?" The suggestion is an adversary document. It is not the place to attack one's opponent or quibble with the panel whose members are, after all, colleagues of the judges one is trying to reach. As with any another petition, suggestion, or motion, this kind of internal dialogue will greatly improve the product.

In keeping with this approach, the suggestion must be short. Rule 35 limits rehearing petitions to 15 pages in absence of a circuit rule or leave of court. This is a workable maximum for Rule 40 suggestions.[46]

§11.05 How the Court Decides Rehearing Petitions and Suggestions

Even in circuits that permit a party to mail a brief and appendix on the due date, rehearing petitions must be actually received in the clerk's office on the fourteenth day after the judgment is entered unless an extension is requested within the 14 days. Failure to follow this rule means that the time for seeking further review in the Supreme Court runs from the date of judgment and not from the date the rehearing petition is denied.[47]

---

[45] **§11.01.**

[46] Robert L. Stern, *supra* note 37 has for years suggested 20 pages as optimal for a certiorari petition.

[47] One also should note two (seldom used) procedural devices. First, a party may request en banc consideration as an initial matter in the court of appeals. Such a suggestion, absent a contrary local rule or order, must be filed on or before the date the appellee's brief is filed. Fed R App P 35(b). Second, a party may seek to abort court of appeals review by petitioning the Supreme Court for certiorari before judgment in the court of appeals. 28 USC §1254(1). United States v Mistretta, 486 US 1054 (1988), *affd,* 488 US 361 (1989), involved a grant of certiorari before judgment on cross-petitions by the defendant and the government; at issue was the constitutionality of the sentencing guidelines legislation. *See* James Lindgren & William P. Marshall, *The Supreme Court's Extraordinary Power to Grant Certiorari Before Judgment in the Court of Appeals,* 1986 Sup Ct Rev 259.

A petition for rehearing is sent to the panel that rendered the opinion. A suggestion of the appropriateness of rehearing en banc is handled differently in different circuits, but will in every case be sent to the panel that decided the case and to every active (that is, nonsenior) judge on the court, these being the judges eligible to sit on the en banc court.[48] Typically, the suggestion will be held open for a period established by the rules or procedures of the circuit for a judge or judges to vote or to request a poll as provided in Rule 35(b).[49]

Rule 40 states that the court ordinarily will not grant rehearing without soliciting a response from the winning party, and the practice under Rule 35 is to follow the same procedure. Therefore, the opponent may not file an opposition as a matter of course. A party who has not moved for rehearing, and who is dissatisfied with portions of the panel opinion, should consider a conditional cross-petition for rehearing. If the time for filing a petition has elapsed, the party may seek an extension under Rule 35(a).

If the court requests an opposition to a rehearing petition, the advocate should consider the following approaches:

1. Obviously, defend the correctness of the panel's treatment of the law and the facts to the maximum extent possible.
2. If the panel has misstated the record, this is not fatal; the advocate should note that, while the petitioner arguably is right about the facts, the result would not be any different under his or her view.
3. If the petitioner seems to have a well-founded or potentially persuasive observation about the breadth or application of the legal rules relied upon by the panel, the opponent should suggest, as an alternative to outright denial of the petition, a reformulation or minor amendment to the opinion that leaves the result intact.

To this list may be added, in responding to a suggestion of appropriateness of rehearing en banc, the tactic of arguing that the panel opinion simply applies well-settled (albeit perhaps important) principles of law to facts that, to the extent they are dispositive, are not seriously subject to question.

---

[48] *See* **§4.01.** *See also* Moody v Albemarle Paper Co, 417 US 622 (1974) (senior judges ineligible to vote on whether to grant rehearing). However, a senior judge who was on the panel may sit on the en banc court. In United States v Nixon, 827 F2d 1019 (5th Cir 1987), *cert denied,* 484 US 1026 (1988), the Fifth Circuit interpreted its rule that a majority of judges in regular active service is required to grant a suggestion of the appropriateness of rehearing en banc. Nixon, a federal judge, had been convicted and his conviction affirmed, 816 F2d 1022 (5th Cir 1987). It was impossible to summon a majority for en banc reconsideration because 11 of the 14 judges on the Fifth Circuit recused themselves. The Fifth Circuit, nonetheless, sustained its procedure against constitutional challenge. The Ninth Circuit, as noted at **§4.11,** has established a limited en banc review procedure because of the number of active judges in that circuit.

[49] This period will be determined by local rule, internal operating procedure, or practice. Counsel should consult the clerk's office if it is important to gauge the time that decision may consume. Also, it is safe to assume that when the initial open period passes without a decision, the odds of the petition being granted rise slightly.

If rehearing is granted, the panel sometimes simply issues an amended opinion or an amendment to its opinion. In other rehearing situations, and in almost all cases of rehearing en banc, the advocate will receive an order setting a schedule for filing supplemental briefs and (usually) for reargument.

En banc briefing and argument follows the same forms and techniques as the initial appeal—with one important difference. On en banc rehearing, the advocate knows much better the views of at least some of the judges and the key issues on which the decision is likely to turn. Because an en banc court can overrule panel opinions and even prior en banc decisions, the field of argument is broader than on the initial appeal.

Unless and only to the extent the order granting rehearing or rehearing en banc expressly provides otherwise, the grant vacates the panel opinion and renders it of no precedential value.[50] Although counsel should make sure to check with the clerk, the grant will in most circuits stay the mandate.[51]

§11.06 Further Review—Supreme Court

If the advocate has petitioned for rehearing and suggested rehearing en banc, the two items will usually be disposed of in the same order. In most cases, the request and suggestion are denied; the clerk's office will send out a standard form reflecting the denial. The denial of the Fed R App P 40 petition, assuming it was timely filed, starts the clock running for Supreme Court review.[52] As noted at **§11.01**, a petition for certiorari is the method of seeking such review in almost all cases.[53]

Petitioning for certiorari involves costs, though a quick survey of petitions filed shows that most filers have not weighed the costs carefully or are not greatly concerned with them. In cases from the federal courts of appeals, it is not difficult to identify issues worthy of consideration on certiorari.

First, a petition by the United States is more likely to be granted than one by a private litigant. The Court's members expect the United States not to bring cases unless there is a substantial reason for doing so, and government lawyers receive deference at the Court's hands.

Second, an intercircuit conflict helps make a case cert-worthy, but is no guarantee of review. The Court often lets such conflicts mature, to see if the weight of authority will push the dissenting circuits into uniformity. An intercircuit conflict must be real, not simply arguable or hypothetical. Throughout this treatise, and particularly in Chapter 2, the reader will find citations to dissents

---

[50] *See, e.g.,* Internal Operating Procedure under 5th Cir R 35.

[51] *Id.*

[52] *See* **§11.01.**

[53] *See generally* Robert L. Stern, Supreme Court Practice (6th ed 1986). A very small number of cases—limited to those involving reapportionment, the Civil Rights and Voting Rights Act, the antitrust laws, or the Presidential Campaign Fund Act—are subject to appellate review or review as of right. Such review usually is sought after judgment in the court of appeals, although the statute does permit a petition for certorari before judgment in the court of appeals. Needless to say, such petitions are rarely granted.

from denial of certiorari in which a Justice or Justices will note a conflict among circuits and urge that it be resolved. Analyzing these dissents can help one understand how an intercircuit conflict should be evaluated and portrayed.

Third, identifying an issue significant enough to merit review on certiorari requires a detailed knowledge of the Supreme Court's work for the past several terms. There is no other way to know what the Justices have found significant than to study their opinions. It will sometimes be wise to consult with counsel who appear often before the Supreme Court to help identify such issues.

§11.07 —Collateral Attack

An appeal from the district court is termed *direct review.* Once the direct review process is over, or the chance for direct review has been forgone, the judgment becomes final.[54] For purposes of this section, further challenge to the judgment may be termed *collateral attack.*[55]

There are many forms of collateral attack on judgments. Most of these involve filing a proceeding in the district court, rather than in the court of appeals. For example, Fed R Civ P 60(b) permits a party to move for relief from a judgment obtained as a result of mistake, fraud, excusable neglect, newly discovered evidence, and other grounds.[56] A motion based on mistake, newly discovered evidence, or fraud must be made within one year. Federal Rules of Civil Procedure 60(b) expressly authorizes using the traditional device of an independent action in equity to set aside a judgment. Moreover, a party may not be bound by a judgment obtained without personal or subject matter jurisdiction; the preclusive scope of a former judgment will be tested in a subsequent proceeding to enforce that judgment.[57] Federal Rules of Civil Procedure 60(b) also acknowledges "the power of a court . . . to set aside a judgment for fraud upon the court."[58]

In federal criminal cases, collateral attack is governed by 28 USC §2255, which provides for a motion to vacate a sentence similar to habeas corpus.[59] A convicted defendant no longer in custody may bring a petition for writ of error coram nobis.[60] In addition, certain motions under Fed R Crim P 33 for

---

[54] *See* Fleming James, Jr, Geoffrey Hazard & John Leubsdorf, Civil Procedure §12.14 (4th ed 1992).

[55] *Id.*

[56] *Id* §12.15.

[57] *See id* §§11.1-11.32 (claim preclusion and issue preclusion); *id* §§2.3-2.9 (sister state must give full faith and credit to judgment only if the judgment was obtained consistent with due process). As a related example, a putative member of a class is not bound by a judgment against the class if the judgment was not obtained by means consistent with due process, and that may raise this issue in a subsequent proceeding. Hansberry v Lee, 311 US 32 (1940).

[58] The full text of Fed R Civ P 60(b) is in **app B.**

[59] *See generally* 2 James S. Liebman, Federal Habeas Corpus Practice & Procedure ch 36 (1988).

[60] United States v Morgan, 346 US 502, 511 (1954). Fed R Civ P 60(b) abolishes the writ of error coram nobis for civil cases.

new trial, or Fed R Crim P 35 for correction or reduction of sentence, may be made as provided in the criminal rules.[61]

Appeals from denial of relief under these provisions of law are taken and conducted as described in the earlier chapters of this book.

The question remains what power a court of appeals has to set aside its own judgment, on its own motion or on a party's application directly to the court of appeals. As noted at **§§10.15** and **11.01,** the court can recall its mandate when justice so requires, although the precise contours of this power are uncertain.

A court of appeals also has the power—shared by all federal courts—to accept, initiate, investigate, hear, and decide a claim of fraud on the court. In *Hazel-Atlas Glass Co v Hartford-Empire Co,*[62] Hazel-Atlas filed an action in the court of appeals nine years after a patent judgment had become final, claiming that Hartford had defrauded the patent office and the court of appeals in obtaining the earlier judgment. The Supreme Court upheld the court of appeals' power to entertain such an action and to grant relief, including vacatur of the earlier judgment.[63]

Today, the mechanism for making such a challenge probably would be a motion to vacate the court of appeals judgment, and in the alternative a petition for mandamus, to direct the lower court to vacate its judgment.[64] If the irregularity in the earlier judgment does not rise to the level of fraud, the court of appeals still should have the power to direct the lower court to vacate its judgment under any proper ground, such as those enumerated in Fed R Civ P 60(b). It would possess this power in consequence of its jurisdiction to review a judgment by the lower court accepting or rejecting a Fed R Civ P 60(b) challenge—including a challenge authorized by that rule such as an independent action in equity.[65]

---

[61] *See generally* 3 Charles A. Wright, Federal Practice & Procedure: Criminal 2d §§551-559, 581-587 (1982 & Supp 1993).

[62] 322 US 238 (1944).

[63] The decision was reaffirmed in Universal Oil Prods Co v Root Ref Co, 328 US 575, 580 (1946), and Chambers v NASCO, Inc, 111 S Ct 2123, 2132 (1991).

[64] *See* **ch 3.**

[65] On the question of All Writs Act power dependent solely on the jurisdiction to review an eventual judgment, see **§§3.01-3.03.**

Appendix A
Federal Rules of Appellate Procedure

TITLE I. APPLICABILITY OF RULES

Rule 1. Scope of rules

(a) Scope of rules.—These rules govern procedure in appeals to United States courts of appeals from the United States district courts and the United States Tax Court; in appeals from bankruptcy appellate panels; in proceedings in the courts of appeals for review or enforcement of orders of administrative agencies, boards, commissions and officers of the United States; and in applications for writs or other relief which a court of appeals or a judge thereof is competent to give. When these rules provide for the making of a motion or application in the district court, the procedure for making such motion or application shall be in accordance with the practice of the district court.

(b) Rules Not to Affect Jurisdiction. These rules shall not be construed to extend or limit the jurisdiction of the courts of appeals as established by law. [*See* **§§6.01, 6.11.**]

(As amended Apr. 30, 1979, eff. Aug. 1, 1979. As amended Apr. 25, 1989, eff. Dec. 1, 1989.)

Rule 2. Suspension of Rules

In the interest of expediting decision, or for other good cause shown, a court of appeals may, except as otherwise provided in Rule 26(b), suspend the requirements or provisions of any of these rules in a particular case on application of a party or on its own motion and may order proceedings in accordance with its direction. [*See* **§6.03.**]

TITLE II. APPEALS FROM JUDGMENTS AND ORDERS OF DISTRICT COURTS

Rule 3. Appeal as of Right—How Taken

(a) Filing the notice of appeal.—An appeal permitted by law as of right from a district court to a court of appeals shall be taken by filing a notice of appeal with the clerk of the district court within the time allowed by Rule 4. Failure of an appellant to take any step other than the timely filing of a notice of appeal does not affect the validity of the appeal, but is ground only for such action as the court of appeals deems appropriate, which may include dismissal of the appeal. Appeals by permission under 28 U.S.C. § 1292(b) and appeals in bankruptcy shall be taken in the manner prescribed by Rule 5 and Rule 6 respectively.

(b) Joint or Consolidated Appeals. If two or more persons are entitled to appeal from a judgment or order of a district court and their interests are such as to make joinder practicable, they may file a joint notice of appeal, or may join in appeal after filing separate timely notices of appeal, and they may thereafter proceed on appeal as a single appellant. Appeals may be consolidated by order of the court of appeals upon its own motion or upon motion of a party, or by stipulation of the parties to the several appeals.

(c) Content of the Notice of Appeal.—

A notice of appeal must specify the party or parties taking the appeal by naming each appellant in either the caption or the body of the notice of appeal. An attorney representing more than one party may fulfill this requirement by describing those parties with such terms as "all plaintiffs," "the defendants," "the plaintiffs A, B, et al.," or "all defendants except X." A notice of appeal filed pro se is filed on behalf of the party signing the notice and the signer's spouse and minor children, if they are parties, unless the notice of appeal clearly indicates a contrary intent. In a class action, whether or not the class has been certified, it is sufficient for the notice to name one person qualified to bring the appeal as representative of the class. A notice of appeal also must designate the judgment, order, or part thereof appealed from, and must name the court to which the appeal is taken. An appeal will not be dismissed for informality of form or title of the notice of appeal, or for failure to name a party whose intent to appeal is otherwise clear from the notice. Form 1 in the Appendix of Forms is a suggested form for a notice of appeal.

(d) Serving the Notice of Appeal.—The clerk of the district court shall serve notice of the filing of a notice of appeal by mailing a copy to each party's counsel of record (apart from the appellant's), or, if a party is not represented by counsel, to the party's last known address. The clerk of the district court shall forthwith send a copy of the notice and of the docket entries to the clerk of the court of appeals named in the notice. The clerk of the district court shall likewise send a copy of any later docket entry in the case to the clerk of the court of appeals. When a defendant appeals in a criminal case, the clerk of the district court shall also serve a copy of the notice of appeal upon the defendant, either by personal service or by mail addressed to the defendant. The clerk shall note on each copy served the date when the notice of appeal was filed and, if the notice of appeal was filed in the manner provided in Rule 4(c) by an inmate confined in an institution, the date when the clerk received the notice of appeal. The clerk's failure to serve notice does not affect the validity of the appeal. Service is sufficient notwithstanding the death of a party or the party's counsel. The clerk shall note in the docket the names of the parties to whom the clerk mails copies, with the date of mailing. (Amendments to Rule 3(c) & (d) to be effective December 1, 1993 unless changed by Congress)

(e) Payment of Fees. Upon the filing of any separate or joint notice of appeal from the district court, the appellant shall pay to the clerk of the district court such fees as are established by statute, and also the docket fee prescribed by the Judicial Conference of the United States, the latter to be received by the clerk of the district court on behalf of the court of appeals. [*See* **§§6.02, 6.09, 8.01.**]

(As amended Apr. 30, 1979, eff. Aug. 1, 1979; Mar. 10, 1986, eff. July 1, 1986.)

(As amended Apr. 25, 1989, eff. Dec. 1, 1989.)

Rule 3.1. Appeal from a Judgment Entered by a Magistrate Judge in a Civil Case

When the parties consent to a trial before a magistrate judge under 28 U.S.C. § 636(c)(1), any appeal from the judgment must be heard by the court of appeals in accordance with 28 U.S.C. § 636(c)(3), unless the parties consent to an appeal on the record to a district judge and thereafter, by petition only, to the court of appeals, in accordance with 28 U.S.C. § 636(c)(4). An appeal under 28 U.S.C. § 636(c)(3) must be taken in identical fashion as an appeal from any other judgment of the district court.

(Amendments to Rule 3.1 to be effective December 1, 1993 unless changed by Congress)

Rule 4. Appeal as of Right—When Taken

(a) Appeal in a Civil Cases.

(1) Except as provided in paragraph (a)(4) of this Rule, in a civil case in which an appeal is permitted by law as of right from a district court to a court of appeals the notice of appeal required by Rule 3 must be filed with the clerk of the district court within 30 days after the date of entry of the judgment or order appealed from; but if the United States or an officer or agency thereof is a party, the notice of appeal may be filed by any party within 60 days after such entry. If a notice of appeal is mistakenly filed in the court of appeals, the clerk of the court of appeals shall note thereon the date when the clerk received the notice and send it to the clerk of the district court and the notice will be treated as filed in the district court on the date so noted.

(2) A notice of appeal filed after the court announces a decision or order but before the entry of the judgment or order is treated as filed on the date of and after the entry.

(3) If one party timely files a notice of appeal, any other party may file a notice of appeal within 14 days after the date when the first notice was filed, or within the time otherwise prescribed by this Rule 4(a), whichever period last expires.

(4) If any party makes a timely motion of a type specified immediately below, the time for appeal for all parties runs from the entry of the order disposing of the last such motion outstanding. This provision applies to a timely motion under the Federal Rules of Civil Procedure:

(A) for judgment under Rule 50(b);

(B) to amend or make additional findings of fact under Rule 52(b), whether or not granting the motion would alter the judgment;

(C) to alter or amend the judgment under Rule 59;

(D) for attorney's fees under Rule 54 if a district court under Rule 58 extends the time for appeal;

(E) for a new trial under Rule 59; or

(F) for relief under Rule 60 if the motion is served within 10 days after the entry of judgment.

A notice of appeal filed after announcement or entry of the judgment but before disposition of any of the above motions is ineffective to appeal from the judgment or order, or part thereof, specified in the notice of appeal, until the date of the entry of the order disposing of the last such motion outstanding. Appellate review of an order disposing of any of the above motions requires the party, in compliance with Appellate Rule 3(c), to amend a previously filed notice of appeal. A party intending to challenge an alteration or amendment of the judgment shall file an amended notice of appeal within the time prescribed by this Rule 4 measured from the entry of the order disposing of the last such motion outstanding. No additional fees will be required for filing an amended notice.

(5) The district court, upon a showing of excusable neglect or good cause, may extend the time for filing a notice of appeal upon motion filed not later than 30 days after the expiration of the time prescribed by this Rule 4(a). Any such motion which is filed before expiration of the prescribed time may be ex parte unless the court otherwise requires. Notice of any such motion which is filed after expiration of the prescribed time shall be given to the other parties in accordance with local rules. No such extension shall exceed 30 days past such prescribed time or 10 days from the date of entry of the order granting the motion, whichever occurs later.

(6) The district court, if it finds (a) that a party entitled to notice of the entry of a judgment or order did not receive such notice from the clerk of any party within 21 days of its entry and (b) that no party would be prejudiced, may, upon motion filed within 180 days of entry of the judgment or order or within 7 days of receipt of such notice, whichever is earlier, reopen the time for appeal for a period of 14 days from the date of entry of the order reopening the time for appeal.

(7) A judgment or order is entered within the meaning of this Rule 4(a) when it is entered in compliance with Rules 58 and 79(a) of the Federal Rules of Civil Procedure.

(b) Appeal in a Criminal Case. In a criminal case, a defendant shall file the notice of appeal in the district court within 10 days after the entry either of the judgment or order appealed from, or of a notice of appeal by the Government. A notice of appeal filed after the announcement of a decision, sentence, or order—but before entry of the judgment or order—is treated as filed on the date of and after the entry. If a defendant makes a timely motion specified immediately below, in accordance with the Federal Rules of Criminal Procedure, an appeal from a judgment of conviction must be taken within 10 days after the entry of the order disposing of the last such motion outstanding, or within 10 days after the entry of the judgment of conviction, whichever is later. This provision applies to a timely motion:

(1) for judgment of acquittal;

(2) for arrest of judgment;

(3) for a new trial on any ground other than newly discovered evidence; or

(4) for a new trial based on the ground of newly discovered evidence if the motion is made before or within 10 days after entry of the judgment.

A notice of appeal filed after the court announces a decision, sentence, or order but before it disposes of any of the above motions, is ineffective until the date of the entry of the order disposing of the last such motion outstanding, or until the date of the entry of the judgment of conviction, whichever is later. Notwithstanding the provisions of Rule 3(c), a valid notice of appeal is effective without amendment to appeal from an order disposing of any of the above motions. When an appeal by the government is authorized by statute, the notice of appeal must be filed in the district court within 30 days after (i) the entry of the judgment or order appealed from or (ii) the filing of a notice of appeal by any defendant.

A judgment or order is entered within the meaning of this subdivision when it is entered on the criminal docket. Upon a showing of excusable neglect, the district court may—before or after the time has expired, with or without motion and notice—extend the time for filing a notice of appeal for a period not to exceed 30 days from the expiration of the time otherwise prescribed by this subdivision.

The filing of a notice of appeal under this Rule 4(b) does not divest a district court of jurisdiction to correct a sentence under Fed.R.Crim.P. 35(c), nor does the filing of a motion under Fed.R.Crim.P. 35(c) affect the validity of a notice of appeal filed before entry of the order disposing of the motion.

(c) Appeal by an Inmate Confined in an Institution.—If an inmate confined in an institution files a notice of appeal in either a civil case or a criminal case, the notice of appeal is timely filed if it is deposited in the institution's internal mail system on or before the last day for filing. Timely filing may be shown by a notarized statement or by a declaration (in compliance with 28 U.S.C. § 1746) setting forth the date of deposit and stating that first-class postage has been prepaid. In a civil case in which the first notice of appeal is filed in the manner provided in this subdivision (c), the 14-day period provided in paragraph (a)(3) of this Rule 4 for another party to file a notice of appeal runs from the date when the district court receives the first notice of appeal. In a criminal case in which a defendant files a notice of appeal in the manner provided in this subdivision (c), the 30-day period for the government to file its notice of appeal runs from the entry of the judgment or order appealed from or from the district court's receipt of the defendant's notice of appeal.

These provisions effectively preserve the right of appeal based on a timely notice, even if motions are filed to alter or amend the judgment. The only consequence of not noticing that the motion to alter or modify has been filed is that a party may lose the right to challenge the alteration or modification, unless an appropriate amendment is filed to the notice of appeal. [*See* **§§2.04, 6.03, 6.04, 6.07, 6.09, 6.10, 8.07.**]

(As amended Apr. 30, 1979, eff. Aug. 1, 1979; Nov. 18, 1988, Pub.L. 100-690, Title VII, § 7111, 102 Stat. 44191; Apr. 30, 1991, eff. Dec. 1, 1991.)

(Amendments to Rule 4(a)(1), 4(a)(2), 4(a)(3), 4(a)(4)(A), 4(a)(4)(B), 4(a)(4)(C), 4(a)(4)(D), 4(a)(4)(E), 4(a)(4)(F), 4(b), and 4(c) to be effective December 1, 1993 unless changed by Congress.)

Rule 5. Appeals by Permission Under 28 U.S.C. § 1292(b)

(a) Petition for Permission to Appeal. An appeal from an interlocutory order containing the statement prescribed by 28 U.S.C. § 1292(b) may be sought by filing a petition for permission to appeal with the clerk of the court of appeals within 10 days after the entry of such order in the district court with proof of service on all other parties to the action in the district court. An order may be amended to include the prescribed statement at any time, and permission to appeal may be sought within 10 days after entry of the order as amended.

(b) Content of Petition; Answer. The petition shall contain a statement of the facts necessary to an understanding of the controlling question of law determined by the order of the district court; a statement of the question itself; and a statement of the reasons why a substantial basis exists for a difference of opinion on the question and why an immediate appeal may materially advance the termination of the litigation. The petition shall include or have annexed thereto a copy of the order from which appeal is sought and of any findings of fact, conclusions of law and opinion relating thereto. Within 7 days after service of the petition an adverse party may file an answer in opposition. The application and answer shall be submitted without oral argument unless otherwise ordered.

(c) Form of Papers; Number of Copies. All papers may be typewritten. Three copies shall be filed with the original, but the court may require that additional copies be furnished.

(d) Grant of Permission; Cost Bond; Filing of Record. Within 10 days after the entry of an order granting permission to appeal the appellant shall (1) pay to the clerk of the district court the fees established by statute and the docket fee prescribed by the Judicial Conference of the United States and (2) file a bond for costs if required pursuant to Rule 7. The clerk of the district court shall notify the clerk of the court of appeals of the payment of the fees. Upon receipt of such notice the clerk of the court of appeals shall enter the appeal upon the docket. The record shall be transmitted and filed in accordance with Rules 11 and 12(b). A notice of appeal need not be filed. [*See* **§§2.09, 6.05, 6.07, 6.09, 6.10, 8.07.**]

(As amended Apr. 30, 1979, eff. Aug. 1, 1979.)

Rule 5.1. Appeal by Permission Under 28 U.S.C. § 636(c)(5)

(a) Petition for Leave to Appeal; Answer or Cross Petition.—An appeal from a district court judgment, entered after an appeal under 28 U.S.C. § 636(c)(4) to a district judge from a judgment entered upon direction of a magistrate judge in a civil case, may be sought by filing a petition for leave to appeal. An appeal on petition for leave to appeal is not a matter of right, but its allowance is a matter of sound judicial discretion. The petition shall be filed with the clerk of the court of appeals within the time provided by Rule 4(a) for filing a notice of appeal, with proof of service on all parties to the action in the district court. A notice of appeal need not be filed. Within 14 days after service of the petition, a party may file an answer in opposition or a cross petition. (Amendments to Rule 5.1(a) to be effective December 1, 1993 unless changed by Congress)

(b) Content of Petition; Answer. The petition for leave to appeal shall contain a statement of the facts necessary to an understanding of the questions to be presented by the appeal; a statement of those questions and of the relief sought; a statement of the reasons why in the opinion of the petitioner the appeal should be allowed; and a copy of the order, decree or judgment complained of and any opinion or memorandum relating thereto. The petition and answer shall be submitted to a panel of judges of the court of appeals without oral argument unless otherwise ordered.

(c) Form of Papers; Number of Copies. All papers may be typewritten. Three copies shall be filed with the original, but the court may require that additional copies be furnished.

(d) Allowance of the Appeal; Fees; Cost Bond; Filing of Record. Within 10 days after the entry of an order granting the appeal, the appellant shall (1) pay to the clerk of the district court the fees established by statute and the docket fee prescribed by the Judicial Conference of the United States and (2) file a bond for costs if required pursuant to Rule 7. The clerk of the district court shall notify the clerk of the court of appeals of the payment of the fees. Upon receipt of such notice, the clerk of the court of appeals shall enter the appeal upon the docket. The record shall be transmitted and filed in accordance with Rules 11 and 12(b).

(Added Mar. 10, 1986, eff. July 1, 1986.)

Rule 6. Appeals in Bankruptcy Cases from Final Judgements and Orders of District Courts or of Bankruptcy Appellate Panels

(a) Appeal From a Judgment, Order or Decree of a District Court Exercising Original Jurisdiction in a Bankruptcy Case. An appeal to a court of appeals from a final judgment, order or decree of a district court exercising jurisdiction pursuant to 28 U.S.C. § 1334 shall be taken in identical fashion as appeals from other judgments, orders or decrees of district courts in civil actions.

(b) Appeal From a Judgment, Order or Decree of a District Court or Bankruptcy Appellate Panel Exercising Appellate Jurisdiction in a Bankruptcy Case.

(1) Applicability of Other Rules. All provisions of these rules are applicable to an appeal to a court of appeals pursuant to 28 U.S.C. § 158(d) from a final judgment, order or decree of a district court or bankruptcy appellate panel exercising appellate jurisdiction pursuant to 28 U.S.C. § 158(a) or (b), except that:

(i) Rules 3.1, 4(a)(4), 4(b), 5.1, 9, 10, 11, 12(b), 13-20, 22-23, and 24(b) are not applicable;

(ii) the reference in Rule 3(c) to "Form 1 in the Appendix of Forms" shall be read as a reference to Form 5; and

(iii) when the appeal is from a bankruptcy appellate panel, the term "district court" as used in any applicable rule, means "appellate panel".

(2) Additional Rules. In addition to the rules made applicable by subsection (b)(1) of this rule, the following rules shall apply to an appeal to a court of appeals pursuant to 28 U.S.C. § 158(d) from a final judgment, order or decree of a district court or of a bankruptcy appellate panel exercising appellate jurisdiction pursuant to 28 U.S.C. § 158(a) or (b):

(i) Effect of a Motion for Rehearing on the Time for Appeal. If any party files a timely motion for rehearing under Bankruptcy Rule 8015 in the district court or the bankruptcy appellate panel, the time for appeal to the court of appeals for all parties runs from the entry of the order disposing of the motion. A notice of appeal filed after announcement or entry of the district court's or bankruptcy appellate panel's judgment, order, or decree, but before disposition of the motion for rehearing, is ineffective until the date of the entry of the order disposing of the motion for rehearing. Appellate review of the order disposing of the motion requires the party, in compliance with Appellate Rules 3(c) and 6(b)(1)(ii), to amend a previously filed notice of appeal. A party intending to challenge an alteration or amendment of the judgment, order, or decree shall file an amended notice of appeal within the time prescribed by Rule 4, excluding 4(a)(4) and 4(b), measured from the entry of the order disposing of the motion. No additional fees will be required for filing the amended notice.

(ii) The Record on Appeal. Within 10 days after filing the notice of appeal, the appellant shall file with the clerk possessed of the record assembled pursuant to Bankruptcy Rule 8006, and serve on the appellee, a statement of the issues to be presented on appeal and a designation of the record to be certified and transmitted to the clerk of the court of appeals. If the appellee deems other parts of the record necessary, the appellee shall, within 10 days after service of the appellant's designation, file with the clerk and serve on the appellant a designation of additional parts to be included. The record, redesignated as provided above, plus the proceedings in the district court or bankruptcy appellate panel and a certified copy of the docket entries prepared by the clerk pursuant to Rule 3(d) shall constitute the record on appeal.

(iii) Transmission of the Record. When the record is complete for purpose of the appeal, the clerk of the district court or the appellate panel, shall transmit it forthwith to the clerk of the court of appeals. The clerk of the district court or of the appellate panel shall number the documents comprising the record and shall transmit with the record a list of documents correspondingly numbered and identified with reasonable definiteness. Documents of unusual bulk or weight, physical exhibits other than documents, and such other parts of the record as the court of appeals may designate by local rule, shall not be transmitted by the clerk unless the clerk is directed to do so by a party or by the clerk of the court of appeals. A party must make advance arrangements with the clerk for the transportation and receipt of exhibits of unusual bulk or weight. All parties shall take any other action necessary to enable the clerk to assemble and transmit the record. The court of appeals may provide by rule or order that a certified copy of the docket entries shall be transmitted in lieu of the redesignated record, subject to the right of any party to request at any time during the pendency of the appeal that the redesignated record be transmitted.

(iv) Filing of the Record. Upon receipt of the record, the clerk of the court of appeals shall file it and shall immediately give notice to all parties of the date on which it was filed. Upon receipt of a certified copy of the docket entries transmitted in lieu of the redesignated record pursuant to rule or order, the clerk of the court of appeals shall file it and shall immediately give notice to all parties of the date on which it was filed. [*See* **§§6.06, 6.07, 6.09, 7.01, 8.04.**]

(Added Apr. 25, 1989, eff. Dec. 1, 1989, and amended Apr. 30, 1991, eff. Dec. 1, 1991.)

(Amendments to Rule 6(b)(2)(i) to be effective December 1, 1993 unless changed by Congress.)

Rule 7. Bond for Costs on Appeal in Civil Cases

The district court may require an appellant to file a bond or provide other security in such form and amount as it finds necessary to ensure payment of costs on appeal in a civil case. The provisions of Rule 8(b) apply to a surety upon a bond given pursuant to this rule. [*See* **§§6.07, 6.09, 6.11.**]

(As amended Apr. 30, 1979, eff. Aug. 1, 1979.)

Rule 8. Stay or Injunction Pending Appeal

(a) Stay Must Ordinarily Be Sought in the First Instance in District Court; Motion for Stay in Court of Appeals. Application for a stay of the judgment or order of a district court pending appeal, or for approval of a supersedeas bond, or for an order suspending, modifying, restoring or granting an injunction during the pendency of an appeal must ordinarily be made in the first instance in the district court. A motion for such relief may be made to the court of appeals or to a judge thereof, but the motion shall show that application to the district court for the relief sought is not practicable, or that the district court has denied an application, or has failed to afford the relief which the applicant requested, with the reasons given by the district court for its action. The motion shall also show the reasons for the relief requested and the facts relied upon, and if the facts are subject to dispute the motion shall be supported by affidavits or other sworn statements or copies thereof. With the motion shall be filed such parts of the record as are relevant. Reasonable notice of the motion shall be given to all parties. The motion shall be filed with the clerk and normally will be considered by a panel or division of the court, but in exceptional cases where such procedure would be impracticable due to the requirements of time, the application may be made to and considered by a single judge of the court.

(b) Stay May Be Conditioned Upon Giving of Bond; Proceedings Against Sureties. Relief available in the court of appeals under this rule may be conditioned upon the filing of a bond or other appropriate security in the district court. If security is given in the form of a bond or stipulation or other undertaking with one or more sureties, each surety submits to the jurisdiction of the district court and irrevocably appoints the clerk of the district court as the surety's agent upon whom any papers affecting the surety's liability on the bond or undertaking may be served. A surety's liability may be enforced on motion in the district court without the necessity of an independent action. The motion and such notice of the motion as the district court prescribes may be served on the clerk of the district court, who shall forthwith mail copies to the sureties if their addresses are known.

(c) Stays in Criminal Cases. Stays in criminal cases shall be had in accordance with the provisions of Rule 38(a) of the Federal Rules of Criminal Procedure. [*See* **§§6.07, 6.08, 6.09, 6.11, 8.01, 8.04, 9.09.**]

(As amended Mar. 10, 1986, eff. July 1, 1986.)

Rule 9. Release in Criminal Cases

(a) Appeals from Orders Respecting Release Entered Prior to a Judgment of Conviction. An appeal authorized by law from an order refusing or imposing conditions of release shall be determined promptly. Upon entry of an order refusing or imposing conditions of release, the district court shall state in writing the reasons for the action taken. The appeal shall be heard without the necessity of briefs after reasonable notice to the appellee upon such papers, affidavits, and portions of the record as the parties shall present. The court of appeals or a judge thereof may order the release of the appellant pending the appeal.

(b) Release Pending Appeal From a Judgment of Conviction. Application for release after a judgment of conviction shall be made in the first instance in the district court. If the district court refuses release pending appeal, or imposes conditions of release, the court shall state in writing the reasons for the action taken. Thereafter, if an appeal is pending, a motion for release, or for modification of the conditions of release, pending review may be made to the court of appeals or to a judge thereof. The motion shall be determined promptly upon such papers, affidavits, and portions of the record as the parties shall present and after reasonable notice to the appellee. The court of appeals or a judge thereof may order the release of the appellant pending disposition of the motion.

(c) Criteria for Release. The decision as to release pending appeal shall be made in accordance with Title 18, U.S.C. § 3143. The burden of establishing that the defendant will not flee or pose a danger to any other person or to the community and that the appeal is not for purpose of delay and raises a substantial question of law or fact likely to result in reversal or in an order for a new trial rests with the defendant. [*See* **§§2.15, 6.07, 6.09, 6.12, 8.08.**]

(As amended Apr. 24, 1972, eff. Oct. 1, 1972; Oct. 12, 1984, Pub. L. 98-473, Title II, § 210, 98 Stat.1987.)

Rule 10. The Record on Appeal

(a) Composition of the Record on Appeal. The original papers and exhibits filed in the district court, the transcript of proceedings, if any, and a certified copy of the docket entries prepared by the clerk of the district court shall constitute the record on appeal in all cases.

(b) The Transcript of Proceedings; Duty of Appellant to Order; Notice to Appellee if Partial Transcript is Ordered.

(1) Within 10 days after filing the notice of appeal the appellant shall order from the reporter a transcript of such parts of the proceedings not already on file as the appellant deems necessary, subject to local rules of the courts of appeals. The order shall be in writing and within the same period a copy shall be filed with the clerk of the district court. If funding is to come from the United States under the Criminal Justice Act, the order shall so state. If no such parts of the proceedings are to be ordered, within the same period the appellant shall file a certificate to that effect.

(2) If the appellant intends to urge on appeal that a finding or conclusion is unsupported by the evidence or is contrary to the evidence, the appellant shall include in the record a transcript of all evidence relevant to such finding or conclusion.

(3) Unless the entire transcript is to be included, the appellant shall, within the 10-day time provided in paragraph (b)(1) of this Rule 10, file a statement of the issues the appellant intends to present on the appeal, and shall serve on the appellee a copy of the order or certificate and of the statement. An appellee who believes that a transcript of other parts of the proceedings is necessary shall, within 10 days after the service of the order or certificate and the statement of the appellant, file and serve on the appellant a designation of additional parts to be included. Unless within 10 days after service of the designation the appellant has ordered such parts, and has so notified the appellee, the appellee may within the following 10 days either order the parts or move in the district court for an order requiring the appellant to do so.

(4) At the time of ordering, a party must make satisfactory arrangements with the reporter for payment of the cost of the transcript.

(c) Statement of the Evidence or Proceedings When No Report Was Made or When the Transcript is Unavailable. If no report of the evidence or proceedings at a hearing or trial was made, or if a transcript is unavailable, the appellant may prepare a statement of the evidence or proceedings from the best available means, including the appellant's recollection. The statement shall be served on the appellee, who may serve objections or proposed amendments thereto within 10 days after service. Thereupon the statement and any objections or proposed amendments shall be submitted to the district court for settlement and approval and as settled and approved shall be included by the clerk of the district court in the record on appeal.

(d) Agreed Statement as the Record on Appeal. In lieu of the record on appeal as defined in subdivision (a) of this rule, the parties may prepare and sign a statement of the case showing how the issues presented by the appeal arose and were decided in the district court and setting forth only so many of the facts averred and proved or sought to be proved as are essential to a decision of the issues presented. If the statement conforms to the truth, it, together with such additions as the court may consider necessary fully to present the issues raised by the appeal, shall be approved by the district court and shall then be certified to the court of appeals as the record on appeal and transmitted thereto by the clerk of the district court within the time provided by Rule 11. Copies of the agreed statement may be filed as the appendix required by Rule 30.

(e) Correction or Modification of the Record. If any difference arises as to whether the record truly discloses what occurred in the district court, the difference shall be submitted to and settled by that court and the record made to conform to the truth. If anything material to either party is omitted from the record by error or accident or is misstated therein, the parties by stipulation, or the district court either before or after the record is transmitted to the court of appeals, or the court of appeals, on proper suggestion or of its own initiative, may direct that the omission or misstatement be corrected, and if necessary that a supplemental record be certified and transmitted. All other questions as to the form and content of the record shall be presented to the court of appeals. [*See* **§§6.09, 6.13, 6.14, 6.16, 6.17, 8.08.**]

(As amended Apr. 30, 1979, eff. Aug. 1, 1979; Mar. 10, 1986, eff. July 1, 1986; Apr 30, 1991, eff. Dec. 1, 1991.)

(Amendments to Rule 10(b)(3) to be effective December 1, 1993 unless changed by Congress.)

Rule 11. Transmission of the Record

(a) Duty of Appellant. After filing the notice of appeal the appellant, or in the event that more than one appeal is taken, each appellant, shall comply with the provisions of Rule 10(b) and shall take any other action necessary to enable the clerk to assemble and transmit the record. A single record shall be transmitted.

(b) Duty of Reporter to Prepare and File Transcript; Notice to Court of Appeals; Duty of Clerk to Transmit the Record. Upon receipt of an order for a transcript, the reporter shall acknowledge at the foot of the order the fact that the reporter has received it and the date on which the reporter expects to have the transcript completed and shall transmit the order, so endorsed, to the clerk of the court of appeals. If the transcript cannot be completed within 30 days of receipt of the order the reporter shall request an extension of time from the clerk of the court of appeals and the action of the clerk of the court of appeals shall be entered on the docket and the parties notified. In the event of the failure of the reporter to file the transcript within the time allowed, the clerk of the court of appeals shall notify the district judge and take such other steps as may be directed by the court of appeals. Upon completion of the transcript the reporter shall file it with the clerk of the district court and shall notify the clerk of the court of appeals that the reporter has done so.

When the record is complete for purposes of the appeal, the clerk of the district court shall transmit it forthwith to the clerk of the court of appeals. The clerk of the district court shall number the documents comprising the record and shall transmit with the record a list of documents correspondingly numbered and identified with reasonable definiteness.

Documents of unusual bulk or weight, physical exhibits other than documents, and such other parts of the record as the court of appeals may designate by local rule, shall not be transmitted by the clerk unless the clerk is directed to do so by a party or by the clerk of the court of appeals. A party must make advance arrangements with the clerks for the transportation and receipt of exhibits of unusual bulk or weight.

(c) Temporary Retention of Record in District Court for Use in Preparing Appellate Papers. Notwithstanding the provisions of (a) and (b) of this Rule 11, the parties may stipulate, or the district court on motion of any party may order, that the clerk of the district court shall temporarily retain the record for use by the parties in preparing appellate papers. In that event the clerk of the district court shall certify to the clerk of the court of appeals that the record, including the transcript or parts thereof designated for inclusion and all necessary exhibits, is complete for purposes of the appeal. Upon receipt of the brief of the appellee, or at such earlier time as the parties may agree or the court may order, the appellant shall request the clerk of the district court to transmit the record.

(d) [Abrogated.]

(e) Retention of the Record in the District Court by Order of Court. The court of appeals may provide by rule or order that a certified copy of the docket entries shall be transmitted in lieu of the entire record, subject to the right of any party to request at any time during the pendency of the appeal that designated parts of the record be transmitted.

If the record or any part thereof is required in the district court for use there pending the appeal, the district court may make an order to that effect, and the clerk of the district court shall retain the record or parts thereof subject to the request of the court of appeals, and shall transmit a copy of the order and of the docket entries together with such parts of the original record as the district court shall allow and copies of such parts as the parties may designate.

(f) Stipulation of Parties That Parts of the Record be Retained in the District Court. The parties may agree by written stipulation filed in the district court that designated parts of the record shall be retained in the district court unless thereafter the court of appeals shall order or any party shall request their transmittal. The parts thus designated shall nevertheless be a part of the record on appeal for all purposes.

(g) Record for Preliminary Hearing in the Court of Appeals. If prior to the time the record is transmitted a party desires to make in the court of appeals a motion for dismissal, for release, for a stay pending appeal, for additional security on the bond on appeal or on a supersedeas bond, or for any intermediate order, the clerk of the district court at the request of any party shall transmit to the court of appeals such parts of the original record as any party shall designate. [*See* **§§6.09, 6.11, 6.13, 6.14, 7.01, 8.04, 8.07, 10.07.**]

(As amended Apr. 30, 1979, eff. Aug. 1, 1979; Mar. 10, 1986, eff. July 1, 1986.)

Rule 12. Docketing the Appeal; Filing of the Record

(a) Docketing the Appeal. Upon receipt of the copy of the notice of appeal and of the docket entries, transmitted by the clerk of the district court pursuant to Rule 3(d), the clerk of the court of appeals shall thereupon enter the appeal upon the docket. An appeal shall be docketed under the title given to the action in the district court, with the appellant identified as such, but if such title does not contain the name of the appellant, the appellant's name, identified as appellant, shall be added to the title.

(b) Filing a Representation Statement.—Within 10 days after filing a notice of appeal, unless another time is designated by the court of appeals, the attorney who filed the notice of appeal shall file with the clerk of the court of appeals a statement naming each party represented on appeal by that attorney.

(c) Filing the Record, Partial Record, or Certificate.—Upon receipt of the record transmitted pursuant to Rule 11(b), or the partial record transmitted pursuant to Rule 11(e), (f), or (g), or the clerk's certificate under Rule 11(c), the clerk of the court of appeals shall file it and shall immediately give notice to all parties of the date on which it was filed. [*See* **§§6.09, 7.01, 8.04.**]

(As amended Apr. 30, 1979, eff. Aug 1, 1979; Mar. 10, 1986, eff. July 1, 1986.)

(Amendments to Rule 12(b) & 12(c) to be effective December 1, 1993 unless changed by Congress.)

TITLE III—REVIEW OF DECISIONS OF THE TAX COURT OF THE UNITED STATES

Rule 13. Review of Decisions of the Tax Court

(a) How Obtained; Time for Filing Notice of Appeal. Review of a decision of the United States Tax Court shall be obtained by filing a notice of appeal with the clerk of the Tax Court within 90 days after the decision of the Tax Court is entered. If a timely notice of appeal is filed by one party, any other party may take an appeal by filing a notice of appeal within 120 days after the decision of the Tax Court is entered.

The running of the time for appeal is terminated as to all parties by a timely motion to vacate or revise a decision made pursuant to the Rules of Practice of the Tax Court. The full time for appeal commences to run and is to be computed from the entry of an order disposing of such motion, or from the entry of decision, whichever is later.

(b) Notice of Appeal—How Filed. The notice of appeal may be filed by deposit in the office of the clerk of the Tax Court in the District of Columbia or by mail addressed to the clerk. If a notice is delivered to the clerk by mail and is received after expiration of the last day allowed for filing, the postmark date shall be deemed to be the date of delivery, subject to the provisions of § 7502 of the Internal Revenue Code of 1954, as amended, and the regulations promulgated pursuant thereto.

(c) Content of the Notice of Appeal; Service of the Notice; Effect of Filing and Service of the Notice. The content of the notice of appeal, the manner of its service, and the effect of the filing of the notice and of its service shall be as prescribed by Rule 3. Form 2 in the Appendix of Forms is a suggested form of the notice of appeal.

(d) The Record on Appeal; Transmission of the Record; Filing of the Record.

The provisions of Rules 10, 11 and 12 respecting the record and the time and manner of its transmission and filing and the docketing of the appeal in the court of appeals in cases on appeal from the district courts shall govern in cases on appeal from the Tax Court. Each reference in those rules and in Rule 3 to the district court and to the clerk of the district court shall be read as a reference to the Tax Court and to the clerk of the Tax Court respectively.

If appeals are taken from a decision of the Tax Court to more than one court of appeals, the original record shall be transmitted to the court of appeals named in the first notice of appeal filed. Provision for the record in any other appeal shall be made upon appropriate application by the appellant to the court of appeals to which such other appeal is taken. [*See* **§§6.07, 6.09, 6.14, 7.07.**]

(As amended Apr. 30, 1979, eff. Aug. 1, 1979.)

TITLE III—REVIEW OF DECISIONS OF THE TAX COURT OF THE UNITED STATES

Rule 14. Applicability of Other Rules to Review of Decisions of the Tax Court

All provisions of these rules are applicable to review of a decision of the Tax Court, except that Rules 4-9, Rules 15-20, and Rules 22 and 23 are not applicable. [*See* **§§6.07, 6.09, 6.10.**]

TITLE IV—REVIEW AND ENFORCEMENT OF ORDERS OF ADMINISTRATIVE AGENCIES, BOARDS, COMMISSIONS AND OFFICERS

Rule 15. Review or Enforcement of Agency Orders—How Obtained; Intervention

(a) Petition for Review of Order; Joint Petition.—Review of an order of an administrative agency, board, commission, or officer (hereinafter, the term "agency" will include agency, board, commission, or officer) must be obtained by filing with the clerk of a court of appeals that is authorized to review such order, within the time prescribed by law, a petition to enjoin, set aside, suspend, modify, or otherwise review, or a notice of appeal, whichever form is indicated by the applicable statute (hereinafter, the term "petition for review" will include a petition to enjoin, set aside, suspend, modify, or otherwise review, or a notice of appeal). The petition must name each party seeking review either in the caption or in the body of the petition. Use of such terms as "et al.," or "petitioners," or "respondents" is not effective to name the parties. The petition also must designate the respondent and the order or part thereof to be reviewed. Form 3 in the Appendix of Forms is a suggested form of a petition for review. In each case the agency must be named respondent. The United States will also be a respondent if required by statute, even though not designated in the petition. If two or more persons are entitled to petition the same court for review of the same order and their interests are such as to make joinder practicable, they may file a joint petition for review and may thereafter proceed as a single petitioner.

(b) Application for Enforcement of Order; Answer; Default; Cross-Application for Enforcement. An application for enforcement of an order of an agency shall be filed with the clerk of a court of appeals which is authorized to enforce the order. The application shall contain a concise statement of the proceedings in which the order was entered, the facts upon which venue is based, and the relief prayed. Within 20 days after the application is filed, the respondent shall serve on the petitioner and file with the clerk an answer to the application. If the respondent fails to file an answer within such time, judgment will be awarded for the relief prayed. If a petition is filed for review of an order which the court has jurisdiction to enforce, the respondent may file a cross-application for enforcement.

(c) Service of Petition or Application. A copy of a petition for review or of an application or cross-application for enforcement of an order shall be served by the clerk of the court of appeals on each respondent in the manner prescribed by Rule 3(d), unless a different manner of service is prescribed by an applicable statute. At the time of filing, the petitioner shall furnish the clerk with a copy of the petition or application for each respondent. At or before the time of filing a petition for review, the petitioner shall serve a copy thereof on all parties who shall have been admitted to participate in the proceedings before the agency other than respondents to be served by the clerk, and shall file with the clerk a list of those so served.

(d) Intervention. Unless an applicable statute provides a different method of intervention, a person who desires to intervene in a proceeding under this rule shall serve upon all parties to the proceeding and file with the clerk of the court of appeals a motion for leave to intervene. The motion shall contain a concise statement of the interest of the moving party and the grounds upon which intervention is sought. A motion for leave to intervene or other notice of intervention authorized by an applicable statute shall be filed within 30 days of the date on which the petition for review is filed.

(e) Payment of Fees.—When filing any separate or joint petition for review in a court of appeals, the petitioner must pay the clerk of the court of appeals the fees established by statute, and also the docket fee prescribed by the Judicial Conference of the United States. [*See* **§§2.16, 6.07, 6.09, 7.01, 8.04.**]

(Amendments to Rule 15(a) and (e) to be effective December 1, 1993 unless changed by Congress.)

Rule 15.1. Briefs and Oral Argument in National Labor Relations Board Proceedings

Each party adverse to the National Labor Relations Board in an enforcement or a review proceeding shall proceed first on briefing and at oral argument unless the court orders otherwise.

(Added Mar. 10, 1986, eff. July 1, 1986.)

Rule 16. The Record on Review or Enforcement

(a) Composition of the Record. The order sought to be reviewed or enforced, the findings or report on which it is based, and the pleadings, evidence and proceedings before the agency shall constitute the record on review in proceedings to review or enforce the order of an agency.

(b) Omissions From or Misstatements in the Record. If anything material to any party is omitted from the record or is misstated therein, the parties may at any time supply the omission or correct the misstatement by stipulation, or the court may at any time direct that the omission or misstatement be corrected and, if necessary, that a supplemental record be prepared and filed. [*See* **§§6.07, 6.09, 7.01.**]

Rule 17. Filing of the Record

(a) Agency to File; Time for Filing; Notice of Filing. The agency shall file the record with the clerk of the court of appeals within 40 days after service upon it of the petition for review unless a different time is provided by the statute authorizing review. In enforcement proceedings the agency shall file the record within 40 days after filing an application for enforcement, but the record need not be filed unless the respondent has filed an answer contesting enforcement of the order, or unless the court otherwise orders. The court may shorten or extend the time above prescribed. The clerk shall give notice to all parties of the date on which the record is filed.

(b) Filing—What Constitutes. The agency may file the entire record or such parts thereof as the parties may designate by stipulation filed with the agency. The original papers in the agency proceeding or certified copies thereof may be filed. Instead of filing the record or designated parts thereof, the agency may file a certified list of all documents, transcripts of testimony, exhibits and other material comprising the record, or a list of such parts thereof as the parties may designate, adequately describing each, and the filing of the certified list shall constitute filing of the record. The parties may stipulate that neither the record nor a certified list be filed with the court. The stipulation shall be filed with the clerk of the court of appeals and the date of its filing shall be deemed the date on which the record is filed. If a certified list is filed, or if the parties designate only parts of the record for filing or stipulate that neither the record nor a certified list be filed, the agency shall retain the record or parts thereof. Upon request of the court or the request of a party, the record or any part thereof thus retained shall be transmitted to the court notwithstanding any prior stipulation. All parts of the record retained by the agency shall be a part of the record on review for all purposes. [*See* **§§6.07, 6.09, 6.14, 7.01.**]

Rule 18. Stay Pending Review

Application for a stay of a decision or order of an agency pending direct review in the court of appeals shall ordinarily be made in the first instance to the agency. A motion for such relief may be made to the court of appeals or to a judge thereof, but the motion shall show that application to the agency for the relief sought is not practicable, or that application has been made to the agency and denied, with the reasons given by it for denial, or that the action of the agency did not afford the relief which the applicant had requested. The motion shall also show the reasons for the relief requested and the facts relied upon, and if the facts are subject to dispute the motion shall be supported by affidavits or other sworn statements or copies thereof. With the motion shall be filed such parts of the record as are relevant to the relief sought. Reasonable notice of the motion shall be given to all parties to the proceeding in the court of appeals. The court may condition relief under this rule upon the filing of a bond or other appropriate security. The motion shall be filed with the clerk and normally will be considered by a panel or division of the court, but in exceptional cases where such procedure would be impracticable due to the requirements of time, the application may be made to and considered by a single judge of the court. [*See* **§§6.02, 6.09, 8.01, 8.04.**]

Rule 19. Settlement of Judgments Enforcing Orders

When an opinion of the court is filed directing the entry of a judgment enforcing in part the order of an agency, the agency shall within 14 days thereafter serve upon the respondent and file with the clerk a proposed judgment in conformity with the opinion. If the respondent objects to the proposed judgment as not in conformity with the opinion, the respondent shall within 7 days thereafter serve upon the agency and file with the clerk a proposed judgment which the respondent deems to be in conformity with the opinion. The court will thereupon settle the judgment and direct its entry without further hearing or argument. [*See* **§§6.07, 6.09.**]

(As amended Mar. 10, 1986, eff. July 1, 1986.)

Rule 20. Applicability of Other Rules to Review or Enforcement of Agency Orders

All provisions of these rules are applicable to review or enforcement of orders of agencies, except that Rules 3-14 and Rules 22 and 23 are not applicable. As used in any applicable rule, the term "appellant" includes a petitioner and the term "appellee" includes a respondent in proceedings to review or enforce agency orders. [*See* **§§6.07, 6.09.**]

TITLE V. EXTRAORDINARY WRITS

Rule 21. Writs of Mandamus and Prohibition Directed to a Judge or Judges and Other Extraordinary Writs

(a) Mandamus or Prohibition to a Judge or Judges; Petition for Writ; Service and Filing. Application for a writ of mandamus or of prohibition directed to a judge or judges shall be made by filing a petition therefor with the clerk of the court of appeals with proof of service on the respondent judge or judges and on all parties to the action in the trial court. The petition shall contain a statement of the facts necessary to an understanding of the issues presented by the application; a statement of the issues presented and of the relief sought; a statement of the reasons why the writ should issue; and copies of any order or opinion or parts of the record which may be essential to an understanding of the matters set forth in the petition. Upon receipt of the prescribed docket fee, the clerk shall docket the petition and submit it to the court.

(b) Denial; Order Directing Answer. If the court is of the opinion that the writ should not be granted, it shall deny the petition. Otherwise, it shall order that an answer to the petition be filed by the respondents within the time fixed by the order. The order shall be served by the clerk on the judge or judges named respondents and on all other parties to the action in the trial court. All parties below other than the petitioner shall also be deemed respondents for all purposes. Two or more respondents may answer jointly. If the judge or judges named respondents do not desire to appear in the proceeding, they may so advise the clerk and all parties by letter, but the petition shall not thereby be taken as admitted. The clerk shall advise the parties of the dates on which briefs are to be filed, if briefs are required, and of the date of oral argument. The proceeding shall be given preference over ordinary civil cases.

(c) Other Extraordinary Writs. Application for extraordinary writs other than those provided for in subdivisions (a) and (b) of this rule shall be made by petition filed with the clerk of the court of appeals with proof of service on the parties named as respondents. Proceedings on such application shall conform, so far as is practicable, to the procedure prescribed in subdivisions (a) and (b) of this rule.

(d) Form of Papers; Number of Copies. All papers may be typewritten. Three copies shall be filed with the original, but the court may direct that additional copies be furnished. [*See* **§§3.01, 3.15, 3.16, 3.17, 8.04.**]

TITLE VI. HABEAS CORPUS; PROCEEDINGS IN FORMA PAUPERIS

Rule 22. Habeas Corpus Proceedings

(a) Application for the Original Writ. An application for a writ of habeas corpus shall be made to the appropriate district court. If application is made to a circuit judge, the application will ordinarily be transferred to the appropriate district court. If an application is made to or transferred to the district court and denied, renewal of the application before a circuit judge is not favored; the proper remedy is by appeal to the court of appeals from the order of the district court denying the writ.

(b) Necessity of Certificate of Probable Cause for Appeal. In a habeas corpus proceeding in which the detention complained of arises out of process issued by a state court, an appeal by the applicant for the writ may not proceed unless a district or a circuit judge issues a certificate of probable cause. If an appeal is taken by the applicant, the district judge who rendered the judgment shall either issue a certificate of probable cause or state the reasons why such a certificate should not issue. The certificate or the statement shall be forwarded to the court of appeals with the notice of appeal and the file of the proceedings in the district court. If the district judge has denied the certificate, the applicant for the writ may then request issuance of the certificate by a circuit judge. If such a request is addressed to the court of appeals, it shall be deemed addressed to the judges thereof and shall be considered by a circuit judge or judges as the court deems appropriate. If no express request for a certificate is filed, the notice of appeal shall be deemed to constitute a request addressed to the judges of the court of appeals. If an appeal is taken by a state or its representative, a certificate of probable cause is not required. [*See* **§§3.14, 6.07, 6.08, 6.09.**]

Rule 23. Custody of Prisoners in Habeas Corpus Proceedings

(a) Transfer of Custody Pending Review. Pending review of a decision in a habeas corpus proceeding commenced before a court, justice or judge of the United States for the release of a prisoner, a person having custody of the prisoner shall not transfer custody to another unless such transfer is directed in accordance with the provisions of this rule. Upon application of a custodian showing a need therefor, the court, justice or judge rendering the decision may make an order authorizing transfer and providing for the substitution of the successor custodian as a party.

(b) Detention or Release of Prisoner Pending Review of Decision Failing to Release. Pending review of a decision failing or refusing to release a prisoner in such a proceeding, the prisoner may be detained in the custody from which release is sought, or in other appropriate custody, or may be enlarged upon the prisoner's recognizance, with or without surety, as may appear fitting to the court or justice or judge rendering the decision, or to the court of appeals or to the Supreme Court, or to a judge or justice of either court.

(c) Release of Prisoner Pending Review of Decision Ordering Release. Pending review of a decision ordering the release of a prisoner in such a proceeding, the prisoner shall be enlarged upon the prisoner's recognizance, with or without surety, unless the court or justice or judge rendering the decision, or the court of appeals or the Supreme Court, or a judge or justice of either court shall otherwise order.

(d) Modification of Initial Order Respecting Custody. An initial order respecting the custody or enlargement of the prisoner and any recognizance or surety taken, shall govern review in the court of appeals and in the Supreme Court unless for special reasons shown to the court of appeals or to the Supreme Court, or to a judge or justice of either court, the order shall be modified, or an independent order respecting custody, enlargement or surety shall be made. [*See* **§§6.07, 6.08, 6.09.**]

(As amended Mar. 10, 1986, eff. July 1, 1986.)

Rule 24. Proceedings in Forma Pauperis

(a) Leave to Proceed on Appeal in Forma Pauperis From District Court to Court of Appeals. A party to an action in a district court who desires to proceed on appeal in forma pauperis shall file in the district court a motion for leave so to proceed, together with an affidavit, showing, in the detail prescribed by Form 4 of the Appendix of Forms, the party's inability to pay fees and costs or to give security therefor, the party's belief that that party is entitled to redress, and a statement of the issues which that party intends to present on appeal. If the motion is granted, the party may proceed without further application to the court of appeals and without prepayment of fees or costs in either court or the giving of security therefor. If the motion is denied, the district court shall state in writing the reasons for the denial.

Notwithstanding the provisions of the preceding paragraph, a party who has been permitted to proceed in an action in the district court in forma pauperis, or who has been permitted to proceed there as one who is financially unable to obtain adequate defense in a criminal case, may proceed on appeal in forma pauperis without further authorization unless, before or after the notice of appeal is filed, the district court shall certify that the appeal is not taken in good faith or shall find that the party is otherwise not entitled so to proceed, in which event the district court shall state in writing the reasons for such certification or finding.

If a motion for leave to proceed on appeal in forma pauperis is denied by the district court, or if the district court shall certify that the appeal is not taken in good faith or shall find that the party is otherwise not entitled to proceed in forma pauperis, the clerk shall forthwith serve notice of such action. A motion for leave so to proceed may be filed in the court of appeals within 30 days after service of notice of the action of the district court. The motion shall be accompanied by a copy of the affidavit filed in the district court, or by the affidavit prescribed by the first paragraph of this subdivision if no affidavit has been filed in the district court, and by a copy of the statement of reasons given by the district court for its action.

(b) Leave to Proceed on Appeal or Review in Forma Pauperis in Administrative Agency Proceedings. A party to a proceeding before an administrative agency, board, commission or officer (including, for the purpose of this rule, the United States Tax Court who desires to proceed on appeal or review in a court of appeals in forma pauperis, when such appeal or review may be had directly in a court of appeals, shall file in the court of appeals a motion for leave so to proceed, together with the affidavit prescribed by the first paragraph of (a) of this Rule 24.

(c) Form of Briefs, Appendices and Other Papers. Parties allowed to proceed in forma pauperis may file briefs, appendices and other papers in typewritten form, and may request that the appeal be heard on the original record without the necessity of reproducing parts thereof in any form. [*See* **§§6.15, 8.04.**]

(As amended Apr. 30, 1979, eff. Aug. 1, 1979; Mar. 10, 1986, eff. July 1, 1986.)

TITLE VII. GENERAL PROVISIONS

Rule 25. Filing and Service

(a) Filing.—Papers required or permitted to be filed in a court of appeals must be filed with the clerk. Filing may be accomplished by mail addressed to the clerk, but filing is not timely unless the clerk receives the papers within the time fixed for filing, except that briefs and appendices are treated as filed on the day of mailing if the most expeditious form of delivery by mail, except special delivery, is used. Papers filed by an inmate confined in an institution are timely filed if deposited in the institution's internal mail system on or before the last day for filing. Timely filing of papers by an inmate confined in an institution may be shown by a notarized statement or declaration (in compliance with 28 U.S.C. § 1746) setting forth the date of deposit and stating that first-class postage has been prepaid. If a motion requests relief that may be granted by a single judge, the judge may permit the motion to be filed with the judge, in which event the judge shall note thereon the date of filing and thereafter give it to the clerk. A court of appeals may, by local rule, permit papers to be filed by facsimile or other electronic means, provided such means are authorized by and consistent with standards established by the Judicial Conference of the United States.

(b) Service of All Papers Required. Copies of all papers filed by any party and not required by these rules to be served by the clerk shall, at or before the time of filing, be served by a party or person acting for that party on all other parties to the appeal or review. Service on a party represented by counsel shall be made on counsel.

(c) Manner of Service. Service may be personal or by mail. Personal service includes delivery of the copy to a clerk or other responsible person at the office of counsel. Service by mail is complete on mailing.

(d) Proof of Service. Papers presented for filing shall contain an acknowledgment of service by the person served or proof of service in the form of a statement of the date and manner of service and of the names of the person served, certified by the person who made service. Proof of service may appear on or be affixed to the papers filed. The clerk may permit papers to be filed without acknowledgment or proof of service but shall require such to be filed promptly thereafter. [*See* **§§8.07, 9.02.**]

(As amended Mar. 10, 1986, eff. July 1, 1986; Apr. 30, 1991, eff. Dec. 1, 1991.)

(Amendments to Rule 25(a) to be effective December 1, 1993 unless changed by Congress.)

Rule 26. Computation and Extension of Time

(a) Computation of Time.—In computing any period of time prescribed or allowed by these rules, by an order of court, or by any applicable statute, the day of the act, event, or default from which the designated period of time begins to run shall not be included. The last day of the period so computed shall be included, unless it is a Saturday, a Sunday, or a legal holiday, or, when the act to be done is the filing of a paper in court, a day on which weather or other conditions have made the office of the clerk of the court inaccessible, in which event the period runs until the end of the next day which is not one of the aforementioned days. When the period of the time prescribed or allowed is less than 7 days, intermediate Saturdays, Sundays, and legal holidays shall be excluded in the computation. As used in this rule "legal holiday" includes New Year's Day, Birthday of Martin Luther King, Jr., Washington's Birthday, Memorial Day, Independence Day, Labor Day, Columbus Day, Veterans Day, Thanksgiving Day, Christmas Day, and any other day appointed as a holiday by the President or the Congress of the United States. It shall also include a day appointed as a holiday by the state wherein the district court which rendered the judgment or order which is or may be appealed from is situated, or by the state wherein the principal office of the clerk of the court of appeals in which the appeal is pending is located.

(b) Enlargement of Time. The court for good cause shown may upon motion enlarge the time prescribed by these rules or by its order for doing any act, or may permit an act to be done after the expiration of such time; but the court may not enlarge the time for filing a notice of appeal, a petition for allowance, or a petition for permission to appeal. Nor may the court enlarge the time prescribed by law for filing a petition to enjoin, set aside, suspend, modify, enforce or otherwise review, or a notice of appeal from, an order of an administrative agency, board, commission or officer of the United States, except as specifically authorized by law.

(c) Additional Time After Service by Mail. Whenever a party is required or permitted to do an act within a prescribed period after service of a paper upon that party and the paper is served by mail, 3 days shall be added to the prescribed period. [*See* **§§2.09, 8.01, 8.04, 8.07, 9.02, 9.03, 10.06.**]

(As amended Mar. 1, 1971, eff. July 1, 1971; Mar. 10, 1986, eff. July 1, 1986; Apr. 25, 1989, eff. Dec. 1, 1989; Apr. 30, 1991, eff. Dec. 1, 1991.)

Rule 26.1. Corporate Disclosure Statement

Any non-governmental corporate body party to a civil or bankruptcy case or agency review proceeding and any non-governmental corporate defendant in a criminal case shall file a statement identifying all parent companies, subsidiaries (except wholly-owned subsidiaries), and affiliates that have issued shares to the public. The statement shall be filed with a party's principal brief or upon filing a motion, response, petition or answer in the court of appeals, whichever first occurs, unless a local rule requires earlier filing. The statement shall be included in front of the table of contents in a party's principal brief even if the statement was previously filed.

(Added Apr. 25, 1989, eff. Dec. 1, 1989, and amended Apr. 30, 1991, eff. Dec. 1, 1991.)

Rule 27. Motions

(a) Content of motions; response.—Unless another form is elsewhere prescribed by these rules, an application for an order or other relief shall be made by filing a motion for such order or relief with proof of service on all other parties. The motion shall contain or be accompanied by any matter required by a specific provision of these rules governing such a motion, shall state with particularity the grounds on which it is based, and shall set forth the order or relief sought. If a motion is supported by briefs, affidavits or other papers, they shall be served and filed with the motion. Any party may file a response in opposition to a motion other than one for a procedural order [for which see subdivision (b)] within 7 days after service of the motion, but motions authorized by Rules 8, 9, 18 and 41 may be acted upon after reasonable notice, and the court may shorten or extend the time for responding to any motion.

(b) Determination of Motions for Procedural Orders. Notwithstanding the provisions of (a) of this Rule 27 as to motions generally, motions for procedural orders, including any motion under Rule 26(b), may be acted upon at any time, without awaiting a response thereto, and pursuant to rule or order of the court, motions for specified types of procedural orders may be disposed of by the clerk. Any party adversely affected by such action may by application to the court request consideration, vacation or modification of such action.

(c) Power of a Single Judge to Entertain Motions. In addition to the authority expressly conferred by these rules or by law, a single judge of a court of appeals may entertain and may grant or deny any request for relief which under these rules may properly be sought by motion, except that a single judge may not dismiss or otherwise determine an appeal or other proceeding, and except that a court of appeals may provide by order or rule that any motion or class of motions must be acted upon by the court. The action of a single judge may be reviewed by the court.

(d) Form of Papers; Number of Copies. All papers relating to motions may be typewritten. Three copies shall be filed with the original, but the court may require that additional copies be furnished. [*See* **§§8.01, 8.02, 8.03, 8.04, 8.05, 8.08, 10.14.**]

(As amended Apr. 30, 1979, eff. Aug. 1, 1979.)

(As amended Apr. 25, 1989, eff. Dec. 1, 1989.)

Rule 28. Briefs

(a) Brief of the Appellant. The brief of the appellant shall contain under appropriate headings and in the order here indicated:

(1) A table of contents, with page references, and a table of cases (alphabetically arranged), statutes and other authorities cited, with references to the pages of the brief where they are cited.

(2) A statement of subject matter and appellate jurisdiction. The statement shall include: (i) a statement of the basis for subject matter jurisdiction in the district court or agency, with citation to applicable statutory provision and with reference to the relevant facts to establish such jurisdiction; (ii) a statement of the basis for jurisdiction in the court of appeals, with citation to applicable statutory provisions and with reference to the relevant facts to establish such jurisdiction; the statement shall include relevant filing dates establishing the timeliness of the appeal or petition for review and (a) shall state that the appeal is from a final order or a final judgment that disposes of all claims with respect to all parties or, if not, (b) shall include information establishing that the court of appeals has jurisdiction on some other basis.

(3) A statement of the issues presented for review.

(4) A statement of the case. The statement shall first indicate briefly the nature of the case, the course of proceedings, and its disposition in the court below. There shall follow a statement of the facts relevant to the issues presented for review, with appropriate references to the record (see subdivision (e)).

(5) An argument. The argument may be preceded by a summary. The argument shall contain the contentions of the appellant with respect to the issues presented, and the reasons therefor, with citations to the authorities, statutes and parts of the record relied on.

(6) A short conclusion stating the precise relief sought.

(b) Appellee's Brief.—The brief of the appellee must conform to the requirements of paragraphs (a)(1)-(5), except that none of the following need appear unless the appellee is dissatisfied with the statement of the appellant:

(1) the jurisdictional statement;

(2) the statement of the issues;

(3) the statement of the case;

(4) the statement of the standard of review.

(c) Reply Brief. The appellant may file a brief in reply to the brief of the appellee, and if the appellee has cross-appealed, the appellee may file a brief in reply to the response of the appellant to the issues presented by the cross appeal. No further briefs may be filed except with leave of court. All reply briefs shall contain a table of contents, with page references, and a table of cases (alphabetically arranged), statutes and other authorities cited, with references to the pages of the reply brief where they are cited.

(d) References in Briefs to Parties. Counsel will be expected in their briefs and oral arguments to keep to a minimum references to parties by such designations as "appellant" and "appellee". It promotes clarity to use the designations used in the lower court or in the agency proceedings, or the actual names of parties, or descriptive terms such as "the employee," "the injured person," "the taxpayer," "the ship," "the stevedore," etc.

(e) References in Briefs to the Record. References in the briefs to parts of the record reproduced in the appendix filed with the brief of the appellant (see Rule 30(a)) shall be to the pages of the appendix at which those parts appear. If the appendix is prepared after the briefs are filed, references in the briefs to the record shall be made by one of the methods allowed by Rule 30(c). If the record is reproduced in accordance with the provisions of Rule 30(f), or if references are made in the briefs to parts of the record not reproduced, the references shall be to the pages of the parts of the record involved; e.g., Answer p. 7, Motion for Judgment p. 2, Transcript p. 231. Intelligible abbreviations may be used. If reference is made to evidence the admissibility of which is in controversy, reference shall be made to the pages of the appendix or of the transcript at which the evidence was identified, offered, and received or rejected.

(f) Reproduction of Statutes, Rules, Regulations, etc. If determination of the issues presented requires the study of statutes, rules, regulations, etc. or relevant parts thereof, they shall be reproduced in the brief or in an addendum at the end, or they may be supplied to the court in pamphlet form.

(g) Length of Briefs.—Except by permission of the court, or as specified by local rule of the court of appeals, principal briefs shall not exceed 50 pages, and reply briefs shall not exceed 25 pages, exclusive of pages containing the corporate disclosure statement, table of contents, tables of citations and any addendum containing statutes, rules, regulations, etc.

(h) Briefs in Cases Involving Cross Appeals. If a cross appeal is filed, the party who first files a notice of appeal, or in the event that the notices are filed on the same day, the plaintiff in the proceeding below shall be deemed the appellant for the purposes of this rule and Rules 30 and 31, unless the parties otherwise agree or the court otherwise orders. The brief of the appellee shall conform to the requirements of subdivision (a)(1)-(6) of this rule with respect to the appellee's cross appeal as well as respond to the brief of the appeallant except that a statement of the case need not be made unless the appellee is dissatisfied with the statement of the appellant.

(i) Briefs in Cases Involving Multiple Appellants or Appellees. In cases involving more than one appellant or appellee, including cases consolidated for purposes of the appeal, any number of either may join in a single brief, and any appellant or appellee may adopt by reference any part of the brief of another. Parties may similarly join in reply briefs.

(j) Citation of Supplemental Authorities. When pertinent and significant authorities come to the attention of a party after the party's brief has been filed, or after oral argument but before decision, a party may promptly advise the clerk of the court, by letter, with a copy to all counsel, setting forth the citations. There shall be a reference either to the page of the brief or to a point argued orally to which the citations pertain, but the letter shall without argument state the reasons for the supplemental citations. Any response shall be made promptly and shall be similarly limited. [*See* **§§1.01, 8.04, 9.03, 9.04, 9.09, 9.10, 9.11, 9.12, 9.14, 9.18, 9.19, 9.20.**]

(As amended Apr. 30, 1979, eff. Aug. 1, 1979; Mar. 10, 1986, eff. July 1, 1986; Apr. 25, 1989, eff. Dec. 1, 1989; Apr. 30, 1991, eff. Dec. 1, 1991.)

(Amendments to Rule 28(b) to be effective December 1, 1993 unless changed by Congress.)

Rule 29. Brief of an Amicus Curiae

A brief of an amicus curiae may be filed only if accompanied by written consent of all parties, or by leave of court granted on motion or at the request of the court, except that consent or leave shall not be required when the brief is presented by the United States or an officer or agency thereof, or by a State, Territory or Commonwealth. The brief may be conditionally filed with the motion for leave. A motion for leave shall identify the interest of the applicant and shall state the reasons why a brief of an amicus curiae is desirable. Save as all parties otherwise consent, any amicus curiae shall file its brief within the time allowed the party whose position as to affirmance or reversal the amicus brief will support unless the court for cause shown shall grant leave for later filing, in which event it shall specify within what period an opposing party may answer. A motion of an amicus curiae to participate in the oral argument will be granted only for extraordinary reasons. [*See* **§2.02.**]

Rule 30. Appendix to the Briefs

(a) Duty of Appellant to Prepare and File; Content of Appendix; Time for Filing; Number of Copies. The appellant shall prepare and file an appendix to the briefs which shall contain: (1) the relevant docket entries in the proceeding below; (2) any relevant portions of the pleadings, charge, findings or opinion; (3) the judgment, order or decision in question; and (4) any other parts of the record to which the parties wish to direct the particular attention of the court. Except where they have independent relevance, memoranda of law in the district court should not be included in the appendix. The fact that parts of the record are not included in the appendix shall not prevent the parties or the court from relying on such parts.

Unless filing is to be deferred pursuant to the provisions of subdivision (c) of this rule, the appellant shall serve and file the appendix with the brief. Ten copies of the appendix shall be filed with the clerk, and one copy shall be served on counsel for each party separately represented, unless the court shall by rule or order direct the filing or service of a lesser number.

(b) Determination of Contents of Appendix; Cost of Producing. The parties are encouraged to agree as to the contents of the appendix. In the absence of agreement, the appellant shall, not later than 10 days after the date on which the record is filed, serve on the appellee a designation of the parts of the record which the appellant intends to include in the appendix and a statement of the issues which the appellant intends to present for review. If the appellee deems it necessary to direct the particular attention of the court to parts of the record not designated by the appellant, the appellee shall, within 10 days after receipt of the designation, serve upon the appellant a designation of those parts. The appellant shall include in the appendix the parts thus designated with respect to the appeal and any cross appeal. In designating parts of the record for inclusion in the appendix, the parties shall have regard for the fact that the entire record is always available to the court for reference and examination and shall not engage in unnecessary designation. The provisions of this paragraph shall apply to cross appellants and cross appellees.

Unless the parties otherwise agree, the cost of producing the appendix shall initially be paid by the appellant, but if the appellant considers that parts of the record designated by the appellee for inclusion are unnecessary for the determination of the issues presented the appellant may so advise the appellee and the appellee shall advance the cost of including such parts. The cost of producing the appendix shall be taxed as costs in the case, but if either party shall cause matters to be included in the appendix unnecessarily the court may impose the cost of producing such parts on the party. Each circuit shall provide by local rule for the imposition of sanctions against attorneys who unreasonably and vexatiously increase the costs of litigation through the inclusion of unnecessary material in the appendix.

(c) Alternative Method of Designating Contents of the Appendix; How References to the Record May be Made in the Briefs When Alternative Method is Used. If the court shall so provide by rule for classes of cases or by order in specific cases, preparation of the appendix may be deferred until after the briefs have been filed, and the appendix may be filed 21 days after service of the brief of the appellee. If the preparation and filing of the appendix is thus deferred, the provisions of subdivision (b) of this Rule 30 shall apply, except that the designations referred to therein shall be made by each party at the time each brief is served, and a statement of the issues presented shall be unnecessary.

If the deferred appendix authorized by this subdivision is employed, references in the briefs to the record may be to the pages of the parts of the record involved, in which event the original paging of each part of the record shall be indicated in the appendix by placing in brackets the number of each page at the place in the appendix where that page begins. Or if a party desires to refer in a brief directly to pages of the appendix, that party may serve and file typewritten or page proof copies of the brief within the time required by Rule 31(a), with appropriate references to the pages of the parts of the record involved. In that event, within 14 days after the appendix is filed the party shall serve and file copies of the brief in the form prescribed by Rule 32(a) containing references to the pages of the appendix in place of or in addition to the initial references to the pages of the parts of the record involved. No other changes may be made in the brief as initially served and filed, except that typographical errors may be corrected.

(d) Arrangement of the Appendix. At the beginning of the appendix there shall be inserted a list of the parts of the record which it contains, in the order in which the parts are set out therein, with references to the pages of the appendix at which each part begins. The relevant docket entries shall be set out following the list of contents. Thereafter, other parts of the record shall be set out in chronological order. When matter contained in the reporter's transcript of proceedings is set out in the appendix, the page of the transcript at which such matter may be found shall be indicated in brackets immediately before the matter which is set out. Omissions in the text of papers or of the transcript must be indicated by asterisks. Immaterial formal matters (captions, subscriptions, acknowledgments, etc.) shall be omitted. A question and its answer may be contained in a single paragraph.

(e) Reproduction of Exhibits. Exhibits designated for inclusion in the appendix may be contained in a separate volume, or volumes, suitably indexed. Four copies thereof shall be filed with the appendix and one copy shall be served on counsel for each party separately represented. The transcript of a proceeding before an administrative agency, board, commission or officer used in an action in the district court shall be regarded as an exhibit for the purpose of this subdivision.

(f) Hearing of Appeals on the Original Record Without the Necessity of an Appendix. A court of appeals may by rule applicable to all cases, or to classes of cases, or by order in specific cases, dispense with the requirement of an appendix and permit appeals to be heard on the original record, with such copies of the record, or relevant parts thereof, as the court may require. [*See* **§§5.03, 7.01, 7.02, 7.03, 7.04, 8.04.**]

(As amended Mar. 30, 1970, eff. July 1, 1970; Mar. 10, 1986, eff. July 1, 1986; Apr. 30, 1991, eff. Dec. 1, 1991.)

Rule 31. Filing and Service of Briefs

(a) Time for Serving and Filing Briefs. The appellant shall serve and file a brief within 40 days after the date on which the record is filed. The appellee shall serve and file a brief within 30 days after service of the brief of the appellant. The appellant may serve and file a reply brief within 14 days after service of the brief of the appellee, but, except for good cause shown, a reply brief must be filed at least 3 days before argument. If a court of appeals is prepared to consider cases on the merits promptly after briefs are filed, and its practice is to do so, it may shorten the periods prescribed above for serving and filing briefs, either by rule for all cases or for classes of cases, or by order for specific cases.

(b) Number of Copies to be Filed and Served. Twenty-five copies of each brief shall be filed with the clerk, unless the court by order in a particular case shall direct a lesser number, and two copies shall be served on counsel for each party separately represented. If a party is allowed to file typewritten ribbon and carbon copies of the brief, the original and three legible copies shall be filed with the clerk, and one copy shall be served on counsel for each party separately represented.

(c) Consequence of Failure to File Briefs. If an appellant fails to file a brief within the time provided by this rule, or within the time as extended, an appellee may move for dismissal of the appeal. If an appellee fails to file a brief, the appellee will not be heard at oral argument except by permission of the court. [*See* **§9.02**]

(As amended Mar. 30, 1970, eff. July 1, 1970; Mar. 10, 1986, eff. July 1, 1986.)

Rule 32. Form of Briefs, the Appendix and Other Papers

(a) Form of Briefs and the Appendix. Briefs and appendices may be produced by standard typographic printing or by any duplicating or copying process which produces a clear image on white paper. Carbon copies of briefs and appendices may not be submitted without permission of the court, except in behalf of parties allowed to proceed in forma pauperis. All printed matter must appear in at least 11 point type on opaque, unglazed paper. Briefs and appendices produced by the standard typographic process shall be bound in volumes having pages 6 ⅛ by 9 ¼ inches and type matter 4 ⅙ by 7 ⅙ inches. Those produced by any other process shall be bound in volumes having pages not exceeding 8 ½ by 11 inches and type matter not exceeding 6 ½ by 9 ½ inches, with double spacing between each line of text. In patent cases the pages of briefs and appendices may be of such size as is necessary to utilize copies of patent documents. Copies of the reporter's transcript and other papers reproduced in a manner authorized by this rule may be inserted in the appendix; such pages may be informally renumbered if necessary. If briefs are produced by commercial printing or duplicating firms, or, if produced otherwise and the covers to be described are available, the cover of the brief of the appellant should be blue; that of the appellee, red; that of an intervenor or amicus curiae, green; that of any reply brief, gray. The cover of the appendix, if separately printed, should be white. The front covers of the briefs and of appendices, if separately printed, shall contain: (1) the name of the court and the number of the case; (2) the title of the case (see Rule 12(a)); (3) the nature of the proceeding in the court (e.g., Appeal; Petition for Review) and the name of the court, agency, or board below; (4) the title of the document (e.g., Brief for Appellant, Appendix); and (5) the names and addresses of counsel representing the party on whose behalf the document is filed.

(b) Form of Other Papers. Petitions for rehearing shall be produced in a manner prescribed by subdivision (a). Motions and other papers may be produced in like manner, or they may be typewritten upon opaque, unglazed paper 8 ½ by 11 inches in size. Lines of typewritten text shall be double spaced.

Consecutive sheets shall be attached at the left margin. Carbon copies may be used for filing and service if they are legible.

A motion or other paper addressed to the court shall contain a caption setting forth the name of the court, the title of the case, the file number, and a brief descriptive title indicating the purpose of the paper. [*See* **§§6.11, 7.02, 8.03, 8.04, 8.07, 9.03, 9.04, 11.03.**]

Rule 33. Prehearing Conference

The court may direct the attorneys for the parties to appear before the court or a judge thereof for a prehearing conference to consider the simplification of the issues and such other matters as may aid in the disposition of the proceeding by the court. The court or judge shall make an order which recites the action taken at the conference and the agreements made by the parties as to any of the matters considered and which limits the issues to those not disposed of by admissions or agreements of counsel, and such order when entered controls the subsequent course of the proceeding, unless modified to prevent manifest injustice. [*See* **§8.06.**]

Rule 34. Oral Argument

(a) In General; Local Rule. Oral argument shall be allowed in all cases unless pursuant to local rule a panel of three judges, after examination of the briefs and record, shall be unanimously of the opinion that oral argument is not needed. Any such local rule shall provide any party with an opportunity to file a statement setting forth the reasons why oral argument should be heard. A general statement of the criteria employed in the administration of such local rule shall be published in or with the rule and such criteria shall conform substantially to the following minimum standard:

Oral Argument will be allowed unless

(1) the appeal is frivolous; or

(2) the dispositive issue or set of issues has been recently authoritatively decided; or

(3) the facts and legal arguments are adequately presented in the briefs and record and the decisional process would not be significantly aided by oral argument.

(b) Notice of Argument; Postponement. The clerk shall advise all parties whether oral argument is to be heard, and if so, of the time and place therefor, and the time to be allowed each side. A request for postponement of the argument or for allowance of additional time must be made by motion filed reasonably in advance of the date fixed for hearing.

(c) Order and Content of Argument.—The appellant is entitled to open and conclude the argument. Counsel may not read at length from briefs, records, or authorities.

(d) Cross and Separate Appeals. A cross or separate appeal shall be argued with the initial appeal at a single argument, unless the court otherwise directs. If a case involves a cross appeal, the party who first files a notice of appeal, or in the event that the notices are filed on the same day the plaintiff in the proceeding below, shall be deemed the appellant for the purpose of this rule unless the parties otherwise agree or the court otherwise directs. If separate appellants support the same argument, care shall be taken to avoid duplication of argument.

(e) Non-Appearance of Parties. If the appellee fails to appear to present argument, the court will hear argument on behalf of the appellant, if present. If the appellant fails to appear, the court may hear argument on behalf of the appellee, if present. If neither party appears, the case will be decided on the briefs unless the court shall otherwise order.

(f) Submission on Briefs. By agreement of the parties, a case may be submitted for decision on the briefs, but the court may direct that the case be argued.

(g) Use of Physical Exhibits at Argument; Removal. If physical exhibits other than documents are to be used at the argument, counsel shall arrange to have them placed in the court room before the court convenes on the date of the argument. After the argument counsel shall cause the exhibits to be removed from the court room unless the court otherwise directs. If exhibits are not reclaimed by counsel within a reasonable time after notice is given by the clerk, they shall be destroyed or otherwise disposed of as the clerk shall think best. [*See* **§§8.04, 10.02, 10.03, 10.04, 10.07, 10.09, 10.12.**]

(As amended Apr. 30, 1979, eff. Aug. 1, 1979; Mar. 10, 1987, eff. July 1, 1986; Apr 30, 1991, eff. Dec. 1, 1991.)

(Amendments to Rule 34(c) to be effective December 1, 1993 unless changed by Congress.)

Rule 35. Determination of Causes by the Court in Banc

(a) When Hearing or Rehearing in Banc Will be Ordered. A majority of the circuit judges who are in regular active service may order that an appeal or other proceeding be heard or reheard by the court of appeals in banc. Such a hearing or rehearing is not favored and ordinarily will not be ordered except (1) when consideration by the full court is necessary to secure or maintain uniformity of its decisions, or (2) when the proceeding involves a question of exceptional importance.

(b) Suggestion of a Party for Hearing or Rehearing in Banc. A party may suggest the appropriateness of a hearing or rehearing in banc. No response shall be filed unless the court shall so order. The clerk shall transmit any such suggestion to the members of the panel and the judges of the court who are in regular active service but a vote need not be taken to determine whether the cause shall be heard or reheard in banc unless a judge in regular active service or a judge who was a member of the panel that rendered a decision sought to be reheard requests a vote on such a suggestion made by a party.

(c) Time for Suggestion of a Party for Hearing or Rehearing in Banc; Suggestion Does Not Stay Mandate. If a party desires to suggest that an appeal be heard initially in banc, the suggestion must be made by the date on which the appellee's brief is filed. A suggestion for a rehearing in banc must be made within the time prescribed by Rule 40 for filing a petition for rehearing, whether the suggestion is made in such petition or otherwise. The pendency of such a suggestion whether or not included in a petition for rehearing shall not affect the finality of the judgment of the court of appeals or stay the issuance of the mandate. [*See* **§§8.05, 11.01, 11.02, 11.03, 11.04, 11.05.**]

(As amended Apr. 30, 1979, eff. Aug. 1, 1979.)

Rule 36. Entry of Judgment

The notation of a judgment in the docket constitutes entry of the judgment. The clerk shall prepare, sign and enter the judgment following receipt of the opinion of the court unless the opinion directs settlement of the form of the judgment, in which event the clerk shall prepare, sign and enter the judgment following final settlement by the court. If a judgment is rendered without an opinion, the clerk shall prepare, sign and enter the judgment following instruction from the court. The clerk shall, on the date judgment is entered, mail to all parties a copy of the opinion, if any, or of the judgment if no opinion was written, and notice of the date of entry of the judgment. [*See* **§10.15.**]

Rule 37. Interest on Judgments

Unless otherwise provided by law, if a judgment for money in a civil case is affirmed, whatever interest is allowed by law shall be payable from the date the judgment was entered in the district court. If a judgment is modified or reversed with a direction that a judgment for money be entered in the district court, the mandate shall contain instructions with respect to allowance of interest. [*See* **§10.16.**]

Rule 38. Damages for Delay

If a court of appeals shall determine that an appeal is frivolous, it may award just damages and single or double costs to the appellee. [*See* **§§5.02, 6.11, 8.09, 10.16.**]

Rule 39. Costs

(a) To Whom Allowed. Except as otherwise provided by law, if an appeal is dismissed, costs shall be taxed against the appellant unless otherwise agreed by the parties or ordered by the court; if a judgment is affirmed, costs shall be taxed against the appellant unless otherwise ordered; if a judgment is reversed, costs shall be taxed against the appellee unless otherwise ordered; if a judgment is affirmed or reversed in part, or is vacated, costs shall be allowed only as ordered by the court.

(b) Costs For and Against the United States. In cases involving the United States or an agency or officer thereof, if an award of costs against the United States is authorized by law, costs shall be awarded in accordance with the provisions of subdivision (a); otherwise, costs shall not be awarded for or against the United States.

(c) Costs of Briefs, Appendices, and Copies of Records. By local rule the court of appeals shall fix the maximum rate at which the cost of printing or otherwise producing necessary copies of briefs, appendices, and copies of records authorized by Rule 30(f) shall be taxable. Such rate shall not be higher than that generally charged for such work in the area where the clerk's office is located and shall encourage the use of economical methods of printing and copying.

(d) Bill of Costs; Objections; Costs to be Inserted in Mandate or Added Later. A party who desires such costs to be taxed shall state them in an itemized and verified bill of costs which the party shall file with the clerk, with proof of service, within 14 days after the entry of judgment. Objections to the bill of costs must be filed within 10 days of service on the party against whom costs are to be taxed unless the time is extended by the court.

The clerk shall prepare and certify an itemized statement of costs taxed in the court of appeals for insertion in the mandate, but the issuance of the mandate shall not be delayed for taxation of costs and if the mandate has been issued before final determination of costs, the statement, or any amendment thereof, shall be added to the mandate upon request by the clerk of the court of appeals to the clerk of the district court.

(e) Costs on Appeal Taxable in the District Courts. Costs incurred in the preparation and transmission of the record, the cost of the reporter's transcript, if necessary for the determination of the appeal, the premiums paid for cost of supersedeas bonds or other bonds to preserve rights pending appeal, and the fee for filing the notice of appeal shall be taxed in the district court as costs of the appeal in favor of the party entitled to costs under this rule. [*See* **§§6.11, 9.04, 10.16.**]

(As amended Apr. 30, 1979, eff. Aug. 1, 1979; Mar. 10, 1986, eff. July 1, 1986.)

Rule 40. Petition for Rehearing

(a) Time for Filing; Content; Answer; Action by Court if Granted. A petition for rehearing may be filed within 14 days after entry of judgment unless the time is shortened or enlarged by order or by local rule. The petition shall state with particularity the points of law or fact which in the opinion of the petitioner the court has overlooked or misapprehended and shall contain such argument in support of the petition as the petitioner desires to present. Oral argument in support of the petition will not be permitted. No answer to a petition for rehearing will be received unless requested by the court, but a petition for rehearing will ordinarily not be granted in the absence of such a request. If a petition for rehearing is granted the court may make a final disposition of the cause without reargument or may restore it to the calendar for reargument or resubmission or may make such other orders as are deemed appropriate under the circumstances of the particular case.

(b) Form of Petition; Length. The petition shall be in a form prescribed by Rule 32(a), and copies shall be served and filed as prescribed by Rule 31(b) for the service and filing of briefs. Except by permission of the court, or as specified by local rule of the court of appeals, a petition for rehearing shall not exceed 15 pages. [*See* **§§8.04, 8.05, 10.15, 11.01, 11.02, 11.03, 11.04, 11.05, 11.06.**]

(As amended Apr. 30, 1979, eff. Aug. 1, 1979.)

Rule 41. Issuance of Mandate; Stay of Mandate

(a) Date of Issuance. The mandate of the court shall issue 21 days after the entry of judgment unless the time is shortened or enlarged by order. A certified copy of the judgment and a copy of the opinion of the court, if any, and any direction as to costs shall constitute the mandate, unless the court directs that a formal mandate issue. The timely filing of a petition for rehearing will stay the mandate until disposition of the petition unless otherwise ordered by the court. If the petition is denied, the mandate shall issue 7 days after entry of the order denying the petition unless the time is shortened or enlarged by order.

(b) Stay of Mandate Pending Application for Certiorari. A stay of the mandate pending application to the Supreme Court for a writ of certiorari may be granted upon motion, reasonable notice of which shall be given to all parties. The stay shall not exceed 30 days unless the period is extended for cause shown. If during the period of the stay there is filed with the clerk of the court of appeals a notice from the clerk of the Supreme Court that the party who has obtained the stay has filed a petition for the writ in that court, the stay shall continue until final disposition by the Supreme Court. Upon the filing of a copy of an order of the Supreme Court denying the petition for writ of certiorari the mandate shall issue immediately. A bond or other security may be required as a condition to the grant or continuance of a stay of the mandate. [*See* **§§8.01, 10.15, 11.01, 11.02.**]

Rule 42. Voluntary Dismissal

(a) Dismissal in the District Court. If an appeal has not been docketed, the appeal may be dismissed by the district court upon the filing in that court of a stipulation for dismissal signed by all the parties, or upon motion and notice by the appellant.

(b) Dismissal in the Court of Appeals. If the parties to an appeal or other proceeding shall sign and file with the clerk of the court of appeals an agreement that the proceeding be dismissed, specifying the terms as to payment of costs, and shall pay whatever fees are due, the clerk shall enter the case dismissed, but no mandate or other process shall issue without an order of the court. An appeal may be dismissed on motion of the appellant upon such terms as may be agreed upon by the parties or fixed by the court. [*See* **§8.09**.]

Rule 43. Substitution of Parties

(a) Death of a Party. If a party dies after a notice of appeal is filed or while a proceeding is otherwise pending in the court of appeals, the personal representative of the deceased party may be substituted as a party on motion filed by the representative or by any party with the clerk of the court of appeals. The motion of a party shall be served upon the representative in accordance with the provisions of Rule 25. If the deceased party has no representative, any party may suggest the death on the record and proceedings shall then be had as the court of appeals may direct. If a party against whom an appeal may be taken dies after entry of a judgment or order in the district court but before a notice of appeal is filed, an appellant may proceed as if death had not occurred. After the notice of appeal is filed substitution shall be effected in the court of appeals in accordance with this subdivision. If a party entitled to appeal shall die before filing a notice of appeal, the notice of appeal may be filed by that party's personal representative, or, if there is no personal representative by that party's attorney of record within the time prescribed by these rules. After the notice of appeal is filed substitution shall be effected in the court of appeals in accordance with this subdivision.

(b) Substitution for Other Causes. If substitution of a party in the court of appeals is necessary for any reason other than death, substitution shall be effected in accordance with the procedure prescribed in subdivision (a).

(c) Public Officers; Death or Separation From Office.

(1) When a public officer is a party to an appeal or other proceeding in the court of appeals in an official capacity and during its pendency dies, resigns or otherwise ceases to hold office, the action does not abate and the public officer's successor is automatically substituted as a party. Proceedings following the substitution shall be in the name of the substituted party, but any misnomer not affecting the substantial rights of the parties shall be disregarded. An order of substitution may be entered at any time, but the omission to enter such an order shall not affect the substitution.

(2) When a public officer is a party to an appeal or other proceeding in an official capacity that public officer may be described as a party by the public officer's official title rather than by name; but the court may require the public officer's name to be added. [*See* **§8.04.**]

(As amended Mar. 10, 1986, eff. July 1, 1986.)

Rule 44. Cases Involving Constitutional Questions Where United States Is Not a Party

It shall be the duty of a party who draws in question the constitutionality of any Act of Congress in any proceeding in a court of appeals to which the United States, or any agency thereof, or any officer or employee thereof, as such officer or employee, is not a party, upon the filing of the record, or as soon thereafter as the question is raised in the court of appeals, to give immediate notice in writing to the court of the existence of said question. The clerk shall thereupon certify such fact to the Attorney General. [*See* **§3.15.**]

Rule 45. Duties of Clerks

(a) General Provisions. The clerk of a court of appeals shall take the oath and give the bond required by law. Neither the clerk nor any deputy clerk shall practice as an attorney or counselor in any court while continuing in office. The court of appeals shall be deemed always open for the purpose of filing any proper paper, of issuing and returning process and of making motions and orders. The office of the clerk with the clerk or a deputy in attendance shall be open during business hours on all days except Saturdays, Sundays, and legal holidays, but a court may provide by local rule or order that the office of its clerk shall be open for specified hours on Saturdays or on particular legal holidays other than New Year's Day, Birthday of Martin Luther King, Jr., Washington's Birthday, Memorial Day, Independence Day, Labor Day, Columbus Day, Veterans Day, Thanksgiving Day, and Christmas Day.

(b) The Docket; Calendar; Other Records Required. The clerks shall maintain a docket in such form as may be prescribed by the Director of the Administrative Office of the United States Courts. The clerk shall enter a record of all papers filed with the clerk and all process, orders and judgments. An index of cases contained in the docket shall be maintained as prescribed by the Director of the Administrative Office of the United States Courts.

The clerk shall prepare, under the direction of the court, a calendar of cases awaiting argument. In placing cases on the calendar for argument, the clerk shall give preference to appeals in criminal cases and to appeals and other proceedings entitled to preference by law.

The clerk shall keep such other books and records as may be required from time to time by the Director of the Administrative Office of the United States Courts with the approval of the Judicial Conference of the United States, or as may be required by the court.

(c) Notice of Orders or Judgments. Immediately upon the entry of an order or judgment the clerk shall serve a notice of entry by mail upon each party to the proceeding together with a copy of any opinion respecting the order or judgment, and shall make a note in the docket of the mailing. Service on a party represented by counsel shall be made on counsel.

(d) Custody of Records and Papers. The clerk shall have custody of the records and papers of the court. The clerk shall not permit any original record or paper to be taken from the clerk's custody except as authorized by the orders or instructions of the court. Original papers transmitted as the record on appeal or review shall upon disposition of the case be returned to the court or agency from which they were received. The clerk shall preserve copies of briefs and appendices and other printed papers filed. [*See* **§§8.03, 10.15.**]

(As amended Mar. 1, 1971, eff. July 1, 1971; Mar. 10, 1986, eff. July 1, 1986.)

Rule 46. Attorneys

(a) Admission to the Bar of a Court of Appeals; Eligibility; Procedure for Admission. An attorney who has been admitted to practice before the Supreme Court of the United States, or the highest court of a state, or another United States court of appeals, or a United States district court (including the district courts for the Canal Zone, Guam and the Virgin Islands), and who is of good moral and professional character, is eligible for admission to the bar of a court of appeals.

An applicant shall file with the clerk of the court of appeals, on a form approved by the court and furnished by the clerk, an application for admission containing the applicant's personal statement showing eligibility for membership. At the foot of the application the applicant shall take and subscribe to the following oath or affirmation:

I, ________________, do solemnly swear (or affirm) that I will demean myself as an attorney and counselor of this court, uprightly and according to law; and that I will support the Constitution of the United States.

Thereafter, upon written or oral motion of a member of the bar of the court, the court will act upon the application. An applicant may be admitted by oral motion in open court, but it is not necessary that the applicant appear before the court for the purpose of being admitted, unless the court shall otherwise order. An applicant shall upon admission pay to the clerk the fee prescribed by rule or order of the court.

(b) Suspension or Disbarment. When it is shown to the court that any member of its bar has been suspended or disbarred from practice in any other court of record, or has been guilty of conduct unbecoming a member of the bar of the court, the member will be subject to suspension or disbarment by the court.

The member shall be afforded an opportunity to show good cause, within such time as the court shall prescribe, why the member should not be suspended or disbarred. Upon the member's response to the rule to show cause, and after hearing, if requested, or upon expiration of the time prescribed for a response if no response is made, the court shall enter an appropriate order.

(c) Disciplinary Power of the Court Over Attorneys. A court of appeals may, after reasonable notice and an opportunity to show cause to the contrary, and after hearing, if requested, take any appropriate disciplinary action against any attorney who practices before it for conduct unbecoming a member of the bar or for failure to comply with these rules or any rule of the court. [*See* **§§4.01, 5.02, 5.03.**]

(As amended Mar. 10, 1986, eff. July 1, 1986.)

Rule 47. Rules by Courts of Appeals

Each court of appeals by action of a majority of the circuit judges in regular active service may from time to time make and amend rules governing its practices not inconsistent with these rules. In all cases not provided for by rule, the courts of appeals may regulate their practice in any manner not inconsistent with these rules. Copies of all rules made by a court of appeals shall upon their promulgation be furnished to the Administrative Office of the United States Courts. [*See* **§§1.01, 4.01.**]

Rule 48. Title

These rules may be known and cited as the Federal Rules of Appellate Procedure.

FEDERAL RULES OF APPELLATE PROCEDURE APPENDIX OF FORMS

Form 1. Notice of Appeal to a Court of Appeals From a Judgment or Order of a District Court [See Effective Date note below.]

United States District Court for the
__________ District of __________

File Number __________

A.B., Plaintiff
v.
C.D., Defendant

Notice of Appeal

Notice is hereby given that [(here name all parties taking the appeal), (plaintiffs) (defendants) in the above named cases,*] hereby appeals to the United States Court of Appeals for the _______ Circuit (from the final judgment) (from an order (describing it)) entered in this action on the _______ day of _______, 19__.

(s) ____________________
Attorney for [______________]
[Address: ________________]

* See Rule 3(c) for permissible ways of identifying appellants.

(Amendments to Form 1 to be effective December 1, 1993 unless changed by Congress)
F. R. A. P. Form 1, 28 U. S. C. A. [*See* **§6.02.**]

Form 2. Notice of Appeal to a Court of Appeals From a Decision of the [United States] Tax Court

UNITED STATES TAX COURT
Washington, D.C.

A.B., Petitioner v. Commissioner of Internal Revenue, Respondent	Docket No. ________

Notice of Appeal

Notice is hereby given that [here name all parties taking the appeal*], hereby appeals to the United States Court of Appeals for the ______ Circuit from (that part of) the decision of this court entered in the above captioned proceeding on the ______ day of ______, 19____ (relating to ______).

(s) ____________________
Counsel for [____________]
[Address: ______________]

* See Rule 3(c) for permissible ways of identifying appellants.

(Amendments to FORM 2 to be effective December 1, 1993 unless changed by Congress)
F. R. A. P. Form 2, 28 U. S. C. A. [*See* **§6.07.**]

Form 3. Petition for Review of Order of an Agency, Board, Commission or Officer

United States Court of Appeals for the ________ Circuit

A.B., Petitioner
v.
XYZ Commission, Respondent

Petition for Review

[(here name all parties bringing the petition)*] hereby petitions the court for review of the Order of the XYZ Commission (describe the order) entered on ______, 19____.

[(s)] ____________________
Attorney for Petitioners
Address: ______________

* See rule 15

(Amendments to FORM 3 to be effective December 1, 1993 unless changed by Congress)
F. R. A. P. Form 3, 28 U. S. C. A. [*See* **§§2.16, 6.09.**]

Form 4. Affidavit to Accompany Motion for Leave to Appeal in Forma Pauperis

United States District Court for the __________ District of __________

United States of America
v.
A. B.
} No. __________

Affidavit in Support of Motion to Proceed on Appeal in Forma Pauperis

I, __________ being first duly sworn, depose and say that I am the __________ in the above-entitled case; that in support of my motion to proceed on appeal without being required to prepay fees, costs or give security therefor, I state that because of my poverty I am unable to pay the costs of said proceeding or to give security therefor; that I believe I am entitled to redress; and that the issues which I desire to present on appeal are the following:

I further swear that the responses which I have made to the questions and instructions below relating to my ability to pay the cost of prosecuting the appeal are true.

1. Are you presently employed?
   a. If the answer is yes, state the amount of your salary or wages per month and give the name and address of your employer.
   b. If the answer is no, state the date of your last employment and the amount of the salary and wages per month which you received.
2. Have you received within the past twelve months any income from a business, profession or other form of self-employment, or in the form of rent payments, interest, dividends, or other source?
   a. If the answer is yes, describe each source of income, and state the amount received from each during the past twelve months.
3. Do you own any cash or checking or savings account?
   a. If the answer is yes, state the total value of the items owned.
4. Do you own any real estate, stocks, bonds, notes, automobiles, or other valuable property (excluding ordinary household furnishings and clothing)?
   a. If the answer is yes, describe the property and state its approximate value.
5. List the persons who are dependent upon you for support and state your relationship to those persons.

I understand that a false statement or answer to any questions in this affidavit will subject me to penalties for perjury.

____

SUBSCRIBED AND SWORN TO before me this ______ day of ______, 19____.

Let the applicant proceed without prepayment of costs or fees or the necessity of giving security therefor.

________________________________,
District Judge

(Amendments to FORM 4 to be effective December 1, 1993 unless changed by Congress)
F. R. A. P. Form 4, 28 U. S. C. A. [*See* **§6.15.**]

Form 5. Notice of Appeal to a Court of Appeals from a Judgment or Order of a District Court or a Bankruptcy Appellate Panel

United States District Court for the ____________ District of ____________

In re

______________________________,
Debtor

______________________________,
Plaintiff

v.

______________________________,
Defendant

File No ____________

Notice of Appeal to United States Court of Appeals for the ____________ Circuit

____________, the plaintiff [or defendant or other party] appeals to the United States Court of Appeals for the ____________ Circuit from the final judgment [or order or decree] of the district court for the district of ____________ [or bankruptcy appellate panel of the ____________ circuit], entered in this case on ____________, 19__ [here describe the judgment, order, or decree]

____

The parties to the judgment [or order or decree] appealed from and the names and addresses of their respective attorneys are as follows:

Dated____________________________
Signed____________________________
Attorney for Appellant
Address: ____________________________
____

(Amendments to FORM 5 to be effective December 1, 1993 unless changed by Congress)
F. R. A. P. Form 5, 28 U. S. C. A. [*See* **§6.06.**]

Appendix B
Federal Rules of Civil Procedure 28 U.S.C.A. §§46, 50, 51, 52, 54, 58, 59, 60, 61

VI. TRIALS

Rule 46. Exceptions Unnecessary

Formal exceptions to rulings or orders of the court are unnecessary; but for all purposes for which an exception has heretofore been necessary it is sufficient that a party, at the time the ruling or order of the court is made or sought, makes known to the court the action which the party desires the court to take or the party's objection to the action of the court and the grounds therefor; and, if a party has no opportunity to object to a ruling or order at the time it is made, the absence of an objection does not thereafter prejudice the party. [*See* **§5.03.**]

(As amended Mar. 2, 1987, eff. Aug 1, 1987.)

Rule 50. Judgment as a Matter of Law in Actions Tried by Jury; Alternative Motion for New Trial; Conditional Rulings

(a) Judgment as a Matter of Law.

(1) If during a trial by jury a party has been fully heard with respect to an issue and there is no legally sufficient evidentiary basis for a reasonable jury to have found for that party with respect to that issue, the court may grant a motion for judgment as a matter of law against that party on any claim, counterclaim, cross-claim, or third party claim that cannot under the controlling law be maintained without a favorable finding on that issue.

(2) Motions for judgment as a matter of law may be made at any time before submission or the case to the jury. Such a motion shall specify the judgment sought and the law and the facts on which the moving party is entitled to the judgment.

(b) Renewal of Motion for Judgment After Trial; Alternative Motion for New Trial. Whenever a motion for a judgment as a matter of law made at the close of all the evidence is denied or for any reason is not granted, the court is deemed to have submitted the action to the jury subject to a later determination of the legal questions raised by the motion. Such a motion may be renewed by service and filing not later than 10 days after entry of judgment. A motion for a new trial under Rule 59 may be joined with a renewal for the motion for judgment as a matter of law, or a new trial may be requested in the alternative. If a verdict was returned, the court may, in disposing of the renewed motion, allow the judgment to stand or may reopen the judgment and either order a new trial or direct the entry of judgment as a matter of law. If no verdict was returned, the court may, in disposing of the renewed motion, direct the entry of judgment as a matter of law or may order a new trial.

(c) Same: Conditional Rulings on Grant of Motion for Judgment as Matter of Law.

(1) If the renewed motion for judgment as a matter of law is granted, the court shall also rule on the motion for a new trial, if any, by determining whether it should be granted if the judgment is thereafter vacated or reversed, and shall specify the grounds for granting or denying the motion for the new trial. If the motion for a new trial is thus conditionally granted, the order thereon does not affect the finality of the judgment. In case the motion for a new trial has been conditionally granted and the judgment is reversed on appeal, the new trial shall proceed unless the appellate court has otherwise ordered. In case the motion for a new trial has been conditionally denied, the appellee on appeal may assert error in that denial; and if the judgment is reversed on appeal, subsequent proceedings shall be in accordance with the order of the appellate court.

(2) The party against whom judgment as a matter of law has been rendered may serve a motion for a new trial pursuant to Rule 59 not later than 10 days after entry of the judgment.

(d) Same: Denial of Motion for Judgment as a Matter of Law. If the motion for judgment as a matter of law is denied, the party who prevailed on that motion may, as appellee, assert grounds entitling the party to a new trial in the event the appellate court concludes that the trial court erred in denying the motion for judgment. If the appellate court reverses the judgment, nothing in this rule precludes it from determining that the appellee is entitled to a new trial, or from directing the trial court to determine whether a new trial shall be granted. [*See* **§§5.15, 10.15.**]

(As amended Jan. 21, 1963, eff. July 1, 1963; Mar. 2, 1987, eff. Aug. 1, 1987; Apr. 30, 1991, eff. Dec. 1, 1991.)

Rule 51. Instructions to Jury: Objection

At the close of the evidence or at such earlier time during the trial as the court reasonably directs, any party may file written requests that the court instruct the jury on the law as set forth in the requests. The court shall inform counsel of its proposed action upon the requests prior to their arguments to the jury. The court, at its election, may instruct the jury before or after argument, or both. No party may assign as error the giving or the failure to give an instruction unless that party objects thereto before the jury retires to consider its verdict, stating distinctly the matter objected to and the grounds of the objection. Opportunity shall be given to make the objection out of the hearing of the jury. [*See* **§§5.03, 5.06.**]

(As amended Mar. 2, 1987, eff. Aug. 1, 1987.)

Rule 52. Findings by the Court; Judgment on Partial Findings

(a) Effect. In all actions tried upon the facts without a jury or with an advisory jury, the court shall find the facts specially and state separately its conclusions of law thereon, and judgment shall be entered pursuant to Rule 58; and in granting or refusing interlocutory injunctions the court shall similarly set forth the findings of fact and conclusions of law which constitute the grounds of its action. Requests for findings are not necessary for purposes of review. Findings of fact, whether based on oral or documentary evidence, shall not be set aside unless clearly erroneous, and due regard shall be given to the opportunity of the trial court to judge of the credibility of the witnesses. The findings of a master, to the extent that the court adopts them, shall be considered as the findings of the court. It will be sufficient if the findings of fact and conclusions of law are stated orally and recorded in open court following the close of the evidence or appear in an opinion or memorandum of decision filed by the court. Findings of fact and conclusions of law are unnecessary on decisions of motions under Rules 12 or 56 or any other motion except as provided in Rule 41(b).

(b) Amendment. Upon motion of a party made not later than 10 days after entry of judgment the court may amend its findings or make additional findings and may amend the judgment accordingly. The motion may be made with a motion for a new trial pursuant to Rule 59. When findings of fact are made in actions tried by the court without a jury, the question of the sufficiency of the evidence to support the findings may thereafter be raised whether or not the party raising the question has made in the district court an objection to such findings or has made a motion to amend them or a motion for judgment.

(c) Judgment on Partial Findings. If during a trial without a jury a party has been fully heard on an issue and the court finds against the party on that issue, the court may enter judgment as a matter of law against that party with respect to claim or defense that cannot under the controlling law be maintained or defeated without a favorable finding on that issue, or the court may decline to render any judgment until the close of all the evidence. Such a judgment shall be supported by findings of fact and conclusions of law as required by subdivision (a) of this rule. [*See* **§§5.04, 5.13, 5.15, 6.03, 9.10.**]

(As amended Dec. 27, 1946, eff. Mar. 19, 1948; Jan. 21, 1963, eff. July 1, 1963; Apr. 28, 1983, eff. Aug. 1, 1983; Apr. 29, 1985, eff. Aug. 1, 1985; Apr. 30, 1991, eff. Dec. 1 1991.)

VII. JUDGMENT

Rule 54. Judgments; Costs

(a) Definition; form "Judgment" as used in these rules includes a decree and any order from which an appeal lies. A judgment shall not contain a recital of pleadings, the report of a master, or the record of prior proceedings.

(b) Judgment upon multiple claims or involving multiple parties. When more than one claim for relief is presented in an action, whether as a claim, counterclaim, cross-claim, or third-party claim, or when multiple parties are involved, the court may direct the entry of a final judgment as to one or more but fewer than all of the claims or parties only upon an express determination that there is no just reason for delay and upon an express direction for the entry of judgment. In the absence of such determination and direction, any order or other form of decision, however designated, which adjudicates fewer than all the claims or the rights and liabilities of fewer than all the parties shall not terminate the action as to any of the claims or parties, and the order or other form of decision is subject to revision at any time before the entry of judgment adjudicating all the claims and the rights and liabilities of all the parties.

(c) Demand for Judgment. A judgment by default shall not be different in kind from or exceed in amount that prayed for in the demand for judgment. Except as to a party against whom a judgment is entered by default, every final judgment shall grant the relief to which the party in whose favor it is rendered is entitled, even if the party has not demanded such relief in the party's pleadings.

(d) Costs; Attorneys' Fees.

(1) Costs Other than Attorney's Fees. Except when express provision therefor is made either in a statute of the United States or in these rules, costs other than attorneys' fees shall be allowed as of course to the prevailing party unless the court otherwise directs; but costs against the United States, its officers, and agencies shall be imposed only to the extent permitted by law. Such costs may be taxed by the clerk on one day's notice. On motion served within 5 days thereafter, the action of the clerk may be reviewed by the court.

(2) Attorneys' Fees.

(A) Claims for attorneys' fees and related nontaxable expenses shall be made by motion unless the substantive law governing the action provides for the recovery of such fees as an element of damages to be proved at trial.

(B) Unless otherwise provided by statute or order of the court, the motion must be filed and served no later than 14 days after entry of judgment; must specify the judgment and the statute, rule, or other grounds entitling the moving party to the award; and must state the amount or provide a fair estimate of the amount sought. If directed by the court, the motion shall also disclose the terms of any agreement with respect to fees to be paid for the services for which claim is made.

(C) On request of a party or class member, the court shall afford an opportunity for adversary submissions with respect to the motion in accordance with Rule 43(e) or Rule 78. The court may determine issues of liability for fees before receiving submissions bearing on issues of evaluation of services for which liability is imposed by the court. The court shall find the facts and state its conclusions of law as provided in Rule 52(a), and a judgment shall be set forth in a separate document as provided in Rule 58.

(D) By local rule the court may establish special procedures by which issues relating to such fees may be resolved without extensive evidentiary hearings. In addition, the court may refer issues relating to the value of services to a special master under Rule 53 without regard to the provisions of subdivision (b) thereof and may refer a motion for attorneys' fees to a magistrate judge under Rule 72(b) as if it were a dispositive pretrial matter.

(E) The provisions of subparagraphs (A) through (D) do not apply to claims for fees and expenses as sanctions for violations of these rules or under 28 U.S.C. § 1927. [*See* **§§2.02, 2.06, 2.08, 2.09, 2.10, 2.14, 5.15, 6.03.**]

(As amended Dec. 27, 1946, eff. March 19, 1948; Apr. 17, 1961, eff. July 19, 1961.)

(As amended Mar. 2, 1987, eff. Aug. 1, 1987.)

Rule 58. Entry of Judgment

Subject to the provisions of Rule 54(b): (1) upon a general verdict of a jury, or upon a decision by the court that a party shall recover only a sum certain or costs or that all relief shall be denied, the clerk, unless the court otherwise orders, shall forthwith prepare, sign, and enter the judgment without awaiting any direction by the court; (2) upon a decision by the court granting other relief, or upon a special verdict or a general verdict accompanied by answers to interrogatories, the court shall promptly approve the form of the judgment, and the clerk shall thereupon enter it. Every judgment shall be set forth on a separate document. A judgment is effective only when so set forth and when entered as provided in Rule 79(a). Entry of the judgment shall not be delayed, nor the time for appeal extended, in order to tax costs or award fees, except that, when a timely motion for attorneys' fees is made under Rule 54(d)(2), the court, before a notice of appeal has been filed and has become effective, may order that the motion have the same effect under Rule 4(a)(4) of the Federal Rules of Appellate Procedure as a timely motion under Rule 59. Attorneys shall not submit forms of judgment except upon direction of the court, and these directions shall not be given as a matter of course. [*See* **§§2.02, 6.03.**]

(As amended Dec. 27, 1946, eff. Mar. 19, 1948; Jan. 21, 1963, eff. July 1, 1963.)

Rule 59. New Trials; Amendment of Judgments

(a) Grounds. A new trial may be granted to all or any of the parties and on all or part of the issues (1) in an action in which there has been a trial by jury, for any of the reasons for which new trials have heretofore been granted in actions at law in the courts of the United States; and (2) in an action tried without a jury, for any of the reasons for which rehearings have heretofore been granted in suits in equity in the courts of the United States. On a motion for a new trial in an action tried without a jury, the court may open the judgment if one has been entered, take additional testimony, amend findings of fact and conclusions of law or make new findings and conclusions, and direct the entry of a new judgment.

(b) Time for motion. A motion for a new trial shall be served not later than 10 days after the entry of the judgment.

(c) Time for serving affidavits. When a motion for new trial is based upon affidavits they shall be served with the motion. The opposing party has 10 days after such service within which to serve opposing affidavits, which period may be extended for an additional period not exceeding 20 days either by the court for good cause shown or by the parties by written stipulation. The court may permit reply affidavits.

(d) On initiative of court. Not later than 10 days after entry of judgment the court of its own initiative may order a new trial for any reason for which it might have granted a new trial on motion of a party. After giving the parties notice and an opportunity to be heard on the matter, the court may grant a motion for a new trial, timely served, for a reason not stated in the motion. In either case, the court shall specify in the order the grounds therefor.

(e) Motion to alter or amend a judgment. A motion to alter or amend the judgment shall be served not later than 10 days after entry of the judgment. [*See* **§§2.02, 5.15, 6.03.**]

(As amended Dec. 27, 1946, eff. Mar. 19, 1948; Feb. 28, 1966, eff. July 1, 1966.)

Rule 60. Relief From Judgment or Order

(a) Clerical Mistakes. Clerical mistakes in judgments, orders or other parts of the record and errors therein arising from oversight or omission may be corrected by the court at any time of its own initiative or on the motion of any party and after such notice, if any, as the court orders. During the pendency of an appeal, such mistakes may be so corrected before the appeal is docketed in the appellate court, and thereafter while the appeal is pending may be so corrected with leave of the appellate court.

(b) Mistakes; Inadvertence; Excusable Neglect; Newly Discovered Evidence; Fraud, etc. On motion and upon such terms as are just, the court may relieve a party or a party's legal representative from a final judgment, order, or proceeding for the following reasons: (1) mistake, inadvertence, surprise, or excusable neglect; (2) newly discovered evidence which by due diligence could not have been discovered in time to move for a new trial under Rule 59(b); (3) fraud (whether heretofore denominated intrinsic or extrinsic), misrepresentation, or other misconduct of an adverse party; (4) the judgment is void; (5) the judgment has been satisfied, released, or discharged, or a prior judgment upon which it is based has been reversed or otherwise vacated, or it is no longer equitable that the judgment should have prospective application; or (6) any other reason justifying relief from the operation of the judgment. The motion shall be made within a reasonable time, and for reasons (1), (2), and (3) not more than one year after the judgment, order, or proceeding was entered or taken. A motion under this subdivision (b) does not affect the finality of judgment or suspend its operation. This rule does not limit the power of a court to entertain an independent action to relieve a party from a judgment, order, or proceeding, or to grant relief to a defendant not actually personally notified as provided in Title 28, U.S.C., § 1655, or to set aside a judgment for fraud upon the court. Writs of coram nobis, coram vobis, audita querela, and bills of review and bills in the nature of a bill or review, are abolished, and the procedure for obtaining any relief from a judgment shall be by motion as prescribed in these rules or by an independent action. [*See* **§11.07.**]

Rule 61. Harmless Error

No error in either the admission or the exclusion of evidence and no error or defect in any ruling or order or in anything done or omitted by the court or by any of the parties is ground for granting a new trial or for setting aside a verdict or for vacating, modifying or otherwise disturbing a judgment or order, unless refusal to take such action appears to the court inconsistent with substantial justice. The court at every stage of the proceeding must disregard any error or defect in the proceeding which does not affect the substantial rights of the parties. [*See* **§5.03.**]

Appendix C
Federal Rules of Criminal Procedure 18 U.S.C.A. §§30, 38, 51, 52

[VIII. APPEAL] (ABROGATED DEC. 4, 1967, EFF. JULY 1, 1968)

Rule 30. Instructions

At the close of the evidence or at such earlier time during the trial as the court reasonably directs, any party may file written requests that the court instruct the jury on the law as set forth in the requests. At the same time copies of such requests shall be furnished to all parties. The court shall inform counsel of its proposed action upon the requests prior to their arguments to the jury. The court may instruct the jury before or after the arguments are completed or at both times. No party may assign as error any portion of the charge or omission therefrom unless that party objects thereto before the jury retires to consider its verdict, stating distinctly the matter to which that party objects and the grounds of the objection. Opportunity shall be given to make the objection out of the hearing of the jury and, on request of any party, out of the presence of the jury. [*See* **§5.03.**]

Rule 38. Stay of Execution

(a) Death. A sentence of death shall be stayed if an appeal is taken from the conviction or sentence.

(b) Imprisonment. A sentence of imprisonment shall be stayed if an appeal is taken from the conviction or sentence and the defendant is released pending disposition of appeal pursuant to Rule 9(b) of the Federal Rules of Appellate Procedure. If not stayed, the court may recommend to the Attorney General that the defendant be retained at, or transferred to, a place of confinement near the place of trial or the place where an appeal is to be heard, for a period reasonably necessary to permit the defendant to assist in the preparation of an appeal to the court of appeals.

(c) Fine. A sentence to pay a fine or a fine and costs, if an appeal is taken, may be stayed by the district court or by the court of appeals upon such terms as the court deems proper. The court may require the defendant pending appeal to deposit the whole or any part of the fine and costs in the registry of the district court, or to give bond for the payment thereof, or to submit to an examination of assets, and it may make any appropriate order to restrain the defendant from dissipating such defendant's assets.

(d) Probation. A sentence of probation may be stayed if an appeal from the conviction or sentence is taken. If the sentence is stayed, the court shall fix the terms of the stay.

(e) Criminal Forfeiture, Notice to Victims, and Restitution. A sanction imposed as part of the sentence pursuant to 18 U.S.C. 3554, 3555, or 3556 may, if an appeal of the conviction or sentence is taken, be stayed by the district court or by the court of appeals upon such terms as the court finds appropriate. The court may issue such orders as may be reasonably necessary to ensure compliance with the sanction upon disposition of the appeal, including the entering of a restraining order or an injunction or requiring a deposit in whole or in part of the monetary amount involved into the registry of the district court or execution of a performance bond.

(f) Disabilities. A civil or employment disability arising under a Federal statute by reason of the defendant's conviction or sentence, may, if an appeal is taken, be stayed by the district court or by the court of appeals upon such terms as the court finds appropriate. The court may enter a restraining order or an injunction, or take any other action that may be reasonably necessary to protect the interest represented by the disability pending disposition of the appeal. [*See* **§§6.11, 6.12.**]

(As amended Dec. 27, 1948, eff. Jan. 1, 1949; Feb. 28, 1966, eff. July 1, 1966; Dec. 4, 1967, eff. July 1, 1968; Apr. 24, 1972, eff. Oct. 1, 1972.)

(As amended Oct. 12, 1984, Pub.L. 98-473, Title II, § 215(c), 98 Stat. 2016; Mar. 9, 1987, eff. Aug. 1, 1987.)

RULE APPLICABLE TO OFFENSES COMMITTED PRIOR TO NOV. 1, 1987

This rule as in effect prior to amendment by Pub.L. 98-473 read as follows:

Rule 38. Stay of Execution, and Relief Pending Review

(a) Stay of Execution.

(1) Death. A sentence of death shall be stayed if an appeal is taken.

(2) Imprisonment. A sentence of imprisonment shall be stayed if an appeal is taken and the defendant is released pending disposition of appeal pursuant to Rule 9(b) of the Federal Rules of Appellate Procedure. If not stayed, the court may recommend to the Attorney General that the defendant be retained at, or transferred to, a place of confinement near the place of trial or the place where an appeal is to be heard, for a period reasonably necessary to permit the defendant to assist in the preparation of an appeal to the court of appeals.

(3) Fine. A sentence to pay a fine or a fine and costs, if an appeal is taken, may be stayed by the district court or by the court of appeals upon such terms as the court deems proper. The court may require the defendant pending

appeal to deposit the whole or any part of the fine and costs in the registry of the district court, or to give bond for the payment thereof, or to submit to an examination of assets, and it may make any appropriate order to restrain the defendant from dissipating such defendant's assets.

(4) Probation. An order placing the defendant on probation may be stayed if an appeal is taken. If not stayed, the court shall specify when the term of probation shall commence. If the order is stayed the court shall fix the terms of the stay.

[(b) Bail.] (Abrogated Dec. 4, 1967, eff. July 1, 1968)

[(c) Application for Relief Pending Review.] (Abrogated Dec. 4, 1967, eff. July 1, 1968)

For applicability of sentencing provisions to offenses, see Effective Date and Savings Provisions, etc., note, section 235 of Pub.L. 98-473, as amended, set out under section 3551 of Title 18, Crimes and Criminal Procedure.

Rule 51. Exceptions Unnecessary

Exceptions to rulings or orders of the court are unnecessary and for all purposes for which an exception has heretofore been necessary it is sufficient that a party, at the time the ruling or order of the court is made or sought, makes known to the court the action which that party desires the court to take or that party's objection to the action of the court and the grounds therefor; but if a party has no opportunity to object to a ruling or order, the absence of an objection does not thereafter prejudice that party. [*See* **§5.03.**]

(As amended Mar. 9, 1987, eff. Aug. 1, 1987.)

Rule 52. Harmless Error and Plain Error

(a) Harmless Error. Any error, defect, irregularity or variance which does not affect substantial rights shall be disregarded.

(b) Plain error. Plain errors or defects affecting substantial rights may be noticed although they were not brought to the attention of the court. [*See* **§5.03.**]

Appendix D
Crimes and Criminal Procedure 18 U.S.C.A. §§3145, 3731, 3742

18 U.S.C.A. § 3145
TITLE 18. CRIMES AND CRIMINAL PROCEDURE
PART II—CRIMINAL PROCEDURE
CHAPTER 235—APPEAL

§ 3145. Review and appeal of a release or detention order

(a) Review of a release order. If a person is ordered released by a magistrate, or by a person other than a judge of a court having original jurisdiction over the offense and other than a Federal appellate court—

(1) the attorney for the Government may file, with the court having original jurisdiction over the offense, a motion for revocation of the order or amendment of the conditions of release; and

(2) the person may file, with the court having original jurisdiction over the offense, a motion for amendment of the conditions of release.

The motion shall be determined promptly.

(b) Review of a detention order. If a person is ordered detained by a magistrate, or by a person other than a judge of a court having original jurisdiction over the offense and other than a Federal appellate court, the person may file, with the court having original jurisdiction over the offense, a motion for revocation or amendment of the order. The motion shall be determined promptly.

(c) Appeal from a release or detention order. An appeal from a release or detention order, or from a decision denying revocation or amendment of such an order, is governed by the provisions of section 1291 of title 28 [28 USCS § 1291] and section 3731 of this title [18 USCS § 3731]. The appeal shall be determined promptly. A person subject to detention pursuant to section 3143(a)(2) or (b)(2), and who meets the conditions of release set forth in section 3143(a)(1) or (b)(1), may be ordered released, under appropriate conditions, by the judicial officer, if it is clearly shown that there are exceptional reasons why such person's detention would not be appropriate. [*See* **§2.11.**]

(Added Oct. 12, 1984, P.L. 98-473, Title II, ch I, § 203(a) in part, 98 Stat. 1976; Nov. 29, 1990, P.L. 101-647, Title IX, § 902(c), 104 Stat. 4827.)

18 U.S.C.A. § 3731
TITLE 18. CRIMES AND CRIMINAL PROCEDURE
PART II—CRIMINAL PROCEDURE
CHAPTER 235—APPEAL

§ 3731. Appeal by United States

In a criminal case an appeal by the United States shall lie to a court of appeals from a decision, judgment, or order of a district court dismissing an indictment or information or granting a new trial after verdict or judgment, as to any one or more counts, except that no appeal shall lie where the double jeopardy clause of the United States Constitution prohibits further prosecution.

An appeal by the United States shall lie to a court of appeals from a decision or order of a district courts (sic) suppressing or excluding evidence or requiring the return of seized property in a criminal proceeding, not made after the defendant has been put in jeopardy and before the verdict or finding on an indictment or information, if the United States attorney certifies to the district court that the appeal is not taken for purpose of delay and that the evidence is a substantial proof of a fact material in the proceeding.

An appeal by the United States shall lie to a court of appeals from a decision or order, entered by a district court of the United States, granting the release of a person charged with or convicted of an offense, or denying a motion for revocation of, or modification of the conditions of, a decision or order granting release.

The appeal in all such cases shall be taken within thirty days after the decision, judgment or order has been rendered and shall be diligently prosecuted.

The provisions of this section shall be liberally construed to effectuate its purposes. [*See* **§§2.05, 2.11, 3.12.**]

(June 25, 1948, c. 645, 62 Stat. 844; May 24, 1949, c. 139, § 58, 63 Stat. 97; June 19, 1968, Pub.L. 90-351, Title VIII, § 1301, 82 Stat. 237; Jan. 2, 1971, Pub.L. 91-644, Title III, § 14(a), 84 Stat. 1890; Oct. 12, 1984, Pub.L. 98-473, Title II, §§ 205, 1206, 98 Stat. 1986, 2153.)

(As amended Pub.L. 99-646, § 32, Nov. 10, 1986, 100 Stat. 3598.)

18 U.S.C.A. § 3742
TITLE 18. CRIMES AND CRIMINAL PROCEDURE
PART II—CRIMINAL PROCEDURE
CHAPTER 235—APPEAL

§ 3742. Review of a sentence

(a) Appeal by a defendant.—A defendant may file a notice of appeal in the district court for review of an otherwise final sentence if the sentence—

(1) was imposed in violation of law;

(2) was imposed as a result of an incorrect application of the sentencing guidelines; or

(3) is greater than the sentence specified in the applicable guideline range to the extent that the sentence includes a greater fine or term of imprisonment,

probation, or supervised release than the maximum established in the guideline range, or includes a more limiting condition of probation or supervised release under section 3563(b)(6) or (b)(11) than the maximum established in the guideline range; or

(4) was imposed for an offense for which there is no sentencing guideline and is plainly unreasonable.

(b) Appeal by the Government.—The Government, may file a notice of appeal in the district court for review of an otherwise final sentence if the sentence—

(1) was imposed in violation of law;

(2) was imposed as a result of an incorrect application of the sentencing guidelines;

(3) is less than the sentence specified in the applicable guideline range to the extent that the sentence includes a lesser fine or term of imprisonment, probation, or supervised release than the minimum established in the guideline range, or includes a less limiting condition of probation or supervised release under section 3563(b)(6) or (b)(11) than the minimum established in the guideline range; or

(4) was imposed for an offense for which there is no sentencing guideline and is plainly unreasonable.

The Government may not further prosecute such appeal without the personal approval of the Attorney General, the Solicitor General, or a deputy solicitor general designated by the Solicitor General.

(c) Plea agreements.—In the case of a plea agreement that includes a specific sentence under rule 11(e)(1)(C) of the Federal Rules of Criminal Procedure—

(1) a defendant may not file a notice of appeal under paragraph (3) or (4) of subsection (a) unless the sentence imposed is greater than the sentence set forth in such agreement; and

(2) the Government may not file a notice of appeal under paragraph (3) or (4) of subsection (b) unless the sentence imposed is less than the sentence set forth in such agreement.

(d) Record on review.—If a notice of appeal is filed in the district court pursuant to subsection (a) or (b), the clerk shall certify to the court of appeals—

(1) that portion of the record in the case that is designated as pertinent by either of the parties;

(2) the presentence report; and

(3) the information submitted during the sentencing proceeding.

(e) Consideration.—Upon review of the record, the court of appeals shall determine whether the sentence—

(1) was imposed in violation of law;

(2) was imposed as a result of an incorrect application of the sentencing guidelines;

(3) is outside the applicable guideline range, and is unreasonable, having regard for—

(A) the factors to be considered in imposing a sentence, as set forth in chapter 227 of this title; and

(B) the reasons for the imposition of the particular sentence, as stated by the district court pursuant to the provisions of section 3553(c); or

(4) was imposed for an offense for which there is no applicable sentencing guideline and is plainly unreasonable.

The court of appeals shall give due regard to the opportunity of the district court to judge the credibility of the witnesses, and shall accept the findings of fact of the district court unless they are clearly erroneous and shall give due deference to the district court's application of the guidelines to the facts.

(f) Decision and disposition

If the court of appeals determines that the sentence—

(1) was imposed in violation of law or imposed as a result of an incorrect application of the sentencing guidelines, the court shall remand the case for further sentencing proceedings with such instructions as the court considers appropriate;

(2) is outside the applicable guideline range and is unreasonable or was imposed for an offense for which there is no applicable sentencing guideline and is plainly unreasonable, it shall state specific reasons for its conclusions and—

(A) if it determines that the sentence is too high and the appeal has been filed under subsection (a), it shall set aside the sentence and remand the case for further sentencing proceedings with such instructions as the court considers appropriate;

(B) if it determines that the sentence is too low and the appeal has been filed under subsection (b), it shall set aside the sentence and remand the case for further sentencing proceedings with such instructions as the court considers appropriate;

(3) is not described in paragraph (1) or (2), it shall affirm the sentence.

(g) Application to a sentence by a magistrate.—An appeal of an otherwise final sentence imposed by a United States magistrate may be taken to a judge of the district court, and this section shall apply (except for the requirement of approval by the Attorney General or the Solicitor General in the case of a Government appeal) as though the appeal were to a court of appeals from a sentence imposed by a district court.

(h) Guideline not expressed as a range.—For the purpose of this section, the term "guideline range" includes a guideline range having the same upper and lower limits. [*See* **§§2.03, 2.11.**]

(Added Pub.L. 98-473, Title II, § 213(a), Oct. 12, 1984, 98 Stat. 2011.)

(As amended Pub.L. 99-646, § 73(a), Nov. 10, 1986, 100 Stat. 3617; Pub.L. 100- 182, §§ 4 to 6, Dec. 7, 1987, 101 Stat. 1266, 1267; Pub.L. 100-690, Title VII, § 7103(a), Nov. 18, 1988, 102 Stat. 4416, 4417; Pub.L. 101-647, Title XXXV, §§ 3501, 3503, Nov. 29, 1990, 104 Stat. 4921.)

Appendix E Judiciary and Judicial Procedure 28 U.S.C.A. §§1291, 1292, 1295, 1651, 1915, 2106, 2107, 2112

28 U.S.C.A. § 1291
TITLE 28. JUDICIARY AND JUDICIAL PROCEDURE
PART IV—JURISDICTION AND VENUE
CHAPTER 83—COURTS OF APPEALS

§ 1291. Final decisions of district courts

The courts of appeals (other than the United States Court of Appeals for the Federal Circuit) shall have jurisdiction of appeals from all final decisions of the district courts of the United States, the United States District Court for the District of the Canal Zone, the District Court of Guam, and the District Court of the Virgin Islands, except where a direct review may be had in the Supreme Court. The jurisdiction of the United States Court of Appeals for the Federal Circuit shall be limited to the jurisdiction described in sections 1292(c) and (d) and 1295 of this title. [*See* **§§2.01, 2.02, 2.04, 2.05, 2.06, 2.07, 2.08, 2.09, 2.10, 2.11, 2.13, 2.14, 2.15, 3.04, 3.08, 3.16, 4.14, 6.06, 8.01, 9.09.**]

(June 25, 1948, c. 646, 62 Stat. 929; Oct. 31, 1951, c. 655, § 48, 65 Stat. 726; July 7, 1958, Pub.L. 85-508, § 12(e), 72 Stat. 348.)

(As amended Apr. 2, 1982, Pub.L. 97-164, Title I, § 124, 96 Stat. 36.)

28 U.S.C.A. § 1292
TITLE 28. JUDICIARY AND JUDICIAL PROCEDURE
PART IV—JURISDICTION AND VENUE
CHAPTER 83—COURTS OF APPEALS

§ 1292. Interlocutory decisions

(a) Except as provided in subsections (c) and (d) of this section, the courts of appeals shall have jurisdiction of appeals from:

(1) Interlocutory orders of the district courts of the United States, the United States District Court for the District of the Canal Zone, the District Court of Guam, and the District Court of the Virgin Islands, or of the judges

thereof, granting, continuing, modifying, refusing or dissolving injunctions, or refusing to dissolve or modify injunctions, except where a direct review may be had in the Supreme Court;

(2) Interlocutory orders appointing receivers, or refusing orders to wind up receiverships or to take steps to accomplish the purposes thereof, such as directing sales or other disposals of property;

(3) Interlocutory decrees of such district courts or the judges thereof determining the rights and liabilities of the parties to admiralty cases in which appeals from final decrees are allowed.

[(4) Repealed. Pub.L. 97-164, Title I, § 125(a) (3), Apr. 2, 1982, 96 Stat. 36]

(b) When a district judge, in making in a civil action an order not otherwise appealable under this section, shall be of the opinion that such order involves a controlling question of law as to which there is substantial ground for difference of opinion and that an immediate appeal from the order may materially advance the ultimate termination of the litigation, he shall so state in writing in such order. The Court of Appeals which would have jurisdiction of an appeal of such action may thereupon, in its discretion, permit an appeal to be taken from such order, if application is made to it within ten days after the entry of the order: Provided, however, That application for an appeal hereunder shall not stay proceedings in the district court unless the district judge or the Court of Appeals or a judge thereof shall so order.

(c) The United States Court of Appeals for the Federal Circuit shall have exclusive jurisdiction—

(1) of an appeal from an interlocutory order or decree described in subsection (a) or (b) of this section in any case over which the court would have jurisdiction of an appeal under section 1295 of this title; and

(2) of an appeal from a judgment in a civil action for patent infringement which would otherwise be appealable to the United States Court of Appeals for the Federal Circuit and is final except for an accounting.

(d) (1) When the chief judge of the Court of International Trade issues an order under the provisions of section 256(b) of this title, or when any judge of the Court of International Trade, in issuing any other interlocutory order, includes in the order a statement that a controlling question of law is involved with respect to which there is a substantial ground for difference of opinion and that an immediate appeal from that order may materially advance the ultimate termination of the litigation, the United States Court of Appeals for the Federal Circuit may, in its discretion, permit an appeal to be taken from such order, if application is made to that Court within ten days after the entry of such order.

(2) When the chief judge of the United States Court of Federal Claims issues an order under section 798(b) of this title, or when any judge of the United States Claims Court, in issuing interlocutory order, includes in the order a statement that a controlling question of law is involved with respect to which there is a substantial ground for difference of opinion and that an immediate appeal from that order may materially advance the ultimate termination of the litigation, the United States Court of Appeals for the Federal Circuit

may, in its discretion, permit an appeal to be taken from such order, if application is made to that Court within ten days after the entry of such order.

(3) Neither the application for nor the granting of an appeal under this subsection shall stay proceedings in the Court of International Trade or in the Claims Court, as the case may be, unless a stay is ordered by a judge of the Court of International Trade or of the Claims Court or by the United States Court of Appeals for the Federal Circuit or a judge of that court.

(4) (A) The United States Court of Appeals for the Federal Circuit shall have exclusive jurisdiction of an appeal from an interlocutory order of a district court of the United States, the District Court of Guam, the District Court of the Virgin Islands, or the District Court for the Northern Mariana Islands, granting or denying, in whole or in part, a motion to transfer an action to the United States Claims Court under section 1631 of this title.

(B) When a motion to transfer an action to the Claims Court is filed in a district court, no further proceedings shall be taken in the district court until 60 days after the court has ruled upon the motion. If an appeal is taken from the district court's grant or denial of the motion, proceedings shall be further stayed until the appeal has been decided by the Court of Appeals for the Federal Circuit. The stay of proceedings in the district court shall not bar the granting of preliminary or injunctive relief, where appropriate and where expedition is reasonably necessary. However, during the period in which proceedings are stayed as provided in this subparagraph, no transfer to the Claims Court pursuant to the motion shall be carried out.

(e) The Supreme Court may prescribe rules, in accordance with section 2072 of this title, to provide for an appeal of an interlocutory decision to the courts of appeals that is not otherwise provided for under subsection (a), (b), (c), or (d). [*See* **§§2.02, 2.04, 2.06, 2.07, 2.08, 2.09, 2.10, 2.12, 2.13, 2.14, 2.17, 3.04, 3.07, 3.08, 4.14, 5.15, 6.05, 8.01.**]

(June 25, 1948, c. 646, 62 Stat. 929; Oct. 31, 1951, c. 655, § 49, 65 Stat. 726; July 7, 1958, Pub.L. 85-508, § 12(e), 72 Stat. 348; Sept. 2, 1958, Pub.L. 85-919, 72 Stat. 1770.)

(As amended Apr. 2, 1982, Pub.L. 97-164, Title I, § 125, 96 Stat. 36; Nov. 8, 1984, Pub.L. 98-620, Title IV, § 412, 98 Stat. 3362; Nov. 19, 1988, Pub.L. 100-702, Title V, § 501, 102 Stat. 4652; Oct. 29, 1992, Pub.L. 102-572, Title I, § 101, Title IX, § 906(c), 106 Stat. 4506, 4518.)

28 U.S.C.A. § 1294
TITLE 28. JUDICIARY AND JUDICIAL PROCEDURE
PART IV—JURISDICTION AND VENUE
CHAPTER 83—COURTS OF APPEALS

§ 1294. Circuits in which decisions reviewable

Except as provided in sections 1292(c), 1292(d), and 1295 of this title, appeals from reviewable decisions of the district and territorial courts shall be taken to the courts of appeals as follows:

(1) From a district court of the United States to the court of appeals for the circuit embracing the district;

(2) From the United States District Court for the District of the Canal Zone, to the Court of Appeals for the Fifth Circuit;

(3) From the District Court of the Virgin Islands, to the Court of Appeals for the Third Circuit;

(4) From the District Court of Guam, to the Court of Appeals for the Ninth Circuit. [*See* **§4.01.**]

(June 25, 1948, c. 646, 62 Stat. 930; Oct. 31, 1951, c. 655, § 50(a), 65 Stat. 727; July 7, 1958, Pub.L. 85-508, § 12(g), 72 Stat. 348; Mar. 18, 1959, Pub.L. 86-3, § 14(c), 73 Stat. 10; Aug. 30, 1961, Pub.L. 87-189, § 5, 75 Stat. 417.)

(As amended Apr. 2, 1982, Pub.L. 97-164, Title I, § 126, 96 Stat. 37.)

28 U.S.C.A. § 1295
TITLE 28. JUDICIARY AND JUDICIAL PROCEDURE
PART IV—JURISDICTION AND VENUE
CHAPTER 83—COURTS OF APPEALS

§ 1295. Jurisdiction of the United States Court of Appeals for the Federal Circuit

(a) The United States Court of Appeals for the Federal Circuit shall have exclusive jurisdiction—

(1) of an appeal from a final decision of a district court of the United States, the United States District Court for the District of the Canal Zone, the District Court of Guam, the District Court of the Virgin Islands, or the District Court for the Northern Mariana Islands, if the jurisdiction of that court was based, in whole or in part, on section 1338 of this title, except that a case involving a claim arising under any Act of Congress relating to copyrights, exclusive rights in mask works, or trademarks and no other claims under section 1338(a) shall be governed by sections 1291, 1292, and 1294 of this title;

(2) of an appeal from a final decision of a district court of the United States, the United States District Court for the District of the Canal Zone, the District Court of Guam, the District Court of the Virgin Islands, or the District Court for the Northern Mariana Islands, if the jurisdiction of that court was based, in whole or in part, on section 1346 of this title, except that jurisdiction of an appeal in a case brought in a district court under section 1346(a) (1), 1346(b), 1346(e), or 1346(f) of this title or under section 1346(a) (2) when the claim is founded upon an Act of Congress or a regulation of an executive department providing for internal revenue shall be governed by sections 1291, 1292, and 1294 of this title;

(3) of an appeal from a final decision of the United States Claims Court;

(4) of an appeal from a decision of—

(A) the Board of Patent Appeals and

Interferences of the Patent and Trademark Office with respect to patent applications and interferences, at the instance of an applicant for a patent or any party to a patent interference, and any such appeal shall waive the right of such applicant or party to proceed under section 145 or 146 of title 35;

(B) the Commissioner of Patents and Trademarks or the Trademark Trial and Appeal Board with respect to applications for registration of marks and other proceedings as provided in section 21 of the Trademark Act of 1946 (15 U.S.C. 1071); or

(C) a district court to which a case was directed pursuant to section 145 or 146 of title 35;

(5) of an appeal from a final decision of the United States Court of International Trade;

(6) to review the final determinations of the United States International Trade Commission relating to unfair practices in import trade, made under section 337 of the Tariff Act of 1930 (19 U.S.C. 1337);

(7) to review, by appeal on questions of law only, findings of the Secretary of Commerce under U.S. note 6 to subchapter X of chapter 98 of the Harmonized Tariff Schedule of the United States (relating to importation of instruments or apparatus);

(8) of an appeal under section 71 of the Plant Variety Protection Act (7 U.S.C. 2461);

(9) of an appeal from a final order or final decision of the Merit Systems Protection Board, pursuant to sections 7703(b) (1) and 7703(d) of title 5;

(10) of an appeal from a final decision of an agency board of contract appeals pursuant to section 8(g) (1) of the Contract Disputes Act of 1978 (41 U.S.C. 607(g) (1));

(11) of an appeal under section 211 of the Economic Stabilization Act of 1970;

(12) of an appeal under section 5 of the Emergence Petroleum Allocation Act of 1973;

(13) of an appeal under section 506(c) of the Natural Gal Policy Act of 1978; and

(14) of an appeal under section 523 of the Energy Policy and Conservation Act.

(b) The head of any executive department or agency may, with the approval of the Attorney General, refer to the Court of Appeals for the Federal Circuit for judicial review any final decision rendered by a board of contract appeals pursuant to the terms of any contract with the United States awarded by that department or agency which the head of such department or agency has concluded is not entitled to finality pursuant to the review standards specified in section 10(b) of the Contract Disputes Act of 1978 (41 U.S.C. 609(b)). The head of each executive department or agency shall make any referral under this section within one hundred and twenty days after the receipt of a copy of the final appeal decision.

(c) The Court of Appeals for the Federal Circuit shall review the matter referred in accordance with the standards specified in section 10(b) of the Contract Disputes Act of 1978. The court shall proceed with judicial review on the administrative record made before the board of contract appeals on matters so referred as in other cases pending in such court, shall determine the issue of finality of the appeal decision, and shall, if appropriate, render judgment thereon, or remand the matter to any administrative or executive body or official with such direction as it may deem proper and just. [*See* **§§2.02, 2.12, 4.14.**]

(Added Pub.L. 97-164, Title I, § 127(a), Apr. 2, 1982, 96 Stat. 37, and amended Pub.L. 98-622, Title II, § 205(a), Nov. 8, 1984, 98 Stat. 3388; Pub.L. 100-418, Title I, § 1214(a)(3), Aug. 23, 1988, 102 Stat. 1156; Pub.L. 100-702, Title X, § 1020(a)(3), Nov. 19, 1988, 102 Stat. 4671; Pub.L. 102-572, Title I, § 102(c), Oct. 29, 1992, 106 Stat. 4507.)

28 U.S.C.A. § 1651
TITLE 28. JUDICIARY AND JUDICIAL PROCEDURE
PART V—PROCEDURE
CHAPTER 111—GENERAL PROVISIONS

§ 1651. Writs

(a) The Supreme Court and all courts established by Act of Congress may issue all writs necessary or appropriate in aid of their respective jurisdictions and agreeable to the usages and principles of law.

(b) An alternative writ or rule nisi may be issued by a justice or judge of a court which has jurisdiction. [*See* **§§3.01, 3.05, 6.09.**]

(June 25, 1948, c. 646, 62 Stat. 944; May 24, 1949, c. 139, § 90, 63 Stat. 102.)

28 U.S.C.A. § 1915
TITLE 28. JUDICIARY AND JUDICIAL PROCEDURE
PART V—PROCEDURE
CHAPTER 123—FEES AND COSTS

§ 1915. Proceedings in forma pauperis

(a) Any court of the United States may authorize the commencement, prosecution or defense of any suit, action or proceeding, civil or criminal, or appeal therein, without prepayment of fees and costs or security therefor, by a person who makes affidavit that he is unable to pay such costs or give security therefor. Such affidavit shall state the nature of the action, defense or appeal and affiant's belief that he is entitled to redress.

An appeal may not be taken in forma pauperis if the trial court certifies in writing that it is not taken in good faith.

(b) Upon filing of an affidavit in accordance with subsection (a) of this section, the court may direct payment by the United States of the expenses of (1) printing the record on appeal in any civil or criminal case, if such printing is required by the appellate court; (2) preparing a transcript of proceedings before a United States magistrate in any civil or criminal case, if such transcript is required by the district court, in the case of proceedings conducted under section 636(b) of this title or under 340(b) of title 18, United States Code; and (3) printing the record on appeal if such printing is required by the appellate court, in the case of proceedings conducted pursuant to section 636(c) of this title. Such expenses shall be paid when authorized by the Director of the Administrative Office of the United States Courts.

(c) The officers of the court shall issue and serve all process, and perform all duties in such cases. Witnesses shall attend as in other cases, and the same remedies shall be available as are provided for by law in other cases.

(d) The court may request an attorney to represent any such person unable to employ counsel and may dismiss the case if the allegation of poverty is untrue, or if satisfied that the action is frivolous or malicious.

(e) Judgment may be rendered for costs at the conclusion of the suit or action as in other cases, but the United States shall not be liable for any of the costs thus incurred. If the United States has paid the cost of a stenographic transcript or printed record for the prevailing party, the same shall be taxed in favor of the United States. [*See* **§6.15.**]

(As amended May 24, 1949, c. 139, § 98, 63 Stat. 104; Oct. 31, 1951, c. 655, § 51(b,c), 65 Stat. 727; Sept. 21, 1959, Pub. L. 86-320, 73 Stat. 590; Oct. 10, 1979, Pub.L. 96-82, § 6, 93 Stat. 645.)

28 U.S.C.A. § 2106
TITLE 28. JUDICIARY AND JUDICIAL PROCEDURE
PART V—PROCEDURE
CHAPTER 133—REVIEW—MISCELLANEOUS PROVISIONS

§ 2106. Determination

The Supreme Court or any other court of appellate jurisdiction may affirm, modify, vacate, set aside or reverse any judgment, decree, or order of a court lawfully brought before it for review, and may remand the cause and direct the entry of such appropriate judgment, decree, or order, or require such further proceedings to be had as may be just under the circumstances. [*See* **§10.15.**]

(June 25, 1948, c. 646, 62 Stat. 963.)

28 U.S.C.A. § 2107
TITLE 28. JUDICIARY AND JUDICIAL PROCEDURE
PART V—PROCEDURE
CHAPTER 133—REVIEW—MISCELLANEOUS PROVISIONS

§ 2107. Time for appeal to court of appeals

(a) Except as otherwise provided in this section, no appeal shall bring any judgment, order or decree in an action, suit or proceeding of a civil nature before a court of appeals for review unless notice of appeal is filed, within thirty days after the entry of such judgment, order or decree.

(b) In any such action, suit or proceeding in which the United States or an officer or agency thereof is a party, the time as to all parties shall be sixty days from such entry.

(c) The district court may, upon motion filed not later than 30 days after the expiration of the time otherwise set for bringing appeal, extend the time for appeal upon a showing of excusable neglect or good cause. In addition, if the district court finds—

(1) that a party entitled to notice of the entry of a judgment or order did not receive such notice from the clerk or any party within 21 days of its entry, and

(2) that no party would be prejudiced, the district court may, upon motion filed within 180 days after entry of the judgment or order within 7 days after receipt of such notice, whichever is earlier, reopen the time for appeal for a period of 14 days from the date of entry of the order reopening the time for appeal.

(d) This section shall not apply to bankruptcy matters or other proceedings under Title 11. [*See* **§6.03.**]

(June 25, 1948, c. 646, 62 Stat. 963; May 24, 1949, c. 139, §§ 107, 108, 63 Stat. 104; Dec. 9, 1991, Pub.L. 102-198, § 12, 105 Stat. 1627.)

28 U.S.C.A. § 2112
TITLE 28. JUDICIARY AND JUDICIAL PROCEDURE
PART V—PROCEDURE
CHAPTER 133—REVIEW—MISCELLANEOUS PROVISIONS

§ 2112. Record on review and enforcement of agency orders

(a) The rules prescribed under the authority of section 2072 of this title may provide for the time and manner of filing and the contents of the record in all proceedings instituted in the courts of appeals to enjoin, set aside, suspend, modify, or otherwise review or enforce orders of administrative agencies, boards, commissions, and officers. Such rules may authorize the agency, board, commission, or officer to file in the court a certified list of the materials comprising the record and retain and hold for the court all such materials and transmit the same or any part thereof to the court, when and as required by it, at any time prior to the final determination of the proceeding, and such filing of such certified list of the materials comprising the record and such subsequent transmittal of any such materials when and as required shall be deemed full compliance with any provision of law requiring the filing of the record in the court. The record in such proceedings shall be certified and filed in or held for and transmitted to the court of appeals by the agency, board, commission, or officer concerned within the time and in the manner prescribed by such rules. If proceedings are instituted in two or more courts of appeals with respect to the same order, the following shall apply:

(1) If within ten days after issuance of the order the agency, board, commission, or officer concerned receives, from the persons instituting the proceedings, the petition for review with respect to proceedings in at least two courts of appeals, the agency, board, commission, or officer shall proceed in accordance with paragraph (3) of this subsection. If within ten days after the issuance

of the order the agency, board, commission, or officer concerned receives, from the persons instituting the proceedings, the petition for review with respect to proceedings in only one court of appeals, the agency, board, commission, or officer shall file the record in that court notwithstanding the institution in any other court of appeals of proceedings for review of that order. In all other cases in which proceedings have been instituted in two or more courts of appeals with respect to the same order, the agency, board, commission, or officer concerned shall file the record in the court in which proceedings with respect to the order were first instituted.

(2) For purposes of paragraph (1) of this subsection, a copy of the petition or other pleading which institutes proceedings in a court of appeals and which is stamped by the court with the date of filing shall constitute the petition for review. Each agency, board, commission, or officer, as the case may be, shall designate by rule the office and the officer who must receive petitions for review under paragraph (1).

(3) If an agency, board, commission, or officer receives two or more petitions for review of an order in accordance with the first sentence of paragraph (1) of this subsection, the agency, board, commission, or officer shall, promptly after the expiration of the ten-day period specified in that sentence, so notify the judicial panel on multidistrict litigation authorized by section 1407 of this title, in such form as that panel shall prescribe.

The judicial panel on multidistrict litigation shall, by means of random selection, designate one court of appeals, from among the courts of appeals in which petitions for review have been filed and received within the ten-day period specified in the first sentence of paragraph (1), in which the record is to be filed, and shall issue an order consolidating the petitions for review in that court of appeals. The judicial panel on multidistrict litigation shall, after providing notice to the public and an opportunity for the submission of comments, prescribe rules with respect to the consolidation of proceedings under this paragraph. The agency, board, commission, or officer concerned shall file the record in the court of appeals designated pursuant to this paragraph.

(4) Any court of appeals in which proceedings with respect to an order of an agency, board, commission, or officer have been instituted may, to the extent authorized by law, stay the effective date of the order. Any such stay may thereafter be modified, revoked, or extended by a court of appeals designated pursuant to paragraph (3) with respect to that order or by any other court of appeals to which the proceedings are transferred.

(5) All courts in which proceedings are instituted with respect to the same order, other than the court in which the record is filed pursuant to this subsection, shall transfer those proceedings to the court in which the record is so filed. For the convenience of the parties in the interest of justice, the court in which the record is filed may thereafter transfer all the proceedings with respect to that order to any other court of appeals.

(b) The record to be filed in the court of appeals in such a proceeding shall consist of the order sought to be reviewed or enforced, the findings or report upon which it is based, and the pleadings, evidence, and proceedings before the agency, board, commission, or officer concerned, or such portions thereof

(1) as the rules prescribed under the authority of section 2072 of this title may require to be included therein, or (2) as the agency, board, commission, or officer concerned, the petitioner for review or respondent in enforcement, as the case may be, and any intervenor in the court proceeding by written stipulation filed with the agency, board, commission, or officer concerned or in the court in any such proceeding may consistently with the rules prescribed under the authority of section 2072 of this title designate to be included therein, or (3) as the court upon motion of a party or, after a prehearing conference, upon its own motion may by order in any such proceeding designate to be included therein. Such a stipulation or order may provide in an appropriate case that no record need be filed in the court of appeals. If, however, the correctness of a finding of fact by the agency, board, commission, or officer is in question all of the evidence before the agency, board, commission, or officer shall be included in the record except such as the agency, board, commission, or officer concerned, the petitioner for review or respondent in enforcement, as the case may be, and any intervenor in the court proceeding by written stipulation filed with the agency, board, commission, or officer concerned or in the court agree to omit as wholly immaterial to the questioned finding. If there is omitted from the record any portion of the proceedings before the agency, board, commission, or officer which the court subsequently determines to be proper for it to consider to enable it to review or enforce the order in question the court may direct that such additional portion of the proceedings be filed as a supplement to the record. The agency, board, commission, or officer concerned may, at its option and without regard to the foregoing provisions of this subsection, and if so requested by the petitioner for review or respondent in enforcement shall, file in the court the entire record of the proceedings before it without abbreviation.

(c) The agency, board, commission, or officer concerned may transmit to the court of appeals the original papers comprising the whole or any part of the record or any supplemental record, otherwise true copies of such papers certified by an authorized officer or deputy of the agency, board, commission, or officer concerned shall be transmitted. Any original papers thus transmitted to the court of appeals shall be returned to the agency, board, commission, or officer concerned upon the final determination of the review or enforcement proceeding. Pending such final determination any such papers may be returned by the court temporarily to the custody of the agency, board, commission, or officer concerned if needed for the transaction of the public business. Certified copies of any papers included in the record or any supplemental record may also be returned to the agency, board, commission, or officer concerned upon the final determination of review or enforcement proceedings.

(d) The provisions of this section are not applicable to proceedings to review decisions of the Tax Court of the United States or to proceedings to review or enforce those orders of administrative agencies, boards, commissions, or officers which are by law reviewable or enforceable by the district courts. [*See* **§§6.09, 8.01.**]

(Added Pub.L. 85-791, § 2, Aug. 28, 1958, 72 Stat. 941, and amended Pub.L. 89- 773, § 5(a), (b), Nov. 6, 1966, 80 Stat. 1323.)

(As amended Pub.L. 100-236, § 1, Jan. 8, 1988, 101 Stat. 1731.)

Cases

A

Abatti v Commissioner, 859 F2d 115 (9th Cir 1988) **§2.13**

Abbott Labs v Gardner, 387 US 136 (1967), *overruled on other grounds sub nom* Califano v Sanders, 430 US 99 (1977) **§2.16**

Abbs v Sullivan, 963 F2d 918 (7th Cir 1992) **§2.16**

Abdallah, *In re,* 778 F2d 75 (1st Cir 1985), *cert denied,* 476 US 1116 (1986) **§2.14**

Abel v Miller, 904 F2d 294 (7th Cir 1990) **§2.04**

Abercrombie v City of Catoosa, 896 F2d 1228 (10th Cir 1990) **§1.06**

Abney v United States, 431 US 651 (1977) **§§2.05, 2.17**

Acosta v Louisiana Dept of Health & Human Resources, 478 US 251 (1986) **§6.03**

Adams, *In re,* 809 F2d 1187 (5th Cir 1987) **§2.15**

Admiral Ins Co v United States Dist Court, 881 F2d 1486 (9th Cir 1989) **§3.06**

Aerojet-General Corp v Machine Tool Works, 895 F2d 736 (Fed Cir 1990) **§4.14**

Aetna Casualty & Sur Co v Cunningham, 224 F2d 478 (5th Cir 1955) **§2.02**

Aetna Life Ins Co v Alla Medical Servs, 855 F2d 1470 (9th Cir 1988) **§§2.04, 6.02**

Afram Lines Intl, Inc v M/V Capetan Yiannis, 905 F2d 347 (11th Cir 1990) **§2.08**

Air Crash at Dallas/Fort Worth Airport on Aug 22, 1985, *In re,* 852 F2d 842 (5th Cir 1988) **§6.03**

Air Line Pilots Assn, Intl v UAL Corp, 897 F2d 1394 (7th Cir 1990) **§§2.18, 5.16**

AJ Indus v United States Dist Court, 503 F2d 384 (9th Cir 1974) **§3.07**

Alabama v EPA, 871 F2d 1548 (11th Cir 1989) **§6.03**

Alabama Power Co v Interstate Commerce Commn, 852 F2d 1361 (DC Cir 1988) **§2.19**

B

C

D

E

F

G

H

Hanna v Plumer, 380 US 460 (1965) **§2.02**

Harkins Amusement Enter v General Cinema Corp, 850 F2d 477 (9th Cir 1988), *cert denied,* 488 US 1019 (1989) **§6.14**

Hardie v Cotter & Co, 819 F2d 181 (8th Cir 1987) **§2.10**

Harlow v Fitzgerald, 457 US 800 (1982) **§2.04**

Harris v Board of Governors, 938 F2d 720 (7th Cir 1991) **§2.18**

Harris Truck Lines v Cherry Meat Packers, Inc, 371 US 215 (1962) **§6.03**

Harte-Hanks Communications, Inc v Connaughton, 491 US 657 (1989) **§5.13**

Hartford Fin Sys v Florida Software Servs, 712 F2d 724 (1st Cir 1983) **§2.02**

Hatchell v Heckler, 708 F2d 578 (11th Cir 1983) **§6.15**

Hattaway v McMillian, 903 F2d 1440 (11th Cir 1990) **§2.02**

Hawaii-Pacific Venture Capital Corp v Rothbard, 564 F2d 1343 (9th Cir 1977) **§2.02**

Hazel-Atlas Glass Co v Hartford-Empire Co, 322 US 238 (1944) **§§5.02, 11.07**

Heat & Control, Inc v Hester Indus, 785 F2d 1017 (Fed Cir 1986) **§§2.02, 2.04, 2.12, 4.14**

Helstoski v Meanor, 442 US 500 (1979) **§§2.05, 3.04, 8.01**

Helton v Clements, 787 F2d 1016 (5th Cir 1986) **§2.04**

Henco, Inc v Brown, 904 F2d 11 (7th Cir 1990) **§§2.06, 2.18**

Henderson v Kibbe, 431 US 145 (1977) **§5.08**

Henry v Independent Am Sav Assn, 857 F2d 995 (5th Cir 1988) **§6.03**

Her Majesty the Queen in Right of Ontario v United States EPA, 912 F2d 1525 (DC Cir 1990) **§2.16**

Herring v New York, 422 US 853 (1975) **§5.06**

Herzog Contracting Corp v McGowen Corp, 976 F2d 1062 (7th Cir 1992) **§6.03**

Hicks v Miranda, 422 US 332 (1975) **§11.04**

Hicks v NLO, Inc, 825 F2d 118 (6th Cir 1987) **§2.02**

Hill v Bache Halsey Stuart Shields, Inc, 790 F2d 817 (10th Cir 1986) **§2.02**

Hill v Rose, 579 F Supp 1080 (MD Tenn 1983) **§6.08**

Hilmon Co (VI) v Hyatt Intl, 899 F2d 250 (3d Cir 1990) **§5.02**

Hilton v Braunskill, 481 US 770 (1987) **§6.11**

Hoffa v Gray, 323 F2d 178 (6th Cir), *cert denied,* 375 US 907 (1963) **§3.13**

Hoffman v Blaski, 363 US 335 (1960) **§3.07**

Hohri v United States, 782 F2d 227 (DC Cir 1986) **§4.14**

Holcomb v Colony Bay Coal Co, 852 F2d 792 (4th Cir 1988) **§9.11**

Holmberg v Baxter Healthcare Corp, 901 F2d 1387 (7th Cir 1990) **§9.11**

Holmes v Silver Wings Aviation, Inc, 881 F2d 939 (10th Cir 1989) **§2.19**

Hollywood v City of Santa Maria, 886 F2d 1228 (9th Cir 1989) **§2.02**

I

J

L

N

O

P

S

St Louis Baptist Temple, Inc v FDIC, 605 F2d 1169 (10th Cir 1979) **§7.01**

St Paul Fire & Marine Ins Co v United States, 959 F2d 960 (Fed Cir 1992) **§2.02**

Salazar v Atlantic Sun, 881 F2d 73 (3d Cir 1989) **§2.08**

Samaad v City of Dallas, 940 F2d 925 (5th Cir 1991) **§2.10**

Sambo's Restaurants, Inc, *In re,* 754 F2d 811 (9th Cir 1985) **§2.14**

Sampson v Commissioner, 710 F2d 262 (6th Cir 1983) **§2.13**

Samuels v American Motors Sales Corp, 969 F2d 573 (7th Cir 1992) **§2.19**

Sandahl, *In re,* 980 F2d 1118 (7th Cir 1992) **§3.08**

Sanders v Sullivan, 863 F2d 218 (2d Cir 1988) **§5.09**

Sanderson v Winner, 507 F2d 477 (10th Cir 1974), *cert denied,* 421 US 914 (1975) **§3.06**

Sandwiches, Inc v Wendy's Intl, Inc, 822 F2d 707 (7th Cir 1987) **§2.10**

Sanko SS Co v Galin, 835 F2d 51 (2d Cir 1987) **§2.04**

SB McLaughlin & Co v Tudor Oaks Condominium Project, 877 F2d 707 (8th Cir 1989) **§2.04**

SCA Servs v Morgan, 557 F2d 110 (7th Cir 1977) **§3.08**

Schetz v United States, 901 F2d 85 (7th Cir 1990) **§2.03**

Schiavone v Fortune, 477 US 21 (1986) **§5.06**

Schlagenhauf v Holder, 379 US 104 (1964) **§§3.02, 3.03, 3.04, 3.05, 3.06, 3.10, 3.12, 3.16**

Schoenamsgruber v Hamburg Am Line, 294 US 454 (1935) **§2.08**

School Asbestos Litig, *In re,* 977 F2d 764 (3d Cir 1992) **§3.08**

Schrader v Commissioner, 916 F2d 361 (6th Cir 1990) **§2.13**

Scott v Lacy, 811 F2d 1153 (7th Cir 1987) **§2.04**

Sckolnick v Harlow, 820 F2d 13 (1st Cir 1987) **§6.11**

Sealed Case, Sealy, Inc, *In re* v Easy Living, Inc, 743 F2d 1378 (9th Cir 1984) **§5.04**

Sears, Roebuck & Co v Mackey, 351 US 427 (1956) **§2.10**

Seattle Times Co v Rhinehart, 467 US 20, *cert denied,* 467 US 1230 (1984) **§3.09**

SEC v American Principals Holdings, Inc, 817 F2d 1349 (9th Cir 1987) **§2.07**

SEC v Bartlett, 422 F2d 475 (8th Cir 1970) **§2.07**

SEC v Chenery Corp, 318 US 80 (1943) **§5.05**

SEC v ESM Govt Sec, Inc, 645 F2d 310 (5th Cir 1981) **§2.16**

SEC v Lincoln Thrift Assn, 577 F2d 600 (9th Cir 1978) **§2.07**

SEC v Samuel H. Sloan & Co, 369 F Supp 994 (SDNY 1973) **§6.15**

SEC v Thomas, 965 F2d 825 (10th Cir 1992) **§§7.04, 8.01**

SEC v Universal Fin, 760 F2d 1034 (2d Cir 1985) **§2.07**

SEC v Youmans, 729 F2d 413 (6th Cir), *cert denied,* 469 US 1034 (1984) **§6.03**

See v City of Seattle, 387 US 541 (1967) **§5.11**

Segni v Commercial Office of Spain, 816 F2d 344 (7th Cir) **§2.04**

Seligson v OPM, 878 F2d 369 (Fed Cir 1989) **§10.13**

cert denied, 493 US 848 (1989) **§2.15**

Swift & Co v United States, 276 US 311 (1928) **§2.02**

Swift & Co Packers v Compania Colombiana Del Caribe, SA, 339 US 684 (1950) **§2.04**

T

Talbott Big Foot, Inc, *In re,* 854 F2d 758 (5th Cir 1988) **§2.08**

Tapper v Commissioner, 766 F2d 401 (9th Cir 1985) **§2.13**

Tatelbaum v United States, 749 F2d 729 (Fed Cir 1984) **§4.14**

Tavoulareas v Washington Post Co, 737 F2d 1170 (DC Cir 1984) **§3.09**

Taylor, *In re,* 916 F2d 1027 (5th Cir 1990) **§2.18**

TCL Investors, *In re,* 775 F2d 1516 (11th Cir 1985) **§2.14**

Technitrol, Inc v McManus, 405 F2d 84 (8th Cir 1968), *cert denied,* 394 US 997 (1969) **§3.07**

Teleport Oil Co, *In re,* 759 F2d 1376 (9th Cir 1985) **§2.14**

TeleSTAR, Inc v FCC, 888 F2d 132 (DC Cir 1989) **§2.16**

Teradyne, Inc v Mostek Corp, 797 F2d 43 (1st Cir 1986) **§2.06**

Texaco, Inc v Louisiana Land & Exploration Co, 995 F2d 43 (5th Cir 1993) **§2.04**

Texas v United States, 837 F2d 184 (5th Cir), *cert denied,* 488 US 821 (1988) **§6.09**

Thames v Dugger, 848 F2d 149 (11th Cir 1988) **§§6.04, 6.08**

Theis v Smith, 827 F2d 260 (7th Cir 1987) **§2.04**

Thermtron Prods, Inc v Hermansdorfer, 423 US 336 (1976) **§2.15**

Thomas v Arn, 474 US 140 (1985) **§2.15**

Thomas v Capital Sec Servs, 836 F2d 866 (5th Cir 1988) **§§2.04, 5.02**

Thomas v Computax Corp, 631 F2d 139 (9th Cir 1980) **§§6.15, 6.16**

Thomas E. Hoar, Inc v Sara Lee Corp, 882 F2d 682 (2d Cir 1989) **§2.04**

Thompson v INS, 375 US 384 (1964) **§6.04**

T.H. Richards Processing Co, *In re,* 910 F2d 639 (9th Cir 1990) **§5.04**

Tideland Welding Serv v Department of Labor, 817 F2d 1211 (5th Cir 1987) **§2.16**

TK-7 Corp v Estate of Barbouti, 966 F2d 578 (10th Cir 1992) **§9.04**

TMI Litig Cases Consol II, 940 F2d 832 (3d Cir 1991), *cert denied,* 112 S Ct 1262 (1992) **§2.15**

Toepfer v DOT, 792 F2d 1102 (Fed Cir 1986) **§5.02**

Toliver v Community Action Commn to Help the Economy, Inc, 613 F Supp 1070 (SDNY 1985), *affd,* 800 F2d 1128 (2d Cir), *cert denied,* 489 US 863 (1986) **§6.15**

Topco, Inc, *In re,* 894 F2d 727 (5th Cir 1990) **§2.14**

Torres v Oakland Scavenger Co, 487 US 312 (1988) **§§6.02, 6.03**

Trinity Broadcasting Corp v Eller, 827 F2d 673 (10th Cir), *affd on rehg,* 835 F2d 245 (10th Cir 1987), *cert denied,* 487 US 1223 (1988) **§2.10**

U

United States v Werker, 535 F2d 198 (2d Cir), *cert denied,* 429 US 926 (1976) **§3.12**

United States v West, 672 F2d 796 (10th Cir), *cert denied,* 457 US 1133 (1982) **§3.13**

United States v Wheeler, 795 F2d 839 (9th Cir 1986) **§6.12**

United States v Williams, 112 S Ct 1735 (1992) **§5.03**

United States v Williams, 952 F2d 418 (DC Cir 1991), *cert denied,* 113 S Ct 148 (1992) **§§5.02, 9.11**

United States v Williams, 809 F2d 1072 (5th Cir), *corrected on rehg,* 828 F2d 1 (5th Cir), *cert denied,* 484 US 896 (1987) **§§5.09, 8.06, 9.19, 10.02**

United States v Wilson, 420 US 332 (1975) **§2.11**

United States v Wilson, 750 F2d 7 (2d Cir 1984), *cert denied,* 479 US 839 (1986) **§2.11**

United States v Winner, 666 F2d 447 (10th Cir 1981) **§3.12**

United States v Wyatt, 680 F2d 1080 (5th Cir 1982) **§4.15**

United States v Zang, 645 F2d 999 (Temp Emer Ct App 1981) **§4.15**

United States v Zherebchevsky, 849 F2d 1256 (9th Cir 1988) **§2.15**

United States v Zolin, 491 US 554, *cert denied,* 492 US 926 (1989) **§2.18**

United States Catholic Conference v Abortion Rights Mobilization, Inc, 487 US 72 (1988), *cert denied,* 495 US 918 (1990) **§§2.04, 2.19**

Universal Oil Prods Co v Root Ref Co, 328 US 575 (1946) **§11.07**

UNR Indus, Inc, *In re,* 725 F2d 1111 (7th Cir 1984) **§2.14**

Uppercu, *Ex parte,* 239 US 435 (1915) **§3.05**

V

Valenzuela-Gonzalez v United States Dist Ct, 915 F2d 1276 (9th Cir 1990) **§3.04**

Van Cauwenberghe v Biard, 486 US 517 (1988) **§§2.04, 10.15**

Van Drasek v Lehman, 762 F2d 1065 (DC Cir 1985) **§4.14**

Van Dusen v Barrack, 376 US 612 (1964) **§§3.02, 3.05, 3.07, 3.17**

Van Gemert v Boeing Co, 590 F2d 433 (2d Cir 1978), *affd,* 444 US 472 (1980) **§11.04**

Vargas, *In re,* 723 F2d 1461 (10th Cir 1983) **§3.13**

Varsic v United States Dist Court, 607 F2d 245 (9th Cir 1979) **§3.07**

Velsicol Chem Corp v Parsons, 561 F2d 671 (7th Cir 1977), *cert denied,* 435 US 942 (1978) **§§2.05, 2.19, 3.13**

Venegas v Mitchell, 495 US 82 (1990) **§5.14**

Virginia Land Co v Miami Shipbuilding Corp, 201 F2d 506 (5th Cir 1953) **§6.03**

Vogelsang v Patterson Dental Co, 904 F2d 427 (8th Cir 1990) **§6.03**

Volvo N Am Corp, Men's Intl Professional Tennis Council, 839 F2d 69 (2d Cir), *cert denied,* 487 US 1219 (1988) **§2.06**

Vuitton v White, 945 F2d 569 (3d Cir 1991) **§2.06**

Vuitton et Fils SA, *In re,* 606 F2d 1 (2d Cir 1979) **§§3.01, 3.02, 3.04, 3.06**

W

Y

Z

Index

A

C

F

G

H

I

J

L

M

N

O

P

Q

R

S

T

U

V

W